COLLECTED WORKS OF ERASMUS

VOLUME 56

COLLECTED WORKS OF
ERASMUS

NEW TESTAMENT SCHOLARSHIP

General Editor Robert D. Sider

ANNOTATIONS ON ROMANS

edited by Robert D. Sider

translated and annotated by
John B. Payne, Albert Rabil Jr,
Robert D. Sider, and Warren S. Smith Jr

University of Toronto Press

Toronto / Buffalo / London

The research and publication costs of the
Collected Works of Erasmus are supported by the
Social Sciences and Humanities Research Council of Canada.
The publication costs are also assisted by
University of Toronto Press.

ISBN 0-8020-2803-9

Printed on acid-free paper

Canadian Cataloguing in Publication Data

Erasmus, Desiderius, d. 1536
[Works]
Collected works of Erasmus

Includes bibliographical references.
Partial contents: v. 56. New Testament scholarship:
Annotations on Romans / edited by Robert D. Sider.
ISBN 0-8020-2803-9 (v. 56)

1. Erasmus, Desiderius, d. 1536. I. Title.

PA8500 1974   876'.04   C74-006326-X

Collected Works of Erasmus

The aim of the Collected Works of Erasmus
is to make available an accurate, readable English text
of Erasmus' correspondence and his
other principal writings. The edition is planned
and directed by an Editorial Board, an Executive Committee,
and an Advisory Committee.

Contents

Preface

The nature and scope of the series of volumes to be published as the New Testament scholarship of Erasmus have been described in the preface to volume 42. Apart from the prolegomenous volume (CWE 41) the series is to be completed in two sequences, one of the *Paraphrases* (CWE 42–50), one of the *Annotations* (CWE 51–60). The volumes devoted to the *Annotations* will differ in important respects from those in which the *Paraphrases* are appearing, for the *Annotations* were a project quite distinct from the *Paraphrases* and have a very different publication history.

The *Paraphrases* originally appeared independently of Erasmus' New Testament, and in a sequence that stretched over a period of years: beginning in 1517 with the *Paraphrase on Romans*, the sequence was not completed until the *Paraphrase on Acts* was published in 1524. The *Paraphrases* were unaccompanied by any biblical text apart from some marginal catchwords – most of which were brief excerpts (only a few words) from the Vulgate. Changes to the text of the paraphrases made in editions subsequent to the first were modest, sometimes negligible.

The *Annotations*, on the other hand, were published as notes to accompany Erasmus' editions of the New Testament, and were intended to justify and clarify Erasmus' text and translation; hence readers of the *Annotations* had available to them the Greek text and the Latin translation of the New Testament (and, for the third edition, the Vulgate translation as well). The *Annotations* on all the books of the New Testament were necessarily published together at the same time, and in the traditional sequence of the biblical books. Five editions were published – in 1516, 1519, 1522, 1527, and 1535; each publication saw major additions to, and significant changes in, the text of the *Annotations*. By 1535 the *Annotations* had become a highly complex text, an intricately woven fabric. In establishing the sequence and form appropriate to the publication of the *Annotations* in this series, the Editorial Board has taken into account the character of the *Annotations*, a character fundamentally shaped by the original edition and maintained thereafter.

It may be noted first that the volumes devoted to the *Annotations* will follow the sequence of the New Testament books, as the *Annotations* were originally published. Hence this volume on Romans, CWE 56, though first to be published, does not formally initiate the series, and the introductory material in this volume is confined therefore to the Translators' Note.

The annotations are, with rare exceptions, individual units, each introduced by a cue phrase, or lemma, that normally represents a text of the Vulgate. We have taken advantage of the well-defined boundaries of the individual annotations to have the translators' notes placed immediately after each annotation so that the reader may have easy access to them. Such access seemed particularly desirable in a work that required frequent notation of changes in the various editions, elucidation of the multitudinous references, and explication of the argument in other ways. Further, since many annotations undertake a defence of Erasmus' translation, it is essential that our reader knows how Erasmus translated the passages in question. Accordingly every cue phrase is matched with the corresponding portion of Erasmus' translation. For each chapter of the Bible standard verse numbers are provided, though these had not yet come into use in Erasmus' day. Besides facilitating cross-reference, the verse numbers should be an advantage to those who wish to read the annotations with an open Bible beside them.

In this volume the translators have described in a prefatory essay the programme Erasmus undertook to fulfil in the *Annotations*, and have shown in outline how this programme underlies the *Annotations on Romans*. Their notes fill in the outline with many details; but it is, of course, to the annotations themselves that the reader must turn to grasp the nature of Erasmus' enterprise.

RDS

Translators' Note

The *Annotations on Romans* share the general character of the annotations Erasmus wrote to accompany his Greek text and Latin translation of all the books of the New Testament. These annotations attempted to explain and defend both his text and his translation, particularly where either represented a change from the Vulgate. The *Annotations* are, therefore, in the first instance, a roll-call of witnesses, one after another, to the readings of the text: Greek manuscripts, Latin manuscripts, and an array of early Christian writers, Latin and Greek, illustrating in any particular case both Erasmus' preferred reading and variants.[1] In the second place, the work of translating demanded frequent explication of the semantics of New Testament language: discussion was required on the connotation of words, on the identification and meaning of Greek idioms, sometimes of Hebrew idioms underlying the Greek, on the significance of syntax and style. Furthermore, translating called for an analysis of Latin idiom and style to show how Erasmus' translation in any particular case represented the appropriate Latin equivalent for a Greek expression. Moreover, the study of language that was implicitly theological inevitably led to theological issues which had to be addressed, sometimes (and particularly in the later editions) at considerable length. Again, the text of Scripture, even when 'corrected,' does not always yield an obvious reading: punctuation must be supplied, the sequence of thought determined, and in some cases sentences have to be completed; the annotations sought also, therefore, to clarify the obscurities and ambiguities of the text. Then, too, we have Erasmus' word that he deliberately set out to compare the Septuagint version with the original Hebrew of the Old Testament passages cited in the New.[2] Finally, the *Annotations* reflect Erasmus' advice (in the *Ratio*) to the aspiring theologian that Scripture can be wonderfully illuminated by an understanding of the historical setting of the books of the Bible.[3] It is towards these goals that a large part of the annotations on Romans, as indeed those on all the New Testament books, is directed.[4]

In the *Annotations on Romans* much of the discussion – the reader may, in fact, be surprised at the extent – is devoted to the correct reading of the biblical text. To validate his Greek text of Romans, Erasmus often refers generically to the Greek and Latin manuscripts, and especially so in the first edition.[5] While the Greek manuscripts were of great importance in establishing the text of his New Testament,[6] in the annotations on Romans they remain somewhat faceless throughout the five editions. On the other hand Erasmus called attention in these annotations to several of the Latin manuscripts he used. Among these were a manuscript from the library of St Paul's, London; two codices from the library of St Donatian's in Bruges – one of the entire New Testament, one with only Paul's Epistle to the Romans and the Epistles of James, Peter, John, and Jude; and two manuscripts of the 'apostolic Epistles' from the library of the cathedral chapter at Constance.[7] From such manuscripts one could attempt to conjecture the Greek text underlying the Latin translation. These manuscripts came into Erasmus' hands as he prepared successive editions, the Donatian codices in time for the edition of 1522, those from Constance for the edition of 1527. Though Erasmus claims to have seen the manuscript from St Paul's before his 1516 edition was published,[8] all of the allusions to it in the annotations on Romans appear first in the edition of 1519, though in one annotation (on Rom 15:4) Erasmus made a small but interesting change in 1535: in 1519 he had spoken of the value of this manuscript 'when I added this'; in 1535 the passage reads, 'when I first published this.' Each of these manuscripts is described more fully in the appropriate place in our notes.

Erasmus' appeal to the 'Fathers' as witnesses to the text of Romans is impressive for the variety of authors cited and for the wide range of works canvassed, as a brief glance at the index of patristic and medieval authors in this volume will reveal. Equally striking is Erasmus' persistent reading of a few central patristic texts – ancient commentaries and homilies on Romans – to determine both from their citation and from their interpretation the correct reading of Scripture.[9] By the final edition of 1535 the commentaries of Origen and Ambrosiaster, the homilies of Chrysostom, and the exposition of Theophylact, all on Romans, had become a part of the very fabric of the *Annotations*.[10] Their effect is compelling, inasmuch as Erasmus forces their authors into dialogue with himself and his reader, but their use was not without problems. He had to unmask the translator of Origen – Rufinus – and he lamented the latter's unfaithfulness to what must have been Origen's original text. Throughout the annotations on Romans Ambrosiaster is everywhere called Ambrose (though in Erasmus' edition of Ambrose [1527] he raised a question about the authenticity of the *Commentary on Romans*). On the assumption that the author of the commentary was the great bishop of Milan, Erasmus could wonder why Ambrose, who knew Greek, did not consult the Greek texts. Chrysostom's *Homilies on Romans* were not available to Erasmus for his first three editions; it was only when he was preparing his fourth (1527) that a copy was made for him. As for Theophylact, not only did Erasmus mistakenly name him 'Vulgarius' in the first two editions; he was compelled at times to follow his commentary in Porsena's translation. In Erasmus' hands, these commentaries do not appear as mere sources for variant readings; the commentaries become closely associated with their authors in such a way that author and text together acquire a sort of persona as witness to the true readings of Scripture or to variants. Indeed, if modern scholarship has gone well beyond the textual criticism of Erasmus, the intellectual drama so vividly revealed in Erasmus' search for the true reading gives permanent value to his work.

In the *Annotations on Romans* Erasmus sought also to bring clarity to the text. The work of translation in any case required a careful study of the nuances of the words, and one will find in the annotations some extensive discussions of the language of Romans: on the precise meaning, for example, of ὁρίζω (1:4) – is the word to be understood as 'predestine,' 'ordain,' or 'declare,' 'mark out'? of λογίζομαι 'impute' (4:6, 5:13); of χάρις 'grace' (1:7); of φρονέω 'to have an affection for' (8:5–7); and perhaps the most important of all, of πίστις 'faith' (1:17). More arresting are the vivid images that emerge in Erasmus' exploration of the scriptural language. For example, in the annotations on 8:26, the Spirit is portrayed as a helper, stretching out a hand to one weary with struggle, and as an intercessor who makes an appeal for us just as one might approach a prince to commend the cause of a friend; the phrase 'sheep for the slaughter' (8:36) is, in the annotation, set within a picture of the slaughterer feeling the animal with his hands to determine whether it is fit to be slain.

The Epistle to the Romans contains some passages notoriously difficult to construe. Two of these led Erasmus into very serious debate, and consequently into radical revision and enormous enlargement of annotations written for the earlier editions. The problematical ἐφ' ᾧ of 5:12 ('*in whom* all have sinned' DV; '*for that* all have sinned' AV; '*because* all have sinned' RSV) elicited what became the longest annotation of those on Romans. Here Erasmus defended himself against the charge of Pelagianism while refusing to deny an exemplarist interpretation of the passage: all have sinned after the pattern of Adam. Similarly, Erasmus' discussion on the reading of 9:5 appeared to some to be insufficiently decisive against Arianism, particularly after the additions of *1519* and *1522*, and Erasmus responded with a radical revision of the annotation in 1535.[11] Elsewhere, too, though theological issues were less crucially at stake, the annotations seek to establish an authentic reading for ambiguous passages. The reading of 8:34 as it was sometimes heard in the churches of Erasmus' day seemed to him simply blasphemous – it was read, as he says, 'with insolence towards Christ' (1516–1527; removed 1535) – because it appeared to make 'Jesus Christ who died' the one who will condemn (cf DV). He himself preferred the reading of Origen: God is the one who justifies; who therefore will condemn? Christ is the one who died and is seated at God's right hand; who therefore will accuse his chosen?

Though Romans is primarily a theological text, it does not come to us without a historical context, and the annotations repeatedly address questions about the author and his audience. The perspective is not always that of our own day. It is the paradigmatic aspects of Paul's character and experience that draw the attention of Erasmus: the Apostle's call illustrates the divine grace, and the separation he knew as a Pharisee was extended to his new life as a Christian but in a new way, as he was set apart for the gospel of God. In the annotations Paul's dominant characteristics appear to be his civility and his humility: distinguished though he may be, he knows only the humility of Christ, possesses none of the arrogance of the ecclesiastical hierarchy. As a master rhetorician and stylist he knows his audience well and writes to them always conscious of their own self-esteem.[12] Indeed, the Paul of these annotations sees his audience as not only Romans, but proud Romans, who are aware that they live in the noblest city on earth. To the modern reader, however, the *Annotations on Romans* do not appear to reconstruct an authentic picture of the early Christian community in Rome; even those discussions – inevitable in a commentary on this Epistle – that concern the relation between Jews and gentiles are rather generalized and take little account of the particular components of the church in Rome.

If, as we have said above, Erasmus was in dialogue with Christian authors of late antiquity, he was also in dialogue with his contemporaries and near-contemporaries. He observed closely the *Annotations* on Romans by Lorenzo Valla (1406–57), and there are several explicit allusions, none of them hostile,[13] to the scholarship of Erasmus' contemporary, Jacques Lefèvre d'Etaples, who published, first in 1512, a commentary on the Pauline Epistles, a work in which the commentary was preceded by Lefèvre's own Latin translation placed in columns parallel with the Vulgate. Our notes attempt to trace points of similarity between the comments of Erasmus on the one hand and the notes of Valla and Lefèvre on the other – fairly exhaustively in the case of Valla, whose annotations were relatively sparse; more selectively in the case of Lefèvre, whose commentary is much more extensive.[14] John Colet had been a source of inspiration for Erasmus and had written an exposition of Romans. His commentary, however, was a very different enterprise from the *Annotations* of Erasmus, much less philological in orientation, and the lines of thought between the two works are only occasionally contiguous.[15]

The early editions of the *Annotations* also aroused open hostility in some quarters, and in his own mind, at least, Erasmus' critics seem to have spoken with a louder voice than his friends. Our notes will show how the annotations on Romans reflect Erasmus' response to his critics, especially Edward Lee, Diego López Zúñiga, and above all, Frans Titelmans. Whereas the criticisms of Lee and Zúñiga were directed against Erasmus' work on the entire New Testament, Titelmans directed his *Collationes* specifically to the discussion of Romans, and indeed to that not only of Erasmus but of Valla and Lefèvre as well.

A few words about our translation and our notes. In keeping with the general policy of CWE's New Testament Scholarship series, our translation endeavours to follow faithfully the original language; indeed, we have attempted to render the Latin as literally as English prose will allow. Paraphrase too easily conceals linguistic features that carry nuances important in discussions devoted to the thought and style of a text, especially of a biblical text. Where consistency of argument and clarity in cross-reference required, we have maintained one translation for a given Latin word. Otherwise, though we have not sought abundance, we have had no fear of variety. The English language sometimes failed, we felt, to have words that corresponded equally well to each of the Latin words Erasmus might use to explain a Greek word. The translation of the cue phrase could be particularly problematic. For each annotation we have placed the corresponding portion of Erasmus' translation immediately above the cue phrase from the Vulgate. The comparison of the two is often helpful in understanding the discussion in the annotation, and we have endeavoured in our English translation to reflect as far as possible the difference in each case between the two Latin translations. We have been willing sometimes to sacrifice the *mot juste* to keep the difference clear. On occasion we have deliberately attempted to suggest by our English translation that the Vulgate, from Erasmus' point of view, was something less than elegant. Finally, we may note here that Erasmus frequently refers indefinitely to the 'translator' (Latin *interpres*, literally 'interpreter') of the Vulgate; in such cases we have capitalized 'Translator' to mark more clearly the distinction from other translators, for example, the 'translator' of Origen's work.

The notes that accompany our translation have several functions. In the first place, they indicate the development and change that occurred in the text of the *Annotations*. Erasmus published the *Annotations on the New Testament* in five editions, those of 1516, 1519, 1522, 1527, and 1535; in each edition he added new material, so that the final edition of 1535 was vastly larger than the first edition of 1516. Occasionally comments made in the early editions were omitted in the later; sometimes substitutions were made, whether of a simple word or a phrase – primarily perhaps for elegance or clarity – or of a passage of some length with political or theological import. The reflective reader will want to trace the development of Erasmus' thought and, further, to be aware of Erasmus' sensitivity to style. We have collated the five editions and have checked our collation against the facsimile edition of the final Latin text edited by Anne Reeve and M.A. Screech.[16] Differences between their collation and ours remain only after verification of our own collation by appeal to the original editions. In the course of preparing the five editions Erasmus made a few changes so minor that they lose virtually all significance in translation; these we have not recorded.

A word of caution. As we indicated above, it was not until *1522* that Erasmus corrected the name 'Vulgarius' to Theophylact. Since the name appears without exception as Vulgarius in the annotations of the first two editions, as Theophylact thereafter, we have not burdened the notes by repeatedly observing the change, but ask the reader to understand that wherever 'Theophylact' appears as part of a passage published in *1516* or *1519*, those editions in fact printed 'Vulgarius.'

In the second place our notes endeavour to explain historical and literary allusions as well as allusions to Erasmus' own contemporaries and to identify references to biblical, classical, patristic, and medieval literature. The indexes that follow our notes will indicate the extent to which Erasmus drew upon such literature. In accordance with editorial policy, we have used the standard sources for reference to patristic literature. However, Erasmus' text of Origen and Chrysostom differed at points from modern critical editions. Our notes trace some of Erasmus' special readings of Origen to the Merlin edition (Paris 1512).[17] The source of Erasmus' special readings of Chrysostom remains to be identified. Though the Verona edition of the homilies on the Pauline Epistles was available to Erasmus for the 1535 edition (cf the annotation on 14:9), that edition generally agrees with the edition of J.P. Migne at those points where we have found Erasmus' text to disagree with Migne. Perhaps these readings belong to the text copied for Erasmus before the 1527 edition.[18]

Finally, for some of the longer annotations, we have attempted to clarify the argument for the reader. The process of growth towards the text of the final edition included additions, changes, and substitutions in the text. Together, these rendered the discourse increasingly complex and sometimes brought ambiguity, even obscurity, to the argument. It seemed appropriate in these circumstances to help the reader find a way through the most difficult texts.

ACKNOWLEDGMENTS

The translators wish to express their gratitude to the Social Sciences and Humanities Research Council of Canada for its generous support of the Collected Works of Erasmus. We also acknowledge with deep appreciation the help of many colleagues in the preparation of this translation; particular thanks are owed to John J. Bateman, Alexander Dalzell, and Henk J. de Jonge for numerous contributions towards the solution of difficult problems in translation, to Erika Rummel for twice checking the entire text against the Latin with many suggestions for the improvement of both translation and notes, to Elizabeth Huweiler for checking the Hebrew, and to Mary Baldwin for her keen editorial eye. The preparation of this volume for printing has required many skills; those of Barbara McDonald, who typed the manuscript in its final form, of Lynn Child, who corrected and coded the computer disks, and of Philippa Matheson, who set the Greek, are much appreciated.

JBP, AR Jr, RDS, WSS Jr

NOTES

1 For the manuscripts Erasmus used cf Bentley *Humanists* 124–37; Rummel *Erasmus' 'Annotations'* 35–42; and Ep 384 introduction. For the patristic writers as witnesses to the text see Rummel ibidem 52–74.

2 Erasmus himself knew little Hebrew, and he acknowledged the help of Johannes Oecolampadius 'in this department' (Ep 373:72–83; cf Ep 324:31n). As our notes will show, a large part of the Hebrew quoted in *1516* did not appear in subsequent editions (in this volume the dates *1516, 1519, 1522, 1535*, in italics, signify the editions of Erasmus' New Testament with the *Annotations* published in those years).

3 Cf the *Ratio* in Holborn 184:23–185:18.

4 For a description of Erasmus' 'program' in writing the *Annotations*, cf Bentley *Humanists* 123–4; and for Erasmus' own statement thereof, Ep 373:44–83 and the preface to the *Annotations* addressed to 'the pious reader' (LB VI ***4 recto–verso).

5 Cf Rummel *Erasmus 'Annotations'* 35.

6 Cf Bentley *Humanists* 124–37.

7 Cf Allen Ep 1761:12–13 and 10n; also the annotations on Eph 1:7 (*in remissionem peccatorum*) and Col 1:19 (*omnem plenitudinem divinitatis*).

8 Cf Ep 373:20–5.

9 Cf Rummel *Erasmus' 'Annotations'* 67, who cites André Godin 'Fonction d'Origène dans la pratique exégètique d'Erasme: les Annotations sur l'épître

aux Romains' in *Histoire de l'exégèse au xvie siècle* (Geneva 1978) 26–7 for the fact that 'four-fifths of the notes referring to [Origen] served the purpose of textual criticism and of elucidating grammatical or stylistic points.'

10 For the growth of allusions to patristic writers in the *Annotations on Romans* in the course of the five editions (*1516–1535*) cf Albert Rabil *Erasmus and the New Testament: The Mind of a Christian Humanist* (San Antonio 1972; repr New York 1993) 115–18.

11 For Erasmus' thought in relation to Arianism and Pelagianism see Payne *Erasmus: His Theology* 54–9.

12 In his *Annotations on Romans* Erasmus frequently observes the 'rhetoric' of Paul in this Epistle; cf the annotation on 1:1 ('set apart for the gospel of God') n3 below.

13 They were 'not hostile' in spite of the quarrel between Erasmus and Lefèvre; on which see Rummel *Erasmus' 'Annotations'* 124.

14 For a comparison of the exegesis of Erasmus and Lefèvre see John B. Payne 'Erasmus and Lefèvre d'Etaples as Interpreters of Paul' *Archiv für Reformationsgeschichte* 65 (1974) 54–82.

15 For contiguous lines of thought between Erasmus' *Annotations* and Colet's commentaries on the New Testament see Catherine A.L. Jarrott 'Erasmus's *Annotations* and Colet's Commentaries on Paul: A Comparison of Some Theological Themes' in *Essays on the Works of Erasmus* ed Richard DeMolen (New Haven 1978) 125–44.

16 Anne Reeve and M.A. Screech *Erasmus' Annotations on the New Testament: Acts, Romans, I and II Corinthians*. Facsimile edition of the final Latin text with all the earlier variants (Leiden 1990).

17 On this edition see Godin *Erasme* 417–18.

18 Cf the annotation on 13:5; and for Chrysostom in Erasmus generally, see Robert D. Sider ' "Searching the Scriptures": John Chrysostom in the New Testament Scholarship of Erasmus' in *Within the Perfection of Christ: Essays ... in honor of Martin Schrag* ed Terry L. Brensinger and E. Morris Sider (Nappanee, IN 1990) 83–105.

ANNOTATIONS ON THE EPISTLE TO THE ROMANS

Annotationes in epistolam ad Romanos

The Annotations of Erasmus of Rotterdam,

least[1] among the professors of theology,

on the Epistles of the apostle Paul, which have been

carefully revised by the same hand,[2] [revised] first of all

according to the true Greek text, then according to the

reliable tradition of the most ancient Latin manuscripts, and,

finally, according to the quotations as well as the interpretations

of authors fully and universally approved.[3]

1 least ... theology] 1519 only
2 Latin *ab eodem*, literally 'by the same,' ie Erasmus
3 This paragraph introducing the annotations on all the Pauline Epistles
  immediately preceded the first annotation on Romans. A similar, but
  longer, paragraph preceding the first annotation on Matthew introduces the
  Annotations on the New Testament as a whole.
  With this statement of Erasmus' work in 'revising' the New Testament
  compare the more elaborate description in Epp 373 and 384; and see H.J.
  de Jonge 'Novum Testamentum a nobis versum: The Essence of Erasmus'
  Edition of the New Testament' *Journal of Theological Studies* NS 35 part 2
  (1984) 394–413.

CHAPTER 1

1:1 [ER VG] *Paulus* **'Paul.'** There are those who think that Saul's name had been changed following his conversion; among[1] these is Ambrose.[2] St Jerome, however, commenting on the Epistle to Philemon, supposes that he began to be called Paul instead of Saul because of the proconsul Sergius Paulus, the first of all the gentiles whom this apostle gained for Christ, as we read in the thirteenth chapter of the Acts of the Apostles.[3] Chrysostom[4] thinks his name was changed by the divine will, like that of the chief of the apostles, who was called Cephas or Peter instead of Simon.[5] There are those who think he had two names;[6] and this in my opinion is closer to the truth, though I believe that the Hebraic name Saul was originally given to Paul, who was first a Hebrew. For by that name Christ addresses him on the road: Σαοὺλ Σαοὺλ τί με διώκεις, that is, 'Saul, Saul, why do you persecute me?'[7] Then, since for the most part by that time Egypt, Cilicia, and the part of Syria that bordered it spoke Greek – a result of Alexander the Great's empire and the later Roman administration[8] – the Hebrew word was changed to a Greek form. For Greeks have no word ending in λ [*l*], so that Saul became Saulus, as even today Latin speakers say Adamus for Adam, Abrahamus for Abraham, and Josephus for Joseph. Finally, since the name Paul was equally familiar to Greeks and Romans, Saulus was further changed to Paulus, so that they whose teacher he claimed to be would with even greater pleasure recognize his name, and in this, too, he would be all things to all men.[9] Certainly he himself used this name constantly in his writings.[10]

Saul in Hebrew is שָׁאוּל meaning 'sought,' a passive from שָׁאַל, for he had been admitted into apostolic service.[11] Ambrose points out that Saul means 'tribulation' or 'restlessness.'[12] Elsewhere likewise people give interpretations of all kinds for Hebrew names that have only a tenuous play on words;[13] I shall not analyse these closely as it is not part of this enterprise. But the Greek word σαῦλος, if the υ is removed, becomes σάλος, which means 'agitation' and 'disturbance,' properly of the sea and the waves; whereas Paul in Greek means 'at rest' – from the verb παύομαι [*pauomai* 'I cease, rest from'], whence also the name παῦλα [*Paula*] 'rest.' To the Romans [*paulus*] means 'paltry.' Now[14] as to Jerome's point, that in Hebrew Paul means 'wonderful' – it is a wonder to me that he commits the very fault he elsewhere criticizes in others who sought the etymologies of words from a different language.[15] Since, indeed, it is clear that *Paulus* is a Latin word, or at least Greek, it was not appropriate to derive its etymology from Hebrew. I have pointed this out in passing, so that what saintly expositors in their commentaries discuss concerning the explanation of names – or the puns they make – might be understood more easily.

1 among ... Acts of the Apostles] Added in 1519, except 'the gentiles,' added in 1527
2 Ambrosiaster *Comm in Rom* 1:1 (1). The commentaries on the Pauline Epistles that Erasmus ascribes to Ambrose are, in fact, the work of Ambrosiaster; cf CWE 42 7 n13, and the annotation on 12:11 ('serving the Lord') n7.
3 Acts 13:6–12. Cf Jerome *Commentarius in epistulam ad Philemonem* 1 PL 26 (1883) 640A–641A.
4 Chrysostom ... Simon.] Added in 1527
5 Commenting on Acts 13:9, where the two names of the Apostle appear, Chrysostom writes: 'Here [Paul's] name is changed after his appointment to ministry, as in the case of Peter [Matt 16:17] also' (*In Acta apostolorum homiliae* 28.1 PG 60 209). Cf also Chrysostom *Hom in Rom* 1.1 PG 60 395.
6 See for example Origen *Comm in Rom* praefatio PG 14 836A–838A.
7 Cf Acts 9:4.
8 A vigorous policy of Hellenization followed Alexander's conquests (331–324 BC) in Asia Minor and the Levant, which made Greek the common language of administration, commerce, and higher education. Rome acquired these territories only gradually, a process virtually completed in the first century BC. Roman policy encouraged the continued use of Greek in these provinces for commercial and administrative purposes, but among the common people native languages and dialects persisted as the normal mode of communication.
9 Cf 1 Cor 9:22.
10 writings] In 1516, 1519, and 1522 only, there followed here the words: 'But I discuss these matters more carefully in the commentary on Paul that I began some time ago and will soon finish, with the help of Christ. Now, as far as the present undertaking is concerned, what I have said is sufficient.' For this projected commentary on the Pauline Epistles see CWE 42 xiii–xiv.
11 Erasmus evidently wishes to see in the word 'Saul' a connection with the Hebrew שָׁאַל [sha'al] 'to ask,' an analogy to the Latin *peto* 'to ask,' 'seek' (passive *petitum* 'something sought,' 'petition'), which can be used as a technical political term: 'to apply for office,' 'to be a candidate.' Similarly the related phrase *dare petitionem* means 'to admit to candidacy.' Cf Jerome *Commentarius in epistulam ad Philemonem* 1 PL 26 (1883) 641A, who says that Saul means *expetitus* 'sought,' but explains the significance of the term differently: ' "sought" because the devil had desired that he persecute the church.'
12 Ambrosiaster *Comm in Rom* 1:1 (1): 'Since Saul ... means "restlessness" or "tribulation" ... he says he is Paul, that is, "quiet" ... for though he once brought tribulations ... to the servants of God, he himself later suffered tribulations because of his hope.'
13 Cf below, the allusion to the 'saintly expositors.' The interpretation of Hebrew names was held in high regard in both patristic and medieval exegesis. Cf Origen *Commentaria in evangelium Joannis* 2.27 and 6.24 PG 14 172B–C and 269B–C; Jerome *Liber interpretationis Hebraicorum nominum* praefatio CCL 72

59–60; and Augustine *De doctrina christiana* 2.16.23 PL 34 47. See also J.N.D.
Kelly *Jerome: His Life, Writings, and Controversies* (New York 1975) 153–5.
14 Now ... from Hebrew.] Added in *1519*
15 Erasmus evidently refers to the word פֶּלֶא [*Pele*] 'wonder.' Jerome found it
    'a wonder that ... from being a persecutor he [Paul] had become a vessel
    of election' (*Commentarius in epistulam ad Philemonem* 1 PL 26 [1883] 641A).
    Erasmus here turns Jerome's pun on the word 'wonder' against him.

1:1 [ER *vocatus ad munus apostolicum* 'called to apostolic service']
[VG] *vocatus apostolus* 'called an apostle'; κλητὸς ἀπόστολος. 'Called' in
this passage is not the participle 'said' or 'named' – as today certain men
for the sake of modesty commonly write 'called a bishop,' indicating not
so much with modesty as with truth that they are bishops in name more
than in fact.[1] Even St Bernard,[2] in general a man of Christian learning, holy
eloquence, and devout geniality, falls into this κακόζηλος [affectation]: he
qualifies his own title by writing 'called an abbot.'[3] The designation is a
substantive – [he is], as an apostle, κλητός [a 'called one'], not κληθείς or
κεκλημένος [was, or has been, called (an apostle)]. So also a little below the
'called of Jesus Christ,' κλητοί,[4] and just afterwards κλητοῖς ἁγίοις, that is,
'to those called, to the saints.'[5] So 'called' is a term with a sense complete
in itself – just as long ago among the Romans those who were summoned
to war as friends were said to be 'the ones called forth,'[6] and today as well
in France[7] some who are close to senatorial dignity are called 'the elect.'[8]
The word has virtually the same force as though you said 'an apostle with
a calling,' or 'an apostle by calling,' and 'to those who are saints by calling.'

At the outset, in the very preface to the Epistle,[9] Paul looks to his
own interest and secures trustworthiness and authority for himself. First,
with his very name he sets in sharp relief his altered mode of life. Then, by
calling himself a 'servant' he indicates that he is attending to the interest
not of himself, but[10] of him who had sent him. When to this he adds 'of
Jesus Christ' he excludes Moses, who had become so deeply fixed in the
minds of the Jews that there was a danger that the gentiles too might be
led away into the servitude of the law of Moses. This clearly would have
happened if Paul had not most vehemently resisted with might and main,
so that the gospel of Christ can appear as revived through this champion.
Then he adds 'apostle,' which means 'envoy' or 'one sent by another.'[11]
And since at that time there were many pseudo-apostles who were thrust-
ing themselves into this office for the sake of glory and gain, he adds κλητός
'called,' which has a double meaning: either that he was called, that is, 'summoned,' to this office by Christ himself, and had not claimed for himself
the work of an apostle – indeed, he had assumed this obligation not from
men but from Christ himself; or that with this word he is excluding the

merit and works of the Law and declaring the grace of the gospel, which is given to all, not from the ceremonies of the Mosaic law, in which the Jews trusted, not from human wisdom, on which the Greeks relied, but at the call of deity. For the blessed Paul's chief concern in this letter is to take away from both groups their pride: to deprive the Jews of their confidence in the law of Moses and the Greeks of their security in philosophy, and consequently to unite both groups on an equal basis in Christ. The apostles have certain special words of their own – grace, calling, election, foreknowledge, destination, and predestination[12] – and these are virtually always opposed to trust in the Law, a danger, paramount at that particular time, that seemed to threaten. I am not[13] unaware that Origen, using the opportunity afforded by this word, discourses – with shrewdness and erudition, no doubt – concerning those who are indeed called, but who fall short of the reward of their service.[14] It is not my intention to reject such an interpretation; but in divine literature the simplest and the least forced interpretations are more satisfactory. Yet I would certainly not deny that this word κλητός [called] is sometimes used in a way not much different from a participle, as in Matthew: 'Many are called, but few are chosen' [22:14], where ἐκλεκτοί [chosen] and κλητοί [called] are read. This word[15] belongs especially to Paul, who is eager to remove from everyone trust in human works, and to transfer all the glory to the God who calls. Whoever heeds God when he calls is saved. Thus Paul soon obeyed after he had been called from heaven.[16]

1 In medieval Latin, *vocatus* 'called' can be used of bishops elected but not yet consecrated. See *vocatus* in Niermeyer. Irony is perhaps intended in the use of the word here in the sense of 'so-called.'

2 Even St Bernard ... abbot.'] Added in 1519

3 The expression is found frequently in the salutation of the letters of St Bernard (1090–1153), abbot of the Cistercian monastery at Clairvaux, often accompanied by other expressions of humility, eg Ep 14: 'To Pope Honorius, from brother Bernard, abbot so-called of Clairvaux, greetings and whatever else the prayer of a sinner can avail' (PL 182 117B); Ep 189: '[To Pope Innocent] from brother Bernard, abbot so-called of Clairvaux, small as that is (PL 182 354A); similarly Epp 251, 346.

4 Rom 1:6

5 Rom 1:7

6 Latin *evocati*. The *evocati* appear generally to have been veterans who rejoined the troops of a beloved commander. Crastinus of Caesar's army (*De bello civili* 3.91.1) and T. Flavius Petro of Pompey's army (Suetonius *Vespasian* 1.2) were vivid examples. Suetonius records, however, that Galba's bodyguard was comprised of young men who were knights and were called *evocati* (*Galba* 10.3). Valla also alludes to the Roman *evocati* in his *Annot in Rom* 1 (1 855).

7 in France] Added in *1519*

8 For the French use of perfect participles of the verb *élire* (from Latin *eligere*) to indicate nobility see E. Huguet *Dictionnaire de la langue française du xvi siècle* (Paris 1925) under *élire: élit, le plus éleu, esleu.*

9 Latin *exordium*, a technical term for the preface or introduction to a speech. According to classical theory it was here that the speaker was to gain the good will, respect, and confidence of his audience. See Cicero *De inventione* 1.15.20 and Quintilian 4.1.5–51; also Lausberg I 263.

10 but of him who had sent him] Added in *1519*

11 So Valla, in *Annot in Rom* 1 (I 855). For modern scholarship on the meaning of 'apostle,' see M.H. Shepherd Jr 'Apostle' in IDB I 170–2.
In what immediately follows, and elsewhere, Erasmus characteristically defines Paul's apostleship as a *munus*, translated in this volume variously as 'office,' 'task,' 'obligation,' 'duty,' 'service'; cf the annotation on 1:5 ('grace and apostleship') below.

12 For the distinction between *destinatio* and *praedestinatio*, see the annotation on 1:4 ('who was predestined') below.

13 I am not … satisfactory.] Added in *1519*

14 Origen *Comm in Rom* 1.2 PG 14 840A–842A. Origen contrasts the 'called' and the 'elect.' Many are called to a particular service, but only those who faithfully fulfil their duty to the end are the 'elect.'

15 This word … heaven.] Added in *1527*

16 Cf Gal 1:15–23.

1:1 [ER VG] *segregatus in evangelium dei* 'set apart for the gospel of God'; ἀφωρισμένος. With an admirably increasing emphasis he commends his own position as one who not only has been called to perform the service of an apostle, but, as[1] a chosen vessel, has also been selected and separated for the duty of preaching the gospel. For ἀφωρίζειν [*aphōrizein*] not only means 'to separate' but also 'to distinguish and select with judgment.' Thus physicians call rules stated briefly and complete in themselves ἀφορισμοί [*aphorismoi* 'aphorisms'], as the ἀποφθέγματα [*apophthegmata*] of the wise are called.[2]

This expression does not have a simple significance.[3] For in the first place, he seeks to avert the charge of inconstancy, because he appeared to be deserting the law of Moses. He says 'called' and 'set apart,' as though he were some chosen and special instrument; Christ himself bears witness: 'He is my chosen vessel, to bear my name before the gentiles.'[4] Second, he makes an allusion to the party to which he adhered in Judaism, playing on its name. For the Jewish people, although they embraced the same Law, were divided[5] into various schools; Josephus, in the second chapter of the eighteenth book of *Antiquities*, mentions the chief of these – Essenes, Sadducees, and Pharisees.[6] Paul belonged to the Pharisaic sect, which receives its name from the Hebrew word פָּרַס, *pharas* [separate], because they wanted to appear separated and removed from the common people due to their noteworthy holiness of life and their superior doctrine. Paul therefore began to be in the gospel what he had been in Judaism, but in a different way. Under Judaism his title was one of pride; in the gospel he had been marvellously separated from Moses unto Christ, from the letter unto the spirit, from trust in works unto grace.

1 as a chosen vessel] Added in 1527
2 the wise are called] First in 1535; from 1516 to 1527, 'the wise also are called.' Seven 'sections' of 'aphorisms' are found in the *corpus* of the Greek physician Hippocrates; see *Hippocrates* IV trans W.H.S. Jones, Loeb Classical Library (London and Cambridge, MA 1959) 99–221. Plutarch's *Moralia* offer a large collection of the 'apophthegms' of famous men; see *Plutarch's Moralia* III trans F.C. Babbitt, Loeb Classical Library (London and New York 1931) 9–469. For the *Apophthegmata* of Erasmus' friend Michael Apostolius, see Ep 1232A n2. In his letter of 26 Feb 1531 to William Duke of Cleves, to whom he dedicated his own *Apophthegmata*, Erasmus noted that the characteristics of the apophthegm are brevity, subtlety, wit, and polish (Allen Ep 2431:58–9); cf Cicero *De officiis* 1.29.104.
3 Erasmus uses here the Greek rhetorical term ἔμφασις [*emphasis*], which he normally transliterates. Quintilian defines 'emphasis' as 'words that mean more than they say' (8.2.11, and cf 9.2.64); Erasmus explains it in *Ecclesiastes* III as an expression that 'suggests more to the thought of the listeners than the words denote' (LB V 1005B–C). For Erasmus' interest in the stylistic features of this Epistle, see Robert D. Sider 'Erasmus on the Epistle to the Romans: A Literary Reading' in *Acta Conventus Neo-Latini Torontonensis* Medieval and Renaissance Texts and Studies (Binghamton 1991) 129–35.
4 Acts 9:15
5 were divided ... Pharisees] The reading of 1535. From 1516 to 1527 this passage read 'were divided into various schools: Samaritans, Essenes, Nazarenes, Sadducees, Herodians, Pharisees.'
6 Cf Josephus *Jewish Antiquities* 18.1.2–5 (11–22).

1:3 [ER *qui genitus fuit* 'who was begotten']

[VG] *qui factus est ei* 'who was made to him'; τοῦ γενομένου. Lorenzo Valla prefers 'begotten' [*genitus*] or 'born' [*natus*] rather than 'made';[1] in the present case, I neither approve nor disapprove his opinion. It would certainly be 'begotten' if the Greek were γεννηθείς or[2] γεννόμενος.[3] Augustine, in the eleventh book *Against Faustus*, chapter 4, testifies that some Latin manuscripts read 'born' instead of 'made.'[4] And yet elsewhere the same author explains why the Apostle preferred to say 'was made' rather than 'was born,' namely, because he was conceived and born not from the seed of a man, but from the work of the Holy Spirit.[5] Nevertheless, this reason does not prevent the word 'born' from being used elsewhere.[6]

The pronoun 'to him,' which is added in the Latin manuscripts, is found in none of the Greek.[7] Yet since the expression would seem rather absurd if he had said 'who was made from the seed of David,' 'to him' was added by way of explanation. But the addition of this pronoun not only fails to help the sense, it actually obstructs it. Paul's concern here is not to bring to light the one to whom Christ was born, but to make clear that the one by whom he had been set apart to preach the gospel was true God, and also true man: man, because he was born from the seed of David according to the flesh; God, because his divine power was revealed through the spirit of sanctification and the resurrection from the dead. But if there had been any point in determining to whom Christ was born or made, he was born to us, with whose welfare he was concerned, rather than to the Father.

If anyone does not very much like that word 'born,' and prefers 'made' as the Vulgate edition reads, I shall have no strong objection, provided he understands that 'made' here means 'began to be.' It is similar to the verse 'He who came after me was made before me';[8] that is, he who followed me began to be before, and preceded me, as I have pointed out in the annotations on the Gospels. For he who never began to be God did nevertheless begin to be a man.[9]

1 In his *Annot in Rom* 1, Valla mentions only 'begotten' (1 855). Both Diego López Zúñiga and Frans Titelmans challenged Erasmus on his own translation here. See *Apologia ad annotationes Stunicae* ASD IX-2 162 and *Responsio ad collationes* LB IX 967F–969B. On Zúñiga, see the annotation on 5:13 ('was not imputed') n8. Titelmans (1502–37) as a relatively young man published his *Collationes quinque super epistolam ad Romanos* (1529) defending the Vulgate against the criticisms of Valla, Lefèvre d'Etaples, and Erasmus – to which Erasmus replied with his *Responsio ad collationes* (1529); see *Contemporaries* III 326–7; also CWE 42 xviii.

2 or ... used elsewhere] Added in 1522

3 The reading γενομένου, with single ν (from γίγνομαι 'to be,' 'become') may be ambiguous, but γεννομένου (for γεννωμένου, with double ν, from γεννάω) can only mean 'begotten.' The Greek witnesses almost universally support γενομένου (Tischendorf II 364 3n). For γίγνομαι in the sense of 'was made' (AV), 'became' (RSV), see John 1:14, where Erasmus translated, like the Vulgate, *factum est*; and see Erasmus' explanation 'began to be' in the concluding sentences of this annotation. For γεννάω see n6 below.

4 Augustine *Contra Faustum Manichaeum* 11.4 PL 42 248

5 See, for example, Augustine *Enchiridion* 38.12 PL 40 251–2.

6 *natus* (*nasci* 'to be born') is used of the birth of Jesus in the Vulgate of the Gospels (eg Matt 1:16, 2:1; Luke 1:35, 2:11 – where in all these passages the Greek verb γεννάω is found); cf also Gal 4:4, where the Vulgate renders γενόμενον by *factus*, and Gal 4:29, where γεννηθείς is rendered by *natus*.

7 Tischendorf (II 364 3n) cites no Greek witnesses for the reading 'to him'; it is, however, the better attested reading of the Latin manuscripts (Wordsworth and White II 63 3n).

8 Cf John 1:15 and 30, where the Vulgate translated the verb γίγνομαι by *factus est* 'was made' [before me] (AV 'is preferred before me').

9 From *1519* to *1527* Erasmus made very significant changes in his original annotation on John 1:15 (*qui post me venturus est ante me factus est*); he never, however, departed from his fundamental interpretation of this Johannine verse, that though John preceded Christ in time both in his birth and ministry, Christ overtook John in glory and authority – and in this sense began to be before him. In *1527* Erasmus showed how the Arians used John 1:15 to support their view that Christ was a creature: the Christ who had followed John had been 'made' before him. The final sentence in this annotation on Rom 1 eliminates the possibility of an Arian interpretation of Rom 1:3.

1:4 [ER *qui declaratus fuit* 'who was shown']

[VG] *qui praedestinatus est* 'who was predestined.' The Greek codices largely agree in reading ὁρισθέντος, that is, 'who was marked out' or 'defined.' According to the interpretation of the scholia of the Greeks,[1] this means 'surely and openly proclaimed,' 'pointed out,' and 'revealed.' So read Chrysostom[2] and Theophylact;[3] and Origen, in his commentary on this passage, even expressly advises that it must be so read.[4]

With respect to this, however, one is led to wonder, in passing, how it is that Origen cites the Latin witnesses in this instance; he admits that in most of these the reading is 'predestined' rather than 'destined.' Perhaps the translator has added something on his own;[5] or else Origen, not satisfied with so many [Greek] editions,[6] tracked down not only the Hebrew sources, but with the same zeal scanned the Latin manuscripts as well. It is strange how Thomas Aquinas agonizes over this passage – on any count a great man, and not only in his own time. For there is no recent theologian,[7] at least in my opinion, who is his equal in diligence, more distinguished in ability, more solid in learning; and he certainly deserved to obtain a knowledge of languages as well,[8] and everything else belonging to the study of good literature, inasmuch as he so skilfully used the resources available to him in his own day. Thus, if great writers are sometimes at a loss in the Pauline Epistles, this must in part be ascribed to the obscurity of the wording and of the sense, in part to the infelicity of the times, when good literature had almost completely perished. Therefore this diligent and clever man moves every stone in this passage, and, like a kind of Proteus, changes himself into all things in his efforts to escape.[9] Now he follows Origen's reading, now he retreats to our own; at one point he interprets 'destine' to mean 'send,' at another 'ordain'; again, he interprets 'predestine' at one point as 'to foreknow,' at another he wants it to be something else; and he introduces various relationships implied by destination and predestination.[10] But Origen distinguishes without difficulty between predestination and destination, when he declares: ' "To destine" is used of one who already exists; "to predestine" is used of one who does not yet exist.'[11] Consequently St Jerome, in his commentary on the first chapter of the Epistle to the Ephesians, remarks (following, I believe, [Origen's] opinion) that Paul does not use the word προορίζειν [to predestine] except when he speaks of us, and he points out plainly that in this passage ὁρισθέντος, not προορισθέντος, is said of the Son – that is, 'destined,' not 'predestined.'[12] But if we stumble over this, that with the prepositional prefix 'pre'destined' refers to something that does not yet exist,[13] the same difficulty remains in the simple verb ['destined']. For since 'destine' means, not 'send,' as the unlettered rabble think,[14] but 'to fix something firmly in the mind beforehand,' clearly the word by its very nature has a future signification, as have 'hope,' 'fear,' 'determine,' 'resolve,' 'decide.'[15] All of these refer to something in the future. Further, if we prefer to turn this future aspect in another direction rather than to apply it to the actual nature of the Son of God, so that he who was begotten Son of God from eternity was 'destined' and 'ordained' for doing this or that, then the prefix 'pre-' is no obstacle at all. [When the matter is considered] in this way, nothing prevents us from calling the Son of God 'predestined' to that which later occurred. Or perhaps[16] you prefer what Origen seems to have thought, that 'predestine' has a double aspect of futurity and 'destine' merely a single. For if I 'destine' a bride for a son of mine already born, the person for whom I destine belongs to the present time, what I am destining belongs to the future. But if I resolve to dedicate to the study of theology the son who will be born first, then both the person and the thing belong to future time; and Origen would have the word 'predestine' refer to cases of the latter type.[17]

But whether you read 'destine' or 'predestine,' and to whatever you apply the future reference, the words that follow clamour for attention: 'The Son of God according to the spirit of sanctification' and 'from the resurrection of the dead.' Grant that the 'destination' was eternal, so that he was always 'destined' for this – to be the Son of God; what, then, is the connection of [the words] 'through the spirit of sanctification,' and 'from the resurrection of the dead'? What do these words have to do with that destination? Hence Ambrose, toiling also in these straits, adds a couple of words (I have no idea from where) – ut manifestaretur – [that he might be revealed] as the Son of God.[18] And Thomas points out that sometimes in divine literature the word fieri [to be done] is used when some things[19] are understood to be done and to become known.[20] And when they say such things, they foresee, as it were, what we observe.

And yet it was not necessary to seek from elsewhere what is present in the very words of Paul. For the Greek word ὁρίζειν itself means not

only 'to define' and 'to determine,' but also 'to make a fixed pronouncement' and 'to make public' what you have determined; therefore, a fixed
judgment about the nature of a thing is called a ὅρος.[21] And the grammarians use the term ὁριστικός to refer to the indicative mood, because
it points out and shows something fixed and sure. Consequently, if you
read 'shown' rather than 'predestined,' the whole thought will be everywhere as straight as a ruler; no rough spots will remain in the way. The
evidence is clear that Christ was a man, because he was born from the
seed of David; this is verified by the senses themselves. But it had to be
shown that he was also the Son of God as he always had been, though
this was unknown to the world. He, therefore, who clearly was a man,
was shown to be the Son of God. The flesh showed that he was a man;
his power and the spirit of sanctification show that he is the Son of God
and God. This was shown both by other means indeed – namely, by the
oracles of the prophets, by innumerable signs – but especially through
the resurrection of the dead. The scholia of the Greeks also interpret the
word in this way, as I said.[22] I will quote their actual words in case anyone distrust me: ὁρισθέντος τοῦτ' ἐστὶν ἀποδειχθέντος, ἀποφανισθέντος, διά
τε τῶν προφητῶν, διά τε τῶν τοσούτων θεοσημειῶν, διά τε τῆς ἀναστάσεως
– in translation: 'defined, that is, demonstrated, shown, first through the
prophets, then through so many signs of divinity, then through the resurrection itself.' To this point, the Greek scholia. So far[23] is Theophylact
from disagreeing with these words that he does not adduce any other interpretation than this. He explains ὁρισθέντος υἱοῦ τοῦ θεοῦ to mean 'recognized as Son of God,' then 'set forth,' 'established,' and 'disclosed';[24]
for these words are used by the translator of the work falsely ascribed
to Athanasius. (As I had earlier suspected, I discovered once I had compared the Greek and Latin that this was the work of Theophylact.[25]) His
words[26] are: ἀποδειχθέντος, βεβαιωθέντος, κριθέντος, that is, 'demonstrated'
or 'shown,' 'established,' 'judged,' or 'determined.' Chrysostom explains
with these words: δειχθέντος, ἀποφανθέντος, κριθέντος, ὁμολογηθέντος, that
is, 'demonstrated, shown, judged, acknowledged.'[27] He had always been
the Son of God but known to few, namely the Jews, and few even of
them. But afterwards he was shown to the whole world to be such. To
make it even clearer, however, that eternal predestination is not intended
here, Chrysostom adds: 'Judged on the assent of all, from [the witness of]
the prophets, from his miraculous nativity according to the flesh, from the
power of signs, from the spirit through whom he gave holiness, from the
resurrection, through which he broke the tyranny of death.'[28] This is evidence enough that ὁρισθέντος means to the Greeks something other than
the Latin translations suggest.

1 By 'the scholia of the Greeks' Erasmus is probably referring to the catenae
  of brief exegetical comments of the Eastern Fathers which began to be
  compiled towards the end of the patristic period. H.J. de Jonge (ASD
  IX-2 194:539n) identifies these scholia with the anonymous commentary,
  wrongly ascribed to Oecumenius, contained in MS 7 of the Pauline Epistles
  (A.N.III.11) in the Basel University Library and accessible in Migne PG 118–19.
  Bentley *Humanists* 128–9 also identifies these scholia with those contained
  in A.N.III.11. Karl Staab *Die Pauluskatenen nach den handschriftlichen Quellen
  untersucht* (Rome 1926) 151–8 has shown that the Migne text reproduces
  without critical assessment an earlier edition (1532) by Donatus Veronensis,
  who attributed to Oecumenius, a sixth-century Greek philosopher and rhetor,
  three eighth-century commentaries in the form of catenae, one of them on
  the Pauline Epistles; cf Staab ibidem 93–6 and *The Encyclopedia of the Early
  Church* ed Angelo Di Berardino, trans Adrian Walford (New York 1992) II
  610. But for a different opinion on the identity of these scholia, see Godin
  Erasme 143 n12, where the author asserts that the scholia to which Erasmus
  refers cannot be represented by the 'Oecumenius-catena' in PG 118–19. For
  the quotation from the scholia here, see Pseudo-Oecumenius *Comm in Rom*
  1:4 PG 118 325B–C.
2 So read ... Theophylact; and] Added in *1519*, except that 'Chrysostom
  and' was added in *1527*. For Theophylact, and for 'Vulgarius' in place of
  'Theophylact' in the editions prior to *1522*, see n25 below and the Translators'
  Note xvi above.
3 Chrysostom *Hom in Rom* 1.2 PG 60 397; Theophylact *Expos in Rom* 1:4 PG 124
  341. As the immediately subsequent reference to Origen indicates, Erasmus
  wishes to disallow προορισθέντος 'marked out *beforehand, pre*destined' as an
  alternative reading.
4 Origen *Comm in Rom* 1.5 PG 14 849A
5 On the identification of the translator (Rufinus), see the annotation on 3:5 ('is
  God unfair who inflicts wrath') n11.
  Origen was a Greek-speaker, and citations from the Latin Bible were therefore
  unexpected in his work. Erasmus surmises that these were added by the
  translator, but grants that Origen might well have sought out the Latin
  manuscripts for himself. On the extent to which Rufinus changed the text of
  Origen see the annotation on 3:5 (cited above) n14.
6 Evidently a reference to the *Hexapla*, in which Origen attempted to establish
  a text of the Bible in a comparison of the Septuagint with other Greek
  translations of the Old Testament and by reference to the original Hebrew.
  See Pierre Nautin *Origène: sa vie et son oeuvre* (Paris 1977) 303–61; and, for a
  briefer account, Trigg *Origen* 82–6.
7 Erasmus refers to the *recentiores*, the scholastics of the Middle Ages, as
  opposed to the writers of the patristic period, the ancients (*vetustiores*).
  For Erasmus' attitude to Thomas Aquinas and the 'moderns,' see Rummel
  Erasmus' 'Annotations' 74–85 and n109.
8 Of the classical languages Thomas knew only Latin. Erasmus alludes here to
  his failure to obtain a knowledge of the languages prized by the humanists,
  Greek especially, but also Hebrew. Cf the annotation on 4:17 ('that I have
  made you the father of many nations').

9 Proteus is the old man of the sea who transformed himself into different shapes to escape those who tried to lay hold of him to compel him to tell them the unknown. He appears in *Odyssey* 4.384–570, and Virgil *Georgics* 4.387–529. See *Adagia* II ii 74, III iv 1.

10 Thomas Aquinas *Super Rom lect* cap 1 lectio 3.43–57. Thomas uses the various terms cited by Erasmus to explain the implications of *praedestinare*. This in turn leads to an analysis of the terms *destinare* and *praedestinare* to discover the breadth of applicability they enjoy (ie the relationships they imply): *destinare* can imply both mission and purpose, including the end ordained. *Praedestinare* is not applied to natural constitutions (eg one is not 'predestined' to have hands) but to the use made of something. Christ was predestined not in his eternal nature as Son of God, but to the end ordained that he should manifest power as the Son of God.

11 Origen *Comm in Rom* 1.5 PG 14 849A

12 Jerome *Commentarius in epistulam ad Ephesios* 1 (on 1:5) PL 26 (1883) 478B–C

13 An objection countered by Thomas Aquinas, who also quotes Origen's solution (*Super Rom lect* cap 1 lectio 3.49–50)

14 Thomas Aquinas (see n10 above) had accepted 'send' as a common meaning of *destinare*, and attempted to illustrate the meaning from the Vulgate of 1 Macc 1:14.

15 See the annotation on Rom 8:29 ('whom he foreknew') for a further discussion of the sense of futurity implied in ὁρίζειν-*destinare*.

16 Or perhaps ... type.] Added in *1519*

17 Origen *Comm in Rom* 1.5 PG 14 849B. Origen-Rufinus (cf n5 above) seeks to show that in spite of the Latin witnesses, the meaning here is properly conveyed only by the Latin *destinare*, since *praedestinare* can refer only to those who do not yet exist; but it is blasphemy to say there was a time when the Son did not exist. The images of the bride destined for a son and of a son destined for theology belong to Erasmus' exposition of Origen. Frans Titelmans responded with the image of the mother who predestines her unborn son to literature, then 'destines' him to a teacher. In this analogy, Erasmus countered, 'destine' merely means 'send' (*Responsio ad collationes* LB IX 969C–E).

18 Ambrosiaster *Comm in Rom* 1:4 (1). The two words *ut manifestaretur* 'that he might be revealed' appear in Ambrosiaster as a single word, the infinitive *manifestari* 'to be revealed.' The word, however, is not in the biblical text Ambrosiaster quotes, but belongs to his own exposition of the text.

19 some things] Added in *1519*; in *1516*, 'they'

20 Cf Thomas Aquinas *Super Rom lect* cap 1 lectio 3.50: 'But since all Latin Scriptures have in common "who was predestined" some have wanted to explain this in a different way, according to the scriptural manner of saying that something is done when it becomes known. Thus, after his resurrection, the Lord says in the last chapter of Matthew, "All power has been given to me" [28:18], since after the resurrection it became known that such power had been given to him from eternity.'

21 For Erasmus' definition of ὅρος here see Theophylact, who, in explaining this passage, says that a 'ὅρος is a judgment, a vote, a decision of the court' (*Expos in Rom* 1:4 PG 124 341A). For the allusion, immediately following, to the grammarians, see LSJ, who cite Dionysius Thrax and

Apollonius Dyscolus as witnesses for ἡ ὁριστική used to refer to the indicative mood.

22 As I said] Added in *1519*. See n1 above and the reference there to PG 118 325B–C.

23 So far ... work of Theophylact.] Added in *1519*

24 Theophylact *Expos in Rom* 1:4 PG 124 341A. The 1529 Porsena edition (cf n25 below) has *iudicatus* 'judged' for *indicatus* 'disclosed.' Cf the text immediately below, where Erasmus translates the Greek κριθέντος by *iudicati* 'judged.'

25 We know that for his first edition of the New Testament (*1516*) Erasmus had used a Greek manuscript of the Gospels that contained the commentary of Theophylact (died c 1108), archbishop of Ochrida (modern Ohrid, Yugoslavia), seat of the Bulgarian Orthodox patriarchate. Erasmus found the manuscript in the Dominican library at Basel. It is possible that he also consulted Theophylact's commentary on the Pauline Epistles, likewise present in that library, for there are several references to 'Vulgarius' in the *1516* annotations on Romans. When he was preparing his second edition (*1519*) in Louvain during 1517 and 1518, Erasmus used a Latin version of Theophylact's commentary on the Pauline Epistles falsely attributed to Athanasius. This version, made by Porsena, was first published in Rome in 1477, with subsequent editions in Erasmus' lifetime (1519, 1529); for the 1529 edition see the annotation on 5:12 ('in whom [or, in which] all have sinned') n54. Though Erasmus suspected that the work was a commentary of Theophylact, it was evidently not until May of 1518, when he returned to the Dominican library in Basel, which possessed a Greek manuscript of it, that he was able to compare Porsena's translation with the Greek and verify that the translation of 'Athanasius' was in fact the commentary of Theophylact. In his first edition, Erasmus had called the author of these commentaries 'Vulgarius' rather than Theophylact. He later claimed that the mistake had arisen from the poor condition of the manuscript of the Gospels, which had a parchment leaf attached to the cover with the words (barely legible, he said) *Vulgarius* [ie Bulgarius] *archiepiscopus super evangelia quattuor*; see ASD IX-2 130:435–7 and LB IX 311D–E; also Ernst Staehelin 'Die Vaterübersetzungen Oekolampads' *Schweizerische theologische Zeitschrift* 33 (1916) 64–6. In *1519*, though the name 'Vulgarius' is used in the annotations, the correct name appears on the title-page of the volume containing Erasmus' text of the New Testament (Ep 846 n9), and in 1522 the name was systematically corrected in the annotations (see Translators' Note xvi above).
   For further details see H.J. de Jonge *Apologia ad annotationes Stunicae* ASD IX-2 92–3:64n, 192–3:493n, and 131:43n; also Rummel *Erasmus' 'Annotations'* 36–7, 67–8.

26 His words ... translations suggest.] The remainder of the annotation was added in *1527*.

27 Chrysostom *Hom in Rom* 1.2 PG 60 397

28 Chrysostom *Hom in Rom* 1.2 PG 60 397–8

1:4 [ER *cum potentia* 'with power']
   [VG] *in virtute* 'in power';[1] ἐν δυνάμει. [The Translator] has rendered this correctly if only we understand it correctly. For the Latin word is ambiguous.

Sometimes it is taken as the opposite of vice, and corresponds to the Greek ἀρετή [virtue]; occasionally it is the contrary of weakness. Accordingly, I have preferred elsewhere[2] to translate it as *potentia* [ability, power] or *potestas* [authority, power]; for δύναμις [ability, power] is derived from δύναμαι [I am able].

By a wonderful plan, Paul has opposed contraries to contraries. For first he set in contrast 'Paul' with Saul; he set 'a servant of Jesus Christ' in contrast with the servitude of the Mosaic law; an 'apostle called' with those who were taking the office upon themselves; 'set apart for the gospel' with the Pharisaism that he professed before. Thus far he has commended himself and the office he filled. The words that follow relate to the commendation of Christ, who was promised not by just anyone, but by God himself; and promised not through just anyone but through his own prophets, that is, men who were true and inspired by God; and not with[3] just any instruments, but in the Holy Scriptures. Then with words wonderful in their suggestive power, he describes the double nature of Christ in the same *hypostasis*:[4] concerning the man, he says he 'was made,' so that you may understand that something which was not came into existence; concerning the divinity he says 'he was shown.' To the former clause he adds 'according to the flesh,' whose companions are weakness and impurity – hence: 'The spirit is willing, but the flesh is weak.'[5] And the desires of the flesh are called affections that incite us to sins.[6] Accordingly, he set in contrast to the flesh the power of God and the spirit of sanctification, that is, power in contrast to weakness, holiness to uncleanness. [Christ] assumed, therefore, our flesh; and he demonstrated his power, above all by the fact that through his own power he rose from the dead, and the life which by his own will he had laid down at his death he received back again in his own good time. Further, because mortality belongs to the flesh, to this, too, [Paul] opposed the resurrection of the dead, which is immortality.

Now,[7] with respect to the phrase ἐν δυνάμει, that is, 'in power,' I thought I should point out that the preposition 'in' is sometimes used in the Gospels and the Epistles of the apostles in almost the same sense as 'through,'[8] so that the meaning is 'in the power of God,' that is, 'through the divine power,' or[9] 'from the power,' as Chrysostom interprets.[10] That he was able to die was [an inheritance] received from David; that he was able to make us immortal, he received from the Father.

1 As the annotation reveals, Erasmus' preference for *potentia* arises from the ambiguity of *virtus*. When Erasmus refers in his discussion to the biblical term, however, he uses the Vulgate translation, not his own, on the understanding that *virtus* is being read as 'power.' Accordingly, we have

found distinction in translation impractical and we have throughout this
annotation rendered both *virtus* and *potentia* as 'power.'

2 See, for example, Erasmus' translation of Luke 4:36; Rom 1:16, 15:13; Heb
7:16. Even when, as frequently occurs, Erasmus retains the Vulgate *virtus*
in his translation (cf eg Luke 1:17, 35; Acts 1:8, 4:7; 1 Cor 4:20; 2 Cor 4:7),
he appears to be conscious of the ambiguity of the Latin *virtus*, as his
annotations on Acts 1:8 (*accipietis virtutem*) and 2 Cor 4:7 (*ut sublimitas*) show,
where he notes, as in this annotation on Rom 1:4, that *virtus* must not be
understood as 'virtue,' but as 'strength.' Cf the annotation on 1:16 ('for it is
the power of God').

3 Though LB prints *nec in quibuslibet instrumentis*, all editions consulted read
nec id quibuslibet instrumentis.

4 Erasmus retains (though transliterating) the Greek term authoritative since
its adoption by the Council of Chalcedon in 451 to express the unity of
Christ's person in two natures. For the term, see J.N.D. Kelly *Early Christian
Creeds* 3rd ed (New York 1972) 240–50 and Frances M. Young *From Nicaea to
Chalcedon* (Philadelphia 1983) passim.

5 Cf Mark 14:38; Matt 26:41.

6 Cf Thomas Aquinas *Summa theologiae* pars prima secundae, quaest 77 art 5.
Thomas shows that the concupiscence of the flesh, the concupiscence of the
eyes, and pride of life may be appropriately described as 'passions' that are
the cause of sin. See also CWE 42 10 n30.

7 *Vero*, in 1535 only. In all other editions, *verbo* 'in a word,' which, if not a
printer's error, is to be taken with the verb 'I thought I should point out in a
word'

8 For cases in point, and with significance for Erasmus' New Testament
translation, see Robert D. Sider 'Χάρις and Derivatives in the Biblical
Scholarship of Erasmus' in *Diakonia: Studies in Honor of Robert T. Meyer* ed
Thomas Halton and Joseph P. Williman (Washington 1986) 245–6.

9 or ... interprets] Added in 1527. Before 1527 the preceding phrase ('through
the divine power') had been expressed as 'through the power of the divinity,'
changed to 'divine power' in 1527.

10 Cf Chrysostom *Hom in Rom* 1.2 PG 60 397: 'From the wonders he wrought,
he gave proof of his great power, for that is the meaning of "in power."'

**1:4 [ER *secundum spiritum sanctificationis* 'according to the spirit of
sanctification']**

[VG] *per spiritum sanctificationis* 'through the spirit of sanctification.'[1]
Thomas points out that there were those who twisted these words to apply
to the clause concerning the Incarnation, 'who was made from the seed
of David,' and this not by common physical intercourse, but through the
spirit of sanctification from which that marvellous progeny was conceived.
But this opinion is too absurd even to deserve refutation. Hence, I shall not
exert myself to knock down what even Thomas himself has cast aside.[2]

The reader should be advised that idioms of this type are peculiar to
the apostles, so that for disobedient sons they say 'sons of disobedience;'

for a stumbling-stone, 'a rock of offence.'[3] Thus here also Paul[4] has said 'the spirit of sanctification' for 'the sanctifying spirit.' But what Origen records here of his distinction among the flesh, the soul, and the spirit,[5] while it was nicely said in its proper place,[6] in this passage is rather foreign and forced.

1 From *1519* to *1535* the four annotations following the preceding one on 'in power' appeared in the order found here: 1/ 'through the spirit of sanctification,' 2/ 'of Jesus Christ our Lord,' 3/ 'grace and apostleship,' 4/ 'from the resurrection of the dead of Jesus Christ.' In *1516* the order was 4, 1, 2, 3. The arrangement of LB (1, 4, 2, 3) places the annotations in the order of the words of the biblical text.

2 Thomas Aquinas *Super Rom lect* cap 1 lectio 3.58–9. Thomas offers two interpretations: 1/ that Christ is Son of God is seen from the fact that he gives the sanctifying Spirit; 2/ Christ, through the Holy Spirit, was conceived in the Virgin's womb. He adds that both interpretations are possible, but the former is the better.

3 For expressions of this type, see Eph 2:2 and 5:6 ('sons of distrust'); Col 3:6 ('sons of unbelief'); Rom 9:33; and 1 Pet 2:8 ('rock of offence'). In his own translation Erasmus generally renders these in the appropriate Latin idiom, eg Eph 5:6, *filii inobedientes* 'disobedient sons' for the Vulgate's *filii diffidentiae* 'sons of distrust,' though he retains the biblical idiom in Rom 9:33.

4 Paul has said] Added in *1519*

5 Origen *Comm in Rom* 1.5 PG 14 849C–850B. Origen says that while flesh and spirit are both mentioned here, soul is omitted, since it is an intermediary between the two and becomes identified with that to which it joins itself – in the case of Christ, with spirit.

6 Cf Origen *De principiis* 3.4.1 PG 11 319C–320B and Erasmus *Enchiridion* CWE 66 51–4, where Erasmus illustrates Origen's distinction.

1:4 [ER *Iesus Christus dominus noster* 'Jesus Christ our Lord']
[VG] *Iesu Christi domini nostri* 'of Jesus Christ our Lord.' This, too, reader, you will find in Paul, as Ambrose[1] has also noted, and likewise in the other apostles: they usually[2] attribute the term 'God' to the Father, 'Lord' to Christ,[3] although either term suits either of them equally, since[4] the same dominion belongs to both Father and Son.

1 as Ambrose ... noted] Added in *1519*

2 usually] Added in *1519*

3 Cf Ambrosiaster *Comm in Rom* 1:7 (2): 'He calls God our Father on account of origin, because all things are from him. Christ, however, he calls Lord, because we have been made sons of God redeemed by his blood.'

4 since ... Son] Added in *1527*

1:5 [ER *gratiam ac muneris apostolici functionem* 'grace and the fulfilment of the apostolic task']
[VG] *gratiam et apostolatum* 'grace and apostleship'; χάριν καὶ ἀποστολήν.

'Grace,' too, is a Pauline word, a word Paul repeatedly emphasizes, desiring to exclude carnal[1] reliance on the Mosaic law. In Greek, however, χάρις sometimes means 'a kindness' that is conferred without recompense – whence also the verb χαρίζεσθαι 'bestow'[2] or 'give freely'; sometimes 'favour,' for example, 'you have found gratiam [favour] with God';[3] sometimes 'an obligation for an act of kindness,' for example, ἔχω χάριν [I owe thanks, am grateful], οἶδα χάριν [I am grateful], καὶ [and] μεμνήσομαι χάριν [I will show gratitude].[4]

Now I am aware that there have been some who are offended by the word apostolatus [apostleship], which sounds unpleasant to Latin ears, and who prefer to retain the Greek word ἀποστολή [apostolē].[5] I would readily subscribe to their view if as many people understood apostolē as apostolatus. In addition, I see that Christian writers, under compulsion, I suppose, have retained this form in many expressions: clericatus, diaconatus, episcopatus.[6] I have translated 'the fulfilment of the apostolic task,' so no one will think that Paul means an office with rank. For just as ἐπισκοπή [bishopric] is the actual fulfilment of the duties of the episcopate, so also ἀποστολή is the actual fulfilment of the duties of the apostolate.[7]

By grace[8] here he means that he was called back from error; and not only called back, but also chosen to call, with authority, others to the grace of the gospel.

1 carnal] Added in 1527
2 'bestow,' or 'give freely'] Added in 1519
3 Luke 1:30; Erasmus explicates the sense of 'favour' more fully in the paraphrase on this verse. See also the annotation on Luke 1:28 (ave gratia plena).
4 The first two idioms are common in Greek literature (see χάρις II 2 in LSJ). For the latter see Euripides Alcestis 299, and the note there in the edition by A.M. Dale (Oxford 1954).
5 These persons are unidentified.
6 The frequency of apostolatus, clericatus, episcopatus in late antique and medieval Latin is attested in Niermeyer. The words frequently imply office, status, or dignity; for the range of meanings, see the words in Niermeyer.
7 In his response to Titelmans, Erasmus distinguished between those who merely hold office and those who carry out the tasks required by their office. By his translation he tried to suggest that the Greek implied the latter (see Responsio ad collationes LB IX 970B–C).
8 By grace ... gospel.] Added in 1527

1:4 [ER ex eo quod resurrexit e mortuis Iesus Christus 'in that he rose from the dead, Jesus Christ']
[VG] ex resurrectione mortuorum Iesu Christi 'from the resurrection of the dead of Jesus Christ.' This passage can be read in a variety[1] of ways. I

shall set forth all the ways simply, as is my purpose in this work; the right to judge and the power to choose will belong to the reader. The ancient commentators seem generally to have followed the first interpretation, where the meaning is this: that the divine power and the spirit of sanctification had been demonstrated by the fact that many bodies of the saints arose with Christ, as the evangelist Matthew has recounted.[2] I am not strongly opposed to this view, particularly because I see that Origen did not disapprove,[3] while Jerome actually approved of it,[4] especially since Paul writing to the Colossians[5] calls Christ the 'first-born from among the dead'[6] and in the First[7] Epistle to the Corinthians calls him 'the first-fruits of those who sleep.' Above all [is the consideration] that there is the same resurrection of the head and of the members, so that (as Origen writes) just as the glory of Christ in a certain sense is complete only when the members of the whole body are brought together, so likewise his resurrection is completed only when the rest of the members also are united with their head.[8] Therefore in Christ resurrection made a beginning, and hope was offered to the members. In this way we understand that the resurrection 'of the dead of Jesus Christ' is the same as that of Christ himself. In any case, what Paul writes to the Corinthians, 'But now Christ has risen, the first fruits of those who sleep,' does not apply only to those very few who had risen at that time when the tombs were opened, but to all the members of Christ in whom Paul is trying to inspire a hope of resurrection through the fact that Christ himself arose. For it is not reasonable that the head – and such a head – since he lives and reigns, will desert his own members.

In the first place, however, I believe it is clear that Paul intends to persuade [his readers] that Christ was a man who sacrificed himself for us, and is also God, by whose power we must be made holy and will gain immortality. And in passing he touches on the principal proofs, namely, the Davidic descent; then the death, which necessarily preceded the resurrection; then the resurrection from the dead, which is the hinge on which our entire faith hangs. Moreover, Paul never elsewhere in his Epistles mentioned these dead who rose with Christ (although he very often tries to build up the resurrection of the dead); nor, for that matter, have any of the writers of the Gospels except Matthew, and even he touches upon it as it were in passing, with few words and unexplained,[9] [not revealing] either who they were who had risen or to whom they appeared. In saying this, I would not be understood to imply that the reliability of Matthew, who tells the story, is less certain than if they all had reported the same thing – for we do not put the reliability of the Gospel writers to the same test as that of other historians; but rather because it is probable that if this story had specific relevance to proving Christ's divinity, the other Gospel writers would not have omitted a matter of such great importance, especially since they were nowhere more diligent than in establishing[10] the evidence for the resurrection.[11]

This is not to mention, meanwhile, that the resurrection of these saints appears from Matthew's account to have preceded the resurrection of Christ. For thus we read in Matthew: 'But Jesus crying out again gave up his spirit. And behold, the veil of the temple was torn in two from top to bottom, and the earth was shaken, and the rocks were split, and the tombs were opened, and many bodies of saints, who had been sleeping, arose, and going out from the tombs after the resurrection came into the holy city and appeared to many' [27:50–3]. And it appears more clearly from the original Greek, as I indicated [in my comments] on that passage,[12] that these words, 'after the resurrection,' are to be taken with what follows, that is, with the phrase[13] 'appeared to many,' or at least with what immediately precedes, 'going out from the tombs,' so that you understand that at once, at his very death, the bodies of the dead came back to life, but did not appear until after the resurrection of Christ.[14] Thus just as John was a forerunner of the preaching and passion of Christ, so these were πρόδρομοι [forerunners][15] of the resurrection. (I am not unaware that Jerome and with him many other interpreters are of the opinion that the tombs had merely been opened at Christ's death but that no one arose until his resurrection was completed. I readily yield to his authority. But if anyone weighs carefully Matthew's actual words, he will discover that this interpretation is rather distorted.)[16] Moreover, if anyone is worried that Christ is not 'the first-fruits of those who sleep,' as Paul wrote, what will he say of the fact that Lazarus and many others[17] as well came back to life before Christ [arose]?[18] But, [he will reply], those arose to die again; these [whom Paul mentions] will live forever. I concede that there is some point to this distinction. But even if we grant that those arose before [Christ arose], still, he will be the 'first-fruits of those who sleep' who was the initiator and author of all resurrection, through whom even those came back to life who were resurrected before him. I will not, however, argue over this. It is more to the point of our discussion that since Paul wished, incidentally and in passing, to assert the divinity and power of Christ, he ought rather, I should think,[19] to have adduced the resurrection of Christ himself than that of others about whom the Romans had possibly heard nothing; and just as he had pointed to the nativity of Christ, in order to show by it that Christ was a man, so he would point to his resurrection also, through which he was revealed the Son of God. These words, therefore, must be understood to refer either to the total resurrection which began in Christ, or to the resurrection of Christ himself.

A second reading, approved, I see, by Lorenzo Valla, a man of very shrewd judgment, comes quite close to this sense. On this reading, the Vulgate's genitive 'of Jesus Christ' is turned into an ablative.[20] For the Greek genitive, Ἰησοῦ Χριστοῦ [Jesus Christ], can refer to either of two phrases: either to 'the dead' [of Jesus Christ]; or to what has preceded, περὶ τοῦ υἱοῦ αὐτοῦ [...] Ἰησοῦ Χριστοῦ, that is, 'concerning his Son [...] Jesus Christ' – so that after the hyperbaton (a figure Paul often uses),[21] [the Greek genitive] is rendered by 'Jesus Christ' [in the ablative].[22] In fact, I am so far from disapproving of this opinion of Valla that I wonder that neither Origen, nor Chrysostom, nor Theophylact,[23] nor Augustine, nor Ambrose ever thought of anything like it, especially since the passage caused them some distress. For Augustine[24] realized the difficulty – that [the words] 'of Jesus Christ' seemed to be added here in such a way that the 'Son of God' was one person and 'Jesus Christ' another; he discussed this matter in his exposition of the sixty-seventh Psalm.[25] But we shall escape this difficulty if we follow the reading of Lorenzo [Valla]. Others[26] cure the passage by saying that this repetition of the same phrase follows Hebraic idiom, for Hebrew repeats a proper noun in place of a pronoun; for example, 'Moses did as the Lord commanded Moses' in place of 'as the Lord commanded him.'[27]

The third reading holds that 'of Jesus Christ' is in the genitive case but refers only to the resurrection[28] [of Christ], not to the other dead; not that we would exclude them from the resurrection, but we are considering what Paul means here. For the fact that 'of the dead' is added does not require that we understand it of the dead other than Christ. But since the Latin word[29] resurrectio and the Greek word ἀνάστασις were ambiguous (for one also 'rises' who has been sitting or lying down, and those ἀνίστανται [rise] who wish to express an opinion in the senate[30]) he added 'of the dead' so that the passage would not be ambiguous. Therefore these two words, resurrectio mortuorum [resurrection of the dead], setting out a single idea in a kind of circumlocution, refer together to [the phrase] 'of Jesus Christ.' Thus the sense here would be this: 'Just as he was made man, born of David according to the flesh, so he was revealed Son of God, in the power of God through the spirit of sanctification – revealed, I say, by the fact that he rose from the dead, which indeed belongs to God alone.' Moreover, if anyone is detained by this concern, that on our interpretation the preposition ἐξ would have to be added: ἐξ ἀναστάσεως ἐκ τῶν νεκρῶν Ἰησοῦ Χριστοῦ [from the resurrection from the dead of Jesus Christ] one can reply that the preposition ['from'], which has preceded [resurrection], can easily be supplied [before 'the dead'], especially since it is a matter of repeating the same preposition, which might seem to have been omitted for this very reason;[31] besides, in Greek prepositions are very often omitted, especially ἐν, σύν, κατά, ἐξ, ἀπό [in, with, down, out of, from] – and this would be easier here because ἀνάστασις [resurrection] in itself has the force of the preposition, and implies motion *from* some place. In words of this kind, Latin writers also not infrequently omit a preposition, if they like, as in *surrexit terra* and *surrexit a terra* [arose from the earth], *deiecit caelo* and *deiecit e caelo* [cast down from the sky]. Finally, if one takes [the words] 'resurrection of the dead' together, as we showed above, there would indeed be no need for any preposition, since[32] the two expressions are used for a single one.

But as for our translation 'Jesus Christ,' in the nominative case: first, it does not change Paul's meaning at all, and yet we avoid two difficulties at once, namely, the ambiguity of the language and the problem of the hyperbaton. Otherwise it could have been rendered literally as follows: 'Concerning his Son born from the seed of David according to the flesh, revealed the Son of God, in power, according to the spirit of sanctification, from the resurrection of the dead, Jesus Christ our Lord.'[33]

But I[34] would like the careful reader to consider this, too, whether here ἀνάστασις [resurrection] can be taken transitively, with the sense conveyed, for example, in the phrase 'by resuscitating the dead.' In fact Chrysostom and his imitator Theophylact[35] hint at something like this when they say: 'It was Christ first of all and alone who raised himself, and from this evidence above all it is clear that he was the Son of God.'[36] Augustine no doubt correctly pointed out that 'from the resurrection of the dead' must refer not to the immediately preceding words but to what was said earlier, 'who was predestined.'[37] But 'was predestined' makes an awkward connection with 'from the resurrection,' unless [instead] we translate 'was revealed.' Augustine also interprets 'predestined from the dead' to mean 'predestined to this, that he should rise first,' so that the preposition *prae* [before] refers to the order of resurrection.[38] But the actual words of Paul do not sufficiently convey this meaning.

And now[39] to conclude with a summary of this long discussion: if we read 'of Jesus Christ' [in the genitive] there are three possibilities, first that we take ἀνάστασις as active or neutral, and this in two parallel senses, either that the Father is understood to have raised the Son from the dead, or that the Son raised himself; for either sense is pious. Second, that 'resurrection' be taken as passive, and that we have in mind the dead who are to be raised[40] at the voice of the Son of God, just as he also raised Lazarus as well as others. And yet nothing prevents 'resurrection' here from being taken to mean the universal resurrection, which is that of both the head and the whole mystic body. Finally, the genitive 'of the dead' refers to Jesus Christ, for those who die in faith are said to be 'his dead,' so that you understand that the reference here is to the resurrection of the righteous alone. [The words] 'the resurrection of the dead' can also be read closely together to mean 'by the resurrection-from-the-dead,' so that [the phrase] 'of Jesus Christ' relates to ἀνάστασις [resurrection], not to the dead. But if we read 'Jesus Christ' [in the ablative], then the reference goes back to the preceding words, 'concerning his Son Jesus Christ who was predestined' etc.[41] I have carried on this discussion longer than the character of this work perhaps allowed; but I have done so advisedly, lest anyone should complain that I have changed the reading of this passage rashly against the opinion of all previous writers. As for the rest, I have fulfilled the task of an informer, leaving judgment to the reader.[42]

1 a variety] First in 1527; from 1516 to 1522, 'in three ways'

2 On this interpretation 'the dead of Jesus Christ' are the saints of Matt 27:53, whose resurrection showed, by the power it implied, that Jesus was the Son of God.

3 Origen speaks of the 'bodies of the saints that came out of the tomb' (Matt 27:52) as being, with Christ, the first-fruits from the dead. For the context see n8 below.

4 Jerome Commentarii in evangelium Matthaei 27:52 PL 26 222A: 'Many bodies of saints arose, pointing to the Lord's resurrection. But though the tombs were opened, they did not rise before the Lord arose, so that he should be the first-born of the resurrection among the dead.'

5 writing to the Colossians] Added in 1519. See Col 1:18.

6 the dead] In 1516 only there followed here the additional words 'and first-born of many brothers' – a reference to Rom 8:29.

7 in the First . . . calls him] Added in 1519. See 1 Cor 15:20.

8 Origen Comm in Rom 1.6 PG 14 852B–C. The image of 'head and members' (for which see Eph 1:19–23) belongs to Erasmus' interpretation of Origen. Origen asks whether the 'first-born' or 'first-fruits' from the dead refers only to Christ, or whether others are not with Christ the 'first-born.' He thinks it is likely that Christ shares the privilege of being 'first-born' with those who 'sit with him in heavenly places [Eph 2:6]' or with those who came forth from the tombs at his death; it is perhaps such as these whom the Apostle calls the 'church of the first-born' (Heb 12:23).

9 unexplained] non explicatis, first in 1535; from 1516 to 1527, non explicans 'not explaining' either who . . .

10 establishing] Added in 1519

11 Edward Lee accused Erasmus of undermining with these remarks the veracity of the writers of the Gospels, an accusation he vigorously denied; cf Responsio ad annotationes Lei LB IX 212C–213C.
   Lee was an Englishman who had gone to Louvain to study Greek. Erasmus received from him some notes for use in preparing the second edition of his New Testament. Bitterness developed between the two men; Lee published his notes in Annotationum libri duo (February 1520), which Erasmus answered with Responsio ad annotationes Lei (April 1520). See Contemporaries II 311–14; also Ep 1061 and the introductions to Ep 1037 and Ep 1080.

12 See the annotation on Matt 27:52 (*et multa corpora quae dormierant*), where Erasmus, citing Jerome, Chrysostom, and Origen, argues that according to the phrasing of the Greek, it appears that the bodies revived immediately upon Christ's death but did not appear until his resurrection. This interpretation is incorporated into his paraphrase on the verse. (For the citation of Chrysostom and Jerome see nn14, 16 below.)

13 the phrase] Added in *1519*

14 Erasmus cites Chrysostom to this effect in the annotation on Matt 27:52 (n12 above), though Chrysostom, in his commentary on this verse, is not so explicit; see *In Matthaeum homiliae* 38.2 PG 58 777.

15 Lee, in the work cited above (n11) also objected that those who came from the tombs were not 'forerunners' but 'witnesses' (LB IX 213D).

16 For Jerome see nn4 and 12 above. In his *1516* annotation on Matt 27:52 Erasmus had cited Jerome as evidence that 'arose' meant the same as 'revived,' 'came to life,' since (according to Erasmus) Jerome says the saints arose though they did not appear until after Christ's resurrection. Here, in Rom 1:4, however, Erasmus appears to have noted more carefully Jerome's words that 'though the tombs were opened, the saints did not arise before the Lord arose.' In this respect, he regards Jerome's interpretation as distorted.
For 'other interpreters' see eg Origen on Matt 27:53 in *Series veteris interpretationis commentariorum Origenis in Matthaeum* 139 PG 13 1791C–D.

17 many others] First in *1527*; previously, 'innumerable others'

18 Jerome had cited the case of Lazarus (cf n4 above); for Origen's solution to the problem, cf n8 above.

19 I should think] Added in *1519*

20 Cf Valla *Annot in Rom* 1 (I 855).

21 A figure Erasmus often notes. Hyperbaton refers generally to a transposition of words from their natural order. Here the hyperbaton consists in separating the words 'Jesus Christ our Lord' (end of verse 4; cf RSV) from their antecedent 'concerning his Son' (beginning of verse 3; cf RSV) by a lengthy list of predicates. For the hyperbaton as an aspect of elegant style cf Quintilian 8.6.62–7.

22 Just as the Greek preposition περί 'concerning' is followed by the genitive, the equivalent Latin *de* is followed by the ablative. The Vulgate had translated 'his Son' (verse 3) quite correctly by an ablative, following *de*, and should therefore have also written 'Jesus Christ,' an appositive (verse 4), in the ablative, to read 'concerning his Son ... Jesus Christ.' Instead, it had in verse 4 followed the Greek literally using a Latin genitive for 'Jesus Christ,' thus breaking the grammatical agreement with 'his Son' and inviting the confused reading 'concerning his Son ... of Jesus Christ.'

23 nor Chrysostom nor Theophylact] Added in *1527*

24 For Augustine ... Lorenzo.] Added in *1519*

25 Augustine *Enarrationes in psalmos* 67.13 PL 36 820

26 Others ... commanded *him.*'] Added in *1527*

27 Cf Exod 40:18–19; Lev 8:13.

28 the resurrection] First in *1519*; in *1516*, 'Christ'

29 the Latin word] Added in 1519

30 The practice of 'rising' to speak in council is as old as Homer; cf *Iliad* 1.58, 2.76.

31 Omitted, that is, because the proximity of the preposition 'from' preceding 'resurrection' would lead one to supply the same preposition before 'the dead'

32 since ... single one] Added in 1519

33 In the translation Erasmus made for his New Testament, he had put 'Jesus Christ' in the nominative case, in apposition to the subject of the verb of the last clause of verse 4: 'Concerning his Son ... who was shown to be the Son of God with power from the fact that he rose again from the dead – Jesus Christ our Lord.' In the translation he offers here in the annotation, which he regards as literal in contrast with his own somewhat free translation, Erasmus renders 'Jesus Christ our Lord' in the ablative, in apposition to 'his Son' (verse 3); cf n21 above.

34 But I ... this meaning.] This paragraph was added in 1519, except for the words 'Chrysostom and his imitator,' which were added in 1527.

35 As Erasmus here and elsewhere notes, Theophylact was very much dependent upon Chrysostom for his interpretations. Karl Staab has shown, however, that Theophylact draws little of his exegesis of Chrysostom directly out of his *Homilies*, but rather for the most part from the unknown authors in the ninth and tenth centuries who are represented in the Pseudo-Oecumenius type of Greek catenae on the Pauline Epistles. To be sure, Theophylact supplemented these catenae with some material directly from Chrysostom's *Homilies*; see Karl Staab *Die Pauluskatenen nach den handschriftlichen Quellen Untersucht* (Rome 1926) 234–45; also Rummel *Erasmus' 'Annotations'* 67–8 and n92.

36 Chrysostom *Hom in Rom* 1.2 PG 60 397; Theophylact *Expos in Rom* 1:4 PG 124 341B. While the first clause is a precise translation of Theophylact and Chrysostom, the second part of the sentence appears to be an inference by Erasmus.

37 Augustine *Epistulae ad Romanos inchoata expositio* 1.5 PL 35 2091

38 Augustine ibidem PL 35 2091: 'Christ was "designated" to rise before the rest of the dead.' Cf the annotation on 1:4 ('who was predestined').

39 And now ... etc.] Added in 1527

40 The future passive participle *suscitandos* stresses the passive sense here of 'resurrection'; but the time frame is left ambiguous, presumably to include both those who 'were to be raised' at the cry of Christ before his death and those who 'are to be raised' in the universal resurrection of 'head and members.'
   In this 'passive' sense, the 'resurrection ... of Christ' is understood to refer to those who are resurrected *by Christ*; whereas in the active and neutral sense, the resurrection of Christ refers to his own rising, whether the Father raised him (active) or he raised himself (neutral).

41 The details of Erasmus' summary may obscure its relation to the main exposition. In his exposition Erasmus had discussed three options: 1/ Following the Vulgate reading – 'the resurrection of the dead of Jesus Christ' – we may understand the expression to refer to Christ's own resurrection, ie the resurrection of Jesus Christ from the dead, implying, if taken in an

active sense, that the Father raised Christ; or, if in a neutral sense, that the
Son raised himself. This is identified in the exposition as the 'third reading.'
2/ Following the Vulgate reading – 'the resurrection of the dead of Jesus
Christ' – we may understand the expression in the 'passive' sense to refer to
the dead raised by Jesus Christ, whether those specifically mentioned in the
New Testament who arose at the 'cry of Christ' or all the dead-in-Christ (ie
'his dead'), who will arise at the time of the universal resurrection. This is
the 'first interpretation' of the main exposition. 3/ We may reject the Vulgate
reading and render 'concerning his Son ... Jesus Christ.' This is the solution
of Valla (which Erasmus adopts) and appears as the second reading in the
main exposition.

42 In *Responsio ad collationes* LB IX 969F–970B Erasmus affirms again that he
merely shows here the various senses of which the Greek is capable, without
disapproving of any. He accepts Titelman's proposition that fecundity of
Scripture is good, but contrasts fecundity with obscurity and ambiguity,
which are merely troublesome.
Erasmus says that his role here is that of an *index* – an 'informer.' The Latin
word had both a good and a bad sense: a guide or a witness, and a betrayer
or a spy.

1:5 [ER *ut obediatur fidei* 'that the faith might be obeyed']

[VG] *ad obediendum fidei* 'to the obeying of the faith.' In Greek this is a
noun, not an infinitive, εἰς ὑπακοὴν πίστεως, that is, *ad obedientiam fidei* [to
the obedience of faith]. But since this expression is ambiguous in Latin, the
Translator has clarified it with a gerund, I with a verb: 'that the faith might
be obeyed.' By 'obedience of faith' he means, as Chrysostom explains,[1]
that [faith] is not obtained by a painstaking process of logical reasoning,
but by simple obedience and quiet compliance. And this applies to both
peoples: to the Jews who sought for signs, and to the gentiles who demanded philosophical arguments; and perhaps[2] today it applies to the convoluted labyrinths of the questions of the scholastics concerning those matters of which it is pious to be ignorant.

> 1 as Chrysostom explains] Added in 1527. See Chrysostom *Hom in Rom* 1.3
> PG 60 398.
> 2 and perhaps ... ignorant] Added in 1519. This sentiment is also expressed
> in the *Ratio* (Holborn 297–301). Cf, in addition, the famous portrait of
> theologians as quibblers and wordspinners in the *Moria* CWE 27 126–30.

1:5 [ER *super ipsius nomine* 'regarding his name']

[VG] *pro nomine eius* 'for his name'; ὑπὲρ τοῦ ὀνόματος αὐτοῦ, that is, 'concerning his name' [*de nomine eius*] or 'regarding his name' [*super nomine
eius*]. For the Greek preposition has a double significance (as is true of
many prepositions in Greek), so that [here] the sense is: We have received the task of an apostle for this purpose, that in all nations, not just

among the Jews, the faith that concerns the name of Jesus Christ should be obeyed. The Greek scholia likewise suggest that these words 'concerning his name' refer to the obedience of faith.[1] Theophylact[2] explains ὑπέρ by using περί [concerning]. Nevertheless that outstanding man and my incomparable friend Jacques Lefèvre d'Etaples, whom I never mention except to do him honour, disagrees.[3] To be sure, I strongly approve of his most ardent zeal to restore good literature; I admire his erudition, so varied, and so different from that of the common herd; I sincerely love his unusual cordiality and affability; moreover I revere and greatly praise his singular holiness of life. And yet has there ever been anyone either so learned or careful that from time to time his mind did not wander, or he did not nod, especially when engaged with so many volumes and so many difficulties of interpretation? I should have no doubt that if he reread his own work he would occasionally do what Augustine did in his books.[4] Accordingly, no one should take it as an insult if I disagree with him on a few passages in defending the truth to the utmost of my ability. Not only would I bear with equanimity the same kind of treatment in turn, but I would even consider it the greatest of favours, provided malice is absent. And yet in this passage I certainly do not disapprove of Lefèvre's opinion that the words 'regarding his name' refer to the preceding phrase, 'we have received apostleship,' that is, the task of an apostle and this mission that we are now performing. But [a mission] concerning what? Obviously, concerning the preaching of the name of Jesus. Therefore either interpretation fits well, so well that it is hard to decide which is preferable. Chrysostom[5] in his commentary seems to follow the second interpretation. He explains: 'I was not sent to spin out syllogisms, but to perform the task committed to me.'[6] The Greek[7] reads: εἰς ὑπακοήν, οὐκ εἶπε ζήτησιν καὶ κατακραυγήν, ἀλλὰ ὑπακοήν. οὐδὲ γὰρ ἐπέμφθημέν, φησι, συλλογίζεσθαι, ἀλλ᾽ ὅπερ ἐνεχειρίσθημεν ἀποδοῦναι.

1 Cf Pseudo-Oecumenius *Comm in Rom* 1:5 PG 118 328A. For the 'two senses' of the Greek preposition ὑπέρ (1/ for, on behalf of; 2/ concerning), see BAG 846–7.
2 Theophylact ... περί.] Added in 1535. Cf *Expos in Rom* 1:5 PG 124 341D.
3 Cf Lefèvre *Pauli epistolae* fol 69 verso. Lefèvre retains the Vulgate translation *pro* 'for,' 'on behalf of,' which he connects with 'apostleship': Paul received apostleship 'for his name,' that is, 'in his place and name.'
Jacques Lefèvre d'Etaples (1460–1536) was a leading exponent of Christian humanism in France. After a career teaching philosophy and the liberal arts, he retired in 1508 to take up the study of the Bible (see *Contemporaries* II 315–18). Lefèvre published his commentary on the Pauline Epistles in 1512. His correspondence with Erasmus began in 1514 with a warm and admiring letter to the latter (Ep 315). Erasmus disagreed with Lefèvre's

biblical interpretation not only here but, much more seriously, on Heb 2:7, where the disagreement grew into a public quarrel. It is noteworthy that in spite of the quarrel, Erasmus' warm acclamation of Lefèvre in this 1516 annotation on Rom 1:5 was never modified in the later editions. See Epp 315 introduction and 597:37n, 44n.
4 A reference to the *Retractations*, in which Augustine several years before his death (in 430) reviewed and corrected opinions expressed in earlier writings.
5 Chrysostom ... to me.'] Added in 1527
6 See Chrysostom *Hom in Rom* 1.3 PG 60 398.
7 The Greek ... ἀποδοῦναι.] Added in 1535. The translation that precedes renders only the latter part of the Greek quotation. The first part reads: ' "Unto obedience"; he did not say "unto inquiry and constructive reasoning," but "unto obedience," for I was not sent' etc (reading with Migne κατασκευή 'constructive reasoning,' rather than with Erasmus κατακραυγή, a word that does not appear in LSJ, BAG, or G.W.H. Lampe *A Patristic Greek Lexicon* [Oxford 1961]).

1:6 [ER *quorum de numero estis et vos* 'from whose number are you also'] [VG] *in quibus estis* 'in whom are you'; ἐν οἷς, that is, 'among which' [*inter quas*] or 'from the number of which,' namely, of the nations that have been called. Of the same sort is the phrase *in omnibus gentibus* [in all nations], ἐν πᾶσιν τοῖς ἔθνεσιν, that is, 'among all nations.'[1] Yet I am well aware that Latin authors did sometimes speak according to a Greek idiom. But I have striven for a version that would be clearer. Chrysostom[2] has pointed out that Paul has paid no deference to the Roman masters of the world, but in the reckoning of the gospel he has made them one among the number of other nations.[3]

1 For this expression see eg Deut 30:1 in both the LXX and the Vulgate. For the Greek ἐν, used (as here) in the sense of 'among,' see ἐν I 4 a in BAG.
2 Chrysostom ... nations.] Added in 1527. See Chrysostom *Hom in Rom* 1.3 PG 60 399.
3 For the portrait of the Romans see the annotation on 1:12 ('to be comforted together') below.

1:7 [ER *omnibus qui Romae estis* 'to all of you who are in Rome'] [VG] *omnibus qui sunt Romae* 'to all who are in Rome'; πᾶσι τοῖς οὖσιν ἐν Ῥώμῃ. Since Paul has expressed the Greek verb in the form of a participle, it can be taken as either third or second person – 'to all those who are' or 'to all of you who are.' Literally it means 'to all being at Rome,' but this makes no difference to the sense. And in fact it is customary to write in the third person the name of the one whom we address in a letter: 'Pliny sends greetings to his friend Tacitus.'[1] Up to this point the whole passage has lacked a resolution; now at last the principal period has been completed, and the second part [of the sentence] is begun.

Here one must refute, or rather laugh at, the mistake of those who think that Paul wrote to the Romans in the Roman tongue, just as he wrote to the Hebrews in Hebrew and to the Greeks in Greek.[2] For he was not writing only to the Romans, but to all those who lived in Rome. But at that time virtually all of Greece had flocked to Rome, so that Juvenal calls it a 'Greek city.'[3] Certainly not only Italy, but also Syria, Egypt, Cilicia, and a good part of the world had by then admitted the Greek language.[4] But if he did write in the language of the Romans, Origen complains without cause in his commentary on this Epistle that the Greek style here is involved, obscured by hyperbata, and that due to Cilician idioms some parts are scarcely Greek and have the character not of Greek but[5] of a foreigner's speech.[6]

1 The historian Cornelius Tacitus was frequently the recipient of letters from Pliny; cf eg *Letters* 1.6, 20 and 4.13.

2 Even in antiquity there were those who believed that Paul wrote Hebrew, Greek, and Latin. Jerome, for example, conjectures that Paul may have written the Epistle to the Hebrews in Hebrew, and he accepts the authenticity of the spurious correspondence in Latin between Seneca and Paul (see *De viris illustribus* 5 and 12 PL 23 [1883] 650A and 662A).

3 Juvenal *Satires* 3.60–1

4 Cf the annotation on 1:1 ('Paul') n8 above.

5 but of a foreigner's speech] Added in *1519*

6 Origen *Comm in Rom* praefatio PG 14 833A. Origen notes the difficulty of Paul's speech but does not here attribute the cause to Cilician idioms. Elsewhere Erasmus cites Jerome as one who demonstrated Paul's speech as Cilician; cf the annotation on 1 Cor 4:3 (*aut ab humano die*). See also CWE 42 12 n34.

1:7 [ER VG] **dilectis dei** *'beloved of God'*; ἀγαπητοῖς θεοῦ. This is the word that is frequently translated by *charissimos* [most dear].[1] But in Greek it is not a participle, but a noun, as though you were to say 'friend.' Thus in Greek it joins more naturally with the noun 'God' [in the possessive case].[2]

1 Cf the annotation on 11:28 ('but according to the election most dear').

2 The Latin *dilectis*, a participle, is normally followed by the dative case: dear *to* God.

1:7 [ER VG] *vocatis sanctis* **'called saints'**; κλητοῖς ἁγίοις. I pointed out above that 'called' in this passage is not a participle, but a noun,[1] and has the same force as if you said 'those called to holiness.' For[2] the name of gentiles was hateful to the Jews, because the Jews considered them profane and alien to God and Moses. Therefore Paul refutes this view when he says that the Romans, by right, are counted among the gentiles, but that they are equal to the Jews in that they are loved by the same God and have been called

by the same God to the same holiness. In their own view, the Jews were
holy by birth, were descended from those who were holy, and were born
under the holy Law; but what birth seemed to offer these, the favour and
calling of God offered the gentiles.

What³ he calls 'grace,' however, is spontaneous generosity. First he
had said ἀγαπητοῖς [beloved], then κλητοῖς [called], but since someone can
be called and loved on his own merit he adds 'grace.' Grace given brings
forth forgiveness of sins, which in his customary way he calls 'peace.'⁴ For
sin puts hostility between God and men. He called us, it was not we who
sought him; he loved us first when we were hostile [to him]; he bestowed
the gift of the Spirit upon those who deserved punishment; through the
Spirit, however, he bestowed forgiveness of sins and an abundance of gifts.

1 Cf the annotation on 1:1 ('called an apostle') above.
2 For ... offered the gentiles.] Added in 1519
3 What ... abundance of gifts.] Added in 1527
4 Erasmus' *Paraphrases* frequently reflect the close relation he sees between
grace and peace in the Pauline Epistles. See eg the paraphrases on 1 Cor 1:3
and 1 Pet 1:2.

1:7 [ER *a deo patre nostro et domino Iesu Christo* 'from God our Father
and the Lord Jesus Christ']
[VG] *a deo patre et domino nostro Iesu Christo* 'from God the Father and
our Lord Jesus Christ.' The Greek expression is ambiguous. It can, indeed,
be read: 'from our Father and the Father of the Lord Jesus Christ,' in which
case you would understand that we have the same Father as he; or: 'from
our Father and from the Lord Jesus Christ,' and in this case you would
understand that the grace he invokes for these [the beloved of God] comes
simultaneously from the Father, whom, as I have just said,¹ he customarily
calls 'God' – a word peculiar, as it were [to the Father] – and from the
Son, whom he most often likes to call 'Lord,' but 'God' very rarely.² In fact
in the fifth chapter of this very Epistle he openly calls him a man: 'Much
more has the grace of God and of the Lord³ abounded for many in the
grace of one man, Jesus Christ' [5:15]. And in the Acts of the Apostles Peter
calls him a man – 'a man approved by God' [2:22]; likewise Paul before
the Athenians: 'the man he has appointed' [17:31]. I incline to the second
reading especially⁴ because it has been noted both by Ambrose⁵ and by
Didymus in the second book of his work *On The Holy Spirit*, but in such
a way that this form of expression detracts from neither the lordship of
the Father, nor the deity of the Son: 'For in the same way that the Father
is Lord, and the Son is God, the Holy Spirit is also called Lord' – such
were Didymus' words.⁶ My aim⁷ in this annotation is nothing else than

to point out the character of apostolic speech. Tertullian makes the same observation in the book he wrote against Praxeas. It would be better to quote him directly: 'And so I shall not speak of gods or lords at all, but I follow the Apostle, so that if the Father and Son both must be named, I shall call God "Father," and Jesus Christ I shall name "Lord." Christ alone, however, I shall be able to call "God," as also does the Apostle: "From whom is Christ, who is," he says, "God above all blessed for ever."[8] For the ray of the sun, too, taken by itself, I shall call the sun, but when naming the sun, whose ray it is, I shall not straightway also call the ray "the sun." For even if I make two suns, nevertheless I shall count both the sun and its ray as much two things and two forms of a single and undivided substance, as God and his Word, as Father and Son.'[9]

1 as I have just said] Added in 1519. For the reference see the annotation on 1:4 ('of Jesus Christ our Lord').
2 very rarely ... he has appointed'] Added in 1519. In 1516 instead of 'God very rarely' Erasmus wrote, 'God, so far as I recall, nowhere.'
3 Erasmus misquotes. Both the Greek text and Vulgate read 'the grace of God and the gift.'
4 especially ... Didymus' words] Added in 1519
5 Ambrosiaster *Comm in Rom* 1:7 (3)
6 Didymus of Alexandria *De spiritu sancto* 29 PG 39 1060A. Didymus, also called 'the Blind' (c 313–98), was made head of the catechetical school at Alexandria by Athanasius. Inasmuch as he had been influenced by Origen, he was condemned in 553, and much of his writing disappeared. In his view of the Trinity, however, he followed Nicene orthodoxy. In *Apologia adversus monachos* LB IX 1025E Erasmus cites these words from this annotation as evidence of his own orthodox Trinitarianism.
7 My aim ... Son.'] The remaining portion of the annotation was added in 1527.
8 Rom 9:5
9 Tertullian *Adversus Praxean* 13.9–10 CCL 2 1175–6. Erasmus follows P in reading *nam etsi soles duos faciam* 'for even if I make two suns.' M and F, however, read *nam et soles duos faciam* 'for then I would make two suns' (cf ibidem 1176:74); in this case the clause is to be taken with the preceding sentence.

1:8 [ER VG] *primum quidem gratias ago* 'first[1] indeed I give thanks.' Who can sufficiently admire the care of Origen in examining sacred literature? This, too, exercised the man: since Paul here says 'first,' what can be the second part that corresponds to this? And he questions whether it follows further on: 'And I would not have you ignorant, brethren.'[2] But in the beginning of any argument it would perhaps not be absurd to say 'first,' even if you should add no specific 'second.'

1 First ... second.'] The entire annotation was added in 1519.
2 Rom 1:13. Cf Origen *Comm in Rom* 1.9 PG 14 855C.

1:8 [ER *in toto mundo* 'in all the world']

[VG] *in universo mundo* 'in[1] the entire world.' Since the Greek here reads ἐν
ὅλῳ τῷ κόσμῳ 'in all the world,' and according to the Greek commentators
this is a hyperbole for 'in many parts of the world,'[2] to what purpose did
the Latin Translator compound the exaggeration, by saying 'in the entire
world'? For Origen, after pointing out the hyperbole, goes on to philosophize about the world of the angels,[3] and thereby offers a not inelegant
parallel[4] to our own world. But I am happier with the simple and the γνήσια
[legitimate], which reveals the meaning of the Apostle rather than displays
the cleverness of the interpreter.

　　1　in ... interpreter.] The complete annotation was added in *1519*.
　　2　See eg Origen *Comm in Rom* 1.9 PG 14 855A.
　　3　Origen *Comm in Rom* 1.9 PG 14 855A–B. Origen first takes the passage literally
　　　(*simpliciter*), to mean that the faith of the Romans is proclaimed in many
　　　parts of the earth, then 'goes on' to the 'anagogical' meaning, that the faith
　　　of the Romans is also proclaimed in the heavenly world.
　　4　'Parallel' translates *anagoge*, a transliteration in Erasmus' text of the Greek
　　　word. In patristic exegesis *anagoge* referred in general to the deeper, spiritual
　　　sense as opposed to the literal. During the early Middle Ages, however,
　　　the word came to be applied to the eschatological interpretation of biblical
　　　passages. Parallel to the eschatological were the allegorical and moral
　　　interpretations, and all three came to be known as the 'spiritual sense'
　　　in contrast to the literal. See H. de Lubac *Exégèse médiévale* part 1-2 (Paris
　　　1959) 418 ff, and, for a brief account, K. Grobel 'History and Principles of
　　　Interpretation' in IDB II 720–1.

1:9 [ER VG] *testis enim mihi est deus* 'for God is witness to me'; μάρτυς γάρ μου
ἐστίν,[1] that is, 'for God is my witness'; yet the Translator's version is good.
He has accommodated Latin idiom rather than follow the Greek expression,
unless he read μοι [*moi*, dative] rather than μου [*mou*, genitive].[2]

　　1　After ἐστίν LB adds ὁ θεός 'God,' but without warrant from the editions
　　　1516–1535.
　　2　If the Translator read the Greek dative μοι, then in translating with the
　　　equivalent Latin dative *mihi* it could be said that he has after all 'followed
　　　the Greek,' even though the result is good Latin idiom.

1:9 [ER *cui colo* 'whom I worship']

[VG] *cui servio* 'whom I serve'; ᾧ λατρεύω, that is, whom I worship. For
[λατρεύω] does not mean the same as the Greek δουλεύω [I serve]; hence
worship offered to divinities or to God is called λατρεία [*latreia*]. The Greeks
think that the word is derived from λα [*la*], a particle that to them signifies vehemence, and τρεῖν [*trein*], which means 'to tremble' or 'to fear.'[1]
Although the Translator has rendered λατρεία elsewhere, at one time by *obsequium*, at another by *servitus*, it would be more correctly rendered by *cultus*

[worship].[2] Paul[3] is suggesting that the mode of religion and worship must be changed, since the Jews were urging that pagans be dragged into the ceremonies of the Mosaic law. Accordingly, though Paul himself had advanced from Moses to Christ and no longer sacrificed beasts, he was nevertheless worshipping the same God by a different ritual, that is, by preaching the gospel of the Son, which was a spiritual worship, and consequently by far the most pleasing to God. For when he says 'in my spirit,' he is excluding corporeal victims. Moreover, with respect to [the phrase] 'in the spirit' the preposition ἐν [in] has been followed by a dative of instrument or means in accordance with Hebrew idiom, as I have frequently shown already.[4]

1 The etymology of the word is uncertain. See λάτρον in Chantraine *Dictionnaire* II 622–3.
2 Though he admits the ambiguity of the word, Erasmus defends *cultus* again in his *Responsio ad collationes* LB IX 970D–E. Cf the annotation on 12:1 ('reasonable service').
Obsequium is used with various meanings: 'compliance,' 'obedience,' 'service'; *servitus* is found in the sense of 'servitude,' 'service.' For λατρεία translated in the Vulgate as *obsequium* see John 16:2; Rom 9:4, 12:1. While *servitus* is not found for λατρεία in the New Testament, the verb *servio* translates λατρεύω here and elsewhere, eg Matt 4:10; Heb 9:9, 12:28.
3 Paul ... already.] This remaining portion of the annotation was added in 1519.
4 Cf the annotation on 1:4 ('in power') and n8 above. For the influence of 'Hebrew idiom' on this construction, see ἐν III 1 in BAG.

1:9 [ER *mentionem vestri* 'mention of you']
[VG] *memoriam vestri* 'remembrance of you'; μνείαν ὑμῶν: Since the Greek word has two meanings ['remembrance' and 'mention'], and since in Latin we do not say *facio memoriam* [I make remembrance], [the Translator] would have more suitably rendered [I make] 'mention' – for 'to pray'[1] is nothing else than to converse with God, in case anyone thinks the expression 'I make mention of you' is somewhat harsh.

1 for 'to pray' ... harsh] Added in 1519

1:10 [ER VG] *si quomodo* 'if by any means'; εἴπως ἤδη ποτέ, that is, 'if in any way now at length' or 'now at last.' For ἤδη [already, now] in Greek sometimes has a force of urgency. Moreover, this heaping up of adverbs and conjunctions, πῶς, ἤδη, ποτέ [somehow, now, at length] expresses a kind of strange and impatient desire and eagerness to hurry, as the Greek scholia also point out.[1]

1 Cf Pseudo-Oecumenius *Comm in Rom* 1:10 PG 118 329B.

1:10 [ER *prosperum iter contingat* 'a prosperous journey should be mine']
[VG] *prosperum iter habeam* 'I may have a prosperous journey.'[1] The Greek
is εὐοδωθήσομαι, a word composed of two parts, εὖ 'well' and ὁδός 'road':
εὐοδόω. One uses this word whenever something turns out according to
one's desires. The same word is used in the first Psalm: 'And all things,
whatever he does, will prosper,' εὐοδωθήσονται [1:3].[2] For Paul suggests
that up to now he has not thus prospered.

> 1 In *1516* this and the next two annotations appeared in the sequence: 1/ 'of
> coming to you,' 2/ 'I may have a prosperous journey,' 3/ 'in the will.' In
> *1519* they assumed the order presented here.
> 2 Evidently recalled from the Septuagint, where the word is κατευοδωθήσεται

1:10 [ER *volente* '(God) willing']
[VG] *in voluntate* 'in the will'; ἐν τῷ θελήματι. We have noted a little above,
and[1] elsewhere as well, that this preposition ἐν [in] is sometimes used to
mean 'through,' a figure of speech borrowed, as I believe, from Hebrew.[2]
Accordingly[3] I have translated 'God willing,' conveying the sense rather
than rendering literally.

> 1 a little above, and] Added in *1519*
> 2 See the annotation on 1:9 ('whom I serve') n4 above.
> 3 Accordingly ... literally.] Added in *1519*

1:10 [ER *ut veniam ad vos* 'that I may come to you']
[VG] *veniendi ad vos* 'of coming to you'; ἐλθεῖν. It would be more correct
to say 'to come' or 'that I may come,' so that the infinitive [to come] may
be joined with the participle δεόμενος [praying], which has just preceded:
'Praying that I may come to you, if ever, God willing, a prosperous journey[1]
should be mine.' For this is the meaning of the Greek words.

> 1 journey] Added in *1519*

1:11 [ER *aliquod impartiar donum* 'that I may impart some gift']
[VG] *aliquid impartiar gratiae* 'that I may impart some grace'; ἵνα τι μεταδῶ
χάρισμα, that is, 'gift,' not χάρις 'grace.' And yet in regard to this term the
Translator has sported in his usual way with variety of expression.[1] For
in some places, he translates [the Greek by] *donum* [gift] as in the passage
'but not as the trespass, so also the gift,' ἀλλ' οὐχ ὡς τὸ παράπτωμα, οὕτως
καὶ τὸ χάρισμα.[2] Elsewhere he retains the Greek word, as though he had
no means of rendering it in Latin: 'Pursue the better *charismata* [gifts],'
ζηλοῦτε δὲ τὰ χαρίσματα τὰ κρείττονα.[3] But I leave it to others to define
the difference between χάρις and χάρισμα. It is clear that χάρις means 'a

kindness' and χαρίζομαι⁴ 'I bestow a kindness' or 'I do as a favour.' From this⁵ is derived the noun χάρισμα; χαρίζομαι [I bestow a kindness] comes from χάρις [kindness], χάρισμα [gift] from κεχάρισμαι [I have bestowed a kindness]. Either word ['kindness' or 'gift'] is applicable when something is given freely or benefits someone.

> 1 Frans Titelmans attacked Erasmus both for his criticism of the Translator's fondness for variety and for using the word 'to sport' (ludere) in this annotation. Erasmus responded that variety, when it is not affected and is expressed in good Latin, is acceptable, but the Translator fails on both counts. He excuses his use of the term 'to sport' on the grounds that the word suggests something done for the pleasure it brings, without the constraints of necessity. For Erasmus' fondness for variety in his own translation of the New Testament cf Germain Marc'hadour 'Phobie de la répétition chez S. Jérome, Erasme, et Tyndale' in Les problèmes d'expression dans la traduction biblique ed Henri Gibaud (Angers 1988) 43–56.
>
> 2 Rom 5:15
>
> 3 1 Cor 12:31. As in his editions, Erasmus reads here κρείττονα, and, with the Vulgate printed in 1527, meliora 'better.'
>
> 4 χαρίζομαι ... favour'] In 1516 the passage read: 'χαρίζομαι, which is "I bestow," or "I do as a favour." '
>
> 5 From this ... κεχάρισμαι.] First in 1519. In 1516 the passage read, perhaps with some mistake: 'from this is derived the noun χάρισμα comes from χάρις.'

1:12 [ER *communem capiam consolationem* 'that I might receive a comfort shared']

[VG] *simul consolari* 'to be comforted together.' Lorenzo [Valla] μαστιγοῖ [chastises] the Translator at this point, and not without reason.[1] Since the Greek verb in either case – στηριχθῆναι [to be strengthened] and συμπαρα-κληθῆναι [to be comforted] – is an infinitive, what reason did he have to leave one [as an infinitive] and render the other as a gerundive?[2] It appears that both are related to the accusative ὑμᾶς [you] since it precedes in the construction;[3] so that the sense is 'that you might be strengthened, and to-gether receive mutual comfort among yourselves.' Indeed, the phrase 'to be comforted together' seems to have been added not to make a new point, but to soften, by way of explanation, what he had said ('for strengthening you') for he feared that he might offend the Romans, with their somewhat arrogant disposition, if they appeared to need strengthening, as though they were vacillating or wavering.[4] Thus he explains this strengthening as their 'mutual comfort,' speaking, as usual, with the greatest modesty.

Yet the Greek scholia make Paul as well [as the Romans] the subject of the second verb, συμπαρακληθῆναι.[5] If it is read thus, one understands that the Romans are to be strengthened and supported by the arrival of Paul, whereas Paul will receive comfort in turn by the strengthening of their faith. If one agrees with this, a pronoun of the first person, ἐμέ or ἡμᾶς, that is, 'I' or 'we,' has to be supplied. Indeed, Origen[6] and Theophylact[7] are of this opinion; and I find it the more satisfying for this reason that [Paul] has added the connecting particle δέ – τοῦτο δέ ἐστιν [that is] – which is a clear indication that he is softening and correcting what preceded; similarly, 'This is a great sacrament, but I speak of Christ and the church.'[8] Secondly, if he had meant 'among yourselves,' he would have said ἐν ἑαυτοῖς rather than ἐν ὑμῖν.[9] Finally, this interpretation better suits what follows: διὰ τῆς ἐν ἀλλήλοις πίστεως ὑμῶν τε καὶ ἐμοῦ, that is, 'through mutual faith, both yours and mine.' Their faith was being preached throughout the whole world;[10] and Paul had faith. Thus by making comparison both would be supported by their own, that is, their common, faith, one by the other – as happens whenever two people compare between themselves something learned from different sources, and each believes more firmly what he has heard because of the agreement of the stories they have shared. I should[11] add, lest it escape the reader, that συμπαρακληθῆναι can refer either to 'mutual comfort' or to 'mutual encouragement,' and since he has just spoken about strengthening them, 'mutual encouragement' is more fitting than 'comfort.'

Theophylact notes that in this passage 'comfort' can be understood not inappropriately as 'joy.'[12] Chrysostom[13] refers to the soothing remedy for the afflictions that those who believed the gospel patiently endured for the name of Christ, and at the same time he indicates the steps by which the Apostle softened and tempered his speech. For when he had said 'strengthened,' fearing that the arrogant Romans might reply, 'What? do we waver so that we have to be propped up by your tongue?' he softened this by changing the word 'strengthen' to 'comfort.' And not content with that, he said, not παρακληθῆναι [comfort], but συμπαρακληθῆναι [to comfort together], as though he himself needed their comfort no less. Finally, he spoke of the fellowship of faith, taking off the mask of teacher and assuming that of a fellow pupil.[14] Thus Paul becomes all things to all men that he might win all.[15] This is pious cunning and, if I may use the phrase, holy flattery. The interpretation[16] of Theophylact does not differ from that of Chrysostom.

1 Valla *Annot in Rom* 1 (I 855)
2 Compare the translation of Erasmus (for 1:11b–12) with that of the Vulgate, where the infinitive *consolari* and the gerundive *confirmandos* are used:
   ER *quo confirmemini, hoc est ut communem capiam consolationem in vobis per mutuam fidem vestram simul et meam* 'that you might be strengthened, that is, that I might receive among you a comfort shared through mutual faith, both yours and mine'
   VG *ad confirmandos vos id est simul consolari in vobis per eam quae invicem est fidem vestram atque meam* 'for strengthening you, that is to be comforted together among you through that faith which is in turn yours and mine'

3 Though the pronoun ὑμᾶς 'you' must be taken closely with στηριχθῆναι
  'for you to be strengthened,' the subject of the subsequent verb is more
  ambiguous. Erasmus suggests first that the subject appears to be the same
  ὑμᾶς 'you' – 'that you may be comforted' – but in the next paragraph
  proposes that the subject 'I' or 'we' be supplied from the context.
4 For the portrait of the Romans, see the annotation on 1:6 ('in whom are you')
  above.
5 Cf Pseudo-Oecumenius *Comm in Rom* 1:12 PG 118 329C.
6 Origen *Comm in Rom* 1.12 PG 14 857B–858A
7 and Theophylact] Added in *1519*. See Theophylact *Expos in Rom* 1:12 PG 124
  348B. Frans Titelmans accused Erasmus of misrepresenting the position of the
  'sacred teachers' of the church in claiming that they made Paul the subject
  of the second verb, when in fact such Doctors as Origen and Theophylact
  suggest that both Paul and the Romans may be understood as the subject
  of this verb. In his *Responsio ad collationes* Erasmus contended that he had
  never denied this possibility. His translation, however, clearly makes Paul
  the subject. See LB IX 971C–E.
8 Eph 5:32. See the annotation on this verse (*sacramentum hoc*) where Erasmus
  argues from the use of the Greek particle δέ in the phrase ἐγὼ δὲ λέγω 'but I
  speak' that the second clause 'softens and corrects' the first.
9 The Greek ἐν ἑαυτοῖς is reflexive, implying the subject ὑμᾶς 'you'; ἐν ὑμῖν,
  not being reflexive, allows 'Paul' to be the subject, thus supporting Erasmus'
  argument.
10 Cf Rom 1:8.
11 I should … 'joy.'] Added in *1519*
12 Theophylact *Expos in Rom* 1:12 PG 124 348C
13 Chrysostom … flattery.] Added in *1527*, constituting, except for the last
   sentence, the remaining portion of this annotation
14 Chrysostom *Hom in Rom* 2.3, 4 PG 60 404–5.
15 Cf 1 Cor 9:19–22. This is a frequent characterization of Paul in these
   annotations; cf the annotation on 1:1 ('Paul') and n9.
16 The interpretation … Chrysostom.] Added in *1535*. Cf Theophylact *Expos in
   Rom* 1:12 PG 124 348B–C.

1:13 [ER VG] *nolo autem vos* 'but I would not have you [ignorant].' Origen points
     out in this passage the hyperbaton, that is, the confusion in the order of
     words, thinking that something has even been omitted. But he believes that
     the sequence of language can be restored as follows: 'Just as I have had fruit
     in the other nations (I am debtor to Greeks and barbarians, to the wise and
     foolish), likewise, in so far as it lies in me, I am ready, if it be permitted,
     to preach the gospel also to you who are at Rome.'[1] I have noted this in
     passing because it relates to the way the words of Scripture are construed.

     1 Origen *Comm in Rom* 1.13 PG 14 858A–B. According to Origen the missing
       word is *quibus* 'to whom,' reading 'Just as I have had fruit in other nations,
       Greeks and barbarians, the wise and foolish, to whom I am debtor, likewise
       …' Erasmus represented the missing word by a parenthesis in all editions

except 1522, where the parenthesis was, perhaps inadvertently, omitted. On
the hyperbaton see the annotation on 1:4 ('from the resurrection of the dead
of Jesus Christ') n21.

1:13 [ER *licet praepeditus fuerim* 'though I have been prevented']
[VG] *et prohibitus sum* 'and[1] I have been prohibited'; ἐκωλύθην, which
means 'I was prevented' rather than 'I was prohibited,' no doubt by affairs that stood in the way – the Greek for the latter is ἐμποδίζειν. Strictly
speaking, one 'prohibits' who forbids you to do something; unless[2] we are
to understand that Paul was prohibited by the Holy Spirit, as in Acts 16,
when he wanted to go to Bithynia, but the Holy Spirit did not permit
him to do so.[3] For Chrysostom suggests something like this when he says,
τῷ μὲν θελήματι τοῦ θεοῦ οὐκ ἀντιπίπτων, τὴν δὲ ἀγάπην διατηρῶν [not re-
sisting the will of God, but maintaining love].[4] For Paul, when he is not
given the opportunity to go to Rome, interprets this devoutly as the will of
God.

   1 and ... do something] This was the extent of a new annotation in 1527.
   2 unless ... will of God] Added in 1535
   3 Acts 16:7
   4 Chrysostom *Hom in Rom* 2.5 PG 60 406. Commenting on Rom 1:13, Chrysostom
     represents Paul as saying 'When I was prevented [from seeing you] I did not
     cease trying, but have always been trying, always prevented, nor have I yet
     ceased, not indeed resisting the will of God, but maintaining love.'

1:13 [ER *haberem inter vos quoque* 'that I might have among you also']
[VG] *habeam in vos* 'that I may have in you';[1] σχῶ καὶ ἐν ὑμῖν, that is,
'that I may have also in you.' For the conjunction [καί] 'also' is not without
its special meaning.[2] He had gathered some fruit among all the Greeks;
he desires the same among the Romans. Again 'in you' is used to mean
'among you.'[3]

   1 In 1516 this annotation preceded the annotation on 1:13 ('but I would not
     have you [ignorant]'). It found its present position in 1519.
   2 The conjunction καί 'and' is sometimes used adverbially to mean 'also.'
   3 Cf the annotation on 1:6 ('in whom are you') n1.

1:14 [ER *Graecis simul et barbaris* 'to the Greeks as well as to the barbarians']
[VG] *Graecis ac barbaris* 'to the Greeks and the barbarians.' In Greek the
conjunction is doubled: Ἕλλησί τε καὶ βαρβάροις, that is, 'both to the Greeks
and to the barbarians.'[1] And again, σοφοῖς τε καὶ ἀνοήτοις, that is, 'both to
the wise and to the foolish.' The repetition of the conjunction is not without
significance, indicating that Paul is a debtor equally to all without any distinction of race. He presses this point because of the Jews, who wanted the

preaching of the gospel to extend to themselves alone. Further, σοφοῖς here does not mean 'wise' so much as 'educated,' and ἀνοήτοις means 'dull' and 'unlearned' rather than 'foolish'; for the Greeks made claim to wisdom, that is, erudition. Moreover the 'Greeks,' who,[2] you will find, sometimes stand for the gentiles without differentiation, he has here opposed to 'barbarians,' whom[3] he calls ἀνόητοι [foolish], inasmuch as they are unacquainted with philosophy and are unlearned.[4]

1 Erasmus repeatedly notes the 'double conjunction.' Cf eg the annotations on 1:16 ('To the Jew first and to the Greek') and 2:9 ('of the Jew first and of the Greek').
2 who] Added in 1519
3 whom ... unlearned] Added in 1519
4 For the word ἀνόητος see the annotation on Gal 3:1 (*O insensati*). For the word in the paraphrase on Galatians see especially the Argument and chapter 3 CWE 42 94 and 107–9.

1:15 [ER *ita quantum in me est paratus sum* 'so far as in me lies I am prepared']
[VG] *ita quod in me promptum est* 'thus what in me is ready.' Lorenzo [Valla] points out that in this passage 'ready' must be taken substantively, that is, for 'readiness' itself.[1] In the same way the Greeks speak of χρηστότης [goodness] as χρηστόν [the good], and ταχυτής [swiftness] as ταχύ [the swift], using adjectives as substantive nouns. Then the sense will be: 'Thus so far as I am able, I am ready – I have a readiness of heart – to preach the gospel to you also who are at Rome.' And so indeed reads Ambrose: 'Therefore, as far as it lies in me I am ready' etc.[2]

There are those who would rather refer the infinitive εὐαγγελίσασθαι [to preach the gospel] to ὀφειλέτης [debtor], a noun conveying the verbal force [of owing], and take οὕτως [thus] as an adverb which does not connect this portion of the discourse with what he had said above,[3] but refers to the 'others' to whom Paul had already preached the gospel; so that the sense would be: 'Just as I have already preached to the other gentiles, since I owe it to all, so too [οὕτως], as far as my own readiness of heart is concerned, I owe it to you who live at Rome to preach the gospel of Christ, even though you are wise, powerful, and learned.'[4] And this fits quite nicely with the words that then follow.

1 Valla *Annot in Rom* 1 (1 855–6). Valla had illustrated with Erasmus' first example here, χρηστότης 'goodness,' citing Rom 2:4.
2 Ambrosiaster *Comm in Rom* 1:15
3 By 'above' Erasmus refers to verse 13. On the reading that takes verse 15 closely with verse 13, the sense is: 'I have often determined to come to you to have some fruit among you ... So [οὕτως] I am eager to preach to you at

Rome.' On the alternative reading, verse 15 is taken closely with verse 14, as
Erasmus' paraphrase here in the annotation illustrates.

4 Origen *Comm in Rom* 1.13 PG 14 860A–B and Ambrosiaster (cf n2) appear to
follow this reading; while Chrysostom *Hom in Rom* 2.6 PG 60 407 reads verse
15 closely with verse 13.

1:16 [ER *non enim me pudet evangelii* 'for I am not ashamed of the gospel']
[VG] *non enim erubesco evangelium* 'for I do not feel ashamed of the
gospel'; οὐ γὰρ ἐπαισχύνομαι τὸ εὐαγγέλιον. The Translator sometimes renders [the Greek ἐπαισχύνομαι 'I am ashamed'] by *confundor* [I am con-
founded], sometimes by *erubesco* [I feel shame] followed by the accusative
case. It would be better Latin to say *non enim me pudet evangelii* 'for I am not
ashamed of the gospel.'[1] And yet[2] I know that in Quintus Curtius one reads
'he feels ashamed of fortune' [*erubescit fortunae*].[3] If such an expression frequently occurred in good authors, I would not be reluctant to imitate it.

Some of[4] the Greek manuscripts add 'of Christ': τὸ εὐαγγέλιον τοῦ
Χριστοῦ [the gospel of Christ]. For the name of Christ was still held in con-
tempt by many, especially those who were puffed up by their confidence in
wisdom, among[5] whom the Platos, the Pythagorases, the Zenos, the Aris-
totles were in high esteem. And yet[6] Chrysostom does not add 'of Christ';
but the article makes clear that one must have in mind the gospel about
which he had formerly spoken,[7] the gospel of God.

1 *Pudet* with the genitive (of the cause of shame) and the accusative (of the
person ashamed) is conventional Latin.
2 And yet ... imitate it.] Added in *1519*
3 Quintus Curtius Rufus (fl first century AD) wrote a history of Alexander
the Great in ten books. The text has been transmitted in a somewhat
unsatisfactory condition. The *editio princeps* was published in Venice in 1470
or 1471, and Erasmus published his own edition in 1518 (Strasbourg: Matthias
Schürer), the year preceding the present addition to the *Annotations*. (For
the prefatory letter to Duke Ernest of Bavaria, to whom Erasmus dedicated
his edition, see Ep 704.) The phrase *erubesceret fortunae* (where *erubesco* is
followed by the genitive) is found in his edition on fol 31 verso, though it
is printed in the edition of the Loeb Classical Library (trans John C. Rolfe
[Cambridge, MA and London 1946] I 376) as *erubesceret fortuito*.
4 some of] Added in *1527*
5 among ... esteem] Added in *1519*
6 And yet ... God.] Added in *1527*. Cf Chrysostom *Hom in Rom* 2.6 PG 60 407.
7 In 1:1

1:16 [ER *potentia siquidem est dei* 'since indeed it is the power of God']
[VG] *virtus enim dei est* 'for it is the power of God'; δύναμις γὰρ θεοῦ,[1]
that is, 'for it is the power of God.' He intends to show that [the gospel]
is something that should not be spurned even by the Romans as mean

and ineffective. I have pointed this out because the Latin word *virtus* is
ambiguous;[2] occasionally it is used to correspond to the Greek word ἀρετή
[virtue] and is the opposite of κακία, that is, 'vice'; sometimes it corresponds
to the Greek word δύναμις, and is opposed to 'feebleness' or 'weakness.'
But [Paul] added 'of God,' so that Christ would not be despised, as being a
man, by the weak and unbelieving.[3] He[4] does not add the article, τοῦ θεοῦ,
because here God is spoken of not as a definite person,[5] but as the divine
nature itself, in contrast to mankind.

> 1 θεοῦ] θεοῦ was added in 1519. After θεοῦ LB adds ἐστιν 'is,' but without
>   warrant from the editions 1516–1535.
> 2 Cf the annotation on 1:4 ('in power') above.
> 3 the weak and unbelieving] First in 1527; previously, 'the ungodly'
> 4 He ... mankind.] Added in 1535
> 5 In Greek the article precedes the name of a specific person.

1:16 [ER VG] *omni credenti* **'to everyone who believes'**; παντὶ τῷ πιστεύοντι. It
would be clearer to say *cuivis credenti* [to anyone at all who believes]. For
he does not want to make[1] any distinction of[2] race or fortune, provided
only there is a common faith.

> 1 to make] First in 1527; previously, 'to appear'
> 2 of ... faith] Added in 1519

1:16 [ER *Iudaeo primum simul et Graeco* **'to the Jew first as well as to
the Greek'**]
[VG] *Iudaeo primum et Graeco* **'to the Jew first and to the Greek.'** Here
as well, there is a double conjunction in the Greek,[1] Ἰουδαίῳ τε πρῶτον καὶ
Ἕλληνι, that is, 'to the Jew first, and as well, to the Greek.' 'First,' however,
has here the same sense as 'especially': because Christ was promised to the
Jews, from whom also he was sprung; and the Greeks excelled in wisdom.

By 'Greek' in this passage [the Translator] understands 'pagan,' and so
renders the word elsewhere in more than one place.[2] And yet above [in the
phrase] 'Greeks and barbarians'[3] he has made them stand for a particular
nation.

> 1 Cf the annotation on 1:14 ('to the Greeks and the barbarians') n1 above.
> 2 The Vulgate translates Ἕλλην by both *Graecus* 'Greek' and *gentilis* 'gentile,'
>   but characteristically uses *ethnicus* 'pagan' for ἐθνικός and *gentes* 'nations'
>   for ἔθνη. See, for example, respectively, Rom 1:14; Acts 17:4; Matt 18:17;
>   1 Cor 1:23. In the translation of this annotation, 'pagan' represents the Latin
>   *ethnicus*, the reading of the text from 1519; in 1516 it read *gentilis* 'gentile.'
> 3 Rom 1:14

1:17 [ER VG] *ex fide in fidem* **'from faith**[1] **unto faith.'** The Latin language has
no word exactly corresponding to πίστις. In Latin, one who believes the

words of another is said to have *confidence* [*fides*] in him;[2] one who makes a solemn promise is said to give a *pledge* [*fides*]; and one who binds himself in obligation to another is said to plight his *faith* [*fides*]. One who performs what he has promised, however, is said to fulfil his *trust* [*fides*]. One who is not believed lacks our *trust* [*fides*] – [we have] no *faith* [*fides*] in the appearances [he puts on].[3] One who does not adhere to an agreement breaks *faith* [*fides*]; from this one speaks of the *perfidious* [*perfidus*] and *perfidy* [*perfidia*]. A person who causes another not to be believed diminishes the latter's *credibility* [*fides*]. He who does the opposite, inspires *confidence* [*fides*]. We lose *confidence* [*fides*] in one who fails to be responsible for an obligation assumed; we gain *confidence* [*fides*] in one who has carefully done what he could. And we hand over for *security* [*fides*] what we *entrust* [*fidei committimus*] to someone. One who comes into ownership without deception is said to be the *bona fide* purchaser for value; one who does otherwise, [takes possession] in bad *faith* [*fides*]. We read much about the *faithfulness* [*fides*] of servants towards their masters.[4] One who persuades creates *confidence* [*fides*], and he is called *trustworthy* [*fides*] – also *faithful* [*fidelis*] – who runs affairs conscientiously. In Latin, therefore, *fides* belongs sometimes to one who promises, sometimes to one who fulfils a promise, sometimes to one who believes, sometimes to one who is believed; sometimes it is a general term, as when we say 'there is no *faith* [*fides*] left in the world,' meaning that no one fulfils what he promises, and that no one *trusts* [*fidere*] another.

In Greek, too, πίστις [faith] sometimes means the *reliability* [*fides*] of one promising or fulfilling, sometimes the evidence by which we persuade. One is called πιστός [trustworthy] who does not deceive, ἄπιστος [faithless] who is either *unreliable* [*infidus*] or *untrusting* [*diffidens*]. He trusts [πιστεύει] who gives credence or *relies upon* [*confidit*] or entrusts, and he is without trust [ἀπιστεῖ] who does not *place reliance* [*non fidit*] [on anything].

In Latin, the incredulous person is one who *distrusts* [*diffidit*]; for 'credulous' and 'credulity' have a negative connotation, though 'to give credence' [*credere* 'to believe'] is ambiguous. He believes [*credit*] who gives his assent to what has been said; and he believes [*credit*] who *relies* [*fidit*], and he entrusts [*credit*] his wife to another who gives her into his charge. Now we speak in a positive way of *trusting* [*fidens*] and of *trust* [*fiducia*], which resides only in the believer [*in credente*]; in a positive way likewise [we use the infinitives] *to entrust* [*confidere*] and *to trust* [*fidere*]; but *self-confident* [*confidens*] and *boldness* [*confidentia*] have a negative connotation.[5] But sacred literature frequently uses these words loosely, for it often uses *fides* [faith] for *fiducia* [trust] in God almost in the sense of hope; sometimes for the belief or conviction by which we assent to the things handed down to us about God – by which even the demons believe.[6] Sometimes the word *faith* [*fides*] embraces all these meanings: that assent to the truth both of the historical record and of the promises, and the *trust* [*fiducia*] that arises from his omnipotent goodness, not without the hope, that is, the expectation, of the promises. So far, indeed, does one speak of the *faith* [*fides*] of human beings.

However, one also speaks of the *faith* [*fides*] of God, a faith he manifests in his promises; hence God is said to be *trustworthy* [*fidus*] or *faithful* [*fidelis*], that is, πιστός, because he does not deceive.[7] But a man is said to be *faithful* [*fidelis*] who believes the one who makes a promise.[8] This is not characteristic Latin use, and yet sacred literature frequently speaks in this way. For in Latin a steward is called *faithful* [*fidelis*]; *faithless* [*infidelis*], however, is used in the Scriptures (but not in [secular] Latin) of one who does not believe.[9] The Greek ἄπιστος [unbelieving] or ἀπειθής [not to be persuaded] is better.[10] Sometimes [the Scriptures] speak of the *faith* of God [*fides dei*][11] by which we *trust* [*fidimus*] in him rather than in man; it is said to be 'of God' not only because it is directed towards him, but also because it is given by him;[12] sometimes [the Scriptures speak of the faith] of both [God and man] as in 'The righteous shall live by *faith* [*fides*] – of God who does not deceive in what he has promised, and also of man who *trusts* [*fidit*] in God.'[13] To both belongs the phrase used here, 'from *faith* [*fides*] to *faith* [*fides*].' For just as God at appointed times began to reveal his nature and to fulfil his promises, so man's knowledge of and *trust* [*fiducia*] in God grew by stages. Few believed the prophets until the Lord displayed before their eyes what they had promised. Again, from what we have seen, and now see,[14] our *faith* [*fides*] is strengthened concerning the things that were predicted about his final coming.

1 from faith ... coming.] This entire annotation was added in 1527.
2 The different meanings of *fides* illustrated in this annotation are rendered in our translation by a variety of English words. In this annotation English words translating either *fides* itself, or Latin words with *fid* in the stem, are placed in italics, with the Latin following in square brackets. For the initial contrast between *habere fidem* 'have confidence' and *dare fidem* 'give a pledge' see Valla *Elegantiae* 5.16 (1 167) and *fidem dare* in Erasmus' *Paraphrasis in Elegantias Vallae* ASD I-4 256. John Colet had offered a more extensive definition of faith, in the manner of Erasmus here, in his 'literal exposition' of the Epistle to the Romans, chapter 3. See the *Expositio literalis* (English 92–3, Latin 230–1). For the definitions here see also *fides* in L&S, where most of the uses given by Erasmus in this annotation are exemplified in citations from standard Latin authors.
3 Cf Juvenal *Satires* 2.8 and the translation 'Men's faces are not to be trusted' in *Juvenal and Persius* trans George Gilbert Ramsay, Loeb Classical Library, rev ed (London and Cambridge, MA 1969).
4 For examples of the faithful servant in classical literature cf Eumaeus in the

Odyssey, the watchman in Aeschylus' *Agamemnon*, the nurse in Euripides' *Medea*, Tyndarus in Plautus' *Captivi*, and Messenio in his *Menaechmi*. For the 'faithful servant' in biblical literature cf eg Matt 24:45, 25:14–30; 1 Cor 4:2; Heb 3:5.

5 *confidens* and *confidentia* are used both with a positive and with a negative connotation in Latin. *Confidens* 'self-confident' with a negative connotation suggests audacity.

6 Cf James 2:19.

7 Cf 1 Cor 1:9; Heb 10:23, 11:11.

8 Cf Gal 3:8–9.

9 Cf Luke 12:46; 1 Cor 7:14, 15.

10 ἄπιστος is frequently rendered in the Vulgate by *infidelis*, though ἀπειθής more regularly by *incredibilis* (Luke 1:17; Titus 1:16) or *incredulus* (Acts 14:2).

11 Cf Mark 11:22, where Erasmus' annotation indicates that the phrase means 'towards God,' ie 'trust in God.'

12 Erasmus correctly notes the ambiguity of the Greek as well as the Latin genitive, which may be used to refer either to my faith towards God, ie the faith of which God is the object, or to the faith that comes from God.

13 Cf Hab 2:4 and Rom 1:17. See the following annotation ('lives by faith'), where Erasmus quotes both the Septuagint, 'the righteous one shall live by *my* faith,' and the translation of Symmachus, 'the righteous one shall live by *his* faith.'

14 Cf Matt 13:16–17 and Luke 10:23–4.

1:17 [ER *ex fide victurus est* 'is going to live by faith']

[VG] *ex fide vivit* 'lives by faith.' 'Shall live' must be read, with the verb in the future tense,[1] ἐκ πίστεως ζήσεται [shall live by faith]; and so it is cited both in Paul's Epistle to the Galatians and in the Epistle of St James.[2] So Chrysostom[3] interprets, explaining it in terms of the future life: since here in the meantime we face afflictions and death, on this account [Scripture] said 'shall live,' not 'lives.'[4] But the passage that Paul cites comes from the second chapter of the prophet Habakkuk, which the LXX[5] rendered thus: 'But the righteous shall live by my faith.' Symmachus alone has expressed the thought more clearly: ὁ δὲ δίκαιος τῇ ἑαυτοῦ πίστει ζήσεται, that is, 'but the righteous shall live, or, is about to live, through his own faith.'[6] Jerome thinks that the LXX erred on account of the similarity of the Hebrew letters, which are distinguished only by length. For in Hebrew בֶּאֱמוּנָתוֹ means *in fide sua* [in *his* faith], because the letter ו, *vau*, when added to a word, has the force of the pronoun *sui* [his (reflexive)] or *eius* [his]. Likewise, the addition of *jod*, י, has the force of the pronoun *mei* [my]: בֶּאֱמוּנָתִי that is, *in fide mea* [in *my* faith].[7] Furthermore, that the verb is 'shall live' in the future tense, not only does the Greek edition[8] indicate (which Jerome cites, and which is found in the published codices of the Greeks) but also the Hebrew verb[9] יִחְיֶה, for the addition of י at the beginning forms the third person of a masculine future.[10] I imagine, however, that Paul did not include either pronoun ['my' or 'his'] because the Septuagint was known to the Romans and he was not willing therefore to contradict it or, on the other hand, to bring in the Hebrew, of which they were ignorant; or because pronouns of this kind are often understood from the context; or to make a more absolute and universal statement.[11]

1 So Valla *Annot in Rom* 1 (I 856)

2 Gal 3:11. The reference to James is apparently erroneous; cf instead Heb 10:38.

3 So Chrysostom ... 'lives.'] Added in *1527*

4 Chrysostom *Hom in Rom* 2.6 PG 60 409–10. In his exposition of 1:17 Chrysostom insists primarily on the importance of faith in contrast to the endless questioning of the faithless heretics. But he alludes to Abraham and Rahab, prominent among the *exempla* of faith in Hebrews 11 who faced affliction and death.

5 Though Erasmus sometimes speaks of the 'Septuagint edition' he more frequently writes simply *septuaginta* 'the seventy'; indeed, when he uses the word as subject, he normally puts the verb in the plural, and in the past. We have attempted to retain the ambiguity of this use by the Roman numeral LXX, suggesting both the edition and the hypothetical seventy translators.

6 Symmachus is known to us almost solely from the fragments of his Greek translation of the Hebrew Bible incorporated into Origen's *Hexapla* (see the annotation on 1:4 ['who was predestined'] n6 above). Possibly of Jewish origin, he lived perhaps in the late second and early third centuries AD. The fragments have been edited by F. Field, *Origenis Hexaplorum quae supersunt; sive veterum interpretum Graecorum in totum vetus testamentum fragmenta* 2 vols (Oxford 1867–71). For this citation see II 1005. Erasmus appears to have derived this text from Jerome *Commentarii in Abacuc* 1.2 PL 25 (1845) 1289C.

7 Jerome ibidem

8 Ie the Septuagint

9 Literally 'but also *in* the Hebrew verb.' Erasmus' syntax appears to be faulty here.

10 future] In *1516* only, an additional sentence followed here: 'The text of the prophet – if anyone asks – reads like this: וְצַדִּיק בֶּאֱמוּנָתוֹ יִחְיֶה.'

11 For a discussion of the problem of the reading of Hab 2:4 see Otto Kuss *Der Römerbrief* 2 vols, 2nd ed (Regensburg 1963) I 24–5.

1:17 [ER VG] ἐκ πίστεως; **by faith.**[1] The preposition signifies source. For life has its beginning in this, that we subordinate our human understanding and trust the divine words. This phrase is directed against the philosophers.[2]

1 This annotation, added in *1527*, appeared both in *1527* and *1535* as a separate entry, introduced, quite unusually, by a lemma from the Greek text. In LB it is coalesced with the previous annotation ('lives by faith').

2 For a similar interpretation by Chrysostom, see the preceding annotation, n4.

1:18 [ER *palam fit* 'is made known to all']

[VG] *revelatur* 'is revealed'; ἀποκαλύπτεται, that is, 'is uncovered and disclosed' – when that which had before been concealed is made known to
all. For[1] before the gospel of Christ was revealed, the wrath of God seemed
to lie open and disclosed to the Jews alone, if they sinned. And he adds
'upon *all* ungodliness,'[2] because the grace of the gospel belonged equally
to all. I think it will be understood, even without anyone to point it out,
that 'wrath' is frequently used in Hebrew idiom to mean vengeance and
punishment.[3]

    1 For ... punishment.] The remaining portion of the annotation was added in
      1519.
    2 The discussion here extends beyond the cue phrase:
      ER *palam fit enim ira dei de caelo adversus omnem impietatem* 'for the wrath
      of God from heaven against all ungodliness is made known to all'
      VG *revelatur enim ira dei de caelo super omnem impietatem* 'for the wrath of
      God is revealed from heaven upon all ungodliness'
    3 For *ira* 'wrath,' in the Vulgate as 'vengeance,' cf eg Exod 15:7; Josh 22:20.

1:18 [ER *veritatem* 'truth']

[VG] *veritatem dei* 'the truth[1] of God.' 'Of God' is not added in the Greek
or in the old Latin copies; nor does Chrysostom mention it.[2] For [Paul]
is thinking of the truth known to the philosophers, which is rather their
own truth than that of God. For[3] the truth of God bestows life; the truth of
the philosophers puffs up. But the truth through which they should have
advanced to higher things, they held in unrighteousness.[4]

    1 the truth ... that of God.] These sentences comprised the annotation of
      1519, except that the words 'nor does Chrysostom mention it' were added in
      1527.
    2 Though some witnesses, chiefly Latin, read 'of God,' the preferred reading
      omits the expression. See Tischendorf II 366 18n; Wordsworth and White II
      66 18n. Cf Chrysostom *Hom in Rom* 3.1 PG 60 411–12.
    3 For ... unrighteousness.] Added in *1527*
    4 Except for the omission of *dei* [of God], Erasmus followed the Vulgate
      in translating the last words of 1:18: *qui veritatem in iniustitia detinent* 'who
      hold the truth in unrighteousness.'

1:19 [ER *quod de deo cognosci potest* 'what can be discerned about God']

[VG] *quod notum est dei* 'what is known of God'; τὸ γνωστὸν τοῦ θεοῦ, that
is, 'what of God is discernible,' that is, what can be known and discerned
about God – this has the support of the interpreters also.[1] For in God there
is something that no imagination of the human mind can fathom by any
means.

1 Cf Theophylact *Expos in Rom* 1:19 PG 124 353B–C. Theophylact distinguishes the essence of God, which cannot be known, and his attributes, which can. So similarly Thomas Aquinas *Super Rom lect* cap 1 lectio 6.117.

1:19 [ER VG] *manifestum est in illis* 'is¹ manifest in them.' 'In them' is used, strangely, for 'to them' or 'among them.' For 'in them' cannot refer to created things, which² have not yet been mentioned, but to the philosophers. Furthermore, he adds 'in them' to distinguish these from the barbarians and the uneducated common people.

1 is ... people.] With the exception noted below, this entire annotation was added in 1522.
2 which ... mentioned] Added in 1527. Paul speaks of 'created things' in 1:20.

1:20 [ER *ex creatione mundi* 'from the creation of the world']
[VG] *a creatura mundi* 'by the creature¹ of the world.' κτίσις is an ambiguous word in Greek. It can mean either *creatio* itself,² that is, the act of creating or founding, or the actual *creatura*, that is, the thing created. The Translator seems to apply κτίσις [creation] to man, and τὰ ποιήματα [things made] to created things, so that you understand that 'by the creature,' that is, by created man, things can be perceived by the mind that cannot be seen with bodily eyes, and this [perception comes] through created things, in which are found the traces of divinity. Others on the contrary prefer to apply the latter [ie things made] to man and the former to the creation of the world.³ But⁴ the sense is the same in either case. It seems to me that both words [κτίσις and ποιήματα] can refer not unreasonably to the created world: thus you would understand that the invisible things of God are perceived in the very creation of the world, while they are recognized through the works that display the power, wisdom, and goodness of God the creator. On this reading the Greek dative, ποιήμασιν [by things made], is related not to the verb καθορᾶται [are perceived], but to the participle νοούμενα, that is, '[the unseen things are] recognized' – through what? – τοῖς ποιήμασιν, that is, 'through the works,' as the instrument.⁵ For in Greek the dative case expresses instrument, as does the ablative in Latin.

Now it is not of any great importance to point out that νοούμενα [being recognized], which [the Translator] renders 'having been recognized,' is a participle of the present tense, not past. For they are not perceived after they have been recognized, but are perceived at the same time they are recognized from created things – as though he were explaining what he meant when he said 'are perceived.'⁶ For they are recognized from created things, just as you might perceive an image in a mirror; hence the origin of the word κάτοπτρον [mirror].⁷ Indeed,⁸ the pronoun αὐτοῦ [of him] also can refer to either of two phrases: to τὰ ἀόρατα [the invisible things], so that you take these to be the nature of God and the powers that cannot be seen [the invisible things 'of him']; or to what follows almost immediately, τοῖς ποιήμασιν αὐτοῦ [through the works 'of him'], that is, 'through his works.'

1 Our translation reflects Erasmus' interpretation of the Vulgate reading, but it is possible to translate the Vulgate in the same way we have rendered Erasmus' translation; cf eg the annotation on 8:19 ('for the expectation of the creation'), where Erasmus adopts (all editions) the Vulgate's *creatura* for the Greek κτίσις.
Erasmus' discussion extends beyond the cue phrase:
ER *siquidem quae sunt invisibilia illius ex creatione mundi dum per opera intelliguntur pervidentur* 'for the invisible things of him are discerned from the creation of the world, in so far as they are recognized through his works'
VG *invisibilia enim ipsius a creatura mundi per ea quae facta sunt intellecta conspiciuntur* 'for the invisible things of that one are perceived by the creature of the world, recognized through those things which have been made'

2 Valla prefers *creatio*: 'I do not understand,' he says, 'what "creature of the world" means': *Annot in Rom* 1 (I 856).

3 The sense would be: 'The invisible things recognized in the creation of the world are perceived by those made [ie mankind].'

4 But ... case.] Added in *1519*

5 In place of the reading 'the invisible things, having been recognized, are perceived by those made' (cf n3 above, where 'those made' is 'related to' the verb 'are perceived'), the construction suggested here would be rendered 'the invisible things are perceived, recognized through the things made.'

6 The present participle in Greek expresses time contemporaneous with the main verb; hence here Erasmus wishes to read 'they are perceived, being recognized through the works.'

7 The Greek κάτοπτρον 'mirror' is a derivative of the verb καθοράω, used above in the form καθορᾶται 'are seen.'

8 Indeed ... works'] Added in *1527*

1:20 [ER *ipsaque aeterna* 'both (his) eternal (power) itself']
[VG] *sempiterna quoque* 'also [his] everlasting [power]'; ἥ τε ἀίδιος αὐτοῦ δύναμις. The Greek here is not 'also' (a connective that language entirely lacks) but [the connective] -*que* 'and.'[1] Yet the Translator has rendered it well provided Origen's interpretation is correct, that 'invisible' refers to invisible creatures, that is,[2] distinct essences, not to God himself, whom [Paul] then adds separately.[3] I certainly[4] do not disapprove of the diligence of Origen, who philosophizes everywhere, but I think that view which Ambrose and Chrysostom[5] hold is more straightforward.

1 Cf Valla *Annot in Rom* 1 (I 856). The Latin connective -*que* attached to a word has the significance of the conjunction 'and'; when followed by another -*que*,

and sometimes by *et* or *ac*, it can mean 'both ... and,' and so represent the force of the τέ ... καί of the Greek of this clause.

2 that is, distinct essences] Added in *1519*

3 Origen *Comm in Rom* 1.17 PG 14 864B–C. Origen calls the invisible things the (heavenly) 'creatures,' citing Col 1:16, and says that beyond them is the eternal power, ie God. On this reading, 'his invisible things' as well as (ie also) his eternal power and godhead are seen, recognized through the things made.

4 I certainly ... straightforward.] The remainder of the annotation was added in *1519*, except for the reference to Chrysostom, added in *1527*.

5 Ie the view that the 'invisible things of him' and the 'eternal power' both refer to attributes of God to which the works of creation give witness; cf Ambrosiaster *Comm in Rom* 1:20 (1); Chrysostom *Hom in Rom* 3.2 PG 60 412–13. On this reading, the invisible things are 'both his eternal power and godhead.'

1:20 [ER *in hoc ut sint* 'to this end that they might be']

[VG] *ita ut sint* 'so that they are.' 'So' is not only redundant, but it actually undermines the sense if it is added. The Greek reads εἰς τὸ εἶναι αὐτοὺς ἀναπολογήτους, that is, 'that they might be inexcusable' or 'to this end that they might be inexcusable' – either because they have been led to such a point through the knowledge of God that they cannot use their ignorance as a pretext when they sin; or because God granted them knowledge of himself for this very purpose, that they should afterwards have no excuse for their disbelief if they should reject Christ. And yet[1] Theophylact points out that Paul uses this type of construction when he is not thinking of purpose, but result. There is the same sort of thing in the psalm: 'For I have done evil in your presence, so that you might be justified in your words' [51:4]. For [the Psalmist] does not mean that he has sinned with the purpose of making God appear just; this, rather, is the result, so that while *he* does not cease from sinning, the righteousness of God shines forth, who fulfils his promises even for a sinner.[2]

1 And yet ... sinner.] Added in *1519*

2 Theophylact *Expos in Rom* 1:20 PG 124 353D–356A. Citing Ps 51:4, Theophylact notes the special idiom of Scripture in which a purpose clause directs attention to the ultimate outcome of an event. Though in the Vulgate the construction of the two passages is similar, in the Greek different constructions are used: in Ps 51:4b (LXX 50:6b, cited in Rom 3:4) ὅπως ἄν, a phrase that normally indicates purpose; here, in Rom 1:20 the preposition εἰς with the articular infinitive τὸ εἶναι, a phrase used to indicate both purpose and result – see A.T. Robertson *A Grammar of the Greek New Testament in the Light of Historical Research* 3rd ed (New York 1919 [1914]) 1002–3.
On the problem of determing purpose and result in the Pauline Epistles, see the annotation on Rom 11:11 ('can it be that they have so stumbled that they fell').

Whether purpose or result is intended here in 1:20 is still disputed; see Cranfield I 116 n1.

1:21 [ER *frustrati sunt* 'were deceived']

[VG] *sed evanuerunt* 'but became vain'; ἐματαιώθησαν, that is, 'they were rendered empty [*vani*]' or 'superfluous' or 'were deceived,' for μάτην means *frustra* [to no purpose], hence μάταιος means 'superfluous' and 'of no use' and ματαιόομαι [means] *frustror* [I am deceived, cheated of]. *Vanum* [vain] is commonly used to mean boastful and proud, and [Nicholas of] Lyra explains it in this sense.[1] Those who are practised in Latin use *vanum* either of what is not true or of what is frivolous and empty,[2] having nothing solid. Now *evanescere* is used of something which, since it was presented to our eyes first through an unreal likeness, later disappears like smoke. Now Paul means that they have been deceived by their own deliberations, that is, things had turned out quite otherwise than they supposed. This becomes clear from the words that soon follow: 'claiming to be wise, they became fools.'[3] For 'to be deceived' is this: when you have hoped for the highest wisdom, to fall into the most abysmal stupidity; or when you have dreamed of the brightest light, to be sunk in the deepest darkness; or when[4] you have set before yourself some glory rare among mortals, then to fall into desires that are so shameful that even the irrational animals instinctively shrink from them.

Διαλογισμός,[5] however, is not mere thinking, but the thinking of one who deliberates, [who] weighs alternatives and judges among them, something completely alien to the faith in Christ to which Paul[6] is calling them. For in passing he censures the dialectical subtleties of the philosophers, vainly relying on which they both claimed perfect wisdom for themselves and promised it to others.

1 Cf Lyra *Postilla* IV fol aa iii verso.
2 and empty] Added in *1519*
3 Cf 1:22.
4 or when ... from them] Added in *1519*
5 Erasmus extends the discussion to the phrase following the lemma:
   ER *per cogitationes suas* 'through their deliberations'
   VG *in cogitationibus suis* 'in their thoughts'
6 Paul] Added in *1519*; in *1516*, 'he'

1:22 [ER *cum se crederent esse sapientes* 'since they thought they were wise']

[VG] *dicentes se esse sapientes* 'saying that they were wise'; φάσκοντες εἶναι σοφοί. If one may change nothing in mystic literature, why did the Translator dare here to change a Greek idiom into a Latin one?[1] And yet not even so did he fully express the sense. For φάσκοντες εἶναι means rather 'who, though they thought themselves' or 'claimed' to be wise. Because of the close relationship of the concepts, [the Greeks] often use φημί [I say] for οἶμαι [I think]. Now[2] the conjunction 'for,' which is added in most of our manuscripts, is not found in the Greek volumes, or in the old Latin volumes, specifically in those made available to me by the cloister library of St Donatian at Bruges.[3]

1 The Greek idiom here leaves the subject of the infinitive unexpressed, with the predicate in the nominative; Latin idiom requires, as in the Vulgate here, a reflexive pronoun in the accusative case as subject of the infinitive, with accusative predicate in agreement.
2 Now ... Bruges.] Added in 1522
3 In August 1521 Erasmus went to Bruges to see some English friends in the company of Cardinal Wolsey, who had arrived to negotiate with the emperor Charles. Erasmus was the guest of his friend, Marcus Laurinus, dean of the college at the church of St Donatian in Bruges. He thus acquired access to the cloister library, where he found several Latin manuscripts of the New Testament, two of which are described in his annotation on Matt 3:16 (baptizatus autem Iesus). These manuscripts appear as textual witnesses in the third edition of Erasmus' New Testament (1522); see the Translators' Note xii above. See also Ep 1223 introduction and H.J. de Jonge in ASD IX-2 168:73–4n.

1:22 [ER VG] *stulti facti sunt* 'they became fools.' The Greek uses a single word, ἐμωράνθησαν, that is, 'they were infatuated.'

1:23 [ER *immortalis dei* 'of the immortal God']
[VG] *incorruptibilis dei* 'of the incorruptible God'; ἀφθάρτου, which he else-where translates 'immortal,' as in[1] the first chapter of First Timothy, 'to the immortal God,' ἀφθάρτῳ θεῷ,[2] and certainly in this passage [immortal] would have been more appropriate. For he is contrasting 'the immortal God' with the likeness of a mortal (φθαρτός) man, except[3] that ἄφθαρτος [incorruptible] means somewhat more than ἀθάνατος [deathless]. For the rational souls of human beings are ἀθάνατοι [deathless] but by no means ἄφθαρτοι [incorruptible].

1 as in ... θεῷ] Added in 1527
2 1 Tim 1:17. Cf the annotation on Rom 2:7 ('to those seeking life') and n22.
3 except ... ἄφθαρτοι] Added in 1527

1:23 [ER *per imaginem non solum ad ... similitudinem effictam* 'through an image fashioned not only according to ... the likeness']
[VG] *in similitudinem imaginis* 'into the likeness of the image'; ἐν ὁμοιώματι εἰκόνος 'in the likeness of an image' or rather 'in the fashioning' or 'repre-senting[1] of an image.' For he does not mean that they had turned the glory

of God into the image of a man, but that they had thought about God not as
they should when they devised the image of a man for him who is² similar
to nothing among corporeal things. Thus the expression 'in the likeness [of
an image]' has the sense '*through* the representation of an image.' A little
below, in the same manner, μετήλλαξαν τὴν ἀλήθειαν αὐτοῦ ἐν τῷ ψεύδει,
that is, 'they transformed his truth³ *in* a lie.' In both phrases⁴ the case is
ablative, not accusative.⁵ For they did not turn the truth of God *into* a lie, but
since they themselves were engaged in a lie, they changed for themselves
the truth of God by preaching about him otherwise than he is. Certainly⁶ the
very old codex from the library of St Donatian reads 'in a lie.' If they⁷ had
worshipped man in place of God, the affront to the creator would be great,
but the madness would have been slighter. Now [Paul] calls the likeness,
which in appearance counterfeits a man or some other animal, though it
neither lives nor feels, a 'lie.' For a living monkey is preferable to the statue
of a man.

1 Latin *assimilatio*; cf the annotation on 5:14 ('unto the likeness') below – where
  Erasmus again distinguishes between *similitudo* and *assimilatio* – and nn14
  and 15.
2 who is ... corporeal things] Added in *1527*
3 his truth] First in *1519*; in *1516*, 'the truth of God'
4 in both phrases] Added in *1519*. The reference is to the phrases 'in the
  likeness' (1:23) and 'in a lie' (1:25).
5 Cf 1:25, where the Vulgate of *1527* read *in* followed by the accusative, '*into*
  a lie' (cf Wordsworth and White II 67 25n). The Greek ἐν is used here to
  express means. Cf the annotation on 1:10 ('in the will'), where the Greek ἐν
  'in' is to be translated by the Latin *per* 'through.'
6 Certainly ... 'in a lie.'] Added in *1522*; 'in a lie' is the preferred Vulgate
  reading (Wordsworth and White II 67).
7 If they ... man.] Added in *1527*

1:24 [ER *per cupiditates cordium suorum* 'through the passions¹ of their
      hearts']
[VG] *in desideria cordis* 'to the desires of the heart'; ἐν ταῖς ἐπιθυμίαις τῶν
καρδιῶν αὐτῶν, that is, 'in the lusts of their hearts,' not 'heart' and not
'to the desires.' Certainly in this passage [the Translator] might seem to
have misconstrued the preposition ['in'], as he does elsewhere,² too, except
that here the preposition is used more suitably – provided we understand
'handed over' in the sense of 'abandoned.'³ For God did not force them
into foul lusts, but abandoned them as they went thither by their own vice.
So also⁴ one can take 'in the lusts' to mean 'through lusts.' Into such great
deeds of shame did they fall, enticed and drawn away by their own passions
– God permitting.⁵ The plural, 'hearts,' is not without special meaning: you

are to understand that the affections of fools are diverse; among these there is not a single and united heart, or any concord.[6]

> 1 In *1516* Erasmus translated *in desideriis cordium* 'in the desires of their hearts.' He changed the translation in *1519*, a change reflected in the *1519* addition to the annotation (see n4 below).
> 2 Cf the previous annotation, n5.
> 3 Erasmus followed the Vulgate in translating *tradidit* 'handed over': 'Wherefore God handed them over ...'
> 4 So also ... permitting.] Added in *1519*. See nn1 and 2 above.
> 5 Commentators in antiquity and the Middle Ages in their discussion of this verse undertook to relieve God of the responsibility for making man sin. See Ambrosiaster *Comm in Rom* 1:24 (2): 'To hand over is to permit, not to incite'; Pelagius *Expos in Rom* 1:24: 'In Scripture God is said to "hand over" when he does not prevent those who sin of their own will' (Souter II 15:15–16); Thomas Aquinas *Super Rom lect* cap 1 lectio 7.139: 'God hands human beings over to sin – indirectly, in so far as he rightly withdraws his grace ...' Cf Chrysostom *Hom in Rom* 3.3 PG 60 414–15. Cf also the paraphrase on this and the succeeding verses, CWE 42 18 and n20.
> 6 For the torment of conflicting passions in the person who lacks wisdom see Plato *Republic* 9.6 (579D–E) and Cicero *Tusculan Disputations* 5.20.60.

1:24 [ER *corpora sua inter se mutuo* 'their bodies, mutually[1] among themselves']
[VG] *corpora sua in semetipsis* 'their bodies in themselves'; ἐν ἑαυτοῖς, that is, 'among themselves' [*inter sese*]. For he means, if I am not mistaken,[2] a mutual debauchery of the males among themselves, and likewise a mutual intercourse of the women among themselves.[3]

> 1 mutually among themselves] The translation of *1519* and thereafter. In *1516*, *inter seipsos* 'among themselves'
> 2 if I am not mistaken] Added in *1519*
> 3 In the paraphrase primary responsibility is given to men, not to women (in spite of the sequence in 1:26 and 27) for this 'unnatural' use of sex. Cf CWE 42 18 n19.

1:25 [ER *veritatem eius* 'his truth']
[VG] *veritatem dei* 'the truth of God'; τὴν ἀλήθειαν αὐτοῦ, that is, 'his truth,' namely, God's. Besides, since 'God' has just preceded, it is a little harsh to repeat it in such close succession. But[1] the Greek codices vary here.

> 1 But ... here.] Added in *1527*. Tischendorf offers no alternative to the standard τὴν ἀλήθειαν τοῦ θεοῦ 'the truth of God'; cf II 367.

1:25 [ER *et venerati sunt* 'and venerated']
[VG] *et coluerunt* 'and worshipped'; ἐσεβάσθησαν, that is, 'venerated,' a word properly used of those things to which we attribute majesty, and

something divine. They are also called σεβαστά, that is,[1] 'august.' The word which follows, ἐλάτρευσαν 'served,'[2] I have preferred to translate 'worshipped.'[3]

1 that is, 'august'] Added in 1527
2 For the extended passage, compare the translations of Erasmus and the Vulgate:
ER *et venerati sunt colueruntque ea quae condita sunt* 'both venerated and worshipped created things'
VG *et coluerunt et servierunt creaturae* 'and worshipped and served the creature'
3 On λατρεία as 'worship,' see the annotations on 1:9 ('whom I serve') and 12:1 ('reasonable service').

1:25 [ER *supra eum qui condidit* 'beyond him who created']
[VG] *potius quam creatori* 'rather than the creator'; παρὰ τὸν κτίσαντα, that is, 'beyond him' or 'above him who created.' That is, they offered more honour to things created than to him who created. Hilary[1] well conveys the sense in his twelfth book *On the Trinity*: 'They served the creature,' he says, 'passing over the creator.'[2]

1 Hilary ... creator.] Added in 1527
2 Hilary *De Trinitate* 12.3 PL 10 435C

1:25 [ER *qui est laudandus* 'who is to be praised']
[VG] *qui est benedictus* 'who is blessed'; εὐλογητός. For the sake of the simpler folk, I have translated this as 'to be praised.'[1] For in Greek εὐλογεῖν [to speak well] is to speak honourably about someone; whence also, I think, we speak of the *benedictiones* [blessings] of bishops, for they pray a blessing upon the people and pronounce words of good promise [on their behalf].[2] And yet[3] this word [*benedictus*] is so generally used in sacred literature that one can scarcely change it.

1 Challenged by Zúñiga on this rendering, Erasmus replied that he wanted to clarify Paul's meaning for the common folk, who think that *benedicere* means to make the sign of the cross or to pronounce a blessing; he also wished to translate the Bible into proper Latin. See *Apologia ad annotationes Stunicae* ASD IX-2 164 and the note on lines 15–16.
2 Erasmus understands the Latin *benedictiones* (literally 'well-sayings') as analogous to the Greek εὐλογεῖν, εὐλογίαι.
From the early medieval period the blessing upon the people placed in the mass after the Lord's Prayer and before the communion belonged to the bishop alone. Sometimes the priest would administer a modified form of this blessing, but he could not usurp the longer version by the bishop. See D.D. DuCanges *Glossarium infimae et mediae latinitatis* I (Paris 1937) 625.
3 And yet ... it.] Added in 1519

1:26 [ER *in cupiditates ignominiosas* 'to shameful desires']

[vg] *in passiones ignominiae* 'to passions of shame'; εἰς πάθη ἀτιμίας. The Greek πάθη sometimes means 'disturbances of the soul' or 'emotions' or 'diseases' or (a word that Fabius[1] strongly prefers) 'affections.'[2] In such a great abundance of acceptable terms, where was the need for the strange and artificial word *passio* [suffering, passion]? 'Diseases' would have been especially fitting in this place, since Horace, too, calls effeminate lust a 'disease': 'With her herd of filthy men [corrupted] by disease.'[3] Further, the addition of *ignominiae* [of shame] appears to have been derived from Hebrew idiom, to mean ' "disgraceful" or "reproachful" or "shameful"[4] affections.' For he calls lust a 'reproach' to the body, as above, τοῦ ἀτιμάζεσθαι σώματα αὐτῶν [the dishonouring of their bodies].[5] And Peter, in the[6] interpretation of Jerome, calls it an 'honour' to the wife if she is not defiled by sexual intercourse. But ἀτιμία [shame] is the opposite of honour.[7]

1 Ie Marcus Fabius Quintilian. See n2.

2 Erasmus describes the πάθη in similar terms in *Ecclesiastes* III LB V 977C–D. For the definitions here see Cicero *Tusculan Disputations* 3.4.7–9, 4.5.10 and *De finibus* 3.10.35; Quintilian 6.2.8. Valla had cited both Cicero and Quintilian in defining the πάθη of this passage. See *Annot in Rom* 1 (I 856). See also the annotation on 1:31 ('without disposition'). For Erasmus' objection in the next sentence to *passio*, see L&S, especially II B.

3 Horace *Odes* 1.37.9–10. 'Corrupted' (*contaminato* in the text of Horace) appears in LB, but is not part of the quotation in any edition from 1516 to 1535. The ode expresses joy in Roman relief from the threat of Cleopatra. Though it is generally admitted that *morbo* 'disease' in the text refers to unnatural vice, and often assumed that the allusion is to Cleopatra's eunuch slaves, the precise interpretation of the passage is disputed. See D.R. Shackleton Bailey *Profile of Horace* (Cambridge, MA 1982) 116.

4 or "shameful"] Added in 1519. For the 'Hebrew idiom' see the annotation on 1:4 ('through the spirit of santification') and n3.

5 Cf Rom 1:24, where Erasmus' annotation ('their bodies in themselves') failed to discuss the verb ἀτιμάζεσθαι, which the Vulgate translated *contumeliis afficiant* 'bring shameful things upon,' and he rendered *ignominia afficiant* 'bring shame upon.' Valla, too, had correlated the ἀτιμία of this verse with the ἀτιμάζεσθαι of 1:24 (*Annot in Rom* 1 [I 856]).

6 in the ... Jerome] Added in 1522

7 Though the identification of Jerome was not added until 1522, Erasmus' interpretation of this passage (1 Pet 3:1–7) was apparently derived already in 1516 from Jerome's *Adversus Jovinianum* 1.7 PL 23 (1883) 230C–231A. Jerome, beginning with 1 Pet 3:7, notes that husbands are to bestow honour upon their wives. He continues: 'If we abstain from intercourse, we bestow honour upon our wives; if we do not abstain, it is clear that "reproach" is the opposite of honour.'

1:26 [ER *nam et foeminae illorum mutaverunt naturalem usum* 'for their women also changed the natural use']

[VG] *nam et foeminae illorum commutaverunt naturalem usum foeminae* 'for¹ their women also wholly changed the natural use of a woman.' The last word, θηλείας 'of a woman,' is added in some Greek codices, but falsely – no doubt inserted here, if I am not mistaken, from the subsequent clause.²

> 1 for ... clause.] This note is a *1519* addition. The Vulgate printed in *1527* did not add the second *foeminae* 'of a woman'; the majority Vulgate reading omits the word (cf Wordsworth and White II 28 26n).
> 2 Ie from the expression 'the natural use of the woman' in verse 27. Erasmus had accepted the word in his *1516* text and translation, but omitted it in all subsequent editions.

1:27 [ER *per appetentiam sui* 'through longing for themselves']

[VG] *in desideriis suis* 'in their desires'; ἐν τῇ ὀρέξει αὐτῶν,¹ that is, *in appetentia sua* [in their longing] or, as I should prefer, *sui* [(longing) for themselves]. So you would understand a mutual longing of males for one another.

> 1 For the Greek text of his New Testament Erasmus printed the reflexive αὐτῶν in all editions after *1516*.

1:27 [ER *et praemium quod* 'and the reward which']

[VG] *et mercedem quam* 'and the pay which.' The Greek word ἀντιμισθία has a fuller significance. It has the meaning of 'compensation' or 'repayment' or 'due reward' or 'pay corresponding to deserts.' For some¹ outrages are such that they are not only crimes in themselves but also the punishment for the crimes. Augustine,² in *Against Julian*, book 5, chapter 3, cites several times [the phrase] *mercedem mutuam* [payment in turn]³ as though to convey the force of the preposition ἀντί, for ἀντικατηγορία means 'countercharge.'⁴ But the word [ἀντί] does not always have this force; sometimes it indicates only a 'return,' like the Latin prefix *re-* in *respondere* [reply] and *rependere* [pay back]. And yet, it would not be absurd to say 'in turn' if payment were made in turn for payment, just as one who returns love 'loves in turn'; but here punishment is paid back to the sinner, not sin in return for sin.⁵ It would be much more absurd to understand 'in turn' of the persons sharing obscene pleasure.

> 1 For some ... for the crimes.] Added in *1519*
> 2 Augustine ... pleasure.] The remaining portion of the annotation was added in *1535*.

3 Cf Augustine *Contra Julianum* 5.3.10 PL 44 789, where the phrase is cited three times. It is found elsewhere in Augustine as well; cf *De natura et gratia* 22 PL 44 259.
4 The Greek word is cited in Quintilian 3.10.4, where it is translated *mutua accusatio*.
5 Except for replacing *merces* with *praemium* Erasmus followed the Vulgate closely: 'and receiving in themselves the reward which they deserved for their error.'

1:28 [ER *et quemadmodum non probaverunt* 'and as they did not think it right']

[VG] *et sicut non probaverunt* 'and just as they did not think it right.' [The Vulgate here] has a double sense,[1] but this is inherent in the Greek words: καὶ καθὼς οὐκ ἐδοκίμασαν τὸν θεὸν ἔχειν ἐν ἐπιγνώσει. For if you take these words in this sense: 'and just as they did not think it right' (that is, 'were unwilling') 'to hold God in acknowledgment' – for the meaning here is 'acknowledgment' rather than 'knowledge' ('and they were unwilling to acknowledge him, however known') – [the phrase 'to hold God'] seems to require the article τό: τὸ τὸν θεὸν ἔχειν. But if [you take the words] in this sense: 'and just as they did not think it right that God acknowledged and knew all' – for, supposing he knew nothing, they sinned without restraint – [then] an object seems to be lacking, [an object] required by the verb ἔχειν [to have, to hold] in order to express what God had in cognizance. And although [the Greeks] seem elsewhere to use ἐπίγνωσις for γνῶσις, that is, 'acknowledgment' for 'knowledge,' the difference between these nouns is noted by our Jerome as well as by the Greek interpreters.[2] In this passage at least, 'acknowledged' would be very suitable. For [Paul] had said earlier that God was 'known' by them; but here he says that God was not 'acknowledged.' 'To know' [*cognoscere*] is [said] of one who understands; 'to acknowledge' [*agnoscere*] of one who is grateful and mindful. An ungrateful person 'knows' an act of kindness; but when he pretends that he owes nothing in return, he fails to 'acknowledge' it. Theophylact[3] points out that ἐδοκίμασαν [they thought it right] is here used for ἔκριναν [they judged, determined], that is, 'it did not seem good to them,' so that you see it is not their lack of knowledge that is being blamed, but their perverse will. For the verb *probare* is ambiguous in Latin; one *probat* [approves] who thinks something right, one *probat* [proves] who tests, one *probat* [proves, demonstrates] who teaches by arguments.[4] Thus according to the Greek interpreters[5] the sense is something like this: 'It did not seem good to them to acknowledge and venerate God, whom they knew.'

1 The extended passage in Erasmus and the Vulgate reads:
   ER *et quemadmodum non probaverunt ut deum agnoscerent* 'and as they did
   not think it right that they should acknowledge God'
   VG *et sicut non probaverunt deum habere in notitia*
   As Erasmus notes, the syntax of the Vulgate allows two interpretations:
   1/ 'and just as they did not think it right that they hold God in cognizance';
   and 2/ 'and just as they did not think it right that God held in cognizance.'
   However, as Erasmus also notes, the second can be read only if an object is
   supplied for 'held' ('held *all things* in cognizance').
2 For ἐπίγνωσις in the sense of 'knowledge' see ἐπίγνωσις 1 2 in LSJ and
   Cranfield 1 128.
   Origen, Chrysostom, and Theophylact do not make a distinction in their
   commentary on Rom 1:28. Jerome, however, in his commentary on Eph
   1:17 PL 26 (1883) 489B says that certain people understand the distinction
   thus: γνῶσις is knowledge newly learned, ἐπίγνωσις is knowledge of things
   once known, forgotten, then recollected; and such interpreters 'suppose
   there was a former life in heaven, but afterwards, we were sent into bodies,
   and, forgetful of the Father, came to know him through revelation; [these
   interpreters] adduce such scriptures as Ps 22:27 "Let all the ends of the earth
   remember and turn to the Lord." '
   Jerome is apparently dependent here upon Origen's *Commentary on
   Ephesians*. See J.A.F. Gregg 'The Commentary of Origen upon the Epistle
   to the Ephesians Part II' *Journal of Theological Studies* 3 (1902) 399. On the
   dependence of Jerome's commentary on that of Origen see A. von Harnack
   Der kirchengeschichtliche Ertrag der exegetischen Arbeiten des Origenes Texte und
   Untersuchungen 42 (Leipzig 1919); also F. Deniau 'Le commentaire de Jérôme
   sur Ephésiens nous permet-il connaître celui d'Origène?' in *Origeniana:
   premier colloque international des études origéniennes (Montserrat, 18–21 septembre
   1973)* ed H. Crouzel et al (Bari 1975) 163–79.
   In 1516 only, and perhaps by mistake, the next sentence read, 'In this
   passage, at least, "known" would be very suitable.'
3 Theophylact ... they knew.'] This remaining portion of the annotation was
   added in 1527. See Theophylact *Expos in Rom* 1:28 PG 124 359B.
4 For *probo* see the annotation on 2:18 ('you approve the more useful things').
5 Theophylact's interpretation had followed that of Chrysostom. See *Hom in
   Rom* 5.1 PG 60 421: 'Sin comes from a corrupted judgment.'

1:28 [ER *in reprobam mentem* 'to a reprobate mind']
   [VG] *in reprobum sensum* 'to a reprobate sense'; εἰς ἀδόκιμον νοῦν. The word
   here is not αἴσθησις 'sense,' such as seeing and hearing, but νοῦς, that is,
   'mind.' Thus it would be clearer to say 'to a reprobate mind.' Moreover,
   there is an engaging likeness in the words ἐδοκίμασαν [edokimasan] and
   ἀδόκιμον [adokimon], that is, *probaverunt* [they thought right, they approved]
   and *reprobum* [reprobate, reproved]. For here *probari* [to be approved] is
   said of that which is acceptable, and ἀδόκιμον [reprobate] of that which is

unacceptable to all. Of such a kind are the things he lists here – monstrous outrages which even pagans[1] themselves abhor.

    1 pagans] *ethnici* in *1519* and subsequent editions; *'gentiles'* in *1516*

1:28 [ER VG] *quae non conveniebant* **'that were not becoming'**; τὰ μὴ καθήκοντα. The sense is, 'unworthy of themselves,' that is, things which disgraced such people to do.

1:29 [ER *repleti* **'filled'**]
[VG] *repletos* **'filled.'** The Translator has connected these accusatives with the verb that preceded, 'handed over.' But they are more properly connected with the infinitive ποιεῖν [to do]. After he had changed this verb into a different mood, the accusatives should have been likewise changed into nominatives: 'That they[1] might do those things which were not becoming, filled with all iniquity.'[2]

    1 'That they ... iniquity'] Added in *1527*
    2 The passage in question reads: 'God handed *them* over to a reprobate mind *to do* things that were unbecoming, *filled* with all injustice ...' As it often did, so here the Vulgate followed closely the Greek construction, in which 'filled' can modify 'them,' object of 'handed over.' But Latin idiom forced the Vulgate to change the Greek infinitive 'to do' into a subjunctive verb in a clause of its own: 'God handed them over to a reprobate mind, so that *they* did (or, might do) what was unbecoming, *filled* with all injustice.' In this construction, 'filled' is now better read as modifying the 'they,' subject of the subordinate clause, therefore nominative, not accusative case. Hence also the adjectives that follow in verses 29–31 are similarly to be read as nominatives rather than the accusatives of the Vulgate, and so they appear in Erasmus' translation.

1:29 [ER VG] *avaritia* **'with avarice'**; πλεονεξία. This word sometimes translates 'plunder,' sometimes 'fraud,' occasionally, 'avarice.' The verb πλεονεκτεῖν, however, is a compound from πλέον ἔχειν, that is, 'having more.' The Greeks use this of someone who acquires more than his due, who seizes the more desirable portions even though others are cheated; hence the words πλεονέκτης [grasping] and πλεονεξία [greediness]. However, not only is every avaricious person also a cheat; but even every rich person is either unjust or the heir to someone unjust, if we[1] believe the proverb.

    Now, whenever a catalogue of nouns of this kind occurs, there are some discrepancies in the manuscripts, whether[2] you consult the Greek or Latin; this is due to forgetfulness on the part of the amanuenses, as it is difficult to keep this sort of thing in mind. I do not always approve of the too anxious care taken in these matters by certain people who think the number as well is to be observed in a thick forest of names. For example, both in some other places and in the Epistle to the Galatians,[3] what is the purpose of counting the fruits of the Spirit when the works of the flesh correspond[4] neither in number nor in kind? Finally, there is added to the catalogue [the phrase] 'and things like these.'[5]

> 1 if we ... proverb] Added in 1522. See the proverb 'The rich man is either unjust or the heir of one who is unjust' *Adagia* I ix 47. For the connotations of 'fraud,' 'undue gain' in πλεονεξία and πλεονεκτέω, see the words in LSJ. Throughout the New Testament the Vulgate translated the noun by *avaritia*, the verb by *circumvenire*, 'to take advantage of,' 'defraud.'
> 2 whether ... Latin] Added in 1519
> 3 Gal 5:22–3. Cf also Eph 5:9, where Erasmus read 'the fruits of the Spirit,' against the Vulgate 'the fruit of light'; see the annotation on Eph 5:9 (*fructus enim lucis*).
> 4 correspond ... these'] Added in 1522. In 1516 the annotation ended with 'when the works of the flesh were not numbered?'
> 5 Cf Gal 5:23. Lee thought it significant that the fruits of the Spirit are numbered while the works of the flesh are not, since the works of the devil are without measure, while the works of God are measured. See *Responsio ad annotationes Lei* LB IX 213F–214B; and Edward Lee *Annotationes in annotationes Erasmi* (Mainz 1520) fol 26 verso.

1:29 [ER *malitia* 'with malice'][1]

[VG] *nequitia* 'with wickedness'; κακία. This word in Greek sometimes means 'vice' and is opposed to ἀρετή [virtue]. Sometimes it means 'sloth,' and hence ἐκκακοῦν 'to fail' or 'grow faint'; occasionally 'suffering,' which is, however, more correctly κάκωσις. In this passage, I should have preferred to translate *malitia* [malice], which in Seneca is used simply for 'vice';[2] in other cases, it means 'perversity,' when someone is spiteful in return for a service rendered. But [the Translator] renders πονηρία by *malitia* though the word sometimes means not only 'malice' but 'craftiness' and 'cunning'; hence it immediately precedes 'avarice,' its sibling, as it were.[3] But *nequitia* [wickedness, or moral worthlessness] properly has reference to lust and luxury, for these vices indicate that one is corrupt and worthless, and those subject to them are accustomed to be scorned by all. To those[4] who read Greek, there is an attractive similarity between πορνεία [*porneia* 'fornication'] and πονηρία [*ponēria* 'wickedness'].

> 1 malice] The translation from 1519; for the 1516 translation see n3 below.
> 2 Cf Seneca *Epistulae morales* 31.5.6, 47.21.6, 81.21.5.
> 3 This annotation reflects not only variants in the textual tradition but the differences in translation between the Vulgate and Erasmus, whose 1516 and 1519 editions themselves varied considerably here:
>> ER [1516] *repleti omni iniustitia, fornicatione, avaritia, malitia* 'filled with all unrighteousness, fornication, avarice, malice'

ER [1519] *repleti omni iniustitia, scortatione, versutia, avaritia, malitia* 'filled with all unrighteousness, whoring, craftiness, avarice, malice'
VG *repletos omni iniquitate, malitia, fornicatione, avaritia, nequitia* 'filled with all iniquity, malice, fornication, avarice, wickedness'
In *1516* Erasmus printed a Greek text with the word πονηρία, though the word is not represented in his Latin translation – perhaps omitted inadvertently – so that in *1516* 'fornication' immediately precedes 'avarice.' In *1519*, however, he translated the word by *versutia* 'craftiness,' following a Greek text in which the word preceded 'avarice.' In the Vulgate the word immediately precedes 'fornication,' not 'avarice.' Thus though Erasmus begins this sentence with reference to the Translator of the Vulgate, it appears that he concludes by describing the order of words in the Greek text.
4 To those ... πονηρία.] Added in *1519*

1:29 [ER *invidia, caede* '(full of) envy, slaughter']
[VG] *invidia, homicidiis* '[full of] envy, murders.' In Greek there is a pleasing similarity in the words φθόνου [*phthonou* 'envy'] and φόνου [*phonou* 'murder']. 'Slaughter' in the singular, however, is a better [translation] than 'murders.'

1:29 [ER *malis praediti moribus* 'possessed of a harsh disposition']
[VG] *malignitate* '[full of] spite'; κακοηθείας. This means, rather, 'a harsh and obstinate disposition.' For in our language 'spite' is opposed to 'kindness' or 'candour.' He praises 'spitefully' who praises sparingly and almost grudgingly. He gives 'spitefully' who gives restrictively.

1:30 [ER *obtrectatores* 'disparagers']
[VG] *detractores* 'detractors.' The Greek word κατάλαλοι has a fuller meaning [than 'detractors']. [It means] 'disparagers';[1] one 'detracts' who diminishes someone's praise; one 'disparages'[2] who speaks spitefully about someone.

> 1 disparagers] In *1516* Erasmus had translated *oblocutores* 'those who cast reproach' and so had used the same term here in the annotation. In *1519* he translated *obtrectatores* and changed the annotation accordingly.
> 2 disparages] First in *1527*; in *1516–1522*, 'disparages or casts reproach'

1:30 [ER *dei osores* 'haters of God']
[VG] *deo odibiles* 'hateful to God.' This is a single word in Greek, θεοστυγεῖς, and means 'those to whom God is hateful' rather than 'those whom God holds in hatred.' And so interpret the Greek scholia,[1] though Theophylact[2] interprets in both ways,[3] while Chrysostom does not touch on it. Likewise Cyprian in the fourth letter of the first book reads 'shunning God';[4] no doubt they are the sort 'who say to God, "Depart from us, we do not want the knowledge of your ways." '[5] Julius Pollux[6] mentions θεοστυγής also among

the words by which we express impiety; he points out that it is a word used in tragedy.[7]

1 Cf Pseudo-Oecumenius *Comm in Rom* 1:30 PG 118 348D.
2 though Theophylact . . . of your ways"'] Added in *1519*, except for the words 'while Chrysostom does not touch on it,' which were added in *1535*.
3 See Theophylact *Expos in Rom* 1:30 PG 124 361A.
4 Cyprian *Epistulae* 67.9 CSEL 3/2 743:6
5 Job 21:14
6 Julius Pollux . . . tragedy.] Added in *1535*. Julius Pollux, a Greek rhetorician, was appointed to a chair of rhetoric at Athens in the late second century AD. His *Onomasticon*, a sort of rhetorical handbook, abounds in word-studies. For the reference, see *Onomasticon* 1.21 (*Pollucis Onomasticon* ed E. Bethe, 2 vols [Leipzig 1900, 1931] I 5).
7 Cf Euripides *Trojan Women* 1213.

1:30 [ER *contumeliosi* 'contumelious']

[VG] *contumeliosos* 'contumelious'; ὑβριστάς, that is, 'insolent' and 'crushing others forcibly,' as though to say 'violators.' Thus he adds next the vice related to this – ὑπερήφανος 'arrogant.'[1]

1 Compare the translations of the word in Erasmus and the Vulgate:
   ER *elati* 'exalted'
   VG *superbos* 'arrogant'

1:30 [ER *gloriosi* 'boastful']

[VG] *elatos* '**exalted**'; ἀλαζόνας. Plautus translates ἀλαζών as *gloriosus* [braggart],[1] one whom you might also rightly call 'pretentious.' The Greek[2] word comes παρὰ τὸ ἐν ἄλῃ ζῆν [from living in wandering],[3] because impostors of this kind are accustomed to go frequently from place to place in order more easily to deceive those who do not know them. ἀλαζών [*alazōn*] is the opposite of εἴρων [*eirōn*] in Greek. The former advertises and vaunts himself to be what he is not; the latter conceals what he is.[4]

1 Plautus *Miles gloriosus* 86–7
2 The Greek . . . know them.] Added in *1527*
3 Erasmus derives ἀλαζών (*alazōn*) from ἄλη and ζῆν (*alē zēn*), but Chantraine *Dictionnaire* I 53 cites Bonfante for the opinion that the word originally designated a Thracian tribe and came into common use like the English word 'vandal.'
4 Cf Aristotle *Nicomachean Ethics* 2.7 (1108a23) where the ἀλαζών and the εἴρων are contrasted as 'buffoon' and 'self-deprecator.'

1:30 [ER *excogitatores malorum* 'contrivers[1] of evils']

[VG] *inventores malorum* 'inventors of evils'; ἐφευρετάς, that is, 'those who invent by bringing something in besides'[2] – either because in things good

in themselves they mix in some evil, or because they always add evil to
evils. For evil always arises out of evil.

1 contrivers] From *1519*; in *1516*, like the Vulgate, *inventores*
2 *adinventores*. So also Cyprian *Epistulae* 67.9; cf the annotation on 1:30 ('hateful
to God') n4 above.

1:30 [ER *immorigeri* 'uncompliant']
[VG] *non obedientes* '**not obedient**'; ἀπειθεῖς, that is, 'uncompliant' or 'disobedient' [*inobedientes*] or 'intractable.' There was no need for the circumlocution here.[1]

1 The Greek is ἀπειθεῖς, a single word not requiring, Erasmus argues, two Latin
words (a circumlocution) to translate.

1:31 [ER *expertes intelligentiae pactorum haudquaquam tenaces* '**devoid of
understanding, not at all faithful to contractual agreements**']
[VG] *insipientes incompositos* '**senseless,**[1] **without covenants.**' Again, in
the Greek there is a very pleasing similarity of words, which the Translator
did not attempt to reproduce, nor was he able to do so: ἀσυνέτους [*asyne-
tous*], ἀσυνθέτους [*asynthetous*]. Theophylact[2] interprets 'without covenants'
to mean 'faithless' and 'in no way holding to agreements,' with a slippery reliability in contracts,[3] because in Greek 'to make an agreement'
is συντίθεσθαι [*syntithesthai*], and [the noun] 'covenants' is συνθῆκαι [*syn-
thēkai*].[4] Moreover, he calls those ἀσύνετοι [devoid of understanding] who
are not restrained by the reason peculiar to humanity, and without which
one ceases to be human.

1 senseless] *insipientes* in *1535* only; in editions from *1516* to *1527*, *sine intellectu*
'without understanding'
2 Theophylact . . . human.] This remaining portion of the annotation was added
in *1519*.
3 Theophylact *Expos in Rom* 1:31 PG 124 361B
4 Erasmus tells Frans Titelmans, however, that one of the chief reasons for
replacing the Vulgate *incompositos* was its ambiguity: the word invited
the reader to think also of the 'indecorous.' See *Responsio ad collationes*
LB IX 971F.

1:31 [ER *alieni a charitatis affectu* '**strangers to the feeling of charity**']
[VG] *sine affectione* '**without disposition**';[1] ἀστόργους. I shall not, by the
way, go into detail over the Translator's use of *affectio* for *affectus*, although
there is a great difference between them;[2] among the Stoics to lack *affectus*
[emotions] merited the highest praise;[3] so with us, to be free from evil
affections is considered praiseworthy.[4] But στοργή does not simply mean
'emotions,' but rather that feeling of piety or charity by which parents are

drawn towards children, their children, in turn, towards the parents, and brother is drawn towards brother. Hence those who have advanced so far in vice that they have become deaf to even these common affections, and to natural instinct itself, are called ἄστοργοι. Such[5] was the man about whom the satirist [said], 'He does not love, and is loved by none.'[6]

In[7] his commentary, Chrysostom brings these words together in this way: ἀσυνθέτους, ἀσπόνδους, ἀστόργους, ἀνελεήμονας [without the bonds of social intercourse, without covenants, without affection, without mercy][8] – as though the first referred to the natural affection by which all living things are united in a common species, such as man to man, wolf to wolf; the second to civic agreements, based on contracts; the third, to the feeling for relations and kin; the fourth, to the feeling of mercy, whereby we sometimes grieve for the afflictions even of our enemies. [Paul] heaps up these examples because the impiety of those people had made them deaf to all these natural affections.[9] Theophylact follows the same order of words, interpreting ἀσυνθέτους to mean τοῖς συμπεφωνημένοις οὐκ ἐμμένοντας, that is, 'not continuing in agreements.'[10]

1 The translation attempts to reflect Erasmus' apparent reading of the Vulgate.
2 Erasmus fails to define specifically the distinction he intends here, but for a similar discussion on the confusion of the two terms cf Valla *Elegantiae* 4.78 (I 147–8), who described *affectio* as a disposition, *affectus* as an emotion, or, in Ciceronian language, a *perturbatio* (a disturbance); but cf Erasmus' *Paraphrasis in Elegantias Laurentii Vallae* ASD I-4 218–19, where the two words are defined. Cf Cicero *Tusculan Disputations* 4.13.29–30 and 15.34; cf also the annotation on 1:26 ('to passions of shame'). We have translated *affectus* variously by 'emotion,' 'affection,' 'feeling.' Cf the annotation on 8:7 ('because the wisdom of the flesh') and n4.
3 Cf Cicero *Tusculan Disputations* 3.6.12–3.10.22.
4 Cf Gal 5:19–24.
5 Such … none.'] Added in 1527
6 Cf Juvenal *Satires* 12.130, speaking of the 'legacy hunter.'
7 In … agreements.'] The remainder of the annotation was added in 1535.
8 So Theophylact *Expos in Rom* 1:31 PG 124 361B, but conflicting with the order printed in the Greek text of Erasmus' New Testament (all editions) – 'without the bonds of social intercourse, without affection, without covenants, without mercy' – which, indeed, is the order in Migne's text of Chrysostom's *Homilies on Romans* (cf 5.1 PG 60 425)
9 The significance Erasmus gives to the four predicates here is apparently an inference from Chrysostom, who had rather commented on the four terms as a single unit that provided an appropriate climax to the entire list beginning with 1:29, since their position here implied that the loss of natural affection was the result of the human evils previously mentioned. See *Hom in Rom* 5.1 PG 60 421–2. Erasmus explained the four terms similarly in the quarrel with Titelmans; cf *Responsio ad collationes* LB IX 972A–C.

10 Theophylact *Expos in Rom* 1:31 PG 124 361B. In the *Responsio ad collationes* Erasmus recognized that the order of the four predicates in Theophylact differed from that printed in his New Testament (cf nn8 and 9 above).

1:31 [ER *nescii foederis* 'unaware of the contractual bond']
[VG] *absque foedere* 'apart from[1] contract.' What, I ask, does this mean, 'without contract?' Is he condemning those who do not draw up contracts, or rather those who are bound by no contracts that would prevent them from doing whatever they like? He ought rather to have called them 'contract breakers.' Yet elsewhere the Greeks use ἄσπονδος [without treaty] to mean 'irreconcilable,' as in ἄσπονδος πόλεμος [a war in which no truce is possible, implacable war],[2] and σπονδή also signifies 'fellowship,' so that [by ἄσπονδοι] you understand 'not to be dealt with,' living to themselves, exercising towards none the right of relationship.

This συναθροισμός [synathroismos], that is, 'piling up of words,' and ἀσύνδετον [asyndeton] add strikingly to the power and force of the discourse. And the προσονομασία [prosonomasia][3] adds to the pleasure, but also to the intensification and to the hatred of what is disliked. It is as though you were to say about a manifest lie 'this has never been described in writing, never portrayed in colour.'

1 apart from] 1535. Previous editions read *sine* 'without.'
2 Cf Demosthenes *On the Crown* 262 and Polybius *Histories* 1.65.6.
3 προσονομασία refers to the play on words in 1:28–31, which Erasmus has noted in several of the preceding annotations, for example, on 'to a reprobate sense' (1:28), '[full of] envy, murders' (1:29), 'senseless, without covenants' (1:31). The term is used in the sense of the *paronomasia* of the classical rhetoricians (for which see Quintilian 9.3.66; see also Lausberg I 637–9 and Chomarat *Grammaire et rhétorique* I 533 n144). For their similarity in the Renaissance, see the entries in Sir Thomas Elyot's dictionary, *Biblioteca Eliotae* (1548) intro Lillian Gottesman (Delmar, NY 1975), and for *prosonomasia* see *George Puttenham, The Arte of English Poesie* ed Gladys Doidge Willcock and Alice Walker (Cambridge 1936) 202–3. For Erasmus' own definition of *prosonomasia* see *Ecclesiastes* III LB V 1000 A–B.

1:31 [ER *immisericordes* 'unmerciful']
[VG] *sine misericordia* 'without mercy'; ἀνελεήμονας, that is, 'unmerciful.' I am surprised that a circumlocution[1] caught the fancy of the Translator here.

1 Cf the annotation on 1:30 ('not obedient') n1.

1:32 [ER *qui cum dei iustitiam* 'who though (they know) the righteousness of God']
[VG] *qui cum iustitiam dei* 'who[1] though [they knew] the righteousness of God.' In this passage the Greek manuscripts vary widely from our own.

They read as follows: οἵτινες τὸ δικαίωμα τοῦ θεοῦ ἐπιγνόντες, ὅτι οἱ τὰ τοιαῦτα πράσσοντες, ἄξιοι θανάτου εἰσίν, οὐ μόνον αὐτὰ ποιοῦσιν, ἀλλὰ καὶ συνευδοκοῦσι τοῖς πράσσουσιν, that is, 'who, though they know the right-eousness of God,' this righteousness, namely, 'that those who do such things are worthy of death, not only do these same things, but even give their consent to those who do them.' On this reading, you understand that to approve of the evil deeds of others is worse than to do evil yourself and keep quiet. But these two words ποιοῦσιν and συνευδοκοῦσιν ['they do' and 'they give their consent'] provided the occasion for corruption [in the text]; in Greek these can be either participles, in the dative plural, or verbs in the third person.[2] For first [Paul] sets down the 'righteousness of God,' then he sets out, as it were, what that righteousness is, namely, 'that those who do such things are worthy of death.' But how these two words *non intellexerunt* [they did not understand] came into our copies, certainly I do not quite understand;[3] though even if they are added the sense will be the same if you read them as a negative question,[4] taking it to mean that it was impossible for them not to have understood this as well. From Origen noth-ing definite can be inferred that relates to this point indeed,[5] except that I suspect this passage in his text is corrupt.[6] The Greek scholia indicate only[7] that some are accustomed to read this passage in a different way, so that 'doing' is the more serious offence, 'consenting' the lighter.[8] But our[9] [Latin writers], I suspect, added these two words, *non intellexerunt*, on their own, because they felt that some words were required to fill out the meaning. But the Greek manuscripts[10] now extant, with large consensus, suggest that Paul's meaning was different, namely, that to approve of the evil deeds of others is more serious than to fall into sin yourself, for the latter is very often due either to chance or to weakness; the former either to a most per-nicious flattery or to a most deplorable malice. It was the duty of the wise to restrain the unlearned common people from these vices; instead, those[11] not only did the same things, but even confirmed by their own authority the madness of the people. Chrysostom[12] and Theophylact[13] interpret [the passage] in this way, but Cyprian disagrees in the fourth letter of the first book,[14] and with him Ambrose.[15]

But because[16] of some who are δυσπειθεῖς [difficult to persuade] it would be better to set down the words of Chrysostom himself: δύο τιθεὶς ἐνταῦθα ἀντιθέσεις ἀνεῖλε αὐτὰς προηγουμένως. τί γὰρ ἂν εἴπῃς, φησίν, ὅτι οὐκ οἶδα τὰ πρακτέα; μάλιστα μὲν ᾔδεις, σὺ αἴτιος, ἀφεὶς τὸν γνωρίζοντά σοι θεόν, νῦν δὲ διὰ πολλῶν δείκνυμί σε εἰδότα, καὶ ἑκόντα πλημμελοῦντα. ἀλλὰ ὑπὸ τοῦ πάθους ἕλκῃ. τί οὖν καὶ συμπράττεις καὶ ἐπαινεῖς; οὐ γὰρ μόνον αὐτὰ ποιοῦσιν, ἀλλὰ καὶ συνευδοκοῦσι τοῖς πράττουσι. τὴν γοῦν χαλεπωτέραν πρότερον θεὶς καὶ ἀσύγγνωστον, ἵνα ἕλῃ, καὶ γὰρ τοῦ πλημμελοῦντος τὴν ἁμαρτίαν ἐπαιρῶν, πολλῷ χαλεπώτερος. τοῦτ᾽ οὖν πρῶτον εἰπὼν διὰ τούτου σφοδρότερον πάλιν ἐν τοῖς ἑξῆς χειροῦται αὐτῶν οὕτως λέγων, διὸ ἀναπολόγητος εἶ ὦ ἄνθρωπε, that is, 'Here he removes two proposed objections at the start. For, says he, what reason do you have to say, "I do not know what should be done"? You certainly knew very well. You are at fault for departing from God, through whom you knew these things. But now with much evidence I convict you of sinning knowingly and willingly. But [you further object] desire drags you towards sin. Why therefore do you both do these things and praise them? For they not only do these things, but also approve of those who do the same. First, therefore, he has set forth the more serious fault, one that can by no means be forgiven, in order to convict them. For one who magnifies the sin of the offender is much more forceful.[17] Therefore, having first said this, he closes in upon them the more forcefully through it in these words which follow, when he says, "Therefore you are without excuse, O man."' Theophylact [interprets the passage] in this way: ἔδειξεν ὅτι ἀπὸ τοῦ μὴ θέλειν γνῶναι θεὸν ἐπληρώθησαν πάσης κακίας. δείκνυσι νῦν ὅτι οὐδὲ συγγνώμης εἰσὶν ἄξιοι. οὐ γὰρ ἔχουσιν εἰπεῖν, ὅτι ἠγνοοῦμεν τὸ καλόν. οἴδασι γὰρ τὸ δικαίωμα τοῦ θεοῦ. ἑκόντες ἄρα ποιοῦσι, καὶ ὃ χεῖρον τούτου, ἐπευδοκοῦσι τοῖς πράττουσι, τοῦτ᾽ ἔστι συνηγοροῦσι τῷ κακῷ, ὅπερ ἀνίατα νοσεῖν ἐστίν, that is, 'He has shown that because they were unwilling to acknowledge God they have been filled with all wickedness. He now shows that they do not even deserve forgiveness. For they cannot say, "We did not know what was right"; for they know the righteousness of God. Therefore they act willingly, and, what is worse, in addition they also approve of those who do [evil], that is, they become patrons of wickedness – an incurable disease.'

The very[18] tenor of the discussion supports this view: 'For this reason, you are without excuse, O man' etc.

    1 who ... Ambrose.] The annotation was introduced first in 1516 with this paragraph (for minor additions later see nn5–14). It was placed, however, under the rubric 'From the second chapter,' though a second rubric 'From the second chapter,' under which the annotations on chapter 2 were placed, beginning with 'because of which,' immediately followed this annotation. In 1519 the first of the two rubrics was omitted, and this annotation became the last of those on chapter 1.

    2 Cf the annotation on 2:1 ('because of which') n4.

    3 The 1527 Vulgate read: *qui cum iustitiam dei cognovissent, non intellexerunt, quoniam qui talia agunt digni sunt morte, non solum qui ea faciunt sed etiam qui consentiunt facientibus* 'who though they knew the righteousness of God did not understand that those who do such things are worthy of death, not only those who do them, but also those who consent to those who do them.' But the Vulgate texts offer several variants; the preferred reading is that of 1527, except that *qui* 'who' is entirely omitted from the last two clauses, with a consequent disruption in the sense; cf Wordsworth and White II 70 32n. For

his New Testament Erasmus printed the Greek as in this annotation with essentially the same translation: 'who, though they know' etc.

4 For an explanation of *non intellexerunt* 'did not understand' in the text, see Cranfield I 134. Against Frans Titelmans, Erasmus denied that the added words changed the sense if they were read as a question: 'Since they knew the righteousness of God, did they not understand ...?' See *Responsio ad collationes* LB IX 972 C–F.

5 indeed] Added in *1535*

6 Origen *Comm in Rom* 1.19 PG 14 869C–D. The Migne text of Origen favours the Vulgate reading; the text of Merlin (Paris 1512) omits *non intellexerunt* (cf fol CXXXVII verso) from the commentary, though the words are included in the introductory citation from the biblical text.

7 only] Added in *1519*

8 See Pseudo-Oecumenius *Comm in Rom* 1:32 PG 118 349B–C.

9 our ... suspect] Added in *1519*

10 manuscripts ... consensus] Added in *1519*

11 those] Added in *1535*; in previous editions, 'they'

12 Chrysostom] Added in *1527*; previously the text read 'Theophylact also interprets.'

13 For the passages quoted see Chrysostom *Hom in Rom* 5.1 PG 60 423 and Theophylact *Expos in Rom* 1:32 PG 124 361C. In both cases the quotations offer only minor variations from the Migne text.

14 but ... Cyprian] Added in *1519*. Cf Cyprian *Epistulae* 67.9 CSEL 3/2 743.

15 Cf Ambrosiaster *Comm in Rom* 1:32 (3–4), who condemns two kinds of people: those who do not themselves sin, but refuse to rebuke others who do, and those who both sin themselves and encourage others to do so.

16 But because ... disease.'] The remainder of this annotation, except for the last sentence, was added in *1527*. For the references to Chrysostom and Theophylact see n13 above.

17 Erasmus evidently interprets Chrysostom's Greek in this and the previous sentence somewhat differently from the translators of these homilies in NPNF; see NPNF 1st series, XI 360 col 2.

18 The very ... etc.] Added in *1535*

2:1 [ER *quapropter* 'wherefore']

[VG] *propter quod* 'because of which.' Origen points out the correct sequence of Paul's entire argument here, since it is in any case rather confusing, because[1] the verb 'hand over' is repeated three times,[2] and some reasons are given for 'handing over' that do not, however, seem to fit very well the particular [consequences].[3] Accordingly [Origen] thinks it is better to gather together all the reasons for 'handing over,' which are advanced separately in each case, and then to bring together the cases of 'handing over,' so that we arrange in this way: 'Since men changed the glory of the immortal God through an image fashioned in the likeness of a mortal man and of birds and beasts and serpents; and since they corrupted the truth of God with a lie, and revered and worshipped the creature instead of the creator, and did not wish to acknowledge God' – so far extends the accumulation of reasons; then, the forms of evil to which [God] has handed them over are thus brought together: 'Because of all these things God handed them over to the desires of their hearts and to impurity, that they might dishonour their own bodies; and God handed them over to shameful affections, so that their women perverted [the] natural use to a use contrary to nature, and the men did likewise. But God also handed them over to a reprobate mind, so that they might do things that are not fitting – they who were filled with all manner of wickedness, lust, deceit, avarice, malice, and were full of envy, murder, strife, guile, and the other evils that he recounts. And since they knew this was the righteousness of God, that those who do such things are worthy of death – those not only who do them, but who assent to those who do them – on this account also they will be without excuse for all these evils, inasmuch as they judge and condemn others for the acts that they themselves commit. For he who punishes another for things that he himself commits pronounces [judgment] against himself.' This is the arrangement Origen has described for reading the text.

One may gather from this passage that [Origen] read the text otherwise than do the Greek manuscripts today, for he does not end the sentence where we conclude the chapter, but joins it with the beginning of the next chapter – 'Because of which you are inexcusable, O man.' This interpretation might well stand if it could be elicited from the Greek. Now it would be possible by the addition of the single pronoun οἵ [who] to read [as Origen's text requires]: οὐ μόνον οἷ αὐτὰ ποιοῦσιν, ἀλλὰ καὶ συνευδοκοῦσι τοῖς πράσσουσι [those not only who do them, but also assent to those who do them]. For it is not, I think, appropriate to attribute to Paul such a crude solecism as the use of the dative for the nominative, that is, ποιοῦσιν [to those who do] and συνευδοκοῦσι [to those who assent] in place of ποιοῦντες [those who do] and συνευδοκοῦντες [those who assent].[4] Perhaps[5] the translator[6] has changed the Greek reading. Certainly in some cases he takes the liberty of a paraphraser.

1 because ... συνευδοκοῦντες.] Except for the last sentence, the remainder of the annotation was added in 1519. In 1516 a single sentence followed the first sentence ('Origen ... confusing'): 'Since I cannot comment on this briefly, and it does not really belong to this undertaking, I have noted it in passing, and anyone who wishes can turn to the author himself.'
2 In 1:24, 26, and 28
3 For example, Origen notes that those who were 'handed over' because they 'served the creature' (1:26) became guilty of more serious sins than those who were handed over because they worshipped images (1:24), while those who did not have God in cognizance (1:28) were handed over to a 'swarm of evils' worse than anything yet mentioned. As there seems to be no appropriate correspondence between cause and consequence, it is better to understand the causes as essentially one; while the consequences, too, belong together as though flowing from a single cause. See Origen *Comm in Rom* 1.19 PG 14 868B–869D.
4 Cf the annotation on 1:32 ('who though they knew the righteousness of God'). The words ποιοῦσιν and συνευδοκοῦσιν in 1:32c will not construe as participles in the dative, and so must be read as verbs. They are usually read with subject οἴτινες in verse 32a: 'though they know ... they not only do, but also assent.' This reading implies a full stop at the end of 1:32. If, however, the relative pronoun οἵ 'who' is inserted before these words, they become the verbs of a subordinate clause, leaving the sentence to be completed in 2:1. According to the Merlin text (Paris 1512), this seems to be the way Origen read the passage, in his commentary making the connection with 2:1 thus: 'Who, since they knew that this is the righteousness of God, that those who do such things are worthy of death – not only those who do them but also who assent to those who do them – on this account also will be inexcusable while they both judge and condemn others for those sins which they themselves commit' (fol CXXXVIII verso); cf *Comm in Rom* 1.19 PG 14 869C–D.
5 Perhaps ... paraphraser.] Added in 1527
6 Ie the translator of Origen whom Erasmus elsewhere accuses of paraphrasing; see the annotation on 2:7 ('to those seeking life') n17.

2:1 [ER *quisquis es qui iudicas* 'whoever you are who judge']
[VG] *omnis qui iudicas* 'every one of you who judge'; πᾶς ὁ κρίνων, that is, 'you, whoever judge' [*quisquis judicas*] or 'whoever you are who judge' [*quisquis es qui judicas*].

2:1 [ER *nam hoc ipso quod ... alterum* 'for by[1] the very fact that (you judge) another']

[VG] *in quo enim alterum* 'for in what [you judge] another'; ἐν ᾧ γάρ. The sense is: in judging another you condemn yourself, that is, 'by the very fact that you judge, you condemn yourself.' This [ἐν ᾧ] is a characteristic Greek idiom. Thus,[2] 1 Peter 2: ἐν ᾧ καταλαλοῦσι [in that they speak against you] [2:12]. For this is characteristically said in relation to magistrates and censors of morals: in bringing judgment against another, you bring it against yourself – just as we read that David pronounced a sentence of death against himself.[3] There is, besides, something rather harsh [in the Vulgate reading] about the unexpected change of number; first 'in what' [singular], then 'for you do the same *things*' [plural].[4] Moreover, when he adds 'for you do the same things' etc, he repeats virtually the same thought, unless you read according to our annotation.[5]

1 by] First in 1519; in 1516, *in hoc ipso* 'in the very fact'
2 Thus ... annotation.] This remaining portion of the annotation was added in 1535.
3 Cf 2 Sam 12:1–15.
4 In *Responsio ad collationes* LB IX 973A–C Erasmus defends his translation here on the grounds of its elegance.
5 Compare, on Erasmus' interpretation, the Vulgate reading with his own:
    VG for in what thing you judge another, you condemn yourself, for you do the same things which [*quae*] you judge
    ER now by the very fact that you judge another, you condemn yourself, for you who [*qui*] judge do the same things

2:1 [ER *eadem enim ... tu qui iudicas* 'for you who judge (do) the same things']

[VG] *eadem enim quae iudicas* 'for [you do] the same things which you judge'; τὰ γὰρ αὐτὰ πράσσεις ὁ κρίνων, that is, 'you who judge,' or 'you, the very one judging, do the same things.' Yet[1] this mistake has entered even the oldest codices, either because it is very easy to slip when writing *qui* [who] and *quae* [which],[2] or because some have read ἃ κρίνεις [things which you judge] in place of ὁ κρίνων [the one judging]. But it is not clear from the interpretation of Origen, or Chrysostom, or Theophylact, or Ambrose, what they read at this point;[3] but[4] the Greek [manuscripts] without exception read ὁ κρίνων.

1 Yet ... this point] Added in 1519, except that the phrase 'or Chrysostom' was added in 1527
2 Cf the preceding annotation ('for in what [you judge] another') n5.
3 In their commentaries at this point only Ambrosiaster and Theophylact cite these words. The Latin text of the former presupposes ἃ κρίνεις, while the latter reads ὁ κρίνων. Origen offers no discussion of 2:1, while the actual

commentary of the others gives no decisive evidence for their reading. Cf
Chrysostom *Hom in Rom* 5.1 PG 60 423; Theophylact *Expos in Rom* 2:1 PG 124
362D–365A; Ambrosiaster *Comm in Rom* 2:1.

4 but ... κρίνων] Added in 1527. For ὁ κρίνων as the preferred reading see
Tischendorf II 370 1n.

2:3 [ER VG] *iudicas condemnas* 'you judge, you condemn';[1] κρίνεις, κατακρίνεις
[*krineis, katakrineis*]. The charm of the Greek figure of speech could not be
reproduced by the Translator, for the *prosonomasia*[2] has no correspondence
in the Latin words.

    1 A separate annotation in all editions from 1516 to 1535, but coalesced in LB
      with the preceding annotation
    2 Cf the annotation on 1:31 ('apart from contract') n3.

2:4 [ER *divitias bonitatis illius* 'the riches of his[1] goodness']
[VG] *divitias bonitatis eius* 'the riches of his goodness'; ἢ τοῦ πλούτου
τῆς χρηστότητος. 'Riches' is a word much loved by Paul, as shown by his
quite frequent use of it whenever[2] he wants to suggest a great supply and
abundance of anything.[3] Now [the word here translated] 'goodness' is not
ἀγαθωσύνη, denoting that goodness [*bonitas*] which is opposed to πονηρία,
that is, to wickedness, but χρηστότης, for which the Latin word is *benignitas*;[4]
philosophers define it thus: *benignitas* [kindness] is a virtue freely offered
for doing good.[5] Hence the Greek word is derived from [a word meaning]
'use.'[6] And yet the same word is used for the courtesy and compliance by
which we make ourselves agreeable in social intercourse. In Latin, too, *usus*
expresses intimacy or companionship. And the Greeks call those who are
extremely affable and charming in conversation χρηστολόγοι [*chrēstologoi*].
Goodness is not much different from kindness. For when they call the gods
'good,' they want them to be regarded as beneficent. But I have preferred
to follow [the rendering] which, besides the fact that it was unequivocal,
was clearer, and more suited to this context. In any case, by χρηστότης he
means the gentleness and clemency of God, and the fact that he is in no
way harsh.

    1 Erasmus' *illius* 'his' is more emphatic than the Vulgate's *eius*, also 'his,' and
      points more directly to 'God' in 2:3.
    2 whenever ... anything] Added in 1519
    3 Cf eg Rom 9:23, 11:33; Eph 1:7, 3:8.
    4 For the definition see the annotations on 11:22 ('goodness and severity') and
      15:14 ('you are full of love').
    5 For the sentiment see Seneca *De beneficiis* 4.14.3.
    6 χρηστότης from χράομαι 'I use,' more specifically 'I use as a friend, I am
      intimate with'

2:4 [ER *ignorans* 'not knowing']

[VG] *ignoras*: **'do you not know'**; ἀγνοῶν, that is, 'not knowing,' a reading[1] supported by the very old Donatian codex. It is a participle in the Greek, and depends on the preceding construction. And[2] Jerome, writing on Ezekiel, so reports it.

  1 a reading ... codex] Added in 1522. For this codex, see the annotation on 1:22 ('saying that they were wise') n3.
  2 And ... it] Added in 1527. See Jerome *Commentarii in Ezechielem* 5 (on 16:53–4) PL 25 157B.

2:4 [ER VG] *quod bonitas dei* **'that the goodness[1] of God'**; ὅτι τὸ χρηστόν. [Paul] has used an adjective as a substantive. This is the same word that I have just explained.[2]

  1 Though the cue phrase reads *bonitas* 'goodness,' the 1527 Vulgate reads *benignitas* 'kindness.' Wordsworth and White read *benignitas*, but note the reading *bonitas* (II 71 4n).
  2 For χρηστότης, of which χρηστός is the corresponding adjective, see above on this verse ('the riches of his goodness').

2:4 [ER *ad poenitentiam te invitat* **'invites you to repentance'**]

[VG] *ad poenitentiam te adducit* **'leads you to repentance'**; ἄγει, that is, 'leads' [*ducit*], that is, 'entices and invites.' Jerome, writing on Ezekiel, translates *provocat* [calls forth, invites].[1] Besides, *adducere* [to lead to] is the same as *perducere*.[2]

  1 See Jerome *Commentarii in Ezechielem* 5 (on 16:53–4) PL 25 157B.
  2 In response to Frans Titelmans, Erasmus argued that not the compound of the Vulgate, *adducere*, but the simple *ducere* is the correct literal translation of the Greek ἄγειν. He also defended his interpretation that the intent here is to stress the benignity of God, so that the language of invitation and enticement is appropriate. See *Responsio ad collationes* LB IX 973C–F.

2:5 [ER *cor poenitere nescium* **'a heart unable to repent'**]

[VG] *cor impoenitens* **'unrepenting heart.'** The Greek word ἀμετανόητος is more meaningful, as though one said *impoenitibile* [incapable of repentance]. [It signifies] a heart that no beneficence of God can lead to repentance. Moreover, you would correctly translate μετάνοια by *resipiscentia* [a return to one's senses], and μετανοεῖν by *resipiscere* [to return to one's senses]. The word is derived from the fact that after committing a crime, a man realizes he has sinned – from μετά 'after' and νοεῖν 'to understand.'[1]

  1 Cf the discussion in the annotation on Matt 3:2 (*poenitentiam agite*), where the Greek μετανοεῖν is explained and *resipiscere* is proposed as a good translation.

2:5 [ER *colligis tibiipsi* 'you are gathering up for your own self']
[vg] *thesaurizas tibi* 'you treasure up for yourself'; θησαυρίζεις σεαυτῷ, that
is, 'you treasure up for your own self.' The compounding of the pronoun
is not superfluous here, indicating that he himself is the cause of such
great evil, since the goodness of God calls him elsewhere. But I wonder
why the Translator is so very fond of the Greek word [*thesaurizo*],[1] when
he could have said, 'you collect, store up, put away.' [Paul] means that the
divine wrath accumulates little by little, all to be brought forth at last in
the manner of a hoard.

> 1 Elsewhere Erasmus complains that *thesaurizo* is neither proper Latin nor
> proper Greek; cf *Responsio ad collationes* LB IX 973F–974A. See also the
> annotation on Matt 6:19 (*thesaurizate*), where he offers the same alternatives
> as here.

2:5 [ER *patefiet iustum iudicium* 'the just judgment will be disclosed']
[vg] *revelationis iusti iudicii* 'of the revelation of the just judgment.' In
Greek the phrase is divided by a conjunction, ἀποκαλύψεως καὶ δικαιοκρισίας,
that is, 'of the revelation *and* of the just judgment.' However in Greek
'just judgment' is a single word, and more elegant for the reason that it
distinguishes, by a word newly coined,[1] the divine judgment from human
judgments, in which the guilty not infrequently escape and the innocent
are condemned. He marks the one day with three attributes: 'of wrath,'
because then there will be no place for pity; 'of revelation,' because all
will be laid bare which now lies hidden; and 'of just judgment,' because
a pronouncement is to be made without error in relation to the deserts of
each. Whoever[2] reads carefully the interpretation of Theophylact will gather
that he read [the passage] thus. Certainly[3] the text quoted reads thus, both
in his work and in that of Chrysostom. And yet[4] in some of the Greek
manuscripts a third conjunction is not added, so that the sense is: on that
day in which the impious will experience, not the goodness of God, which
they have scorned, but the wrath, that is, the justice and vengeance, and in
which will be disclosed the divine judgment, which meanwhile lies hidden
to mortals.[5]

> 1 The word is not attested in LSJ before its occurrence here in Romans.
> 2 Whoever ... thus.] Added in 1519. See Theophylact PG 124 364D.
> 3 Certainly ... Chrysostom.] Added in 1527. For Chrysostom, see *Hom in Rom*
> 5.2 PG 60 425.
> 4 And yet ... mortals.] Added in 1519
> 5 The 1519 additions to this annotation reflect some uncertainty about the
> better reading. In 1516 Erasmus' translation followed the Greek text he
> printed, which read: 'But according to your hardness *and* impenitent heart,
> you gather up for yourself wrath in the day of wrath *and* of revelation *and*

of the just judgment of God.' In 1519, however, in spite of Theophylact,
he changed his Greek text to read: 'But according to your hardness *and*
impenitent heart you gather up for yourself wrath in the day of wrath,
and of the revelation of the just judgment of God.' This latter reading (like
that of the Vulgate) has only two, not three, conjunctions (placed here in
italics), and this remains the better attested reading; cf Cranfield I 141 n21.
(For his translation, from 1519, Erasmus turned the latter part of the sentence
into a relative clause: '... day of wrath in which the just judgment of God
will be disclosed.')

2:6 [ER *iuxta facta sua* 'according to his deeds']
[VG] *secundum opera eius* 'according to the works of him'; κατὰ τὰ ἔργα
αὐτοῦ, that is, *iuxta facta sua* [according to his deeds], not *eius* [(deeds) of
him]; unless[1] [instead of *sua*] you prefer *ipsius* [his own], a pronoun which
has virtually the force of a reflexive.

    1 unless ... reflexive] Added in 1519

2:7 [ER *perseverantes* 'persevering']¹
[VG] *secundum patientiam* 'according to [their] patience'; καθ᾽ ὑπομονήν,
that is, 'the perseverance in,' or 'the maintaining of' good work; that is,
'because he has persevered in good work.'

    1 persevering] First in 1519; in 1516, *iuxta tolerantiam* 'according to [their]
      endurance'

2:7 [ER *his quidem qui ... quaerunt, vitam* 'to those indeed who seek
(he will give eternal) life']
[VG] *quaerentibus vitam* 'to those seeking life.' Here[1] the passage has been
rendered rather awkwardly, though the Greek reading, if you will note,
is elegant: ὃς ἀποδώσει ἑκάστῳ κατὰ τὰ ἔργα αὐτοῦ, τοῖς μὲν καθ᾽ ὑπομονὴν
ἔργου ἀγαθοῦ, δόξαν καὶ τιμὴν καὶ ἀφθαρσίαν ζητοῦσι, ζωὴν αἰώνιον, that is,
'who will render to each man according to his works: to those who through
perseverance in good work seek (or, have sought) glory and honour and
immortality,[2] eternal life'; so that ζωὴν αἰώνιον [eternal life] is joined with
ἀποδώσει, that is, 'he will render,' and the article τοῖς [to those] is joined with
the participle ζητοῦσι [seeking]; the sense is: to those who here seek that
glory and honour and immortality, persevering in the good works through
which those things are procured, he will give eternal life, which is the very
thing they have sought. On the other hand, to those[3] who have preferred to
be contentious and have not obeyed the truth will come wrath etc. Origen
seems to have read [the passage] in this way, since he says: 'To those,'
says [Paul], 'seeking glory and honour and incorruption, for their patience
in good work eternal life will be given.' And shortly[4] after, 'Now indeed

let us seek glory and honour.'[5] Theophylact, the Bulgarian archbishop,[6] reads and interprets in the same way,[7] and Chrysostom,[8] and the other scholia of the Greeks,[9] so that[10] we are to understand that this outstanding reward is given to those who strive, and that the striving is through good deeds. The witnesses follow this reading with great consensus.[11] In either[12] case, indeed, the sentence is divided the same. Theophylact, however, more clearly relates the accusatives 'glory and honour and incorruption' to the participle ζητοῦσι [to those seeking] than does Chrysostom.

Rufinus,[13] in the third book of Περὶ ἀρχῶν [*On First Principles*] (following some [text] I have no idea which) gives the passage thus: 'To those, indeed, who according to their endurance in good work – who seek eternal life – glory and incorruption. But to those who are from the contention, and do not believe in the truth but believe in unrighteousness, wrath and indignation' etc.[14] On this reading, the verb 'will be' is understood in each sentence.[15] But it[16] is evident that Rufinus is not a very conscientious translator.[17] And this version offers the opportunity for another reading, which will arise from moving the comma back one word, so that the first accusatives, 'glory, honour, and incorruption' are joined with the preceding verb 'will give'; 'eternal life' is joined with the participle 'to those seeking.'[18] This, then, is the order: 'To those who are according to their endurance of good work, to those seeking eternal life, he will give glory, honour,' etc. In this construction, a comma is placed after 'good work,' and the verb 'are' is supplied, a verb the translator has expressed in the second part: τοῖς δὲ ἐξ ἐριθείας 'but to those who *are* from the contention.' Ambrose seems to have followed this reading, and, at least in this passage, Rufinus.[19] I do indeed find this acceptable; but the Translator has expressed clearly neither reading, in that though he has turned the article into a pronoun,[20] he has not turned the participle into an active verb, [which would read] 'to those who seek,' so that it corresponds to the contrasting clause, 'but to those who are from the contention.' For [Paul] has contrasted 'contention' with 'patient endurance.' There is not much difference between the ways of understanding [the passage] created by the altered position of a comma. For it makes no difference whether by good works one strives for eternal life, or for glory, honour, and immortality, since God is all these things to us.[21]

No one should be offended that I translate [ἀφθαρσία as] 'immortality' in place of [the Vulgate's] 'incorruption'; Ambrose translates it in the same way in the First Epistle to Timothy, chapter 1 – ἀφθάρτῳ 'to the immortal' God [1:17] – and the church reads it in this way.[22] In fact this is the meaning of the Greek word. I do[23] not know whether *incorruptio* [incorruption] is a Latin word.[24]

1 Here ... awkwardly] First in *1535*; previously, 'The thought in this passage too has been strangely distorted.'
The annotation discusses closely the text of an extended passage, 2:6–9. We translate the Vulgate (which Erasmus characterizes as awkward) following closely the text and punctuation of the Vulgate printed in *1527*.

> VG [6] who renders to each according to his works. [7] To those indeed seeking according to the patience of good work glory and honour and incorruption eternal life. [8] To those however who are from the contention, and who do not give assent to the truth, but believe in unrighteousness, anger and indignation, [9] tribulation and distress, to every life of man working evil, the Jew first and the Greek
> ER [6] who will render to each according to his deeds, [7] to those who, persevering in well-doing, seek glory and honour and immortality, eternal life; [8] but to those who are contentious and who do not obey the truth, but obey unrighteousness, will come indignation and wrath, [9] suffering and distress against every soul of man committing evil, the Jew first and also the Greek

2 immortality] From *1519*; in *1516*, 'incorruption'
3 to those] Added in *1522*
4 And shortly ... honour.'] Added in *1535*
5 Origen *Comm in Rom* 2.5 PG 14 880A–C. Erasmus quotes correctly according to the Merlin edition (fol CXLI); in Migne, however, the passage reads, 'Now let us investigate what it is to seek glory and incorruption.'
6 Bulgarian archbishop] First in *1527*; from *1516* to *1519*, 'Vulgarius the bishop'; in *1522*, 'Theophylact the bishop.' For Theophylact as Bulgarian archbishop see the annotation on 1:4 ('who was predestined') n25.
7 Theophylact *Expos in Rom* 2:7 PG 124 365B
8 and Chrysostom] Added in *1527*. See Chrysostom *Hom in Rom* 5.3 PG 60 425.
9 Not, however, Pseudo-Oecumenius, who makes 'eternal life' object of 'seek' and 'glory and honour and incorruption' objects of 'render.' See *Comm in Rom* 2:7 PG 118 353A.
10 so that ... good deeds] Added in *1519*
11 consensus] A sentence followed here in all editions except *1535*: The Translator's mistake was due to the participle ζητοῦσι "seeking," which has exactly the same form as the third person plural of the verb, "they seek." '
12 In either ... Chrysostom.] Added in *1535*. For the references see above nn7, 8.
13 Rufinus ... sentence.] Added in *1527*
14 Origen *De principiis* 3.1.6 PG 11 258C.
15 Ie in the main clause: '... there will be glory and incorruption ... there will be wrath and indignation.'
16 But it ... things to us.] The remaining portion of this paragraph was added in *1535*.
17 On Rufinus as a translator of Origen, see the annotation on 3:5 ('is God unfair who inflicts wrath') nn11, 14, 15.
18 In the Greek quoted at the beginning of this annotation Erasmus had placed a comma *after* ζητοῦσι 'seeking,' thus clarifying his own reading, 'who will give eternal life to those seeking glory etc'; by placing the comma *before*

ζητοῦσι 'seeking,' one could read, 'who will give glory etc to those seeking eternal life.'

19 Ambrosiaster *Comm in Rom* 2:7; for Rufinus see above n14.
20 Ie the Vulgate renders the Greek article τοῖς in verse 7 by the phrase 'to those'
21 Similarly, in *Responsio ad collationes* LB IX 974A
22 The Vulgate reading of 1 Tim 1:17 is 'immortal.' While Ambrosiaster in his *Commentarius in epistulam ad Timotheum primam* 1:17 reads *immortalis*, here at Rom 2:7 *incorruptio* is found in both his text and commentary (CSEL 81/3 257). Cf the annotation on 1:23 ('of the incorruptible God'). To the Greek ἀφθάρτῳ LB adds θεῷ 'God,' without warrant, however, from the editions 1516–1535.
23 I do ... word] Added in 1522
24 L&S cite no examples from classical Latin of *incorruptio*. In *Responsio ad collationes* Erasmus admits he himself elsewhere used *incorruptio*, but only when he preferred to speak ecclesiastical rather than correct Latin. He also describes the scriptural meaning of *immortalitas* as 'that life which is free from all evils' (LB IX 974C–D).

2:8 [ER *contentiosi* 'contentious']

[VG] *ex contentione* 'from the contention'; τοῖς δὲ ἐξ ἐριθείας, that is con-*tentiosis* [contentious], as Theophylact also has noted,[1] or 'those who are "from the contention."' For the Greeks call οἱ ἐκ στοᾶς [those from the Stoa] 'Stoics,' and Paul calls οἱ ἐκ περιτομῆς [those from circumcision] 'the circumcised.'[2]

1 as Theophylact also has noted] Added in 1519. See Theophylact *Expos in Rom* 2:8 PG 124 365C.
2 Cf Rom 4:12; Gal 2:12; Col 4:11; Titus 1:10.

2:8 [ER *non obtemperant* 'do not obey']

[VG] *non acquiescunt* 'do not give assent to.' In Greek this is a single word, and a participle, ἀπειθοῦσι, that is, 'to those not submitting to' or 'obeying.' Our Latin version does not convey the pleasure of the Greek expression produced[1] by the figure of ἐναντίωσις [opposites]:[2] ἀπειθοῦσι [apeithousi] and πειθομένοις [peithomenois], that is, 'to those not obeying' and 'to those obeying.'[3]

1 produced ... ἐναντίωσις] Added in 1527
2 Quintilian speaks of ἐναντιότης as a form of argument from opposites (κατ' ἐναντίωσιν) and identifies it with the figure 'contrarium' in Cicero's *De oratore* 3.52.201ff (Quintilian 9.2.106 and 9.3.90). Cf *Ecclesiastes* II LB V 938D–F and especially III LB V 996D–F, where Erasmus shows that the 'opposition' may lie either in the words or the ideas; cf the annotation on 15:1 ('we the more robust').
3 Valla *Annot in Rom* 2 (I 856) had pointed to the delight conveyed by the similarity of sounds in the Greek. Against Frans Titelmans Erasmus defended

his annotation, submitting that the Translator was not often able, or easily able, to capture Greek sound-effects in Latin, but one cannot deny that such effects are found in Pauline discourse (LB IX 974E).

2:9 [ER *Iudaei primum simul et Graeci* 'first, both of the Jew as well as of the Greek']

[VG] *Iudaei primum et Graeci* 'of the Jew first and of the Greek.' Here also is the double conjunction that I pointed out above,[1] τε καί[2] 'of the Jew first "and also" of the Greek.' But[3] I think the adverb 'first' applies to both races, 'of the Jews and of the Greeks,' so that we understand thus: 'Just as the grace of Christ was extended in the first place to the Jews and the Greeks, so these especially must be punished if they spurn the gift offered.[4]

> 1 Cf annotation on 1:16 ('to the Jew first and to the Greek'); cf also the annotation on 10:12 ('of the Jew and the Greek').
> 2 LB adds to τε καί the contextual words Ἰουδαίου τε καὶ Ἕλληνος 'of the Jew first and also of the Greek,' without warrant, however, from the editions *1516–1535*.
> 3 But ... offered.] Added in *1519*
> 4 Cf the annotation on 1:16 ('to the Jew first and to the Greek'), where he understands 'first' in the sense of 'especially.'

2:11 [ER *personarum respectus* 'regard for persons']

[VG] *acceptio personarum* 'acceptance of persons'; προσωποληψία. This is a single word which means 'regard for the person,'[1] when we favour this one more than that, making our judgment on the basis of the person, not the matter in hand. This is the opposite of the word used a little above,[2] δικαιοκρισία, that is, 'just judgment.'[3] *Acceptio*[4] *personae* [acceptance of the person] signifies nothing to Latin ears, even though it is frequently used in sacred literature.[5] But προσωπόληπτοι [respecters of persons] seems to designate those who are taken by fondness for a person rather than those who receive [the favour of another], just as one speaks of the ἐρωτόληπτοι [smitten, that is, seized by love] and νυμφόληπτοι [literally 'caught by nymphs,' that is, frenzied].[6] This word is concerned with 'appearance' as much as with 'person.' Certainly elsewhere he says that God does not judge 'according to appearance.'[7]

> 1 So Valla *Annot in Rom* 2 (I 856)
> 2 In 2:5. See the annotation ('of the revelation of the just judgment').
> 3 that is, just judgment] Added in *1519*
> 4 *Acceptio* ... appearance.] This remaining portion of the annotation was added in *1527*.
> 5 The idiom is found more frequently in the Vulgate of the New Testament than of the Old, though it appears there occasionally in the form *accipere personam*; cf Deut 1:17, 16:19; 2 Chron 19:7; Job 34:19; Eph 6:9; Col 3:25; James 2:1, 9; 1 Pet 1:17. In response to Frans Titelmans, Erasmus contended that

accipere personam (as he himself had translated in Gal 2:6) is good Latin, but *acceptor* and *acceptio personae* were not (*Responsio ad collationes* LB IX 975A–C).

6 Like προσωπόληπτοι, these words are compounded with -ληπτοι from the verb λαμβάνω, meaning 'to take, receive, catch, seize.'

7 For the phrase see the Vulgate of John 7:24, 'Do not judge according to appearance,' and for the sentiment, Gal 2:6; Eph 6:9; and Col 3:25.

2:12 [ER VG] *sine lege peccaverunt* '**have sinned without the Law.**' The Greek expression is more engaging because of the adverb ἀνόμως [without the Law], as though you were to say *illegaliter* or *exlegaliter* [law-lessly] – the word used in both clauses[1] – for we read *exlex* [law-less] for ἄνομος.[2] This whole[3] sentence is made vivid by the repetition of the words and by the contraries answering to one another, and rhythmic by the pattern of the phrases: ἀνόμως, ἀνόμως, ἐν νόμῳ, διὰ νόμου, ἥμαρτον, ἥμαρτον, ἀπολοῦνται, κριθήσονται [*anomōs, anomōs, en nomō, dia nomou, hēmarton, hēmarton, apolountai, krithēsontai*].

1 the word used in both clauses] Added in *1519*. The two clauses are represented by the cue phrases of this and the next annotation.

2 In *illegaliter* and *exlegaliter* Erasmus recognizes adverbs formed analogously to the Greek ἀνόμως. Neither term is attested in classical Latin literature (though the adjective *exlex* is found), but for *exlegalitas*, *exlex* and *illegalis* in medieval literature see these words in Niermeyer.

3 This whole ... κριθήσονται.] Added in *1527*

2:12 [ER *sine lege et peribunt* '**shall also perish without the Law**']
[VG] *sine lege peribunt* '**shall perish**[1] **without the Law.**' The Greek is καὶ ἀπολοῦνται, that is, 'shall also perish,' so that you can see a comparison is being made: their end would be as their life had been.

1 shall perish ... had been] This annotation was added in *1522*.

2:13 [ER *qui legem factis exprimunt* '**who fulfil the Law by their deeds**']
[VG] *sed factores legis* '**but the doers of the Law**'; ποιηταί,[1] that is, 'who perform and do the precepts of the Law.' In any case, the phrase *faciunt legem* is used of those who 'make the law.'[2]

1 After ποιηταί LB adds τοῦ νόμου 'of the Law,' but without warrant from the editions *1516–1535*. In *1516* only, the placement of this and the next annotation was reversed.

2 the law] Added in *1519*. Cf the *Responsio ad collationes* LB IX 975C: 'To one who knew only Latin, what else would *factor legis* mean but "lawmaker"?'

2:14 [ER *eae legem* '**these (nations not having) a Law**']
[VG] *eiusmodi legem* '**a law of this kind.**' The Greek is οὗτοι, that is, 'these,' not 'of this kind.'[1] The Translator[2] seems to have read τοιοῦτοι. It makes no difference to the sense.

1 So Valla *Annot in Rom* 2 (I 856)
2 The Translator ... sense.] Added in *1535*

2:15 [ER VG] *scriptum in cordibus* **'written in their hearts.'** *Scriptum* [something written] is, in Greek, the noun γραπτόν, not a participle, as if you were to say *scriptitium* [a writing]. It is the opposite of that which the law experts call ἄγραπτον 'unwritten law.'[1]

> 1 unwritten law] Added in *1519*. For ἄγραπτα νόμιμα 'unwritten laws' see Sophocles *Antigone* 454–5; for ἄγραφα νόμιμα 'unwritten laws' see Aristotle *Nicomachean Ethics* 1180b1 and Plato *Laws* 793A.

2:15 [ER *attestante illorum* **'their (conscience) confirming'**]
[VG] *testimonium illis reddente* **'[the conscience] bearing witness to them'**; συμμαρτυρούσης αὐτῶν τῆς συνειδήσεως, that is, 'their conscience also testifying.' For 'to them' is not in the Greek.[1] Thus you are to understand that their conscience agrees with the judgment of God.

> 1 So Valla *Annot in Rom* 2 (I 856)

2:15 [ER *cogitationibus ... accusantibus* **'thoughts accusing'**]
[VG] *cogitationum accusantium* **'thoughts accusing.'** The Translator was quite fast asleep when he translated the one Greek genitive συμμαρτυρούσης [also testifying] by a Latin ablative, but left the other [κατηγορούντων 'accusing'] in the genitive.[1] He should have translated [with ablatives], *cogitationibus invicem accusantibus aut etiam defendentibus* [their thoughts in turn accusing or also defending]. And so it is in Jerome's quotation, where he is commenting on the sixteenth chapter of Ezekiel.[2] In the same[3] way reads Ambrose in the translation [of this text].[4] So does Augustine both in the twentieth book of *The City of God*, chapter 26, and frequently elsewhere.[5] And yet[6] he cites it differently when he expounds the Lord's Sermon on the Mount – at least if the codex is free from error.[7] For scribes[8] are accustomed to emend the citations of the ancients according to our Vulgate edition. Nor did[9] the translator of Origen's work on this Epistle, whoever he was, read otherwise.[10] Those who would like the Translator of the Vulgate never to have made a mistake, and to have translated at the prompting of the Holy Spirit, should explain, if they can, this one passage. But[11] such extraordinary slackness and the dozing so evident in this one passage can be sufficient indication of how far we should trust him in other passages. I am speaking[12] of the propriety of language, not of thoughts. It is not necessary to ascribe everything to the Holy Spirit. Some[13] try to make the genitive *cogitationum* refer to the preceding word, *conscientia*: 'the conscience [ie the knowledge] of the thoughts.'[14] But this is extremely harsh. In my opinion

the best excuse we can make for the Translator is to say that in his day the common people were accustomed to speak thus in imitation of the Greeks; and it was they rather than the educated whom he endeavoured to serve.

1 In the Greek these are parallel clauses in the genitive absolute construction; a literal translation would therefore render both into equivalent ablatives absolute in Latin. But for the second clause the Translator kept the Greek genitive absolute construction, however impossible this is to construe in proper Latin:

VG *testimonium reddente illis conscientia ipsorum et inter se invicem cogitationum accusantium aut etiam defendentium* 'their conscience bearing witness to them and of [Latin genitive] their thoughts mutually in turn accusing or also defending'

ER *attestante illorum conscientia et cogitationibus inter se accusantibus aut etiam excusantibus* 'their conscience confirming and their thoughts mutually accusing or also excusing'

Valla also asked for a correction here; cf *Annot in Rom* 2 (I 856).

2 Jerome *Commentarii in Ezechielem* 5 (on 16:35–43) PL 25 151B

3 In the same ... elsewhere.] Added in *1519*

4 Ambrosiaster *Comm in Rom* 2:15–16

5 See Augustine *De civitate dei* 20.26 CSEL 40/2 500:30. For 'elsewhere' see *Enarrationes in psalmos* 9.9 PL 36 121.

6 And yet ... error.] Added in *1527*

7 Augustine *De sermone domini in monte* 2.9.32 PL 34 1283. In this instance, as Augustine cites the passage, the first Greek genitive ('also testifying') is turned into a Latin ablative, while the second Greek genitive ('accusing') is translated by a Latin genitive – like the Vulgate.

8 For scribes ... edition.] Added in *1535*

9 Nor did ... otherwise.] Added in *1519*

10 Origen *Comm in Rom* 2.9 PG 14 892A. On the translator of Origen see the annotation on 3:5 ('is God unfair who inflicts wrath') nn11, 14.

11 But ... passages.] Added in *1519*

Frans Titelmans rebuked Erasmus for the attitude displayed in this annotation towards the Translator of the Vulgate, and particularly objected to Erasmus' characterization of the Translator as 'slack and sleepy.' In a lengthy response, Erasmus distinguished the unknown Translator from the apostles who were the original writers, and further argued that though the Holy Spirit inspired the minds of the apostles, he allowed them to use their own human faculties of speech; see *Responsio ad collationes* LB IX 975D–976E.

12 I am speaking ... Spirit.] Added in *1527*

13 Some ... serve.] The remainder of the annotation was added in *1535*.

14 A solution proposed by Frans Titelmans and refuted in the lengthy response cited in n11 above

2:17 [ER *ecce* 'behold!']

[VG] *si autem* 'but if.' The truer and older reading of the Greek codices is ἰδέ,[1] that is, 'behold,' not εἰ δέ 'but if.' Otherwise, there is not a proper

sequence in what follows, 'you, therefore, who teach another.'² And yet
Ambrose reads εἰ δέ, unless there is an error in the books, as do Origen
and Theophylact.³ There is no difficulty as far as the sense is concerned,
except that, as⁴ I have just said, the words join a little harshly with what
follows, 'you, therefore, who teach another.' Yet this, too, is not new in
Paul,⁵ and is in any case tolerable.

1 The reading of late manuscripts. Challenged by Titelmans, Erasmus defended
the claim that the reading was older on the grounds that he found this
reading in the oldest manuscripts, the claim that it was truer on the grounds
that it made better sense (*Responsio ad collationes* LB IX 976E).
2 Rom 2:21
3 Cf Ambrosiaster *Comm in Rom* 2:11; Origen *Comm in Rom* 2.17 PG 14 894C;
and Theophylact *Expos in Rom* 2:17 PG 124 372C. Zúñiga preferred the
evidence of Origen and Theophylact (whom he thought to be Athanasius).
See ASD IX-2 164 and the notes on lines 23–5 by H.J. de Jonge. In fact εἰ δέ
'but if' is the preferred reading in spite of the anacoluthon; cf Metzger 507
and Cranfield I 163.
4 as ... said] Added in 1519
5 For Erasmus' comments elsewhere on the defective sentence sequence
in Paul see the annotation on 5:12 ('therefore just as through one man')
and n4.

2:18 [ER *probas eximia* 'you approve the excellent things']
[VG] *probas utiliora* 'you approve the more useful things'; τὰ διαφέροντα
[*ta diapheronta*, things with a 'difference'], that is, 'excellent' or 'outstanding things.' The Translator seems to have read συμφέροντα, that is, 'useful' or 'advantageous things.' I cannot imagine, however, why Theophylact
wanted to interpret διαφέροντα as συμφέροντα,¹ unless perhaps the Greeks
speak after the Latin manner in saying 'it makes a difference to someone'
to refer to what relates to his interest [ie is advantageous to him].

Finally, *probas* [you approve] here is δοκιμάζεις, that is, *comprobas*,
which is to give your approval with discretion, and after reconnoitering, as
it were.²

1 Theophylact *Expos in Rom* 1:18 PG 124 372D–374A: 'One is to understand
διαφέροντα as that which is appropriate to each, that is, what is advantageous.'
2 For *probo* = δοκιμάζω see the annotation on 1:28 ('and just as they did not
think it right').

2:18 [ER *institutus ex lege* 'taught from the Law']
[VG] *instructus per legem* 'instructed through the Law.' The Greek is κατηχούμενος, that is, 'trained' or 'initiated' and 'taught.' It is, however, a word
used especially by Paul;¹ it seems to have come from the term used long ago
for handing down the mysteries, which were forbidden to be entrusted to

books.[2] His disciple Luke[3] uses the same word in his preface to his Gospel, as I[4] have pointed out there.

1 Though not by Paul exclusively in the New Testament; cf eg Acts 18:25.
2 Erasmus had already affirmed in his annotation on Luke 1:4 (*de quibus eruditus es*) that the word referred to instruction in both pagan and Christian mysteries handed down orally because it was too sacred to be committed to writing. But the word appears, especially in late classical literature, for instruction generally; cf Cicero *Epistulae ad Atticum* 15.12.2 and Dionysius of Halicarnassus *De Demosthenis dictione* (*On the Style of Demosthenes*) 50.
3 In the dedicatory epistle to Henry VIII that prefaced the *Paraphrase on Luke*, Erasmus says of the physician Luke that 'he was friendly with all the apostles, but in particular a follower of Paul, and in fact his sole companion on his journeys' (Ep 1381:73–5). Cf also the annotation on Col 4:14 (*Lucas medicus*).
4 as I ... there] Added in 1519. Cf n2 above.

2:20 [ER *doctorem imperitorum* 'teacher of the unlearned']
[VG] *magistrum infantium* 'master of infants'; διδάσκαλον νηπίων. As I have already pointed out in several places, νήπιος when it refers to age means 'infant'; when it refers to the mind it means 'insufficiently instructed, not much developed in ability and experience.'[1] Here it would have been more fitting to translate 'of fools,'[2] 'of the simple,'[3] or 'of boys.' For who teaches infants? 'Of children,'[4] as he often translates, would have been more tolerable. For in this case it is not a master who rules, but a διδάσκαλος, that is, [one] who teaches. Further παιδευτήν, which just precedes,[5] is ambiguous; it is used both of one who instructs boys, and of one who punishes and corrects them when they err. Paul[6] appears to be making a tacit allusion here to Isaiah 33: 'Where is the scribe? Where is he who weighs the words of the Law? Where is the teacher of children?'[7]

1 Cf the annotations on Matt 11:25 (*parvulis*), Matt 21:16 (*ex ore lactantium et infantium*), and Luke 10:21 (*parvulis*).
2 On the meaning of *stulti* 'fools,' see the annotation on Matt 11:25 (n1 above).
3 'of the simple'] Added in 1522
4 'Of children' ... tolerable] Added in 1527. The Vulgate translated νήπιοι as 'children' in eg Matt 11:25 and Luke 10:21 (cited n1 above). So Valla *Annot in Rom* 2 (I 856): 'I should have preferred "children [*parvuli*]," as νήπιοι is often translated [in the Vulgate].'
5 Erasmus follows the Vulgate in translating παιδευτής as *eruditor* in the phrase *eruditorem insipientium* 'instructor of the simple.'
6 Paul ... children?'] Added in 1519
7 Cf the Vulgate of Isa 33:18.

2:20 [ER VG] *habentem formam* 'having the form'; μόρφωσιν, that is, 'formation,' as though you were to speak of a method of training and shaping that one

might prescribe for others, just as even today there are some who claim
to be able to shape the consciences of individuals.[1] Likewise[2] the Jews
prided themselves on teaching a pattern of life to proselytes as if they were
stupid. Theophylact also expounds [the phrase] according to this view, but
he adds that there were those who interpreted μόρφωσις in this passage
to mean not 'form' but 'a false and counterfeit image of righteousness'[3] –
when they teach thus: 'Do not touch, do not taste, do not handle.'[4]

1 Apparently a reference to the scholastics, indicated by a sentence that
    followed here in the first three editions but was omitted in 1527: 'For some –
    I should not say theologians but idlelogians [mataeologi, from Greek mataios
    "empty," "idle," "vain"] – take pleasure in these words.' See the annotation
    on 1 Tim 1:6 (in vaniloquium), where Erasmus condemns scholastic debates
    as mataeologia.
2 Likewise ... handle.] Added in 1519
3 Theophylact Expos in Rom 2:20 PG 124 373B–C
4 Cf Col 2:21.

2:23 [ER dehonestas 'do you discredit']
    [VG] inhonoras 'do you dishonour'; ἀτιμάζεις, that is, 'you discredit,' or 'you
    bring disgrace upon.'

2:24 [ER male audit 'is in bad repute']
    [VG] blasphematur 'is blasphemed.' The Greek word is βλασφημεῖται,
    which you could translate into Latin as male audit [is in bad repute] or
    maledictis afficitur [is slandered].[1] Origen refers the text that Paul adduces[2]
    to Isaiah, chapter 52,[3] where you read: 'Since my people have been carried
    away for nothing, their oppressors act unjustly, says the Lord, and all day
    long my name is blasphemed' [52:5]. Further, the two words in gentibus
    [in the nations] are added from the Septuagint edition, which Paul seems
    to have used here. The original Hebrew reads otherwise:[4] 'And all day
    long my name is blasphemed.' In[5] discussing this passage of Isaiah, Jerome
    indicates that reference can be made to Ezekiel also,[6] where you read in
    chapter 36: 'And they came unto the nations, among whom they entered
    and profaned my holy name, when it was said of them, "That is the people
    of the Lord," and they profaned my holy name' [36:20].
        Now as for Lyra, only he knows what he intended in regard to this
    passage.[7] For our edition conforms both to the Septuagint and to the original
    Hebrew, nor in this passage, at least, is there any difference, if we are to
    trust printed texts.[8] I am, in truth, less surprised about Lyra, but Aquinas,
    who was far more assiduous in this passage, for some reason refers to a
    double reading. I am not reluctant to quote his words, so that the reader
    might more easily either judge or investigate the matter. For when he had

cited the passage of Isaiah – 'Their oppressors act unjustly, and all day long my name is blasphemed' – he adds (from Jerome no doubt)[9] another text with these words: '[...] and Ezekiel 36, according to another reading, where our text reads thus: "Not because of you will I act, O house of Israel, but because of my holy name, which you have profaned in the nations"' [36:22].[10] So far Aquinas. Now, pray tell me, what is the other reading, or, to use their word, 'letter,'[11] that differs from the first? Examine, search; you will find nothing of the kind. Accordingly, I guess that Thomas, working in haste, did not take this from the original texts,[12] but from collections [of texts] of others.[13] For in the same chapter of Ezekiel there are two different passages that have a similar sense.[14] The first passage is the one I cited above, in which there is no conflict between the original Hebrew and the Septuagint edition. The other follows shortly thereafter, repeating what had just been said; this Aquinas cites: 'Not because of you will I act, O house of Israel, but because of my holy name, which you have profaned in the nations unto which you came.' And not even here is there any disagreement between Jerome's translation and the Septuagint. But if[15] anyone distrusts me, let him compare both versions, which are juxtaposed in the works of Jerome in the most recent Basel edition.[16]

Now, in truth, we Christians must heed much more [carefully] Paul's admonition to the Jews, for if our life is different from that of the pagans only by the profession of the Christian name and by ceremonies, while in all other respects it is the same, or even more impure, there is a danger that the most holy name of Christ will be profaned and disgraced among the enemies of the faith, the Jews and the Turks – if they look upon us serving lust no less despicably, grasping for gain no less greedily, no less eager for revenge, no less fearful of death and desirous of life, no less mad in waging wars, in rousing tumults, in fierce contention, for the most trivial reasons.[17]

1 For a similar definition, see the annotation on 3:8 ('as we are reviled').
2 Erasmus extends the discussion beyond the cue phrase:
    ER *nam nomen dei propter vos male audit inter gentes, quemadmodum scriptum est. Nam circumcisio* ... 'for because of you the name of God is in bad repute among the nations, as it is written. For circumcision ...'
    VG *nomen enim dei per vos blasphematur inter gentes. Sicut scriptum est: circumcisio* ... 'for through you the name of God is blasphemed among the nations. As it is written: circumcision ...
3 Origen *Comm in Rom* 2.11 PG 14 898B
4 In *1516* only Erasmus quoted the Hebrew here. Jerome, too, notes that *in gentibus* is not in the Hebrew (*Commentarii in Isaiam* 14 [on 52:4–5] PL 24 498B).
    In citing the words in the text of 2:24 as *in gentibus* Erasmus is perhaps influenced by Jerome's discussion of Isa 52:4–5. *In gentibus* does appear as a minority reading of the Vulgate of Rom 2:24, but the preferred Vulgate

reading is *inter gentes* 'among the nations' (Wordsworth and White II 74 24n), the reading found in the Vulgate printed in *1527*.

5 In ... of Isaiah] Added in *1519*

6 Jerome *Commentarii in Isaiam* 14 (on 52:4–5) PL 24 499C. In his commentary at this point Jerome addresses Christians who have figuratively 'descended into Egypt.' 'To these,' he adds, 'it is said in Ezekiel, "You have sullied my name among the nations."' Though Erasmus quotes Ezek 36:20, Jerome's citation apparently refers to Ezek 36:22: '... for the sake of my holy name, which you have profaned among the nations ...(RSV).

7 Nicholas of Lyra thought the Septuagint translated Ezek 36:20 thus: 'And they came unto the nations and profaned my name.' Erasmus says, however, that the Septuagint and the Vulgate understand the Hebrew in the same way. See Lyra *Postilla* IV fol aa v recto

8 printed texts] In *1516* Erasmus quoted the Hebrew at this point, and added: 'If any one asks for a literal rather than a polished translation, this can be read: "They came to the nations to which they came there, and profaned this my holy name, while it was said to them, 'That people of the Lord.'"' This was omitted in *1519* and in subsequent editions. For the Latin *vulgata exemplaria* here as 'printed texts' cf Chomarat *Grammaire et rhétorique* I 487.

9 Cf Jerome *Commentarii in Isaiam* 14 (on 52:4–5) PL 24 499C. Aquinas quotes Ezek 36:22, the passage found in Jerome. Cf n6 above.

10 Thomas Aquinas *Super Rom lect* cap 2 lectio 4.236. Aquinas cites both Isa 52:5 and Ezek 36:22 as the reference for Paul's quotation: 'Paul says "As it is written," referring to Isa 52 ... and Ezek 36 according to another reading, where ours reads, "Not because of you will I act, house of Israel, but because of my holy name, which you have profaned in the nations."'

11 *littera*, the customary scholastic expression for textual reading

12 texts] In *1516* and *1519* only, there followed here 'which he alone of all the more recent theologians was accustomed to do.'

13 *collectanea*; a reference evidently to the compilations of biblical and patristic texts in some medieval commentaries. On the *collectanea* see Beryl Smalley, *The Study of the Bible in the Middle Ages* (South Bend, IN 1964) 36–41; on the *Gloss* ibidem 46–66. Erasmus himself cites Augustine from the *Gloss* and the *collectanea* in his *Apologia ad Caranzam* LB IX 419B–C.

14 Ie Ezek 36:20 and 22

15 But if ... edition.] Added in *1519*. In the place of this sentence, *1516* quoted the Hebrew and added: 'If anyone should scrupulously desire that this be translated, the words mean pretty much this: "Not because of you am I acting, house of Israel, but for my holy name, which you have profaned in the nations to whom you entered there."'

16 Johann Froben published the works of Jerome in 1516, for which edition Erasmus edited the letters. In his commentaries on the prophets Jerome frequently set down a translation of the Septuagint along with his own Latin version. According to the Migne text, however, the Septuagint version of these verses is not given (see *Commentarii in Ezechielem* 11 [on 36:16–38] PL 25 340–1).

17 John Colet, like Erasmus in this annotation, had concluded his commentary on Romans 2 by drawing from Paul's words to the Jews admonition

for contemporary Christians; see Colet *Expositio literalis* (English 88–90, Latin 226–9). Elsewhere, too, Erasmus draws out the religious and ethical implications of the profession of the Christian name. See, for example, the paraphrase on Rom 12:1–2 CWE 42 69–70 and the *Enchiridion*, where the nominal and the true Christian are frequently contrasted; cf eg CWE 66 70–3 and 93–104.

2:24 [ER *propter vos male audit* 'because of you is in bad repute']
[VG] *per vos blasphematur* 'through you is blasphemed.'[1] The Greek phrase is δι' ὑμᾶς [through you], that is, 'because of you,' indicating cause, not instrument.

> 1 A separate annotation in all editions from 1516 to 1535, though coalesced in LB with the preceding annotation

2:28 [ER *non is qui in manifesto Iudaeus* 'not he who is outwardly a Jew']
[VG] *non enim qui in manifesto Iudaeus* 'for not [he] who is outwardly a Jew.' In this passage, the prepositive articles in the Greek afford a brevity which, to make the meaning clearer, I have expanded by the addition of several words,[1] but without making the slightest change in the sense, as follows: Not he, who is outwardly a Jew, is a Jew; nor is that which is outwardly circumcision of the flesh, circumcision; but he who has been[2] a Jew inwardly is a Jew;[3] and circumcision is[4] circumcision of the heart, which is found[5] in the spirit, not in the letter.[6]

> 1 In the Greek here the article precedes both the noun and its modifiers and provides a very abbreviated expression: for not the [one] manifestly a Jew is [a Jew] etc. Additional words are necessary in Latin.
> 2 has been] Added in 1522
> 3 is a Jew] Added in 1519. In 1516 the last two clauses read: 'But he who [is] a Jew inwardly, and circumcision [is] of the heart in the Spirit, not the letter.'
> 4 circumcision is] Added in 1519
> 5 which is found] Added in 1519
> 6 Though Erasmus' translation of 2:28 found its finished form in 1516, Erasmus departed only modestly from the Vulgate of 2:29 in 1516; it was in 1519 that he offered the translation he has given in this annotation. The Vulgate had followed the Greek closely in translating these verses: '[28] For not [he] who is manifestly a Jew [is a Jew], nor the circumcision which is manifestly in the flesh [is circumcision] [29] but [he] who is a Jew in the depths; and circumcision [is] of the heart in the Spirit, not the letter.'
> To Frans Titelmans, who contended that the Vulgate was no more obscure than the Greek, Erasmus replied that it was surely permitted to add what had to be supplied, 'especially in an edition prepared for the purpose of understanding the Vulgate more correctly' (*Responsio ad collationes* LB IX 976F–977A).

3:1 [ER *quid igitur ... in quo praecellat* 'what then (has the Jew) in which he is superior']

[VG] *quid ergo amplius* 'what more therefore [does the Jew possess']. περισσόν in Greek sometimes means 'superfluous,' sometimes 'extraordinary,' that is, ἐξαίρετον. Here 'the extraordinary' is understood as the excellent, for τοῦ Ἰουδαίου follows, that is, 'in which the Jew excels.'[1]

> 1 Titelmans evidently complained that terms like 'extraordinary' and 'excellent' do not catch the sense of comparison implied in the Vulgate *amplius*: 'What more therefore does the Jew possess?' Erasmus replied that the Vulgate 'more' is ambiguous, meaning either 'further' or 'better.' His translation attempted to clarify the ambiguity: 'What does the Jew have in which he excels?' (*Responsio ad collationes* LB IX 977A–B).

3:2 [ER VG] *multum* 'much'; πολύ [*poly*]. Thus it is found also in Greek with an upsilon [*y*]. Yet it appears that πολλή [*pollē*] should be read, with a double λ [*l*] and with η[1] [*ē*], to modify the [feminine] noun[2] ὠφέλεια 'advantage.' πρῶτον 'first' here signifies the order of the discussion, rather than 'chiefly.'[3]

> 1 η] First in *1535*; previously, *ita* for *eta*, the name of the letter η
> 2 the noun ... 'advantage'] Added in *1519*; previously, 'to modify ὠφέλεια.' Translating neuter πολύ, *multum* modifies *quid amplius* and responds to 3:1a, 'what more has the Jew?' The feminine πολλή, Erasmus' conjectural emendation, would refer to 'advantage' (feminine in Greek) in 3:1b: 'What is the advantage of circumcision? – Much in every way.' There is, however, no basis in the Greek manuscripts for this conjecture (see Tischendorf II 374 2n). Erasmus himself printed πολύ (*multum*) in all editions.
> 3 Erasmus follows the Vulgate in translating *primum* 'first.'

3:2 [ER *illis oracula* 'to them the oracles']

[VG] *illis eloquia* 'to them, the utterances.'[1] 'To them' is not in the Greek, but the Translator added it out of necessity. ἐπιστεύθησαν[2] [they were entrusted the oracles of God], that is, the utterances were 'trusted,' which is to say, 'the utterances of God were "entrusted" or "committed" to them.' For[3] the Greeks speak thus: ἐνεχειρίσθην[4] ταύτην τὴν ἐπιμέλειαν, ἐπιτέτραμμαι τὴν δίαιταν, that is, 'this province has been committed to me, this judicial inquiry has been assigned,' as though you should say – adopting the Greek idiom – 'he was[5] entrusted this thing' and 'I was committed this task,' just as[6] the Latins say 'I was taught grammar.'[7]

Further,[8] the word in our text, *eloquia* [utterances], is λόγια in Paul; Origen philosophizes somewhat on this word.[9] But by λόγια [Paul] meant 'oracles,' because this people preserved the oracles (which would profit others more than themselves), and kept [the words] they did not understand. For so Hesychius interprets λόγια: θεόσφατα, μαντεύματα, φῆμαι, χρησμοί, that is, 'responses of the divine powers, prophecies, sayings, oracles.'[10] And in[11] this sense it is repeatedly found in Aristophanes' *Knights*. Among Latin writers, Juvenal used *eloquium* to mean 'eloquence': 'The eloquence and fame of Demosthenes.'[12]

1 The full clause reads:
    ER *quod illis commissa sunt oracula dei* 'that to them were committed the oracles of God'
    VG *quia credita sunt illis eloquia dei* 'that the utterances of God were entrusted to them'
2 After ἐπιστεύθησαν LB adds τὰ λόγια τοῦ θεοῦ 'the oracles of God,' but without warrant from the editions *1516-1535*.
3 For ... speak thus] Added in *1519*
4 ἐνεχειρίσθην ... Greek idiom] Added in *1535*
5 'he was ... task'] Added in *1519*. Erasmus had turned the Greek expressions cited into conventional Latin. Had he 'adopted the Greek idiom,' he might have translated 'I have been committed this province; I have been assigned this judicial inquiry.'
6 just as ... grammar'] Added in *1535*. Just before this clause Erasmus inserted, in *1519* and *1522*, the words 'Lyra seems to understand the passage as though the utterances were believed by the Jews, and in this they excel us.' For Lyra cf *Postilla* IV fol aa v verso.
7 In his reply to Titelmans, Erasmus adduced this example to show that Latin idiom did have a parallel to the Greek construction here, where 'oracles' functions as object of the verb: 'They were entrusted the oracles of God' (LB IX 977C). For the construction cf Allen and Greenough 396b.
8 Further ... Demosthenes.'] With the exception noted (n11) this remaining portion of the annotation was added in *1519*.
9 Cf Origen *Comm in Rom* 2.14 PG 14 915B-918A. Origen distinguishes between those who do not understand the word given through Moses, and therefore do not believe in Christ, and those who do. To the former, the Scriptures are merely 'the letter,' to the latter, they are the *eloquia*, the oracles of God (PG 14 916B).
10 Cf *Hesychii Alexandrini Lexicon* ed M. Schmidt III (Jena 1861) 47. Hesychius, lexicographer probably of the fifth century AD, based his lexicon on the work of previous scholars. The abridged version that has come down to us is a valuable glossary of proverbs, biblical names, and Attic Greek. This lexicon was published first in 1514, edited by Marcus Musurus; see *Contemporaries* II 472-3 and Deno John Geanakoplos *Greek Scholars in Venice* (Cambridge 1962) 154-5.
11 And in ... *Knights*.] Added in *1535*. Cf Aristophanes *Knights* 120, 1015.
12 Cf Juvenal *Satires* 10.114.
    Erasmus defended his choice of *oracula* in place of the Vulgate's *eloquia* on the grounds that it was a loftier word, and more appropriate, since *eloquium*

was used of the words of human beings, but *oracula* of the words of God.
See *Responsio ad collationes* LB IX 977D.

3:3 [ER *faciet irritam* 'will make without effect']
[VG] *evacuavit* 'has made void.' The Greek is in the future tense, καταργήσει,
that is, will 'abolish,' 'obliterate,' 'render without effect,' or 'make obsolete';[1]
[it is] a word frequently used by St Paul. The Translator very often renders
it *destruere* [destroy].[2] ἀργός 'idle,' hence καταργεῖν 'to render useless and
unnecessary.'

    1 Latin *antiquabit*. For this word see the annotation on Heb 8:13 (*veteravit prius*),
      and for the connotations of 'cancel,' 'annul' associated with the word, see the
      paraphrase on the same verse.
    2 For example in Rom 3:31; 1 Cor 1:28; 2 Tim 1:10; but the Vulgate often uses
      evacuare (as here), eg 2 Cor 3:7, 11, 13, 14; Gal 5:4.

3:4 [ER *imo sit* 'rather let (God) be (true)']
[VG] *est autem* 'but [God] is [true].'[1] The Greek is γινέσθω, that is, 'but let
God be (or, become) true.' Perhaps the Translator had written *esto*,[2] as the[3]
translator of Theophylact (until now falsely called Athanasius)[4] renders.[5]
But[6] γινέσθω is used to mean φανερούσθω, ἀποδεικνύσθω, that is, 'let him
be revealed,' 'let him be shown.' For it[7] cannot be that God *is* not true, but
what matters to us is that people *understand* him to be such. And yet[8] [this]
can be used in an expression of praise, as when we say 'Glory to you, O
Lord.'

    1 For the sequence of this annotation see the following annotation, n1.
    2 Ie, using an imperative form ('let him be') rather than the subjunctive.
      Titelmans nevertheless preferred the indicative *est* because he thought it
      was implied in the Vulgate of Ps 115:11 (Ps 116:11 AV) – 'all men are liars' –
      words echoed here in the phrase 'every man a liar'; cf *Responsio ad collationes*
      LB IX 978A.
    3 as the ... renders] Added in *1519*
    4 Cf the annotation on 1:4 ('who was predestined') n25.
    5 The 1529 Porsena edition has *est*, not *esto*.
    6 But ... shown.'] The reading of *1535*. The first four editions read here simply:
      'But it [ie the verb] is read in the sense of "let [God] appear." '
    7 For it ... such.] Added in *1519*
    8 And yet ... O Lord.'] Added in *1535*

3:4 [ER VG] *absit* 'God forbid!'[1] [a word] frequently met in Paul.[2] The Greek is
μὴ γένοιτο, that is, 'may it not be' or 'not happen,' or 'may God avert' or
'prevent'; it is an expression of abhorrence.[3]

    1 In all editions from *1516* to *1535* this annotation followed the annotation
      above, 'but [God] is true,' In LB the two annotations are in reversed position.

2 Especially in Romans, eg 3:6, 31; 6:2, 15, etc; but also in 1 Corinthians (6:15) and Galatians, eg 2:17; 3:21; 6:14.

3 Latin *abominantis sermo*; for *abominatio* as a rhetorical figure, see *De copia* 1.32 ASD I-6 76:69 (cf CWE 24 347, where the word is translated as 'vehement rejection').

3:4 [ER VG] *ut iustificeris in sermonibus* 'that you may be justified in your words.' The text is from the fiftieth Psalm: 'That you may be justified'[1] [51:4]. 'And when you are judged'[2] is a passive verb in Greek, ἐν τῷ κριθῆναι, or,[3] as others read, κρίνεσθαι. But it is uncertain whether the Hebrew word בְשָׁפְטֶךָ speaks of God as 'judged' or 'judging.' Jerome in his interpretation of this passage seems to understand that God is judged,[4] but that[5] in being judged by unbelievers his own reliability in promises is made clear, as is their deception in judging.[6] Thus[7] 'every man is a liar,' either because no one can fulfil a promise so far as it is in his own power, or because everyone is a liar who distrusts the promises of God, since God fulfils everything.

1 justified] In *1516* only, Erasmus added here a sentence citing the two Hebrew words and explaining: 'The Hebrew means "that you might appear just," and (in the next word) "conquering," or, as others read, "pure," because of the daghes (a dot inserted) – that is, that you might prove yourself just and victor, or "pure."'

2 In his translation Erasmus follows the Vulgate in the first clause of the text: *et vincas cum iudicaris* 'and overcome when you are judged.'

3 or ... κρίνεσθαι] Added in *1519*. κριθῆναι is aorist passive; κρίνεσθαι present passive. Erasmus printed κρίνεσθαι in all editions. Tischendorf does not cite κριθῆναι as a variant for Rom 3:4, nor is any variant cited in the editions of the Septuagint by Swete and Rahlfs; see on Ps 51:6 Swete II 278 and Rahlfs II 53.

4 judged] At this point, in *1516* only, Erasmus quoted from the Hebrew of this psalm.

5 but that ... in judging] Added in *1527*

6 Pseudo-Jerome *Breviarium in psalmos* 50 PL 26 1031B

7 Thus ... everything.] Added in *1519*

3:5 [ER *quod si iniustitia nostra dei iustitiam commendat* 'but if our unrighteousness commend the righteousness of God']
[VG] *si autem iniquitas nostra iustitiam dei commendat* 'however[1] if our wickedness[2] commend the righteousness of God'; συνίστησι, that is, 'establish,' that is, 'strengthen and confirm,' and 'prop up.' Yet 'commend' is also a correct translation. For if we believe Hesychius, the Greek word συνιστάνειν has many meanings, ἐπαινεῖν, φανεροῦν, βεβαιοῦν, παρατιθέναι, that is, 'to praise,' 'to make clear,' 'to confirm,' 'to add to' or 'to commend.'[3] Origen himself, commenting a little later on Paul's words 'But God

commends his love in us,'[4] points out that 'commends' has the same force
as 'confirms' or 'makes lovable.'[5]

    1 however ... lovable.'] This entire annotation was added in 1519.
    2 however if our wickedness] First in 1527; previously, *quod si iniustitia* 'but if
      our unrighteousness'
      In his reply to Zúñiga Erasmus explained the change from the Vulgate
      iniquitas to *iniustitia* in his own translation as an attempt to simulate in Latin
      the effect of the repetition of the sounds in Greek: *adikia dikaiosyne, iniustitia
      iustitia* (*Apologia ad annotationes Stunicae* ASD IX-2 166).
    3 *Hesychii Alexandrini Lexicon* ed M. Schmidt IV (Jena 1862) 105. On Hesychius,
      see the annotation on 3:2 ('to them the utterances') n10.
    4 Rom 5:8
    5 Origen *Comm in Rom* 4.11 PG 14 1000A

3:5 [ER *num iniustus deus qui inducat iram* 'is God unjust who brings his
wrath to bear']
[VG] *numquid iniquus deus qui iram infert* 'is God[1] unfair who inflicts
wrath.' In discussing this passage, Origen (or, if you prefer, Jerome or
Rufinus)[2] shows that some Greek manuscripts[3] read 'who brings wrath
against man.'[4] On this reading, the text would be κατ᾽ ἀνθρώπου [*kat' an-
thrōpou*], that is, 'against man' (without the verb λέγω [*legō*] 'I speak') instead of κατὰ ἄνθρωπον λέγω [*kata anthrōpon legō*], that is, 'I speak in the
manner of men.' It is[5] the translator of Origen, I believe, who adds that
this latter reading is found in the Latin manuscripts as well as in some
of the Greek. But since[6] he rejects neither of these readings,[7] everyone is
free to follow whichever he prefers. Clearly[8] Chrysostom and Theophylact
both read and interpret κατὰ ἄνθρωπον λέγω, that is, 'I speak according to
human reasoning,' in responding on God's behalf, since his judgments are
inscrutable.[9]

    The title[10] and the concluding note to Origen's commentaries on the
Epistle to the Romans led me to believe that they had been translated into
Latin by Jerome, though I had some doubt about the style, which, however,
I thought purer here than in other translations by Rufinus.[11] But what struck
me even more was the admixture of many things that in some cases could
never have been written by a Greek writer ignorant of Roman speech, [and
that] in other cases were diametrically opposed to the doctrines of Origen.[12]
Now Jerome is a more scrupulous translator than Rufinus, who not only
permits himself to work in some opinions of his own, but even omits whole
books and substitutes his own for them.[13] Thus I am ready to go over to the
side of those who think this translation is by Rufinus.[14] For it is probable
that its title was altered by the scribe to make the book easier to sell through
the enticement of a name that pleased. By his device, the name Rufinus was

changed twice, in the concluding note, to the name Jerome.[15] But evidence remained to expose the fraud. For [the author] says that he was being urged by Gaudentius to finish the translation of Clement that he had begun.[16] Now it is evident that Clement was translated by Rufinus, and dedicated to Gaudentius. Rufinus was widely reputed to be an Origenist,[17] and for this reason he advises in the concluding note that the scribe omit the name of the translator and place the name of the author [on the work].[18]

1 is God ... manner of men.'] Added in 1519 when the annotation was introduced, except that 'or Rufinus' was added in 1535. For the conclusion of the 1519 annotation see n6.
2 Cf n11 below.
3 manuscripts] Editions from 1519 to 1527 add here 'as well as the Latin.'
4 Origen *Comm in Rom* 3.1 PG 14 923D–924A
5 It is ... of the Greek.] Added in 1535
6 But since ... prefers.] The concluding sentence of the annotation as it was introduced in 1519
7 It appears that Origen intended to comment on this verse with both readings in mind. Cf PG 14 923–4 and 926B.
8 Clearly ... inscrutable.] Added in 1527
9 Cf Chrysostom *Hom in Rom* 6.5 PG 60 439. Theophylact regards Rom 3:4–5 as an apologia made on God's behalf to the implied charge of 3:3. See *Expos in Rom* 3:5 PG 124 380D–381A. Erasmus turns the 'hidden but excelling reasons of God' of which Chrysostom and Theophylact speak into the phrase 'God's inscrutable judgment,' using the words of his own translation of 11:33 – *inscrutabilia sunt iudicia* (see the annotations on 11:33).
10 The title ... author.] The remainder of the annotation was added in 1535.
11 When this annotation first appeared in 1519, Erasmus believed that Jerome was the translator of Origen's *Commentary on Romans* (cf n1 above). It was not until the annotation took its present form in 1535 that Erasmus gives any indication he has changed his mind; but in the preface to his own edition of Origen's works, published posthumously in 1536, Erasmus repeated the argument given here for Rufinus as translator (LB VIII 436A–437B). For an account of Erasmus' progress towards this discovery see Godin *Erasme* 620–4. For Erasmus' evaluation elsewhere of Rufinus as a translator see the annotations on 2:1 ('because of which') and n6; 2:7 ('to those seeking life') and n17; 5:12 ('in whom [or, in which] all have sinned') n29; and 9:5, 1535 version ('who is above all things God') and n11.
12 See the examples cited by Godin *Erasme* 621 nn105, 106.
13 See n14 below on Rufinus' statement that he reduced the fifteen books of the *Commentary on Romans* to ten. On the other hand, in translating Eusebius' *Ecclesiastical History* he added two books of his own.
14 Rufinus, born in Italy near Aquileia c 345, lived for some time as a monk on the Mount of Olives while Jerome was in his monastery in Bethlehem. Rufinus returned to Italy in 397 and was asked to translate Origen's *On First Principles*. But Origen and Origenist doctrines had been severely attacked in the late fourth century. Consequently, in the preface to his translation

Rufinus says he followed the method of Jerome, who had translated some of the homilies and commentaries of Origen but in such a way that everything offensive to orthodox faith had been removed. Rufinus had published his translation in Rome, but about 399 he moved to Aquileia where he was asked to continue his translations of Origen. It was here that he translated Origen's *Commentary on Romans*, and the *Clementine Recognitions*, which he dedicated to Gaudentius, who had become bishop of Brescia about 397 (see n16 below). In the preface to his translation of the *Commentary on Romans* Rufinus says that he was asked to abbreviate the original fifteen books (PG 14 831–2); in his translation, the *Commentary* appears in ten books. In the *peroratio* (the concluding note) he reports the complaint of some contemporaries that since so much in his translation is his own composition, the *Commentary* should appear under his own name (PG 14 1293–4). Scholars, however, assess variously the degree to which the translation is faithful to the sense of Origen. See Henry Chadwick 'Rufinus and the Tura Papyrus of Origen's *Commentary on Romans' Journal of Theological Studies* 10 (1959) 10–42 for a positive assessment, but for a more sceptical view see Jean Scherer *Le commentaire d'Origène sur Rom. III.5–v.7 d'après les extraits du papyrus no 88748 du Musée du Caire et les fragments de la Philocalie et du Vaticanus gr 762: essai de reconstitution du texte et de la pensée des tomes v et vi du 'Commentaire sur l'épître aux Romains'* Institut français d'archéologie orientale, Bibliothèque d'Etude XXVII (Cairo 1957).

15 For title and concluding note see PG 14 831–2 and 1291–4, and the translation by W.H. Fremantle in NPNF 2nd series, III 566–8.

16 The Pseudo-Clementine literature, originating possibly in the third century AD, is comprised chiefly of twenty *Homilies* and ten books of *Recognitions*. In both the *Homilies* and the *Recognitions* the protagonist is Clement of Rome who, according to the list of the bishops of Rome, was third in succession to St Peter. The *Recognitions* have come to us in their entirety only in Rufinus' translation. On the Clementine literature, see Quasten *Patrology* I 59–61 and IV 253; for Erasmus' evaluation of the literature see the annotation on 16:14 ('Hermas, Patroba, Hermes').

17 For Origenism in the fourth century cf n14 above.

18 Rufinus writes that some are asking him to set his own name rather than Origen's on his translation of the latter's *Commentary on Romans*, since the work has become so much his own. He adds that they 'bestow this whole work on me not because they love me, but because they hate the author' (PG 14 1293–4).

3:6 [ER *iudicabit deus mundum* '(how) will God judge the world']
[VG] *iudicabit deus hunc mundum* '[how] will God judge this world'; τὸν κόσμον, that is, 'the world,' not 'this world,' as if there were some other world; though [in Greek] the addition of the article sometimes implies that a specific thing is being designated.[1]

1 Erasmus changed the Vulgate here, he tells Frans Titelmans, because he feared the philosophers would assume other worlds like our own were meant (*Responsio ad collationes* LB IX 978B).

In *1516* only this annotation preceded that on 3:4 ('that you may be justified in your words').

3:8 [ER *quemadmodum de nobis male loquuntur* 'as they say in reproach of us']
[VG] *sicut blasphemamur* 'as we are reviled.' [The Translator] has used the Greek word βλασφημούμεθα [*blasphēmoumetha*], that is, 'we are maligned,' or 'people say in reproach of us.'[1]

    1 Cf the annotation on 2:24 ('is blasphemed').

3:8 [ER VG] *faciamus mala* 'let us do evil.' [The Translator] has, appropriately, omitted ὅτι [that],[1] which he is accustomed to add freely elsewhere, although there is, in any case, no need for it.[2]

    1 In the Greek, following the verb λέγειν 'affirm'; literally 'as some say we affirm *that* "let us do evil"'
    2 Cf the annotations on 3:10 ('that there is not [anyone] righteous') and 4:17 ('that I have made you the father of many nations').

3:9 [ER VG] *praecellimus eos* 'do we excel them'; προεχόμεθα. 'Them' is not added in the Greek, which is simply 'we are superior to' or 'we excel.' Indeed, the Greek makes a full stop after the words 'What then?' Otherwise [the words] could have been read together: 'In what then do we excel?'

3:9 [ER *ante causis redditis ostendimus* 'we have shown before with reasons given]'
[VG] *causati sumus* 'we have made the case';[1] προῃτιασάμεθα, that is, 'earlier, we made the claim.'[2]

    1 case] In all editions before *1535*, *praecausati sumus* 'we have made the case before,' though the Vulgate printed in *1527* read *causati sumus*, a reading supported by virtually all the textual evidence; cf Wordsworth and White II 76 9n.
    2 Valla argued that the Latin equivalent was *praecausati* (his Vulgate evidently read *causati*), and, in translating, rendered the prefix προ- by *supra* 'above': 'above we pleaded the case'; *Annot in Rom* 3 (I 856).

3:9 [ER *omnes peccato esse obnoxios* 'all are guilty of sin']
[VG] *et omnes sub peccato* 'and they [are] all under sin.' The conjunction 'and' is redundant.[1]

    1 The conjunction does not, however, appear at this point either in the Vulgate printed in *1527* or as a variant reading in Wordsworth and White (II 76 9n).

3:10 [ER *non est iustus* 'there is not (even one) righteous']

[VG] *quia non est iustus* 'that there is not [anyone] righteous'; ὅτι 'that' is redundant; certainly in this passage [the Translator] should have omitted it, as he did just above.[1]

> 1 Cf the annotation on 3:8 ('let us do evil') and nn1 and 2.

3:10 [ER *iustus ne unus quidem* 'righteous, not even one']

[VG] *iustus quisquam* '[not] any one righteous';[1] οὐδὲ εἷς, that is, 'not even one.'

> 1 This appeared as a separate annotation in all editions from 1516 to 1535, though it is conflated in LB with the preceding annotation.

3:11 [ER *qui exquirat* 'who seeks out']

[VG] *requirens* 'seeking'; ὁ ἐκζητῶν, that is, *qui exquirat* [who seeks out]. For we 'seek' [*requirimus*] not something we are tracking down, but something whose absence we deplore: *requirimus in amico fidem* [we look for fidelity in a friend].

3:14 [ER *execratione* 'execration']

[VG] *maledictione* 'reviling'; ἀρᾶς, that is, a solemn curse, execration, or invocation of evil.

    I wish to advise the reader in passing that this text, which Paul has taken from the Old Testament,[1] has been woven together from various passages – perhaps I should say patched together. For the first part[2] is taken from Psalm 13, but in such a way that the Apostle renders the thought rather than the words.[3] The next two lines, 'Their throat is an open tomb' [and] 'With their tongues they dealt deceitfully,' come from the fifth Psalm.[4] What follows, however, 'The venom of asps is under their lips,' is from the one hundred thirty-ninth Psalm.[5] Next he attaches 'Whose mouth is full of reviling and bitterness,' which is drawn from the ninth Psalm.[6] Then from Isaiah he gathers the three short lines that follow: 'Their feet are swift to shed blood,' 'Misery and misfortune are in their paths,' and 'They have not known the way of peace' etc.[7] But the last line, 'There is no fear of God before their eyes,' is from the beginning of the thirty-fifth Psalm.[8] Someone has bound these eight quotations together with Psalm 13, because he found no suitable place to which to refer these texts of Paul, as they are not contained in the Hebrew manuscripts. Jerome[9] pointed this out when he discussed the passage of Isaiah just cited, and again at more length in his preface to the sixteenth book of his commentary.[10] What [Paul] borrowed from Isaiah reads, in chapter 59 of the book of that prophet, as follows – according to the original Hebrew: 'Their thoughts are unprofitable thoughts, in their paths are desolation and misery. The way of peace they do not know, and there is no judgment in their steps.'[11]

1 Erasmus calls the Old Testament here *Vetus instrumentum*, evidently following
  Jerome in his discussion of these verses in the preface to his *Commentarii
  in Isaiam* 16 (see n10 below). He published his first edition of the New
  Testament with the name *Novum instrumentum* but, thereafter, as *Novum
  Testamentum*. For the use of the term *instrumentum* in the first centuries AD to
  designate the Scriptures see J.E.L Van der Geest *Le Christ et l'Ancien Testament
  chez Tertullien* (Nijmegen 1972) 16–24.
2 part ... the next] Added in *1519*
3 Cf Ps 14:1–3. Erasmus refers throughout to the Vulgate numbering of the
  Psalms.
4 Cf Ps 5:9.
5 Cf Ps 140:3.
6 Cf Ps 10:7.
7 etc] Added in *1519*. Cf Isa 59:7–8.
8 Cf Ps 36:1.
9 Jerome ... commentary.] Added in *1519*, except that 'again' was added in
  1527.
10 Jerome *Commentarii in Isaiam* 16 (on 59:7–8) and preface PL 24 579B and (for
   the preface) 547A–548B. In his exposition of the sources of this catena of
   quotations in Paul, Erasmus follows Jerome (in the preface to *Commentarii
   in Isaiam* 16) almost word for word. Following the Septuagint, the Vulgate
   had inserted between verses 3 and 4 of Ps 14 (VG Ps 13) the texts quoted in
   Rom 3:13–17. Modern scholarship agrees with Jerome (PL 24 548B) that the
   verses were not originally in the Septuagint of Ps 14, but were taken from
   the passage in Romans and inserted there by a later hand. See W.E. Barnes
   The Psalms Westminster Commentaries (London 1931) 59 and Cranfield I 193
   n1.
11 Our translation reflects the fact that linguistically the differences between the
   Vulgate of Rom 3:16–17 and what Erasmus quotes 'according to the original
   Hebrew' are minimal. Though his quotation supplies the full text of Isa
   59:7b–8a, he makes no note of the wide variations in language between Rom
   3:15 and Isa 59:7a.

3:19 [ER *obnoxius* 'guilty']

[VG] *subditus* 'subject'; ὑπόδικος, that is to say, 'guilty and condemned' –
for in Greek δίκη signifies the charge, and the trial,[1] and the punishment or
penalty – as though liable to punishment.[2]

1 and the trial] Added in *1519*
2 Erasmus later insisted, against Titelmans, that the context required here a
  word with a more forensic connotation than the Vulgate's 'subject to.' See
  Responsio ad collationes LB IX 978D.

3:20 [ER *agnitio peccati* 'acknowledgment of sin']

[VG] *cognitio peccati* 'knowledge of sin'; ἐπίγνωσις. 'Acknowledgment'
would be more elegant and precise.[1]

1 Cf the annotation on 1:28 ('and just as they did not think it right') and n2.

3:23 [ER *ac destituuntur* 'and are bereft of']

[VG] *et egent* 'and are in need of.' The Greek is ὑστεροῦνται, that is, 'lack' or 'are bereft of.' Literally,[1] it is equivalent to *posteriorantur* [fall short of] as though they did not gain what they desired.[2] The word is 'glory,' in Greek δόξης τοῦ θεοῦ [the glory of God], not 'grace' as we[3] read even in the more corrected Latin codices.[4] For God[5] is glorified in [this], that of his goodness he saves the human race.

> 1 Literally ... desired.] Added in *1535*
> 2 In his reply to Titelmans Erasmus confirmed the definitions offered here in both *1516* and *1535*. He defended *destituo* as a strong word which, however, does not imply the loss of all hope for the one who is bereft (*Responsio ad collationes* LB IX 978F–979A).
> 3 as we ... codices] Added in *1519*
> 4 Perhaps a simple error on Erasmus' part: 'grace' does not appear as a variant for 'glory' in the Vulgate of 3:23, but the first clause of 3:24 has both *gratis* and *gratiam*. Cf Wordsworth and White II 77–8 and 23n.
> 5 For God ... race.] Added in *1527*. Cf *Responsio ad collationes* LB IX 978E: 'It is not surprising that some have spoken of grace, since God's free kindness towards us takes away the glory of our works and illuminates his own glory.'

3:24 [ER *iustificantur autem gratis* 'but they are justified freely']

[VG] *iustificati gratis* 'justified freely'; δικαιούμενοι. The participle is passive, but in the present tense; so I have translated 'but are justified,' adding an unimportant conjunction on my own to make the sense clearer.

3:21 [ER *nunc vero absque lege iustitia dei manifesta est* 'but now apart from the Law the righteousness of God is manifest']

[VG] *nunc autem sine lege iustitia dei manifestata est* 'now,[1] however, without the Law the righteousness of God has been manifested.' Augustine points out in his work against Pelagius and Celestius *On the Grace of Christ*, book 1, chapter 8, a way to construe this sentence. It is to be read: *iustitia dei sine lege, nunc manifestata est* [the righteousness of God which is without the Law, now has been manifested].[2] There would be something in what he says if an article [ἡ 'the'] had been placed before the preposition [χωρίς 'without'], νυνὶ δὲ ἡ χωρὶς νόμου δικαιοσύνη. Since this is not the case, we must understand that the righteousness of God has been made known to all and will be of benefit without the help of the Law. But how you write the phrase makes little difference to the sense. I shall quote Augustine's words: 'How then' he says 'has [the righteousness of God] been manifested *without* the Law, if it has been attested *by* the Law? So here the righteousness which is of God is not "manifested without the Law" but is the righteousness without the Law.' Thus Augustine. But the difficulty that disturbs Augustine is of no importance. The righteousness of God through faith and grace was manifested in the advent of Christ, but the Law had foretold that this would be.

1 now ... would be.] The entire annotation was added in 1535, in the sequence indicated here, though in LB it precedes the previous two annotations.
2 Augustine *De gratia Christi et de peccato originali* 1.8.9 PL 44 365

3:24 [ER VG] *per redemptionem* 'through redemption'; διὰ τῆς ἀπολυτρώσεως. This is, properly, the redemption of a captive, when a price has been paid for his freedom; the French[1] call this a 'rançon.'

Τῆς[2] ἐν Χριστῷ Ἰησοῦ [which is in Jesus Christ]. Here too ἐν [in] seems to have been written for διά [through];[3] this redemption comes through Jesus Christ; he repeats this to exclude again the glory of human works.

1 the French ... 'rançon'] Added in 1519
2 Τῆς ... works.] Added in 1527
3 Cf the annotation on 1:4 ('in power').

3:25 [ER *reconciliatorem* 'a reconciler']

[VG] *propitiatorem* 'propitiator'; ἱλαστήριον, that is, 'propitiation,' or rather *propitiatorium* [the place, or instrument of propitiation],[1] so that[2] as Origen holds [Paul] has in mind the image of the Jewish place of propitiation,[3] the type of our Christ; just as[4] he also mentions the blood.[5] Theophylact explains it in the same way,[6] as did Chrysostom before him;[7] so, finally,[8] does Augustine in his book *On the Spirit and the Letter*, chapter 13.[9] Perhaps the Translator takes ὁ ἱλαστήριος as a masculine like[10] ὁ σωτήριος [saviour].

1 Cf Valla *Annot in Rom* 3: 'Some codices read "propitiation" [*propitiatio*], but the Greek is rather "propitiatorium," ἱλαστήριον' (I 856). In fact, the Latin reading is quite divided between *propitiationem* and *propitiatorem* (Wordsworth and White II 78 25n). Origen-Rufinus apparently knows all three readings. See n5 below. For Origen-Rufinus see the annotation on 3:5 ('is God unfair who inflicts wrath') n14.
2 so that ... Christ] Added in 1519
3 Cf Exod 25:17–22.
4 just as ... before him] Added in 1527
5 Origen *Comm in Rom* 3.8 PG 14 946A–952A. Origen compares the 'mercy-seat' (RSV) of Exod 25:17–22 to the soul of Christ, as mediator placed between God and man, sharing in humanity and divinity. But he adds that there is little difference among *propitiatorium, propitiator,* and *propitiatio* (PG 14 951A). Cf CWE 42 25 and n13.
6 Theophylact *Expos in Rom* 3:25 PG 124 387B. Theophylact equates the ἱλαστήριον here with the mercy-seat as the 'covering' of the ark, and interprets it as the human nature that covered the divinity of Christ.
7 Chrysostom *Hom in Rom* 7.2 PG 60 444 has only a brief allusion to the ἱλαστήριον as an Old Testament 'type' foreshadowing the truth.

8 So, finally ... chapter 13] Added in 1535
9 Augustine *De spiritu et littera* 13.21 CSEL 60 174. The Migne text (PL 44 213) reads *propitiatorium*, but notes the variant *propitiatorem*.
10 like ... ὁ σωτήριος] Added in 1535. ἱλαστήριος (like σωτήριος) is an adjective that can be used as a substantive; in Heb 9:5 for example, it is clearly a neuter, as the article indicates: τὸ ἱλαστήριον. Here in Rom 3:25 it is used without the article and may be taken as a neuter substantive (reflected in the Latin neuter *propitiatorium*) or as a masculine adjective modifying the preceding pronoun 'whom' referring to 'Christ Jesus' in 3:24.

3:25 [ER VG] *propter remissionem* 'for[1] the remission.' I wonder what witness Ambrose follows in reading *propter propositum praecedentium delictorum* [on account of the purpose of former sins].[2] For the Greek reads πάρεσις [remission], not πρόθεσις [purpose, plan, a setting forth], unless perhaps there is an error in the Ambrose codex.[3] And yet in his commentary he adds, 'God knowing the purpose of his kindness,' implying that he did read 'purpose,' not 'remission.' Augustine[4] reads in the same way in the passage that I mentioned just above.[5]

1 for ... 'remission.'] All but the last sentence of this annotation was added in 1519.
2 Ambrosiaster *Comm in Rom* 3:26 (1). Ambrosiaster's commentary suggests that he understood this phrase in the context of 3:25: God set forth Christ as a propitiator, to manifest his grace, knowing the purpose of his own kindness: that he wished to deliver all from their sins, those above and those below the earth, Jew and gentile alike. For the sense of *propositum* here in Ambrosiaster see Schelkle 117.
3 Schelkle 117 n2 points out that the translators of the old Latin appear to have read διὰ τὴν πρόθεσιν, and he notes that Augustine and Pelagius have the same reading as Ambrosiaster.
Modern critics dispute the identification of πάρεσις with ἄφεσις 'remission' made by both Erasmus and the Vulgate. The meaning here of πάρεσις is 'passing over' rather than 'remitting.' See Michel 109–10 and Cranfield I 211.
4 Augustine ... above.] Added in 1535.
5 Cf the preceding annotation, n9.

3:25 [ER *quae deus toleravit* 'which God bore']
[VG] *in sustentatione [dei]* 'in the forbearance [of God]'; ἐν τῇ ἀνοχῇ, that is, 'in patient endurance.'

3:27 [ER *ubi igitur (gloriatio)* 'where then (the boasting)']
[VG] *ubi est ergo [gloriatio tua]* 'where is therefore [your boasting].' The words 'is' and 'your' have been added by the Translator. The Greek is ποῦ οὖν ἡ καύχησις 'Where then the boasting?' In this way [the question] is clearly more universal and inclusive.[1] Questions[2] of this kind add

much sharpness to a discourse, especially in a matter already proven by arguments.

    1 In response to the criticism of Titelmans, Erasmus explained that the omission of 'your' allows the question to be directed not merely to Jews but to gentiles also. See *Responsio ad collationes* LB IX 979C. But cf the paraphrase on this verse CWE 42 25 and n16.

    2 Questions ... arguments.] Added in 1527. 'Questions' here translates the Latin *percontationes*. In *Ecclesiastes* III LB V 988D–F Erasmus notes a distinction between *interrogatio* and *percontatio*: 'Certain people distinguish the two thus: *interrogatio* is [used] of one who wishes to learn and expects a reply; *percontatio* of one who is pressing a point to which no reply can be made.' Cf Lausberg I 354, who observes that the *interrogatio*, as a 'Wechselspiel' of question and answer, is called the *percontatio*. Cf also the annotations on 8:33 ('who will make accusation against the elect of God') and n8; and on 8:35 ('who therefore will separate us') and n15.

3:28 [ER *arbitramur igitur* 'we judge then']

[VG] *arbitramur enim* 'for we judge'; λογιζόμεθα οὖν, we 'reckon' or 'conclude,' then.[1] For Theophylact interprets [the word as] συλλογιζόμεθα [we draw the conclusion], as though [Paul] has now reached this conclusion by argumentation.[2]

    1 For the meaning and use of this Greek word see the annotation on 4:3 ('and it was considered') and n5.

    2 Theophylact *Expos in Rom* 3:28 PG 124 389B

3:29 [ER *certe et gentium* 'by all means, of the gentiles also']

[VG] *imo et gentium* 'on the contrary, of the gentiles also.' For *imo* the Greek reads ναί (which is an affirmative adverb) as though you were to say 'beyond doubt, of the gentiles also.'

3:30 [ER *qui iustificabit* 'who will justify']

[VG] *qui iustificat* 'who justifies'; δικαιώσει 'who will justify,' in the future tense.[1] For he was thinking of those who were still in Judaism or paganism.[2] In[3] the codex of St Donatian *iustificavit* [has justified] was written with *b* changed into *v*, a similar sound [ie *iustificabit* 'will justify']. It is a mistake scribes frequently make.

    1 So Valla *Annot in Rom* 3 (I 856)

    2 paganism] In 1516 and 1519 only, 'heathenism.' Erasmus had later to explain that while the future tense implied a distinction between the time before and the time since evangelical grace, he himself did not exclude from evangelical grace those who had lived before the gospel was proclaimed to all (*Responsio ad collationes* LB IX 979D).

    3 In ... make.] Added in 1522. For this codex see the annotation on 1:22 ('saying that they were wise') n3.

3:31 [ER *legem igitur irritam facimus* 'do we then make the Law without
effect']

[VG] *legem ergo destruimus* 'do we therefore destroy the Law'; καταργοῦμεν,
that is, 'do we make without effect' or 'abolish,' as I pointed out a little
above.[1]

Further, the [Vulgate] phrase that follows, *legem statuimus* [we establish the Law], ἱστῶμεν [in the Greek], is used for *fulcimus* [we prop up, sup-
port] or *stabilimus* [we make firm] – to make something stand that would
otherwise be tottering. In[2] any case, in Latin *statuere* has a different meaning, namely, 'to determine.'[3]

1 Cf the annotation on 3:3 ('has made void') and n1.
2 In ... 'to determine.'] Added in 1527
3 But for *statuere legem* in the sense of 'to impose a law,' see *statuo* II B 2 in
L&S.

CHAPTER 4

4:1 [ER *quid igitur dicemus invenisse Abraham patrem nostrum secundum carnem* 'what[1] then shall we say that Abraham our father according to the flesh found?']

[VG] *quid ergo dicemus invenisse Abraham patrem nostrum secundum carnem* 'what[2] therefore shall we say that Abraham our father according to the flesh found?'** It is uncertain whether the phrase 'according to the flesh' refers to 'our father Abraham' or to 'found.' I know that in most Greek codices the order is: 'What therefore shall we say that our father Abraham found according to the flesh?' But Origen reads otherwise, Ambrose otherwise; it is otherwise in the ancient Latin codices; that is[3] to say, it is construed so that 'our father' joins closely with the phrase[4] 'according to the flesh.'[5] For Paul believes that Abraham, in respect to the call to faith, is the father even of the gentiles; but of the Jews he is father only in respect to the flesh. So also[6] interprets Theophylact; he says: πατέρα δὲ κατὰ σάρκα καλεῖ τοῦτον, ἐκβάλλων αὐτοὺς τῆς κατὰ πνεῦμα συγγενείας, μᾶλλον δὲ καὶ ἀνάγκην αὐτοῖς περιτιθεὶς τοῦ μιμήσασθαι αὐτὸν κατὰ πάντα, that is, 'but [Paul] calls him father according to the flesh, excluding them from a kinship according to the spirit, or rather compelling them to imitate him in all things.'[7] Likewise Chrysostom: πατέρα δὲ αὐτὸν κατὰ σάρκα ἐκάλεσεν ἐκβάλλων αὐτοὺς τῆς πρὸς αὐτὸν γνησίας συγγενείας, καὶ προοδοποιῶν τοῖς ἔθνεσι τὴν πρὸς αὐτὸν ἀγχιστείαν, that is, 'but he called him father [according to the flesh], excluding them from a true kinship with Abraham, and at the same time opening up a way for the gentiles to gain a relationship with Abraham.'[8] Nevertheless, the word order in the Greek suggests a different sense in which we must assume a *hyperbaton*; otherwise the reading would have to be τί οὖν ἐροῦμεν Ἀβραὰμ τὸν κατὰ σάρκα πατέρα εὑρηκέναι.[9] Accordingly[10] I was not afraid to return this passage to its original order of words.[11] And yet I was aware that when Ambrose explains this passage he makes 'according to the flesh' modify 'found,' giving us to understand that the Mosaic law is so far from being able to confer salvation that not even Abraham himself would have gained anything 'according to the flesh,' that is, through circumcision, if he had not pleased God by the merit of his faith.[12]

1 what ... found?] First in *1519*. For the *1516* translation see n11 below.
2 what ... in respect to the flesh.] These sentences (with the exception of the phrases noted in nn2 and 3 below) comprised the first portion of the annotation when it was introduced in *1519*; cf n10 below.
3 that is ... construed] Added in *1527*
4 with the phrase] Added in *1522*

5 Cf Origen *Comm in Rom* 4.1 PG 14 959B and 961C–962A and Ambrosiaster *Comm in Rom* 4:1. From Origen's commentary it is clear that he read 'our father according to the flesh' (961C–962A). While the scriptural text (as we have it) in Ambrosiaster reads 'our father according to the flesh,' the commentary suggests that he understood 'found according to the flesh': '[Paul] adds that Abraham was unable to merit anything according to the flesh.'
The original reading of the text is still disputed, though most modern critics are inclined to link 'according to the flesh' with Abraham and not with 'found.' See Michel 115 n1; Metzger 509–10; and Cranfield I 226–7.

6 So also ... εὑρηκέναι.] Added in 1527

7 Theophylact *Expos in Rom* 4:1 PG 124 389D–392A

8 Chrysostom *Hom in Rom* 8.1 PG 60 455A. Erasmus translates αὐτόν 'him' in both cases as Abraham.

9 Ie 'What then shall we say that Abraham our father according to the flesh found?' This would be the natural order of the Greek for the meaning Origen, Ambrosiaster, and Chrysostom give the passage. But since the Greek codices, in fact, give a different word order (illustrated at the beginning of the annotation), one must suppose these commentators assumed, for their interpretation, a hyperbaton, that is, that the phrase 'according to the flesh' is, in the Greek codices, deliberately set out of its natural order. For 'hyperbaton' see the annotation on 1:4 ('from the resurrection of the dead of Jesus Christ') and n21.

10 Accordingly ... faith.] Added as the final portion of the annotation in 1519

11 In 1516, Erasmus' translation had followed closely the word order in his Greek codices – *Quid igitur dicemus Abraham patrem nostrum invenisse secundum carnem* 'What then shall we say that Abraham our father found according to the flesh?' (For this word order, which is not that of the preferred reading, see Tischendorf II 379 1n.) In 1519, influenced evidently by Origen, Ambrosiaster, and the Latin manuscripts, he decided that the Vulgate read the passage properly, and so restored the Vulgate reading in his own text.

12 Cf n5 above.

4:2 [ER *habet quod glorietur* 'he has[1] something of which he might boast']
[VG] *habet gloriam* 'he has glory.' καύχημα means 'boasting' rather than 'glory' (as does καύχησις), that is, 'he has something to boast and brag about.'

1 he has ... boast] First in 1519; in 1516, *habet gloriationem* 'he has boasting'

4:3 [ER *credidit autem Abraham* 'but Abraham believed']
[VG] *credidit Abraham* 'Abraham[1] believed.' Origen raises a subtle question[2] whether the reading here is 'Abraham' instead of 'Abram' due to the mistake of the copyists – a trisyllabic name in place of a disyllabic; for at the time when he believed God who was making the promise he was not yet Abraham, but Abram.[3] Thus it is reasonable that at that point in the Hebrew

the reading is not 'Abraham believed God,' but 'Abram believed.' And so[4] the LXX rendered it – 'Aβράμ. I certainly praise the man's diligence, and am ashamed of my own slackness. And yet in this passage at least, if the language is recognized as the author's, whether he was Moses, Esdras,[5] or anyone else, to him it was certainly 'Abraham.'[6] But when in the narrative God addresses him by name, he says 'Abram,' not 'Abraham,' until his name was lengthened by the addition of a syllable. There are[7] some who say that in the very old Latin codices also, the reading in this passage is Abram, not Abraham.[8]

1 Abraham ... syllable.] This annotation was introduced in 1519 in almost its full extent. Only two sentences were added later (see nn4 and 7).
2 raises a subtle question] From 1522; in 1519, 'raises a quibble'
3 Origen *Comm in Rom* 4.2 PG 14 969C–970A; cf also 4.1 PG 14 962B. The text quoted here in 4:3 is taken from Gen 15:6, where the name is Abram; the name is changed in the narrative at Gen 17:5.
4 And so ... 'Aβράμ.] Added in 1535
5 Cf 2 Esd 14:19–22, 37–48 where Ezra dictates in a trance the books of Hebrew Scriptures that had been lost in the destruction of Jerusalem; see *Harper's Bible Dictionary* ed Paul J. Achtemeier (New York 1985) 279.
6 Origen, too, appeals to the authority of the later name, though on different grounds. Since by God's pronouncement the trisyllabic form of the name had become sacred, the Apostle used the form of the name thus rendered holy (*Comm in Rom* 4.2 PG 14 970A).
7 There are ... Abraham.] Added in 1535
8 Though 'Abram' is found as a variant reading of the Vulgate of 4:1–2, it is not given for 4:3; see Wordsworth and White II 79 1–3nn.

4:3 [ER *et imputatum est* 'and it was imputed']
[VG] *et reputatum est* 'and it was considered'; ἐλογίσθη, that is, 'it was imputed,' at least in this passage. For the Greek word is ambiguous. But *reputare* means something quite different from *imputare*. *Reputare*[1] means to consider, *imputare* means to count to one's credit, or to add to the account, generally with no pejorative connotation.[2] *Deputare* has the meaning of *supputare* [to count, calculate], or of *existimare* [to suppose] or *aestimare* [to judge, esteem];[3] while the Greek word corresponds variously to 'consider,' 'impute,' 'reckon.' Strictly speaking, *imputare* corresponds to ἐλλογεῖσθαι [rather than λογίζεσθαι], and this word, too, the Apostle has used elsewhere.[4]

Valla not unjustly censures the Translator's childish striving for variety here, for in the same passage he translates the same Greek word now by *reputare*, now *accepto ferre* [count as credit], now *imputare*, as though it were forbidden to repeat the same word very often.[5]

1 *Reputare* ... elsewhere.] Added in 1535

2 Challenged by Titelmans on the meaning of *imputare*, Erasmus expressed disagreement with Valla, who taught that *imputare* was used in a negative context ('evils are "imputed"'; *Elegantiae* 6.43 [I 223]). See *Responsio ad collationes* LB IX 979E–980D.

3 In the annotation on 8:18 ('for I suppose') Erasmus distinguishes between *existimare* and *aestimare*: *existimare* often implies a doubt, as in supposition; *aestimare* is the judgment made on the basis of careful consideration. In the same annotation he associates *reputo* with *perpendo* and *cogito*. See the annotation on 8:18 n2.

4 Cf Rom 5:13 and the annotation 'was not imputed.'

5 Valla *Annot in Rom* 4 (I 856). The Greek λογίζεσθαι appears seven times in verses 3–11, and in the Vulgate is translated once by *accepto ferre*, twice by *imputare*, four times by *reputare*. Valla says: 'Who would think there was only one word in the Greek for all of these?'

4:5 [ER *porro ei qui non operatur sed credit* 'now to him who does not work, but believes']

[VG] *ei vero qui non operatur credenti autem* 'to him, however, who does not work, yet believing.' In the Greek, a participle is used in both cases: μὴ ἐργαζομένῳ πιστεύοντι δέ, that is, 'to him not working, but believing.' And again, *reputatur* for *imputatur*.[1]

1 Cf the preceding annotation.

4:5 [ER omitted]

[VG] *secundum propositum gratiae dei* 'according to the purpose of the grace of God.'[1] This clause[2] is not in the Greek codices. But Ambrose so reads, and expounds these words specifically; thus it is clear that he used a different witness.[3] In a very[4] old codex, which John Colet made available from St Paul's Library,[5] the words were not in the text but in the bottom margin, added by a different and more recent hand.

1 A separate annotation in all editions from *1516* to *1535*, though coalesced in LB with the preceding annotation

2 This clause] From *1519*; in *1516*, 'of God' instead of 'this clause.' Though it is omitted from the text of Wordsworth and White, this clause, tacked on to the end of verse 5, is abundantly attested in their critical apparatus; cf II 79 5n. It does not have the support of the Greek witnesses; cf Tischendorf II 381 5n.

3 Ambrosiaster *Comm in Rom* 4:5 (2–3)

4 In a very ... hand.] Added in *1519*, except that Erasmus added to the text in *1522* Colet's Christian name, 'John'

5 John Colet, dean of St Paul's in London, had made available to Erasmus from the chapter house two ancient manuscripts of the Latin Bible, one containing the Epistles, the other the Gospels. Erasmus briefly describes the manuscripts in the preface to the *Annotations* for his first edition of the New

Testament; they were written, he says, in a script so old that he had, as it were, to learn the alphabet all over again (cf Ep 373:20–5). Allen believes these manuscripts perished in the fire of 1561 or the great fire of London in 1666, since nothing is now known of them (Allen Ep 373 introduction). For some other references to the 'manuscripts of St Paul's' see the annotation on Matt 1:18 (*mater Iesu Maria*), where Erasmus says that one of them (ie the one containing the Gospels) was available for the 1519 edition; the annotation on Rom 4:23 ('that it was considered to him'), where Erasmus says the other was the oldest of all he had seen; and the annotation on 1 Cor 8:6 (*ex quo omnia*), where Erasmus claims that it was the 'most corrected' of all he had seen. For a more detailed description of the manuscripts see ASD IX-2 165:997–1000nn.

4:6 [ER *imputat* 'imputes']

[VG] *accepto fert* 'counts to his credit'; λογίζεται, that is, 'imputes' or 'counts to his credit.' But to count to one's credit is to regard as received what you have not received. This, if[1] I am not mistaken, law experts call *acceptilatio* [a formal discharge from a debt].[2]

    1 if ... mistaken] Added in 1519
    2 Cf Valla *Annot in Rom* 4 (I 856); for the legal provenance of *acceptilatio* see
      L&S.

4:8 [ER *non imputabit* 'will not impute']¹

[VG] *non imputavit* 'has not imputed.'[2] λογίσεται is in the future tense, although it can be an aorist subjunctive if written[3] with an η – λογίσηται, *imputaverit* in Latin,[4] though[5] these also may be used as futures.[6]

    1 will not impute] First in 1519; in 1516, *imputarit* 'has (or, will have) imputed.' See n6 below.
    2 Though *imputavit*, past tense, is abundantly attested as a Latin reading, Wordsworth and White print *imputabit*, future (cf Wordsworth and White II 80 8n). *Imputavit* is the reading of the Vulgate of 1527.
    3 if written ... λογίσηται] Added in 1519
    4 In all editions from 1516 to 1535 Erasmus printed the words in his text as an aorist subjunctive, and so it is found in Tischendorf, who lists, however, a few Greek manuscripts in support of the future tense; cf II 381 8n.
    5 though ... futures] Added in 1519
    6 In Greek the aorist subjunctive with the negative particles οὐ μή (as here) can be used to express an 'emphatic denial' of a future possibility (Smyth 1804). In Latin the perfect subjunctive (here *imputaverit*) has the same spelling as the future perfect indicative in the third person singular.

4:9 [ER *tantum ... devenit* 'does it come only']¹

[VG] *tantum manet* 'does it remain only.' I do not find the word 'remain' in the Greek. The Greek codices read: ὁ μακαρισμὸς οὖν οὗτος ἐπὶ τὴν περιτομὴν, ἢ ἐπὶ τὴν ἀκροβυστίαν 'Now this blessedness (or, this being made blessed;

or, being blessed)² to the circumcision, or to the uncircumcision?'– you must supply 'does it come,' 'belong,'³ or some similar word; and so the scholia of the Greek read and interpret. For⁴ the missing verb, which the Translator gives as *manet* [remain], Theophylact in his exposition supplies πίπτει, that is, 'falls upon'⁵ or⁶ 'belongs to,' as when we say 'wrath does not befall the wise.'⁷ Consequently it is possible that the Translator, desiring to explicate Paul's intent, wrote ' "does it flow" [*manat*] to the circumcision,' which was later changed to 'does it remain' [*manet*]. Otherwise⁸ the preposition ἐπί would join harshly with the accusative case.⁹ It is possible also to supply the verb from the words above: 'David declared the blessedness etc;¹⁰ this blessedness, then, was it declared with regard to the circumcision only, or with regard also to the uncircumcision?'

This¹¹ too should be noted, that the word 'only' is added in Origen and Ambrose,¹² but I do not find it in the common Greek codices, or even in the old Latin witnesses. Certainly in that codex from St Paul's¹³ I find written: 'This blessedness, therefore, [is it] in circumcision, or also in uncircumcision?' And yet I would not deny that this adverb ['only'] is, in effect, implied by the conjunction καί,¹⁴ 'or also in uncircumcision'; to make this clearer, [Origen and Ambrosiaster] have added 'only.'

I think¹⁵ we should not overlook even this, that μακαρισμός [blessedness] here is not perceived as an actual quality possessed by one who is blessed, but rather as a declaration of blessedness, a pronouncement David makes upon one not as the result of works, but of the grace of God, who (through faith) does not reckon up sins. For in Greek, those are said μακαρίζεσθαι [to be blessed] who are declared to be such, even though falsely. But what he calls righteousness here is not general virtue,¹⁶ but the innocence that results from the free forgiveness of sins. Moreover, 'blessedness' and 'righteousness' are by nature interconnected;¹⁷ thus it follows that whoever is declared righteous is attested as blessed also. But the epithet 'righteous' was given to Abraham before he was circumcised. To him, therefore, still uncircumcised, and, through him, to the uncircumcised gentiles belongs the epithet 'blessed,' which the circumcised David commends.¹⁸ Thus not only does uncircumcision come even with circumcision, but it is actually superior in that it merited this praise before circumcision arose.

> 1 come only] First in 1519. In 1516 Erasmus omitted both the verb and adverb:
> ER [1516] *beatificatio igitur haec in praeputium an in circumcisionem* 'this being made blessed, then, to uncircumcision or to circumcision?'
> ER [1519] *beatificatio igitur haec in praeputium tantum an et in circumcisionem devenit* 'this being made blessed, then, does it come to uncircumcision only or also to circumcision?'

vg *beatitudo ergo haec in circumcisione tantum manet an etiam in praeputio*
'this blessedness therefore does it remain only in the circumcision or in
the uncircumcision as well?'
On the words of the cue phrase, the Latin manuscripts vary: some omit
manet, some include it, some have *tantum manet;* cf Wordsworth and White
II 80 9n. On the Greek witnesses, Erasmus remains correct; cf Cranfield I 234
n3.
2 or, being blessed] Added in *1519*
3 'belong'] Added in *1535.* For the evidence of the Greek scholia, see
Pseudo-Oecumenius *Comm in Rom* 4:9 PG 118 393D–396A.
4 For ... 'falls upon'] Added in *1527*
5 Theophylact *Expos in Rom* 4:9 PG 124 393A
6 or ... wise'] Added in *1535*
7 For the sentiment cf Cicero *Tusculan Disputations* 3.9.19: 'To grow angry does
not befall the wise'; cf Seneca *Epistulae morales* 85.15–17.
8 Otherwise ... uncircumcision?'] The remainder of this paragraph was added
in *1535.*
9 Ie in the phrase 'to [ἐπί] the circumcision and to [ἐπί] the uncircumcision';
for ἐπί with the accusative cf Smyth 1689 (3).
10 Cf 4:6.
11 This ... added 'only.'] This paragraph was added in *1519.*
12 Origen *Comm in Rom* 4.2 PG 14 966A. Merlin's text (fol CLX recto) reads *tantum,*
but Migne gives the reading only in a footnote. The word does appear in
Ambrosiaster's text: *Comm in Rom* 4:9 (1).
13 For the antiquity of this codex see the annotation on 4:5 ('according to the
purpose of the grace of God') and n5.
14 Above, in quoting the Greek, Erasmus omitted the καί: ἐπὶ τὴν περιτομὴν ἢ
καὶ ἐπὶ τὴν ἀκροβυστίαν 'to the circumcision or *also* to the uncircumcision.'
He printed the καί in all editions of the Greek text.
15 I think ... arose.] The remainder of the annotation was added in *1535.* For
the Greek verb μακαρίζεσθαι in the sense of 'to be pronounced happy' cf LSJ.
16 On 'general virtue' as virtuousness in everyday life see ASD IX-2 166 and 36n.
17 That the virtues are essential for happiness is a common theme in classical
authors. See for example Seneca *De vita beata* passim, and *Epistulae morales*
85.17–19. Cf also Erasmus' paraphrase on Mark 1:1 CWE 49 13–14.
18 Cf the paraphrase on Rom 4:11 CWE 42 28, where Erasmus speaks of the
'felicity of [Abraham's] title.'

4:10 [ER *cum esset in circumcisione* 'when he was in circumcision']
[vg] *in circumcisione* 'in circumcision'; ἐν περιτομῇ ὄντι, that is, 'when he
was in circumcision,' which[1] has the same force as if he had said ἐμπεριτόμῳ,
that is, 'circumcised,' like ἐν ἀκροβυστίᾳ [in uncircumcision] for ἀκροβύστῳ
[uncircumcised]. The δίλημμα [dilemma][2] adds, beside its grace of form,
much clarity: the rejection of the first part demonstrates the second. No
type of argumentation is more clear or more forceful.

1 which ... forceful] Added in *1527*

2 In *Ecclesiastes* II LB V 942C–E Erasmus defines dilemma as a figure in which a pair of alternative questions forces an unavoidable conclusion; cf also *Ecclesiastes* III LB V 996C.

4:11 [ER VG] *signaculum* 'seal.'[1] Paul[2] uses two words, σημεῖον and σφραγίς (the one used second is σφραγίς), that is, *signum* [sign, σημεῖον] and *nota impressa* [impressed mark, σφραγίς].[3] For to ensure reliability we are accustomed to 'seal' [*obsignare*] what we wish to be established. And in the same way we 'seal' what we desire[4] to put away and store up for a time, to be brought forth in its proper place. Otherwise,[5] it could appear that Paul had said the same thing twice, when he had just now said *signum* [mark, or sign] then spoke again of *signaculum* [mark, or seal]. The first of these is, in Greek, σημεῖον, 'a sign' by which something else is designated. For even at that time the carnal circumcision bore the figure of the Christian circumcision, which does not remove the foreskin from the glans but cuts away all harmful desires from the heart.[6] It was also a 'seal,' because for a time it concealed the mystery which was to be opened up later, namely,[7] [the mystery] of righteousness, which is conferred through faith. But it is possible for something to be a 'sign' that is not a 'seal,' as a statue is a 'sign,' but the symbol on a ring, marked on a promissory note, is a σφραγίς [seal]. These two terms, however, are in apposition to each other. For the same thing is said to be a σημεῖον [sign], in so far as it points to the righteousness from faith that was in Abraham before circumcision, and also a σφραγίς [seal], in so far as by the example of Abraham righteousness from faith without circumcision was promised to all who believe. This[8] has been carefully noted by Origen.[9]

1 seal] In *1516* only, Erasmus translated '*obsignaculum,*' evidently by analogy with the verb *obsignare*, which he presently explains, but *obsignaculum* is not attested in L&S, OLD, or Niermeyer.
2 Paul ... second is] Added in *1527*
3 With the exception noted above (n1) Erasmus follows the Vulgate in his translation of the two clauses that provide the context for the discussion in this annotation: *et signum accepit circumcisionis, signaculum justitiae fidei* 'and he received the sign of circumcision, the seal of the righteousness of faith.'
4 desire] First in *1519*; in *1516*, 'what we wish'
5 Otherwise ... opened up later] Added in *1519*
6 Cf the paraphrase on Rom 4:12 CWE 42 29: '... true circumcision is ... accomplished by ... the spirit which cuts away all the perverse desires of the mind.'
7 namely ... all who believe] Except for the last sentence the remainder of the annotation was added in *1527*.
8 This ... Origen.] Added in *1519*
9 Origen *Comm in Rom* 4.2 PG 14 967D–969A. For Origen a 'sign' points to something else; a 'seal' is a mark of identification placed upon something so that it can be opened only by the one whose mark it is.

4:12 [ER *iis qui non solum genus ducerent a circumcisis* 'to those who not
only derived their descent from the circumcised']

[VG] *non his tantum qui sunt ex circumcisione* 'not to those only who are of
the circumcision.'[1] The Greek is quite different: τοῖς οὐκ ἐκ περιτομῆς μόνον,
ἀλλὰ καὶ τοῖς στοιχοῦσι, that is, 'who not only are of the circumcision, but
also walk in the footsteps' etc. From this, you understand that to be a son
of Abraham it is not enough to have been born a Jew, unless you follow in
his footsteps, which is the characteristic of sons. Ambrose[2] agrees with me,
reading as follows: 'That he might be the father of the circumcision – of
those who not only are of the circumcision, but also of those who follow in
the footsteps of faith.'[3] Origen's interpretation is not inconsistent with this
reading, indicating that the Jews would then indeed have Abraham as a father if they held to the faith which had gained for him the epithet 'righteous'
when he was not yet circumcised.[4] Certainly[5] Chrysostom agrees with me,[6]
though the passage is somewhat different in Theophylact's exposition.[7] In
the codex that I used,[8] the scribe had carelessly omitted οὐ [not]. Someone
had added this particle, but not in its proper place, οὐ τοῖς μόνον [not to
those only who], whereas Chrysostom reads τοῖς οὐ μόνον [to those who not
only], and his[9] exposition reflects this order.[10] For [Paul] means by these
words[11] not that Abraham is the father of both the Jews and the gentiles,
but that he is not the father of the Jews unless they follow in his footsteps.
For he[12] said before that he is the father of all races, not of all indiscriminately, but of those who believe.[13] Here he says that he is likewise father
of the Jews, and, lest they should think it enough to have sprung from the
stock of Abraham, he shows that the relation by blood is useless unless, by
imitating his faith, they show themselves his true sons. The conjunction καί
repeated unusually soon, ἀλλὰ καὶ τοῖς [but *also* to those], is something of
an obstacle, but some scribe could possibly have added that syllable.[14]

I obtained again the Greek codex of Theophylact, and checked the
passage more carefully. In his commentary he repeats the same reading
clearly, as I have indicated, with οὐ [not] added above the line, and he even
points out how it must be read, although he does not differ in his view from
Chrysostom. The translator of Theophylact rendered the Greek in such a
way that I doubt if he fully understood it; consequently, I shall not hesitate
to render this passage faithfully: 'He removes an objection that arises. For
perhaps someone would say: If Abraham was justified when he was uncircumcised, why was he circumcised? To this he answers that he received
the sign of circumcision as a seal, which pledged and proclaimed that he
had been justified by faith, the faith he had shown before when he was
uncircumcised. And so since these two things are observed in Abraham,
uncircumcision and circumcision, he is indeed shown through uncircumci-

son [to be] the father of the uncircumcised. But of which [of the uncircum-
cised]? Of those who believed as he himself had believed, so that to them
also faith might be imputed for righteousness, that is, [imputed] to this end,
that they might become righteous. On the other hand, through circumcision
he is shown [to be] father of the circumcision, that is, of the circumcised. But
he is father not to those only who have circumcision, but also to those who
walk in the footsteps of his faith, the faith that he had in uncircumcision. It
should be read, then, in this manner: "And that he might be father of the circumcision, not to those who resemble him in circumcision only, but also to
those who proceed in the footsteps of faith," that is, who believe, as he did,
in the resurrection of dead bodies' etc.[15] The translator has omitted some
words and added one. But I suspect that this passage in Theophylact is not
free from error. For since he points out how it should be read, it is probable
that he had adopted the same reading Chrysostom followed, inasmuch as
the rest of his comments show that he held the same view [as Chrysostom].

I think, however, that I see a way out of this difficulty, so that neither
the repetition of the conjunction nor the transposition of the negative will be
an obstacle. This is that μόνον [only] modify not the negative, as Chrysostom
understands, but ἐκ περιτομῆς [of the circumcision],[16] so that we recognize
two groups among the Jews: on the one hand [are] those who have nothing
in common with Abraham except that they have been circumcised – it is
denied that Abraham is the father of these; on the other hand are those who,
in addition to circumcision, imitate also his faith – of these only will [Paul]
have Abraham be father. This is the sense, and this the reading Theophylact
followed, nor did he diverge from Chrysostom's opinion. Here, however,
the conjunction καί [also] raises an obstacle, since it is not in the proper
position – ἀλλὰ καὶ τοῖς [but also to those who]; but if we read ἀλλὰ τοῖς καί
[but to those who also] not the slightest difficulty remains. This is probably
a mistake made through the carelessness of the scribes.

Either reading has almost the same – and a Catholic – sense. Yet in
each there is a difficulty: in the first, the repetition of [the article] τοῖς; in the
second, the transposition of καί.[17] If we remove the article, the first reads as
follows: τοῖς οὐκ ἐκ περιτομῆς μόνον, ἀλλὰ καὶ στοιχοῦσι τοῖς ἴχνεσι πίστεως,
τῆς ἐν τῇ ἀκροβυστίᾳ, that is, 'to those who not only have been circumcised,
but who follow also in the footsteps of faith, the faith [Abraham] had in
the time of uncircumcision.'[18] The second reads: οὐ τοῖς ἐκ περιτομῆς μόνον,
ἀλλὰ τοῖς καὶ στοιχοῦσι τοῖς ἴχνεσι πίστεως, that is, 'not to those who are
nothing other than circumcised, but to those who also walk in the footsteps
of faith,' so that the word 'also' recalls the circumcision. I prefer the second
reading. But the Translator has given us neither reading, though I suspect
the passage was corrupted by copyists.

1 The passage continues:
    ER *verum etiam ingrederentur vestigiis fidei* 'but also followed in the footsteps of faith'
    VG *sed et his qui sectantur vestigia fidei* 'but also to those who follow after the footsteps of faith'
In *1516* only, however, Erasmus translated *iis qui non solum essent ex circumcisione sed etiam ingrederentur vestigiis fidei* 'to those who not only were of the circumcision, but also followed in the footsteps of faith.' The Greek citation that immediately follows concludes, in all lifetime editions, with στοιχοῦσι 'walk,' though τοῖς ἴχνεσι 'in the footsteps' is added in LB.

2 Ambrose .. not yet circumcised.] Added in *1519*

3 Ambrosiaster *Comm in Rom* 4:12 (2)

4 Origen *Comm in Rom* 4.2 PG 14 969A–B: 'One is called a son not only of the man who is his natural father ... but also of him whose works and deeds he imitates ... they are not sons who do not have the father's faith.'

5 Certainly ... follow in his footsteps.] Added in *1527* with the exceptions noted below (nn9 and 11)

6 Chrysostom *Hom in Rom* 8.3 PG 60 457–8

7 Theophylact *Expos in Rom* 4:12 PG 124 393A–C. According to Migne, Theophylact quotes, prior to his exposition, a biblical text identical with the text Erasmus cites at the beginning of this annotation. In Theophylact's exposition, however, the biblical text undergoes some changes – specifically, Erasmus will note the position of the negative – to read: '[He is father] not to those who have circumcision alone, but also to those who walk in the footsteps of his faith.'

8 For this Greek manuscript see the annotation on 1:4 ('who was predestined') n25.

9 and his ... this order] Added in *1535*

10 Chrysostom comments: 'If he is the father of the uncircumcised, not because he was uncircumcised (even though he was declared righteous in uncircumcision) but because they have emulated his faith, much less will he, though circumcised, be the progenitor of the circumcised, unless they come to faith.' Erasmus, chided by Titelmans for his failure to quote directly from Chrysostom, supplied this quotation in his *Responsio ad collationes* LB IX 981A–B.

11 by these words] Added in *1535*

12 For he ... copyists.] The remainder of this annotation was added in *1535*.

13 Cf Rom 3:29–30 and 4:11.

14 A καί 'and' (Latin *et*), clearly supported by the Greek manuscript tradition, appears at the beginning of 4:12a. It is 'repeated' at the beginning of 4:12b (ie the clause discussed here). This second καί does not have an equivalent in some Latin manuscripts (eg in the *1527* Vulgate). Erasmus himself, however, rendered it by *et* with the sense of 'also': '*And* [*et*] father of the circumcision to those who not only derived their descent from the circumcised, but *also* [*et*] walked in the footsteps of faith.' For the witnesses, see Tischendorf II 382 and Wordsworth and White II 80 12n.

15 In the text of Migne, Theophylact follows Chrysostom when he quotes Rom 4:11–12 to introduce his commentary – 'to those not only of the circumcision.'

In the commentary, however, the phrase is given first in the form 'not to those who have the circumcision only,' and repeated 'not to those who resemble him from the circumcision only.' In both of the readings in the commentary, 'only' is taken closely with 'circumcision,' rather than with 'not' – a solution Erasmus will presently suggest for the text he has in hand.

16 Ie in place of 'to those not only from the circumcision' read 'not to those who are of the circumcision only.'

17 The textual witnesses unanimously support the reading ἀλλὰ καὶ τοῖς 'to those not only from the circumcision, *but also to those* who walk in the footsteps of faith.' Modern critics agree with Erasmus that a scribal error is probable, but it must have occurred very early to have entered into all the extant manuscripts. It has been suggested that the error might have been that of Tertius, Paul's amanuensis, or of Paul himself. See Michel 120 n2 and Cranfield I 237.

18 This is, essentially, the way Erasmus translated the passage for his New Testament (cf nn1 and 14 above) – though for his Greek text he retained the article τοῖς (before στοιχοῦσι), as in the citation at the beginning of this annotation.

4:13 [ER *non enim per legem promissio contigit Abrahae* 'for not through the Law did the promise come to Abraham']
[VG] *non enim per legem promissio Abrahae* 'for the promise [is] not through the Law[1] to Abraham'; τὸ κληρονόμον αὐτὸν εἶναι τοῦ κόσμου. It would have been better if [the Translator] had added here, 'did come':[2] [not through the Law did the promise come] that he was (or, would be) heir of the world.

1 through the Law] Added in 1535
2 'did come'] Added in 1519; perhaps inadvertently omitted in 1516

4:14 [ER *irrita facta est* 'has become void']
[VG] *abolita est* 'has been abolished';[1] κατήργηται With what variation has [the Translator] rendered the same word – 'has become void,' 'has been abrogated,' 'has been annulled.'[2] Nevertheless, in this instance he is right.

1 In 1516 this annotation was preceded by the one that now follows. They assumed their present order in 1519.
2 For the Translator's 'variety' in rendering this Greek word see the annotation on 3:3 ('has made void') and n2.

4:16 [ER *non ei quod est ex lege tantum* 'not to that (seed) which is of the Law only'[1]]
[VG] *non ei qui ex lege est solum* 'not to him who is of the Law only.'[2] In the Greek, 'Abraham' appears to be in the dative case, modifying the pronoun 'that' – [to that Abraham].[3] Otherwise, [Paul] might have added [the definite article in the possessive case] τοῦ Ἀβραάμ [of Abraham].[4] [The Greek is] οὐ τῷ ἐκ τοῦ νόμου μόνον, ἀλλὰ καὶ τῷ ἐκ πίστεως Ἀβραάμ, that is,

[the promise is firm] not only to that Abraham who belongs, on the ground of the Law, specifically to the Jews, but also to that [Abraham] who is, on the ground of faith, common to all races; so that you imagine two Abrahams in one. Though I am not dissatisfied with the one sense, this second seems to me more penetrating. For just as [Paul] makes two Adams, the earthly[5] and the heavenly, so he makes two Abrahams (so to speak):[6] one, justified in uncircumcision through faith, who is the spiritual father of the gentiles; and one, justified through faith in circumcision, who by a twofold right is the father of the Jews who believe. And yet I see that most people follow a different interpretation.[7]

With[8] respect to the [Vulgate] reading, 'not to him who is of the Law merely,' 'which' [instead of 'who'] would be preferable, since 'seed' is the antecedent. Now by 'seed' here he means posterity, in accordance with Hebrew idiom.

1 only] In 1516 only, Erasmus translated: *non solum ei quod est ex lege* 'not only to that which is from the Law.'
2 See preceding annotation, n1.
3 Erasmus extends the discussion here beyond the cue phrase:
   ER *verum etiam ei quod est ex fide Abrahae* 'but also to that (seed) which is of the faith of Abraham'
   VG *sed et ei qui ex fide est Abrahae* 'but also to him who is of the faith of Abraham'
4 In the Greek there is no article before 'Abraham,' which makes it possible to construe as Erasmus does in the next sentence, taking the name with the dative article, 'to that Abraham.' If the possessive article had been inserted before the name, the Greek would have yielded unambiguously the translation of Erasmus, 'the faith of Abraham' (cf n3 above).
5 the earthly and the heavenly] Added in 1535. Cf 1 Cor 15:45.
6 (so to speak) ... who believe] Added in 1535
7 Titelmans charged that no one at all had ever adopted Erasmus' interpretation here. Erasmus replied that perhaps work from the past will yet come to light to support him (*Responsio ad collationes* LB IX 981E–F). In his paraphrase, however, Erasmus appears to have adopted the traditional interpretation only; and this, too, he follows in his translation.
   For the image of 'two in one' see the Argument to the Paraphrase on Romans, and also paraphrases on 6:6 and 8:3 CWE 42 10, 37, 45.
8 With ... idiom.] Added in 1527

4:17 [ER *patrem multarum gentium constitui te* 'I have established you the father of many nations']
[VG] *quia patrem multarum gentium posui te* 'that I have made you the father of many nations.' If it is not right to omit anything, why did [the Translator] elsewhere omit the superfluous conjunction ὅτι [that]? But if it is permitted anywhere, certainly it should have been omitted here.[1]

Thomas Aquinas indicates that some codices have *constitui* [I have established] instead of *posui* [I have made].[2] No doubt he would have also made other observations of more importance if his knowledge of languages had allowed, but he knew only one language, and not even that one fully.[3] But in Greek [the word τίθημι] 'to place' [Latin *ponere*], is frequently used in the sense of 'to make.'

The quotation is from Genesis 13.[4] It should also be noted in passing that in this passage the past tense is used, in the prophetic manner, for the future – 'I have established' for 'I will establish.'

1 Cf the annotation on 3:8 ('let us do evil') and n2.
2 Thomas Aquinas *Super Rom lect* cap 4 lectio 3.363. Here in the first two editions, Erasmus spoke of 'St' Thomas Aquinas; from 1522, simply 'Thomas Aquinas.'
3 For Thomas' knowledge of languages, see the annotation on 1:4 ('who was predestined') and n8.
4 Genesis 13] From 1522 to 1535. In 1516 and 1519 Erasmus wrote 'Genesis 17.' The passage is in fact from Gen 17:5.

4:17 [ER *cui crediderat* 'in whom he had believed']
[VG] *cui credidisti* **'in whom you believed.'** The Greek is κατέναντι οὗ ἐπίστευσε θεοῦ, that is, 'before the God in whom he believed'[1] – so Augustine[2] – or 'after the example of the God in whom he believed.' [*He* believed,] for Paul has returned here to [speaking in] his own person. For he means that just as God is not the God of this or that nation only, but is common to all, so Abraham as well was to be the father of all who believe. In this way Chrysostom,[3] Theophylact, and[4] the scholia of the Greeks interpret κατέναντι τοῦ θεοῦ – lest anyone should reject this as my own dream.[5] For we[6] reproduce an original [an exemplar] which has been 'set opposite.' And yet[7] Ambrose read ἐπίστευσας, that is, 'in whom you [singular] believed,' so that the reference is to the pagan whom [Paul] is addressing. For he says: 'In order to teach that he is the one God of all, he addresses the gentiles.'[8] There is no reason why the singular[9] should be an obstacle, for ἑτερώσεις[10] of this kind are frequent in Paul. Origen likewise points out that the clause 'before God in whom he believed' was added as from the persona of Paul – but he read 'in whom he believed,' not 'in whom you believed.'[11]

1 The annotation extends the discussion to the words preceding the cue phrase:
ER *nimirum ad exemplum dei cui crediderat* 'that is, after the example of the God in whom he had believed'
VG *ante deum cui credidisti* 'before the God in whom you have believed'
For witnesses to the reading *credidisti* (Greek ἐπίστευσας) 'you have believed' see Wordsworth and White II 81 17n and Tischendorf II 383 17n.

2 so Augustine] Added in *1535*. Cf Augustine *Expositio quarundam propositionum ex epistula ad Romanos* 24 PL 35 2067. The Greek κατέναντι, meaning 'opposite, over against' is used in the sense of 'before,' 'in the presence of,' for example in Exod 19:2 (LXX) and Mark 11:2, and this is the sense of Augustine.

3 Chrysostom] Added in *1527*

4 Theophylact, and] Added in *1519*

5 Chrysostom *Hom in Rom* 8.4 PG 60 460; Theophylact *Expos in Rom* 4:17 PG 124 396C-D; and Pseudo-Oecumenius *Comm in Rom* 4:17 PG 118 401C. For Chrysostom's interpretation see Schelkle 136. This interpretation has influenced Erasmus' paraphrase on this verse. See CWE 42 30 ('On the contrary . . .').

6 For we . . . 'set opposite'] Added in *1527*. The sentence evidently attempts to explain how κατέναντι 'before' (Vulgate), 'opposite,' can be understood in the sense of Erasmus' translation 'after the example of.'

7 And yet . . . believed.'] The remainder of this annotation was added in *1519*.

8 Ambrosiaster *Comm in Rom* 4:17 (2). Thus for Ambrosiaster the 'you' of 'you believed' does not refer to Abraham.

9 'You believed' is singular, in spite of the plural 'gentiles.'

10 Erasmus describes ἑτέρωσις (= *enallage*) in *De copia* 1.13 as the use of related forms of words to achieve variety; for example, interchanges of singular and plural (CWE 24 321-9, and especially 324). Cf also Quintilian 9.3.12.

11 Origen *Comm in Rom* 4.5 PG 14 977B. Like Ambrosiaster, Origen understands the words 'in the presence of the God in whom he believed' (4:17 RSV) as a comment by Paul, but unlike Ambrosiaster reads 'he believed.'

4:17 [ER *tamquam sint* 'as though they were']

[VG] *tamquam ea quae sunt* 'as those which are'; ὡς ὄντα, that is, 'as if they were,' and not τὰ ὄντα [those which are].[1] However, he has implied that[2] 'not to be' is something more than 'to be dead.'[3] Augustine[4] cites this passage in explicating Psalm 104 and follows the original Greek; 'For "he called forth hunger" who "calls forth those things which are not as though they were." The Apostle did not say "who calls forth those things which are not, in order that they might be," but "as though they were." '[5] For ancient[6] writers, too, used to say that things of no weight 'were not.' Marcus Tullius [Cicero] seems to call the will of a certain Minucius 'nothing,' because it was invalid and rejected by law;[7] and the Greeks, when speaking of laws that are abrogated and of no effect, call them νόμοι οὐκ ὄντες [laws that are not].[8] St Jerome, [commenting] on the first chapter of Jeremiah, quotes this passage as follows: 'Who has called those things that were not, as if [they were] things that were.'[9] Though his words differ from mine, in substance, he agrees.

1 Erasmus makes the distinction on the grounds that the first phrase (ὡς ὄντα) does not have the article, the second (τὰ ὄντα) does. Cf Valla *Annot in Rom* 4 (I 856-7).

2 he has implied that] Added in *1527*

3 Ie there is a gradation in the significance of the ideas expressed in 4:17: (Abraham believed God) who restores the dead to life, and calls those things that are not as though they were.

4 Augustine ... but "as though they were." '] Added in *1519*

5 Cf Augustine *Enarrationes in psalmos* 104.11 PL 37 1396, where Augustine cites Rom 4:17 in Latin but according to the original Greek. For the brief quotation from the Psalms, see 105:16. Erasmus recognized in response to Titelmans that elsewhere (cf eg *Enchiridion* 29 PL 40 246) Augustine follows the reading of the Vulgate (*Responsio ad collationes* LB IX 982C). But the reading of Rom 4:17 cited by Erasmus is not confined in Augustine to his exposition of Ps 105:16. Cf eg *Tractatus in evangelium Ioannis* 105.7 PL 35 1907 and *Sermones* 69.2.3 PL 38 441.

6 For ancient ... agrees.] Added in *1535*

7 Cicero *In Verrem* 1.45.115

8 For the use of εἰμί 'to be' in the sense of 'be in effect' see LSJ A II 2, and the reference there to Thucydides' *Peloponnesian War* 4.118, where a truce is to 'be in effect' for one year.

9 Jerome *Commentarii in Hieremiam prophetam* 1 (on 1:4–5) PL 24 682D

4:18 [ER *praeter spem* 'beyond hope']

[VG] *contra spem* 'against hope'; παρ' ἐλπίδα, that is, 'beyond hope' or 'past hope,' that is, 'although it was not apparent what could be hoped for, nevertheless, he maintained the utmost faith in[1] the God who was promising.'

1 in ... promising] Added in *1519*

4:18 [ER *sub spe* 'in dependence upon hope']

[VG] *in spem* 'unto hope'; ἐλπίδι ἐπίστευσεν, that is, 'he relied upon hope' or 'he believed hope,' though some codices read ἐπ' ἐλπίδι 'in hope' or 'in[1] dependence upon hope.'[2] But[3] the repetition of the same word is pleasant,[4] as is the mutual relationship of contraries, as though you were to say, 'he hoped in the hopeless, and though hope was gone he still hoped, not trusting himself but trusting God.' And this faith is most pleasing to God precisely when we are destitute of our own resources and depend entirely on God. For Chrysostom[5] neatly marks the distinction thus: παρ' ἐλπίδα τὴν ἀνθρωπίνην, ἐπ' ἐλπίδι τῇ τοῦ θεοῦ, that is, 'beyond the hope of man, in the hope of God.'[6] By 'the hope of God' he means the hope that Abraham had in the promises of God.

1 or 'in ... entirely on God] Added in *1519*, with the exception noted in n3

2 Though Erasmus printed ἐπ' ἐλπίδι in all editions, in *1516* he translated *in spe* 'in hope,' changing to *sub spe* in *1519*. For the expression, see Cranfield I 246 and nn2 and 3.

3 But ... contraries] Until *1527* this read: 'But the mutual relationship of contraries is pleasant.' In *Ecclesiastes* III Erasmus distinguishes 'contraries' as, on the one hand, a figure designed to achieve forcefulness, and, on the other,

an argument designed to persuade (see LB V 1002B–C and 976B–D). Cf the
annotation on 1:4 ('in power'). See also Quintilian 5.11.31.
4 Ie in 4:18: 'who beyond hope, in dependence upon hope, believed that he
would be the father of many nations ...'
5 For Chrysostom ... of God.] The remainder of the annotation was added in
1527.
6 Chrysostom *Hom in Rom* 8.5 PG 60 461

4:18 [ER *se fore* 'that he would be']

[VG] *ut fieret* 'that he might become'; εἰς τὸ γενέσθαι.[1] 'That he would be
father' would be better. For this is what he hoped for beyond hope.

And 'according to that which *had been said*'[2] would be clearer than
'was said.'[3] Further, the Translator added the pronoun *ei* [to him] by way
of explication.

1 Though LB prints εἰς τὸ γενέσθαι αὐτὸν πατέρα 'unto his being father,' all
editions from 1516 to 1535 quote simply εἰς τὸ γενέσθαι 'unto being.' Erasmus
observes in *Responsio ad collationes* LB IX 982C that the frequent use of εἰς in
Paul's letters derives from Hebrew idiom.
2 With the concluding sentences of this annotation the discussion has covered
almost the full extent of verse 18:
ER *qui praeter spem sub spe credidit, se fore patrem multarum gentium, iuxta
id quod dictum est* 'who beyond hope, in dependence upon hope believed
that he would be the father of many nations according to that which was
said'
VG *qui contra spem in spem credidit ut fieret pater multarum gentium secundum
quod dictum est ei* 'who against hope, unto hope believed that he might
become the father of many nations according to that which was said to
him'
3 *Dictum fuerat* rather than *dictum est*, ie pluperfect rather than perfect,
representing clearly, as in the Greek participle it translates, the time (past)
relative to the main verb 'believed': 'believed as it had been said.'

4:18 [ER omitted]

[VG] *sicut stellae coeli et arena maris* 'as the stars of the sky, and the sand
of the sea.' None of these words appears in the Greek codices; there is[1]
only 'so shall be your seed.'[2] The rest are added neither in Chrysostom
nor in Theophylact nor in Ambrose, though the translator of Theophylact
inserts them from the Vulgate edition.[3] It appears that they were added by
someone who wanted to make the sense clearer. For Paul was quoting the
words of God when he showed the stars of the sky to Abraham, as you
read in Genesis, the fifteenth chapter: 'Count[4] the stars if you can, so shall
be your seed' [15:5]. But here the sentence does not cohere well: 'So shall
be your seed as the sand of the sea' etc.[5] It was enough to say: 'Your seed
shall be as the stars of the sky.'

1 there is ... Vulgate edition] Added in 1527

2 Though some manuscripts do have the additional words, the evidence of the witnesses supports their omission; see Tischendorf II 383 18n.
3 Cf Chrysostom *Hom in Rom* 8.5 PG 60 460; Ambrosiaster *Comm in Rom* 4:18; Theophylact *Expos in Rom* 4:18 PG 124 398B. For the translator of Theophylact see the annotation on 1:4 ('who was predestined') n25.
4 'Count . . . sky.'] Added in *1527*
5 The two images of sand and stars appear together in Gen 17:22, but not with the words 'so shall your seed be,' which belong to Gen 15:5. Titelmans denied that the word 'so' disturbed the coherence of the sentence (*Responsio ad collationes* LB IX 982D).

4:19 [ER *non infirmatus fide* 'not weakened in faith']
[VG] *non est infirmatus in fide* 'he was not weakened in faith'; μὴ ἀσθενήσας τῇ πίστει, that is, 'not weakened in faith,' that is, 'not at all enfeebled' and 'very firm and solid in faith.' In Latin[1] the preposition 'in' is superfluous.

1 In Latin] Added in *1527*. In fact, *in* is omitted in the preferred reading, though *in fide* is the reading of the *1527* Vulgate; cf Wordsworth and White II 82 19n.

4:19 [ER *suum ipsius corpus* 'his own body']
[VG] *suum corpus* 'his body'; ἑαυτοῦ σῶμα, that is, 'his own body.' Though it is customary for Paul freely to use the personal pronoun for the reflexive,[1] nevertheless, here [the reflexive] has some significance.

1 Ie αὐτοῦ for ἑαυτοῦ, 'his' (personal pronoun) for 'his own' (reflexive). On αὐτοῦ for αὑτοῦ (= ἑαυτοῦ) in the Pauline writings see ἑαυτοῦ in BAG 211 and in C.L.W. Grimm and J.H. Thayer *Greek-English Lexicon of the New Testament* (Edinburgh 1901) 163. For Erasmus' translation of ἑαυτοῦ by *suum ipsius* see his translation of Theodorus Gaza's *Grammar* LB I 161B. For Theodorus Gaza, see the annotation on 11:11 ('can it be that they have so stumbled that they fell') n6.

4:19 [ER *centum fere natus esset* 'was about the age of one hundred']
[VG] *fere centum esset* 'was about a hundred';[1] ἑκατονταέτης που. The addition of the qualifying adverb που makes the number of years indefinite. For at that time Abraham was ninety-nine years old, as the Greek scholia indicate,[2] and it[3] is so recorded in Genesis.[4]

1 In *1516* only, this annotation was preceded by the annotation 'dead womb.' The position of the two annotations was reversed in *1519*.
2 Cf Pseudo-Oecumenius *Comm in Rom* 4:19 PG 118 404C.
3 and it . . . Genesis] Added in *1519*
4 Gen 17:1

4:19 [ER VG] *emortuam vulvam* 'dead womb';[1] νέκρωσιν τῆς μήτρας, that is as if to say, 'the womb in a state of death.'

Here it is [Abraham's] worn-out [body] he calls 'dead' (νενεκρωμένον),[2] so that no one should suppose he was already a corpse; rather he was impotent through old age – not completely, for afterwards he fathered children from Keturah without any special miracle,[3] but to this extent was he dead, that without divine help he could not produce children from an old woman. For we read that he married Keturah when she was still in the flower of her age.[4] Augustine [says] something of the same kind in the first book of his *Questions on Genesis*.[5] But what [the Translator] calls *vulva* is not the female sexual organ, as the uneducated masses understand, but the womb in which the fetus is conceived.[6] When this is deprived of the power of attracting and retaining the seed, the woman becomes barren.

1 Cf the preceding annotation, n1.
2 νενεκρωμένον ... *on Genesis*] Added in 1519.
   This annotation begins as a comment on 4:19c, where the reference is to Sarah, but with this sentence Erasmus returns to the discussion of 4:19a, where Abraham is the subject, as in the preceding annotations. Erasmus reads 4:19a with two negatives: 'And not weakened in faith, he [Abraham] did not consider his own body now dead' (so AV, but cf RSV).
3 Cf Gen 25:1–2.
4 Cf Gen 25:1–4; also Josephus *Jewish Antiquities* 1.15 (238–40). Keturah's youth is evidently inferred from the fact that she gave birth to several children. For the expression 'in the flower of her age' see Terence *Andria* 72.
5 Augustine *Quaestiones in Heptateuchum* 1.35 PL 34 557–8
6 For *vulva* in the sense of both *uterus* and *vulva* see J.N. Adams *The Latin Sexual Vocabulary* (Baltimore 1982) 100–6.

4:20 [ER *verum ad promissionem dei* 'but rather at the promise of God']
[VG] *in repromissione etiam dei* 'indeed, in the counter-promise of God';[1] εἰς δὲ τὴν ἐπαγγελίαν,[2] that is, '*but* in the promise of God.' And so reads Ambrose,[3] so that this part marks a contrast with the preceding words: 'He was not weakened, he did not consider' etc, '*but* he[4] was not at all distrustful, did not hesitate in the promises of God,' or rather 'at the promises of God.' For[5] the Greek is εἰς ἐπαγγελίαν [with respect to the promise].

1 The passage continues:
     ER *non haesitabat ob incredulitatem* 'he was not hesitant because of unbelief'
     VG *non haesitavit diffidentia* 'he did not hesitate through distrust'
   See the following annotation.
   For *repromissio* in classical Latin as 'counter-promise' see L&S. Pelagius (*Expos in Rom* 4:20) and Ambrosiaster (*Comm in Rom* 4:20 [1–2]) speak only of *promissio* in their comments on the verse, but Thomas Aquinas sees a special meaning in the prefix – *repromissio* is a 'promise repeated' (*Super Rom lect* cap 4 lectio 3.375).
2 LB adds here τοῦ θεοῦ 'of God,' without warrant, however, from the editions 1516–1535.

3 Ambrosiaster *Comm in Rom* 4:20, though Ambrosiaster uses *autem* (however) rather than Erasmus' *vero* to mark the contrast with the preceding words
4 'but he ... in the promises of God'] Added in *1519*
5 For ... ἐπαγγελίαν.] Added in *1519*

4:20 [ER *non haesitabat* 'he was not hesitant']

[vg] *non haesitavit* 'he did not hesitate'; οὐ διεκρίθη, that is, 'he did not make distinctions or ask questions,' as a distrustful person does. For one who does not fully trust investigates carefully and makes calculated decisions.

4:20 [ER *robustus factus est* 'he became firm']

[vg] *confortatus est* 'he was strengthened'; ἐνεδυναμώθη, that is, 'he grew strong and became powerful,' to correspond to the phrase above, μὴ ἀσθενήσας τῇ πίστει, that is, 'not become feeble in faith.'[1] The preposition[2] 'in' is not added here,[3] not even[4] in the old Latin codices, though it is contained in the compound [Greek] verb.

  1 Cf 4:19.
  2 preposition] In *1535*; in all previous editions 'conjunction'
  3 Ie before *fide*:
       ER *robustus factus est fide* 'he became firm in faith'
       vg *confortatus est fide* 'he was strengthened in faith'
  4 not even ... codices] Added in *1522*. But *in* is found in some witnesses; cf Wordsworth and White II 82 20n and the edition of Ambrosiaster by Vogels (CSEL 81/1 146:5, 147:7 and 7n).

4:21 [ER *certa persuasione concepta* 'having laid hold of a firm conviction']

[vg] *plenissime sciens* 'knowing full well'; πληροφορηθείς, that is, 'having been assured' and 'having acquired a firm conviction' as if to say 'fully satisfied,' as I have explained more fully in the preface to the Gospel of Luke.[1]

  1 Cf the annotation on Luke 1:1 (*quae in nobis completa sunt rerum*), where Erasmus reviews the biblical use of this Greek word. Cf also the annotation on Rom 14:5 ('in his understanding').

4:21 [ER *quod is qui promiserat* 'that he who had promised']

[vg] *quaecunque promisit deus* 'whatever God has promised'; ὅτι ὃ ἐπήγγελται, δυνατός ἐστι καὶ ποιῆσαι 'that what has been promised, he is able also to do.' And here [in the Vulgate] the conjunction *quia* ['that' or 'because'] translates ὅτι, which I take εἰδικῶς [specifically], not αἰτιολογικῶς [causally],[1] that is, not to point out the reason, but to specify the conviction he held.

1 Like *quia* in post-classical Latin, ὅτι in Greek can mean either 'that' or 'because.' For εἰδικῶς see the annotations on 8:36 ('as sheep of the slaughter') n8 and 10:5 ('for Moses wrote') n12.

For this sentence, our translation follows the text of LB, which places the comma after ὅτι. The 1535 edition omits the comma altogether, but all previous editions read 'ὅτι *quod,* εἰδικῶς *accepto,'* which is apparently to be rendered '[*quia* translates] ὅτι "that," [the word] being understood specifically.'

4:23 [ER *imputatum fuisse illi* 'it had been imputed to him']

[VG *quia reputatum est ei*[1] 'that it was considered to him.' Here, where[2] for the third time now[3] the text from Genesis is repeated, the Latin codices add *ad iustitiam* 'for righteousness.' The Greek reads only ὅτι ἐλογίσθη αὐτῷ, 'it was imputed to him.'[4] And that was enough, for [Paul] writes in abbreviated form what was previously said as though it was now known. And the[5] copy from St Paul's Library, which is the oldest of all those I have seen,[6] agrees with the Greek witnesses.

1 The Vulgate printed in 1527 reads *illi* in both 4:22 and 4:23; so also Wordsworth and White, who, however, cite *ei* as a minor variant in both verses (II 83 22–3nn); cf n3 below.
2 where ... repeated] Added in 1519
3 Elsewhere above in 4:3 and 4:9. If one includes the quotation in 4:22, this is the fourth time the text is quoted.
4 Most of the Greek witnesses omit 'for righteousness' (Tischendorf II 384 23n); Wordsworth and White do not print the phrase in their text, but provide abundant witnesses for the reading in the Latin manuscripts (II 83 23n).
5 And the ... witnesses.] Added in 1519
6 On this manuscript see the annotation on 4:5 ('according to the purpose of the grace of God') and n5.

4:24 [ER *quibus imputabitur* 'to whom it will be imputed']

[VG *quibus reputabitur* 'to whom it will be considered'; οἷς μέλλει λογίζεσθαι, that is, 'to whom it will be imputed.' I am surprised that Jacques Lefèvre, in his discussion, translated 'it *ought* to be imputed,' as though *debet* [ought] signified the future tense, as does the Greek μέλλει [is about to], and as though 'ought to be imputed' and 'will be imputed' are the same thing, as the uneducated crowd thinks. Perhaps he thought he should speak in this way in order to instruct.[1]

1 Cf Lefèvre *Pauli epistolae* fol 78 verso (though in his translation itself Lefèvre left the Vulgate unchanged; cf fol 3 verso). On μέλλω, see Chantraine *Dictionnaire* II 682. For μέλλω and *debeo* used to connote a future destiny see μέλλω I c in LSJ and *debeo* II A 2 in L&S.

4:24 [ER *qui excitavit Jesum* 'who raised Jesus']
[VG] *qui suscitavit Jesum Christum* 'who raised up Jesus Christ.' Χριστός
[Christ] is not added in the Greek.

CHAPTER 5

5:1 [ER *pacem habemus erga deum* 'we have peace towards God']
[VG] *pacem habeamus ad deum* 'let us[1] have peace in regard to God.' In
most[2] of the Greek codices the reading is ἔχομεν [we have], in others the
reading varies;[3] for example, in Theophylact the [biblical] text [cited] has
ἔχομεν 'we have,' but the exposition ἔχωμεν 'let us have.'[4] In Chrysostom
the text [cited] has ἔχωμεν 'let us have,' and likewise the commentary; but
that this is a mistake made through the carelessness of copyists is implied
by what follows, τοῦτ᾽ ἔστιν, οὐκ ἔτι ἁμαρτάνομεν, that is, 'we sin no more,'
where [the copyist] has not changed the omicron [to omega].[5] I do not
know whether the first person of τὰ αὐτοπαθητικά[6] has the same form as
the indicative, as the second [person] has: ἔχομεν, ἔχετε, [we have, you
have].

Granted that it does, the sense here does not allow the imperative
mood. For the Apostle is speaking here about those who, justified through
faith, now have peace with God; if he had wished to deter them from
sinning, so that they would not lose the peace they had received, he would
have said more fittingly τηρῶμεν [let us keep] rather than ἔχωμεν. For here
he is not warning those who are justified, but he is expressing joy in their
felicity, because as a result not of their own merits but of the freely offered
kindness of God they have been freed from their sins and reconciled to
him with whom formerly they were at enmity. This sense is reflected in the
words that follow about the assurance of access to God, about the hope of
the glory of the sons of God – a hope that perseveres even in the afflictions
of this world – and about the love of God who reconciled the world to
himself by the death of the Only-Begotten.

It is clear that Ambrose read 'we have,' not 'let us have,' as is shown
by these words: 'Faith, not law, makes [us] have peace with God. For this
reconciles us to God – the sins taken away that had made us enemies
to God; and because the Lord Jesus is the minister of this grace, through
him we have made peace with God' etc.[7] In Origen we read 'we have' in
the [biblical] text, and he repeats it in his commentary: 'If we have cast
away the arms of the devil and taken up the standard of Christ and the
banner of his cross, assuredly we have peace with God.'[8] And his exposition
reflects this reading. He says, 'Through these things that he has perceived
– what it is to be justified by faith and not by works – [Paul] very clearly
invites to the peace of God that passes all understanding, and in which also
consists the fullness of perfection.'[9] So far Origen. In the same way one who
extols the tranquillity of the monastic life proclaims the praises of virginity

[and] invites to this manner of life those who have not yet embraced it. There follows at that point in Origen: 'When we were enemies of God we were reconciled to God'[10] etc. But Origen shows the consequence, that one who has been freely reconciled to God thinks no more those things that are hostile to God.[11] It is not strange if thereupon Origen, using [Paul's] words to express his own thought, changes the indicative mood into the imperative, 'let us have peace': 'let there not be in us yes and no.'[12]

There is no need, then, of a verb in the imperative for this exhortation, but the situation itself exhorts us, once freed from our sins and reconciled to God, not to fall back again into those things that sever the friendship between God and men. What Chrysostom writes agrees with this account, and Theophylact, too, who borrowed his material from him.[13] And this kind of admonishing suits better the modesty and civility of Paul. It is a familiar figure of speech: we say something is being done that (we wish to have understood) ought to be done. For example, 'one who is born of God does not sin,'[14] and 'a mother cannot hate her son,' and 'a ruler measures everything by the good of the state.'[15] I have argued my case without, however, absolutely condemning the other reading. For this statement can apply to those baptized who are still weak in spirit, and from time to time fall back into sin, so that the Apostle, to soften his admonition, included his own person.[16]

1 let us ... God.] This annotation appeared first in 1519, but in 1516 a brief comment on the proper form of the verb (*habemus, habeamus*) was included in the next annotation. See the annotation on 5:2 ('[we have] an access') n1.

2 In most ... ἔχετε.] The entire annotation was printed in its present form first in 1535. In 1519 and 1522 the annotation consisted of the following: '[The reading] is ἔχομεν in most of the Greek codices, that is, "we have"; in others, however, ἔχωμεν "let us have." Origen seems to have followed the second reading, understanding by these words that we are called to peace with one another. I do not know whether in the Greek the first person of τὰ αὐτοπροστακτικά has the same form as the indicative, as has the second [person], ἔχομεν.' To this 1527 added a further sentence: 'In Theophylact the text had ἔχομεν, the exposition, ἔχωμεν; in Chrysostom ἔχωμεν is found in both [text and exposition].'
For the reference to Origen see *Comm in Rom* 4.8 PG 14 988–9, especially 989B–C, where Origen explains that to have peace is to have no dissension within or without. For the references to Theophylact and Chrysostom see nn4 and 5 below.

3 Contrary to Erasmus' assertion, the vast majority of the Greek codices have the reading ἔχωμεν 'let us have.' Nevertheless, most modern interpreters prefer here the minority reading ἔχομεν 'we have' on grounds similar to Erasmus', that it better renders the Pauline sense. See Michel 130 n2; Metzger 511; and Cranfield I 257 n1.

4 Theophylact *Expos in Rom* 5:1 PG 124 400B–C. In the Migne text, however,

ἔχωμεν 'let us have' is read in both the introductory citation from the Bible and in the commentary.

5 Chrysostom *Hom in Rom* 9.1 PG 60 467–8. Chrysostom asks what Paul can mean by the words 'let us have peace,' and suggests that because Paul wished no one, after his discussion in chapter 4 on faith and works, to find an occasion for laziness, he adds 'Let us have peace, that is, let us sin no more.' The Migne text of Chrysostom does not read with Erasmus 'we sin no more' (οὐκ ἔτι ἁμαρτ[άν]ομεν, with an omicron), but 'let us sin no more' (μηκέτι ἁμαρτάνωμεν, with an omega), and the contextual discussion indicates that Chrysostom understood the imperative 'let us have.' (1535 printed ἁμάρτομεν, evidently for ἁμαρτάνομεν.)

6 τὰ αὐτοπαθητικά] First in 1535; in previous editions, τὰ αὐτοπροστακτικά (see n2 above). αὐτοπροστακτικός does not appear in LSJ, but προστακτικός is cited as a grammatical term referring to the imperative mood; αὐτοπαθής is cited as a grammatical term referring to the reflexive; here τὰ αὐτοπαθητικά evidently means 'commands to oneself.'
In the conclusion of the sentence, 1535 has ἔχομεν, ἔχετε 'we have,' 'you have'; LB ἔχωμεν, ἔχετε 'let us have,' 'you have.'
In his response to Titelmans Erasmus affirmed that 'For a Greek who understands αὐτοπαθητικά verbs, it makes no difference to the sense [whether you read ἔχομεν or ἔχωμεν]' (*Responsio ad collationes* LB IX 982E).

7 Ambrosiaster *Comm in Rom* 5:1. In the response to Titelmans Erasmus quoted this passage as the witness 'of one very weighty authority' (*Responsio ad collationes* LB IX 982F). In fact, Ambrosiaster's is the only patristic interpretation that presupposes the indicative as the reading. See Schelkle 150–1.

8 Origen *Comm in Rom* 4.8 PG 14 988C. In the passages quoted throughout this annotation, Erasmus cites accurately the Merlin text (fol CLXV recto-verso) and suggests that Origen read this verb as an indicative (Erasmus explains away the one citation in the imperative; cf n12 below). The text printed in Migne, however, suggests that Origen did indeed understand the verb as an imperative (cf Schelkle 150–1).

9 Origen *Comm in Rom* 4.8 PG 14 988B; the reading of the Merlin edition (fol CLXV recto). In Migne, the passage reads: 'Through this the one who has perceived what it is . . . perfection.'

10 Origen *Comm in Rom* 4.8 PG 14 988C

11 Origen *Comm in Rom* 4.8 PG 14 988D–989B

12 Origen *Comm in Rom* 4.8 PG 14 989C

13 See above nn4 and 5. But on Theophylact as an epitomator of Chrysostom see the annotation on 1:4 ('from the resurrection of the dead of Jesus Christ') n35.

14 Cf 1 John 3:9.

15 With the first of these common sentiments, compare Erasmus in *Ecclesiastes* III LB V 977D: 'Parents love their children, but the mother loves more fondly'; with the second, compare Pompey's claim that he had always considered the good of the state more compelling than personal relationships (Caesar *De bello civili* 1.8.3).

16 The argument of this 1535 addition is substantially the same as that of the earlier *Responsio ad collationes* LB IX 982E–983C, where, however, the

concession made here in the final sentences does not appear.

5:2 [ER *perduceremur* 'we were led']

[VG] [*habemus*] *accessum* '[we have] an access'; προσαγωγὴν ἐσχήκαμεν, that is, 'we had'[1] or[2] 'we obtained an entry.' And yet I am aware that in Greek the past tense of some verbs is used as a present, particularly those expressing a state of mind or body such as γέγηθα, δέδια [I rejoice, I fear] and in the word which follows just below, ἐστήκαμεν 'we have stood' for 'we stand'[3] – where[4] this should be noted, that in [the phrase] ἐν ᾗ ἐστήκαμεν 'in which we stand,'[5] it is uncertain whether the relative pronoun ['which'] refers to 'grace' or 'faith.'[6] Ambrose seems to refer it to faith when he says: 'For this reason [Paul said that we are] "standing," because formerly we lay prostrate, but on believing, we were raised up' etc.[7]

> 1 'we had'] At this point in 1516 only, Erasmus added: 'and a little before, εἰρήνην ἔχομεν, that is, "we have peace," not ἔχωμεν, that is, "let us have," although on this latter [ie whether ἔχομεν or ἔχωμεν] the Greek copies vary.' See the preceding annotation, nn1 and 2.
>
> 2 or ... obtained] Added in 1519
>
> 3 In his own translation here Erasmus used the present tense for 'we stand,' but changed the Vulgate 'we have an access' into past time (cf n5 below) to reflect more precisely the Greek; see *Responsio ad collationes* LB IX 983C–D.
>
> 4 where ... etc] Added in 1519
>
> 5 Cf the context in the Latin translation:
> ER *per quem et contigit nobis ut fide perduceremur in gratiam hanc in qua stamus* 'through whom also it happened that we were led by faith into this grace in which we stand'
> VG *per quem habemus accessum per fidem in gratiam istam in qua stamus* 'through whom we have an access through faith into that grace in which we stand'
>
> 6 'faith'] In 1535 only; in previous editions, 'hope,' but probably by mistake
>
> 7 Ambrosiaster *Comm in Rom* 5:2

5:2 [ER *sub spe gloriae dei* 'with[1] the hope of the glory of God']

[VG] *in spe filiorum dei* 'in the hope of the sons of God.' The Greek reads 'in the hope of the glory of God,' ἐπ᾽ ἐλπίδι τῆς δόξης τοῦ θεοῦ. It does[2] not add 'of the sons.' It is clear from his exposition that Origen read 'in the hope of the glory of God.'[3] Nor from the interpretation of Ambrose can any hint be gathered from which one might assume that he added 'of the sons.' For he writes: 'But, believing we are raised up, boasting in the hope of the splendour that God has promised us.'[4] He does not differ from Origen, who interprets: 'Boasting in the hope of seeing the glory of God.'[5] Theophylact[6] interprets: 'In the hope of the good things that will come to us not from our own merit, but that God might be glorified.'[7] Chrysostom reads likewise.[8]

1 with] First in *1519*; in *1516, in spe* 'in the hope.' For the phrase *sub spe* see the annotation on 4:18 ('in dependence upon hope').
2 It does ... seeing the glory of God.'] Added in *1519*
3 Origen *Comm in Rom* 4.8 PG 14 891A
4 Ambrosiaster *Comm in Rom* 5:2
5 See n3 above.
6 Theophylact ... likewise.] Added in *1527*
7 Theophylact *Expos in Rom* 5:2 PG 124 400D
8 Chrysostom *Hom in Rom* 9.2 PG 60 468

5:3 [ER *nec id solum* 'and not only this']

[VG] *non solum autem* 'and not only'; οὐ μόνον δέ. The Latin language does not allow this form of speech;[1] it would be smoother if [the Translator] had added a pronoun, 'And not only this' or[2] 'and not only these things' – for Origen believes that this phrase must be referred not only to what has just been said, 'we boast in the hope of the glory of God,' but also to the other things [Paul] had taught that we gained through Jesus Christ, namely, that we have been justified by faith through him; through him an entry into that grace was given; through him it has come about that we can boast in and hope for the glory of God.[3] To me, [the phrase] seems to fit neatly if referred to the last of these.

1 The comment gave occasion to Frans Titelmans to affirm that 'Scripture pays no heed to elegance of expression'; see *Responsio ad collationes* LB IX 983C–D. On the idiom see the annotation on 8:23 ('and not only that') n3.
2 or ... last of these] Added in *1519*
3 Origen *Comm in Rom* 4.9 PG 14 993A

5:5 [ER *non pudefacit* 'does not make ashamed']

[VG] *non confundit* 'does not confound'; οὐ καταισχύνει, that is, *non pudefacit* [does not make ashamed] or *pudore afficit* [bring shame upon]. What[1] Latin-speaker would take *confundit* to mean *pudefacit*? *Suffundi*[2] [to be embarrassed] is a term applied to those who blush, *confundi* [to be confused, confounded] to those who are thrown into mental confusion. A deep shame certainly can sometimes produce this [confusion] in one, but *confundere* and *pudefacere* do not, on this account, mean the same, just as it is one thing 'to drink wine' another 'to become drunk.' In the passage in Acts 'and he confounded the Jews' [9:22], the verb is not κατῇσχυνεν [*katēischynen*] but κατέχυνεν [*katechynen*],[3] that is, 'threw into confusion' and 'put at a loss.' However, it is probable that at that time the common people spoke thus, and the New Testament was long ago handed down in the language of the common people.

Augustine,[4] in the fourth book of *De doctrina christiana*, the seventh chapter, points out the figures in this passage, one of which is called κλῖμαξ in Greek, *gradatio* [gradation] in Latin,[5] [a figure] that greatly enhances the pleasure [we receive] from the discourse. A 'gradation' occurs whenever the last word of a preceding clause is taken up by the next clause, so as to arrive at the final clause through a sort of [sequence of] steps. Here for example, 'tribulation' is joined with 'endurance,' 'endurance' with 'testing,' 'testing' with 'hope.' He points out also the structural grace [of the passage], in that the period completes a sentence measured by rhythmical clauses and phrases. The first clause is 'since tribulation brings endurance'; the second, 'and endurance testing'; the third, 'and testing hope.' Then a 'period' is added, itself also consisting of three clauses, of which the first is 'but hope does not confound'; the second, 'because love[6] has been shed abroad in our hearts'; the third, 'through the Holy Spirit who has been given to us.' Something of this sort is what Augustine says.[7] And yet in my opinion nothing prevents us from rounding out the first [part of the] arrangement with four clauses, where the fourth becomes 'but hope does not confound'; for this is the end of the gradation. Then a period comes in, consisting of either one or two members, 'because the love of God has been shed abroad in our hearts, through the Holy Spirit who has been given to us.' Indeed even the preceding clauses can be divided into two sections; the first is 'since tribulation,' then, after the slightest pause, 'brings endurance,' and likewise with the rest. St Augustine confesses that these [effects] were in no way deliberately sought by the Apostle, but that eloquence was of its own accord a companion to wisdom, and wisdom does not disdain such a companion.[8]

1 What ... *pudefacit?*] Added in 1527

2 *Suffundi* ... of the common people.] Added in 1535. The addition renders the substance of the defence made to Titelmans, who at this point had treated with disdain Erasmus' desire to translate the Scriptures into 'elegant' Latin. See *Responsio ad collationes* LB IX 984E–985C.

3 The verb in Acts 9:22 is not κατέχυνεν, but συνέχυνεν, from συγχέω (Hellenistic form συγχύν(ν)ω), for which the Latin *confundere* 'throw into confusion' is indeed a close equivalent (see συγχέω in BAG). LSJ cite καταχύννω as a late form of καταχέω, with the meaning 'pour down,' 'pour over.' In his own editions, Erasmus printed συνέχυνεν in Acts 9:22.
For *confundere* and *pudefacere* see further the annotations on Acts 9:22 (*et confundebat*) and Rom 10:11 ('every one who believes upon him will not be confounded') and n3.

4 Augustine .. companion.] This remaining portion of the annotation was added in 1527, with the exception noted in n6 below.

5 For κλῖμαξ or *gradatio* in classical rhetoric see *Rhetorica ad Herennium* 4.25.34–5 and Quintilian 9.3.54–7; also Lausberg I 623–4. In *Ecclesiastes* III LB V 1002F–1003C Erasmus demonstrates the pleasure and the force this figure can lend to expression.

6 LB adds 'of God,' but without warrant from the editions of 1527 and 1535.

7 Augustine *De doctrina christiana* 4.7.11 PL 34 93–4

8 Cf Augustine *De doctrina christiana* 4.7.11 PL 34 94

5:5 [ER *effusa sit* 'has been poured out']

[VG] *diffusa est* 'has been shed abroad'; ἐκκέχυται, that is, 'has been poured out' or 'was poured out,' so that you understand it has been 'poured out' – bountifully.

5:6 [ER *enim* 'for']

[VG] *ut quid enim* 'for in order that what.' It is different in the Greek: ἔτι γὰρ Χριστὸς ὄντων ἡμῶν ἀσθενῶν, that is, 'for Christ, when we were still weak.' It appears that the codex the Translator followed had εἰς τί, that is, 'to what end?'[1] Either sense is tolerable. 'For to what end?' – the implied answer is: 'That hope should not confound.'[2] And Ambrose[3] also reads *ut quid*. Theophylact[4] reads ἔτι [still] and so interprets.

1 Latin *ad quid*. Erasmus' conjecture supposes that in place of the (preferred) reading ἔτι 'still' the Translator read εἰς τί 'to what end?' 'why?' which Erasmus would render by *ad quid* rather than the *ut quid* of the Vulgate. Valla, too, had criticized the Latin reading, but wished to render *etiam enim* 'for even'; see *Annot in Rom* 5 (I 857). *Ut quid* is frequently found in the Vulgate for the Greek ἵνα τί – literally 'in order that what,' though commonly written ἱνατί and meaning 'wherefore,' 'why'; see ἱνατί in BAG. For the reading εἰς τί see Tischendorf II 385–6 6n.

2 Ie if one adopts the Vulgate reading, then *ut quid enim*? (or Erasmus' emendation, *ad quid enim*?) may make verse 6 a question: Why did Christ die? The reader may then infer the answer from verse 5: 'That hope should not confound.'

3 And Ambrose ... *quid*.] Added in 1519. See Ambrosiaster *Comm in Rom* 5:6.

4 Theophylact ... interprets.] Added in 1527. See Theophylact *Expos in Rom* 5:6 PG 124 401C.

5:6 [ER *iuxta temporis rationem* 'in accordance with the order of the time']

[VG] *secundum tempus* 'according to the time'; κατὰ καιρόν. If the words [according to the time] refer to 'the weak,' they soften what has been said, as though their weakness is to be imputed to the time in which the grace of the gospel had not yet appeared. But if they refer to 'he died,' you[1] will understand that [Christ] met his death at the fitting time, a time appointed by the Father.[2] The Greek scholia interpret thus,[3] and Ambrose[4] follows the same opinion. He writes: 'If, for the sake of the unbelievers and enemies of God, Christ surrendered to death for a time – for he died "for a time," since he rose on the third day.' Shortly thereafter: 'And so in the eyes of men – that is, "according to time" – he seemed to die.'[5] Origen agrees with this,[6] and Theophylact virtually accords with it when he interprets 'according to the time' to mean 'at the designated and opportune time.'[7]

And yet[8] Ambrose refers more to the brevity of the time than to the opportunity. Chrysostom does not mention the phrase κατὰ καιρόν in his exposition.[9] Origen appears to take up both readings.[10] For in the text he divides the passage as follows: 'When we were still weak according to the time, he died even for the ungodly.'[11] On the other hand, when he says in his exposition, 'Who according to that time in which he suffered, did not shrink from enduring death on behalf of the ungodly and unjust,' he appears to hold the same opinion that Ambrose expressed. A little later when he adds, 'Particularly if he understood that when still according to the time we were ungodly and weak, he himself first died for us,' he comes back to the first way of construing the passage.[12] Either reading has a pious sense. The man whose scholia on the Epistles of Paul go under the name of Jerome[13] accepts three senses: weak according to the time when we were still faint under the burden of sins and wickedness, and weak according to the time in which righteousness had then virtually disappeared; or (he adds a second [interpretation]) that Christ suffered in the last time; or (he adds a third, which belongs to Ambrose[14]) that [Christ] died for a three-day period, as was prophesied.[15] Thomas also touches upon the varied construction.[16]

1 you ... the Father] First in 1519, for which the Latin reads: *intelleges illum idoneo tempore et a patre praescripto mortem oppetisse*. In 1516, in place of this clause there appeared only the words *defectus oppetisse*. We find these words difficult to construe, and it is our conjecture that the word *defectus* 'something missing' came into the text in the process of production to mark the apparent omission of a line, ie the words from *intelleges* to *mortem*.

2 For his Greek text (all editions) and for his Latin translation from 1519 to 1527 Erasmus punctuated to include the phrase with the words that precede: 'when we were weak in accordance with the order of the time.' But in his translation of 1516 and 1535 he set the phrase off with a comma before and after so that it could be read equally well with what precedes (as above), or what follows: 'in accordance with the order of the time he died.' He maintained, against Frans Titelmans, that he translated to allow the phrase to be taken either way. See *Responsio ad collationes* LB IX 984C–D.

3 Cf Pseudo-Oecumenius *Comm in Rom* 5:6–7 PG 118 413B.
At this point in 1516 only, there followed, as though a new annotation, the words: 'His love; τὴν ἑαυτοῦ ἀγάπην, that is, "his own love" – obviously

[the love] with which he loved us.' The words are omitted from LB. For the position of this annotation in 1516 see the succeeding annotation, n1.

4 and Ambrose ... opportune time] Added in 1519

5 Ambrosiaster *Comm in Rom* 5:6–7 (1)

6 Origen *Comm in Rom* 4.10–11 PG 14 998A–999C

7 Theophylact *Expos in Rom* 5:6 PG 124 401D

8 And yet ... construction.] This remaining portion of the annotation was added in 1535.

9 See Chrysostom *Hom in Rom* 9.3 PG 60 470–1.

10 Here Erasmus corrects his earlier statement of 1519. See n6 above.

11 The reading of Merlin's text (fol CLXVII recto), which Erasmus both used for his *Annotations* and followed for his own edition of Origen (Basel 1536); cf Godin *Erasme* 598–600. Migne places the comma after 'weak.'

12 For these two quotations see Origen *Comm in Rom* 4.10 PG 14 998A and 998C.

13 On the identification of Pseudo-Jerome as Pelagius, see the annotation on 5:12 ('in whom [or, in which] all have sinned') n22.

14 See the reference to Ambrosiaster n5 above.

15 Pelagius *Expos in Rom* 5:6 (Souter II 43:12–16). Erasmus appears to offer four, not three interpretations. In fact he cites accurately, except that in Pelagius only the last three alternatives ('... time in which righteousness ... prophesied') belong to the interpretation of 'according to the time.' The first clause ('when we were still faint ... wickedness') is an exposition of the words 'when we were still weak.'

16 Thomas Aquinas *Super Rom lect* cap 5 lectio 2.395. Thomas Aquinas clearly takes the phrase with 'he died' and interprets it to mean 'for a fixed time,' since Christ would rise on the third day.

5:7 [ER *pro iusto morietur* 'for the righteous, will one die']
[VG] *pro iusto moritur* 'for the righteous, one dies';[1] ἀποθανεῖται, that is, 'will die.'

Further, 'righteous' and 'good' in this passage do not signify some person, but a thing, that is, righteousness and goodness themselves.[2] They are not of the masculine gender; they are neuters, as St Jerome holds in his letter to Algasia, the seventh question.[3] Origen[4] speaks [of these] in both ways: for a righteous man and a righteous cause.[5] Ambrose takes the former[6] meaning, referring[7] the word 'righteous' to a person.[8]

1 In 1516 this annotation, and the next, immediately preceded the annotation on 5:6 ('according to the time'). They found their present position in 1519.

2 So Valla *Annot in Rom* 5 (I 857)

3 Jerome *Epistulae* 121.7 CSEL 56 29:10–12

4 Origen ... meaning] Added in 1519, but see n6 below.

5 Origen *Comm in Rom* 4.10 PG 14 998A–C

6 the former] In 1535 only; before 1535, 'a different'

7 referring ... person] Added in 1527

8 Ambrosiaster *Comm in Rom* 5:6–7 (2)

5:7 [ER *etiam mori sustinet* 'even endures to die']

[VG] *audeat mori* 'would dare to die';[1] 'also dares,' or 'might even dare to die,' καὶ τολμᾷ ἀποθανεῖν.[2] And yet here [the Translator] would more correctly have rendered 'endures' [to die], a word Suetonius used in the same sense.[3]

    1 For the sequence of this annotation in 1516 see the preceding annotation, n1.
    2 Erasmus' reading both restores the emphasis in the Greek καί (= *etiam* 'even') and places the verb (*sustinet*) in the indicative rather than in the subjunctive as the Vulgate did (*audeat*). In the annotation, however, he recognizes the ambiguity of the Greek verb τολμᾷ, which may be either indicative or subjunctive, 'dares' or 'might dare' (rendered in the annotation by the Latin perfect subjunctive rather than the Vulgate's present subjunctive).
    3 See for example Suetonius *Augustus* 66.4, *Vespasian* 13.

5:8 [ER *quod* 'that']

[VG] *quoniam si* 'since if.' It is different in the Greek: ὅτι ἔτι ἁμαρτωλῶν ὄντων ἡμῶν, that is, '[in] that when we were still sinners,'[1] so that[2] this clause is dependent on the preceding words: 'Perhaps there will be someone who might die for the good. But God's love towards us is superior to human love, no matter how great, and is distinguished in this, that he wanted his only Son to die for the ungodly and unworthy.' After a colon, [the passage] continues, 'much more, therefore, now justified' etc.[3] If you do not believe me, this construction [of the passage] appears in the manuscript at St Paul's that I have often mentioned:[4] 'But God commends his love in us,' then, after a comma, [the passage] continues, 'since when we were still sinners, Christ died for us.' Then a period; what follows begins with a capital letter: 'Much more, then' etc. But someone later, wanting, I suppose, to emend the text, wrote 'if' in the interlinear space: 'Since if when we were still sinners' etc. My copy,[5] in old type,[6] construed in this way, and 'if' is not added.[7]

    1 sinners] In 1516 only, the annotation continued (and concluded) with the following words: 'etc, much more then. And yet the sense is the same either way.' The words 'much more then. And yet' are incorporated below in the 1519 text.
    2 so that ... sinners' etc] Except for the last sentence and for the words indicated in n1 above, the remaining portion of the annotation was added in 1519.
    3 Cf the Vulgate, whose 'since if' clause could be read less closely with what precedes and more closely with what follows: 'Perhaps someone might die for the good. But Christ commended his love to us. Since if, when we were sinners, Christ died for us, much more now that we are justified will we be saved.'
    4 Cf the annotation on 4:5 ('according to the purpose of the grace of God') n5.
    5 My copy ... added.] Added in 1527

6 In a 1527 addition to the annotation on Rom 13:1 ('those, however, which are from God') Erasmus speaks in the same terms of what is apparently this codex. Cf also his reference in the *Apologia adversus debacchationes Petri Sutoris* LB IX 766E to an 'edition, in my possession, of both Testaments, printed, I would guess, some sixty years ago.'

7 A few manuscripts include *si*, but the majority omit the word; cf Wordsworth and White II 84 8n.

5:11 [ER *verum etiam gloriantes* 'but also boasting']

[VG] *sed et gloriamur* 'but we boast also'; ἀλλὰ καὶ καυχώμενοι, that is, 'but also boasting,' though it is not of much importance to the meaning. And in some Greek copies I have found written καυχώμεθα [we boast], as in the one that was shown to me at the Dominican monastery in Basel.[1]

1 When Erasmus was preparing his first edition of the New Testament, he had access to the library of the Dominican monastery in Basel, which had received from a bequest of John of Ragusa (a prominent figure at the Council of Basel [1431–9] who died in 1443) some manuscripts of the Greek New Testament. Erasmus used chiefly five of these, including a manuscript of the Pauline Epistles (MS 7; University of Basel MS A.N.III.11), which contained anonymous scholia; cf the annotation on 1:4 ('who was predestined') n1. For descriptions of the manuscripts in the Dominican library that Erasmus used, see Epp 384 introduction, 300:35n; Allen Ep 373 introduction; and Bentley *Humanists* 126–32.

5:12 [ER *propterea quemadmodum per unum hominem* 'therefore as through one man'[1]]

[VG] *propterea sicut per unum hominem* 'therefore just as through one man.' In Greek this is διὰ τοῦτο ὥσπερ δι' ἑνὸς ἀνθρώπου, but what follows does not respond to the ὥσπερ [just as (ie does not complete the comparison)], unless ὡς is read in the sense of 'because' or ὥσπερ as ὡς; or unless you take ὥσπερ to mean 'as though'; or unless anyone prefers [to think] that this sentence, too, is ἀναπόδοτος[2] [lacking an apodosis],[3] of which kind there appear to be many in Paul.[4]

Origen records two opinions. According to the first, he maintains that Paul did not leave this sentence incomplete due to his ignorance of Greek speech, but deliberately suppressed what otherwise should have followed because he judged it better that both clauses[5] be implied than openly expressed. For if he had added that part[6] which answers to the 'as' clause – 'So through one man righteousness came into the world, and through righteousness life was passed down to all' – there was the danger that some, on hearing this, would become quite unconcerned and negligent or would begin to expect even now what will come later; or[7] they might think that there falls here to those who are lazy what we gain only by effort and zeal.

Accordingly, in other examples, [Paul] changes tense in the second part [of the comparison] and renders the verb in the future: 'Just as in Adam all die, so in Christ all will be made alive.'[8] According to the second view, [Origen] would have the second part completed in the words that follow, though only after a considerable interval – there, in fact, [where he says]: 'But not as the sin, so likewise the gift. For if many died through the trespass of one, much more has the grace of God and the gift through[9] grace of one man, Jesus Christ, abounded for many' [5:15].[10]

But I think there is still another possible way to remedy this difficulty in the passage if, as often in Greek, we understand οὕτως [so] implied in the conjunction καί [and].[11] There is an example of this in the Gospel, ὡς ἐν οὐρανῷ καὶ ἐπὶ τῆς γῆς, that is, 'as in heaven, so also on earth';[12] οὕτως is understood. This, then, will be the sense: 'Therefore just as through one man sin entered into the world, so also through one man death entered' – so that you understand that both of these have come to us from Adam. Adam sinned, and because of his sin fell into death. So likewise we, since (following him) we sin, are hastening to death; and the result is that both sin and death have spread to all.[13]

1 through one man] First in 1527; in the first three editions, 'on account of one man.' But Erasmus later insisted that the reading of the first three editions was due to collaborators who had prepared the text for the printer. His annotation clearly implied that he had always read 'through one man.' See *Responsio ad collationes* LB IX 985E–986C; and on the preparation of the text for the printer Ep 384 introduction.

2 ἀναπόδοτος] First in 1519; in 1516, ἀνακόλουθος [anacoluthos]

3 Most contemporary scholars adopt the last of Erasmus' alternatives, that the comparison begun in verse 12 is interrupted at verse 13. The protasis of verse 12 is not completed with its apodosis until verse 18. See Cranfield I 269–70. The annotation does not explain the effect of the first two alternatives on the reading.

4 For other points where Erasmus notes difficulties in the sequence of the Pauline sentence, see the annotations on 2:17 ('but if') and 9:22 ('but if God wishing'). See also the annotation on 15:24 ('that in passing by') and n3.

5 Ie the two clauses defined in the next sentence as 'that part which answers to the "as" clause'; these two clauses appear to be equivalent to the 'so' clause of verses 18 and 19.

6 that part ... 'as' clause] Added in 1519

7 or ... zeal] Added in 1519

8 1 Cor 15:22. Cf Origen *Comm in Rom* 5.1 PG 14 1005A–1006A; cf 1007A–B. Erasmus summarizes Origen's argument. Origen quotes 1 Cor 15:22 to show that Paul constructs the apodosis of a comparison with care to give no one grounds to cease efforts to win the final goal. Thus though Paul uses the present tense in the first part of the comparison, he carefully changes tense in the second. He does not say 'has been made alive' or 'is made alive,' but

'will be made alive.' So here in Rom 5:12, Origen suggests, the apodosis is deliberately suppressed to give no one grounds for thinking he 'has life' without further effort.

9 through] In *1519*; in *1516*, 'by' grace; Vulgate 'in' grace
10 Origen *Comm in Rom* 5.1 PG 14 1006B. On this view the apodosis is found in verse 15; cf n3 above.
11 Ie the conjunction connecting the two clauses 'sin entered the world' and 'through sin death [entered the world].' On this reading one would understand the καί not as 'and' but as 'so also,' as in Matt 6:10.
12 Matt 6:10
13 Though Erasmus' solution does not commend itself to modern scholars, a similar solution has been proposed by some, namely, to begin the apodosis with the καὶ οὕτως of the next clause, reading it not as 'and so,' but as 'so also': 'As through one man sin entered the world, and through sin [came] death, so also to many came death.' For the debate see Cranfield I 272–3.

5:12 [ER *quatenus omnes peccaverunt* 'inasmuch as[1] all have sinned']
[VG] *in quo omnes peccaverunt* 'in whom [or, in which] all have sinned'; ἐφ' ᾧ πάντες ἥμαρτον. Some refer *in quo* [in whom] to Adam,[2] in whom a latent posterity was concealed, as though in a lump,[3] and in him all have sinned. Augustine thinks it can refer to sin, so we understand that in some way we all sinned in that one sin of Adam.[4] This reading does not hold up, because the Greek word for sin, ἁμαρτία, is feminine. In any case it has very little relation to the point. Others interpret *in quo* to mean 'by this, that' or 'inasmuch as.' Those who insist upon the first sense [ie 'in whom'] furnish, from this passage above all, support for [the doctrine of] original sin, of which St Augustine is the staunchest defender, especially after the battle with Pelagius and Julian was raging.[5] St Ambrose did not disagree with his opinion. As usual, he followed Origen here too, philosophizing that the Apostle did not say ἐφ' ᾗ, that is, 'in whom' [feminine], but ἐφ' ᾧ 'in whom' [masculine], that is, in the man not the woman, because the man is the principal author of posterity, even though the woman was the first to fall.[6]

Those who like the second sense refer ἐφ' ᾧ neither to Eve nor to Adam, but to the thing itself without qualification, that is, 'in this, that all have sinned.' And yet this reading does not completely exclude [all reference to] original sin, for it is possible to assume that all have sinned in Adam, in whom they have also died before they were born. But here, a figure of speech cannot be avoided: the fact is that they do not sin who do nothing, nor do those die who do not yet exist; besides, since not only the death of the body but eternal death also was the debt to be paid for the sin of Adam, this sin did not pass down to all, nor does that death pass down to infants if they die without the laver of regeneration (if, that is, we believe the theologians of our own times).[7] Hence it is clear that there is in the language a figure of speech; if we exclude the figure, a great many absurdities follow. For if we wish to follow either the definition of the theologians, or common sense, sin is something said or done,[8] and there is nothing of this sort with newborn infants. But if sin here is understood as the withdrawal of the divine grace that was in Adam before he sinned, or a certain natural propensity to commit sin, which seems ingrown in all[9] (although I think [this propensity] proceeds from example rather than from nature) – these are the *punishments* for sin more truly than they are sin [itself]. And so those who say that all posterity sinned in Adam, as in a lump,[10] seem to be saying nothing else than this, that the sin of Adam brought harm and injury to all his descendants: if Adam had not violated the precept of God, he would have begotten [children] immortal like himself, full of knowledge, reverence, love, and faith, attentive to and eager for every good; now he begets those who are subject to very many evils. Those [evils], however, the scholastics do not allow to be called sin; they allow not even the 'desires of the flesh' to be named sin, though others strongly object.[11] In any case baptism does not take away these evils from infants: for there remains the necessity to die, a body subject to sickness, and a propensity to sin[12] – although for the pious each of these is turned to good. Other [evils] they excuse through the infused habits of the graces.[13] I shall not here enter more deeply into this labyrinth;[14] I have said only enough to demonstrate that the Apostle's expression is not free from figures of speech.

Moreover, I doubt whether the Greek can bear this meaning, that all may be said to sin in Adam, as though latent in him. For [Paul] did not say ἐν ᾧ, but ἐφ' ᾧ. A pregnant woman is said ἐν γαστρὶ ἔχειν [to have in the womb], but not ἐπὶ γαστρί. Something which is contained in a space is said to be ἐν τόπῳ [in the place] rather than ἐπὶ τόπῳ (although you can say ἐπ' οἴκου καὶ ἐπὶ τῆς χώρας [at home and in its place]). For whenever ἐπί means 'above' or 'on' it is followed by the genitive case: ἐπὶ κεφαλῆς [on the head], καὶ ἐπὶ τῆς γῆς [and on the earth], ἐπὶ πάντων 'above all'; likewise when it indicates time or authority, such as ἐπὶ Καίσαρος Ὀκταβίου 'in the time of Caesar Octavius,' and in Acts 26, μέλλων ἀπολογεῖσθαι ἐπὶ σοῦ [about to make my defence before you] [26:2]. When it indicates a cause, or imminence, it is followed by the dative, as ἐπὶ θανάτῳ, that is, 'in expectation of death.' Likewise when it expresses proximity, ἐπὶ γήραος οὐδῷ [on the threshold of old age]; or again, power, ἐπὶ τῷ βασιλεῖ, that is, 'in the power of the king'; likewise, addition, as ἐπὶ τούτοις, that is, 'in addition' or 'besides'; or condition, as ἐπὶ τούτοις ἀφίημί σε, that is, 'I dismiss you on these terms,' and ἐπὶ ῥητοῖς, that is, 'on fixed conditions'; finally, when [it means] 'above,' ἐπὶ στύλῃ 'upon a pillar,' which is very close to the usage in ἐπὶ γήραος οὐδῷ [on the threshold of old age].[15] It takes the accusative case whenever it signifies motion to a place.

Since, then, the use of Greek prepositions is so varied, I should not dare to assert that ἐπί is never found with the dative case when one thing is said to be in another, as a tree is in the seed; but I, at least, have not thus far happened to come upon any such thing. For in Hebrews 7, when Paul says that Levi was in the loins of Abraham he does not say ἐπ' ὀσφύι, but ἐν ὀσφύι.[16] Further, in First Corinthians 15, 'Just as in Adam all die, likewise in Christ shall all be made alive' [15:22], the expressions are not ἐπὶ τῷ Ἀδάμ, ἐπὶ τῷ Χριστῷ, but rather ἐν τῷ Ἀδάμ, ἐν τῷ Χριστῷ. Now suppose we grant that the correct reading is ἐν ᾧ, what is more common in sacred literature than to find 'in' used for 'through'?[17] The sense then could be, 'death passed to all, through this, that all have sinned,' or 'by this, that all have sinned.'

In addition, the Translator rendered the Greek διῆλθεν by *pertransiit* [passed through]; I preferred to translate *pervasit* [broke through],[18] not only to avoid ambiguity, but at the same time to express both the swiftness and the violence of the evil spreading out to all – and especially since I noticed that the blessed Augustine made an error in this case, who thought *pertransire* [to pass through] meant the same as *praeterire* [to pass by]. From this he infers that even the Virgin Mother wavered somewhat at the death of the Lord, but it was as though a sword 'passed through' her without touching her. The passage is in the book *Questions on the Old and New Testament*, question 73, as I indicated in a note on Luke, chapter 2.[19] The διελεύσεται in Luke and the διῆλθεν in this passage are of the same nature, and could have been translated very well by 'flowed down to' or 'was channelled into,' had one not wished to express the force and power of the evil leaping down upon all. Besides, I had doubts whether *pertransit* [passed through] would be found in good Latin usage, whereas *pervadere* [to break through, pervade] is an elegant word and suited to the meaning here. Moreover since in the Greek word there is but a single preposition, *transit* would have been more fitting than *pertransit*.[20] *Transire* [go across, be contagious] is used of things that spread from one to another by contact. Hence in Ovid: 'And many things harm bodies by contagion [*transitione*].'[21]

There is, then, nothing in the words here that cannot be accommodated to sin of imitation. Two syllables alone – ἐφ' ᾧ – appeared to stand in the way, and I have shown that they scarcely convey that sense which is the only one some would have. Even if the words were ἐν ᾧ 'in whom,' there would be no great obstacle to the opinion of those who think that here Paul is talking about the sins that individuals have committed in imitation of Adam. I am not the first to advance this interpretation, for this whole passage is explicated in the same way by whoever he was whose scholia on all the Epistles of Paul bear the name of Jerome.[22] For to these words, 'Sin entered, and death through sin,' he appends this comment, 'by example or pattern.' Then after these words, 'and thus it passed through to all,' he follows with, 'while they thus sin, they also likewise die.' And so that you might understand that he is talking about a mortal sin and the death of the soul, he adds: 'For it did not pass through to Abraham, Isaac, and Jacob, about whom the Lord says "All these live." Here, however, [Paul] says that "all have died," simply because in [speaking of] the multitude of sinners, a few righteous will not be specifically excluded, as in the passage, "There is no one who does good, not so much as one," and "every one is a liar." '[23] Now Origen's reflection on the word 'world' – to the effect that sin was passed down only to the world, that is, to those of a worldly spirit – seems to me rather forced;[24] and yet [Pelagius] also touches upon this argument when he says: 'Or [as an alternative interpretation] it passed to all those who lived in a human way, rather than divine.'[25] Shortly thereafter he adds: 'For it passed down also to all who transgressed the natural law.'[26] Now to those words of the Apostle, *in quo omnes peccaverunt* [in which all have sinned], he adds a comment like this: 'That is, in this, that all have sinned, they sin through the example of Adam.'[27] So far [Pelagius]. There remains then no question that this man, whoever he was, interprets this whole passage in terms of the sin of imitation and the death of the soul. I acknowledge that this work is not by Jerome, as its inept preface falsely claims;[28] but its content bespeaks the work of a learned man, and those who contend that all labels are to be trusted and reject my assessment should certainly regard it as Jerome's.

From Origen, however, it is not so easy to gather what his view was, for he is, of himself, often slippery in argument, [and is so] especially since we have him translated freely with many things added, removed, or changed.[29] First he has some words about the *massa* in which all have sinned: 'Therefore if Levi, born in the fourth generation after Abraham, is said to have been in Abraham's loins,[30] surely all who are born and have been born in this world were in the loins of Adam when he was still in paradise; and all were expelled with him or in him when he was driven out from thence. And the death that came to him from transgression was through him consequently passed down also to those who were contained in his loins. For this reason the Apostle rightly says, "For just as in Adam all die, so also in Christ shall all be made alive" [1 Cor 15:22]. Not, therefore, from the serpent who had sinned before the woman, or from the woman who transgressed before her husband, but through Adam, from whom all mortals trace their origin, is sin said to have entered, and through sin, death.

He, then, clearly, is the only person through whom sin entered, and through sin, death'[31] etc. These words seem to have in view original sin, although on closer inspection it appears otherwise. [Origen] is only showing why the blessed Paul makes neither the devil nor Eve the author of sin – though in reality death entered into the world by the envy of the devil, through the devil it was passed on to Eve, through Eve to Adam; and though the serpent was the first author of sin, Eve soon enticed her husband into sin.[32] But it is because descendants are called by the name of the father that he says all have sinned in Adam, who passed on to his descendants the example of sinning, and [Adam once] corrupted, begot those who were corrupted. The words that immediately follow are sufficient proof that Origen is not speaking here specifically about original sin: 'When he urges us to cast off the image of the earthly and to bear the image of the heavenly, that is, as we live according to the word of God, to be restored and fashioned anew in accordance with the inner man after the image of God who created him'[33] etc. When he says 'as we live,' he implies that he is speaking about the sin of imitation. Again, in the course of the same argument a little below: 'having [your] association not in this world but in heaven.' Then soon: 'He walks with the image of the earthly and he walks according to the image of the earthly, and he has his mind on the flesh, and he minds the things of the flesh'[34] etc. None of this is appropriate to infants. Here follow certain things, either, as it seems, about the fall of Satan, or about souls which, according to Plato, sinned before they were sent into bodies.[35] This the translator has omitted.[36] In fact, although there is nothing that he does not touch on, he nevertheless makes no mention at all of the sin of infants, to whom some want this passage specifically to pertain. Then when he adds[37] that Paul is speaking here about the death of the soul, and cites the saying of the prophet, 'the soul which sins will itself die' [Ezek 18:4], it is clear that he is discussing personal sin. It is even more clear, when he poses the question 'Why did Christ suffer death, when he never sinned?' His answer: 'Christ did not owe death to anyone, for he was free from sin; but he voluntarily laid down his life for our sins.' He does not mention original sin here, but says 'he did not commit sin.' The passage that follows is still clearer, for he addresses the very clause that some urge in support of the sin of infants. He says: 'But let us see in what way death passed through to all – "in whom all," [Paul] says, "have sinned." The Apostle has declared in an unqualified statement that the death resulting from sin has passed through to all – *in eo in quo omnes peccaverunt* [in that in which all have sinned].' I suspect there is a mistake here, and that there had been written *in eo quod* or *quo*, '[in this, that] all have sinned,' so that ἐφ' ᾧ is taken αἰτιολογικῶς [in a causal sense]. But that you might understand that [Origen] is talking about the sins of individuals, he says: ' "All have sinned and fall short of the glory of God."[38] And therefore if you were to mention even that righteous man Abel, he cannot be excused, for "all have sinned." ' [Origen] passes on from Abel to Enosh, from Enosh to Enoch, from Enoch to Methuselah, from Methuselah to Noah, from Noah to Abraham, demonstrating with proofs that individuals have sinned by their own sins. Then, fearing to recount the others lest he should offend someone by attributing sin to those whom the world holds in the highest regard, he comes to Christ. To him, he says, sin came (I suppose when he was tempted by Satan), but by him alone was it repulsed, and so death was conquered, whose sting is sin; whence it is written: 'Oh death, where is your sting?' [1 Cor 15:55] etc. I think it is clear enough from these words that Origen interpreted this passage in terms of the sin of imitation, just as did that scholiast. [Origen] puts to a searching examination even the individual words, as when he distinguishes 'the world' from 'men': that sin *entered* 'the world' and is not said to have departed, but it *passed through* to 'men' – since, that is, repentance offers a way out.[39] There is not even a word about the sin of infants, to whom this passage was specifically to have referred.

I do not say this to call into question whether there was some original sin, but to point out that those lie who say that I alone record this interpretation, and that it is a fabrication peculiar to Pelagius and me.[40] I condemn the opinion of Pelagius, and I am aware of the consensus of the ancients on this matter; [but] the dispute is concerned only with the sense of this passage, whether properly it refers to original sin. In the first place, it is generally acknowledged that the beginning of this whole disputation [in Romans] arose from a point other than the question of original sin; and that the thrust of the disputation moves towards a different end. For in the first chapter [Paul] reproaches the gentiles because, contrary to the law of nature and to their knowledge of philosophy, they had degenerated to every kind of wickedness; in the second chapter he reproves the Jews because they did not observe the Law, in which they boasted; in the third chapter he concludes that both the Jews and gentiles are equally guilty and in need of the grace of God; in the fourth, he teaches that Jews and gentiles are saved not as a result of their own works, but through faith, and that the promise made to Abraham belongs to all who resemble him in their faith; in the fifth he teaches that forgiveness of sins and the gift of righteousness, that is, of innocence, comes to all through the freely given love of God, who has washed away the sins of all through the blood of his Only-Begotten. Up to this point there is nothing that is not applicable to personal sins (to use a scholastic term).[41] Now Chrysostom points out that in the fifth chapter Paul is approaching [the question] how those who have been justified by baptism ought to regulate their lives, that is, to abstain from sin in the future so that we do not tear asunder the peace with God that had been restored.[42] There is nothing here yet about original sin.

It is clear that the words that soon follow – 'For until the Law sin was in the world, but sin was not imputed' [5:13] etc – most of the Doctors explain as referring to the 'sin of imitation.' For St Ambrose writes thus: 'Until the Law was given sin was not imputed, for people supposed that before their fellows they sinned with impunity, but not before God. For the natural law deep within was not lifeless, because they were not ignorant that they should not do to others what they did not want done to themselves' etc.[43] This discussion attests Ambrose's feeling that this passage speaks of personal sins committed. Now whether you read 'in the likeness of Adam' or 'not in the likeness' [5:14],[44] [the Doctors] refer both readings to the sin of imitation. In fact even that passage[45] – 'For if many died through the trespass of one' [5:15] etc – which again it seemed possible to refer to original sin – [Ambrose] interprets thus: 'That is, if by the trespass of one, many died imitating his transgression, much more the grace of God' etc. And just a little further on he says: 'Nor did death hold sway over all, but over those who died through Adam's trespass – those who, [Paul] says, have sinned after the likeness of Adam's transgression.' And on the words 'For the judgment from the one [was] for condemnation' etc [5:16] he comments thus: 'It is clearly dissimilar that those have been condemned by Adam's sin alone who sinned after the likeness of his transgression.'[46] Again, these words, 'As through the trespass of one, [the judgment was] for condemnation upon all' [5:18] etc, he explains thus: 'That is, just as through the trespass of one all who likewise sinned deserved condemnation, so also by the righteousness of one all who believe will be justified.' From here on, [Paul] orders the discussion in such a way that you understand he is talking about the sins specifically of individuals. But in the middle [of the discussion Ambrosiaster] writes: 'And so it is clear that all have sinned in Adam as though in a lump;[47] for he himself was corrupted by sin, and those whom he begot were all born under sin; we are all sinners, for this reason, then, that we are all [descended] from him.' Shortly thereafter: 'There is also another death, which is called the second death – in hell; we do not suffer this through the sin of Adam, but from the opportunity [he created] we procure it through our own sins'[48] etc. Here he distinguishes the sin of Adam from personal sins, and the death of the body from the death of hell.[49]

But the question now is not whether Ambrose acknowledges original sin (it is clear from many passages that he does), but whether it is necessary to understand this passage to refer to original sin. For if this passage, 'and so death spread to all *in quo omnes peccaverunt*,' must be understood to refer to original sin, then it is necessary that we understand in a similar sense the clause attached to it – 'for until the Law sin was in the world' [5:13] – because this clause gives the reason for the previous statement. But Ambrose interprets this clause to refer to the sins committed by each individual.[50] How then will [Paul's] discussion remain firmly on course if the words that both precede and follow are understood to refer to the sins of individuals, while suddenly in the middle a sin of a different kind is thrown in, especially when the conjunction 'for' connects the later clauses with the earlier in such a way that the same thing appears to be under discussion? But just as the conjunction γάρ [for] [5:13] binds together what follows with the preceding words, so διὰ τοῦτο, that is, 'therefore' [5:12], connects its clause with the words that had preceded [it]. Now [this] had preceded: that Christ died for us [though] enemies and sinners, by whose blood we have been freed from the wrath of God, and have attained life in place of death and the glory of sons in place of shame. There is no difference between ['for' and 'therefore'] except that when we say 'therefore' the cause precedes and the result follows; when we say 'for' the reverse is true. If Titius owed to Actius[51] a thousand silver coins taken as a loan and ten drachmas as a deposit, would [Titius'] words seem coherent if he were to say: 'I have never had a more obliging creditor than Actius. I owed him a thousand silver coins, but when he saw I was in difficult financial straits he voluntarily forgave me that sum and put me – no longer in debt to his money – more deeply in debt to his kindness. For me, deserving of nothing, he embraced with singular kindness, and for this reason released me from the obligation; he could have sued me for the loan, and if I had not paid he could have thrown me in prison or seized my property for the mortgage.' Here, when the first and last parts speak of the loan, who would suspect that the words in the middle, 'and released me from the obligation,' refer to the deposit? Now the effect of these two connectives, 'wherefore' and 'for,' is that the connection of thought will be much harsher unless we take the whole to refer to original sin or the whole to personal sin, or the whole to both. But there are parts that cannot be understood of original sin, and parts that cannot be understood of both.

Now on this clause, which, as they would have it, *must* be taken to refer to original sin, St [John] Chrysostom makes no other comment than this: τί δέ ἐστιν, ἐφ᾽ ᾧ πάντες ἥμαρτον; ἐκείνου πεσόντος, καὶ οἱ μὴ φαγόντες ἀπὸ τοῦ ξύλου, γεγόνασιν ἐξ ἐκείνου θνητοί, that is, 'What is the meaning of "in whom all sinned"? When [Adam] fell, even those who had not eaten from the tree became mortal from him.' This statement can refer to either kind of sin. Moreover, he explains the adjoining passage in two ways. I will set down his words [on verse 13] – 'For until the Law sin was in the world, but sin is not imputed when there is no Law' – rendered faithfully into Latin: 'With respect to the words "until the Law," some think the Apostle had in mind the time before the Law was given, for example the time of Abel, Noah, and Abraham right up to the time when Moses was born. What sin, then, was there at that time? Some say he is speaking of the sin in paradise: For (he says) it had not yet been abolished, rather its fruit still flourished, for it was sin that brought in the death common to all, which conquered and reigned. Why, then, does he add, "but sin is not imputed when there is no Law?" Those who have spoken on our side say that the Apostle had put forward this statement from the standpoint of Jews who objected, "If there is no sin without the Law, how did death take away those who lived before the Law?" But it seems to me that what I am now about to say is a more probable [interpretation], and more in accordance with the Apostle's thought. What, then, is this? When he says: "Sin was in the world until the Law," I think he means that after the Law was given, sin – manifestly, sin arising from transgression – held sway, and held sway so long as there was Law. For there can be no sin if there is no Law. And so (he says), if this sin begot death from transgression of the Law, how did it happen that all who lived before the Law died? For if death took its origin from sin, and sin is not imputed when there is no Law, how did death rule? Hence it is clear that it was not this sin of violating the Law but that committed through the disobedience of Adam which corrupted all things. What is the evidence for this? The fact that all died, even before the Law. "For death reigned from Adam until Moses, even over those who did not sin"' etc.[52] With these words Chrysostom does not attribute any sin to infants, but he says that the death of the body spread out to them, just as though they had eaten from the forbidden tree along with their ancestor Adam; that is, they paid the penalty for another's sin.

But, when Theophylact (in translation)[53] speaks thus: 'For when he fell even those who had eaten nothing from the tree became mortal by their wickedness, just as though they themselves were guilty of sin, because he had sinned,'[54] is he not declaring that infants are not guilty of sin? And yet if we understand this passage to refer to the death of hell – a death that Adam deserved – infants are not punished by that death;[55] if [we understand it] to refer to the death of the body, baptism does not release them from this. Perceiving this, Origen retreated to [a third interpretation], the death of the soul – a death that through sin separates God from the soul.[56] If we take the death [to be] this, the passage cannot be taken to refer to original sin. But this passage, which Chrysostom seems to interpret as referring to the transgression of Adam, Ambrose interprets of personal sin, as we have shown.[57] The reckless claim made by someone, that all the ancients, both Greek and Latin, with striking agreement interpret this passage to refer to original sin, is, then, false, since the Greek Origen and the Latin scholiast interpret it otherwise. Consequently, it is not true that this opinion is peculiar to Pelagius and me, since Ambrose, too, interprets what both precedes and follows to refer to the sins of individuals and seems to touch upon the sin of Adam only in the middle. But it is even more false [to say] that this interpretation is in conflict with the special character of Pauline speech and the proper sense of the Greek words, since I have made it clear that both the character of the language, and the sequence and course of the discussion, fit more smoothly the view that I am showing to be possible. I will not now carefully examine what others repeat in order to force this passage to [refer to] original sin; for they speak in ambiguous figures. Certainly none of them attributes sin to infants, but they say that some part of the punishment has been passed on to the descendants.[58]

There remains the uproar over this, that I supposedly aid the Pelagians by disarming the church, since the most powerful weapon of all, as they say, has been wrenched away. First of all, I have shown that there are other passages that are more effective weapons.[59] Second, how do I support the Pelagians when I openly denounce their view? 'But' [you say] 'I show that both readings are valid.' Even if I keep silent, the evidence cries out that the passage is more easily understood to refer to the sin of individuals. One passage of Scripture was enough against Pelagius, and the church would be safe if it lost even this weapon.[60] 'But the whole church interprets the passage in this way!' Do three or four Doctors constitute the whole church? The whole church teaches that all the descendants of Adam are born subject to punishment because of the sin of Adam; but nowhere does the universal church teach that this passage can be understood only of original sin. And yet this was the only point I made in my annotation. 'But,' they reply, 'in the African council' (of Milev, I suppose) 'anathema is pronounced upon those who interpreted this passage of Paul otherwise.' No! anathema is pronounced upon those who taught that infants have no need of baptism because they have no contagion from Adam; and after the anathema it is added 'that it should not be understood otherwise.'[61] I am not examining here the many anathemas of those provincial councils that Hilary, in some manner, translated,[62] and I do not think I am much bound by synods of that kind. Otherwise, if anyone should urge that all their decisions must be observed, I shall bring forth from them some dogmas that the church now condemns as heresy; and I shall bring forth regulations that the church now nowhere keeps. Let them bring forth[63] [decrees] from the ecumenical council which forbade this passage to be expounded otherwise. Grant that the Council of Milev did, to be sure, condemn the Pelagian interpretation; that has no bearing on me. [Pelagius] builds up this interpretation so as to support [a view] of which the church disapproved; I, in demonstrating that this passage does not at all effectively refute the Pelagians, send the disputant to other passages more decisive than this. This is not to snatch away a weapon from the church, but to point to surer weapons in place of one unlikely to hit its mark. This is not to open a breach for the enemy, but to warn us not to press the enemy at a point where he can escape. I acknowledge that the church has the authority to interpret the Scriptures, but the Doctors of the church, however celebrated, hesitate over many passages of Scripture, and have interpreted many of them diversely, some of them even incorrectly.[64] Not one of them contends that this passage cannot be interpreted in a different sense – except St Augustine, after he became embroiled in the conflict with the Pelagians.[65]

But if here they do not permit dissent from Augustine far enough to allow that one may interpret this passage of Paul in two ways, why not bestow the same honour on everything [Augustine] taught and affirmed in this same dispute? For in it he repeatedly insists that infants are baptized in vain unless they are given the body and blood of the Lord.[66] He derived this opinion from John, chapter 6: 'Truly, truly I say to you, unless you eat the flesh of the Son of Man and drink his blood, you shall not have life in you' [6:53]. The earliest writers interpreted this passage to refer to the teaching of Christ; later writers added a second sense, concerning the taking of the Eucharist.[67] But now the church neither does nor allows to be done what Augustine – and with him, probably, the whole Western church – judged necessary for salvation, and it has rejected his interpretation, which would be regarded as heretical if anyone should wish to cling tenaciously to it.[68] In the same dispute [Augustine] insists that Christ alone was free from all sin, and he demonstrates this with many witnesses.[69] But the ranks of the theologians, particularly of Paris, condemn this opinion; they openly reject both the doctrine and the scriptural interpretation of such men.[70] In the same dispute [Augustine] cites Ambrose, who interprets the washing of feet among the apostles[71] as referring to original sin, although today it may be interpreted otherwise.[72] For Peter, already circumcised, was not guilty of that sin. He cites Cyprian, who had written that in baptism infants are forgiven the sins of another, although today the church teaches that the only sin imputed to newborns is that first unparalleled sin of Adam, and not that wholly.[73] In the same dispute, to prove original sin [Augustine] adduces 1 Corinthians 15: 'Just as in Adam all die, so also in Christ will all be made alive' [15:22].[74] Why did Chrysostom dare to interpret this passage of the sins of individuals? For he comments: 'Why then, pray tell, have all died with the death brought by sin in Adam? How then was Noah a righteous man in his generation, or Abraham, or Job, or all the others?' etc.[75] In vain does he recount these things if the passage is considering original sin, since none of those was free from it. But St Augustine believes so firmly that this passage of Paul must be understood to refer to original sin that [he thinks] anyone who tries to interpret it otherwise is striving to undermine our whole belief in Christ – since it pertains to the foundations of our faith.[76] Enlisted also against the Pelagians is the passage 'We were by nature sons of wrath.'[77] Why did St Jerome dare to interpret it as referring to something other than original sin? Why did he dare to point out that φύσει [by nature] can be taken to have the same force as 'utterly' or 'entirely'?[78] Why here does no one cry out that a weapon has been snatched from the defenders of the church? Or will they bind us by this law, that it is impious and forbidden for anyone to interpret any testimony of Scripture in any other way than did the ancient teachers of the church in their conflict with the heretics? But what will they say when we produce from those conflicts so many judgments, so many interpretations of the ancients, which the modern theologians not only reject but judge impious and heretical?

But if the whole church is on the verge of falling because I have remarked that this passage can be interpreted in another way – without condemning the [traditional] interpretation – why has no one as yet cried out against the scholia handed down under the name of Jerome, which explain this whole passage as referring to sins committed voluntarily?[79] It is clear that this whole disputation of Paul is full of obscurities, as Origen truly remarks in his preface;[80] it is clear that many things are said in figures of speech. I affirm original sin not only here, but in many passages of my lucubrations;[81] and even in my paraphrase I include both senses, when I said: 'For if the author of sin so far prevailed that so many are liable to death on account of the deeds of one man' etc; then, '[. . .] in such a way that, by the kindness of God, Adam's loss has worked out to our advantage. Again, though the destruction of sinners has been brought in through one man, Adam, and salvation through the innocence of Christ, nevertheless the two are not alike. For in fact destruction began in such a way that the sin of one man was spread to all his descendants, thus finally rendering all guilty; conversely,' etc; and then, 'But if the one sin of one man was so effective that it bound all under the tyranny of death' etc.[82] What then? Is this to exclude original sin? Now my translation 'inasmuch as' for ἐφ' ᾧ can fit either sense, or rather both: death was passed on through this, that all have sinned – in Adam, surely. Then what do they have to fear? Will the Pelagians suddenly spring back to life because I have interpreted this one passage otherwise than did Augustine in his fight, when there are many other passages by which heretics can be more effectively refuted? But how is it less permissible [to do] here what the orthodox have been allowed [to do] in other passages cited by the same [Augustine]? Or will they say that we must conceal the fact that this passage is explained in two ways? As though, if I were silent, the heretics would not perceive this, or rather, as though they had not perceived it a thousand years ago?

But if we resort to silence as a defence for our faith, what is the point of so many volumes of questions with which the modern theologians have filled the world, calling everything into doubt with the arguments they set forth – Scotus especially, whose arguments opposing the truth, which they call 'previously opposed,' sometimes have more strength than those with which he refutes them.[83] Why do they not fear that here a handle is offered to the heretics? 'But those,' they say, 'are questions debated among the scholastics.' Well, it is hardly in bedrooms that my [annotations] are read, for I have written them for theologians, not for schoolteachers.[84] A single text of Scripture suffices for me; and sometimes the authority of the church even without Scripture.[85] But against the heretics, how would it help to rule that this passage may not be understood in a different sense, when the evidence cries out that it can be understood otherwise? In conclusion, if here there is some small offence, who is more to blame, the one who annotated the passage in just a few words, or those who rail at such little notes in fierce and terrible tones and bring them forth upon the public stage?

1 inasmuch ... sinned] The translation of 1519 and thereafter. In 1516, *in eo quod omnes peccavimus* 'in this, that we all have sinned.' Erasmus excuses the reading '*we* have sinned,' like the reading questioned in the previous annotation (cf n1), on the grounds that it was unintended. See *Responsio ad collationes* LB IX 986E–987A.

2 Adam] Erasmus' interpretation of Rom 5:12 evoked the criticism, at an early point from Edward Lee, later from Frans Titelmans, that it was Pelagian and constituted an attack on the doctrine of original sin. Titelmans also criticized his translation at four specific points: Erasmus had translated 1/ 'on account of one man' instead of 'through one man'; 2/ 'broke through upon' instead of 'passed through to'; 3/ 'inasmuch as' instead of 'in whom'; and 4/ 'we all have sinned' instead of 'all have sinned.' See *Responsio ad annotationes Lei* LB IX 214B–F and *Responsio ad collationes* LB IX 984E–993B. As a result, though in editions from 1519 to 1527 Erasmus amplified somewhat his original brief note of 1516, in 1535 he replaced the earlier form of the annotation with a new and lengthy discussion. The annotation in the earlier editions reads as follows (additions from 1519 to 1527 are inserted in angle brackets, with dates):

Some refer *in quo* [in whom] to Adam; <1519 among these is Ambrose, who philosophizes as well on this, why [Paul] said *in quo* [masculine] meaning Adam, and not *in qua* [feminine], since sin arose from Eve – no doubt following Origen as he generally did;> some to the particular sin

of each person <*1519* which is the view, I see, <*1527* of Chrysostom and>
of Theophylact>. <*1527* And yet both views amount to the same thing.>
I do not think it unreasonable to take ἐφ᾽ ᾧ in the sense of 'inasmuch
as' or 'since,' so that the meaning is that through one man sin came into
the world; death, however, was the companion of sin; accordingly, death
came to all inasmuch as all had sin. For one may find other passages, too,
in St Paul, <*1519* if I am not mistaken,> where ἐν ᾧ or ἐφ᾽ ᾧ has the sense
of 'in this,' that' or 'to whatever extent' or 'inasmuch as.' <*1527* I had less
confidence in this opinion before I discovered it had been proposed by
the man whose scholia we have on all the Pauline Epistles, a learned man,
as his text shows, though an impostor has added a preface, pretending
the author was Jerome – to make the work more saleable. Here is the
scholion: 'In whom all have sinned, that is, in this, that all have sinned,
they sin by the example of Adam.'>

For the references in this passage, see respectively Ambrosiaster *Comm in
Rom* 5:12 (2a); Origen *Comm in Rom* 5.1 PG 14 1009B–C; Chrysostom *Hom
in Rom* 10.1 PG 60 473–5; and Theophylact *Expos in Rom* 5:12–14 PG 124
404C–406B (though Chrysostom and Theophylact speak in general of sin as
stemming from Adam); Pseudo-Jerome (on Rom 5:12) Souter III 8:14 (on
Pseudo-Jerome see n22 below). For ἐν ᾧ or ἐφ᾽ ᾧ elswhere in Paul in the
sense of 'in this, that,' see the annotation on 2:1 ('for in what [you judge]
another').

In the *1535* form of the annotation Erasmus attempts to answer the charges
of his critics and especially the charge of Pelagianism. Of the four criticisms
Titelmans levelled against his translation Erasmus concentrates in this
annotation on the third and the second, since he had admitted mistakes in
the case of the first and fourth (see n1 above and the preceding annotation,
n1). This *1535* annotation reflects in essential points the arguments Erasmus
used in his 1529 response to Titelmans.

3 Latin *massa.* For the patristic use of the word in the exposition of Rom 5:12,
see Ambrosiaster *Comm in Rom* 5:12 (3): 'It is clear that all sinned in Adam
quasi in massa'; also Augustine *De gratia Christi et de peccato originali* 2.29.34
PL 44 402, and Pelagius *Expos in Rom* 5:15 (Souter II 47:10). For the phrase
massa in early medieval theology see Seeberg II 33. In general, the word has
the sense of a cohering and inclusive mass. See the annotation on Gal 5:9
(*totam massam corrumpit*).

4 Augustine *Contra duas epistulas Pelagianorum* 4.4.7 PL 44 614, where, however,
Augustine recognizes the difficulty of the gender (the relative pronoun
is masculine, the Greek word for sin feminine) and reviews two other
possibilities, that the pronoun might refer to 'death' or to 'Adam.'

5 Augustine began his attack upon Pelagian doctrines with his books *De
peccatorum meritis et remissione et de baptismo parvulorum* and *De spiritu et
littera*, published in 412. These were written in the wake of the condemnation
of Celestius by the Council of Carthage in 411. Augustine treated Pelagius
himself with respect until 415, but in 416 both Pelagius and Celestius
were condemned in councils at Carthage and Milev, and Pope Innocent
excommunicated them both in 417. Though Innocent's successor, Zosimus,
was at first sympathetic to them, he too eventually condemned them (418).

Julian, the youthful bishop of Eclanum in Italy, refused, however, to endorse
the condemnation, and a bitter debate ensued between him and Augustine,
resulting in the latter's lengthy treatise *Contra Julianum* in 421. Augustine
continued to write against Pelagian doctrines until his death in 430, leaving
unfinished yet another work against Julian. For the anti-Pelagian writings
of Augustine see NPNF 1st series, V and, for the work *Against Julian*, the
translation of Matthew A. Schumacher, Fathers of the Church 35 (New York
1957).
Augustine appeals frequently to Rom 5:12 in various anti-Pelagian writings.
See, for example, *Contra Julianum* 1.3.8 and 1.7.33 PL 44 645 and 663–4. For
further examples see the Index of Texts in NPNF 1st series, V 564.

6 Ambrosiaster *Comm in Rom* 5:12 (2a) and Origen *Comm in Rom* 5.1 PG 14
1009B–C. For the similar statement of 1519 see n2 above.

7 Erasmus may have in mind here Jean Gerson (1363–1429), chancellor of the
University of Paris (from 1395), distinguished churchman, theologian, and
mystic. He refers to Gerson in two other passages as favouring the view
that unbaptized children of Christian parents may be saved by the immense
mercy of God through the supplications of their parents (*Institutio christiani
matrimonii* LB V 622C and *Hyperaspistes* II LB X 1534E). In fact, Gerson refers
only to unborn infants; see Gerson *Sermo de nativitate Mariae virginis* in *Opera
omnia* ed L.E. Du Pin (Paris 1706) III 1350A–B.

8 So defined, for example, by Augustine *Contra Faustum Manichaeum* 22.27 PL
42 418: 'Sin is something said or done or desired against the eternal law';
quoted by Peter Lombard *Sententiae* 2.35 PL 192 734 and Thomas Aquinas
Summa theologiae pars prima secundae, quaest 71, art 6. Cf also Jerome
Commentarii in Ezechielem 13 (on 43:23–7) PL 25 427B: 'We sin by either
thought or word or deed'; so also Thomas Aquinas *Summa theologiae* pars
prima secundae, quaest 72, art 7.

9 See n11 below.

10 See n3 above.

11 In this passage Erasmus' discussion reflects some of the efforts made
throughout the Middle Ages to define original sin. There were those who
stressed the absence of an original righteousness possessed by Adam which
had made it possible for him to live in loving obedience to God (Anselm,
Duns Scotus, William of Occam); others saw original sin primarily as a
sickness of the soul, an inveterate vice of concupiscence, that is, of the
'desires of the flesh' (Peter Lombard and apparently Gregory of Rimini).
Some of those who held the former view rejected the possibility that
'concupiscence,' the 'desires of the flesh,' could be called original sin; they
regarded concupiscence rather as the punishment for sin. Some theologians,
such as Thomas Aquinas, attempted to find a middle ground: 'the absence
of original righteousness is the form, concupiscence the matter, of original
sin.' See Oberman *Harvest* 122 (Thomas Aquinas), 124 (Gregory of Rimini);
see also Seeberg II 114–18, 153–4.

12 In his response to Titelmans Erasmus listed these same evils as the common
lot of humanity and illustrated their relation to Adam's sin with what he
calls the 'French disease': the children of syphilitic parents are not themselves
guilty of sin, but as a result of their parents' sin are born with an unhealthy

body, and so 'in some way have sinned in their parents.' So infants who
have not sinned share in the troubles Adam brought upon himself as a result
of his sin (LB IX 990D).

Erasmus spoke elsewhere also of the relation between baptism and original
sin. See eg *Enchiridion*: 'These rules ... will be especially effective against
three evils, which are the vestiges of original sin. For even if baptism has
removed the stain, nevertheless a residue of the old malady remains in us
both as a safeguard of humility, and as raw material and a fertile terrain for
virtue. The three evils are blindness, the flesh, and weakness' (CWE 66 54).
Also in *Hyperaspistes* II, written against Luther, Erasmus argues that baptism
does not remove the inclination to sin (LB X 1401D–E), following in this
respect scholastic teaching, which stressed that baptism weakened but did
not destroy the inclination to sin. On baptism and original sin in Erasmus, see
Payne *Erasmus: His Theology* 42–3, 164, 177; and for the scholastic teaching,
Oberman *Harvest* 127, 135 and Steven E. Ozment *The Age of Reform* (New
Haven 1980) 30.

13 The phrase 'the infused habits of the graces' reflects the language of scholastic
theology. 'Habits of grace' refers to the forms of grace implanted in human
beings through the sacraments of baptism and penance, which remove
original sin or actual sins and make persons acceptable to God. These infused
habits of grace create a new disposition and make possible the theological
virtues of faith, hope, and love (*charitas*) which are the basis of truly good
actions. In fact, so important is the infused habit of charity that it is virtually
indistinguishable from the habit of grace. Through the sacrament of the
Eucharist venial sins are forgiven and the habit of charity is increased.
Though the truly serious evils of guilt and eternal punishment are removed
by the habit of grace, the lesser evils of subjection to sickness and death and
inclination to sin are not destroyed but weakened. By the plural 'graces'
Erasmus may refer to the various ways in which grace was designated, *gratia
gratum faciens, gratia creata, gratia prima*, etc. See Oberman *Harvest* 69, 74,
166–72, 203, 206, 209–10; Seeberg II 119, 129–30.

14 For the image of the labyrinth used to characterize the arguments both of
philosophers and of the (scholastic) theologians see the *Moria* CWE 27 127;
but for its use to refer to the convoluted argument of Romans cf CWE 42 13.

15 Though Erasmus cites specifically only Acts 26, the phrases listed here are
standard Greek idioms found in the New Testament literature or in classical
Greek literature. For citations from the literature see ἐπί, θάνατος, οὐδός in
BAG and LSJ. The phrase referring to Caesar Octavius has a close analogy in
Acts 11:28 ἐπὶ Κλαυδίου 'in the time of Claudius.'

16 Cf Heb 7:10, where the reading includes the definite article, ἐν τῇ ὀσφύι.

17 Cf the annotation on 1:4 ('in power') and n8.

18 For the context:
    ER *et sic in omnes homines mors pervasit* 'and thus death broke through
    upon all'
    VG *et ita in omnes homines mors pertransit* 'and so death passed through to
    all'

19 This passage from Luke 2:35 became a *locus classicus* of patristic and medieval
biblical interpretation, as Erasmus' list of commentators indicates in his

annotation on the verse (*et tuam ipsius animam*). In the work Erasmus cites here as Augustine's, the 'sword passing through' signified the doubt Mary suffered at the death of her Son, a merely passing doubt, however, since her faith was confirmed by his resurrection; cf *Quaestiones Veteris et Novi Testamenti* 73 PL 35 2267–8. Modern scholarship regards the *Questions* as the work of Ambrosiaster; see Quasten *Patrology* IV 180, 184 and, for a book-length study of the problem, A. Souter *A Study of Ambrosiaster* (Cambridge 1905).

20 The Vulgate *pertransit* is a compound with two prepositions (*per* 'through' + *trans* 'through,' 'across' + *it* 'went'), whereas *transit*, compounded with one preposition (*trans* 'through' + *it* 'went'), reflects more accurately the Greek in so far as the Greek also has only a single preposition in the compound (διά 'through' + ἦλθεν 'went').

21 Ovid *Remedia amoris* 1.616

22 Even though the commentaries on the thirteen epistles of Paul that bore the name of Jerome as author were included in the ninth volume of the Froben edition of Jerome (1516), Erasmus was already then aware that they were pseudonymous, as his preface to that portion of the edition indicates (see the quotation from this preface in Souter I 6). Souter (I 272–82) demonstrates that the manuscript then housed at Echternach Abbey (now Paris BN 9525) is the one from which Erasmus derived the text of Pseudo-Jerome for the Froben *editio princeps* of 1516 and claims that it is superior to the later Vallarsi edition upon which Migne (PL 30) is based.
Souter has shown in his Introduction (Souter I) that the text of 'Pseudo-Jerome' is a commentary by Pelagius with interpolations; he has also attempted to distinguish the interpolations (Souter III) from the commentary of Pelagius (Souter II); but see Hermann Josef Frede *Ein neuer Paulustext und Kommentar* 2 vols (Freiburg 1974) II 7–10. Though Erasmus apparently did not realize that the primary author was Pelagius, we follow Souter here in identifying the primary text as that of Pelagius (Souter II), and the interpolations as those of Pseudo-Jerome (Souter III).

23 Pelagius *Expos in Rom* (Souter II 45:11–22). For the scriptural references quoted see respectively Luke 20:37–8; Rom 3:12 and 3:4.

24 Origen *Comm in Rom* 5.12 PG 14 1010B–1011B, 1012C–1013A

25 Pelagius *Expos in Rom* (Souter II 45:22–3)

26 Pseudo-Jerome (on Rom 5:12) Souter III 8:17–18

27 Pseudo-Jerome (on Rom 5:12) Souter III 8:14

28 Cf Souter III ix and xiii.

29 On the translator of Origen, and his translation, see the annotation on 3:5 ('is God unfair who inflicts wrath') nn11, 14.

30 Cf Heb 7:9–10. On the meaning of *massa* see n3 above.

31 Origen *Comm in Rom* 5.1 PG 14 1009C–1010A

32 Origen *Comm in Rom* 5.1 PG 14 1009A–B

33 Origen *Comm in Rom* 5.1 PG 14 1010B

34 Origen *Comm in Rom* 5.1 PG 14 1010C; Erasmus cites according to the Merlin edition (fol CLXX). In Migne, the passage reads: 'When he bears the image of the earthly and walks according to the image of the earthly, he minds' etc.

35 Cf Plato *Phaedrus* 248A–E.

36 For Origen's view see Trigg *Origen* 107; Jean Daniélou *Origène* (Paris 1948) 207ff; and Kelly *Doctrines* 180–2, who questions the fidelity of Rufinus' translation of Origen's commentary on Rom 5:12. Origen's doctrine of the fall of pre-existent souls as a result of their turning away from God carried the implication of personal responsibility for sin. Erasmus' belief that Rufinus ('the translator') omitted 'certain things' here is apparently derived from the passage itself: 'But consider this, too, within yourself, whence sin entered into this world ... whether it existed before him to whom it was said "... I have cast you forth upon the earth." For us, however, it is not safe to discuss these things further ...' (Origen *Comm in Rom* 5.1 PG 14 1011A).

37 In the discussion of Origen that follows, Erasmus sometimes quotes directly from the text, sometimes paraphrases it, and sometimes merely summarizes the argument; *Comm in Rom* 5.1 PG 14 1011B–1012C.

38 Cf Rom 3:23.

39 Origen *Comm in Rom* 5.1 PG 14 1012C–1013A. Origen returns to an earlier definition (see n24 above): 'the world' represents persons of worldly mind whom sin enters but does not leave; 'men' are those who repent, through whom, therefore, sin merely passes. Origen concludes: 'In the Epistles of Paul not even a single syllable should be thought devoid of mysteries.'

40 For these charges and Erasmus' response see n2 above. Erasmus' paraphrase of this verse had drawn from Béda the charge of Pelagianism (see CWE 42 34 and n12).

41 The term was used by Titelmans (*Responsio ad collationes* LB IX 991F). See also Thomas Aquinas, who distinguishes between *peccatum commune totius humanae naturae* (ie original sin) and *peccatum speciale uniuscuiusque personae* (sin committed by each individual) (*Summa theologiae* pars tertia, quaest 49, art 5).

42 Chrysostom *Hom in Rom* 9.1 PG 60 467–8

43 Ambrosiaster *Comm in Rom* 5:13 (1). But Erasmus quotes inaccurately. In the CSEL edition (81/1 166:4–11, 167:6–10) the first sentence reads: 'Until the Law was given sin was not imputed, for people supposed that before God they sinned with impunity, but not before their fellows.' Ambrosiaster explains that before the Law was given, men imposed penalties for injuries committed, but they were not held guilty by God. The examples he cites from the Old Testament of individuals for whom punishment repaid wrongdoing suggests that in interpreting this verse he is speaking of the sins of individuals. But for Ambrosiaster as an exponent of the doctrine of original sin see n65 below.

44 The alternative is amplified in the first several lines of the annotation on 5:14 ('unto the likeness').

45 For this and the immediately subsequent references to Ambrosiaster's interpretation of Rom 5:15–18 see *Comm in Rom* 5:15 (1), 5:16 (1), and 5:18.

46 The sentence in Ambrosiaster continues: '... while the grace of God through Christ has redeemed human beings, not from one sin alone, but from many.' See Ambrosiaster *Comm in Rom* 5:16 (1).

47 For the phrase 'as though in a lump' see n3 above. With this quotation Erasmus returns to Ambrosiaster's exposition of 5:12 – the 'middle of the discussion' from 5:8 to 5:18; cf *Comm in Rom* 5:12 (3).

48 Ambrosiaster *Comm in Rom* 5:12 (4)

49 This distinction, too, was made by Titelmans (*Responsio ad collationes* LB IX 991F).
50 Cf n43 above.
51 Cf *Adagia* 1 x 76 for the proverb *Idem Accii quod Titii* 'Accius and Titius take alike,' which means, Erasmus explains, that a child born in the tenth month has the same rights as one born in the eleventh month. He states, 'The source is no doubt the lawyers' custom of using the two names Titius and Accius for any two litigants' (CWE 32 269–70); cf Aulus Gellius 3.16.13–14.
52 Chrysostom *Hom in Rom* 10.1 PG 60 474–5. In the *Responsio ad collationes* Erasmus expressed some dissatisfaction with Chrysostom's argument here. He insists that Chrysostom's comments on the phrase 'until the Law' meant not that all had sinned in Adam, but that all had become mortal through him. But he adds that in what follows Chrysostom seems to offer two views, the second correcting the first (LB IX 990E–F).
53 For the translation of Theophylact into Latin cf the annotation on 1:4 ('who was predestined') n25.
54 Theophylact *Expos in Rom* 5:12 PG 124 404C. Titelmans forced Erasmus to defend his brief supporting allusions to Chrysostom and Theophylact added in 1519 and 1527 (see n2 above), suggesting that Erasmus had misread the text, which should be read, not 'became mortal by their wickedness,' but 'became mortal by his [Adam's] wickedness' – which is indeed the correct reading. Erasmus complained that he had used a very poor Greek copy of Theophylact, and that the translation he had was so bad he was still not always able to be sure of the meaning (LB IX 990D–991B). The quotation here from Theophylact matches that of the 1529 edition of Porsena, *In omnes divi Pauli epistolas enarrationes* (Cologne: Peter Quentell) fol VIII verso. However, 'by his wickedness' represents apparently the interpretation of the translator. In Migne, the text of Theophylact reads 'those who had not eaten from the tree became mortal from him [ie Adam].'
55 Cf *Responsio ad collationes* LB IX 992F–993A, where Erasmus notes that theologians have softer things to say about the damnation of infants than Augustine, or rather than the author of *De fide ad Petrum*.
Augustine ascribed to infants who died unbaptized the punishment of the pain of hell, although the mildest kind (see *Enchiridion* 93.23 PL 40 275; *Contra Julianum* 5.11.44 PL 44 809). In contrast, the scholastics by the beginning of the thirteenth century had reached a consensus that attenuated this Augustinian judgment. They distinguished between the withholding of the vision of God (*poena damni*) and the pain of hell fire – a punishment of the senses (*poena sensus*). The first applied to infants dying unbaptized, but not the second. Between the truly damned and the truly blessed, infants who die with the guilt of original but not of actual sin are in a middle state. See Heinrich Köster *Urstand, Fall und Erbsünde in der Scholastik, Handbuch der Dogmengeschichte* ed Michael Schmaus et al II Fasc 3b (Freiburg im Breisgau 1979) 174–9. Köster provides an abundance of references to the scholastic literature. See also A. Gaudel 'Limbes' in *Dictionnaire de théologie catholique* IX-1 765–6 and A. Gaudel 'Péché originel' ibidem XII-1 462, 487–8, 508–9.
56 Cf Origen *Comm in Rom* 5.1 PG 14 1011B.
57 Cf n43 above. The 'Latin scholiast' of the next sentence is evidently a

reference to Pseudo-Jerome; cf n22 above.

58 For the scholastics, see n55 above.

59 Cf the *Responsio ad collationes* LB IX 988A, where Erasmus argues that Pelagianism is more effectively refuted 'in the passage from Job which declares that an infant is not free from sin on the very day of his birth [cf Job 25:4 and 14:4 LXX] ... and in those words of David, "Behold I was conceived in iniquity" [Ps 51:5].' These passages are echoed in Augustine *Confessions* 1.7.11–12 PL 32 665–6.

60 Cf *Responsio ad collationes* LB IX 988A–B: 'Suppose no scriptural passage [opposed Pelagius], does not the church teach many things that cannot be proved from the canonical Scriptures, such as the perpetual virginity of the Blessed Virgin?'

61 In 416 two African councils, one at Carthage and one at Milev (where Augustine was present) independently condemned the Pelagian doctrines. Of the Council of Milev we have only the synodal letter to Innocent, but at this council it was said that Rom 5:12 was rendered vain by those who contended that little children who had not received sacramental grace would obtain eternal life; see Giovanni Domenico Mansi, *Sacrorum conciliorum nova et amplissima collectio* (Florence 1759–98; facsimile ed Paris 1901–27) IV 335D. When Zosimus, who had become bishop of Rome in 417, declared Celestius orthodox, a general council of African bishops was called; it assembled at Carthage in 418. It is to canon 2 of this council that Erasmus appears to refer here; see *Conciliengeschichte* ed Carl Joseph von Hefele et al, 9 vols, 2nd ed (Freiburg im Breisgau 1873–90) II (1875) 113–17.
In the edition of Migne (PL 67 217C–D), there is first the anathema upon those who deny that infants should be baptized, on the ground that they retain nothing of the original sin of Adam. After the anathema there is added 'For not otherwise can be understood what the apostle had said [Rom 5:12 is here quoted] than the Catholic Church everywhere diffused has always understood it' (so translated in NPNF 2nd series, XIV 496–7, where the canon has the number 110, the number it acquired at the Council of Carthage in 419, which established a collection of 138 canons of the African councils).

62 Cf the anathemas in Hilary *De synodis* 1.13ff PL 10 490ff. In the preface to Erasmus' edition of Hilary, published by Froben in 1523 (revised 1535), Erasmus comments on the translation: '[Hilary] translates it, as he himself testifies, from the Greek; he takes the liberty, however, of avoiding everywhere a word-for-word translation and only renders the thought, and where the opportunity presents itself he mixes in his own ingredients' (Ep 1334:365–9). *De synodis* contained Hilary's translation (chapters 10–61) of the credal formulae produced by councils at Antioch (341), Philippopolis (343), Sirmium (351), and Ancyra (358).

63 Let them bring forth] Latin *proferant*; in LB *proferam*, I shall bring forth. Erasmus will presently cite several instances of change and evolution in church doctrine and regulation. See nn66, 68, 70 below. For a similar account of evolution and change in church doctrine and practice, see the annotation on 1 Cor 7:39 (*liberata est a lege cui autem vult nubat*) in which Erasmus discusses the question of divorce (especially LB VI 696B–D).

64 Elsewhere, too, Erasmus argues that the Fathers were not inerrant, and that

their commentaries should be approached certainly with reverence, but also with some caution (see *Ratio* Holborn 295:21–30; *Ecclesiastes* III LB V 1026C–D).

65 Erasmus' claim here is so sufficiently guarded that it is unexceptionable. But there were exegetes other than Augustine who expounded Rom 5:12–21 in terms that suggest a doctrine of original sin, for example, Ambrosiaster (somewhat ambiguously) in the West, and Ephraim in the East; cf Schelkle 174–5 (Ambrosiaster), 165 (Ephraim). Erasmus' discussion in this annotation, however, has fairly shown that there was a strong tradition that interpreted this Pauline passage to refer to an inherited death and personal sins, a tradition found more pervasively in the East than in the West. For an account of the interpretation of Rom 5:12–21 in individual Fathers of both East and West see Schelkle 162–78. See also J. Freundorfer *Erbsünde und Erbtod beim Apostel Paulus* (Münster in Westfalen 1927) 105–43, who points out that Erasmus was the first in the history of Western exegesis to understand the ἐπί of 5:12 as having a causal sense (cf CWE 42 34 n12).

66 See, for example, Augustine *De peccatorum meritis et remissione et de baptismo parvulorum* 1.20.27, 1.24.34 PL 44 124 and 128–9. Cf Erasmus *Enarrationes in psalmos XXXIII* LB V 413B–C.

67 For the 'earliest' writers see Origen *Commentarii in Joannem* 10.17–18 GCS 10 187–9; also Tertullian *De resurrectione mortuorum* 37.1–5 CCL 969–70. For the later writers, in addition to Augustine, see Chrysostom *In Joannem homiliae* 47.1 PG 59 263–4 (but cf 45.2 PG 59 253, where Chrysostom interprets the bread as Christ's divinity). Erasmus incorporates the interpretation of the 'earliest writers' into his paraphrase on John 6; see especially the paraphrases on John 6:35–6 and 53, and CWE 46 83–6 and nn50 and 69. See also Payne *Erasmus: His Theology* 163 n31.

68 The practice of providing infants after baptism with communion (by placing into the mouth the priest's index finger, which had been dipped into the wine) was a universal custom in the West in Augustine's time. It was also and still is the general usage of the Eastern Orthodox church. In the West the custom waned, so that by the thirteenth century it had almost disappeared. The Fourth Lateran Council (1215) proposed the 'year of discretion' as the appropriate time for the beginning of the communion obligation. See Heinrich Denzinger and Adolphus Schönmetzer *Enchiridion symbolorum* (Freiburg im Breisgau 1963) 437 (812). Infant communion as necessary for salvation was rejected already by most early scholastics and finally by the Council of Trent (ibidem 933 [1730]). See J.A. Jungmann 'Kinderkommunion' in *Lexicon für Theologie und Kirche* VI (Freiburg im Breisgau 1961) 154–5; and K. Dienst 'Kinderkommunion' in *Religion in Geschichte und Gegenwart* III (Tübingen 1959) 1284–5.

69 Cf Augustine *De peccatorum meritis et remissione et de baptismo parvulorum* 2.6.7–20.34 PL 44 155–71; *De spiritu et littera* 1.1.1 PL 44 201; *De perfectione iustitiae hominis* 12.29 PL 44 306–7. But see *De natura et gratia* 1.36.42 PL 44 267, where Augustine exempts Mary from sins.

70 Noël Béda, syndic of the faculty of theology at Paris, had earlier charged that Erasmus had in effect denied the doctrine of the Immaculate Conception of the Blessed Virgin, a doctrine which to Erasmus entailed the rejection of the view that Christ alone was free from sin. Under the influence of Duns

Scotus, the great majority of Franciscan theologians had become champions of the doctrine. But as Erasmus points out, both in his response to Béda and also in his annotation on 1 Cor 7:39 (in the passage cited in n63 above), the Dominicans, following Thomas Aquinas, continued to reject the dogma. See the responses to Béda, *Divinationes* LB IX 460E–F and *Supputatio* LB IX 569E–570B. On the doctrine of the Immaculate Conception in the late Middle Ages see Oberman *Harvest* 283–93 and X. Le Bachelet 'Immaculée Conception' in *Dictionnaire de théologie catholique* VII-1 1073–94, 1108–15. On decrees of the University of Paris supporting the doctrine see Le Bachelet 1126–7.

71 John 13:1–17

72 Augustine *Contra duas epistulas Pelagianorum* 4.11.29 PL 44 632; Ambrose *De mysteriis* 6.32 PL 16 398C. For the analogy in Erasmus between circumcision of infants under the Old Law and baptism of infants under the New Law see Payne *Erasmus: His Theology* 158–9.

73 Augustine cites Cyprian *Epistulae* 64 CSEL 3 720:16–721:2 to show that the latter understood original sin was forgiven in baptism. While Cyprian does, as Erasmus notes, speak of 'sins' (in the plural), by the phrase 'sins of another' he apparently refers to Adam's sin. See *The Letters of St. Cyprian of Carthage* trans and annot G.W. Clarke, Ancient Christian Writers, 4 vols (New York 1984–9) III (1986) 112 and n20. For Augustine see *De nuptiis et concupiscentia* 2.29.51 PL 44 466 and *Contra Julianum* 1.2.6 and 3.17.31 PL 44 644 and 718.

74 Cf *De peccatorum meritis et remissione et de baptismo parvulorum* 1.28.55 and 2.30.49 PL 44 140 and 180; *De nuptiis et concupiscentia* 2.27.46 PL 44 462–3; *Contra Julianum* 1.6.22 PL 44 655.

75 Chrysostom *In epistulam primam ad Corinthios homiliae* 39.3 PG 61 337

76 Augustine *Contra Julianum* 1.6.22 PL 44 655

77 Eph 2:3; cf Augustine *Contra Julianum* 6.10.33 PL 44 841.

78 Jerome *Commentarius in epistulam ad Ephesios* 1 (on 2:3) PL 26 498C. Jerome reports this interpretation of φύσει as the view of others, which he, however, can accept. He himself thinks the phrase refers either to the fact that our bodies are subject to death and that everyone from youth is bent towards evil, or to the fact that from the time we can have a knowledge of God we all do in fact sin (PL 26 497C–D).

79 Cf n22 above.

80 Origen *Comm in Rom* praefatio PG 14 833A–B. On Origen's view of the difficulty of this Epistle see the Argument to the Paraphrase on Romans CWE 42 12–14.

81 See the paraphrase on James 1:15 where, however, Erasmus distinguishes the inclination to vice from sin itself: 'A certain propensity to vicious behaviour has been implanted in our souls from the vice of our first parents. This propensity is, as it were, the seed of sin. If this seed has been admitted into the soul and taken root, the mind has now, so to speak, conceived sin, and if the vicious desire is not weeded out of the soul, that evil foetus gradually becomes larger and stronger until birth is given to a mortal sin . . .' (CWE 44 141). See also the *Explanatio symboli* ASD V-1 242:122–243:139, where Erasmus distinguishes between the proclivity to sin, to which all are subject, and

the evils brought by sin, which Christ too suffered; and *Ecclesiastes* III LB
V 1018B–C: 'To infants sin is ascribed, not because there is any sin in them;
but the absence of the original grace, the natural proclivity to sin and the
misfortune of human life is called sin.' Though Erasmus claims to affirm
original sin, it is clear that he sought to qualify the Augustinian doctrine,
and in this respect follows in the tradition of Scotus and Occam. See Seeberg
II 153–4, 197; Oberman *Harvest* 121–31.

82 The four passages here cited are from the paraphrases on Rom 5:15–17.
Erasmus in general quotes accurately the Latin of the paraphrases (as found
in the 1532 edition), and we have therefore followed in general the translation
in CWE 42 35. There is one significant exception: in place of 'the destruction
of sinners,' the 1532 *Paraphrase* (and CWE 42 35) reads: 'destruction through
the sin of one man.' For the considerable difference in meaning, only a very
small change was required in Latin – to read *peccantium* (1535 *Annotations*)
instead of *peccantem* (1532 *Paraphrase*).

83 In his method of *sic et non*, which set forth both the arguments supporting
the truth of a theological proposition and those which denied it, Abelard
established a pattern for theological discussion that was adopted by the
scholastics who followed him. Duns Scotus (d 1308) in particular was known
for his refined dialectic, which gained for him the name 'the Subtle Doctor.'
For introductions to Scotus' life, work, thought, and significance see C. Balić
'Duns Scotus, John' in *New Catholic Encyclopedia* IV 1102–6, and Efrem Bettoni
Duns Scotus: The Basic Principles of His Philosophy trans and ed Bernardine
Bonansea (Washington 1961).

84 Cf *Contra morosos quosdam ac indoctos*: 'I have written these annotations not
for the multitude, but for scholars, and principally for theological candidates'
(LB VI *** recto).

85 On Erasmus' view concerning the authority of Scripture and church see
R.H. Bainton *Erasmus of Christendom* (New York 1969) 191–6; C. Augustijn,
'Hyperaspistes I: la doctrine d'Erasme et de Luther sur la "claritas scripturae"'
in *Colloquia Erasmiana Turonensia* ed J.C. Margolin 2 vols (Paris 1972) II 737–48;
and Payne *Erasmus: His Theology* 15–33.

5:13 [ER VG] *usque ad legem enim peccatum* 'for[1] until the Law sin'; ἄχρι γὰρ
νόμου. Origen interprets, 'right to the end of the Mosaic law,' that is, 'until
Christ.'[2] Likewise[3] Augustine in the sentences he has annotated from the
Epistle to the Romans, says: 'One must understand "up to the time when
grace came," for it was spoken against those who think that sins can be
removed through the Law.' And shortly thereafter: 'Therefore we should
not think [Paul] said "until the Law" as though sin did not exist already
under the Law, but the words "until the Law" were used to include the
whole time of the Law right to the end of the Law, which is Christ.'[4]

In Chrysostom, γάρ [for] is not added, though it is in Theophylact.[5]

1 for ... 'until Christ'] Added in *1519* when the annotation was introduced
2 A conflation evidently of two similar passages in Origen *Comm in Rom* 5.1;
see PG 14 1018A and 1019A.

3 Likewise ... Theophylact] Added in *1535*

4 Augustine *Expositio quarundam propositionum ex epistula ad Romanos* 27–8 PL 35 2067

5 Cf Chrysostom *Hom in Rom* 10.1 PG 60 474 (where, however, the γάρ is present in the text) and Theophylact *Expos in Rom* 5:13 PG 124 404D.

5:13 [ER *non imputatur* 'is not imputed']

[VG] *non imputabatur* 'was not imputed';[1] οὐκ ἐλλογεῖται, that is, 'is not imputed,' in the present tense so that the statement is a more universal one. For μὴ ὄντος νόμου [there being no law] fits both tenses, as though you said in general, 'there being no law sin is not imputed'; that is, sin is not imputed *wherever* there is no law. Clearly[2] Origen reads thus,[3] and I have found it so written in the codex in St Paul's, which is very old and well emended.[4] Here some interpret ἐλλογεῖται not as imputed [*imputatur*] but as 'considered' [*reputatur*], that is, judged,[5] so that you understand that when no law has been set forth, sinners do not regard what they do as sin, since no law prohibits them from acting thus.[6] A certain[7] quite erudite gentleman[8] in a published book[9] considers the Greek reading to be corrupt, and [thinks] ἐλλογεῖτο [was imputed] should be written in place of ἐλλογεῖται [is imputed] – as though truly it were not shameless to disagree with so great a consensus of the Greek volumes, or as though if one were to require the imperfect tense, he should say ἐλλογεῖτο [*ellogeito*] and not rather ἐνελογεῖτο [*enelogeito*].[10] And this is the man who, in vindicating his own marvellous erudition, is constantly throwing in my face that I know nothing at all. In the codex at St Donatian it was written, 'when there is no law.' Thus we may conjecture that 'was imputed' is a corruption of 'is imputed.'[11] ἐλογεῖτο[12] [*elogeito*] could be tolerable if λογέω [*logeō* 'take account'] had the sense of λογίζομαι [*logizomai* 'reckon,' 'impute']; ἐλογεῖτο was written in the commentaries of Chrysostom; in Theophylact it is ἐλλογεῖτο,[13] but both [readings] are corrupt, if I am not mistaken.

It should be noted in passing that Paul in this passage uses the two words ἁμαρτία [sin] and παράπτωμα [trespass] indiscriminately, though Jerome somewhere conjectures that παράπτωμα is less serious than ἁμαρτία.[14]

1 The Vulgate printed in *1527* read a future tense, *non imputabitur* 'will not be imputed.' The present tense, *imputatur*, is the preferred reading of the Vulgate, though some manuscripts have the imperfect; see Wordsworth and White II 86 13n, where only one manuscript is cited with the future.

2 Clearly ... emended.] Added in *1519*

3 Cf Origen *Comm in Rom* 5.1 PG 14 1013A–1016A. Throughout Origen's discussion here the text is quoted with the verb in the present tense, and Origen's commentary in 1015D–1016A shows that he read it so.

4 For this manuscript see the annotation on 4:5 ('according to the purpose of the grace of God') n5.

5 For Erasmus' discussion of the meaning of this word and the proper Latin equivalents see the annotation on 4:3 ('and it was considered').
6 Cf Jacques Lefèvre d'Etaples: 'When you read "sin was not imputed," you understand "not imputed by God" ... but when you say "is not considered sin," one immediately assumes "not considered to be sin by those who commit it"' (*Pauli epistolae* fol 80 verso).
7 A certain ... corruption of 'is imputed.'] Added in *1522*
8 The reference is to Zúñiga. In his *Annotationes contra Erasmum Roterodamum*, written in defence of the Vulgate, Zúñiga claimed to have spent years reading the Old and New Testaments in Hebrew, Greek, and Latin (cf ASD IX-2 19). For the Complutensian Polyglot he made part of the interlinear Latin version of the Septuagint and collated Greek manuscripts of the Gospels with Vulgate manuscripts. He began to collect notes on Erasmus' New Testament as soon as a copy reached him in 1516; his first public attack came in 1520 with his *Annotationes contra Erasmum Roterodamum*, to which Erasmus replied in the *Apologia ad annotationes Stunicae* (October 1521). On Zúñiga's education and his relations with Erasmus see H.J. de Jonge's Introduction to the *Apologia* in ASD IX-2, especially 14–34, and Bentley *Humanists* 196–208; for a general account see *Contemporaries* II 348–9 (López Zúñiga). For the point at issue here see ASD IX-2 166 and 167 46n and 57n.
9 Ie the *Annotationes contra Erasmum Roterodamum* (cf n8 above)
10 Zúñiga's proposed emendation changed only the personal ending (from -ται to -το) but failed to make the change in the prefix (from ἐλ- to ἐνε-), necessary for the imperfect. In the *Apologia* Erasmus commented that every schoolboy with nothing more than elementary Greek would know better (ASD IX-2 166:59; but see De Jonge's note on line 57).
11 Ie a present tense in the subordinate clause ('when there is no law') could argue an original present tense in the main clause.
12 ἐλογεῖτο ... mistaken] Added in *1535*
13 For Chrysostom see *Hom in Rom* 10.1 PG 60 475; for Theophylact *Expos in Rom* 5:13 PG 124 404D. In both cases, however, the Migne text reads ἐλλογεῖται, though for Theophylact ἐλλογεῖτο is noted as a variant.
14 Jerome *Commentarius in epistulam ad Ephesios* 1 (on 2:1) PL 26 (1883) 495C–496A. Jerome distinguishes παράπτωμα (*delictum*) as the 'beginning' of sin, the silent thought conceived; ἁμαρτία (*peccatum*) as the act completed. Throughout this chapter Erasmus followed the Vulgate in translating παράπτωμα by *delictum*, ἁμαρτία by *peccatum*, except in verse 15, where from *1516* he translated παράπτωμα by *peccatum*.

5:14 [ER *ad similitudinem* 'after the likeness'[1]]

[VG] *in similitudinem* 'unto the likeness'; ἐν ὁμοιώματι, that is, 'in the likeness,' not 'unto the likeness of the transgression of Adam.' This[2] phrase, 'unto the likeness,' can belong either to the previous words, 'death reigned [...] in the likeness,'[3] or to the more immediate phrase, 'those who have not sinned in the likeness.'[4]

Origen[5] and Ambrose and even[6] Augustine, in the eleventh chapter of the first book *On the Merits and Remission of Sins* and again[7] in Letter 89, indicate that there were two ways of reading this passage.[8] One is: 'Death reigned also over those who sinned in the likeness of Adam.' And Origen seems to regard this as the better reading, since he places it first, as does Ambrose also. The second reading, which he indicates is found in several manuscripts,[9] is: 'Death reigned from Adam even over those who did not sin.' The meaning of the first reading, in which the negative is omitted, is that death reigned not only over Adam but also over all who sinned after his example. The second reading has a double sense. The first is[10] that death reigned not only over Adam and over those who sinned after his example, but over those also who either had not sinned, or at least had not sinned as gravely as Adam. The second sense is[11] that death reigned also over those who had not sinned; it reigned, however, not because of their offences but in the likeness of the transgression of Adam, that is, just as though they themselves also had transgressed like Adam.[12]

Since [Paul] has already[13] said elsewhere, 'God has confined all things under sin and all have sinned and lack the glory of God' [Rom 3:23], how does he now say, 'Certain ones have not sinned?' But they had not sinned after his likeness, that is, not so mortally [and] not after receiving a commandment – which is, properly speaking, transgression. For sin was deservedly imputed to Adam, since what he ought to follow, what avoid, had been prescribed for him. But before the law of Moses, sin was not imputed, that is, it did not seem right that it should be imputed, because there was no law that prohibited sin. It should be added that the word here is not ὁμοίωσις but ὁμοίωμα, which suggests a 'resembling' rather than a 'resemblance,'[14] so that you understand that those who sin are, in this [very] respect, like their sinning parents. Paul used the same word [ὁμοίωμα] a little earlier, 'in the likeness of the image of man.'[15]

I am not unaware that some relate this whole passage to original sin.[16] I am not indeed totally opposed to them, but I thought it best to point out the other interpretation as well – which Ambrose did not completely overlook,[17] and which[18] Origen follows almost solely.[19] Similarly[20] he whose scholia we read under the name of Jerome,[21] for so he speaks – for when he had set forth [his view] that those who did not sin in the likeness of Adam were those who sinned before the law of Moses, he explains what he means in these words: 'These are those who did not sin after the likeness of the transgression of Adam; they transgressed the natural law, and not, as Adam, a command.' Then soon he adds: 'For just as Adam, the first to transgress the command of God, is an example for those who wish[22] to transgress the law of God, so Christ, who has embraced the will of the Father, is an example for those who desire to imitate him.'[23] But why pursue this, when, as I said,[24] he interprets the whole chapter as referring

to sins that people commit in imitation of the first parent? But if someone
were to bring forward the example of the Virgin, the ancients freed no one
from sin entirely, except Christ alone; if [the example of] infants, Paul does
not appear to be concerned with them here, and this was not a point at
issue in his day, when it was not yet the tradition to baptize infants.[25] We
should[26] see rather to this, that we do not hate the Pelagians too much;
not because I should not wish the opinion of those who deny original sin
to be condemned, but because I should not like this [issue] to be brought
in artificially on whatever occasion, when there is no need – whether because we take pleasure in subtle discussions on this issue, or in order that
we, too, like astronomers who extricate themselves from many difficulties
with the epicycles they have devised,[27] might return with studied purpose
constantly to this κρησφύγετον [place of refuge] from the point at issue.
Unless[28] perhaps we allow ourselves to twist the words of Scripture in any
way at all to gain a victory in disputing with an adversary who must be
vanquished rather than taught. This Jerome appears at times to do in his
struggle against Jovinian; so on occasion does Augustine, and sometimes[29]
also Ambrose.[30] I should[31] have said these things, I say, not because I favour
those who deny original sin, but because I should like no violence, if possible, to be done to divine Scripture. Rather, from the very sequence of the
argument let us weigh carefully what Paul intended, considering[32] what
the issue is here, whence he began, where he is going, and whether it is
likely that he wished immediately to reveal to the gentiles this mystery,
which today also is believed more than understood – common sense, no
doubt, protesting. But[33] in vain do some slanderously charge that with this
annotation I seem to overthrow original sin,[34] when I openly profess and
affirm it in so many places in my writings.[35] But I believe this passage is
more agreeably expounded in terms of the personal sins committed by the
descendants of Adam – not that I would prejudge the view of anyone.

1 after the likeness] First in 1519; in 1516, *in similitudine* 'in the likeness'
2 This ... 'unto the likeness'] Added in 1522; previously, 'It.' In the preceding
   sentence, LB adds to the Greek quotation the words τῆς παραβάσεως 'Αδάμ
   'of the transgression of Adam'; they are not in the lifetime editions.
3 in the likeness'] Added in 1527
4 in the likeness'] Added in 1527
5 Origen ... double sense.] Added in 1519, but with the exceptions noted
   below (nn6 and 7)
6 and even ... *Sins*] Added in 1522
7 and again ... 89] Added in 1535
8 For Origen see *Comm in Rom* 5.1 PG 14 1018A–1019B; for Ambrosiaster *Comm
   in Rom* 5:14 (2–4); for Augustine *De peccatorum meritis et remissione et de
   baptismo parvulorum* 1.11.13 PL 44 116–17, and *Epistulae* 157.3.19 CSEL 44

467ff. Origen, Ambrosiaster, and Augustine are among the most important witnesses attesting that this text was read without the negative. Modern scholars, on the basis of the overwhelming consensus of the Greek witnesses and of the better sense, accept only the reading with the negative. See Michel 139; Cranfield I 283 n1.

9 Cf Origen *Comm in Rom* 5.1 PG 14 1019A.

10 The first is] Erasmus returns here, after the *1519* addition (cf n5), to the original *1516* text, which proceeded to explain the significance of the two ways of construing the phrase 'in the likeness,' taking the second construction first. Consequently, in *1516*, in place of 'The first is' and (below) 'The second sense is' (as in *1519*), Erasmus had written: 'According to the second reading the sense will be [that death reigned not only] ... according to the first, this will be the sense [that death reigned also].'

11 The second sense is] Cf the preceding note.

12 Adam] In *1516* only there followed here the sentence: 'But I prefer the previous reading as less forced.'

13 already] First in *1522*. Previously, 'for': 'For [Paul] has said ...'

14 Latin *assimilatio ... similitudo*. Cf n15 below. Modern scholars understand ἐπὶ τῷ ὁμοιώματι as meaning 'in the same way as' or 'just as.' See ὁμοίωμα in BAG; J. Schneider in G. Kittel *Theological Dictionary of the New Testament* trans and ed G.W. Bromiley, 10 vols (Grand Rapids, MI 1964–76) V (1967) 195; Michel 139; Cranfield I 283.

15 Rom 1:23, on which see the annotation 'into the likeness of the image,' where also Erasmus prefers *assimilatio* (translated there as 'representing') to *similitudo*

16 So for example Augustine *De peccatorum meritis et remissione et de baptismo parvulorum* 1.11.13 PL 44 116 and, later, Thomas Aquinas *Super Rom lect* cap 5, lectio 4.428

17 See Ambrosiaster *Comm in Rom* 5:14, especially section 2, where Ambrosiaster notes that death reigned over those who sinned after Adam's example, but did not reign over all, because some had not sinned after the likeness of Adam. On this reading the negative is omitted, so that the reference is to 'those [only] who sinned after the likeness of Adam.'

18 and which ... solely] Added in *1519*

19 Origen *Comm in Rom* 5.1 PG 14 1018B–C. Like Ambrosiaster, Origen is discussing the text without the negative, and explains 'likeness' in relation to both birth and education: 'They have in themselves a likeness of Adam's transgression assumed not only from seed, but from education.'

20 Similarly ... baptize infants.] Added in *1527*, with the exception noted below (n24)

21 See the annotation on 5:12 ('in whom [or, in which] all have sinned') n22.

22 wish ... those who] These words do not appear in LB, omitted perhaps inadvertently. They are present in the editions of both *1527* and *1535*.

23 Pseudo-Jerome (on Rom 5:14) Souter III 9:1–7

24 as I said] Added in *1535*. Cf the annotation on 5:12 ('in whom [or, in which] all have sinned') and nn22 and 23.

25 On the examples cited here of the Virgin and infants, see Thomas Aquinas, who, to demonstrate that the sin referred to in this passage was not actual sin

but original sin, brought forward the examples of the just and of children; the latter had committed no actual sins, the former no mortal sins, hence it was through original sin that they sinned in the likeness of Adam's transgression (cf n16 above). On the question of the sinlessness of Mary see the annotation on 5:12 ('in whom [or, in which] all have sinned') n69. On Erasmus' view of the baptism of infants, see Payne *Erasmus: His Theology* 177–8. In the *De concordia* Erasmus argues, against the Anabaptists, that the practice of baptizing infants probably dates back to apostolic times, since children are no doubt implied where families are said to have been baptized in eg 1 Cor 1:16; Acts 10:24, 44–8, and 16:34 (ASD V-3 311:889–312:903).

26 We should ... point at issue.] First in *1519*. In *1516* (following the words above, 'Ambrose did not completely overlook'): 'And theologians should see to this, that they do not dislike Pelagius too much, and embrace too willingly that original sin, whether because they take pleasure in subtle discussions thereon, or, like astronomers through the epicycles they have devised, they, too, extricate themselves from many difficulties through original sin.'

27 Erasmus makes the same point with the same analogy in the *Responsio ad annotationes Lei* LB IX 214C. According to Ptolemy (c 140 AD) a planet revolves at a constant velocity in a smaller circle (an epicycle) whose center, in turn, revolves in a larger circle (the deferent) with the earth at its center. See Thomas S. Kuhn *The Copernican Revolution* (Cambridge, MA 1957) 59–69.

28 Unless ... Augustine] Added in *1519*, except that 'on occasion' was added in *1527*

29 and sometimes ... Ambrose] Added in *1535*

30 In the *Ratio* also, Erasmus cites these three, and Bede as well, as ancient authors who twisted Scripture to make a point, and gives examples from each (Holborn 287–90). In *Ecclesiastes* III LB V 1028C–D Erasmus censures Jerome again for his interpretation, in his work against Jovinian, of 1 Cor 7:32–4; for the allusion see *Adversus Jovinianum* 1.13 PL 23 (1883) 241A–C and *Adversus Helvidium de Mariae virginitate perpetua* 20 PL 23 (1883) 213D–214A.

31 I should ... Scripture.] First in *1519*. In *1516*, 'I should not have said this because I deny original sin, but because I should like no violence to be done to divine Scripture.'

32 considering ... going] Added in *1519*

33 But ... anyone.] The remainder of the annotation was added in *1527*.

34 For Erasmus' critics, in particular, Lee, Zúñiga, and Titelmans, see the annotation on 5:12 ('in whom [or, in which] all have sinned') nn2 and 40.

35 See the annotation on 5:12 ('in whom [or, in which] all have sinned') n81.

5:14 [ER *typum illius futuri* 'the type[1] of him who was to come']
[VG] *forma futuri* 'the figure of the one to come'; τύπος τοῦ μέλλοντος, that is, a 'figure (or, a type)[2] of the one to be,' that is, of Christ who was to come, so that[3] the futurity expressed is relative not to the time in which Paul was writing this, but [to the time of] Adam who preceded Christ, and of whom he was a type. With this sort of expression he wrote to the Colossians on the question of sabbaths and new moons, which he said 'are a shadow of things about to be.'[4] Now for Paul such things were not about to be, but were

present. Origen points out that this can also refer to the condition of the coming age,[5] but this idea seems to me somewhat forced, though you may indeed call it subtle. Adam, then, was the form and type of Christ. And yet, this figure carries a reversal and is[6] an analogy rather than a similitude.[7] For as [Adam] was the originator of sinning and dying, so [Christ] was the leader and author of innocence and immortality. Accordingly, Origen has elegantly written (and Ambrose[8] has followed him), 'Generically alike, specifically contrary': generically, in that as from Adam, so from Christ, something has flowed down to all; specifically, in that from Adam [came] death and sin; from Christ innocence and life.[9] Moreover *forma* is in Greek τύπος, which means a kind of exemplar from which another 'likeness' is made. The words τοῦ μέλλοντος [of that to come] can, however, also be taken as neuters, in a general sense, to refer not to the later Adam but to the actual sin of anyone at all who imitates the parent Adam. For he provided for his descendants the example of sinning. I have shown what sense can be gathered from the Greek words; the wise and prudent reader will follow what he judges to be best.

I should add that in this passage the Translator renders the same Greek word, πολλοί, sometimes as 'more,' sometimes as 'many.'[10] Origen thinks it stands for 'all,' to correspond better to 'one.' And truly, where there are 'all,' there are also 'many.'[11]

1 the type ... to come] The translation from 1519. In 1516 Erasmus retained the Vulgate.
2 type] From 1519; in 1516, *opus* 'work' – perhaps a printer's mistake
3 so that ... type of Christ] Added in 1519
4 Col 2:16–17
5 Origen *Comm in Rom* 5.1 PG 14 1019C–1021B. Origen wonders how Adam, who brought sin and death into the world, can be a type of Christ – unless we understand him to be a type in reverse, inasmuch as Christ brought righteousness and life. But Origen continues the discussion by quoting, as Erasmus does here, from Colossians, adding 'subtle' interpretations: if the 'future' refers to the coming of Christ, then the 'new moons,' for example, are Christ and the apostles; if to the coming age, the 'everlasting years' of eternity.
6 and is ... similitude] Added in 1527
7 For the distinction between *similitudo* and *analogia* as forms of argument see Quintilian 5.11.22 and 5.11.34; see also *Ecclesiastes* II LB V 926C–928A for Erasmus' definitions.
8 and Ambrose ... him] Added in 1519
9 Origen *Comm in Rom* 5.2 PG 14 1022A; Ambrosiaster *Comm in Rom* 5:14 (7) and 5:15 (1a). Erasmus reports rather than quotes Origen; Ambrosiaster makes the point only in a general way.
10 The Greek πολλοί, found in 5:15 (twice: 'many died,' 'abounded unto many'), 5:16 ('many trespasses'), 5:19 (twice: 'many made sinners,' 'many made righteous'), Erasmus consistently translates by the Latin *multi* 'many.' The

Vulgate, too, translates the word as *multi* in all of these cases except the second in 5:15, where *plures* is found. *Plures* 'more' (comparative of *multi*), when used of a great number, can also have the sense of 'many' (see *multus* II B 2 in L&S).

11 Origen *Comm in Rom* 5.1 PG 14 1006B–C; cf 1023C and 1030B. See CWE 42 35 n16. Erasmus appeals to Origen's 'explanation of the mystery' in *Responsio ad annotationes Lei* LB IX 215B.

5:16 [ER *et non sicut per unum qui peccaverat* 'and not as through the one who had sinned']

[VG] *et non sicut per unum peccatum* 'and not as through the one sin.' The Greek is somewhat obscure, καὶ οὐχ ὡς δι᾽ ἑνὸς ἁμαρτήσαντος τὸ δώρημα, that is, 'and not as through the one who sinned the gift.'[1] For one may translate it literally thus, and additional words must be understood, as also the scholia of the Greeks suggest: 'And not as through the one who sinned (understand: death entered), so through the one came the gift,' that is, not in the same way.[2] For from one sin, all die; but from many sins, all are justified through the one. While the printed texts[3] read 'through one sin,' Ambrose reads 'sinner,' not 'sin,'[4] δι᾽ ἑνὸς ἁμαρτήσαντος, that is, 'through one who sinned.'[5] From[6] Theophylact's interpretation, one can conjecture that he read this way.[7] Chrysostom[8] certainly so reads, although he goes on to interpret ἑνός as [one] sin: τὸ μὲν κρῖμα ἐξ ἑνὸς εἰς κατάκριμα 'the judgment from one to condemnation,' since there follows [in the biblical texts]: τὸ δὲ χάρισμα ἐκ πολλῶν παραπτωμάτων 'but the gift, from many sins.' When [Chrysostom] says 'one sin,' he means the sin of Adam; when he says 'many sins,' he means the others that each person adds on his own.[9]

1 To the cue phrase add:
   ER *venerat mors, ita donum* 'came death, so the gift'
   VG *ita et donum* 'so also the gift'
2 Cf Pseudo-Oecumenius *Comm in Rom* 5:16 PG 118 425C.
3 Latin, *vulgati codices*; for this as 'printed books' see Chomarat *Grammaire et rhétorique* I 487.
4 Ambrosiaster *Comm in Rom* 5:16
5 The reading ἁμαρτήσαντος 'sinner' is supported by the majority of Greek and Latin manuscripts and is the more difficult reading. Several Greek and Latin manuscripts witness to ἁμαρτήματος 'sin.' See Tischendorf II 389 16n; Wordsworth and White II 87 16n; and Cranfield I 286 n3.
6 From ... way.] This sentence was added in *1519*.
7 Theophylact *Expos in Rom* 5:16 PG 124 405C: 'Will not the gift of God be as great as the condemnation through the one who sinned?'
8 Chrysostom ... on his own.] Added in *1527*
9 Chrysostom *Hom in Rom* 10.2 PG 60 476: 'Lest you suppose, when you hear of Adam, that his sin alone has been taken away, [Paul] says that many sins have been taken away.'

5:16 [ER *nam condemnatio quidem ex uno delicto* 'for the condemnation,[1] indeed, from the one trespass']

[VG] *nam iudicium ex uno* 'for the judgment from one.' 'From one' does not refer to the person of Adam,[2] but to sin – so that[3] you must supply παραπτώματος [transgression], to which the subsequent words 'from many [sins]' correspond. The sense then is: For the judgment, indeed, [came] from the one sin unto condemnation; but the gift, from many sins unto justification. And yet at this point all interpreters agree. Augustine,[4] [writing] to Valerius *On Marriage and Lust*, in the second book, chapter 27, and again[5] in Letter 89, clearly affirms: One must understand 'from one sin,' not 'from one man,' to correspond to what follows, 'but from many offences, grace,' so that we understand that the one sin sufficed to condemn the whole human race, but that the one grace sufficed to obliterate all sins.[6] He makes the same point in the first book *Against Julian the Pelagian*.[7] Again[8] in the book *On the Merits and the Remission of Sins*, book 1, chapter 11: For there follows, 'but from many offences, grace.'[9]

> 1 the condemnation ... trespass] First in *1519*; in *1516*, 'for the judgment indeed from one' (cf the Vulgate)
> 2 person of Adam] First in *1527*; from *1516–1522*, 'person of Christ'
> 3 so that ... παραπτώματος] Added in *1519*
> 4 Augustine ... *the Pelagian*.] Added in *1519*, with the exception in n5 below
> 5 and again ... Letter 89] Added in *1535*
> 6 Cf Augustine *De nuptiis et concupiscentia* 2.27.46 PL 44 463; *Epistulae* 157.3.12 CSEL 44 460:18–27.
> 7 Cf Augustine *Contra Julianum* 1.6.22 PL 44 655–6.
> 8 Again ... grace.'] Added in *1535*
> 9 Augustine *De peccatorum meritis et remissione et de baptismo parvulorum* 1.12.15 PL 44 117: ' "From one" [Paul] says "unto condemnation." What "one" if not "one sin"? This becomes clear when he adds "but from many offences, grace ..." '

5:16 [ER *donum autem ex multis delictis* 'but the gift, from many trespasses']

[VG] *gratia ex multis delictis* 'grace from[1] many trespasses'; [The Translator] had just translated χάρισμα correctly as 'gift'; now he translates it incorrectly as 'grace,' unless we suppose that 'grace' and 'gift' are entirely the same.

> 1 from many trespasses] Added to the lemma in *1519*. In *1516* the cue phrase was simply 'grace however.'

5:17 [ER *qui exuberantiam gratiae et doni iustitiae accipiunt* 'who receive abundance of grace and of the gift of righteousness']

[VG] *abundantiam gratiae et donationis et iustitiae accipientes* 'receiving the abundance of grace, and of the gift, and of righteousness.'[1] We must read 'of the gift of righteousness,' without the conjunction, so that you understand the gift to be righteousness itself: καὶ τῆς δωρεᾶς δικαιοσύνης [and of the gift of righteousness]. Thus there is no need for that distinction of Thomas, who explains the difference in grace, gift, and righteousness.[2] And yet[3] Ambrose adds the conjunction, like our Vulgate reading 'and of righteousness'; but I[4] think there is a mistake in the codex, for his exposition contains no hint of it.[5] Certainly Chrysostom and Theophylact agree with me.[6]

1 The sequence of the annotations at this point shifted somewhat in various editions. In 1516 the order was 1/ 'the Law, however, entered in'; 2/ 'grace over-abounded'; 3/ 'receiving the abundance of grace, and of the gift, and of righteousness.' 1519 began with 4/ 'just as, then, through the trespass of one, unto all' and continued with 3, 1, and 2. In 1522 and 1527 the order was 4, 3, 1, 2, to which 5/ 'for just as through the disobedience of one man, many have been made sinners' was added. In 1535 the order was 3, 4, 5, 1, 2.

2 Thomas Aquinas *Super Rom lect* cap 5 lectio 5.441: ' "Grace" refers to the forgiveness of sins; "gift" to the gifts of graces, which move us towards the good; "righteousness" to the rectitude of works.'

3 And yet ... righteousness] Added in 1519

4 but I ... with me] Added in 1527

5 Ambrosiaster *Comm in Rom* 5:17. The texts printed in CSEL 81 read 'who receive the abundance of grace and of righteousness,' but a footnote cites the reading of one manuscript that, like the Vulgate, reads 'of grace and of the gift and of righteousness'; cf CSEL 81/1 183:4n. Ambrosiaster comments, '... much more will grace reign through the abundance of the gift of God unto life through the one Jesus Christ'; cf 5:17 (2).

6 Chrysostom *Hom in Rom* 10.2. Chrysostom's exposition, too, speaks only of 'grace and righteousness'; see PG 60 476–7. For Theophylact see *Expos in Rom* 5:17 PG 124 405D. Theophylact comments: '... we who have received the abundance and the copious plenty of grace and have been justified ...'

5:18 [ER *itaque sicut per unius delictum propagatum est malum in omnes homines* 'accordingly,[1] just as through the trespass of one, evil spread to all']

[VG] *igitur sicut per unius delictum in omnes homines* 'just as,[2] then, through the trespass of one, unto all.' This is an abbreviated statement and needs something supplied, namely, what was [the trespass and the gift] each brought in. 'Accordingly, just as, through the trespass of one, sin crept in for the condemnation, so through the righteousness of one, salvation came in for the justification of all.' In almost the same way Theophylact supplies[3] in his exposition the words the sentence lacks.[4] See[5] Augustine, Letter 89.

1 accordingly ... all] The translation from 1519. In 1516 Erasmus followed the Vulgate.

2 just as ... Theophylact] Added in 1519 as a new annotation. For the sequence see preceding annotation, n1. 'Unto all' was added to the cue phrase
in 1527.
3 supplies ... lacks] Added in 1527
4 Theophylact *Expos in Rom* 5:18 PG 124 405D–408B
5 See ... Letter 89] Added in 1535. See Augustine *Epistulae* 157.3.13 CSEL 44
469. In the course of the exposition Augustine rephrases and supplies a verb
'... all come to the grace of justification ...'

5:19 [ER *quemadmodum enim per inobedientiam unius hominis peccatores
constituti fuimus multi* 'for as through the disobedience of one man
many of us were made sinners']
[VG] *sicut enim per inobedientiam unius hominis peccatores constituti sunt
multi* 'for[1] just as through the disobedience of one man, many have been
made sinners.' It does not affect the sense that in our Latin texts the third
person is used, '[many] have been made,' as also in some Greek codices,
κατεστάθησαν, although in most Greek codices the reading is κατεστάθημεν
[we were made] as in the Aldine edition.[2]

1 for ... Aldine edition] Added in 1522; for its position in 1522 and subsequent
editions see the annotation on 5:17 ('receiving the abundance of grace ...') n1.
2 Zúñiga attacked Erasmus on his use of the first person here. For Erasmus'
response see *Apologia ad annotationes Stunicae* ASD IX-2 168. On Zúñiga see
annotation on 5:13 ('was not imputed') n8, and on the correct reading here
H.J. de Jonge in ASD IX-2 168:78n and 80n. For the Aldine edition, see the
annotation on 11:6 ('otherwise grace is no longer grace') n10.

5:20 [ER *ceterum lex obiter subiit* 'but the Law stole in by the way']
[VG] *lex autem subintravit* 'the Law,[1] however, entered in'; παρεισῆλθεν,
that is to say, 'crept in by the way' – because of the Greek preposition,
which is added usually with a derogatory sense.[2]

1 See the annotation on 5:17 ('receiving the abundance of grace ...') n1 for the
sequence of this annotation.
2 Ie the preposition παρά, added as a prefix; see παρά G IV 1 in LSJ.

5:20 [ER *magis exuberavit gratia* 'grace came forth more abundantly']
[VG] *superabundavit gratia* 'grace[1] overabounded.' This is χάρις, not χάρισμα, that is, 'grace,' not 'gift.' But the Greeks sometimes take χάρις, that
is, 'grace,' in the sense of 'kindness.' But what[2] the Latin Translator has rendered *superabundavit*, in the Greek is ὑπερεπερίσσευσεν. This has the force,
not as when you say that a liquid 'abounds' to the extent that you pour off
what is not needed; but rather, it is as though to say it is overflowing very
much and beyond measure. For in Greek ὑπέρ lends emphasis in the same

way as the Latin *per*. Thus some people, using an idiom that is Greek but not at all Latin, say *superbenedictus* [over-blessed] for exceedingly blessed, or *superexcelsus* [over-exalted] for 'very highly exalted.'

1 See the annotation on 5:17 ('receiving the abundance of grace ...') n1 for the sequence of this annotation.
2 But what ... exalted.'] This remaining portion of the annotation was added in 1519.

5:21 [ER *ut quemadmodum regnaverat peccatum in morte* 'that as sin had reigned in death']
[VG] *ut sicut regnavit peccatum in morte* 'that[1] just as sin reigned in death';[2] Origen thinks that the devil can be denoted by the word 'death,' in this passage[3] as also in previous ones.[4] This is easier in Greek, where θάνατος [death] is masculine.[5] Ambrose thought the sense was to be related to the death of the soul.[6] Origen interprets it also of the death of the body, in debating the question of Enoch, who did not undergo death.[7]

When Paul says 'sin reigned in death,' ἐν τῷ θανάτῳ, it appears that he used the preposition ἐν [in] for εἰς [unto] – wrongly, for this phrase should be parallel to the one that follows, 'so that grace might reign through righteousness unto eternal life,' where he did not say ἐν ζωῇ αἰωνίῳ [in life eternal] but εἰς ζωὴν αἰώνιον [unto life eternal].

1 that ... αἰώνιον.] The entire annotation was added in 1519.
2 in death] The Vulgate printed in 1527 read *in mortem* 'unto death,' as in the immediately subsequent annotation. Wordsworth and White read *in morte* but cite substantial manuscript support for *in mortem* (II 88 21n).
3 Origen *Comm in Rom* 5.6 PG 14 1034B–1035A
4 See Origen *Comm in Rom* 5.1, 3 PG 14 1016D–1017B, 1028A, where the identification is implied.
5 In Latin, *mors* 'death' is feminine, making an identification with the masculine *diabolus* 'devil' grammatically more strained.
6 The point is not made in Ambrosiaster's commentary on this verse, but cf *Comm in Rom* 5:14 (4c–d) and 5:15 (1) – on which, see Schelkle 174.
7 Origen *Comm in Rom* 5.4 PG 14 1029C; cf 5.1 PG 14 1012A

5:21 [ER *in morte* 'in death']
[VG] *in mortem* 'unto death';[1] ἐν τῷ θανάτῳ, that is, 'in death,' meaning 'through death,' as I have shown above.[2]

1 This appeared as the final annotation in all editions except 1535, where it has the present position.
2 Erasmus has repeatedly indicated that the Greek ἐν in the New Testament may have the meaning of 'through.' See the annotation on 1:4 ('with power') and n8.

5:21 [ER *per Iesum Christum* 'through Jesus Christ']

[VG] *per Iesum Christum dominum nostrum* 'through[1] Jesus Christ our Lord.' 'Our Lord' is not added in this passage in the Greek [manuscripts] or in the old Latin copies, and though it is added in Ambrose, still, from his interpretation it cannot be ascertained that he read thus.[2] And yet in some Greek copies I have found 'our Lord' added – under the same circumstances, I suspect, as in the Latin, where the two words here have been transcribed from elsewhere.[3]

1 through ... elsewhere.] The entire annotation was added in *1519*. In all editions except *1535* this annotation preceded the note 'unto death' (see preceding annotation, n1).

2 Ambrosiaster *Comm in Rom* 5:21. While the full phrase 'through Jesus Christ our Lord' appears in the commentary in recensions α and β, in the γ recension we find only the abbreviated form 'through Christ.'

3 Tischendorf II 390 reads 'through Jesus Christ our Lord,' offering no variants.

CHAPTER 6

6:2 [ER *qui mortui sumus peccato* 'we who have died to sin']

[VG] *qui enim mortui sumus peccato* 'for we who have died to sin.' 'For' is superfluous. οἵτινες ἀπεθάνομεν,[1] that is, 'whoever of us have died' or 'we who have died to sin.' 'Sin' is in the dative case, not the ablative.[2] It is as though someone[3] were to address sin and say, 'I am dead to you, but I am alive to Christ.'[4]

> 1 LB adds here τῇ ἁμαρτίᾳ] 'to sin,' but without warrant from the editions 1516–1535.
> 2 Valla thought *peccato* an ablative – 'we who are dead *through* sin.' Cf *Annot in Rom* 6 (I 857).
> 3 someone . . . say] First in 1519; in 1516, 'he should say to sin'
> 4 This sentence was included in this annotation first in 1519. In 1516 it completed the annotation immediately below, 'shall we live in that.'

6:2 [ER *vivemus in eodem* 'shall we live in the same']

[VG] *vivemus in illo* 'shall we live in that'; ἐν αὐτῇ. 'In that very thing' or 'in the same' would be more precise.[1]

> 1 precise] In 1516 only there followed here the final sentence of the preceding annotation; see n2 there.

6:3 [ER *an ignoratis* 'do you not know']

[VG] *an ignoratis fratres* 'do you not know brothers.' 'Brothers' was added by the Translator or by a scribe.[1] ἢ ἀγνοεῖτε, that is, 'do you not know.' So,[2] indeed, read Origen and Ambrose;[3] and the oldest Latin codices, copied by hand, have the same.

> 1 or by a scribe] Added in 1519. The word is found in several Latin witnesses (Wordsworth and White II 88n), but Tischendorf (II 391 3n) cites no Greek witnesses.
> 2 So . . . same.] Added in 1519
> 3 Cf Origen *Comm in Rom* 5.7 PG 14 1037C–1038A and Ambrosiaster *Comm in Rom* 6:3.

6:3 [ER *baptizati sumus in Christum Jesum* 'we have been baptized into Christ Jesus'[1]]

[VG] *baptizati sumus in Christo Jesu* 'we have been baptized in Christ Jesus.' In Greek this is 'into Christ Jesus' and 'into death,'[2] εἰς Χριστὸν Ἰησοῦν and εἰς τὸν θάνατον. Although this preposition can be used in more than one way in Greek, still,[3] 'into Christ' would be more suitable here because through baptism we are grafted into the mystical body of Christ.

1 into Christ Jesus] First in 1519; in 1516, 'in Christ Jesus.' In the *Responsio ad collationes* LB IX 993C Erasmus defends both translations.
2 In 1516 Erasmus followed the Vulgate in translating the last clause of the sentence 'have been baptized in his death' (*in morte*) but in 1519 changed to 'into his death' (*in mortem*).
3 still ... Christ] Added in 1527

6:5 [ER *nam si insititii facti sumus* 'for if we have become engrafted']
[VG] *si enim complantati facti sumus* 'for if we have become planted together'; σύμφυτοι, that is, 'those grafted on,' and 'partakers.' For there is an allusion to the ingrafting of a shoot, which corresponds to union with the body of Christ. For just[1] as a shoot plucked from its own tree partakes of the sap of the tree into which it is grafted, so those who are grafted into the body of Christ through baptism become sharers in all his goods. But it is possible that the prefix συν- [together] refers to the Jews and gentiles united together into the one Christ.

1 For just ... the one Christ.] Added in 1519. Later, in his *Responsio ad collationes* LB IX 993D, Erasmus defended his choice of 'ingraft' rather than 'plant together' as evoking more precisely the image intended of the shoot that cannot live without the tree into which it is grafted.

6:5 [ER *nimirum et resurrectionis* 'surely also of the resurrection']
[VG] *simul et resurrectionis* 'together also of the resurrection.' The Greek is ἀλλὰ καὶ τῆς ἀναστάσεως, that is, 'therefore also of the resurrection.' The Translator seems to have read ἅμα [together] in place of ἀλλά. But ἀλλά is a conjunction implying argument, which[1] I have translated 'surely.' 'We shall be also of the resurrection'[2] can be taken in two senses, either that we shall belong to the resurrection, or that we shall be planted together in the likeness of his resurrection. I have followed the former interpretation, and have translated with the addition of a word: 'We shall be partakers also of the resurrection.'

1 which ... resurrection.'] This remaining portion of the annotation was added in 1519.
2 A literal translation of the Greek of the last clause; cf AV, omitting the italicized words.

6:8 [ER *quod et vivemus cum illo* 'that we shall also live with him']
[VG] *quia simul etiam vivemus cum illo* 'that we[1] shall also live together with him.' The Greek is συζήσομεν αὐτῷ 'we shall live with him.' But the Translator has conveyed the sense well.

1 that we ... him] Until 1527 the cue phrase for this annotation cited the first part of this verse rather than the second:

ER *quod si mortui sumus* 'but if we have died'
VG *si autem mortui sumus* 'if, however, we have died'

6:9 [ER *excitatus a mortuis* 'raised from the dead']
[VG] *resurgens a mortuis* 'rising again from the dead.' ἐγερθείς, that is,[1] 'raised' or 'who rose again from the dead,' for the participle is in the past tense. And yet elsewhere he uses participles of this sort.[2]

> 1 that is] First in *1519*; in *1516*, 'past [tense].' After ἐγερθείς LB adds ἐκ νεκρῶν, but without warrant from the editions *1516–1535*.
> 2 Cf eg the annotation on 4:21 ('knowing full well').

6:9 [ER *non amplius dominatur* 'no longer rules']
[VG] *ultra non dominabitur* 'shall no more rule'; οὐκέτι κυριεύει, that is, 'no longer rules,' in the present tense, not future, as in[1] the clause '[Christ] does not die.'[2] He is giving the reason why [Christ] does not die, for through him the lordship of death was taken away. Now these words relate not only to Christ, but also to the mystical body of Christ; and the verbs in the present tense better accommodate this sense. So reads[3] Theophylact,[4] and the exposition of Chrysostom is not out of harmony [with it].[5] For he points out that [the phrase] 'he does not die' means that he is immortal; and 'death no longer rules over him' means that death has no authority over him who, by dying, brought forth immortality for himself and his own.

> 1 as in … this sense] Added in *1527*
> 2 Erasmus agreed with the Vulgate in rendering in the present tense the clause that immediately precedes the clause under discussion:
> > ER *non amplius moritur* 'no longer dies'
> > VG *iam non moritur* 'does not henceforth die'
> 3 So reads … his own.] Added in *1535*. In 1529 Titelmans had challenged the present tense here (*Responsio ad collationes* LB IX 993E).
> 4 Theophylact *Expos in Rom* 6:9 PG 124 412C–D
> 5 Chrysostom *Hom in Rom* 11.2 PG 60 485

6:10 [ER *nam quod mortuus fuit* 'for that which he died']
[VG] *quod enim mortuus est* 'for that which he died'; ὃ γὰρ ἀπέθανε. Lorenzo [Valla] corrects in this manner: 'for that which died,' in the neuter.[1] For in Greek the word ὅ is a relative pronoun [what], not a conjunction [because]. And[2] certainly Hilary reads as Lorenzo wishes in *On the Trinity*, book 9 – according to the witness of the old codices;[3] he refers 'died' to the human body [of Christ], and 'lives' to the divine nature. But in my opinion[4] it is better to refer ἀπέθανε simply[5] to Christ, so that the sense is 'that very thing which Christ died, he died once only, and that to sin, but that which he lives' – that is to say, that death which he died, he died to sin, and the life

which he lives, he lives to God. Now in accordance[6] with the punctuation of the Greek, the comma must be placed after ὃ γὰρ ἀπέθανε, so that what follows, 'he died once,' refers to sin, a word which, like 'God,' is in the dative case here, not ablative.[7] In the same way he said in the Epistle to the Galatians, chapter 2, ὃ δὲ νῦν ζῶ ἐν σαρκί, ἐν πίστει ζῶ, that is, 'but that which I now live in the flesh, I live in faith' [2:20]. But what, after all,[8] is the meaning if you read 'that which died' etc? Rather,[9] Paul is urging this, that just as Christ died once to sin and remains forever immortal, so we, having died once to sin, and having been reborn in him through baptism, should not thereafter fall back into sin. In this way the Translator is freed from the double solecism with which our Lefèvre charged him.[10]

1 Valla *Annot in Rom* 6 (I 857). Valla wished to clarify the Latin *quod*, which can mean either 'what' or 'because.' As a translation for the Greek ὅ it can only mean 'what,' 'that which' (neuter).

2 And ... divine nature.] Added in *1527*

3 Hilary *De Trinitate* 9.13 PL 10 292A. In Migne's text, Hilary reads with Erasmus *quod mortuus est*, but a footnote cites Hilary's reading in the form Valla has it, *quod mortuum est*.

4 in my opinion] Added in *1527*

5 simply] Added in *1527*

6 in accordance ... the Greek] Added in *1527*

7 Erasmus wished to correct the Vulgate punctuation (in a prevalent, if not, the preferred reading; see Wordsworth and White II 90 10n):
   ER *nam quod mortuus fuit, peccato mortuus fuit semel* 'for that which he died, he died to sin once'
   VG *quod enim mortuus est peccato, mortuus est semel* 'for that which he died to sin, he died once'
   The Vulgate *peccato* can be translated also as an ablative: 'for that which he died through sin.'

8 after all] Added in *1519*

9 Rather] Added in *1519*

10 In his 1512 edition Lefèvre had translated *quod mortuum est peccato, mortuum est semel* 'that which died to sin, died once.' In this translation *mortuum*, a neuter participle, agrees with the neuter *quod* (cf *Pauli epistolae* fol 4 recto). Lefèvre claimed that the Vulgate committed a 'double barbarism' in writing *quod mortuus, mortuus est*; this, if read as 'that which died,' makes a masculine participle agree with the neuter *quod* (see *Pauli epistolae* fol 83 recto). In his 1517 edition, however, Lefèvre mentions no solecism and in fact follows the Vulgate rendering of this verse both in his translation and commentary; cf fol IIII (text), fol LXV (commentary). Lefèvre was no doubt influenced by Erasmus' reasoning in his *1516* annotation. This annotation is a good example of Erasmus' independent judgment, which here prefers the Vulgate rendering against the criticisms of two humanist interpreters.
   Titelmans evidently chose at this point to associate Erasmus with Valla and Lefèvre – inopportunely, as Erasmus points out, since here he agreed with neither (*Responsio ad collationes* LB IX 993E–F).

6:11 [ER *reputate vos ipsos mortuos* 'consider[1] that you yourselves (are) dead']
[VG] *existimate vos mortuos* 'judge yourselves dead'; ἑαυτούς, that is, 'you
yourselves,' which, though it appears quite often,[2] the Translator seems to
have disregarded. And[3] 'judge' in Greek is λογίζεσθε, which is a verb of
thinking, as Origen notes, for this is a matter which depends especially
on thought: as often as we think that we are dead along with Christ, the
desires of the flesh are checked and disappear.[4] Thus[5] 'consider' would be
more fitting, that is, 'observe,' and[6] 'hold before your eyes.'

    1 consider] First in 1527. Until then, Erasmus translated, with the Vulgate,
      existimate.
    2 Cf eg 4:19 and the annotation 'his body.'
    3 And ... disappear.] Added in 1519
    4 Cf Origen *Comm in Rom* 5.10 PG 14 1054C–1055A.
    5 Thus ... 'observe'] Added in 1527. Erasmus' translation was criticized by
      Titelmans, who thought *reputare* corresponded to the Greek ἀναλογίζεσθαι,
      not λογίζεσθαι, as here (*Responsio ad collationes* LB IX 994A–B). On *reputare* and
      existimare see the annotation on 4:3 ('and it was considered').
    6 and ... eyes'] Added in 1535

6:11 [ER *per Christum Jesum dominum nostrum* 'through[1] Christ Jesus our
Lord']
[VG] *in Christo Jesu* 'in Christ Jesus.' The Greek adds 'our Lord.'[2]

    1 through ... Lord] First in 1519; in 1516, 'in Christ Jesus our Lord'
    2 Though both Greek and Latin manuscripts are divided on the reading here
      (cf Tischendorf II 392 11n and Wordsworth and White II 90 11n) modern
      scholars regard 'our Lord' as a later addition; cf Metzger 513.

6:12 [ER *ut obediatis illi per cupiditates eius* 'that you might obey it through[1]
its desires']
[VG] *ut obediatis concupiscentiis eius* 'so that you obey its lusts'; εἰς τὸ
ὑπακούειν αὐτῇ ἐν ταῖς ἐπιθυμίαις αὐτοῦ, that is, 'to obey it in its lusts' –
the pronoun 'it' referring to sin, 'its' referring to the body.[2] And so you
understand: 'To obey sin through the affections of the body which incite us
to sin.'

    1 through] First in 1519; in 1516, 'in'
    2 To Titelmans, however, Erasmus admitted there was no difference in sense
      between his translation and the Vulgate (*Responsio ad collationes* LB IX 994B).

6:13 [ER *neque accommodetis* 'and do not lend']
[VG] *sed neque exhibeatis* 'but do not present'; μηδὲ παριστάνετε, that is,
'and do not present' or 'lend.'[1] 'But' is superfluous.

    1 For a more careful discussion of Latin equivalents for the Greek verb, see the
      annotation on 12:1 ('that you present your bodies').

6:17 [ER *gratia autem deo* 'but thanks (be) to God']
[VG] *gratias autem deo* 'but [let us give] thanks to God'; χάρις δὲ τῷ θεῷ, that is, 'but thanks to God,' with 'be' understood. Here[1] a certain man is furious, crying out that *diis gratia* 'thanks to the gods,' is a heathen expression, but that Christians say *deo gratias* 'thanks to God.'[2] Indeed, Christians once did speak in that way, understanding [the words] 'we give' or 'let us give,' but they were unskilled in letters. Certainly Paul has not followed that way of speaking, and what is gained by departing from his expression through a solecism that is, as it were, studied? The chant *deo gratias* is most pleasing to God not because of the solecism, but because of the piety of the singer. *Deo gratia* would be no less pleasing, if it were uttered with the same affection.

> 1 Here ... affection.] The remaining portion of this annotation was added in 1535.
>
> 2 The 'certain man' is Frans Titelmans; see *Responsio ad collationes* LB IX 994B–C.

6:18 [ER VG] *servi facti estis iustitiae* 'you have become servants to righteousness.' 'Righteousness' is in the dative case, ἐδουλώθητε τῇ δικαιοσύνῃ, that is, 'you have begun to be servants and bondmen to righteousness.'[1]

> 1 The dative is unambiguous in Greek, but in Latin the form *iustitiae* may be either dative or genitive – 'of righteousness' (cf AV).

6:19 [ER *humanum quiddam dico* 'I speak in a human sort of way']
[VG] *humanum dico* 'I speak the human thing'; ἀνθρώπινον λέγω. With this figure of speech, Paul frequently[1] softens what he seems, perhaps, to say somewhat harshly or inadvisedly – 'I speak according to man.'

> 1 Cf eg Rom 3:5 and Gal 3:15. See the annotation on Rom 3:5 ('is God unfair who inflicts wrath') and on 2 Cor 11:17 (*secundum dominum*).

6:19 [ER *serva immunditiae* 'servants to uncleanness']
[VG] *servire immunditiae* 'to serve uncleanness.' In Greek this is a noun, and more felicitous – δοῦλα, that is, 'servants,' or 'members "serving" ' and,[1] as it were, 'subject to.'

> 1 and ... 'subject to'] Added in 1519

6:20 [ER *liberi eratis iustitiae* 'you were free (in relation) to righteousness']
[VG] *liberi fuistis iustitiae* 'you have been free [in relation] to righteousness.' In the Greek, 'sin' here[1] is in the genitive, 'righteousness' in the dative, that is 'free from righteousness.'[2] And 'you were' is better than 'you have been' because[3] it is preceded by 'when you were.'[4]

> 1 Ie in the preceding clause:
>   ER VG *cum enim servi essetis peccati* 'when you were servants of sin'

2 Valla is uncertain whether the Greek dative should be translated by a Latin
dative or ablative; see *Annot in Rom* 6 (I 857). Erasmus retains the dative in
his translation, but writes the ablative ('free from righteousness') here in the
annotation.
3 because ... were'] Added in *1527*
4 So Valla *Annot in Rom* 6 (I 857)

6:22 [ER *finem autem vitam aeternam* 'but the end[1] everlasting life']
[VG] *finem vero vitam aeternam* '**and the end everlasting life.**' Lefèvre
d'Etaples reads 'unto eternal life.'[2] But in the emended codices I find
'eternal life' without a preposition, and the Greek and Latin manuscripts
agree, so that[3] [eternal life] is in apposition [to 'end']. I think[4] I should
point out to the reader that in this, and also in the[5] preceding passage
('the end of those things is death'), τέλος [end] can be taken in the sense
of a tribute or tax paid on our servitude to sin.[6] For the word ὀψώνια
[wages] soon follows – though Ambrose and Chrysostom[7] interpret it
differently.[8] It seems that ὀψώνιον is something given for the daily support of a soldier, while τέλος is a final remuneration by which he can
live on his own when he has been granted a discharge. Opposing[9] this
sense[10] is Chrysostom's assertion that when sin is mentioned, *obsonia* (that
is, 'wages') are named, but when eternal life is mentioned, a 'payment' is
not named.[11]

1 the end] First in *1519*; in *1516*, 'fruit.' Erasmus acknowledged this
as a 'printer's mistake'; *Apologia ad annotationes Stunicae* ASD IX-2
168:85–7.
2 Lefèvre *Pauli epistolae* fol 5 recto (translation); fol 83 verso (commentary)
3 so that ... apposition] Added in *1519*
4 I think ... discharge.] Added in *1522*, with the exceptions described in nn5
and 7 below
5 in the ... is death')] Added in *1527*, replacing *superioribus* 'in the above,'
part of the *1522* addition. The reference is to the previous verse, where
Erasmus followed the Vulgate translation: *nam finis illorum mors* 'for their
end is death.'
6 τέλος is used in classical Greek with a variety of meanings, including
'end,' 'result,' 'service rendered,' 'tax.' See LSJ. In the previous passage (6:21)
the τέλος would be a payment made to sin; in this passage (6:22) it would
be a payment made for eternal life – which is open to the objection of
Chrysostom (n11 below).
7 and Chrysostom] Added in *1527*
8 Ambrosiaster and Chrysostom both explain ὀψώνια simply as recompense,
though Chrysostom (and Origen, but not Ambrosiaster) appear to recognize
the military connotation of the word: Ambrosiaster *Comm in Rom* 6:23 (1);
Chrysostom *Hom in Rom* 12.1–2 PG 60 495–6; Origen *Comm in Rom* 6.6
PG 14 1067B–C.
9 Opposing ... named] Added in *1527*
10 Ie that τέλος in 6:22 can mean a final remuneration or reward

11 Chrysostom *Hom in Rom* 12.2 PG 60 496. Chrysostom stresses that eternal life is not a reward for our good works but comes solely from the grace of God.

6:23 [ER *etenim auctoramenta peccati mors* 'for the recompense of sin is death']

[VG] *stipendia enim peccati mors* 'for the wages of sin is death'; τὰ γὰρ ὀψώνια, that is, wages in kind. For soldiers were enticed by food and donatives or 'recompense,' as they are by far the most worthless kind of men – who indeed sell their lives for the sake of food and the belly – but [men] upon whom the Roman emperors once[1] bestowed virtually every badge of honor.[2] Ambrose[3] reads 'pay' and 'profit.'[4] What[5] Seneca had first called 'recompense' of vices he later calls the 'pay.'[6]

1 once] From *1519*; in *1516*, 'afterwards'
2 See the colloquies 'Military Affairs' (1523), and 'The Soldier and The Carthusian' (1532) in Thompson *Colloquies* 11–15, 127–33, where Erasmus makes a number of negative judgments on soldiers.
3 Ambrose ... profit.'] Added in *1522*
4 Ambrosiaster *Comm in Rom* 6:23 (1)
5 What ... 'pay.'] Added in *1535*. The addition reflects the discussion in *Responsio ad collationes* LB IX 994F–5E, where Erasmus defends *auctoramenta* against the Vulgate *stipendia* on the grounds that it is appropriate to the military metaphor and has essentially the same meaning as *stipendia*.
6 Cf Seneca *Epistulae morales* 69.4–5.

6:23 [ER *donum autem dei* 'but the gift of God']

[VG] *gratia autem dei* 'but the grace of God'; τὸ δὲ χάρισμα, that is, 'the gift.' The word is opposed to τὰ ὀψώνια [wages in kind] which is a low word, while the former is elevated.

CHAPTER 7

7:1 [ER *lex tantisper dominetur homini quoad ea vixerit* 'the Law rules a person just so long as it shall live']¹
[VG] *lex in homine dominatur quam diu vivit* 'the Law² rules over a person as long as it [or, he] lives.' It is not clear in the Latin whether we should understand 'as long as the person lives' or 'as long as the Law lives'; and there is the same ambiguity in the Greek words. I think the verb 'lives' should refer to 'Law' rather than to 'person'; and the words which follow [the clause] are the reason for my preference. One could avoid the ambiguity in this way: 'The Law rules a person as long as it³ shall live,' or more elegantly 'only while it lives.' After writing my version, I consulted Origen and found he had carefully observed that in making his comparison,⁴ Paul equated the Law with the husband, the person with the wife. Just as the wife is freed by the death of her husband, so a person who has previously been subject to the Law is freed when the Law is no longer in effect.⁵ He means⁶ that the Law is alive only so long as it is valid; it has died when it has ceased to have force. For the Greek word κυριεύει means not only 'rules,' but also 'has legal right and authority.'

It must be noted in passing that the illustration adduced concerns the woman, not the man, because among the Jews husbands had the right to leave their wives, but only death could free the women from the marital bond. There is no reason to conclude particularly from this passage that divorce was forbidden to Christians under all circumstances,⁷ for when [Paul] adds, 'I am speaking to those who know the Law,' he clearly indicates that he is not setting down a law concerning marriage for Christians but is drawing an analogy from the Mosaic law for purposes of illustration. Nor indeed is it necessary that what is introduced as an analogy should fit in all respects; it is enough if it fits the point it is intended to illustrate and confirm. The coming of Christ is compared in the Gospels to a man who breaks into a house at night,⁸ not because the coming of Christ is in every respect like that of a thief, but the two are alike only in this, that both come unexpectedly.

> 1 shall live] First in *1519*; in *1516*, *lex dominatur homini quamdiu vivit* 'the Law rules a person as long as it lives'
> 2 the Law ... unexpectedly.] This annotation, with the exception noted below (n6), was added in *1519*. The cue phrase, however, was printed in its present form first in *1535*. Previous editions had read *lex dominatur homini quam diu vivit* 'the Law rules a person as long as it [or, he] lives.' The Vulgate text printed in *1527* read as the *1535* cue phrase.

In this annotation we capitalize Law to refer to the Mosaic law. Erasmus' paraphrases on 7:1–4 reflect his awareness of the potential ambiguity of the term: the Mosaic law, Mosaic laws, any law; cf CWE 42 40–1.

3 In Latin *ea*, feminine pronoun modifying *lex*, as in Erasmus' version

4 Ie (in Rom 7:1–7) between the relationship of husband and wife on the one hand, and the Law and the baptized on the other

5 Cf Origen *Comm in Rom* 6.7: 'Do you not know that the Law rules over everyone who is bonded to it and serves it, just as a husband rules over his wife; and just as he rules throughout all his life the woman legally joined to him, so the Law rules a man who is under it as long as it is alive and has force.' Origen completes the comparison: 'Just as, if the man dies, the woman is free, so if the Law "dies," one is freed from it' (PG 14 1069D–1070A). For Origen see Schelkle 225. Cf also Lefèvre d'Etaples, whose allegorization of this passage possesses a strong mystical colour: the wife was the synagogue, bound to her husband Moses by the Mosaic law. The maidservant was the gentiles; she had no husband, but fornicated, serving idols, until she became the bride of Christ, to whom she was joined by the evangelical law (*Pauli epistolae* fols 83 verso–84 recto).

6 He means ... force.] Added in 1527

7 Erasmus had an intense interest in the subject of divorce, which he favoured as a solution of last resort to the many clandestine marriages of his time. See the annotation on 1 Cor 7:39 (*liberata est a lege, cui autem vult, nubat*). See also Emile V. Telle *Erasme de Rotterdam et le septième sacrement* (Geneva 1954) 205–23, 349–65; and Payne *Erasmus: His Theology* 121–5.

8 Cf Matt 24:42 and Luke 12:39.

7:2 [ER *viro obnoxia mulier* 'a woman subject to a husband']

[VG] *quae sub viro est* 'who is under a husband'; ἡ γὰρ ὕπανδρος γυνή, that is, 'subject to the husband,' as if you were to say *subviralis*.[1] And γυνή means both 'wife' and 'woman.'

> 1 Here Erasmus appears to be coining a word parallel to the Greek ὕπανδρος 'under' or 'subject to a husband.'

7:2 [ER *viventi viro alligata est per legem* 'she is bound through the law to her husband while he lives']

[VG] *vivente viro alligata est lege* 'the husband living, she is bound by law'; τῷ ζῶντι ἀνδρὶ δέδεται νόμῳ, that is, 'is bound to her living husband[1] by law' that is, 'through law.' The Greeks also call marriage or the 'right' of marriage a 'law,' as, immediately below, 'from the law of her husband.'

> 1 Erasmus justified his translation with the dative ('to her husband') against Titelmans' defence of the Vulgate's ablative absolute ('her husband being alive') on the grounds that a Greek dative can never be represented by an ablative absolute in Latin (*Responsio ad collationes* LB IX 995E–F).

7:3 [ER VG] *adultera vocabitur* 'shall[1] be called[2] an adulteress'; χρηματίσει. That[3] the verb is χρηματίσει [in the active], not χρηματίσεται [in the passive], is due to the character of the Greek idiom. For just as we say *audit pater, audit princeps,* [he hears (the name of) 'father,' he hears 'prince'] of one who is called a father or a prince, so the Greeks say χρηματίζει ῥήτωρ [he takes the name of orator] of one who professes to be an orator or is considered an orator. Luke uses this verb in Acts 11[4].

    1 shall ... χρηματίσει] The annotation was introduced with these words in 1522. For the remainder of the annotation in 1522 see n3 below.
    2 shall be called] In Erasmus' translation, first in 1527; in 1516, 1519, and 1522 Erasmus translated *iudicabitur* 'shall be judged.'
    3 That ... Acts 11.] First in 1527. In its place, in 1522 the annotation read: 'Moreover, since χρηματίζεσθαι and χρηματισμός are used properly of one who gives a judicial decision, or of the response of an oracle, or of one who speaks with authority, I have preferred [to translate] "shall be judged" rather than "shall be called." ' But Erasmus' translation had been challenged by Zúñiga. Erasmus replied in the *Apologia ad annotationes Stunicae* (1521) with the argument that was to be repeated here in the 1522 *Annotations.* But in Hellenistic Greek the word can mean simply 'to be called,' and in 1527 Erasmus returned to the Vulgate. See ASD IX-2 168 and the notes to lines 97 and 98.
    4 Acts 11:26

7:3 [ER *si se iunxerit alteri viro* 'if she has joined herself in wedlock[1] to another husband']

[VG] *si fuerit cum alio viro* 'if she is with another husband'; ἐὰν γένηται ἀνδρὶ ἑτέρῳ, that is, 'if she should be granted to another husband' or 'if she begins to belong to another husband,' unless we prefer to supply the preposition σύν [with]. Augustine,[2] in pointing out figures of speech in the Old Testament, introduces this one also from Leviticus, chapter 22: 'And if the daughter of a priest shall be "to" a foreign husband' [22:12], which is [a figure] for 'if she shall marry a foreign husband.'[3] And yet,[4] though Augustine interprets [the idiom] thus, a certain man in a published book has unjustly blamed [my translation of] this passage; unless perhaps it is one thing to be 'joined in wedlock' to a husband, another to 'marry' a husband.[5] But we[6] find the expression in this form in Terence's *The Mother-in-Law:* 'That she should be "to" another [that is, be another's wife], if she is not "to" this one' – where the father is thinking about the daughter's marriage, not about the sexual union.[7]

    1 has joined herself in wedlock] First in 1519; in 1516, 'has been joined in wedlock'

2 Augustine ... marry a foreign husband.] Added in 1519
3 Augustine *Locutiones in Heptateuchum* 3.53 CSEL 28/1 580:6–7. Erasmus had
   shown just above how to translate the Greek into idiomatic Latin; literally,
   the Greek might have been rendered 'if she should be to another husband.'
4 And yet ... 'marry' a husband.] Added in 1522
5 The critic is Zúñiga; cf his *Annotationes contra Erasmum Roterodamum* (Alcalá
   1520) fol i verso.
6 But we ... sexual union.] Added in 1535
7 Terence *Hecyra* 509

7:2–3 [ER *sin autem mortuus fuerit vir* 'if, however, the husband dies']
[VG] *si autem mortuus fuerit vir eius* 'if, however, her husband dies.' 'Her'
is not added in the Greek. Likewise in what follows, 'she is released from
the law of the husband,' 'of the husband' is not in the Greek and makes
no point. For by[1] adding the article he shows that he is speaking of the
law about which he previously said 'a woman [is] bound to the husband
through the law.' And yet I do find τοῦ ἀνδρός in certain codices.[2] The Greek
does not say *liberata est* [she is freed], but *libera est* [she is free]: ἐλευθέρα
ἐστὶν ἀπὸ τοῦ νόμου. Although[3] this makes little difference to the sense, I
still do not see why [the Translator] decided to depart from the Apostle's
word. But I suspect that copyists changed *libera* [free] into *liberata* [freed].

　　1 For by ... through the law.'] Added in 1535
　　2 τοῦ ἀνδρός 'of the husband' in the phrase 'from the law of the husband'
　　　is attested in Greek manuscripts in both verse 2 and verse 3. It has the
　　　overwhelming support of the Greek manuscripts in verse 2, but is omitted in
　　　the preferred reading of verse 3 (cf Tischendorf II 395 3n). In both verse 2
　　　and verse 3 Erasmus' translation includes the expression, but his Greek text
　　　omits the words in verse 3 only. It is possible that in this annotation the two
　　　verses are confused. Though the annotation begins with a clear reference to
　　　the Vulgate of verse 2 (*soluta est* 'she is released'), it concludes by referring
　　　to the Vulgate of verse 3 (*liberata est* 'she is freed'). Thus, though in this
　　　paragraph Erasmus quotes the Vulgate of verse 2, 'she is released from the
　　　law of the husband,' it is probable that the words τοῦ ἀνδρός 'of the husband'
　　　to which he refers belong to verse 3. See the next annotation, n2. In the
　　　Responsio ad collationes LB IX 995F–996A Erasmus suggests that the expression
　　　was imported into some Greek manuscripts from the Latin copies.
　　3 Although ... *liberata*.] Added in 1535

7:2 [ER *libera est a iure viri* 'she is free from the authority[1] of the husband']
[VG] *liberata est a lege viri* 'she is freed from the law of the husband';[2]
κατήργηται ἀπὸ τοῦ νόμου. The word κατήργηται signifies 'a legal right abolished and without force,' as also just below,[3] νυνὶ δὲ κατηργήθημεν [now we
have been freed].

1 authority] First in 1519; in 1516, lege 'law'
2 Though for the cue phrase Erasmus correctly quotes the Latin Vulgate of 7:3, he cites the Greek for 7:2, a mistake arising no doubt from the similarity of the two clauses. See the preceding annotation, n2.
3 In 7:6

7:4 [ER *ut iungeremini alteri* 'that you may be wedded to another']
[VG] *ut sitis vos alterius* 'that you may be of [that is, belong to] another.' [The Translator] added *vos* [you] in his version – unnecessarily,[1] even though it is added in the Greek. *Ut sitis alterius* [that you may be of another] would be sufficient, though the Greek is 'to another,' not 'of another'; that is, 'that another may have you, and you be not your own master.' In Greek[2] the expression is unobjectionable because the verb does not indicate the person, but in the Latin verb the first and second person is understood[3] – unless it is expressed either to give emphasis or to mark a distinction. In the more corrected Latin copies *vos* is not added, so that this can be put down to the scribes rather than to the Translator.[4]

1 unnecessarily] First in 1535; from 1516 to 1527, 'inappropriately'
2 In Greek ... Translator.] Added in 1535
3 The Greek verb here, γενέσθαι, is in the infinitive. As the Greek infinitive does not in itself indicate the person of the subject, the personal pronoun must be expressed. In Latin, however, the subjunctive verb that translates the Greek infinitive indicates in its form the person, so the personal pronoun need not be otherwise expressed. So Erasmus explains for Titelmans, with some sarcasm (*Responsio ad collationes* LB IX 996A).
4 *vos* is added in only a few Latin manuscripts. See Wordsworth and White II 94 4n.

7:4 [ER *ut fructificemus deo* 'that we may bear fruit to God']
[VG] *ut fructificetis deo* 'that you may bear fruit to God'; ἵνα καρποφορή-σωμεν, that is, 'that we may bear fruit.' For there follows ὅτε γὰρ ἦμεν, in the same person, that is, 'when we were.' There is an allusion to the wife, whom he just mentioned, who bears for her husband.

7:5 [ER *affectus peccatorum* 'the affections of sins']
[VG] *passiones peccatorum* 'passions of sins'; παθήματα, that is, the 'distempers,' 'desires,'[1] or 'affections,' or 'emotional disorders.'

1 'desires'] Added in 1519. For the definition here of παθήματα see above, the annotation on 1:26 ('to passions of shame') n2.

7:5 [ER *qui sunt per legem* 'that are through the Law']
[VG] *quae per legem erant* 'that were[1] through the Law'; τὰ διὰ τοῦ νόμου. In

this passage 'that' refers not to sins but to the passions, παθήματα, so that you understand that the Law aroused in us the lust to sin.

1 In 1516 only, this annotation followed, rather than preceded, the next.

7:5 [ER *vigebant in membris* 'were active[1] within (our) members']
[VG] *operabantur in membris* 'worked in [our] members'; ἐνηργεῖτο. This means rather 'they had potency,' or 'were secretly at work.' For a hidden power is called ἐνέργεια, as in a seed, and the power of the mind in a human being.

1 were active] First in 1519. In 1516 Erasmus followed the Vulgate. For the position of this annotation, see previous annotation, n1.

7:6 [ER VG] *in qua detinebamur* 'in which we were held.' ἐν ᾧ refers to the Law, not to death.[1] In most of[2] the Greek sources it is not 'of death,' but 'having died,' ἀποθανόντες. Origen[3] attests that both readings were known to him, but he favours the reading I am following.[4] Ambrose follows the other reading;[5] either fits well enough with the words that follow. It is called 'the law of death,' meaning 'the Law, which brings death.' Further, the phrase 'in which we were held' can be taken closely either with 'the Law,' so that the sense is, 'we who have now died in Christ are freed from the authority of the Law,[6] in which we were held'; or with 'having died' – understanding the pronoun [that]: 'having died to that Law in which we were held.'[7] St [John] Chrysostom[8] has a third reading, ἀπὸ τοῦ νόμου ἀποθανόντος, that is, 'from the Law, which has died.' Lest anyone attribute this to the scribes, he interprets: ὡσανεὶ ἔλεγεν, ὁ δεσμὸς δι᾽ οὗ κατειχόμεθα ἐνεκρώθη καὶ διερρύη, that is, 'as though [Paul] had said "the bond by which we were held is dead and has been dissolved." '[9]

1 Erasmus' discussion here extends beyond the words of the cue phrase:
    ER *nunc autem liberati sumus a lege, mortui ei in qua detinebamur* 'but now
      we are freed from the Law, having died to that in which we were held'
    VG *nunc autem soluti sumus a lege mortis in qua detinebamur* 'but now we
      are released from the law of death in which we were held'
    Though *mortis* is abundantly attested, the preferred reading of the Latin
    manuscripts is *morientes*: ' "dying," we are released from the Law, in which
    ...'; cf Wordsworth and White II 94 6n.
2 most of] Added in 1519
3 Origen ... brings death.] Added in 1519
4 Origen *Comm in Rom* 6.7 PG 14 1075B
5 Ambrosiaster *Comm in Rom* 7:6 (1)
6 of the Law] First in 1519; in 1516, 'of death'
7 Erasmus evidently intends the alternatives: 1/ having died, we are freed
    from the Law, in which we were held; 2/ we are freed, having died to that
    (that is, the Law) in which we were held.

8 St [John] Chrysostom ... dissolved." '] Added in *1535*
9 Cf Chrysostom *Hom in Rom* 12.3 PG 60 498. Migne, however, reads
ἀποθανόντες. Beza, apparently on the basis of Erasmus' comment here,
included the reading ἀποθανόντος in his 1565 edition on which the AV
probably based its translation. See Tischendorf II 395–6 6n and Cranfield I
338 n5.

7:8 [ER *sed occasione accepta* 'but the opportunity having been taken']
[VG] *occasione autem accepta* 'however, the opportunity having been taken'; ἀφορμὴν δὲ λαβοῦσα ἡ ἁμαρτία. The Translator has not infelicitously
changed the voice of the participle, and turned the [Greek] active into a
[Latin] passive to reflect accurately the tense. For λαβοῦσα [having taken]
is in the past tense. I do not see why [Lefèvre] d'Etaples should have been
offended by this.[1]

> 1 The Greek aorist active participle makes its subject clear: 'sin having taken
> the opportunity,' while the Vulgate's perfect passive participle leaves the
> subject ambiguous: 'the opportunity having been taken, sin worked.' Lefèvre
> objects that the Vulgate leaves open the possibility of thinking that 'the one
> who gave the Law [God], might take the opportunity ... to lead human
> beings to sin – an impious error!' Since Latin lacks a perfect active participle,
> Lefèvre preferred to change the Greek aorist participle to a Latin present
> active participle: sin taking the opportunity (*Pauli epistolae* fols 85 verso–86
> recto).

7:10 [ER *ego vero mortuus sum* 'but I died']
[VG] *ego autem mortuus sum* 'I, however, died'; ἀπέθανον, that is, 'I was
dead,' or 'I died,' making the verb past tense[1] to correspond to '[sin] came
back to life.'[2] To make his point Paul changed to first person and recalled
things mutually contradictory. For the life of sin is the death of man. Accordingly, if sin came back to life, immediately man's death followed.

> 1 So Valla *Annot in Rom* 7 (I 857)
> 2 The phrase immediately preceding: 'But when the commandment came, sin
> revived [Latin *revixit* 'revived,' 'came back to life'] and I died' (RSV).

7:11 [ER *decepit me* 'deceived me']
[VG] *seduxit me* 'seduced me'; ἐξηπάτησέ με, that is, 'deceived me' and 'led
me from the path.' For this is what ἐξαπατᾶν properly means.

7:13 [ER *imo peccatum. Ut appareret* 'no, rather, sin. In order that it
might appear']
[VG] *sed peccatum ut appareat* 'but sin that it might appear.' The punctuation[1] in this passage varies. In the Greek it is thus divided: 'Did then
that which is good become death for me? Not at all, but sin' – and you

understand 'became death for me.' The Greek reads: τὸ οὖν ἀγαθὸν ἐμοὶ
γέγονε θάνατος; μὴ γένοιτο, ἀλλὰ ἡ ἀμαρτία.[2]

1 The punctuation ... varies.] In 1535 only; until then, 'We have spoiled the
   sense of this passage by a faulty punctuation.'
   Compare the reading of the passage as a whole in Erasmus and the Vulgate
   printed in 1527. Erasmus punctuated (both Greek text and Latin translation)
   to read: 'Did that which was good become death for me? Not at all! It was
   sin rather! – in order that it might appear that sin, through the good, begot
   death for me.' The Vulgate read: 'Did that which is good become death for
   me? Not at all! But sin, that it might appear sin, through the good worked
   death for me.'
2 In *Responsio ad collationes* LB IX 996C Erasmus defends his reading against
   Titelmans' criticism not only on the basis of the Greek manuscripts, but of
   the sense as well: it was not the Law that brought death, but sin, through the
   opportunity given by the Law.

7:13 [ER *mihi gignere* 'begot for me']

[VG] *operatum est mihi* 'worked for me'; κατεργαζομένη, that is, 'working,'
a participle used in place of an infinitive, that is, 'so that sin might appear
to work death for me through that which is good' – not 'by working' as
Lorenzo [Valla] prefers.[1] However,[2] Lorenzo's remark, too, will stand, if
ἵνα φανῇ ἁμαρτία is taken as a parenthesis in this way: Did therefore that
which is good become death for me? By no means, but sin (that it might
become more evident how great an evil it is) became death for me, in that
through the life-giving Law it brought forth my destruction and turned the
remedy that had been applied into a worsening of the disease.[3] For that
must be a great evil which turns the best thing into something ruinous.
Origen, Chrysostom, and Theophylact follow this reading, except that the
translator of Origen changes the participle into a verb.[4] For Chrysostom
and Theophylact read κατεργαζομένη [working].[5] The Translator seems to
have read κατηργάζετο [worked], but it makes little difference to the sense.
Further, the clause he adds – 'that sin might become sinful beyond measure'
– drives home and intensifies the preceding words, 'that it might appear
sin.'
    There is no need to take ἵνα γένηται [so that (sin) might become] as
'so that [sin] might appear,'[6] for sin was in actual fact [and not merely in
appearance] increased by the Law; and when the commandments had been
set up like restraining bars, lust became fierce and raw.

1 Valla *Annot in Rom* 7: 'The Greek does not read "worked" but "working,"
   which I would have translated "by working"' (I 857).
2 However ... raw.] The remaining portion of the annotation was added in
   1535.
3 Under attack from Titelmans (see the preceding annotation, n2), Erasmus
   in 1535 showed how the Vulgate punctuation can be retained using Valla's

gerund (n1 above). Erasmus' paraphrase here of this verse would represent the text construed thus: 'Did the good become death for me? By no means, but sin became death in order that it might appear as sin by working death for me through the good.' Compare the readings of Erasmus and the Vulgate (preceding annotation, n1).

4 Cf Origen *Comm in Rom* 6.8 PG 14 1084A: '[Paul] refutes an obvious objection and says: Not that the good in the Law and the commandment brought death to me, "but sin" (says Paul), "in order that it might appear" how unrighteous it is, "through the good brought [*intulit*, for the Greek participle] death to me."' Cf Chrysostom *Hom in Rom* 12.6 PG 60 502–3; Theophylact *Expos in Rom* 7:13 PG 124 425C.

5 In the reference above (n4) Chrysostom does not quote κατεργαζομένη, since this part of the verse does not appear in his exposition here according to Migne's text.

6 Ie in the last clause of 7:13, 'and through the commandment might become sinful beyond measure' (RSV)

7:13 [ER *majorem in modum peccans peccatum* 'sin sinning[1] the more']
[VG] *supra modum peccans peccatum* 'sin, sinning beyond measure'; καθ' ὑπερβολὴν ἁμαρτωλὸς ἡ ἁμαρτία. This has the same effect as to say *scelestum scelus* [criminal the crime] or (to translate with clarity rather than in good Latin) *peccaminosum peccatum* [sinful the sin].[2] What the Translator renders *peccans* [sinning] is, in Greek, not a participle, but an adjective. Origen[3] or his translator has noted carefully that Paul imagines sin as a sort of person; the word in Greek is feminine, so that a Greek can say *peccatrix peccantia*[4] [sin the sinner]. If 'sin' were masculine in Latin, and we could speak of it as though it were a man – *peccatum vehementer peccator* [sin excessively the sinner] – the expression would be less harsh.[5] But I do not see why Jerome says he prefers to allow incorrect language rather than to express inadequately Paul's meaning.[6] For a Greek ἁμαρτωλὸς ἁμαρτία is not a solecism, at least in the Attic dialect. Moreover, what Latin-speaker would understand 'sin, the sinner' to mean a great and evident sin? Or why *peccator peccatum* rather than *peccatrix peccatum*? And yet so Augustine reads in the first question of the first book *To Simplicianus*, except that in the published copies the reading is – falsely – *super modum peccator aut peccatum* [sinner or sin beyond measure] instead of *supra modum peccator peccatum* [sin, the sinner beyond measure].[7] On[8] the other hand, he reads the same way in the fourth of his sermons on the words of the Apostle.[9] This offers the likely conjecture that the author of the version that Augustine there followed read καθ' ὑπερβολὴν ἁμαρτωλὸς ἡ ἁμαρτία.[10]

1 sinning] First in 1519; in 1516, *peccaminosum* 'sinful'
2 This definition is reiterated in *Responsio ad annotationes Lei* LB IX 215C.
3 Origen … *modum peccator peccatum*.] Except for the last two sentences the remainder of the annotation was added in 1519.

This 1519 addition addresses the problem raised in Origen's commentary, which renders the Greek ἁμαρτωλὸς ἡ ἁμαρτία by the Latin *peccator peccatum*. Though ἁμαρτωλός can be a feminine adjective (as here), Origen's translator evidently read it as masculine and insisted therefore on rendering it by the masculine *peccator*, in spite of the fact that its appositive *peccatum* is neuter. The translator defends the phrase in spite of its harshness: 'I have preferred to admit a fault in expression than to reflect less than fully the Apostle's thought.' See Origen *Comm in Rom* 6.8 PG 14 1084B–C.

4 Lefèvre had explained the Greek by this phrase (*Pauli epistolae* fol 86 recto). The two words in apposition are both feminine, representing a possible construction in Greek.

5 See n3 above.

6 In 1519 Erasmus still believed Jerome was the 'translator' of Origen. For his subsequent change of mind see the annotation on 3:5 ('is God unfair who inflicts wrath') nn11 and 14.

7 Augustine *De diversis quaestionibus ad Simplicianum* 1.1.6 and 16 CCL 44 12:100–1 and 20:312. (An alternative reading, *peccans peccatum*, is cited for both references in the critical apparatus.)

8 On . . . ἁμαρτία.] Added in 1535

9 Cf Augustine *Sermones* 154.1.1 and 153.10.13 PL 38 832 and 833. The reading *peccator aut peccatum* appears elsewhere also; cf eg *De gratia et libero arbitrio* 10.22 PL 44 894, a reading, however, Erasmus rejected in his own edition (cf PL 44 894 n2).

10 The sequence of thought here suggests that in 1535 ἁμαρτωλὸς ἡ ἁμαρτία 'sinner *the* sin' was at this point a misprint for ἁμαρτωλὸς ἢ ἁμαρτία 'sinner *or* sin.' In 1519 Erasmus thought the reading of Augustine, 'sinner or sin,' represented a mistake by those who copied Augustine's manuscript. Finding the same reading in a different work, he concluded in 1535 that the reading originated rather in Augustine's copy of the New Testament, which must have read, not ἁμαρτωλὸς ἡ ἁμαρτία 'sinner the sin,' but ἁμαρτωλὸς ἢ ἁμαρτία 'sinner *or* sin.'

7:14 [ER *venditus sub peccatum* 'sold to sin']

[VG] *venundatus sub peccato* '**sold as a slave under sin**';[1] πεπραμένος ὑπὸ τὴν ἁμαρτίαν, that is, 'sold' or 'given over to sin,' that is, 'into the servitude and yoke of sin.' I do not see what obscurity gave Lefèvre difficulty here.[2]

1 In 1516 only, the position of this annotation and the following was reversed.

2 Lefèvre *Pauli epistolae* 86 recto found *venundatus* 'sold' – used equally for the sale of slaves – 'somewhat obscure,' and preferred *negotiatus* 'traded,' 'trafficked' or *acquisitus* 'procured.'

7:15 [ER *non enim quod volo* 'for not what I wish']

[VG] *non enim quod volo bonum* '**for not the good that I wish**';[1] 'good' and 'evil' are not in the Greek: οὐ γὰρ ὃ θέλω τοῦτο πράσσω, ἀλλὰ ὃ μισῶ, that is, 'for I do not do that which I will, but that which I hate.' But a little below,[2] these two words 'good' and 'evil' are added: 'For I do not do what I wish, that is, the good.'

1 For the sequence, see preceding annotation, n1.
2 In 7:19

7:17 [ER *non iam ego* 'no longer I']

[VG] *iam non ego* 'I no longer'; οὐκέτι ἐγώ. The Translator has rendered
this in correct and polished Latin, and I am surprised that anyone thinks it
ought to be changed.[1]

> 1 Lefèvre thought the proper Latin idiom was *non etiam* 'not even' (*Pauli
> epistolae* fol 86 recto), and so translated (ibidem fol 5 verso). Erasmus' fine
> compliment here to the Translator did nothing to mollify Titelmans; see
> *Responsio ad collationes* LB IX 996B.

7:21 [ER *reperio igitur per legem volenti mihi facere bonum* 'I discover
then through the Law[1] for me wishing to do good']

[VG] *invenio igitur legem volenti mihi facere bonum* 'I find[2] then the Law
for me wishing to do good.' Just as Origen elsewhere notices the absence
of clear and sound expression in Paul,[3] so he believes this passage scarcely
holds together, either because the conjunctions are superfluous or because
they have not been properly used.[4] But he believes this difficulty can be
removed if we read the passage arranged in this way: 'Therefore *because*
evil lies at hand, in wishing to do good I find the law of God and delight
in it according to the inward man' etc.[5] In my opinion the conjunction ὅτι
[meaning either 'because,' or 'that'] can also be taken here, not causally as
Origen takes it, but εἰδικῶς [specifically],[6] so that the sense is: 'When I try
to obey the good law, I realize *that* this evil lies in me, not in the law,' and
am dragged away to evil by overpowering desire. And this, indeed, makes
good sense. But if we approve this, we shall have to admit that in this
passage Paul stumbled in his speech and did not complete what he began
[to say]. For he evidently meant to say something like this: 'Whenever, then,
I try to do good, I find the Law has the effect of making me aware that the
source of sinning and of evil is in myself, not in the Law.'

Theophylact has rendered [the passage] in this way: 'I find therefore
that the Law supports me when I want to do what is good; but I do not do
it for the reason that[7] evil lies close at hand.' But he admits that the sentence
is obscure because something seems to be missing. He also points out that
others arrange the passage in this way: 'I find therefore that it is the Law
for[8] no one else but me, when I want to do the good.' For only to him who
desires to act rightly, is the Law 'the law,' as that which prescribes to be
done what he desires to do.[9] And this[10] is the opinion of Chrysostom, with
which the words that follow [in his text] are consistent: 'For I find pleasure
in the Law. Just as the Law supports me when I want what is good, so also
I, when I desire what is honourable, approve the Law.'[11]

1 through the Law] First in *1519*; in *1516*, like the Vulgate, 'I discover then the Law'

2 I find ... desires to do.] With the exceptions noted below (see nn7, 8, 10) this annotation was added in *1519*. Until *1535*, however, the position of this and the following annotation was reversed.

3 See the Argument to the *Paraphrase on Romans*, where Erasmus also cites Origen on the difficulty of Pauline language; CWE 42 12 and nn34 and 36.

4 Erasmus' discussion includes the clause following the cue phrase:
   ER *reperio igitur per legem volenti mihi facere bonum, quod mihi malum adiunctum sit* 'I discover then through the Law, for me wishing to do good, that evil is present to me'
   VG *invenio igitur legem volenti mihi facere bonum, quoniam mihi malum adiacet* 'I find then the Law for me wishing to do good, that [or, since] evil lies at hand for me'

5 Origen *Comm in Rom* 6.9 PG 14 1088A–C. Origen explicates the passage, however, primarily in relation to the 'inner man' (the will and purpose): one wills to be converted and in so doing consents to and delights in the Law, but without long training does not overcome sin.

6 For ὅτι meaning either 'because' or 'that' (εἰδικῶς) see the annotation on 4:21 ('whatever God has promised') n1.

7 for the reason that] First in *1527*; before *1527*, 'since'

8 it is the Law for] First in *1527*; before *1527*, 'the Law was imposed on'

9 Theophylact *Expos in Rom* 7:21 PG 124 429C–D. Theophylact cites John Chrysostom for the second of his interpretations. See n11 below.

10 And this ... approve the Law.] Added in *1527*

11 Chrysostom *Hom in Rom* 13.2 PG 60 510–11. Chrysostom shows that the Mosaic law supports the natural law implanted in each human being. Erasmus and the Fathers had difficulty with this passage because they understood νόμος as the Mosaic law. Most modern scholars agree that it means 'rule' or 'principle,' as in the RSV: 'So I find it to be a law that when I want to do right ...' See Schelkle 256–7. Cranfield I 361–5 links it with the ἕτερος νόμος 'the other law' of 7:23, which he identifies with the 'law of sin.'

7:23 [ER *rebellentem legi* 'doing battle against the Law']

[VG] *repugnantem legi* 'fighting against the Law';[1] ἀντιστρατευόμενον τῷ νόμῳ, as though to say 'waging war against'[2] and doing battle.' Paul[3] enjoys metaphors which smack of the military; as before[4] when he talks about 'wages.'

   1 On the order of this annotation, see the preceding annotation, n2.
   2 So Valla *Annot in Rom* 7 (I 857)
   3 Paul ... military] Added in *1519*
   4 as before ... wages] Added in *1527*. See the annotation on Rom 6:23 ('for the wages of sin is death').

7:23 [ER *captivum reddentem me legi peccati* 'making me captive to the law of sin']

[VG] *captivantem me in lege peccati* 'taking me captive in the law of sin';

αἰχμαλωτίζοντά με τῷ νόμῳ,[1] that is, 'which makes me captive to the law of sin.'

> 1 Here LB adds τῆς ἁμαρτίας 'of sin,' but without warrant from the editions 1516–1535.

7:24 [ER *ex hoc corpore morti obnoxio* 'from this body subject to death'[1]]
[VG] *de corpore mortis huius* 'from the body of this death'; ἐκ τοῦ σώματος τοῦ θανάτου τούτου. The Greek suggests that 'this' modifies the noun 'body'[2] rather than 'death': 'from this body of death.'[3] For the body subject to the passions of sin he calls the 'body of death.' And he adds 'from *this* body,' because he has himself assumed the persona of one who feels passions of this kind.[4] For this indeed is a special key as it were to understanding Paul – if one should notice a change of the persons about whom and to whom he is speaking. It[5] is quite clear that Theophylact has understood the passage as I have indicated, if one will observe his own interpretation and not his translator's version; for he adds 'that is, "subject to death." '[6] Origen[7] interprets similarly, understanding 'death' as sin, and for this reason the place where sin dwells is called 'the body of death.'[8] And the 'moderns' usually agree with this.[9] Someone, it is true, has explained 'the body of death' as the crowd of evils that rush upon us, but this is rather harsh.[10]

> 1 subject to death] First in 1519; in 1516, *ex corpore mortis hoc* 'from this body of death'
> 2 'body'] Added in 1519
> 3 'from this body of death'] Added in 1527
> 4 Cf Origen *Comm in Rom* 6.9 PG 14 1089B: 'This is the cry of the one whom the Apostle describes as having begun to be converted ... but does not yet achieve the good'; cf the annotation on 7:21 ('I find then the Law for me wishing to do good') n5. For Erasmus' appreciation of persona in reading the biblical text, see Chomarat *Grammaire et rhétorique* I 582–6.
> 5 It ... subject to death." '] Added in 1519
> 6 Theophylact *Expos in Rom* 7:24 PG 124 432C
> 7 Origen ... harsh.] Added in 1522
> 8 Origen *Comm in Rom* 6.9 PG 14 1089B
> 9 Cf eg Thomas Aquinas *Super Rom lect* cap 7 lectio 4.593. For the 'moderns' see the annotation on 1:4 ('who was predestined') and n7.
> 10 Cf eg Origen *Comm in Rom* 6.9 PG 14 1089B and 1090C.

7:25 [ER *gratias ago deo* 'I give thanks to God']
[VG] *gratia dei* 'the grace of God'; εὐχαριστῶ τῷ θεῷ, that is, 'I give thanks to God.' In the emended Latin codices the passage is read in such a way that these are the words of[1] one who is showing through whom he has been freed – through him, that is, to whom he gives thanks; though Lorenzo [Valla] points out that in some manuscripts χάρις τῷ θεῷ was written, that

is, *gratia deo* [thanks to God],[2] conveying[3] the same idea in different words. It is not clear from Origen's interpretation what he read, but that he read what we have shown the Greek to be we may conjecture especially from these words: 'But to his question, "Who will deliver me from the body of this death?" a reply is given (not now [in the persona] of that [wretched man], but with apostolic authority): "The grace of God through Jesus Christ our Lord." Whence it appears that the Apostle describes all these things, and has set forth the evils living within us, for this reason, that in the end he could show and teach from what evils and what deaths Christ has snatched us.'[4] So far Origen, who indicates that what Paul has said up to this point has been spoken under the persona of one who is not yet a partaker of the divine grace, who is still struggling with the affections of the flesh, but is no match for them. But the reply to the exclamatory question is spoken under a different persona, namely, of one who has been freed from that most wretched servitude not through the Law, but through the grace of Christ. Accordingly,[5] he gives to one persona the exclamation 'Wretched man that I am, who' etc, to another, the speech of him who gives thanks to God. In the same way, Origen would also have the many things Paul mentioned above – about 'the law of death' and 'of the members,' and about the necessity of sin – spoken under the persona of the former.[6]

In[7] his interpretation, Ambrose likewise says that from these words we must understand that the man *has been* freed by the grace of God from the body of this death; he is not *to be* freed. The words that soon follow support this: 'For the law of the spirit of life in Christ Jesus has freed me from the law of sin and death' [8:2].[8] But if[9] he had followed the reading 'the grace of God,' this phrase would not be suited to Paul, who did not have to be freed, but was freed, and Ambrose's argument is inconsistent.[10] Therefore we must read either 'thanks be to God' or 'I give thanks.' With these words, he gives thanks – now freed – to God, through whose grace he has attained what neither the law of nature, nor the law of Moses, nor conscience,[11] nor works could offer him.

Chrysostom,[12] without question, reads and interprets εὐχαριστῶ. For he says: εἰ γὰρ καὶ τῷ πατρὶ εὐχαριστεῖ ἀλλὰ καὶ εὐχαριστείας ταύτης καὶ ὁ υἱὸς αἴτιος, that is, 'For although he gives thanks to the Father, nevertheless the cause of this thanksgiving is the Son.' And in the rest of his exposition the word εὐχαριστῶ is repeated so often that it cannot seem due to the carelessness of the copyists.[13] Theophylact follows Chrysostom in every respect.[14] In fact, even St Jerome in [the letter] to Algasia, the eighth question, reads 'thanks be to God,' and the exposition itself shows that he read it thus, when he says: 'Turning to himself, the Apostle, or rather the man under whose persona the Apostle speaks, gives thanks to the Saviour, because he has been redeemed by his blood, and has removed the stains in baptism.' And later: 'I give thanks to God through Jesus Christ our Lord, who has freed me from the body of this death.'[15]

It is not to the point that certain interpreters, citing this passage, call to mind the phrase 'the grace of God,' and suggest that here is shown the one who frees from the body of death,[16] since whoever gives thanks to God for his freedom, by this very act indicates the means through which others can also be freed. But all apply to the person of Paul [the words] wherein he gives thanks as one who has been freed; they differ on the exclamatory question. The ancient commentators are unwilling to have it applied to the Apostle;[17] Jerome believes it is said under the persona of 'Everyman.'[18] And yet[19] if we take 'body of death' as a tendency to sin – as though to say 'a dying body' – nothing prevents all this from also fitting Paul, in accordance with the Latin reading. Certainly[20] Augustine, in the first book *Against the Two Letters of the Pelagians*, the eighth and following chapters, contends that this whole passage is appropriate to Paul either as a boy, or under the law of sin, or under grace – sensing the stir of the affections, but not assenting. But he twists many things so harshly[21] that it is more suitable [to say] that Paul assumes the persona of the whole human race: as a pagan, he is outside the Law; as a Jew he is carnal under the Law; and as spiritual he has been freed through grace.

1 these are the words of] First in *1519*; in *1516*, 'the sense presupposes'
2 Valla *Annot in Rom* 7 (I 857). Valla also found codices with the reading Erasmus preferred. Modern critics believe that Valla's reading, 'thanks to God,' is probably the correct one, though Erasmus' reading is possible. See Cranfield I 367 n1.
3 conveying ... through the grace of Christ] Added in *1519*
4 Origen *Comm in Rom* 6.9 PG 14 1089C
5 Accordingly ... of the former.] Added in *1535*
6 This paragraph undertakes to justify Erasmus' 'conjecture' that in the passage quoted from Origen's interpretation, Origen himself really wrote 'thanks to God' instead of 'the grace of God,' which appears in the text. Erasmus' inference depends upon Origen's elucidation of the speaking persona in 7:24–5 (cf *Comm in Rom* 6.9–10 PG 14 1090C–1091B). According to Origen, the question 'who shall deliver me from the body of this death?' represents the voice of one who does not yet know deliverance; the reply on the other hand represents the voice of the Apostle. Erasmus apparently infers that since, in Origen's view, the Apostle clearly has been delivered, Origen must have understood him to reply with a thanksgiving for deliverance (hence, 'thanks to God') rather than with an answer to the question (ie 'the grace of God'). On these grounds, Erasmus evidently assumes that Origen's translator changed his Greek text ('thanks to God') to conform to the Latin reading ('the grace of God'). Taken as a whole, however, Origen's argument does not support Erasmus' inference.

7 In ... sin and death.'] Added in *1519*

8 Ambrosiaster *Comm in Rom* 7:24–5 (2–5)

9 But if ... offer him.] Added in *1527*

10 The charge of inconsistency is evidently based on the assumption (applied to the exposition of Origen, above) that to respond to the question 'who shall deliver me?' with the words 'the grace of God' implies a deliverance still to occur. Since, however, Ambrosiaster's commentary clearly assumes the deliverance has occurred, the only consistent response to the question would have been an expression of thanks, 'thanks to God.'
Ambrosiaster's comments, however, demonstrate clearly that he read 'the grace of God,' as Titelmans claimed. In spite of Titelmans' objections, Erasmus continued to cling to his argument; cf *Responsio ad collationes* LB IX 996D–997A.

11 Cf Chrysostom *Hom in Rom* 13.3 PG 60 512, who responds to the question 'who shall deliver me?' that 'the Law was not able, conscience did not suffice.'

12 Chrysostom ... grace.] With the exception of one sentence (see n19) the remaining portion of the annotation was added in *1535*. In the Greek quoted, Erasmus printed εὐχαριστείας, Migne εὐχαριστίας.

13 Chrysostom *Hom in Rom* 13.3 PG 60 512. For the phrase repeated see also 13.4 PG 60 512.

14 Theophylact *Expos in Rom* 7:25 PG 124 432D

15 Jerome *Epistulae* 121.8.21 CSEL 56 36

16 Cf eg Chrysostom, who comments on the phrase in question: 'Do you see how he has shown the essential presence of grace, the common righteous deeds alike of Father and Son?' (*Hom in Rom* 13.3 PG 60 512); and Ambrose: 'Adam had built the steps on which the pillager climbed against Adam's sons, [but] the most merciful Lord, moved by pity, gave his grace through Christ' (*Comm in Rom* 7:24–5 [1]).

17 Among the ancient commentators (*vetustiores*) who believe the question of 7:24 represents the voice of human beings in general, rather than of Paul in particular, are Origen, Irenaeus, Didymus, Diodore, Chrysostom, and Pelagius (see Schelkle 243, 246–7). On the other hand Hilary, Ambrose, and Augustine believe Paul himself is the speaker (Schelkle 245–6, 247–8). Among those whom Erasmus elsewhere calls 'modern' interpreters (*recentiores*), Thomas Aquinas allows both possibilities, but prefers to apply the passage to Paul (see *Super Rom lect* cap 7 lectio 3.558 and 4.594).

18 Jerome *Epistulae* 121.8.16 CSEL 56 34

19 And yet ... Latin reading.] Added in *1527*

20 For the reference, see Augustine *Contra duas epistulas Pelagianorum* 1.8.14–11.24 PL 44 556–62

21 Augustine himself appears to have recognized that his explanation was somewhat forced: 'It is not so obvious how the passage that follows [Rom 7:14–25] can be understood of Paul,' and accepts the possibility that in Paul himself all persons are understood (1.10.17). See also Augustine *De nuptiis et concupiscentia* 1.30.34–31.35 PL 44 432–3 and Schelkle 248. Erasmus understands these verses as depicting pre-Christian humanity; cf CWE 42 44 and n8.

CHAPTER 8

8:2 [ER *nam lex spiritus vitae* 'for the law of the spirit of life']
[VG] *lex enim spiritus vitae* 'for the law of the spirit of life.' 'Spirit' in
this passage is in the genitive case, so that you understand the law, not of
the 'flesh,' which brings death, but of the 'spirit,' which bestows life: ὁ γὰρ
νόμος τοῦ πνεύματος. And yet the Greek texts are such that the sense can
be 'the law of the spirit which is life,' τοῦ[1] πνεύματος τοῦ ζωῆς, since 'life'
is preceded by a masculine[2] article. 'The law of the spirit' is an expression
based on the Hebrew idiom, for which we would say 'the spiritual law.'
Yet I[3] am aware that Theophylact thinks both genitives depend on the same
noun – 'the law of the spirit, the law of life.' For he is refuting those who
interpret 'the law of life' as the law of Moses.[4] Chrysostom's[5] comments
are in the same vein.

> 1 τοῦ ... 'the spiritual law'] Added in 1527, with the exception noted below
> (n2)
> 2 masculine] Added in 1535. In his text of the New Testament Erasmus
> consistently printed the feminine article τῆς before 'life' with the meaning
> 'the spirit of life'; in the 1527 addition to the annotation, however, he printed
> the neuter article so that the phrase can mean 'the spirit which is life.' The
> qualification 'masculine' might have been an inadvertent mistake (τοῦ, as a
> form, can be either masculine or neuter). But it is also possible that Erasmus
> had in mind his proposed Latin translation, where the force of the Greek
> neuter article is rendered by the Latin *masculine* pronoun 'which,' hence 'the
> law of the spirit which [*spiritus qui*] is life.' The witnesses, however, read the
> feminine article (cf Tischendorf II 399 and 2n).
> 3 Yet I ... Moses.] Added in 1519
> 4 Theophylact *Expos in Rom* 8.2 PG 124 433B–C. Theophylact (following
> Chrysostom) writes: 'By the law of the spirit he means the Holy Spirit ...
> He calls this the law of life to contrast it with the law of sin which brought
> death for us ... [Some] have dared to say that the law of death is the Mosaic
> law; but this the Apostle always spoke of as holy and spiritual. They reply,
> "If even the Mosaic law is spiritual, how does it differ from the law of the
> spirit?" A great deal. The Mosaic law was only conveyed by the Spirit; this
> law also supplied the Spirit.'
> 5 Chrysostom's ... vein.] Added in 1527. See *Hom in Rom* 13.4 PG 60 513 and
> n4 above.

8:2 [ER *iure peccati et mortis* 'from the authority of sin and death']
[VG] *lege peccati et mortis* 'from the law of sin and death'; ἀπὸ τοῦ νόμου
τῆς ἁμαρτίας καὶ τοῦ θανάτου. Here a more appropriate translation would
have been 'from the authority of sin.'[1] The Greek wording is ambiguous. It
can be understood as 'from the law of sin and of death,' so that 'law' refers

equally to both words, or 'from the law of sin and from death, which is the companion of sin.' Further,[2] Chrysostom's reading, 'has freed you,'[3] for 'has freed me,' makes no difference to the sense.

1 Erasmus defended the translation in *Responsio ad collationes* with an analysis of the uses of *lex* and *ius* in Paul (LB IX 997A–B).
2 Further … sense.] Added in *1527*
3 Chrysostom *Hom in Rom* 13.4 PG 60 513. The Greek text of Migne reads 'me' in all three quotations of the phrase in the homily at this point, though the reading 'you' is attested. (See NPNF 2nd series, XI 431 n6). On the readings here see Cranfield I 376–7.

8:3 [ER *etenim quod lex praestare non poterat* 'for what the Law could not accomplish']

[VG] *nam quod impossibile erat legi* 'for what[1] was impossible for the Law'; τὸ γὰρ ἀδύνατον τοῦ νόμου. The Greek is 'of the Law,' genitive case, not 'for the Law,' dative. And so indeed reads Ambrose.[2] But the language here holds some difficulties, for τὸ γὰρ ἀδύνατον τοῦ νόμου could be understood as 'for the impotence of the Law' or 'the helplessness of the Law,' by which it was weak and ineffectual. But in that case what follows does not fit, unless we wish to admit that Paul has not completed the construction, whether through forgetfulness, or through lack of skill, or in disregard of Greek expression.[3] As I reflect on this passage to the best of my ability, it seems to me some words are needed to complete the sense – if, for instance, we were to read: 'For what the Mosaic law could not do according to its carnal part, in respect of which it was weak and ineffectual, God has accomplished by sending his Son, who fulfilled the spiritual part of the Law.'[4] And the conjunction which follows helps to confirm my opinion: 'and from sin condemned sin.' For unless you supply the word 'accomplished' or 'effected' or something similar, the conjunction appears superfluous. Or perhaps you feel that ἀδύνατον is used as a nominative absolute in place of a genitive, so that the sense is 'for since it was impossible' etc. In any case the words 'for what was impossible of the Law, in which it was weak,' would have to be related to what follows, 'from sin he condemned sin' – this is what the Law could not do.

1 for what … could not do.] This entire annotation was added in *1519*.
2 Ambrosiaster *Comm in Rom* 8:3 (1)
3 Critics are still divided as to the intended syntax here; see Cranfield I 378–9 n3. A literal, and unpunctuated, translation of the Greek reveals the problem: 'For the helplessness of the Law in which it was weak through the flesh God having sent his Son in the likeness of the flesh of sin and from sin condemned sin in the flesh.'
Erasmus, 'supplying' some words (as he goes on to say), rendered (from

1519): 'For what the Law could not accomplish, in that respect in which it was weak through the flesh, this God accomplished, sending his own Son in the likeness of flesh subject to sin, and from sin condemned sin in the flesh ...'

The Vulgate printed in *1527* read (punctuated with two colons): 'For what was impossible for the Law in which it was weak through the flesh: God sending his Son after the likeness of the flesh of sin: and from sin condemned sin in the flesh ...'

4 Erasmus follows Origen in this division of the Mosaic law into two parts, carnal and spiritual. See Origen *Comm in Rom* 6.12 PG 14 1094A. See also the paraphrase on 8:3 CWE 42 45 and n2.

8:3 [ER *ea parte qua imbecillis erat* 'in that[1] respect in which it was impotent'] [VG] *in quo infirmabatur* 'in which it was weak'; ἐν ᾧ ἠσθένει. It can also be understood as 'in this, that it was weak,' that is, 'inasmuch as it was weak,' with ἐν[2] [in] used to mean διά [through, on account of]. Further, he said 'was weak,' meaning 'it was powerless and quite ineffectual.' And lest[3] he should seem to find fault with the Law, he added 'through the flesh,' that is, 'through a carnal understanding of the Law,'[4] or [through] 'the weakness of the flesh' that lacked the grace of the gospel.[5]

1 in that ... which] From *1519*; in *1516*, with the Vulgate, *in quo* 'in which'
2 with ἐν ... διά] Added in *1527*
3 And lest ... gospel.] Added in *1527*
4 Cf Origen *Comm in Rom* 6.12 PG 14 1094A–C.
5 So Chrysostom *Hom in Rom* 13.4 PG 60 513

8:3 [ER *sub specie carnis peccato obnoxiae* 'under[1] the appearance of the flesh subject to sin']
[VG] *in similitudinem carnis peccati* 'after[2] the likeness of the flesh of sin'; ἐν ὁμοιώματι, that is, *in similitudine* [in the likeness], which, as was pointed out above, means rather 'similarity' and 'representation.'[3] For that Christ assumed the role of a sinner was a kind of play-acting, if you will forgive the expression. To make[4] this clearer, I have translated 'under the appearance of the flesh subject to sin,' because the word *species* ['appearance' or 'guise'] seems more suited to suggesting a likeness which is unreal.[5] Moreover, following Hebrew idiom, he said 'the flesh of sin,' meaning 'flesh subject to sin.' For this reason Augustine advises in the thirty-first of his sermons on the words of the Apostle that this should be read inferentially: 'Christ truly had flesh; he seemed to have the flesh of sin, although he did not have it.'[6]

1 under ... to sin] First in *1519*; in *1516*, *in assimilatione carnis peccati* 'in a representation of the flesh of sin'
2 after ... did not have it.'] Except for the *1535* addition (see n4 below), this entire annotation appeared first in *1519*.

3 Cf above the annotation on Rom 5:14 ('unto the likeness') and n14; also the
annotation on 1:23 ('into the likeness of the image').

4 To make ... unreal.] Added in *1535*

5 Frans Titelmans thought the word *species* restricted the breadth of meaning
conveyed by the Vulgate, and, moreover, could imply something false.
Erasmus replied: 'Precisely, just as Christ came under the false appearance
of a sinner' (*Responsio ad collationes* LB IX 998C–D).

6 See Augustine *Sermones* 183.8.12 (on 1 John) PL 38 992: 'For Christ came in
the flesh, which was the likeness of the flesh of sin; it was not the flesh of
sin. The Apostle's words are "God sent his Son after the likeness of the flesh
of sin," not "after the likeness of flesh," as though his flesh were not flesh,
but "after the likeness of the flesh of sin," since he was flesh, but he was not
flesh of sin'; cf *Sermones* 155.7.7 (on Rom 8:1–11) PL38 844.
For this type of 'Hebrew idiom' (which Erasmus frequently observes) see
the annotations on 8:2 above ('for the law of the spirit of life') and on 1:4
('through the spirit of sanctification'), especially n3.

8:3 [ER *de peccato condemnavit peccatum* 'from sin condemned sin']

[VG] *de peccato damnavit peccatum* 'from sin[1] condemned sin.' Origen's
translator – for [the translator] added this on his own – pointed out that
the Greek is not '*de peccato*' but '*pro peccato*,'[2] so that we understand that sin
was condemned from sin;[3] for we cannot understand 'sin was condemned
as a result of sin [*ex peccato*],' since the Greek is περὶ ἁμαρτίας [concerning,
from, sin], and yet that is how they seem to interpret it.[4] I think one can,
not unreasonably, take the passage in this sense: 'Christ, having been sent,
condemned even sin from sin,' that is, he convicted and exposed sinners,
so that it was now clear that those who had previously deceived through a
'false image' of righteousness were impious, since they had killed the Christ,
who was the end of the Law, under the pretext of maintaining the Law.
Others explain that *de peccato* refers to the victim which it is the custom,
according to the rites of the Mosaic law, to sacrifice *for* a transgression.[5] This
indeed does fit Christ quite well, but the preposition περί is an obstacle. It
would be easier if the word were παρά.[6] Theophylact's[7] suggestion follows
more closely the sense of the Greek text: sin, by what was in some sense its
own right, raged against sinners, but when it struck against the innocent
Lord, it was, in a way, caught in sin.[8] But the curious reader will weigh
these things more closely. For my part, I am striving in this exposition to
ascertain especially those things which contribute to a sound reading.

1 from sin ... sound reading.] The entire annotation was added in *1519*, with
the two exceptions noted in nn3 and 7 below.

2 Origen *Comm in Rom* 6.12 PG 14 1094C

3 from sin] *de peccato*, first in *1527*; in *1519* and *1522* simply *peccati*, perhaps a
genitive of the charge, 'condemned for sin'; cf Allen and Greenough 352 and
353 (2).

4 Erasmus' comment may arise out of scholastic exegesis, such as that of
Thomas Aquinas, to whom indeed the indefinite 'they' may refer. Thomas
says: 'From sin [de peccato], that is, by virtue of the sin [pro peccato] committed
against [literally, in] the flesh of Christ by his slayers at the instigation of
the devil. He condemned, that is, he destroyed sin, that is, when the devil
attempted to bring to death an innocent man over whom he had no authority,
it was just that he should lose his power. And for this reason [Christ] is
said to have destroyed sin through [per] his own passion and death. But it
is better to say that he condemned sin in the flesh, that is, he smothered
the tinder of sin in our flesh from sin [de peccato], that is, as a result [ex] of
the power of his passion and death, a death that is called sin because of the
likeness of sin' (Super Rom lect cap 8 lectio 1.609).

5 So Origen Comm in Rom 6.12 PG 14 1095A–B. Origen, writing pro peccato (n2
above), explains that Christ became a sacrifice 'for sin' and was offered up
for the cleansing of sinners. He quotes Heb 7:27.

6 But περὶ ἁμαρτίας 'is frequently used in the LXX to denote a sin offering ... or
with the meaning "for a sin offering"' (Cranfield I 382).

7 Theophylact's ... caught in sin.] Added in 1527

8 Theophylact Expos in Rom 8:3 PG 124 436B. Theophylact relies on Chrysostom,
who elaborates the image: 'For as long as [sin] seized sinners, it led them
to death on just grounds. But when it came upon a body without sin, and
handed this over to death, it was condemned as having acted unjustly ...
Having shown that sin acted unjustly, he then condemned it, not simply by
force and power but even by the principle of justice itself' (Hom in Rom 13.5
PG 60 514).

8:5 [ER *quae spiritus sunt* '(care for)[1] the things that are of the Spirit']
[VG] *quae spiritus sunt sapiunt* 'discern[2] the things that are of the Spirit.'
φρονοῦσι [set their minds on] is not repeated in the Greek.[3] And it means
'feel' or 'care for'[4] rather than 'discern.' But it is strange that the Translator
here strove for an unprofitable variety [in expression] which actually im-
pedes our understanding. For[5] the same word that he has just translated
sapiunt [discern] he now translates *sentiunt* [feel].[6] You will say, 'What difference does it make?' A great deal for the one who wishes to philosophize
in treating these matters.

1 'Care for' is understood from the previous clause, 'care for the things of the
flesh.' Erasmus translated φρονοῦσι by *cogitant* 'think of' in 1516; thereafter
by *curant* 'care for.'

2 See n6 below.

3 So Valla Annot in Rom 8 (I 857)

4 or care for] Added in 1527

5 For ... matters.] Added in 1527

6 In 8:5 the Vulgate (majority reading) translates the one Greek verb φρονοῦσιν
by using two Latin verbs, *sapiunt* 'discern' in the first clause, *sentiunt* 'feel'
in the second clause – so the Vulgate printed in 1527. In a minority reading
sapiunt is used in both clauses (Wordsworth and White II 99 5n). Erasmus'

criticism of the Translator here presupposes the majority reading: ('discern [*sapiunt*] the things of the flesh, feel [*sentiunt*] the things of the Spirit'); his cue phrase, however, appears to represent the minority reading, hence, in the second clause, 'discern [*sapiunt*] the things of the spirit.'

Valla had criticized the Vulgate's 'love of variety' in translating the Greek noun φρόνημα of the next verse by using two Latin nouns, *prudentia* and *sapientia* (*Annot in Rom* 8 [1 857]). Frans Titelmans charged that Erasmus' strictures against the Vulgate's 'variety' could be turned against himself, since he translates the Greek verb in 8:5 by *curo*, but the parallel noun form in 8:6 by *affectus*. Erasmus justified his translation on the grounds of good Latin idiom (*Responsio ad collationes* LB IX 997C–D). Cf the annotation on 14:6 ('and he who does not eat, to the Lord he does not eat') and n20.

8:7 [ER *nam affectus carnis* 'for the affection[1] of the flesh']

[VG] *quoniam sapientia carnis* 'because the wisdom of the flesh'; φρόνημα – the same word that he had, repeatedly, just translated 'prudence.'[2] But it is a noun related to the verb that he has just translated 'discern' and 'feel,' although it signifies rather a disposition of mind; just as μέγα φρονεῖν means 'to be high-minded,' and θνητὰ φρονεῖν 'care about human things.' So in this passage φρόνημα means not so much 'wisdom' and 'prudence' as 'affection' and 'regard' or 'taking thought.' This[3] is indicated by φροντίς [thought, care] and φροντίζειν [to take thought, care for], which come from the same root. In Latin, one who is led by carnal affections is said to 'mind the flesh' [*sapere carnem*]; I have nowhere found *sapientia* [wisdom] to mean 'affection.'[4] It is not surprising that Origen philosophizes, in his usual way, about the carnal understanding of the Law, for a base understanding arises out of base affections, and vice versa.[5] St [John] Chrysostom also touches on Origen's idea.[6]

1 affection] From *1519*; in *1516*, *prudentia* 'prudence'
2 The word φρόνημα occurs only four times in the New Testament, all in Romans 8 (6a, 6b, 7, 27). In 8:6 the Vulgate had both times translated *prudentia* 'prudence.' But the noun φρόνησις also appears twice in the New Testament, the adjective φρόνιμος much more frequently. The Vulgate translates the noun by *prudentia*, and prefers *prudens* for the adjective, but also renders it by *sapiens*. Cf the annotation on 11:25 ('minded towards yourselves'). For the verb φρονέω cf the annotation on 12:16 ('minding high things').
3 This ... on Origen's idea.] Added in *1535*
4 These brief sentences reflect a much longer discussion in *Responsio ad collationes* LB IX 997D–998B. Responding to Titelmans' criticism of 'variety' in his translation (cf preceding annotation, n6), Erasmus replied that while the Latin *affectus* is used for the Greek πάθη 'disturbances' in philosophical discussion, the word elsewhere spans a broader range of connotations, and is therefore especially suitable here because it can be used equally well with both 'spirit' and 'flesh.' At the same time, it is to be distinguished from *sapientia* 'wisdom,' for while 'wisdom' implies a love of what one

understands, 'affection' does not imply an understanding of what is loved. For Erasmus' efforts elsewhere to define *affectus*, see the annotations on 1:26 ('to passions of shame') and on 1:31 ('without disposition'), especially n2.

5 Cf Origen *Comm in Rom* 6.12 PG 14 1096A. Cf the annotation on 8:3 ('for what was impossible for the law') and n4.

6 Cf Chrysostom *Hom in Rom* 13.6 PG 60 515–16. Like Origen, Chrysostom understands the 'mind of the spirit' as the life lived under grace, the 'mind of the flesh' as the life 'yearning for base and worldly things.' In his exposition at this point, however, he does not define, as Origen does, the 'mind of the flesh' specifically in terms of the Mosaic law.

Until 1535 this annotation concluded with all the pre-1535 material now found in the next annotation. See next annotation, n1.

8:7 [ER *inimicitia est adversus deum* 'is hostility towards God']

[VG] *inimica est deo* 'is hostile to God.' The Greek is not[1] 'is hostile to God' but 'is hostility towards God,' ἔχθρα εἰς θεόν, and in this form St Jerome cited the passage more than once [in his treatise] *Against Jovinian*.[2] Augustine[3] cites it in the same way, both in explicating some passages in this Epistle, and several times elsewhere, if I am not mistaken.[4] For in printed editions this reading is found: *quia carnis prudentia inimica est in deum* [because the wisdom of the flesh is hostile to God]; it is likely that *inimica* has been changed from *inimicitia*. In addition,[5] the discourse is more neatly ordered if one abstract corresponds to another. For there had preceded: 'The wisdom of the flesh is death; the wisdom of the Spirit is life and peace.' That phrase 'is death' he now recalls and amplifies – 'is hostility towards God' – as though to say that this is something worse than death. So also Chrysostom.[6] To be sure,[7] if in the Greek the accent is transferred to the final syllable, ἐχθρά [feminine], it will mean 'hostile.' But the preceding noun φρόνημα in the neuter does not allow this; one would rather have to write ἐχθρόν [neuter].[8] Thus[9] I am surprised that some argue that 'hostile' is the correct reading, unless perhaps they think we should alter a reading that is consistent in all the manuscripts.[10] Now it is not strange if some Latin writers in the course of exposition say 'wisdom is "hostile" to God';[11] for both readings give almost the same sense, except that 'hostility' is more effective, and better fits Paul's expression.

1 The Greek is not] This annotation did not appear separately until 1535, when the words *inimica est deo* became the cue phrase for a new annotation, with the result that the words 'the Greek is not' became somewhat illogically the final words of the previous annotation. If the 1535 edition were followed precisely, the two annotations would appear together thus:

... touches on Origen's idea. The Greek is not:

[VG] *inimica est deo* 'is hostile to God' but 'is hostility to God' ...

We have adapted the original form for intelligibility.

2 Jerome *Adversus Jovinianum* 1.37 PL 23 (1883) 274A–B

3 Augustine ... *inimicitia.*] Added in *1519*
4 Augustine *Expositio quarundam propositionum ex epistula ad Romanos* 49 PL 35 2073. Cf also *Sermones* 155.10.10–11 PL 38 846–7 and *De natura et gratia* 17.18 PL 44 255. In all these passages Augustine cites *inimica,* not *inimicitia,* but in the *Expositio* he uses the noun *inimicitia* to explain the reading *inimica,* leading Erasmus, evidently, to infer that *inimica* took the place of an original *inimicitia* in the text.
5 In addition ... Chrysostom.] Added in *1535*
6 Chrysostom *Hom in Rom* 13.6 PG 60 516
7 To be sure ... ἐχθρόν.] Added in *1519*
8 ἐχθρα accented on the first syllable is a noun, ἐχθρά accented on the last syllable is an adjective in the feminine and must therefore modify a feminine noun.
9 Thus ... expression.] Added in *1535*
10 Frans Titelmans had defended the Vulgate reading; cf *Responsio ad collationes* LB IX 998F–999A.
11 Cf eg Ambrosiaster *Comm in Rom* 8:7 (1) and Pelagius *Expos in Rom* 8:7 (Souter II 62:16–19).

8:9 [ER *siquidem spiritus dei* 'since the Spirit of God']
[VG] *si tamen spiritus dei* 'if only the Spirit of God.' The Greek is εἴπερ, which generally has the force of '[if], to be sure,' or 'if indeed' – though in this passage it seems to[1] suggest not a doubt but an inference, as though you said 'since indeed the Spirit of God dwells in you.' And yet Origen and[2] Ambrose read and expound the phrase as though it expressed uncertainty.[3] Nevertheless[4] it is more probable that Paul is attributing the Spirit to those whom he is addressing; for when, immediately after, he speaks more harshly, saying, 'But if anyone does not have the Spirit of Christ [...],' he turns away from the direct address – a point Theophylact made,[5] and Chrysostom[6] before him.[7] The latter observes that εἴπερ in Paul frequently has a sense of confirmation, not of doubt, as though you said ἐπείπερ [seeing that]. It is used in this sense in the first chapter of Second Thessalonians: εἴπερ δίκαιον παρὰ θεῷ ἀποδοῦναι τοῖς θλίβουσιν ὑμᾶς θλίψιν [seeing that it is just with God to repay with affliction those who afflict you.] [1:6][8] Theophylact pointed out that here εἴπερ does not suggest doubt, but confidence.[9] Sometimes [the expression] is also used in entreaty: 'If I have done you any kindness, or if I have brought you any pleasure.'[10] Why, when the Translator has eliminated this ambiguity,[11] are those silent here who shout that I am restricting the breadth of meaning, as though the fecundity of Scripture lay in the ambiguity of language, or as though this fertility were not rather produced by ignorance?[12] It is not a fecundity worthy of praise when the jurists say: '*vel dic, vel dic, vel dic.*'[13]

1 seems to] Added in *1535*

2 Origen and] Added in 1519
3 Ambrosiaster thought that Paul spoke 'ambiguously' here because he was addressing those who still possessed an incomplete faith but in whom he saw the hope of a perfected faith (*Comm in Rom* 8:9 [2]). For Origen, the clause stipulates a condition, and the *si tamen* raises a possible doubt: 'You do not follow the carnal understanding of the Law, but the spiritual, through which you have come to the life-giving Spirit, if your deeds and manner of living are such that you deserve the Spirit of God' (*Comm in Rom* 6.12 PG 14 1096c). Erasmus, on the other hand, believes the clause does not imply a condition that might raise a doubt, but states an inference, and thus translates not 'if only' but 'since' – though he recognizes that εἴπερ can mean either 'if' or 'since.' For patristic and modern interpretations of the conjunction see Schelkle 262–4 and Otto Kuss *Der Römerbrief* 2nd ed, 2 vols (Regensburg 1963) II 500ff.
4 Nevertheless . . . Theophylact made] Added in 1527
5 See n9 below.
6 and Chrysostom . . . *vel dic'*] This remaining portion of the annotation was added in 1535.
7 See n8 below.
8 Chrysostom *Hom in Rom* 13.8 PG 60 518
9 Theophylact *Expos in Rom* 8:10 PG 124 440A
10 Virgil *Aeneid* 4.317–18. Dido's 'if' does not express a doubt whether, but an assurance that, she has given Aeneas favours.
11 Ie that the Greek εἴπερ can introduce statements expressing either doubt or confirmation. The Vulgate's translation suggests doubt; Erasmus', confirmation.
12 For Titelmans' complaint see the annotation on 8:3 ('after the likeness of the flesh of sin') n5.
13 We have not discovered the precise juridical context of this idiom, though the verb *dicere* 'to say,' 'pronounce,' is frequently found in Latin legal jargon. The context here suggests Erasmus' disapproval of those who exploit the ambiguity of a law, of a precedent, or of the evidence of a case with numerous alternative interpretations. Erasmus had already made the complaint about jurists in the *Responsio ad collationes* LB IX 970A–B. See also Erasmus' comments on lawyers in the *Moria* CWE 27 125.

8:10 [ER *corpus quidem mortuum est propter peccatum, spiritus autem vita est* 'the body indeed is dead because of sin, but the Spirit is life']
[VG] *corpus quidem mortuum est propter peccatum, spiritus autem vivit* 'the body[1] indeed is dead because of sin,[2] but the spirit lives.' Instead of 'lives,' the Greek has 'is life.'[3] It is so cited by Augustine in explicating questions on this Epistle,[4] and again in discussing the seventy-fifth Psalm;[5] likewise, in the thirteenth book of *The City of God*,[6] and in the twenty-fourth book *Against Faustus*, the second chapter.[7] So also[8] Hilary in the eighth book *On the Trinity*.[9] Similarly Athanasius, in his book to Serapion *On the Holy Spirit*.[10] Likewise Ambrose in elucidating this passage,[11] and he is

supported by the old Latin manuscripts. [The phrase] 'is life' perhaps is a stronger expression than 'lives,' for '[the Spirit] is life' because it gives life. If I am not mistaken, it is a question of the Spirit of Christ, not our own; the words that immediately follow virtually say as much: 'but if the Spirit of him who raised Jesus from the dead dwells in you.' Now an error between ζωή [zōē] and ζῇ [zē], 'life' and 'lives,' is easy, and, according[12] to Hebrew idiom, makes little difference as far as the sense is concerned. It is[13] no wonder that some authors speak here about our spirit,[14] for just as the body of Christ, raised to life, promises resurrection for our bodies, so the immortal Spirit of Christ confers life on our spirit. Theophylact, indeed, not only reads ζωή , but also interprets 'life' in this sense: 'Not only,' says [Theophylact], 'does he himself live, but he can also bestow this on others.' He also points out that there were some who understood 'Spirit' here to mean Christ himself.[15]

1 the body ... concerned.] When introduced in 1519, this passage constituted the entire annotation, with the exceptions noted in nn2, 8, 12 below.

2 because of sin] Added to the cue phrase in 1535

3 So Valla *Annot in Rom* 8 (I 857)

4 Augustine *Expositio quarundam propositionum ex epistula ad Romanos* 50 PL 35 2073

5 Augustine *Enarrationes in psalmos* 75:5 PL 36 960

6 Augustine *De civitate dei* 13.23.1 CSEL 40/1 648:27–8

7 Augustine *Contra Faustum Manichaeum* 24.2 PL 42 476

8 So also ... *Trinity*.] Added in 1527

9 Hilary *De Trinitate* 8.21 PL 10 252B

10 Athanasius *Epistulae ad Serapionem* 1.6 PG 26 545A

11 Ambrosiaster *Comm in Rom* 8:10. 'The Spirit is life' is, in fact, the preferred reading of the Vulgate, though there are numerous witnesses to the reading as given in the cue phrase; cf Wordsworth and White II 100 and 10n.

12 according to Hebrew idiom] Added in 1522

13 It is ... Christ himself.] Added in 1535

14 So, evidently, Origen *Comm in Rom* 6.13 PG 14 1099B. For Ambrosiaster the Spirit here is the 'Holy Spirit' given in baptism (*Comm in Rom* 8:10), for Chrysostom, it is the divine Spirit which is able to give to others its own life (*Hom in Rom* 13.8 PG 60 519).

15 Theophylact *Expos in Rom* 8:10 PG 124 440B. Theophylact refers here to the first clause of 8:10, 'if Christ is in you.' Origen, referring to both this clause and the phrase 'Spirit of Christ' in 8:9 says, 'The Spirit of Christ and Christ in this passage seem to me to be one and the same' (*Comm in Rom* 6.13 PG 14 1099B).

8:10 [ER VG] *propter iustificationem* **'because of justification.'**[1] διὰ τὴν δικαιο-σύνην [dikaiosynēn], that is, 'because of righteousness' [*propter iustitiam*], as he elsewhere often translates.[2] For 'justification' represents, more accurately, δικαίωσις [dikaiōsis].[3]

1 In 1516 only, this annotation immediately followed the annotation on 8:15 ('Abba, Father').
2 The Vulgate quite regularly renders δικαιοσύνη by *iustitia*: cf eg Rom 1:17; 3:5, 21, 22, 25; 4:3, 5, 9, etc. It renders δικαίωσις by *iustificatio* in Rom 5:18. On the translation of these words in the Vulgate and in Erasmus' New Testament cf Robert D. Sider 'The Just and the Holy in Erasmus' New Testament Scholarship' *Erasmus of Rotterdam Society Yearbook* 11 (1991) 4–6.
3 δικαίωσις] In 1516 only, there followed an additional sentence: 'Here most Latin codices have "lives," though "life" ought to be read; ζωή [life] not ζῇ [lives] is to be understood.' The sentence became superfluous after the preceding annotation, which discussed the point, was added in 1519.

8:11 [ER *propter ipsius spiritum inhabitantem in vobis* 'because of his Spirit dwelling in you']

[VG] *propter inhabitantem spiritum eius in vobis* 'because[1] of the Spirit of him dwelling in you.' Hilary in the second book *On the Trinity* reads: '*propter spiritum suum qui habitat in vobis*[2] [because of his Spirit which dwells in you].' And this is better Latin, but it is too small a point to dispute about. Some of the Greek copies differed here. In most it was διὰ τὸ ἐνοικοῦν αὐτοῦ πνεῦμα ἐν ὑμῖν [preposition with accusative], that is, 'because of his Spirit dwelling in you'; in some, διὰ τοῦ ἐνοικοῦντος αὐτοῦ πνεύματος ἐν ὑμῖν [preposition with genitive], that is, 'through his Spirit which dwells in you.'[3] This makes little difference to the sense. For it is true that the preposition διά when followed by the genitive signifies instrument, and when followed by the accusative, cause; but sometimes there is nothing to prevent the same things from being both cause and instrument.

1 because ... instrument.] The entire annotation was added in 1519.
2 Hilary *De Trinitate* 2.29 PL 10 70A
3 Textual authorities are fairly evenly divided on the reading here, and contemporary scholars do not agree on which is more probably the original one. See Cranfield I 391–2.

8:15 [ER *iterum ad timorem* 'again to fear']

[VG] *iterum in timore* 'again in fear';[1] εἰς φόβον, that is, 'to fear' or 'to terror.'

1 In 1516 only, this annotation was placed immediately between the annotations on 8:7 ('because the wisdom of the flesh') and 8:9 ('if only the Spirit of God').

8:15 [ER *spiritum adoptionis* 'spirit of adoption']

[VG] *spiritum adoptionis filiorum dei* 'the spirit of adoption of the sons of God.' Instead of three words [*adoptionis filiorum dei*] there is one in the Greek, υἱοθεσίας, which means 'the adoption of sons,' or rather,[1] the adoption of those who are not sons by nature into the position of sons –

for[2] grandsons, too, are adopted, though this is an adoption most lovingly bestowed. The Greek[3] offers no difficulty, but I do not see how the Latin [translation] can stand. For if 'adoption' is taken in an active sense, as though the sons are adopting, the expression is absurd; if in a passive sense, one does not say that 'sons are adopted' when through adoption they come into another family, in the same way that one says a magistrate is created or a bishop chosen when he becomes a magistrate or a bishop by election; nor do we speak of the adoption of sons in the same way that we speak of the creation of magistrates.[4] Rather, one adopts the sons of others into the position of sons; they are said to become through adoption the sons of the one who adopts them, and he makes the sons of others or his grandsons his own, whether they are children or independent adults.[5] A father or uncle is said to 'give over for adoption.' If we take [the Vulgate's phrase] to mean the adoption of those who were previously sons of Satan, the Scripture does not intend this. If we understand that we are being adopted sons of God, the Latin expression is inappropriate – one would have to say rather the spirit of 'adoption *into* [the place of] the sons of God.' But just as Paulus can adopt the son of Scipio into the position of his own grandson, so he can adopt Scipio's grandson into the position of his own son.[6] To avoid this difficulty,[7] some have translated *spiritum adoptionis* [the spirit of adoption],[8] because the chief kind of adoption is adoption into the position of son. Thus the shorter expression is understood to stand for the primary type. But the very tone of the Apostle's discourse indicates that here it is a question of those adopted into the privileges of sons. A further point: the genitive 'of God' has been added though it is not found in the Greek codices.[9] For[10] he is not distinguishing here the sons of God from the sons of men, but rather the sons of grace from the servants of the Law.

1 or rather ... position of sons] Added in 1522
2 for ... bestowed] Added in 1527
3 The Greek ... privileges of sons.] Added in 1535
4 This is essentially the argument in the *Responsio ad collationes* LB IX 999A–C, where Erasmus replied to Titelmans' suggestion that his objection to the Vulgate here was a mere cavil.
5 Erasmus distinguishes here between *adoptio* and *arrogatio*. *Arrogatio* was the adoption of a man who was himself the head of a family, so that his adoption effected the fusion of his family with the one into which he was adopted.
6 Erasmus apparently takes the names from two distinguished Roman households, those of the Aemilii and the Cornelii, though he has either postulated hypothetical relationships or garbled the facts. Publius Cornelius Scipio Aemilianus, the natural son of Lucius Aemilius Paullus (conqueror of Greece) was adopted by Publius Cornelius Scipio, the son of the conqueror of Africa, Publius Cornelius Scipio Africanus Maior. Thus by adoption Aemilianus became the grandson of Africanus Maior. Scipio Aemilianus

destroyed Carthage in the third Punic War (149–146 BC), and became known
as Publius Scipio Aemilianus Africanus Minor.
7 Ie the ambiguity of the term 'son'
8 So Lefèvre d'Etaples *Pauli epistolae* fol 6 recto and fol 86 verso
9 *dei* appears in the Vulgate printed in 1527 and is attested in Wordsworth
and White II 101 and 15n. There is, however, no support for it in the Greek
witnesses (see Tischendorf II 402 and 15n).
10 For ... Law.] Added in 1527

8:15 [ER VG] *Abba, pater* 'Abba, Father.' אָב or אֲבִי in Hebrew, or rather[1] in Aramaic, as Jerome points out, means 'father';[2] the term is composed of the
first two letters, aleph[3] and beth. He left the Hebrew word to suggest that
there is something special in the very name, a name fathers like to hear,
and children first learn to pronounce, for with this term they instinctively
implore their fathers' help – in Latin the same is true of *pappus* [papa], a
word used especially by little children.

Now with respect to the addition of ὁ πατήρ [father], it is not clear
in the Greek whether this is a repetition designed to emphasize feeling,
or the translation of a word foreign to the Romans, especially since it is
written in the nominative case [rather than vocative]. To me[4] it seems more
probable that it was said κατ' ἀναδίπλωσιν [for repetition], for this manner of speaking is virtually peculiar to Hebrew, which, for the sake of
ἐπίτασις [intensification],[5] sometimes repeats the same word, sometimes
renders it with a different word that has the same meaning. Examples are:
'Not everyone who says to me Lord, Lord';[6] and 'my God, my God';[7] and
'the good figs, [very] good';[8] and 'Lord, our Lord.'[9] In this last example
the two words are different in Hebrew: the first is a designation of God by
the tetragrammaton, consisting of these [four] letters: יהוה, jod, he, vau, he.
This word [the Hebrews] call ἄρρητον, that is, 'ineffable.' The second is אֲדֹנָי
'adonai'; this is a common title, and frequently attributed even to men. But
here the words are the same as those Christ uses in Mark, the fourteenth
chapter, praying to the Father: '*Abba*,[10] Father' [14:36].[11] I think[12] it due to a
mistake of the copyists that Augustine, in the one hundred seventy-eighth
letter, writes that *abba* is a Greek word, and *pater* Latin. For Paul did not
write to the Romans in Latin, and it is beyond dispute that *abba* is an Aramaic or Hebrew word. I shall quote the words of Augustine: 'Let us not
accept Paul, who says, in writing to the Romans: "in which we cry '*Abba*,
Father.'" He uses two languages for one term; for he says *Abba* – "Father"
in Greek – and then repeating, he names him *pater* in Latin.'[13] Indeed[14] I
believe these words have been patched on to the writings of Augustine.
Thomas is better; he says that *abba* is a Hebrew word, *pater* either Greek or
Latin; for the Latins and Greeks use the same word for father.[15]

1 or rather ... points out] Added in *1519*. Zúñiga attacked Erasmus' statement of *1516* that the word was Hebrew, but Erasmus pointed to this correction in the 1519 edition. Cf *Apologia ad annotationes Stunicae* ASD IX-2 170:106–8.

2 Jerome *Commentarius in epistulam ad Galatas* 2 (on 4:6) PL 26 (1883) 400A–B. In both Hebrew and Aramaic אָב means 'father' and אָבִי means 'my father.'

3 aleph and beth] Added in *1519*

4 To me ... attributed even to men.] Added in *1519*, except that the Hebrew for the '[four] letters' was added in *1535*

5 For the rhetorical terms ἀναδίπλωσις and ἐπίτασις see respectively Lausberg I 619 and Chomarat *Grammaire et rhétorique* II 808–9.

6 Matt 7:21

7 Ps 22:1; Mark 15:34; Matt 27:46

8 Jer 24:3

9 Ps 8:1, 9

10 'Abba, Father'] Added in *1527*; likewise, the word 'here' at the beginning of the sentence

11 Valla, also, cites Mark 14:36, noting that the nominative case here, as in Rom 8:15, implies that the Greek ὁ πατήρ is a translation of the Aramaic word. Zúñiga complained that Erasmus had insisted on the nominative; cf *Apologia ad annotationes Stunicae* ASD IX-2 170 and the notes on lines 110 and 113.

12 I think ... *pater* in Latin.] Added in *1519*

13 See Pseudo-Augustine *Epistulae* 20.15 PL 33 1161. Pseudo-Augustine obviously relies on a Latin text. The author cites this passage from Paul to demonstrate that the term ὁμούσιος (for ὁμοούσιος 'of the same substance') should not be rejected as a Trinitarian formula merely because it is Greek. Otherwise, he argues, let us object to the term Christian, which is Greek in origin, and let us not accept Paul in this passage.
The ἀββά of the Greek text is a transliteration of the Aramaic אַבָּא 'abba'; while this is the grammatical form for 'the father' (cf the Greek ὁ πατήρ) it is idiomatic Aramaic for address to one's father.

14 Indeed ... father.] Added in *1527*

15 Thomas Aquinas *Super Rom lect* cap 8 lectio 3.644. The Greek πατήρ transliterates into the Latin *pater*.

8:16 [ER *testatur* 'witnesses'[1]]

[VG] *testimonium reddit* 'renders testimony'; συμμαρτυρεῖ [*symmartyrei*]. We 'render' that which is either 'returned' or 'owed.' Thus urine[2] 'is rendered' [that is, returned, or passed] and an account 'is rendered' [as something owed]. But the Greek is [better represented in the Latin] *attestatur* [witnesses to] or, more literally, *contestatur* [witnesses together], so that you understand the dual testimony of the two spirits, our own and God's. Moreover, the testimony of our spirit is confirmed by the testimony of the divine Spirit. In the same[3] way they are called *symmachi* [supporting allies] who bring aid in battle. And it is customary to say *teste conscientia* [the conscience bearing witness].[4] The testimony of the human spirit is weak, especially in those who are imperfect, unless the testimony of the divine Spirit is added.

Nothing prevents us from saying that there is a mutual love between God and a human being, though love is the gift of God; so [we can say that] there is a mutual testimony between the Spirit of God and our own, not because our spirit confirms God, but because [his Spirit] gives witness of itself within.[5] Chrysostom suggests that the Greek preposition σύν takes us back to the spoken testimony in the preceding sentence, 'in which we cry "*Abba*, Father"'; that is, the testimony [rendered] in this cry is confirmed by the secret testimony of the divine Spirit, which confirms that cry with its own gift.[6] Theophylact agrees.[7]

1 witnesses] First in *1519*; in *1516*, *testimonium perhibet* 'furnishes a testimony.' Also in *1516* only, this and the following annotation appeared in reverse order.
2 Thus urine ... account 'is rendered.'] Added in *1535*. For *reddere* used in the sense of passing urine, see Pliny *Naturalis historia* 8.66.165.
3 In the same ... agrees.] This remaining portion of the annotation was added in *1535*.
4 Erasmus wishes to stress the significance of the Greek prefix συν- (*syn-* or *sym-*) 'with,' which he equates with the Latin prefix *con-* (*cum*) in such words as *contestatur* and *conscientia*, to suggest a 'joint' endeavour. Many exegetes agree with Erasmus' emphasis on the Greek prefix *syn* in the compound verb. See Cranfield I 403.
5 Frans Titelmans had objected to the notion of a 'mutual witness of spirits,' and had shown 'from the mysteries of theology' that there is only a single witness. Erasmus replied that the witness of our spirit is weak unless the witness of the Spirit comes to its support (*Responsio ad collationes* LB IX 999D–E).
6 Chrysostom *Hom in Rom* 14.3 PG 60 527: 'I am strengthened,' says Paul, 'not only by the cry [*Abba*, Father] but by the source of the cry – the Spirit ... What does he mean by "the Spirit bears witness with the spirit"? He means "the Paraclete with the gift given us," for the cry is not only that of the gift, but of the Paraclete who gave the gift.' On this view the gift given is the Christian's new 'spirit.'
7 Theophylact *Expos in Rom* 8:16 PG 124 444D

8:17 [ER *siquidem simul cum eo patimur* 'since we suffer together with him'] [VG] *si tamen compatimur* 'if only we suffer';[1] εἴπερ, that is, 'since indeed'; because here as well[2] it can be taken to imply inference, not doubt.[3] Also, in this passage *compati* [to suffer with] is not what uneducated people commonly understand – 'to be moved by the evils of another' – but 'to be a companion and imitator' and 'to emulate the afflictions[4] of Christ.'

1 For the position in *1516*, see preceding annotation, n1.
2 Cf the annotation on 8:9 ('if only the Spirit of God').
3 Under attack from Titelmans, Erasmus argued that his translation allowed either inference or doubt, or indeed confirmation, and he accordingly

expected that Titelmans should have praised the 'breadth of meaning' he
offered (*Responsio ad collationes* LB IX 999E–F; cf the annotation on 8:9 ('if only
the Spirit of God') n12.

4 afflictions] First in *1519*; in *1516*, 'sufferings'

**8:17 [ER *ut et una cum illo glorificemur* 'that we may also be glorified
along with him']**

[VG] *ut et glorificemur* 'that[1] we may also be glorified';[2] συνδοξασθῶμεν, so
that[3] you understand that the glory is common to us and Christ.

    1 In *1516* only, the position of this and the following annotation was reversed.
    2 The cue phrase represents a minority reading; the preferred reading (and the
      reading of the Vulgate printed in *1527*) is *conglorificemur* 'glorified together';
      cf Wordsworth and White II 102 and 17n.
    3 so that ... Christ] Added in *1519*

8:18 [ER *nam reputo* 'for I consider']

[VG] *existimo enim* 'for I suppose'; λογίζομαι, that is, *perpendo* [I weigh
carefully], or *reputo* [I consider]. For Paul does not hold this merely as an
opinion, as though in doubt, but, certain that it is so, he weighs it carefully in his mind. For[1] he is not speaking of belief – to express which the
word 'suppose' is too weak, inasmuch as it is frequently connected with
doubt. He is talking about the consideration of those things which he has
believed. Through this consideration, he draws up a balance sheet, so to
speak, comparing the troubles of this life, which must be endured because
of the gospel, with the reward of eternal life, which Christ has promised to
all the godly. But the result of the comparison is indeed that our sufferings
here seem trivial when we reflect upon that eternal felicity.[2] I have never
found λογίζεσθαι used in the sense of *existimare*, which the Greeks express
by οἴεσθαι [to suppose], ἡγεῖσθαι [to deem], δοκεῖν [to seem], νομίζειν [to
hold, consider as]. *Aestimare* [to judge, assess] would be more tolerable, for
it is a word appropriate to reckoning. We 'suppose' that to be dear which
we think of great value, but we 'judge' as dear that which, after reflection,
we regard as dear.

    But if λογίζεσθαι means in Greek the same as *existimare* in Latin, Paul
spoke incorrectly in the fourth chapter to the Philippians, ταῦτα λογίζεσθε
[4:8], or at least the Translator was wrong to render it by *haec cogitate* [think
on these things] when he should have translated *haec existimate* [suppose
these things]. And in the tenth chapter of Second Corinthians he translated τοῦτο λογιζέσθω πάλιν as 'let him think on this again' [10:7]. In the
twelfth chapter of the same Epistle, Paul used this word in the sense of
aestimare: μή τις εἰς ἐμὲ λογίσηται, that is, 'so that no one should think of
me more highly than I deserve' [12:6]. In the Epistle to the Romans, the

second chapter, he uses it for 'think': λογίζῃ δὲ τοῦτο ὦ ἄνθρωπε [and do you think this, O man] [2:3]. In the sixth chapter of the same Epistle, οὕτως καὶ ὑμεῖς λογίζεσθε ἑαυτούς [likewise you too consider yourselves] [6:11], he is not teaching these what they ought to believe, for they had long since learned this, but what they should remember and turn over in their minds, so that 'judge' is more suitable than 'suppose.' Again in the fourth chapter of First Corinthians, οὕτως ἡμᾶς λογιζέσθω ἄνθρωπος [so let everyone consider us] [4:1], 'judge' would be more suitable than 'suppose.' For it would be strange if the Corinthians did not yet surmise that Paul was a steward of the mysteries of God.[3] Again in the tenth chapter of Second Corinthians, 'that confidence by which I am supposed to be bold towards some' [10:2], the Translator renders λογίζομαι by *existimor* [I am supposed], while Chrysostom explains it as meaning 'think' [*cogito*]. For with this statement he is threatening certain people who despised Paul as a nobody. He says that he has not yet made a decision, but is only thinking about punishing these, if they do not have a change of mind.[4] Theophylact understands λογίζομαι as ὑπολαμβάνω, στοχάζομαι, that is, 'have in mind' and 'aim at.'[5] One who 'has in mind' that he will act, has not yet assumed a clear resolution; one who 'aims' still holds the weapon in his hand, thinking against whom and how it is to be thrown.[6]

But he who taught that *existimare* [to suppose] referred to a fixed opinion taught what is clearly wrong, for 'supposition' is every bit as doubtful as 'opinion';[7] in fact 'supposition' is often deceptive, as in the clause 'who supposes himself to be something'; and 'they supposed they saw a spirit.'[8]

1 For ... a spirit.'] This remaining portion of the annotation was added in 1535.
2 The discussion here, in this 1535 addition, of the meaning of λογίζεσθαι follows closely the earlier discussion in the *Responsio ad collationes* LB IX 999F–1000B, which was provoked by Titelmans' claim that *existimo* is indeed the correct translation of the word. For a parallel discussion (also from 1535) see the annotation on Rom 4:3 ('and it was considered') and n3.
3 Cf 1 Cor 4:1: 'So let everyone consider us as servants of Christ and stewards of the mysteries of God.'
4 Chrysostom *In epistulam secundam ad Corinthios homiliae* 21.1 PG 61 542.
   In a 1535 addition to the annotation on 2 Cor 10:2 (*absens autem confido in vobis*) Erasmus argues that λογίζομαι has an active sense ('I am thinking about') rather than passive ('I am supposed') as the Vulgate understands. Both active and passive forms (*existimo* and *existimor*) are attested in the Vulgate (cf Weber II 1798 2 and 2n). The Vulgate printed in 1527 translated *existimor*, as did Erasmus until 1535, when he rendered the word by *cogito* (active).
5 Theophylact *Expositio in epistulam secundam ad Corinthios* 10:2 PG 124 900B
6 The interpretation here of 2 Cor 10:2 is found in virtually the same form in Erasmus' annotation on the passage LB VI 784D.

7 In *Responsio ad collationes* LB IX 1000A Erasmus wrote that *existimo* means the same as *opinor*.
8 The two clauses correspond to the Vulgate of Gal 6:3 and Luke 24:37 respectively, where the Vulgate uses the verb *existimare* 'to suppose.'

8:18 [ER *quae revelabitur erga nos* 'that shall be revealed towards us'¹]
[VG] *quae revelabitur in nobis* 'that shall be revealed in us.' It is uncertain in the Greek whether the verb ἀποκαλυφθῆναι [to be revealed] should be taken with the preposition πρός [in relation to, in comparison with] or with the participle μέλλουσαν² [about to be]. For if it is to be taken with the preposition, the sense will be '[are not a match] in comparison with this, that the glory about to come be revealed in us.' But in that case the article τό seems lacking, which is normally put before verbs in the infinitive.³ The Translator seems to construe [with μέλλουσαν] as follows: πρὸς τὴν δόξαν τὴν μέλλουσαν ἀποκαλυφθῆναι, that is, '[not of worth] in relation to the glory that shall be revealed.'

[The Greek] is not 'in us,' but 'to us' or rather⁴ 'towards us,' in accordance with that [promise] 'Now we see through a glass and in a mystery, but then face to face.'⁵ And yet the preposition εἰς, as I have pointed out quite often,⁶ is ambiguous in Greek, and this⁷ reading⁸ also has a pious sense.

1 towards us] In *1516* only, *in nos* 'to us'
2 The discussion assumes the entire sentence as its context:
    ER *nam reputo non esse pares afflictiones praesentis temporis ad gloriam quae revelabitur erga nos* 'for I consider that the afflictions of the present time are not a match for the glory that shall be revealed towards us'
    VG *existimo enim quod non sunt condignae passiones huius temporis ad futuram gloriam quae revelabitur in nobis* 'for I suppose that the sufferings of this time are not of worth in relation to the future glory that will be revealed in us'
3 Normally, ie, when the infinitive is used as a substantive (articular infinitive), here if translated literally, 'the revealing of' the glory ...
4 or rather ... to face'] Added in *1535*
5 1 Cor 13:12
6 See, for example, the annotation on 6:3 ('we have been baptized in Christ Jesus'). Erasmus admitted the ambiguity of the Greek preposition in his *Responsio ad collationes* LB IX 1000B. For the meaning 'towards' see εἰς (5) in BAG.
7 and this ... sense] Added in *1535*
8 Ie the Vulgate reading 'in us'

8:19 [ER *etenim sollicita creaturae exspectatio* 'for indeed, the eager expectation of the creation']
[VG] *nam exspectatio creaturae* 'for the expectation of the creation'; ἡ γὰρ ἀποκαραδοκία, which does not mean simply 'expectation,' but 'eager and

anxious expectation,' as the Greek scholia also attest, which point[1] out the intrinsic significance of the Greek word, [which is used] when something is awaited with great anticipation.[2] Hence I have translated 'eager expectation.'[3] The Greek[4] word is composed of three parts: the preposition ἀπό [from], κάρα 'head,' and δοκεῖν 'to seem,' because those who earnestly desire to see something raise their heads and keep a constant watch.[5] Hence Ambrose speaks of an 'assiduous expectation,'[6] Hilary of one 'far off,'[7] because with head stretched forward we look into the distance. Paul used the same word in the first chapter of the Epistle to the Philippians.[8] Aristophanes in the *Knights* wrote καραδοκεῖν (omitting the preposition): ἐκαραδόκησεν εἰς ἐμ᾽ ἡ βουλὴ πάλιν, that is, 'they turned their eyes towards me, eager for my promise'[9] – if I may render the sense rather than represent the words.

1 which point . . . 'eager expectation'] Added in 1519
2 Cf Pseudo-Oecumenius *Comm in Rom* 8:19 PG 118 481B.
3 expectation] At this point in the annotation, all editions from 1519 print *expectat* 'awaits,' possibly a mistake arising from Erasmus' translation: *sollicita creaturae expectatio . . . expectat*. Here in the annotation LB prints *expectatio* for the *expectat* of the editions.
4 The Greek . . . the words.] This remaining portion of the annotation was added in 1535.
5 δοκέω means 'to expect' and then 'to think' and 'to imagine' (LSJ). It also means 'to seem,' which in Latin is *videri*, the passive of *videre* 'to see.' Chantraine *Dictionnaire* I 496 rejects the type of explanation Erasmus here offers for ἀποκαραδοκία.
6 See n7.
7 The references to Ambrose and Hilary were apparently inspired by Titelmans' comments that 'some have translated "far off," others "assiduous"' (*Responsio ad collationes* LB IX 1000C). Erasmus agrees, but points out that these are all 'Latins,' whereas the Greeks, Chrysostom and Theophylact, support his interpretation. In fact Ambrosiaster does not interpret the word here as 'assiduous' (but see his commentary on Rom 8:25, where he speaks of the 'constant expectation of the kingdom'); for Hilary, see *Tractatus super psalmos* 148.2 PL 9 879C–880A. Chrysostom explains the word as an 'eager expectation' (*Hom in Rom* 14.4 PG 60 529), Theophylact as a 'great expectation' (*Expos in Rom* 8:19 PG 124 445D).
8 Phil 1:20. See the annotation there (*secundum expectationem*).
9 Aristophanes *Knights* 663

8:20 [ER *quippe vanitati creatura subiacet* 'the creation, to be sure, is subject to vanity']
[VG] *vanitati enim creatura subjecta est* 'for[1] the creation was subjected to vanity.' *Vanitas* here does not mean deceit, but rather futility, ματαιότητι.[2] For in the meantime the creation does not achieve what it strives to effect no matter how. For example, as each creature propagates itself – the individual

members in turn dying and being born again – creation protects the species from extinction and intends a kind of immortality, but in vain.

1 for ... vain.] The entire annotation was added in 1519.
2 For a somewhat similar discussion see the annotation on 1:21 ('but became vain').

8:20 [ER *qui subjecit illam* 'who made it (that is, the creation) subject']
[VG *qui subjecit eam* 'who made this subject.' 'This' has been added [by the Vulgate] for the sake of clarification; [the Greek has only] διὰ τὸν ὑποτάξαντα [through the one who made subject]. And 'in hope,' ἐπ' ἐλπίδι, is rather 'under the condition of hope.' Moreover[1] what follows, '*quia* [because, that] the creation itself also will be freed' etc[2] could be joined with the preceding words, 'made it subject under hope,' namely the hope *that* it too is to be freed from servitude. But the repetition of 'creation' makes the passage rather harsh.[3]

1 Moreover ... harsh.] Added in 1519
2 Erasmus proceeds here to Rom 8:21:
    ER *quoniam et ipsa creatura liberabitur a servitute* 'since the creation itself also will be freed from servitude'
    VG *quia et ipsa creatura liberabitur a servitute* 'because the creation itself also will be freed from servitude'
    For *quia* meaning either 'because' or 'that,' see next note.
3 The Greek ὅτι can mean either 'because' or 'that.' The Vulgate regularly translates ὅτι by *quia*, to mean, like the Greek word, either 'because' or 'that.' In classical Latin, however, *quia* is used only in the sense of 'because.' Cf the annotation on 8:36 ['as sheep of the slaughter'] n6. Erasmus eliminates the ambiguity of the Greek by translating *quoniam* 'since.'

8:21 [ER VG] *liberabitur a servitute corruptionis* 'will be[1] freed from the servitude of corruption.' ἐλευθερωθήσεται ἀπὸ τῆς δουλείας τῆς φθορᾶς, that is, 'will be made free' or 'set free.' And φθορά 'corruption,' is also a word with a double meaning in Greek, for it is used both of a thing vitiated and of one perishing; here it signifies destruction. So reads Augustine, in explaining the Epistle to the Galatians.[2] However, the sense is: 'The creation, which is now subject to destruction, is to be given its freedom, to be given, that is, the glory of the sons of God.'

1 will be ... God.] The entire annotation was added in 1519.
2 Augustine *Epistulae ad Galatas expositio* 1.63 PL 35 2147

8:22 [ER *omnis creatura congemiscit simulque nobiscum parturit* 'the whole creation groans and is in labour together with us']
[VG] *omnis creatura ingemiscit et parturit* 'the whole creation groans and is

in labour.' The Greek is, more aptly, συστενάζει καὶ συνωδίνει, that is, 'groans together and travails together' or 'is in pain together [*condolet*],' so to speak. Certainly Jerome cites *congemiscit* in the eighth book of his commentary on Isaiah;[1] and Augustine[2] in the sixty-seventh of his *Eighty-three Questions* reads *congemiscit et dolet* [groans together and is in pain].[3] Ambrose reads 'is in labour,' meaning 'is in pain';[4] thus the prepositional prefix συν- [with] refers either to us (indicating[5] that even the mute elements in some way groan along with us),[6] or to the universal creation as a whole, so that[7] we understand that the entire world is to be changed for the better. For, to express figuratively the magnitude of the evils, Paul imagines this whole world as a single person to which he attributes feeling, though it has none inherently, just as in the Psalms the mountains are said to 'rejoice' and the rivers to 'clap their hands.'[8] Likewise,[9] Origen expressly notes that the word is *congemit* meaning 'groans with another.' And yet he does not conceal the fact that the books vary, and that in some [the reading] was στενάζει [groans].[10]

1 Jerome *Commentarii in Isaiam* 8 (on 24:21–3) PL 24 288B
2 and Augustine ... in pain] Added in 1519
3 Augustine *De diversis quaestionibus* LXXXIII 67.1 PL 40 66
4 Ambrosiaster *Comm in Rom* 8:22 (1): 'To be in labour is to be in pain'
5 indicating ... along with us] Added in 1535
6 Erasmus told Titelmans that he wished to make every effort to draw out the force of the preposition (*Responsio ad collationes* LB IX 1000C–D).
7 so that ... 'clap their hands'] Added in 1535
8 For both references see Ps 98:8 (VG 97:8). Erasmus follows Chrysostom closely in his interpretation here of κτίσις as the whole world (cf *Hom in Rom* 14.4–5 PG 60 529). For a survey of interpretations of κτίσις in this passage see Cranfield I 411–12. See also Erasmus' interpretation in the *Paraphrase on Romans* CWE 42 48 n12.
9 Likewise ... στενάζει] Added in 1519
10 Ie without the prefix συν- 'with.' Cf Origen *Comm in Rom* 7.4 PG 14 1109C–1110A. Origen, as translated by Rufinus, does indeed stress the significance of the prefix συν- (= *cum*) 'with,' though at this point he is attempting to show rather that some copies have *condolet* 'is in pain together,' some *parturit* 'is in labour.'

8:23 [ER VG] *non solum autem illa* **'and not[1] only that.'** 'That' is not added in the Greek, οὐ μόνον δέ. But from the words which immediately follow, it appears that it must be understood. What are those to do here who do not want even a jot to be changed in sacred literature?[2] Origen frequently points out this form of expression in Paul.[3]

1 and not ... Paul.] The entire annotation was added in 1519. Our translation takes *illa* as feminine singular, referring to 'creation' (*creatura*) in 8:22 (cf

rsv); it is possible to understand it as neuter plural – 'not only those things'
– as Erasmus proposes for the similar expression 'not only these things' in
5:3; cf n3 below.

2 The Vulgate had added *illa*, thus 'changing' Sacred Scripture. Even before
Erasmus' New Testament was printed, Martin Dorp had insisted on the
integrity of the Vulgate; see Ep 304:139–56.

3 Cf Origen *Comm in Rom* 7.5 PG 14 1113B, where Origen says that he has often
pointed out the Apostle's fondness for the phrase 'not only this.' For the
idiom, see the annotation on 5:3 ('and not only') and 9:10 ('but not only she').

8:23 [ER *qui primitias spiritus habemus* 'we who have the first-fruits
of the Spirit']

[vg] *primitias spiritus habentes* 'having[1] the first-fruits of the Spirit'; τὴν
ἀπαρχήν. I wonder whatever text it was that Ambrose followed in reading 'but we too, who have the receptacle [*receptaculum*] of the Spirit.'[2]
And yet from his exposition it is not sufficiently clear what he read.[3]
Perhaps[4] he wrote *inceptaculum* 'a small beginning,' which a scribe changed
to *receptaculum*.

1 having ... read.] Added in 1519
2 Ambrosiaster *Comm in Rom* 8:23. But H.J. Vogels has noted a variant for
recension γ which reads *primitias spiritus*; cf CSEL 81/1 283:14n.
3 In his exposition, Ambrosiaster speaks only in passing of 'those of us who
have received the Spirit of God as a helper'; cf *Comm in Rom* 8:23 (4).
4 Perhaps ... *receptaculum*.] Added in 1527. This comment, in which Erasmus
tries to explain how a corruption may have arisen in Ambrosiaster's text, is
an interesting example of Erasmus' contribution to the still primitive science
of textual emendation. Erasmus conjectures that the Greek ἀπαρχή, which
contains the root ἀρχή 'beginning,' may have been rendered by a Latin
translator as *inceptaculum*, a word which, while unattested in classical or
medieval Latin (cf L&s and Niermeyer), looks as though it meant 'beginning.'
Not recognizing this word, possibly coined for the occasion, another scribe
would have altered it to *in receptaculum*, the latter being a word more familiar
to him.

8:23 [ER *nos ipsi in nobisipsis gemimus* 'we ourselves groan in our very
own selves']

[vg] *intra nos gemimus* 'we groan within[1] ourselves'; ἐν ἑαυτοῖς στενάζομεν,
that is, 'we groan[2] in our very own selves' or 'within[3] our very own selves,'
that is, silently.

1 within] First in 1519; in 1516, *inter* 'among'
2 we groan] In 1516 and 1519 only, *congemiscimus* 'we deeply groan'; in 1522
and thereafter, *ingemiscimus*
3 or 'within ... silently] Added in 1527

8:23 [ER *adoptionem* 'adoption']
[VG] *adoptionem filiorum dei* 'adoption of the sons of God'; υἱοθεσίαν,
that is, 'adoption.' But the Translator added some words to clarify the
thought as constantly he does[1] with this expression.[2] Augustine,[3] in the
third book *Against Faustus*, chapter 3, does not add 'of sons,' but cites only
'adoption.'[4] For who adopts his own sons? When[5] members of other families are adopted, they are not adopted as sons, but into the position of sons,
as was said before.[6]

> 1 he does ... expression] Added in 1519
> 2 See the annotation on 8:15 ('the spirit of adoption of the sons of God').
> 3 Augustine ... own sons?] Added in 1522
> 4 Augustine *Contra Faustum Manichaeum* 3.3 PL 42 215
> 5 When ... before.] Added in 1535
> 6 In the annotation on 8:15 (cf n2 above)

8:23 [ER VG] *redemptionem corporis* 'the redemption of the body'; ἀπολύτρωσιν,
which is properly said when captives are redeemed for a price, those for
example, captured by pirates or in war. 'Of the body' is used for 'from the
body' – so that we are freed from that[1] body which before he called 'the
body of death.'[2] It seems, however, that this was added as though [Paul]
wanted to explain υἱοθεσία 'adoption': this adoption is nothing else than
that we are freed from this body and[3] receive an immortal body.

> 1 that] Added in 1527
> 2 See Rom 7:24 and the annotation there ('from the body of this death').
> 3 and ... body] Added in 1527

8:24 [ER *cur idem speret* 'why[1] would he hope for the same']
[VG] *quid sperat* 'wherefore does he hope'; τί καὶ ἐλπίζει 'wherefore does
he yet hope' or 'wherefore does he hope any more?' The adverb [yet] is not
superfluous. It indicates that it is useless to hope for what you already see.

> 1 why ... same] First in 1519; in 1516, 'how does he yet [*etiam*] hope?'

8:26 [ER *consimiliter autem et spiritus auxiliatur infirmitatibus (nostris)* 'in
like manner, also, the Spirit gives aid to (our) infirmities']
[VG] *similiter autem et spiritus adiuvat infirmitatem [nostram]* 'likewise
also the Spirit helps [our] infirmity.' The number is plural in Greek –
our infirmities, or our weaknesses, συναντιλαμβάνεται ταῖς ἀσθενείαις ἡμῶν.
However, συναντιλαμβάνεσθαι means to be present with aid for one who
is struggling in something he has undertaken;[1] and for that reason [Paul]
adds ὡσαύτως, that is, 'in like manner.' Just as we strive, looking forward

with endurance, so also the Spirit gives its aid to the weary, as though
stretching out a hand to those who struggle.

1 In the *Responsio ad collationes* LB IX 1000D Erasmus notes the force of the
prefix συν- 'with' – which suggests that the Spirit is present, stretching out a
hand, as it were, to our spirit as it struggles.

8:26 [ER *siquidem hoc ipsum quid oraturi simus* 'for indeed this very thing,
what we are to pray for']
[VG] *nam quid oremus* 'for what we pray for'; τὸ γὰρ τί προσευξόμεθα.[1] The
Translator has not expressed the force of the article τό, which refers to the
entire phrase immediately following it. Hence I have rendered: 'For indeed
we do not know this very thing, what we are to pray for as is proper.' That
is,[2] we are so far from being able to help ourselves that we do not even
know what kind of help is needed.

1 The verb is in the indicative in Erasmus' text, but the preferred reading is
subjunctive (cf Tischendorf II 404 26n).
2 That is ... needed.] Added in 1519

8:26 [ER *spiritus intercedit* 'the Spirit intercedes']
[VG] *spiritus postulat* 'the Spirit makes request'; ὑπερεντυγχάνει, which he
sometimes translates 'makes request,' sometimes 'appeals' or 'intercedes.'[1]
This occurs whenever one goes to[2] a person on behalf of another's affairs,
as one might approach a prince to commend the cause of a friend. It must[3]
be observed that he has not said simply ἐντυγχάνει but ὑπερεντυγχάνει, as
this preposition [ὑπέρ 'above'] in Greek usually indicates superiority. For
if I am not mistaken, the sense is this: even though one's spirit sometimes
seeks things that would be harmful, nevertheless the Holy Spirit breathes
upon the souls of some and corrects their misguided demands, as one in
charge of all appeals.

1 ὑπερεντυγχάνω is found only here in the New Testament. But ἐντυγχάνω is
rendered in the Vulgate by *interpello* 'appeal' in Acts 25:24; Rom 8:34, 11:2;
and Heb 7:25; by *postulo* in Rom 8:27.
2 goes to] First in 1519; in 1516, 'addresses'
3 It must ... all appeals.] Added in 1527

8:27 [ER *quis sit sensus spiritus* 'what is the feeling of the Spirit']
[VG] *quid desideret spiritus* 'what the Spirit desires'; τὸ φρόνημα, that is,
'the feeling' [of the Spirit] or 'what the Spirit feels,'[1] that is, the 'disposition' [*affectus*] of the Spirit – which Terence terms *sensus* [feeling]: 'I well
understand his feeling.'[2] This[3] is the same Greek word that he has so many
times already translated as *prudentia* [prudence].[4] I do not[5] know what that

man is thinking of who imagines that 'feeling' and 'disposition' are words appropriate to the flesh, not to the divine Spirit.[6] Do we suppose the man was sober when he wrote that? Was it not said of God: 'Who has known the mind of the Lord?'[7] Is pity not a disposition of mind [*affectus*] attributed especially to God? And if the Spirit of God is rightly said to long for, to desire, to groan, and to appeal,[8] is it absurd to attribute states of feeling to it? But in God, the 'affections' are not as they are in us; but neither are understanding and living and taking pity and loving the same in him as they are in us. And yet, frequently in speaking of him Scripture uses words of this sort appropriate to our human condition.

1 Valla offers the same alternatives; *Annot in Rom* 8 (I 857).
2 Terence *Adelphi* 533; cf the note on the word by R.H. Martin in his edition of the play (Cambridge 1975): ' "the way he feels" or (Sloman, Ashmore) "disposition." ' Erasmus cited this passage again in *Responsio ad collationes* to show that in Latin *sensus* could be used with the meaning of *affectus* (LB IX 1000E).
3 This ... *prudentia*.] Added in *1519*
4 Cf the annotation on 8:7 ('because the wisdom of the flesh'), where Erasmus discusses the meaning of φρόνημα and the Latin words capable of representing it, especially n2.
5 I do not ... condition.] This remaining portion of the annotation was added in *1535*.
6 'That man' is Titelmans; cf *Responsio ad collationes* LB IX 1000E.
7 Rom 11:34; 1 Cor 2:16. Though we have translated *sensus* regularly as 'feeling' in the sense of 'inclination,' we have retained here the more familiar English expression for the Vulgate's *sensus domini*.
8 As in Rom 8:26–7

8:28 [ER *simul adiumento sunt in bonum* 'are together an aid to the good']
[VG] *cooperantur in bonum* 'work together unto good.' In the Greek, συν-εργεῖ can have as its subject either 'the Spirit' or 'all things.' If the former, you would understand that the Holy Spirit turns everything into good by its help. If the latter, you would take it to mean that all things, even evil things, are, for the saints, an aid to ultimate happiness. This is the sense I favour, and this[1] Chrysostom and Theophylact follow.[2] There is no reason why the verb συνεργεῖ in the singular should be a concern to anyone, for πάντα [all things] is a nominative in the neuter.[3]

1 and this ... follow] Added in *1519*, except that the reference to Chrysostom was added in *1527*
2 For Chrysostom see *Hom in Rom* 15.1 PG 60 540–1; for Theophylact, *Expos in Rom* 8:28 PG 124 452B–C.
3 In Greek, plural nouns in the neuter take a verb in the singular; so Valla *Annot in Rom* 8 (I 858). On the problems of textual criticism here see Cranfield I 425–8.

8:28 [ER *iuxta propositum* 'according to the purpose']

[VG] *secundum propositum* 'in accordance[1] with the purpose'; κατὰ πρόθεσιν, that is, 'according to a determining judgment,' so that the 'purpose'
does not refer to 'saints,'[2] or to 'a person with a good resolution,' but refers
to 'the predestination of God.' So Origen[3] and Thomas,[4] though Ambrose
seems to refer to both senses.[5] And yet Origen, too, a little further on, when
he distinguishes those who are said to be called and not chosen from those
who are called and chosen, varies his position somewhat, for he explains that
those are said to be 'called according to the purpose' who, before they were
called, were already inclined in heart to the worship of the divine, [and]
whose will, even then ready, needed only the call. This is to say that the
'purpose' belongs not to the God who destines, but to the person who makes
a mental resolution;[6] unless[7] perhaps [Origen's] translator [Rufinus] added
these words on his own. In his book *On Rebuke and Grace*, the seventh chapter,
Augustine follows Ambrose: 'They were chosen,' he says, 'because they were
called according to a purpose, not, however, their own but God's.'[8] For in
the next chapter of this Epistle Paul has spoken of the 'purpose of God' in a
similar sense; and again in the first chapter [of the Epistle] to the Ephesians.[9]

In the Greek,[10] 'saints' is not added;[11] there is only 'the called.' It is
clear from Origen's exposition that he so reads, when he says: 'One must
consider whether perhaps from the fact that he says "to those who have
been called according to the purpose and whom he foreknew and whom
he predestined" etc.'[12] Ambrose reads likewise, for in his discussion he
says: 'But these are called according to the purpose, who, as believers,
God foreknew would be suitable to him, so that they were known before
they believed.'[13] Augustine[14] reads the same in his book *On Rebuke and
Grace*.[15] Chrysostom and[16] Theophylact follow both this reading and this
understanding,[17] though Thomas[18] and many[19] old Latin codices resist it.[20]
But it appears that 'saints' was added from other passages in which these
two words, 'called saints,' are often joined.[21]

1 in accordance ... mental resolution] Added in *1519*, when the annotation
  first appeared
2 The discussion presupposes a more extensive text than the cue phrase:
    ER *his qui iuxta propositum vocati sunt* 'to those who have been called
    according to the purpose'
    VG *his qui secundum propositum vocati sunt sancti* 'to those who have been
    called saints in accordance with the purpose'
3 Origen *Comm in Rom* 7.7 PG 14 1122A; but see n6 below.
4 Thomas Aquinas *Super Rom lect* cap 8 lectio 6.700
5 Ambrosiaster *Comm in Rom* 8:28
6 Origen *Comm in Rom* 7.8 PG 14 1126A–B. In the first passage (7.7; see n3
  above) Origen interprets the phrase as a condition in the heart of the believer,

pointing out that some are called, but not 'according to purpose,' for they still have the spirit of servitude. This interpretation appears in a different form in the later passage (7.8) where Origen says that those who have good will are called according to purpose, others are merely called. He grants that the expression could refer to the 'purpose' of God, but since that purpose is conditioned by the divine knowledge of the good will and mind of the called, 'there is no contradiction with what was formerly said.'

7 unless ... Ephesians] Added in *1527*
8 Augustine *De correptione et gratia* 7.14 PL 44 924
9 For the two references see Rom 9:11 and Eph 1:11.
10 In the Greek ... joined.] The remaining portion of the annotation, with the exceptions noted below (nn14, 16, 19), was part of the original annotation of *1519*.
11 So Valla *Annot in Rom* 8 (I 858)
12 Origen *Comm in Rom* 7.7 PG 14 1122A
13 Ambrosiaster *Comm in Rom* 8:28
14 Augustine ... Grace.] Added in *1527*
15 Augustine *De correptione et gratia* 7.14 PL 44 924
16 Chrysostom and] Added in *1527*
17 Cf Chrysostom *Hom in Rom* 15.1 PG 60 541 and Theophylact *Expos in Rom* 8:28 PG 124 452B.
18 Thomas Aquinas *Super Rom lect* cap 8 lectio 6.700
19 many] Added in *1535*
20 Wordsworth and White print *sancti* 'saints,' but note its omission from several witnesses; cf Wordsworth and White II 104 and 28n.
21 Cf eg Rom 1:7.

8:28 [ER *vocati sunt* 'are the called']

[VG] *vocati sunt sancti* 'are called saints'; κλητοῖς οὖσιν 'who are the called.' First of all,[1] 'saints,' as has been said,[2] is an unnecessary addition. Secondly,[3] 'called' is not a participle here, but a noun,[4] as I pointed out at the beginning.[5] Thus he again excludes the works of the Law, in which the Jews have misguidedly trusted; and he shows that true holiness comes from God who calls.[6]

1 First of all] Added in *1519*
2 as has been said] Added in *1519*. See the preceding annotation.
3 Secondly] First in *1519*; in *1516*, 'Moreover'
4 Cf Valla *Annot in Rom* 8 (I 858).
5 See the annotation on 1:1 ('called an apostle').
6 calls] In *1516* Erasmus added here 'but not without our effort.' The clause was omitted from the last two editions.

8:29 [ER *quos praesciverat* 'whom he had foreknown'[1]]

[VG] *quos praescivit* 'whom he foreknew'; οὓς προέγνωκεν [whom he had foreknown], or[2] as some read, προέγνω [foreknew].[3] I have already noted above[4] that in Greek this verb is sometimes understood in the sense of 'decide' or 'determine,' because coming to a resolution implies knowing.

These words[5] seem not so much to stand apart from one another through some fundamental incompatibility, as to belong together, distinguished from one another in a sort of sequence of time and logic.[6] In this way, Paul[7] can set the matter forth more vividly: προγνῶναι is used of one deliberating and deciding; deciding, however, what could in some way be changed – to speak in a manner appropriate to the human sphere; next, προορίζειν [mark out beforehand] or ὁρίζειν [mark out][8] is used of one who now openly proclaims what he has decided, and this usually occurs when something has been determined in such a way that it cannot be changed. Moreover, when you have proclaimed your resolution it remains that you must deliver and fulfil what you have promised. Now he who calls and invites is beginning to fulfil [his promise]. Then, lest he seem to have called in vain, he also justifies the called, without which we are not capable of receiving the promise. Finally a reward is given to the justified. Therefore God προέγνωκεν [foreknew] from eternity those whom he decided and determined were to be called to immortality; he προώρισεν [marked out beforehand] those concerning whom he proclaimed, making known his decision already through his prophets, and even more through his Son. Now, he has called through the preaching of Jesus, he has justified through his death, he has glorified through the resurrection and the reward of immortality. Or he[9] has called through the teaching of the gospel, he has justified through baptism, he has glorified through the gifts of the Spirit. In this way Paul arrives in a sort of sequence from what is primary to the culminating point so that the matter might be more firmly grounded and more definitive.

But if anyone judges too harshly that in this passage I do away with foreknowledge, he should know that such is the interpretation of Theophylact, the Greek interpreter, and a recent one[10] (for some will more willingly believe a modern), who thinks that the difference between πρόγνωσις [foreknowledge] and προορισμός [predetermination] (or ὁρισμός [determination]) is this, that the former is less firmly, the latter more firmly established.[11] In fact, one can go further: where Peter writes προεγνωσμένους γὰρ πρὸ τῆς καταβολῆς τοῦ κόσμου, which, on this view, should be translated 'foreknown [before the foundation of the world],'[12] Lyra does not scruple to expound as 'foreordained.'[13] And Thomas[14] points out that there were some who interpreted foreknowledge in this passage in a different sense, namely, as the preparation for grace, which God manifests – temporally – in the saints; their intent, no doubt, was to make a distinction between foreknowledge and predestination.[15] But Thomas[16] justly rejects their fabrication.[17] Origen thinks that in this passage we should not take πρόγνωσις (that is, foreknowledge) in the usual sense, according to which God 'foreknew' even those who were to perish – so that the statement that 'all whom he foreknew he had predestined' then becomes false. But just as divine Scripture says, by a customary idiom, that those are 'known' whom God embraces with affection ('I do not know you'; 'the Lord[18] knows the path of the righteous'[19]), so here they are called 'foreknown.'[20]

I am well aware, however, that some have sought from this passage a field for exercising[21] their ingenuity, in which they philosophize about God's foreknowledge and predestination – namely Origen, St Augustine, Thomas Aquinas, and subsequently all the theological schools.[22] I do not criticize their industry, but here the sense I have established seems to me simpler and more genuine.[23] If anyone prefers something different, as far as I am concerned, let each use his own judgment. I am only advising, not dictating; and I[24] am presenting my own opinion, without prejudging that of anyone else at all.

1 had foreknown] First in 1519; in 1516, with the Vulgate, 'foreknew'
2 or ... προέγνω] Added in 1519
3 προέγνω is the reading in all editions of Erasmus' *Novum Testamentum*, and the only one given in the modern critical editions consulted; see Tischendorf II 405.
4 Erasmus comments on the word in the annotations on Rom 11:2 ('whom he foreknew') and on 1 Pet 1:20 (*praecogniti quidem*). Here, however, he appears to refer to his discussion of predestination in the annotation on 1:4 ('who was predestined') where the problem of foreknowledge arises.
5 Erasmus refers to the sequence of words in Rom 8:29–30: foreknew ... predestined ... called ... justified ... glorified. ER (1516) *quos praescivit, eosdem et praedefinivit ... quos praedefinierat eosdem vocavit ... quos vocavit eos et iustificavit, quos autem iustificavit hos et glorificavit* 'whom he foreknew, the same he also marked out beforehand ... whom he had marked out beforehand, the same he called ... whom he called, these he also justified, while those whom he justified he also glorified.'
Erasmus here generally followed the Vulgate, though *praedefinire* 'to mark out beforehand' replaced VG *praedestinare* 'to predestine' and *glorificare* 'to glorify' replaced VG *magnificare* 'magnify.'
6 Cf *De copia* CWE 24 307:28–30: 'In the first place you will hardly find two words anywhere so isodynamic that they are not kept apart by some distinction.'
7 Paul ... forth] First in 1519; in 1516, 'he can set it forth'
8 For Erasmus' discussion of this word, see the annotation on 1:4 ('who was predestined').
9 Or he ... Spirit.] Added in 1527
10 Latin *recens*. On the *recentiores* see the annotation on 1:4 ('who was predestined') n7.
11 Cf Theophylact *Expos in Rom* 8:29–30 PG 124 452D: 'Foreknowledge is first, foreordination subsequent ... God foreknew that Paul was worthy

of the calling of the gospel, and so he foreordained him, that is, he determined without possibility of change ...' Erasmus here finds support for his own view that to foreknow is to come to a decision, to foreordain is to make the decision in such a way that it cannot be changed; thus the former is something less firmly, the latter more firmly established. The vast majority of the early Fathers concur with the understanding that the foreknowledge of those who are worthy of the calling precedes the predestination, though Augustine is an exception. See Schelkle 308–12.

12 Cf 1 Pet 1:20 and the annotation *praecogniti quidem*. Erasmus translated the προεγνωσμένου of 1 Pet 1:20 by *praeordinatus* 'foreordained' in place of VG *praecogniti* 'foreknown.' Here, however, in the annotation on 8:29, Erasmus has misquoted 1 Pet 1:20 to make 'foreknown' plural, προεγνωσμένους, referring to the 'saints,' whereas in fact it is singular, referring to Christ.

13 Nicholas of Lyra *Postilla* IV fol yy recto

14 Thomas] in all editions from 1522; in 1516 and 1519, 'St Thomas'

15 Thomas Aquinas *Super Rom lect* cap 8 lectio 6.702. Thomas refers to those who define predestination, not foreknowledge, as the preparation for grace in the saints, a preparation that occurs within time, so that predestination is temporal, foreknowledge eternal; thus a sharp distinction between the two is maintained.

16 Thomas] Latin *idem*, added in 1519, understood as referring to Thomas

17 In the passage cited above (n15) Thomas insists that both God's foreknowledge and predestination are from eternity. They differ in that foreknowledge implies only knowledge of future events, predestination implies a certain causality – God has foreknowledge of sins, but predestination concerns salvation.

18 'The Lord ... righteous'] Added in 1519

19 For the two quotations see respectively Matt 25:12 and Ps 1:6. These examples are supplied by Erasmus.

20 Origen *Comm in Rom* 7.8 PG 14 1126D–1127B. Origen argues that by 'foreknown' is meant only those whom God has embraced in love; on this reading the 'predestined' will refer not to both the saved and the damned, but only to the saved.

21 exercising] Added in 1519

22 For Origen and Aquinas see above nn15 and 20; for Augustine see *De correptione et gratia* 7.14, 9.23 PL 44 924–5, 929–30; for the view of the 'theological schools' see Payne *Erasmus: His Theology* 80–3.

23 In distinguishing foreknowledge from predestination, the former as logically prior to the latter, Erasmus is in agreement with the late-medieval nominalists, Occam and Biel. For a fuller statement of his position see *Hyperaspistes* II LB IX 1435B–F, 1456C; and see Payne *Erasmus: His Theology* 78–84.

24 and I ... at all] Added in 1519

8:30 [ER *hos et glorificavit* 'these he also glorified']
[VG] *illos et magnificavit* 'those he also magnified.' The Greek is ἐδόξασε, that is, 'he glorified,'[1] no doubt through the gifts of the Spirit and the

celestial adoption. And 'the same' would be more accurate than 'those.' Ambrose[2] reads 'magnified';[3] Origen, in his discussion of the passage, reads 'glorified,'[4] though [both] took the text from our Vulgate edition.[5]

1 In 1521 in the *Apologia ad annotationes Stunicae* Erasmus acknowledged the variety of translations in the Latin Bible for the Greek δοξάζω, but urged that *magnifico* used in the sense of 'exalt,' 'extol,' though Latin, is very infrequent in Latin authors (ASD IX-2 170:115–19; cf 119n). Later, in the *Responsio ad collationes*, he declared that one never finds *magnifico* in the sense of δοξάζω (LB IX 1001A).

2 Ambrose ... edition.] Added in *1519*

3 Ambrosiaster *Comm in Rom* 8:30

4 Origen *Comm in Rom* 7.8. In Migne, Origen reads *glorificavit* in the introductory citation of the text (PG 14 1124B), and also in the exposition (PG 14 1125A, 1126A–D, 1127B). See next note.

5 In the Merlin edition of Origen, the introductory citation of the text of Rom 8:30 has the reading *magnificavit*, though Origen's discussion of the passage throughout presupposes the reading *glorificavit* (see fol CXCII recto–verso). Wordsworth and White II 105 30n read *glorificavit*, but note important manuscripts which read, with Erasmus' Vulgate, *magnificavit*.

8:32 [ER *qui proprio filio* 'who his own Son']

[VG] *qui etiam proprio filio suo* 'who even his own his Son.'[1] *Suo* [his] is redundant in the Latin text; for ἰδίου, either *suo* [his] or *proprio* [his own] is enough. Certainly[2] *suo* is not added in the old copies, or in Augustine, who cites this passage in the fourth book *On Christian Doctrine*, the twentieth chapter.[3] Indeed[4] Ambrose also cites this passage several times in accordance with the wording of the Greek.[5] Hilary, in the sixth book *On the Trinity*, thinks it a matter of note that [Paul] said *proprio filio* [his own Son] rather than *suo* [his (Son)].[6]

1 In the translations of both Erasmus and the Vulgate, the clause is completed with *non pepercit* 'did not spare': ER 'who did not spare his own Son'; VG 'who did not spare even his own *his* Son' (the italics reflect Erasmus' criticism of the superfluous 'his').
etiam 'even' was added to the cue phrase in *1535*.

2 Certainly ... chapter.] Added in *1519*

3 Augustine *De doctrina christiana* 4.20.43 PL 34 110

4 Indeed ... *suo*.] Added in *1535*

5 Ambrosiaster *Comm in Rom* 8:32. In his commentary on this verse Ambrosiaster says twice that God handed over *filius suus* 'his own Son'; see 8:32 (1) and (2) CSEL 81/1 292:20 and 25, and 293:20 and 25.

6 Hilary *De Trinitate* 6.45 PL 10 194A–B: 'Consider the significance of the word *proprius* ... for though many manuscripts read *suus*, ... in the Greek ... *proprius* is intended here rather than *suus*.'

8:32 [ER *omnia nobis donet* 'he will give us all things']

[VG] *omnia nobis donavit* 'he has given us all things'; χαρίσεται, that is, 'will give,' in the future tense.[1] Ambrose interprets thus[2] and Chrysostom,[3] and Theophylact[4] agrees with this,[5] although the ancient codices and the citations of the early Fathers strongly oppose [the reading].[6] Accordingly, I suspect a variation in the Greek manuscripts, in some of which ἐχαρίσατο [has given] had been written instead of χαρίσεται [will give].[7] Both make good sense. I suspect that someone, objecting that 'all things' seem not yet to have been given us by God, changed the tense of the verb. But when an act of giving is rooted in a firm resolve, nothing prevents [the act] from being already completed, even though there is not yet full possession of the gift.

> 1 So Valla *Annot in Rom* 8 (I 858), and Lefèvre *Pauli epistolae* fol 89 recto
> 2 Ambrosiaster *Comm in Rom* 8:32. See CSEL 81/1 292:23 and 26 and 293:23 and 26. The text is uncertain at this point, and the variants allow us to infer from Ambrosiaster's exposition that he read this verb either in the past or in the future. Erasmus evidently read with α and β a text presupposing the future: 'Why should we not believe that he will do what is less?' (cf 292:26).
> 3 and Chrysostom] Added in 1535. Cf *Hom in Rom* 15.2 PG 60 543.
> 4 and Theophylact ... the gift] Added in 1519
> 5 Theophylact *Expos in Rom* 8:32 PG 124 453B–C
> 6 Cf Augustine *De doctrina christiana* 4.20.43 PL 34 110, where *donavit* is read. For other witnesses to the past tense see Wordsworth and White II 105 32n.
> 7 Tischendorf (II 406 32n) offers no variant to the future.

8:33 [ER *quis intentabit crimina adversus electos dei* 'who will bring charges against the elect of God']

[VG] *quis accusabit adversus electos dei* 'who will make accusation against the elect of God'; τίς ἐγκαλέσει κατὰ ἐκλεκτῶν τοῦ θεοῦ, that is, 'Who will make an accusation,' or 'Who will bring a charge against God's elect?' Lefèvre reads in such a way that κατά [against] is taken as ὑπέρ [on behalf of], that is, 'Who will set up an accusation on behalf of God's elect,' to defend the elect against their enemies?[1] But in this passage Paul's meaning is very clear if we understand that the question implies denial, so that the sense is: No one will dare to charge those whom God has not only called, but also chosen.[2] Accordingly the words that follow, up to the clause 'who will separate us from the love [...],' should be read as emerging from the same question and implying the answer 'Impossible!'[3] And yet even in churches we hear these words publicly read as statements, not questions.[4] For most[5] of the printed editions read thus: 'Who is there who condemns?' – to which inquiry there are attached, as though in response, the words

'Christ Jesus, who died and, indeed, who rose again, who is at the right hand of God, who also pleads for us.'[6]

Augustine commented on this passage in the third book *On Christian Doctrine*, chapter 3.[7] However, he punctuates the sentences somewhat differently from the way we usually do. For when he had pointed out the slight distinction between an 'inquiry' and a 'question' – that there are many possible responses to an 'inquiry,' but to a 'question' only yes or no – he adds: 'Therefore [the passage] will be recited in such a way that after an inquiry wherein we say, "Who will make an accusation against God's elect?" what follows is expressed in the tone of one asking a question: "Is it God who justifies?" to which the silent response is no. Then we make another inquiry: "Who is to condemn?" And again we ask a question: "Is it Christ who died? or, rather, who rose again? Who is on the right hand of God? Who also pleads for us?" In every case the silent response [to our question] is no.'[8] Ambrose seems to have divided the passage in the same way, as one can gather from these words in his exposition: 'He says that God, who justifies us, is not accusing us, and that Christ cannot condemn us, because he loved us with such affection that he died for us, and rising again, always pleads our case before the Father.'[9]

Origen seems to bring the two clauses together in the way I do: 'It is God who justifies; who is to condemn?'[10] – for to 'justify' and 'to condemn' are opposites. Then 'Christ Jesus who died' etc seems to read as though spoken by one who is making not an inquiry, but a statement. [It is spoken] not as a response to the previous question, which, assuming the answer 'No one,' is now complete, but as a new and cumulative series of proofs, so that the sense is: 'God is the one who justifies; who will be the one to condemn? Christ is the one who died for us, yes, who also rose again, who is seated at the right hand of God and pleads for us; who will accuse those who have been chosen, or who will condemn them?' Thus from so many proofs heaped up together, the single consequence follows that there will be no one to bring charges against us or to condemn us.[11] To me, at least, this reading seems the truer, especially because otherwise the conclusion would not seem to advance us very far if we deduce that the Father will not accuse the chosen, since he justifies; or that Christ will not condemn, since he pleads on our behalf.[12] It makes[13] a more effective point [to say] that since we have as judge God, who justifies us, and the Son of God, who died for us and continues to plead for us, there is no reason why we should fear the charges brought by anyone. Neither Chrysostom nor Theophylact mentions any 'inquiry' here; instead, they read the words 'Christ Jesus who died' etc as a statement, agreeing with Origen.[14]

This part could be joined with the words that follow, 'Who shall separate us' etc.[15] For it follows that to him who so loved us that he died for
us, rose for us, and now, sitting at the right hand of God, never ceases to
plead our cause – to him we constantly give our love, even though some
hardships must be borne for his sake. But I do not see that any translator
has followed this way of reading [the passage]. Much[16] light would have
been shed on the passage if the Translator had added a single syllable [*est*
'is']: 'God is the one who justifies,' and 'Christ is the one who died' etc. In
the Greek the articles make the passage clear enough: θεὸς ὁ δικαιῶν, τίς ὁ
κατακρινῶν 'God is the one who justifies, who is the one who will condemn?'
Χριστὸς ὁ ἀποθανών 'Christ is the one who died' and so on, repeating here
the preceding words, τίς ὁ κατακρινῶν 'who is the one who will condemn?'

1 Cf Lefèvre *Pauli epistolae* fol 89 recto: 'Who will bring an accusation against
those who oppose God's elect? ... for God does not bring an accusation
against the elect, but against those who oppose them.'
2 Cf Origen *Comm in Rom* 7.10 PG 14 1130C: 'He did not say, "Who will make
an accusation against the called," but [he said] "against the chosen." For
unless you are chosen, unless you show yourself approved in all things
before God, you will have an accuser.'
3 Erasmus refers to 8:34, where the words 'Christ is the one who has died,
or rather has risen again, who is also on the right hand of God, and who
pleads for us' should be read as an answer to the question of 8:34a, 'Who
is to condemn?' – ie this brief recollection in 8:34 of the victory of Christ is
proof that it is impossible that there should be anyone to condemn us.
4 questions] In the first four editions Erasmus continued here, 'and falsely,
indeed with insolence towards Christ, unless ignorance excuses so great a
fault – which is not really a legitimate defence.' This was omitted in 1535.
5 For most ... pleads for us.'] Added in 1527
6 So reads the Vulgate printed in 1527. In the *Responsio ad collationes* LB IX
1001A–C Erasmus repeats his 1516 judgment (n4 above) that the passage read
in this way is blasphemous.
7 chapter 3 ... pleads on our behalf] Added in 1519
8 Augustine *De doctrina christiana* 3.3.6 PL 34 67. Here 'inquiry' and 'question'
represent respectively the Latin *percontatio* and *interrogatio*. For the distinction
elsewhere between the two see the annotations on 3:27 ('where is therefore
[your boasting]) n2, and 8:35 ('who therefore will separate us') and n15.
9 Ambrosiaster *Comm in Rom* 8:34
10 Origen *Comm in Rom* 7.10 PG 14 1130A–B
11 Between 1516 and 1519 Erasmus made a significant change in his translation
of 8:34.
In 1516 he rendered: 'Who is to condemn? Surely not Christ who died, rather
was raised, who also sits on the right hand of God, and who pleads for us.'
In 1519 and thereafter he read: 'Who is to condemn? Christ is the one who
died, rather was raised, who also sits on the right hand of God, and who
pleads for us.' The difference between the 1516 and 1519 versions is reflected

in the slight difference in the exposition Erasmus gives the passage in the
1516 annotation and the *1519* addition (cf n7 above).

The Vulgate printed in *1527* read: 'Who is to condemn? Christ Jesus, who
died, rather who also rose again, who is on the right hand of the Father, who
also pleads for us.'

Modern translations also differ on the punctuation of this passage: the RSV,
for example, follows essentially the reading of Augustine, while the NEB
adopts the reading of Erasmus. Cf Cranfield I 437–8.

12 Such, Erasmus believes, are the implications of the reading of Augustine and
Ambrose.

13 It makes ... condemn?'] With the exception of the one sentence noted below
(n16) this remaining portion of the annotation was added in *1535*.

14 Cf Chrysostom *Hom in Rom* 15.3 PG 60 543 and Theophylact *Expos in Rom*
8:33–4 PG 124 453D–456A.

15 Ie Rom 8:33–4 could be closely associated with 8:35

16 Much ... died' etc.] Added in *1527*

8:35 [ER *quis nos separabit* 'who will separate us']

[VG] *quis ergo nos separabit* 'who therefore will separate us.' 'Therefore'
has been added in the Latin and is better omitted. For if[1] you separate this
passage from the words immediately before, it appears that Paul, suddenly
carried away, as it were, by emotion, burst forth into this 'exclamation,'
so to speak, because[2] of the great and trustworthy proofs which have preceded. So[3] Theophylact thinks, following[4] the opinion of Chrysostom, who
separates [the passages].[5] But if you read them closely together, they cohere
better without the conjunction ['therefore']: since God and Christ are like
this towards us, 'Who will separate us from their love?'

'Love' here seems to have an active sense – ἀγάπη [*agape*],[6] that is, the
love with which God loved us and prompted us to love him in return.[7]
It is[8] of less importance that Ambrose reads 'from the love "of Christ,"'
Origen 'from the love "of God."'[9]

Augustine[10] cites this whole passage in the fourth book *On Christian Doctrine*, chapter 20, as a model of artistic prose that combines force
(δείνωσις) with ornament.[11] The pleasing effect of the prose lies partly in
the climactic sequence[12] 'foreknew, predestined, called, justified, magnified';
partly in words with similar endings and rhythms, προώρισεν [*prohōrisen*],
ἐκάλεσεν [*ekalesen*], and so on; again ὑπὲρ ἡμῶν [*hyper hēmōn*], καθ' ἡμῶν
[*kath hēmōn*]; partly in repetition of the same word, which is called *traductio*,[13] as in the previous example, ἡμῶν [*hēmōn*], ἡμῶν [*hēmōn*]; then, too, in
contraries, 'justifies' and 'condemns'; 'death,' 'life'; 'things present,' 'things
to come'; 'height,' 'depth.' Parallel structure and the absence of connectives contribute also to δείνωσις,[14] as do questions. Now the whole passage
abounds with inquiries and questions.[15] If one distinguishes sharpness or

intensity in speech from sublimity (which among the rhetoricians is the third style of speaking[16]) a question, which is more forceful than even an emphatic assertion, contributes to sharpness. It is more forceful to say: 'How will he not give us all things along with him?' than to say: 'Beyond a doubt, he will give us all things along with him.' For the listener is thus hard pressed by this confidence in the manifest truth – as though he would have nothing to say in reply. Likewise there is more intensity [in the questions]: whether tribulation? or distress? or persecution? or famine? than in statements of denial. Contributing to the intensity are phrases that begin with the same expression, such as I have just now quoted; also, for example, 'neither death, nor life, nor angels' etc. At the same time, it is these phrases in particular that make the speech elevated, because Paul, breathed upon, as it were by the divine power, says nothing in the low style. For loftily does he declare: 'We know that to those who love God all things' etc. Furthermore the whole passage consists of both things and persons that are great and eminent: death, life, might, height, God, Christ, at the right hand of God, angels, principalities, powers. This, too, no doubt, has a grand air: 'In all these things ὑπερνικῶμεν [we are more than conquerors],' and 'for I am certain.' What did Cicero ever say that effected more fully the grand manner?

1 if ... immediately before] Added in 1527
2 because ... preceded] Added in 1519
3 So ... their love?'] Added in 1527, except for the allusion to Chrysostom (see n4)
4 following ... Chrysostom] Added in 1535
5 Cf Theophylact *Expos in Rom* 8:35 PG 124 456C and Chrysostom *Hom in Rom* 15.3 PG 60 544. Chrysostom notes that after showing forth the great providence of God (8:34) 'Paul does not say that you too ought to love him in return, but as though breathed upon by that ineffable providence, he says, "Who will separate us?"' Theophylact, too, speaks of the divine Spirit here breathing upon Paul, but neither is especially concerned with Erasmus' point, that 8:35 should come as a sudden exclamation sharply distinguished from 8:34.
6 Erasmus replaces the Vulgate *charitas* with *dilectio*, a derivative from *diligo* that implies esteem, deliberate choice, active cultivation:
    ER *a dilectione dei* 'from the love of God'
    VG *a charitate Christi* 'from the love of Christ'
  For the connotation of *diligo* and for *dilectio* used to translate ἀγάπη see A. Ernout and A. Meillet *Dictionnaire étymologique de la langue latine* 4th ed rev Jacques André (Paris 1979) 350.
7 In the phrase 'love of God' most of the Fathers read a subjective genitive signifying 'God's love for us' (see Schelkle 320–2). Ambrosiaster, on the other hand, understood the genitive as objective: nothing will separate us from our love for God; see *Comm in Rom* 8:35 (1). Erasmus suggests both the objective

and subjective possibilities of the genitive: God's 'love for us evokes our love for him.' He expressed this understanding in his paraphrase on the verse; see CWE 42 51. So also John Colet *Enarratio* (English 29, Latin 155).

8 It is ... "of God." '] Added in *1519*

9 Ambrosiaster *Comm in Rom* 8.35 (1); Origen *Comm in Rom* 7:11 PG 14 1131A and C. Erasmus followed Origen (cf n6 above), a reading supported by several important witnesses, but the best attested reading is 'from the love of Christ'; see Tischendorf II 407–8 35n and Metzger 519.

10 Augustine ... manner?] This remaining portion of the annotation was added in *1527*.

11 Augustine *De doctrina christiana* 4.20.43 PL 34 110

12 Latin *gradatio*, on which see *Ecclesiastes* III LB V 1002F–1003C and Quintilian 9.3.54–5

13 On *traductio* see *Ecclesiastes* III LB V 999E–1000A; also *Rhetorica ad Herennium* 4.14.20 and Quintilian 9.3.71.

14 Ie 'force,' on which see Quintilian 6.2.24, 8.3.88, 9.2.104; also *Ecclesiastes* III passim (cf eg LB V 967A, 996D, 999E). For 'parallel structure' (*comparia*) see *Rhetorica ad Herennium* 4.20.27.

15 *percontationes* and *interrogationes*, on which see the annotation on 3:27 ('where is therefore [your boasting]') and n2. Cf also *Rhetorica ad Herennium* 4.15.22 and Quintilian 9.2.6.

16 On the three styles, low, middle, and high, see *Rhetorica ad Herennium* 4.8.11–10.15; Quintilian 12.10.58; and Lausberg I 1079. With Erasmus' stylistic criticism here compare his comments in the annotation on 12:21 ('do not be overcome by evil').

8:36 [ER *velut oves destinatae mactationi* 'just like sheep destined[1] for sacrifice']

[VG] *sicut oves occisionis* 'as sheep of the slaughter.' This proof-text has been taken from the forty-third[2] Psalm. Moreover the word which the Translator renders as *occisio* [slaughter] in Hebrew is טִבְחָה, which in that language has rather the sense of *mactatio*. This is when the slaughterer feels the animal and investigates whether it is fit to be slain; for in Latin *mactatio* has a similar connotation. Thus Horace: '[Venus] will come in more genial mood when a victim has been slain.'[3] Hence he said 'sheep of the slaughter,' meaning 'sheep destined for slaughter.'

In this passage[4] the Translator ought to have omitted the conjunction ὅτι [that, because]. For to a Latin-speaker what would the expression 'It is written *quia* [because] on account of you we are put to death' suggest, if not[5] that the scripture has been given for this reason, that we are put to death the whole day because of God? In Greek this conjunction has more than one meaning, but it is not so in Latin;[6] and whenever[7] it has the force of confirmation [meaning 'that'] it would be better to omit it, if we want to speak Latin. I admit that churchmen frequently use *quoniam* and *quia* either to confirm, or to be understood εἰδικῶς [to specify],[8] particularly when they are citing proof-texts from Scripture; but it is not for that reason correct Latin.[9]

1 destined] From 1519; omitted in 1516
2 Ps 44:22
3 Horace *Odes* 1.19.16. For 'a victim has been slain' the Latin is *mactata hostia*.
4 Ie in the first part of 8:36:
    ER *quemodmodum scriptum est*: *propter te morti tradimur tota die* 'as it is written: on account of you we are daily handed over to death'
    VG *sicut scriptum est quia propter te mortificamur tota die* 'just as it is written because on account of you we are daily put to death'
5 if not ... because of God] Added in 1535
6 The Greek ὅτι can mean either 'that' or 'because.' See also the discussion on this conjunction in the annotations on 8:20 ('who made this subject') and 4:17 ('that I have made you the father of many nations').
7 and whenever ... correct Latin] Added in 1535
8 See the annotation on 4:21 ('whatever God has promised').
9 Titelmans had already drawn from Erasmus this admission, but he had responded that even churchmen use this language only when they are 'treating the Scriptures.' It is not surprising, he added, that Lefèvre retained the Vulgate *quia* here, since he frequently indulges in solecisms (*Responsio ad collationes* LB IX 1001E–F).

8:37 [ER *superamus per eum* 'we overcome[1] through him']
[VG] *superamus propter eum* 'we overcome because of him'; ὑπερνικῶμεν διὰ τοῦ, that is, 'we are "more than conquerors,"' so that you understand something more than simply 'conquering'; for[2] rising above all these evils, we win the victory – and with ease – over such great things. So Theophylact.[3] Further, '*through* him who' etc, not '*because* of him' – διὰ τοῦ.[4] Augustine[5] in the twenty-second book on *The City of God*, chapter 23, quotes in this way: 'In all these things we are more than conquerors through him who loved us.'[6] And he cites the passage in the same way in the fourth book *On Christian Doctrine*, chapter 20.[7] Origen, too, reads likewise in his exposition: 'And therefore, he says, in all these things we overcome, not by our own power, but through him who loved us.'[8] Furthermore[9] St Basil, writing to Amphilochius *On the Holy Spirit*, in chapter 8 quotes 'through him';[10] if you read 'because of him,' you spoil his argument. And yet[11] Ambrose reads 'because of,' understanding that in such great afflictions we endure with spirit unbroken through the love of Christ who has paid out so much for us – paying to him, so to speak, the price of dying.[12] Here are the words of Ambrose himself if anyone happens to want them: 'And why is it strange if slaves die for a good lord, when the Lord died for even bad slaves? His kindness conquers, therefore, and exhorts the spirit to persevere because of him who loved us.'[13] Chrysostom[14] and Theophylact agree with us in both

their reading and their interpretation: 'It is no wonder if we come forth from such evils victorious, for we have God as our champion.'[15] And I[16] believe that this is the true reading. For since the Apostle had made some proud claims in his usual way, he gives all the glory to Christ.[17]

1 overcome] First in 1519. In 1516, *supervincimus* 'we are more than conquerors'
2 for ... Theophylact. Further] Added in 1527
3 Theophylact *Expos in Rom* 8:37 PG 124 457A
4 Erasmus correctly adopts the Eastern textual reading (διὰ τοῦ ἀγαπήσαντος 'through him who loved') rather than that favoured in the West (διὰ τὸν ἀγαπήσαντα 'on account of him who loved'). See Tischendorf II 408 37n; cf Schelkle 322–3.
5 Augustine ... through him who loved us.'] Added in 1519
6 Augustine *De civitate dei* 22.23 CSEL 40/2 641:14–15. On Augustine's preference for the 'Eastern reading,' see Wordsworth and White II 107 37n.
7 Augustine *De doctrina christiana* 4.20.43 PL 34 110
8 Origen *Comm in Rom* 7.11 PG 14 1132C
9 Furthermore ... argument.] Added in 1535
10 Basil *De spiritu sancto* 8.18 PG 32 100A–B). LB's italics appear to ascribe the remainder of this sentence ('if ... argument') to Basil – erroneously.
11 And yet ... who loved us.'] Added in 1519
12 Ambrosiaster *Comm in Rom* 8:37 (1–2). Erasmus offers a somewhat free paraphrase here.
13 Ambrosiaster *Comm in Rom* 8:37 (2)
14 Chrysostom ... champion.'] Added in 1527
15 Theophylact *Expos in Rom* 8:37 PG 124 457A follows closely Chrysostom *Hom in Rom* 15.4 PG 60 545.
16 And I ... Christ.] Added in 1535
17 Cf 15:18–19 and the annotations on these verses.

8:38 [ER *nam mihi persuasum habeo* 'for I am convinced']
[VG] *certus sum enim* 'for I am certain'; πέπεισμαι γάρ, that is, 'I am persuaded'; or 'I am confident'[1] [*confido*], as St Jerome translates in [the letter] to Algasia, the ninth question[2] – and[3] so reads Ambrose.[4]

1 Valla *Annot in Rom* 8 (I 858) suggests that the Greek can be translated 'I am convinced,' or 'I am persuaded,' or 'I am confident.'
2 Jerome *Epistulae* 121.9 CSEL 56 38:15
3 and ... Ambrose] Added in 1519
4 Ambrosiaster *Comm in Rom* 8:38

8:38 [ER *neque futura, neque altitudo* 'nor things to come, nor height']
[VG] *neque futura, neque fortitudo* 'nor things to come, nor might.' 'Might' is not in the Greek, nor does it have anything to correspond to it, since *instantia*, that is, 'things present,' corresponds to 'things to come,' and 'height' to 'depth.'[1] Yet in the passage I have just cited, St Jerome adds 'might,' but[2] he omits 'powers' [*virtutes*], which in Greek is δυνάμεις, and which

Jerome, it appears, called *potestates*.[3] In Ambrose[4] a somewhat different reading is found, where only nine members are enumerated: 'neither death, nor life, nor angel, nor power, nor height, nor depth, nor things present, nor things to come, nor any other creation.'[5] Ambrose's interpretation also shows clearly that he read thus. Hence it is apparent that for 'might,' which is out of order in our text, he substituted 'power,' placing it next to 'angels,' which he refers to the miraculous;[6] he does not, however, mention 'principalities.' Origen does touch on 'principalities' in his commentary, though he is not otherwise especially careful in listing the parts of this 'assemblage.'[7] Augustine, in explicating questions on this Epistle, records: 'death, life, angel, principality, things present, things to come, power, height, depth, and other creation.'[8] But it often happens in the case of such catalogues of individual words that variants occur in the codices due to slips in memory by the scribes.

1 The Vulgate printed in 1527 gives the following sequence: death, life, angels, principalities, powers, things present, things to come, might, height, depth, any other creation. Erasmus followed the same sequence, omitting 'might.' For the preferred Vulgate reading see Wordsworth and White II 107.

2 but ... *potestates*] Added in 1527

3 For the reference, see the preceding annotation on 8:38, n2. Jerome adds 'might' and omits 'powers' in citing the text; in commenting on the verse, however, he discusses 'powers' (*potestates*) in place of 'principalities' (*principatus*). Cf the letter to Eustochium *Epistulae* 22.39 CSEL 54 205:17–18, where 'might' is cited in the text, and 'powers' (*potestates*, not *virtutes*) is given as an alternative reading in the critical apparatus.

4 In Ambrose ... scribes.] Added in 1519

5 Ambrosiaster *Comm in Rom* 8:38–9

6 Ambrosiaster sees the things listed here as coming from the devil. Hence it is appropriate in his order to have 'power' follow 'angel,' since he understands the 'angel' as one sent by Satan to seduce us, while the 'power' represents the miraculous deeds done by such seducers as Simon Magus (*Comm in Rom* 8:39 [1–2]).

7 See Origen *Comm in Rom* 7.12 PG 14 1133–7, where Origen cites more than once the 'elements' listed in these verses, apparently without strict concern for the order. Thus we find the sequence: death, angels, principalities, powers, things present, life, things to come, height, any other creation (1133C–D); but he goes on to comment on the list in the sequence: life, death, angels, principalities, powers, things present, things to come, powers (again), height, depth, any other creation (1134A–1136B); and finally he lists: angels, powers, things present, things to come, any other creation (1136B–C).

8 Augustine *Expositio quarundam propositionum ex epistula ad Romanos* 58 PL 35 2077

CHAPTER 9

9:1 [ER *attestante mihi simul conscientia mea* 'my conscience as well[1] witnessing to me']

[VG] *testimonium mihi perhibente conscientia mea* 'my conscience[2] bearing witness to me.' Since [the Greek] is συμμαρτυρούσης, either we understand that the witness of the conscience joins in support of other witnesses,[3] or (following a common manner of speaking) that a persona is attributed to the conscience, as when we address ourselves, or are said to be at odds with ourselves, when it is the mind that is speaking to itself; or else the preposition σύν is superfluous. Certainly none of the ancients, so far as I know, remarked on its force, at least in this passage.[4]

1 as well] *mihi simul* 'as well to me,' was added in 1519.
2 my conscience ... passage.] The entire annotation appeared first in 1535.
3 Erasmus wishes to express the significance of the preposition σύν 'with' prefixed to the verb μαρτυρέω 'to witness.' Cf *Responsio ad collationes* LB IX 1002A: 'To express the force of the preposition, I added *simul*, so that the witness of the conscience should join with the witness of the word.'
4 Frans Titelmans had observed that no one had commented on the signficance of the preposition here. 'No wonder,' said Erasmus, 'for the sense is the same' (*Responsio ad collationes* LB IX 1002A). Elsewhere, Erasmus, citing the Fathers, has stressed the significance of the preposition σύν; see the annotation on Rom 8:16 ('renders testimony').

9:3 [ER *optarim enim ego ipse* 'for I myself should have wished']

[VG] *optabam enim ego ipse* 'for I myself wished.' In Greek, *anathemata* are things dedicated to the gods, and put away for that purpose. Consider, reader, whether ηὐχόμην ἄν can be understood δυνητικῶς [potentially] as 'I could have wished' or 'I should have wished,' even if ἄν is not added; the sense then would be 'I should have wished, if it were possible.'[1]

The phrase 'from Christ' refers to the anathema,[2] as though to say something removed from and foreign to Christ. For gifts dedicated in the temples to divine beings are called ἀναθήματα [*anathēmata*]; whence also the ancients[3] came to use *sacrum* [something sacred] in a bad sense. As Horace says, 'Let him be *sacer intestabilis* [accursed, abominated].'[4] And Virgil:[5] 'Oh cursed hunger for gold!'[6] Jerome, in [the letter] to Algasia, the ninth question, thinks that here anathema can be understood with reference to the killing of the body, but not the death of the soul;[7] but [the phrase] 'from Christ,' which follows, opposes [this view]. Accordingly,[8] Chrysostom ridicules the worthless invention of some who would have ἀνάθεμα taken in the sense of κειμήλιον, that is, something valuable set apart,[9] which we commonly call a *cleinodium*.[10] He also notes that [Paul] said αὐτὸς ἐγώ [I myself], though the second pronoun seems superfluous. But it has an implication:[11] 'I, the very one who has laboured so much in order not to be separated from Christ.'[12] It seems to me also to emphasize Paul's singularity: 'I should have wished that, if it were permitted, only I might die, one on behalf of many.'

1 In Greek, past tenses in the indicative with ἄν express past potentiality (Smyth 1784). Here, however, the Greek text does not have ἄν; but for a verb of wishing followed by the infinitive without ἄν to express an unattainable wish see Smyth 1782.
2 The translation of this verse in both Erasmus and the Vulgate continues with the words *anathema esse a Christo* 'to be "anathema" from Christ.'
3 ancients] Until 1535, 'ancient Latin-speakers.' 'Latin-speakers' was omitted in 1535.
4 Horace *Satires* 2.3.181 (quoted freely)
5 And Virgil ... opposes] Added in 1519
6 Virgil *Aeneid* 3.57
7 Jerome *Epistulae* 121.9.5–6 CSEL 56 39:24–40:7
8 Accordingly ... many.] Added in 1527
9 Chrysostom *Hom in Rom* 16.3 PG 60 551
10 This word, meaning jewel, is first attested in medieval Latin. See *cleinodium* in Niermeyer.
11 'Implication,' for the Latin *emphasis*. For the figure, see the annotation on 1:1 ('set apart for the gospel of God') n3, and cf the annotation on 9:20 below ('O man, who are you who etc').
12 Chrysostom *Hom in Rom* 16.3 PG 60 552

9:4 [ER *quorum est adoptio* 'of whom is the adoption']
[VG] *quorum adoptio filiorum* 'of whom the adoption of sons': ὧν ἡ υἱοθεσία, that is, 'of whom the adoption,' as I pointed out before.[1] The Translator[2] wished to draw out the meaning of the Greek word, because brothers or grandchildren[3] are also adopted. Augustine does not add 'of sons' in the third book *Against Faustus*, chapter 3.[4] I have[5] spoken of this more fully above.[6]

1 See the annotation on 8:23 ('adoption of the sons of God').
2 The Translator ... chapter 3.] Added in 1522; but see n3 below for one change in 1527.
3 grandchildren] 1527; in 1522, 'fathers'
4 Augustine *Contra Faustum Manichaeum* 3.3 PL 42 215
5 I have ... above.] Added in 1535
6 In the annotation on 8:23; cf n1 above.

9:4 [ER *et testamenta* 'and the testaments']
[VG] *et testamentum* 'and testament'; καὶ διαθῆκαι, that is, 'and testaments.' So cites[1] Augustine in the manuscript copies of the twelfth book *Against*

Faustus, and soon after, commenting on this passage, he repeats 'testaments';[2] for the records of a testament pertain to sons. So reads[3] Jerome in
[the letter] to Algasia, the ninth question, understanding the one [testament]
of the letter, the other of the spirit.[4] And it is so written in the oldest Latin
copies,[5] although Jerome thinks that this word in the Hebrew, whence our
writers have derived it, means 'covenants' rather than 'testaments.'[6]

   1 So cites ... repeats 'testaments'] Added in 1522
   2 Augustine *Contra Faustum Manichaeum* 12.3 PL 42 255
   3 So reads ... Latin copies] This addition appeared first in 1519 as a separate
     annotation following the annotation immediately below ('the giving of the
     Law'). It was introduced with the cue phrase *rursus et testamentum* 'again
     also the testament,' and began with a preliminary sentence: 'In Greek the
     word is testaments, in the plural.' In 1535, when this addition was inserted
     into the present annotation, the cue phrase and preliminary sentence were
     omitted.
   4 Jerome *Epistulae* 121.9 CSEL 56 40.18
   5 The manuscripts, both Latin and Greek, attest more or less equally both
     singular and plural. See Wordsworth and White II 108 4n; Tischendorf II 410
     4n; and Metzger 519.
   6 Cf Jerome *Commentarius in epistulam ad Galatas* 2 (on 3.15) PL 26 (1883) 390C:
     'If anyone will carefully compare the Hebrew and the other editions with
     the Septuagint, he will find that wherever 'testament' is written it means not
     'testament' but 'covenant,' for which the Hebrew word is 'berith.'

9:4 [ER *legis constitutio* 'the establishment of the Law']
[VG] *legislatio* 'the giving of the Law'; ἡ νομοθεσία. In the Greek this is a
single word,[1] applicable to the institution of all laws, not just a single law.
Augustine,[2] in the treatise he wrote *Against an Opponent of the Law*, reads
legis constitutio [the establishment of the law].[3] For Paul has in mind that
the glory of the Law instituted by God rested on the Israelites.

   1 In 1516 and 1519 the word *legislatio* appears to be printed in the Vulgate cue
     phrase as two words, *legis latio*.
   2 Augustine ... Israelites.] Added in 1519
   3 Augustine *Contra adversarium legis et prophetarum* 2.2.7 PL 42 643

9:4 [ER *et cultus* 'and the worship']
[VG] *et obsequium* 'and the subservience'; ἡ λατρεία,[1] that is, 'worship' or
'religious observances,' a word he elsewhere translates *servitus* [servitude].[2]
[The word] denotes the priestly duties, and the rites and ceremonies of
divine worship, as Origen interprets.[3] But what speaker of Latin would
understand *obsequium* to mean anything like this? For *obsequium*[4] is used of
one who complies with the wishes of another, and is frequently intended in
a bad sense.[5] Certainly no Latin-speaker has ever used the word to mean the

worship of the divine; but the Translator has used the language of common people.

1 Valla notes that the word transliterated is *latria*; *Annot in Rom* 9 (I 858).
2 The Vulgate nowhere translates the noun by *servitus*, but frequently renders the corresponding verb λατρεύω by *servio* 'to serve'; see the annotations on 1:9 ('whom I serve') and 1:25 ('and worshipped').
3 Origen *Comm in Rom* 7.13 PG 14 1140A
4 For *obsequium* ... people.] Added in *1535*
5 Ie as 'obsequiousness.' Erasmus repeats here his argument against Frans Titelmans; cf *Responsio ad collationes* LB IX 1002A–B. For Erasmus' objections elsewhere to *obsequium* as a translation for λατρεία, see the annotations on 12:1 ('reasonable service') and John 16:2 (*arbitretur obsequium se praestare*).

9:4 [ER *et promissiones* 'and the promises']
[VG] *et promissio* 'and the promise'; ἐπαγγελίαι, that is, *promissiones*, or *promissa*, as Ambrose reads.[1]

1 Cf Ambrosiaster *Comm in Rom* 9:4–5, where the text cited reads *promissa*. In his exposition, however, Ambrosiaster speaks only of *promissiones* and *promissio* (9:5 [1]).

9:5 [ER *qui est in omnibus deus* 'who is in all God']
[1535][1] [VG] *qui est super omnia deus* 'who is above all things God.' This passage can be construed in three ways.[2] First, the clause 'who is above all,' ὁ ὢν ἐπὶ πάντων, may be joined to the preceding words and separated from the subsequent in this manner: 'From whom is Christ according to the flesh – Christ who is above all' or 'who was above all.' To forestall any suspicion that Christ's honour was diminished through the nature of man which he assumed, [Paul] added, with a view to his divinity, 'who is above all.' This construction attributes divinity to Christ, because nothing is above all except God alone. For ἐπί [in, on, over, above] is used in place of ἐπάνω [above]. Then after a period, there would follow 'God [be] blessed forever,' so that this would be an expression of thanks as a result of the contemplation of love towards the human race so great that God wished God the Son to assume a human body for our sake. But on this reading the article in ὁ ὢν [the one being] is virtually superfluous; [while] in θεὸς εὐλογητός [God (be) blessed], it is lacking.[3]

In the second reading the entire passage sticks tightly together: 'From whom is Christ according to the flesh, which Christ, since he is God above all, is (or, be) blessed forever.' This reading very clearly pronounces Christ God; but it would be easier if ὃς ὢν [who being] had been written in place of ὁ ὢν [the one being].[4]

The third reading has no difficulties, at least on linguistic grounds – 'from whom is Christ according to the flesh'; here a period ends the sentence. Then from a consideration of such great goodness of God, an expression of thanks is added: ὁ ἐπὶ πάντων θεὸς, εὐλογητὸς εἰς τοὺς αἰῶνας, that is, 'God who is above all be blessed forever.' Thus we would understand that the Law that was given and the covenant and the prophets and finally Christ sent in a human body – all of these things God, through an ineffable plan, provided to redeem the human race. Here if you take God to be the whole sacred Trinity (a meaning that frequently occurs in sacred literature, as when we are commanded to worship God alone and serve him alone[5]) Christ is not excluded. But if ['God' here] means the person of the Father (as is frequently true in Paul, especially when Christ or the Spirit is mentioned in the same passage) – [then] although from other passages in Scripture it is clearer than day that Christ, no less truly than the Father or the Holy Spirit, is called God, nevertheless this particular passage does not effectively refute the Arians, since nothing prevents it from being referred to the person of the Father. And so those who claim that from this passage it is clearly demonstrated that Christ is openly called God, seem either to place little confidence in the witness of other scriptural texts; or to attribute no intelligence to the Arians; or they have not considered carefully enough the Apostle's language.[6] There is a similar passage in the eleventh chapter of this Epistle,[7] where he says that the Father is blessed forever: 'God and Father of our Lord Jesus Christ, who is blessed forever.' For in the Greek there, 'blessed' can be referred only to the Father.

Ambrose implies that there were some who tried to twist these [words to refer] to the Father, especially since here the Son had been mentioned just before. Whenever this occurs it is the Apostle's custom to designate the person of the begetter by the word 'God.' But it seems that Ambrose, who argues that this passage can be understood only of the Son, was ready to concede if they brought forth another person to whom the language of this passage might apply;[8] – and yet the case speaks for itself that this is very easy to do. After Arius had been overthrown, some strove with great effort to make it impossible to understand this passage in any other way than of the Son. Among these is Theophylact: he points out specifically that the impiety of the Arians, who wanted only the Father to be truly and properly called God,[9] is refuted by this passage.

It is remarkable how similar is Origen's discussion in his commentary; he indicates that in his day there were some who did not dare to call Christ God, lest they should seem to make several gods.[10] But it is probable that this passage in [Origen's] commentary was corrected by Jerome – or whoever was the translator – who at the beginning of the work does not hide that he has added some things of his own.[11] In fact, he took so much liberty that he sometimes compares [the readings of] the Greek and Latin manuscripts.[12] And St Jerome casts up against Rufinus that in the books which he translated from Origen, [Rufinus] let all his errors stand except those concerning the divine Persons, because he knew that a blasphemy so extraordinary would be absolutely intolerable to Roman ears.[13] For Origen taught that the Son was created, and that the Holy Spirit was a minister to the one created.[14] How then does it arise that Origen fights against the dogma of the Arians, a dogma they had derived from his own books – and many years later they were condemned along with their dogma? Someone might say that here [in his commentary] Origen was correcting what he had impiously expressed in his book Περὶ ἀρχῶν [On First Principles]. But Jerome, [in his Apologia] against Rufinus, says that one finds no place in Origen's writings where he spoke like a Catholic about dogmas he interpreted heretically in the book On First Principles.[15]

Chrysostom, though he does not exclude the divinity of the Son, nevertheless does not use this passage as a weapon against the Arians, as he is accustomed to do freely [with other passages] whenever the occasion arises. But since his interpretation of this passage appears somewhat obscure, I will set down his comment on it in a faithful translation. He says: 'For of God's grace were the adoption, and the glory, and the promises, and the Law; and when [Paul] reflected upon all these things and considered how eager God was, along with his Son, to save the Jews, he cried out earnestly, and said: "Who is blessed forever. Amen," giving thanks for all these things to the only-begotten [Son] of God. "For what," says [Paul], "if others curse? We who have come to know his mysteries and ineffable wisdom and great providence know well that he is worthy to be glorified, not to be assailed with insolent reproaches"' etc.[16] First [Chrysostom] interprets this passage of both Father and Son together, although in [Paul's] text there is no mention of the Father unless it is understood in the word 'God.' Second, when he says that thanks is being given to God's Only-Begotten for all the things [Paul] has mentioned, he implies that the words 'blessed forever' must refer to the Son, whom the Jews cursed because he had made the promise to them but delivered it to others. And yet this clause cannot have reference to Christ unless the words 'Who is above all God' refer also to Christ.

A fourth way of reading, which someone could perhaps contrive, is, I think, mere trifling, where the clause 'Who is above all God' is inserted into the text as a parenthesis – as though Paul had been suddenly carried away, so to speak, in amazement at the profundity of the divine counsel which had purposed in this way to redeem the human race – as, for example, the apostle Thomas declared in an uncompleted expression, 'My Lord and my God.'[17] The rest of the passage would then construe: 'From whom is Christ according to the flesh, blessed forever.' From Scripture, which is sometimes corrupted by scribes, we cannot arrive at a certain judgment. I found the passage in Chrysostom divided thus: αἱ ἐπαγγελίαι, ὧν οἱ πατέρες, καὶ ἐξ ὧν Χριστὸς τὸ κατὰ σάρκα [the promises of which the fathers, and from which Christ according to the flesh]; here after a period there follows ὁ ἐπὶ πάντων θεός [God above all]. Then a comma is added, and there follows εὐλογητὸς εἰς τοὺς αἰῶνας [blessed forever] – a punctuation which, as I said, renders this meaning: 'He who is above all, namely God, be blessed forever.'[18] It was the same in Theophylact, except that no comma was added after θεός.[19] The blessed Cyprian cites this passage in the second book *Against the Jews*, chapter 5, omitting all mention of 'God';[20] similarly Hilary in his exposition of the one hundred and twenty-second Psalm[21] – it may seem to have been omitted through the carelessness of the copyists. Even Chrysostom gives no indication that he read 'God' in this passage.[22] It might seem that the word was added by some scholar, as if to explain who it was who was above all, namely God.

There is no reason why we should here cry out that Christ is being robbed of divinity, since the circumlocution[23] means the same thing as the name 'God,' as, for example, if one were to say 'creator of heaven and earth' instead of 'God.' Let those be quiet, then, who, titillated by the love of glory, raise an uproar at every opportunity as though the church is about to fall: if the word 'God' is omitted here it makes no difference to the thought, since the circumlocution conveys the sense more fully than the word 'God' alone. For, to show that all those things he had mentioned – adoption, glory, covenants, the giving of the Law, the rituals of worship, the promises, and the fathers, from whom Christ had sprung according to the flesh – had happened not by chance, but by the wonderful providence of God, who in so many ways took care for the salvation of the human race, [Paul] said not simply 'God,' but 'he who presides over all things,' who arranges and controls all things by his divine counsel. To him, he says, praise is owed forever because of a love so great towards us; him the Jews cursed when they assailed his only Son with blasphemies. Therefore it detracts in no way from the glory of God, even if this word [God] is not added: if this passage refers to the whole Trinity the Son is not excluded, nor is the Holy Spirit; if it refers specifically to the Father, who promised and sent his Son to redeem the human race, the divine nature of Christ is abundantly demonstrated from other passages in Scripture, and I do not think there is today anyone professing to be a Christian who would bear to hear another expressing doubts about this matter. Now if the church teaches that this passage must be interpreted only in relation to the divinity of the Son, then the church must be obeyed, though this [will do] nothing to refute the heretics[24] or those who listen only to Scripture;[25] but if [the church] says that this passage cannot, according to the Greek, be explained in any other way, it affirms what the facts immediately disprove.[26]

Now this, too, is obvious, that ὁ ἐπὶ πάντων can be taken in two ways, 'above all things' and 'above all people'; and the translator of Origen mentions both readings.[27] 'Above all things' is more unqualified, but 'above all people' is more appropriate to Christ, to give him precedence over the patriarchs, the prophets, and Moses, just as an only son takes precedence over slaves, or even over friends.

There remains one other reading, for ἐπὶ πάντων can be related to 'blessed,' so that we understand that we must forever praise Christ above all persons and all things.

In τὸ κατὰ σάρκα the article [τό] seems to me not without force, although in other circumstances it seems superfluous: [here] it marks more clearly the exception to be made. Otherwise Christ could seem simply to have been born from the Jews and to have been nothing else than a man; now the article shuts out, as it were, this thought: τὸ κατὰ σάρκα, that is, only so far as pertains to a human body – for according to his better nature, he was born God from God, just as he was born man from the fathers.

1 The form of this annotation, as it appeared in 1516, provided the base for additions until 1527. In 1535, however, the entire annotation was radically revised. We offer first, therefore, the annotation in its 1535 form, with our notes, after which we give a translation of the annotation as it appeared from 1516 to 1527, with notes on additions and changes in the text.
Erasmus' comments assume a broader context than the cue phrase gives:
ER *ex quibus est Christus, quantum attinet ad carnem, qui est in omnibus deus laudandus in saecula, amen* 'from whom is Christ, as far as pertains to the flesh, who is in all God to be praised forever. Amen.'
VG *ex quibus est Christus secundum carnem qui est super omnia deus benedictus in saecula, amen* 'from whom is Christ according to the flesh who is above all things God blessed forever. Amen.'
2 This long note attempts to show that there are three legitimate ways to punctuate and interpret Romans 9:5.
1/ 'from whom is Christ according to the flesh – Christ who is above all. God be blessed forever.' Erasmus believes that this interpretation attributes divinity to Christ but does not specifically equate him with God.
2/ 'from whom is Christ according to the flesh, which Christ, since he is God above all, is blessed.' This reading specifically equates Christ with God.
3/ 'from whom is Christ according to the flesh. God who is above all be blessed forever.' Erasmus argues that this reading, while not denying or excluding divinity from Christ, cannot be used as a defence against Arianism,

since it is at least possible to understand 'God' here to mean the Father only. Christ's divinity is not in doubt, and is proved by many passages of Scripture, but it would be wrong for anyone to rely on this passage alone as a weapon to refute those who doubt his divinity.

With this long argument may be compared the even longer exposition in the annotation on Romans 5:12 ('in whom [or, in which] all have sinned').

In both annotations the 1535 text represents a major revision of earlier texts; alternative interpretations are offered; and Erasmus shows that the refutation of heresy (there Pelagianism, here Arianism) does not hinge upon a particular reading of the passage.

Scholars remain divided on the issue of the punctuation in this passage (cf eg Metzger 520 and Cranfield II 465–70). Nevertheless, Erasmus' exegesis here, as on Rom 5:12, is historically important, since most patristic and medieval commentators equated Christ with God in this passage and regarded it as a powerful weapon against the Arians (see Cranfield II 469 and Schelkle 331–4). In his own translation (see n1 above) and paraphrase (see CWE 42 53) Erasmus followed the tradition in identifying Christ with God.

Erasmus' comments in this annotation provoked attacks by Lee, Zúñiga, the Spanish monks, and Titelmans. See *Responsio ad annotationes Lei* (1520) LB IX 215F–216C; *Apologia ad blasphemias Stunicae* (1522) LB IX 362F–363B; *Apologia adversus monachos* (1528) LB IX 1043F–1045B; *Responsio ad collationes* (1529) LB IX 1002B–1003C; and see nn24, 26 below. The passage was also discussed in the debate with Zúñiga's supporter Sancho Carranza (*Apologia ad Caranzam* (1522) LB IX 407B–D).

3 Ie in the phrase ὁ ὤν, literally 'the one being' (which both Erasmus and the Vulgate translate by *qui est* 'who is'), 'the one' (which here represents the article), Erasmus says, is not essential: 'from whom is Christ, according to the flesh, being over all.' Moreover, here the expression 'God be blessed' lacks the article, though elsewhere in the New Testament the analogous expression 'Blessed be God' is always accompanied by the article (cf the benedictions of 2 Cor 1:3, Eph 1:3, and 1 Pet 1:3) – as also in the Septuagint of the Psalms (cf 66:20, 68:35). Cf also n7 below.

4 This 'easier' reading would give: 'from whom is Christ according to the flesh who, being God above all, is blessed forever.'

5 Cf Luke 4:8.

6 Throughout much of the fourth century the church was torn by strife arising from the teaching of Arius of Alexandria (c 250–336). Although Arianism was subject to some modifications during this struggle, it always insisted on a subordinationist view of Christ. Arians believed that Christ was created by God as the Son of God before the creation of the world. Because Christ was a creature whose being was derived from God he could never be called God in the full sense of the word. Arianism was condemned at the Council of Nicaea in 325, but flourished under some of the emperors of the fourth century. Nicene orthodoxy is usually thought to have won its decisive victory at the Council of Constantinople in 381. See Kelly *Doctrines* 223–69; Jaroslav Pelikan *The Christian Tradition: A History of the Development of Doctrine* I *The Emergence of the Catholic Tradition (100–600)* (Chicago 1971) 191–210; and R.P.C. Hanson *The Search for the Christian Doctrine of God: The Arian Controversy* (Edinburgh 1988).

7 The reference is rather to 2 Cor 11:31.

8 Ambrosiaster *Comm in Rom* 9:5 (2). In this passage Ambrosiaster is commenting on the clause 'who is God above all blessed for ever.' His commentary clarifies Erasmus' abbreviated report: 'Since therefore no mention is made of the name of Father, while there is a reference to Christ, the conclusion cannot be avoided that it is Christ who is called God. For often, on account of the profession of one God, if the Scripture speaks of God the Father and adds the Son, it calls the Father "God," and the Son "Lord." If however anyone thinks the phrase "who is God" does not refer to Christ, let him name the person he supposes is referred to, since of God the Father no mention is made in this place.'
On the immediately subsequent expression – 'the case speaks for itself' – see CWE 46 45 n5.

9 Theophlact *Expos in Rom* 9:5 PG 124 461A–B

10 Origen *Comm in Rom* 7.13 PG 14 1140C–1141B. Origen speaks of those who fear that there will be 'two' gods.

11 For Erasmus' view of the Latin translation of Origen's commentary see the annotation on Rom 3:5 ('is God unfair who inflicts wrath'), especially nn11, 14, 18, where it is noted that it is in Rufinus' conclusion that he admits he has added certain things on his own. But for a similar statement in the preface to the *De principiis* see n5 (1527 version) below.
On the reliability of Rufinus' translation of *De principiis* compare P. Koetschau in the introduction to his edition of *De principiis* (Origenes Werke 5) GCS 22 (Leipzig 1913) lxxxviii-cxxxvii with G. Bardy *Recherches sur l'histoire du texte et des versions latines du De principiis d'Origène* (Paris 1933). See also J.M. Rist 'The Greek and Latin Texts in *De Principiis* Book III' and H. Crouzel SJ 'Comparaisons précises entre les fragments du *Peri Archon* selon la *Philocalie* et la traduction de Rufin' in *Origeniana: premier colloque international des études origéniennes (Montserrat, 18–21 septembre 1973)* ed. H. Crouzel et al (Bari 1975) 97–111 and 113–21.

12 Cf for example the annotation on 3:5 ('is God unfair who inflicts wrath'). Origen himself obviously followed the Greek text of the New Testament.

13 Jerome *Apologia adversus libros Rufini* 1.6 PL 23 (1883) 420A. Jerome refers here specifically to *De principiis*.

14 So Jerome ibidem 2.12 PL 23 (1883) 455C. But for Origen's doctrine of the Son and the Holy Spirit, see *De principiis* 1.1–2 and 2.6–7 PG 11 121–45, 209–18 / G.W. Butterworth trans *Origen On First Principles* (New York 1966) 13–39; and for a brief interpretation, Trigg *Origen* 95–103.

15 Jerome ibidem 2.12 PL 23 (1883) 455C–456A. Jerome and Rufinus engaged in a heated controversy over Origen's teachings after Jerome gave up his earlier allegiance to Origen as a result of the attack on Origenism that arose in Palestine in 393. The partisanship of both renders suspect the authenticity of their respective interpretations of Origen. On the conflict see J.N.D. Kelly *Jerome: His Life, Writings and Controversies* (New York 1975) 227–42.

16 Chrysostom *Hom in Rom* 16.3 PG 60 552

17 John 20:28

18 Chrysostom *Hom in Rom* 16.1 PG 60 550. The Migne edition, however, reads: 'The promises, of which the fathers, and from which Christ according to the flesh, being above all God blessed forever.'

19 Theophylact *Expos in Rom* 9:5 PG 124 460D. In Migne, the text of Theophylact and Chrysostom are virtually identical (commas after 'fathers' and 'flesh,' but no pause after 'God').

20 The reference is to Cyprian *Ad Quirinum* (*Testimonia*) 2.6, though modern editions do, in fact, include the word *'deus'* (cf CSEL 3/1 70:1). However, in his own edition of the *Opera* (Basel: Froben 1520) 275 Erasmus omitted the word.

21 Hilary *Tractatus super psalmos* 122.7; here, too, modern editions print *'deus'* (PG 9 671B; cf CSEL 22 584:24). But Erasmus omitted the word in his edition of Hilary's works (Basel: Froben 1523) 272.

22 See the citations above (nn16 and 18). The citation referred to in n16 does not contain the word 'God'; that in n18 does, but the word could have been added, Erasmus argues, by someone who wished to explicate the phrase 'who is above all.'

23 Ie the phrase 'who is above all'

24 See the annotation on Rom 5:12 ('in whom [or, in which] all have sinned') (148–51 above) for a similar, but longer, discussion of the authority of the church in matters of doctrine and in the interpretation of Scripture, however insufficient that authority may be to convince heretics. Erasmus expressed frequently, as here, his obedience to the authority of the church on such matters, even against his own judgment: cf *Responsio ad annotationes novas Lei* (on confession) LB IX 259B, 262D–E; *Responsio ad annotationes Lei* (on marriage as a sacrament) LB IX 226B, 228D; and, on the Eucharist, Allen Epp 1637:59–66, 1717:52–6, and 1893:52–71, and the annotation on 1 Cor 11:24 (*hoc est corpus meum*).

25 It is unclear to whom Erasmus refers, if indeed he has in mind a specific group. A reference to the Protestant Reformers here would seem to be inappropriate, since Protestant interpreters understood this passage to identify Christ with God; cf Martin Luther's German translation of the verse in Otto Albrecht ed *Die deutsche Bibel* VII (Weimar 1931) 56; John Bugenhagen's commentary on the verse in his *In epistolam Pauli ad Romanos interpretatio* (Hagenau 1527) fol 6 recto; and Heinrich Bullinger *In omnes apostolicas epistolas commentarii* (Zürich 1537) 78.

26 In his paraphrase on this passage Erasmus emphatically affirms the traditional view that Christ is here declared to be God (cf CWE 42 53 and n2), and he reminded Sancho Carranza of this in his *Apologia ad Caranzam* LB IX 407B–D.

27 See Origen *Comm in Rom* 7.13 PG 14 1140B–1141B. The Migne text gives only one reading, 'above all things,' but in the Merlin text the commentary includes both readings (fol cxcv recto). In his own translation (see the cue phrase above) Erasmus preserved the ambiguity of the Greek. See the cue phrase for the 1527 version and n1.

9:5 [ER *qui est in omnibus deus* 'who is in all God']
[1527] [VG] *qui est super omnia deus* **'who is above all[1] things God.'** Certainly in this passage Paul has clearly pronounced Christ God, and the Greek copies, at least those I have seen, agree. Theophylact points out that here is refuted the impiety of the Arians, who would have the Father alone truly and properly called[2] God. Origen makes similar remarks, indicating that

already then, there were those who did not dare to call Christ God, lest they should seem to make several gods.[3] But I suspect that since Roman ears could not bear to hear it, the passage was changed by the translator of Origen,[4] or by someone else – whoever it was who showed at the beginning of the work that he had on his own added something.[5] Jerome casts up to Rufinus that in the books he had translated, he had let all the errors of Origen stand except those which concerned the divine Persons, because he knew that no Roman ear would bear that blasphemy.[6] Likewise, in these commentaries, you will find certain things interspersed here[7] and there, though somewhat obscurely, concerning the salvation of the devil (in the third chapter),[8] concerning souls that sinned before they were born, and many other things of this kind.[9] But here he even speaks against the doctrine of the Arians, who had taken their errors from the books of Origen.[10] But St Jerome, writing[11] against Rufinus, says that one finds no place in the books of Origen where he spoke like a Catholic about those things he had interpreted heretically in the books Περὶ ἀρχῶν [On First Principles], as Rufinus affirmed.[12] Indeed,[13] Ambrose implies that, in this passage, there were those who tried to twist these [words to refer] to the Father, not to the Son, because elsewhere in Paul it is customary to attribute the word 'God' to the Father, 'Lord' to the Son;[14] not because the term was less appropriate to the Son than the Father, but because [such appellation] was more advantageous in those times for the preaching of the gospel – as I have abundantly shown elsewhere.[15] But here no mention is made of the Father so that this phrase could in any way be applied to him.

Theophylact[16] reads: ὁ ὢν ἐπὶ πάντων θεὸς εὐλογητὸς εἰς τοὺς αἰῶνας ἀμήν.[17] Chrysostom reads in this way: ὅς ἐστιν εὐλογητὸς εἰς τοὺς αἰῶνας ἀμήν.[18] Perhaps he understood 'God' from what preceded. His commentary on this passage reads thus: ἅπερ ἅπαντα ἐννοήσας καὶ λογισάμενος πόσην ὁ θεὸς μετὰ τοῦ ἑαυτοῦ παιδὸς ἐποιήσατο τὴν σπουδὴν σῶσαι αὐτούς, ἀνεβόησε μέγα καὶ εἶπεν, ὅς ἐστιν εὐλογητὸς εἰς τοὺς αἰῶνας, ἀμήν, τὴν ὑπὲρ πάντων εὐχαριστίαν ἀναφέρων αὐτὸς τῷ μονογενεῖ τοῦ θεοῦ. τί γὰρ εἰ ἕτεροι βλασφημοῦσι, φησίν, ἀλλ' ἡμεῖς οἱ τὰ ἀπόρρητα εἰδότες αὐτοῦ καὶ τὴν σοφίαν τὴν ἄφατον, καὶ τὴν πρόνοιαν τὴν πολλήν, ἴσμεν σαφῶς, ὅτι οὐ τοῦ βλασφημεῖσθαι, ἀλλὰ τοῦ δοξάζεσθαι ἄξιος, that is, 'When he had recognized these things and carefully pondered how much care God, along with his Son, had taken to save them, he cried out earnestly and said, "Who is blessed forever. Amen," he himself returning thanks for all these things to the only-begotten Son of God. "For what," says [Paul], "if others curse? For our part, we who have come to know his mysteries, his ineffable wisdom, his exceeding providence, know well that he is worthy to be glorified, and not to be assailed with blasphemies." ' So far Chrysostom.[19] From these words it appears that he did not read 'God' as we do.

However,[20] in some places, clauses of this kind are found to be added, for example at the conclusion of a reading, just as it is customary for us to add 'You, O Lord, glory to the Father, glory to you, Lord,' so among the Greeks, at the end of the Lord's Prayer, there is added as a conclusion 'Yours is the kingdom and the power and the glory forever and ever. Amen.' In a similar way, the clause might seem to have been added to mark the conclusion of the argument and the beginning of a new section, were there not such great agreement among all the witnesses.

Cyprian, however, in his second book *Against the Jews*, chapter 5, makes no mention of 'God' in citing this passage.[21] But[22] I suspect this occurred through the carelessness of the scribes. I have shown elsewhere[23] also that the sentence can be punctuated so that 'who is above all' refers to Christ; then following a pause, as a sort of concluding flourish, 'Blessed be God,' so that we understand Paul to be giving thanks to the Father, who has put his Son over all things.[24]

1 In *1516* only, the cue phrase read *in omnibus,* as Erasmus himself translated in all editions. The Vulgate of *1527* reads *super omnia.* Cf n27 (*1535* version) above.

From *1516* to *1522* the cue phrase was followed by: 'Unless this clause was added – just as we have come upon certain [other] additions –' and then continued: 'Certainly . . .'

2 called] First in *1519*; in *1516,* 'be.' For the reference see Theophylact *Expos in Rom* 9:5 PG 124 461A–B.

3 See n10 (*1535* version) above.

4 of Origen] Added in *1519*

5 See n11 (*1535* version) above. But in his preface to *De principiis* Rufinus claims to have omitted from his translation offensive passages (which he believes had been imported by heretics) and to have glossed other passages with texts from other works of Origen whose orthodoxy was incontestable. While, however, he admits that he has attempted to clarify and restore, he denies that he has added anything of his own. Cf his *Prologus* PG 11 111–14, especially 112B–114A.

6 See n13 (*1535* version) above.

7 here . . . obscurely] Added in *1519*

8 (in the third chapter)] Added in *1519*

9 On the salvation of the devil see *De principiis* 1.6 PG 11 165–70; on the fallen souls 1.4 and 2.8 PG 11 155–7 and 218–25. On Origen's position see Butterworth (cited n14 [*1535* version] above) 56–7 and 56 n44, 57 n1, 123–8, 251 n1; also Trigg *Origen* 89, 106, 208; and Henri Crouzel *Origen* trans A.S. Worrall (Edinburgh 1989) 212–14 and 262–6.

10 Erasmus evidently assumed in *1516* that when Origen spoke of those who feared to make two gods (cf n10 [*1535* version] above) he was referring to the Arians; on this assumption the statement would be anachronistic,

and its source would therefore be the translator. But Origen's words provide an appropriate reference to the Monarchians, who also saw in incipient orthodoxy the implication of two gods. The Monarchians were well established before Origen wrote; cf Kelly *Doctrines* 117.

11 writing against Rufinus] Added in *1519*

12 For the reference see n15 (1535 version) above.

13 Indeed ... applied to him.] Added in *1519*

14 See n8 (1535 version) above.

15 Cf the *1519* addition to the annotation on 1 Tim 1:17 (*soli deo*): 'It is rare in the letters of the apostles for the name "God" to be attributed to Christ or the Holy Spirit, whether to avoid giving offence to some, or because they were keeping it for its own time – for the apostles did not immediately preach Christ as God or as Son of God' (LB VI 930F–931C). Cf also the annotation on Rom 1:4 ('of Jesus Christ our Lord').

16 Theophylact ... as we do.] Added in *1527*

17 Theophylact *Expos in Rom* 9:5 PG 124 460D

18 Chrysostom *Hom in Rom* 16.3 PG 60 552. In this *1527* addition Erasmus appears to quote in the case of Theophylact from the biblical text preceding the commentary, but in the case of Chrysostom from the commentary itself, in which the fragment 'who is blessed forever' is embedded. In Chrysostom's antecedent and fuller quotation of the biblical text, however (n18 [1535 version] above), the word 'God' does precede.

19 Chrysostom *Hom in Rom* 16.3 PG 60 552. *1535* offered a somewhat different translation of the same passage (cf n16 [1535 version] above).

20 However ... citing this passage.] Added in *1519*

21 Cf n20 (1535 version) above.

22 But ... over all things.] Added in *1522*

23 In his *Apologia* to Carranza (1522) Erasmus points to his paraphrase on the passage, which follows the reading proposed here. See LB IX 407B and CWE 42 53 and n3.

24 all things] Following these words, from *1519* to *1527* a further short annotation appeared:

> [VG] *super omnia deus* 'above all things God.' It is unclear whether we should construe 'God above all things,' or 'above all things blessed,' that is, 'to be celebrated and praised.' Secondly, it is unclear whether [to read] 'above all persons' or 'above all things'; finally, it could also be 'in all' – ἐπὶ πάντων.
>
> In *1535* this annotation was absorbed into the longer annotation above, 'who is above all things God.'

9:6 [ER *non autem haec loquor quod exciderit sermo dei* 'I do[1] not say this, however, because the word of God has failed']

[VG] *non autem quod exciderit verbum dei* 'not however that the word of God has failed'; οὐχ οἷον δὲ ὅτι ἐκπέπτωκεν ὁ λόγος τοῦ θεοῦ. You can translate this 'not however as though the word of God has failed.' That is, the fact that I long for [their salvation] in this way – as though despairing of them – does not mean that I think the divine promises have been made void, since God promised salvation for Israel. Also,[2] the figure has an ellipse:[3] 'However, I do not say this because' and so on. So also in Latin *non quod* [not that]; but the addition of the conjunction makes the expression somewhat harsh.[4]

1 I do ... because] First in *1519*; in *1516, non autem tamquam* 'not, however, as though'
2 Also ... harsh.] Added in *1527*
3 Quintilian places the ellipse (the omission of words necessary for the sense) among the faults of expression; cf 1.5.40 and 8.6.21. See Lausberg I 504, 690–1.
4 For the Greek idiom here with the superfluous conjunction ὅτι, see Cranfield II 472 and ὅτι 1c in BAG. Valla, too, comments on this phrase; *Annot in Rom* 9 (I 858).

9:6 [ER VG] *non enim omnes* 'for not all.' 'From the circumcision' is not in the Greek, but rather οὐ γὰρ πάντες οἱ ἐξ Ἰσραήλ, οὗτοι Ἰσραήλ 'for not all those who are from Israel [are] Israel'[1] – in the second clause 'are' is understood, for [it is] the race itself [that] he calls Israel: 'Not[2] all who are sprung from the stock of Israel are Israelites.' Likewise[3] it is not unusual in the sacred books for 'Judah' to stand not for the man, but for the race, and 'Jacob' to be used for the Hebrews themselves.

I see[4] that the ancients (including both Origen and Jerome) for the most part agree on the interpretation of this name, understanding 'Israel' as 'a man who sees God,'[5] although this interpretation of the word does not square with the passage in the thirty-second chapter of Genesis, where Jacob's name is changed: 'Your name shall not indeed be called Jacob, but Israel; for if you have been strong against God, how much more will you prevail against men?' [32:28]. For this shows that his name was changed for the reason that he had prevailed in the struggle against the angel.[6] This is that force by which – to God's delight – we break into the heavenly kingdom[7] and, by faith and persistent prayers, wrest from him the blessing which we did not earn; and by which the martyrs, though assailed by various afflictions, had persevered in professing the name of Jesus, to the point of despising life. Tertullian alone seems to me to put his finger on the correct interpretation in the fourth book *Against Marcion*. He says: 'And another is inscribed by the name of Israel.[8] For what is wiser and more incontrovertible than a simple and clear confession under the name of "martyr" – one prevailing with God, which is the meaning of "Israel." '[9] Josephus[10] was of this opinion;[11] and I do not see why Jerome rejects it, since he himself interprets 'if you were first with God.'[12] But to be first in a struggle with God is to prevail; for here 'with God' means the same as 'against God,' just as we are said to fight *with* a person against whom we are fighting. Theodotion alone renders 'you were strong with God.'[13] St Jerome in *Hebraic Questions* confesses that he is deeply impressed by the authority of celebrated authors who interpreted 'Israel' as 'a man, (or, a mind) seeing God'[14] – an interpretation which, though he follows it elsewhere,[15] he firmly rejects here [in *Hebraic Questions*].

1 The discussion extends beyond the cue phrase:
   ER *non enim omnes qui sunt ex Israel* 'for not all who are from Israel'
   VG *non enim omnes ex circumcisione* 'for not all from the circumcision'
   Though a few late fifteenth- and early sixteenth-century editions read 'from the circumcision,' along with the Vulgate printed in the 1527 edition, most Latin manuscripts read, with Erasmus, 'from Israel.' See Wordsworth and White II 109 6n. In LB the words *ex circumcisione* are added to the cue phrase, without warrant, however, from the editions 1516–1535.
2 'Not ... Israelites.'] Added in 1519
3 Likewise ... themselves.] Added in 1522
4 I see ... meaning of "Israel." '] Added in 1527
5 Cf Origen *Comm in Rom* 7.14 PG 14 1141C; Jerome *Commentarii in Isaiam* 1 (on 1:3) and 12 (on 44:2) PL 24 27B and 435B; and cf n14 below. In his 1517 paraphrase Erasmus adopted the interpretation of Origen and Jerome. Changes in the paraphrase of 1521 and again in that of 1523 reflect the interpretation of this 1527 addition to the annotations. Cf CWE 42 53 n5, and also the paraphrase on Mark 7:30 CWE 49 94.
6 For the meaning of the name see A. Haldar 'Israel' in IDB II 765–6.
7 Cf Matt 11:12.
8 The allusion is to Isa 44:5.
9 Cf Tertullian *Adversus Marcionem* 4.39.6 CCL 1 652.
10 Josephus ... rejects here.] This remaining portion of the annotation was added in 1535.
11 Josephus *Jewish Antiquities* 1.20.2 (333)
12 Jerome *Liber quaestionum Hebraicarum in Genesim* (on 32:27–8) PL 23 (1883) 1038B–1039B
13 Jerome, whom Erasmus evidently follows here, correctly says that the Septuagint also, along with Theodotion, rendered 'you were strong with God' (Jerome ibidem [on Gen 32:27–8] PL 23 [1883] 1038C). Theodotion (second century AD) translated the Old Testament into Greek. His version is placed in Origen's *Hexapla* after that of the Septuagint; on the *Hexapla*, see the annotation on Rom 1:4 ('who was predestined') n6.
14 Jerome ibidem (on Gen 32:27–8) PL 23 [1883] 1039A–B
15 Cf n5 above.

9:7 [ER *neque quia sunt semen* 'nor, since[1] they are the seed']
[VG] *neque qui semen sunt* 'nor who are the seed'; οὐδ' ὅτι, that is, 'nor because' or 'since,' and so reads Ambrose.[2] The very[3] old manuscript from the library of St Paul's agrees. From this reading it was changed by the copyists.[4] In any case the Translator seems to have read ὅστις [whoever] instead of ὅτι [because]: 'Nor[5] are they the sons of Abraham merely because they trace their descent from him.'

1 since] From 1519; in 1516, *quod* 'because'
2 Ambrosiaster *Comm in Rom* 9:7 (1)
3 The very ... agrees.] Added in 1519
4 Erasmus assumes an easy change from *quia* 'since' to *qui* 'who.' There is
  considerable support in the manuscripts and among the Fathers for *qui*. See
  Wordsworth and White II 109 7n, who, however, read with Erasmus *quia*.
5 'Nor ... him'] Added in 1519

9:9 [ER *promissionis enim sermo* 'for the statement of promise']
[VG] *promissionis enim verbum* 'for the word of promise'; ὁ λόγος 'statement' or 'expression,' for [the promise] does not consist of a single word.[1]

> 1 The context here has determined our translation of *sermo, oratio,* and *verbum*
> respectively as 'statement,' 'expression' and 'single word.' For Erasmus'
> preference of *sermo* to *verbum* for translating λόγος in the New Testament,
> see his annotation on John 1:1 (*erat verbum*) LB VI 335A–337C and his *Apologia
> de 'In principio erat sermo'* LB IX 111B–122E. He prefers *sermo* because 1/ the
> word expresses better the meaning of λόγος: *verbum* refers to a single word,
> *sermo* to the coherent expression of language, including conversation; 2/
> *sermo* has in Latin the same masculine gender as λόγος in Greek, whereas
> *verbum* is neuter. Indeed, were it not for the identity of gender in *sermo*
> and λόγος, Erasmus would translate λόγος by the feminine *oratio*, whose
> meaning (thought expressed in speech, 'discourse') he believes most closely
> approximates the Greek λόγος. See especially LB VI 335C and IX 113E–114A.
> See Chomarat *Grammaire et rhétorique* I 40–1 and C.A.L. Jarrott 'Erasmus' *In
> principio erat sermo*: A Controversial Translation' *Studies in Philology* 61 (1964)
> 35–40, and the notes by Jane Phillips in CWE 46, especially 15 nn16 and 19.

9:9 [ER *in tempore hoc* 'in this time']
[VG] *secundum hoc tempus* 'according to this time': κατὰ τὸν καιρὸν τοῦτον,
that is, 'in this time.'

9:10 [ER *non solum autem hoc* 'and not only this']
[VG] *non solum autem illa* 'and not only she'; οὐ μόνον. The Translator has
added the pronoun 'she' to soften the Greek figure, and rightly so; but he
has not dared to do this elsewhere.[1]

> 1 Not all manuscripts add the pronoun here; cf Wordsworth and White II 110
> 10n. For Erasmus' comments on this figure elsewhere, see the annotation on
> 8:23 ('but not only that'); and for the translation 'she' referring to Sarah in
> the preceding verse, the same annotation, n1.

9:10 [ER *ex uno conceperat* 'had conceived from one']
[VG] *ex uno concubitu* 'from intercourse one time only'; ἐξ ἑνὸς κοίτην
ἔχουσα, that is, 'from one, having intercourse.' It can be read in two ways:[1]
'from one – Isaac': on this reading the Greek genitive πατρὸς ἡμῶν, that

is, 'our father,' would have to be translated by a Latin ablative; or 'from one' (understand 'son'), then [Rebecca] 'having intercourse with,' that is, being united in marriage to, our father Isaac. On this reading, you would understand that the promise depended on one descendent, namely Jacob; for[2] Esau was rejected. Finally, unless you supply ἦν [was], that is, 'was having,' the sentence appears incomplete – unless you repeat the words above.[3] [Esau] was counted among the sons of Abraham, so far as sons are concerned, since [Rebecca] had borne them alike from the same father; but the one who was rejected was not considered as a son, and it was of no use to him to have been born from the same father.

Further, he said 'having a bed' [κοίτην ἔχουσα][4] as a term of modesty for 'she conceived.' Lorenzo Valla is perfectly right in refuting those who understand this passage to mean that Rebecca conceived twins from intercourse one time only – as if the question here were the number of sexual unions required to conceive Jacob and Esau.[5] Rather, to take away confidence in [the merit of] their parentage, Paul puts forward two brothers born from the same father, the same mother, and on the same day, and yet one of them was rejected. What of the fact that the [Greek] words for 'one conception' cannot even agree, since κοίτην [bed] is feminine, and ἑνός [one] masculine?[6] And [while ἑνός is genitive] we do not read κοίτης [in the genitive] but κοίτην , that is, 'bed' [in the accusative].[7]

A certain[8] man has most impudently charged me with impudence, because I have counted this passage among those which are manifestly corrupted [in the Vulgate].[9] Listen to the man's haughty words: 'Assuredly, if the other passages which Desiderius includes in his "catalogue of corruptions" are like this, and if other passages in the Latin edition are no more corrupt, I fear it was said with too little respect, not to say with impudence, that this passage was one of an infinite number manifestly corrupted.'[10] Such are his words. But he had undertaken to defend the Translator, and had found a way out: if anything was found that could not be excused, it was all the fault of the copyists. But when I do this here, he becomes really quite bad-tempered, and he does so the more impudently because he himself cannot explain the passage I have called corrupted. He says: 'Who ever has used the phrase "to have a bed" when he means "to conceive"?' Well! – whoever said 'to have' for 'to be pregnant'? And yet so it must be taken here, if we are to read 'from intercourse one time only.'[11] But what would have been so outlandish if [Paul] here had said 'to have a bed' for 'to conceive' or 'to be pregnant,' when for the sake of modesty we say that a woman who has had relations with a man 'was known by the man,' and when Paul in Hebrews 13 calls a chaste union an 'unstained couch' [13:4]? I admit that Latins do not speak so, but it is likely that the

Hebrews spoke that way, and the Apostle frequently reproduces their idioms. '[The translation] "from intercourse one time" is fine,' he says, 'if we
read κοίτου instead of κοίτην.'[12] Hasn't he unravelled the knot beautifully?
I remarked that the word [in the Latin Vulgate] was corrupted by copyists:
concubitu [from intercourse], instead of *concubitum* [having intercourse];[13]
but he prefers to regard the language of the Apostle as corrupt, since no
Greek manuscript has this [reading], nor does any Greek interpret [the
passage] in this way. For Chrysostom and Theophylact talk about the same
parents, and about the same birth of twins, but say nothing whatever about
the same intercourse.[14] Who knows whether twins are engendered by the
same sexual union? As to his assertion that Theophylact seems to be thinking of the same union, the very words he quotes from Theophylact prove
him false. Theophylact, following Chrysostom as is his custom, points out
that there is this difference between the example of Isaac and Ishmael on
the one hand, and Esau and Jacob on the other, that the former had only a
father in common, the latter had both parents, and moreover were twins,
brought forth by a single parturition.[15] In the citation of the scriptural text,
the freely translated Origen has, it is true, 'from intercourse one time,'[16]
but in his exposition there is not a single syllable which indicates that he
read it thus.[17] [We gather] just as much from the words of Irenaeus.[18] Nor
does Ambrose mention anything about 'the same union.'[19] There remain
two Latin writers who seem to have read 'from intercourse one time'; but
they have been misled, as one must conjecture, by a mistake in the codices.
I will not reply to the scholiast who is falsely called Jerome.[20] Augustine is
not infrequently deceived by corrupt [readings of] the scriptural text, especially when he does not consult the Greek manuscripts.[21] Where now is that
chorus of Greeks and Latins who read 'from intercourse one time only'?
The scriptural text in Ambrose reads 'from intercourse one time having
Isaac our father,'[22] but erroneously, if I am not mistaken. For Rebecca did
not bear Isaac, but from him gave birth to the twins, Jacob and Esau. Our
[Vulgate] reading is not much easier. Accordingly some, stumbling over
[these] words, which signified nothing, added other words to read thus:
'But also Rebecca, having twin sons from one union'; Lyra points this out,
and rejects it.[23] And yet[24] so renders the translator of Theophylact, though
in the Greek author there is nothing of this kind.[25]

   Now it seems to me that the difficulty which remains can be removed
if you understand the nominative participle ἔχουσα as a genitive absolute[26]
ἐχούσης, as the Greeks sometimes do. This will then be the construction:
'Not only Sarah, however, but also when Rebecca was pregnant by one man
– and him our father'; then as a kind of parenthesis these words would be
inserted: 'for the boys were not yet born – when they had done nothing

at all either good or bad – so that God's purpose might remain according to election, [depending] not on works but on him who was calling'; there would follow the corresponding part: 'It was said to her,' and then 'The greater shall serve the lesser.' St Augustine[27] in explicating some questions on this Epistle quotes in this way: 'For not yet born, nor doing anything good or evil.'[28] I believe[29] this was the common way of speaking at that time.

1 Erasmus' discussion goes beyond the cue phrase:
  ER *sed et Rebecca ex uno conceperat Isaac patre nostro* 'but Rebecca also had conceived from one – Isaac, our father'
  VG (as printed in 1527) *sed et Rebecca ex uno concubitu habens Isaac patris nostri* 'but Rebecca also having from the one intercourse of Isaac our father'
  The ambiguity of which Erasmus speaks arises from the syntax of the Greek sentence, which, translated literally, reads: 'And not only, but also Rebecca from one having intercourse Isaac our father.'
  On the first reading 'Isaac our father' is in the genitive after the preposition ἐξ 'from.' (In the Latin the genitives become ablatives after the preposition *ex* 'from'). The sense is that Rebecca had intercourse with one – Isaac, our father. This appears to be the sense of Erasmus' translation.
  On the second reading, a comma is placed after 'from one' (which then means 'one son'), and the phrase requires a reference back to the preceding sentence: the word of promise depended upon one; first Sarah gave birth to one son only, Isaac, then in the next generation also the promise depended on one son only, Jacob, after Rebecca had intercourse with Isaac our father. Valla argued for the second reading (*Annot in Rom* 9 [I 858]); Lefèvre as well followed the second reading (*Pauli epistolae* fol 89 verso).
2 for . . . rejected] Added in 1527
3 In Greek the sentence has a participle, but no finite verb. One may supply ἦν 'was' – was having, ie, had intercourse.
4 Though in the Latin text of his New Testament Erasmus had translated the Greek idiomatically, 'had conceived,' here he translates literally, *cubile habens*; cf Lefèvre, who translated *cubile habebat* 'had a bed' (*Pauli epistolae* fols 7 recto and 89 verso). On the Greek idiom see κοίτη 2b in BAG.
5 For Valla see n1 above. Valla noted that this was the 'common reading.' On this interpretation the sentence would read, 'And not only, but also Rebecca having a single union with Isaac our father.'
6 This paragraph represents in general the argument of Valla. Valla pointed out that the disagreement in the gender of the Greek words made the reading impossible (*Annot in Rom* 9 [I 858]).
7 Ie not only do the words disagree in gender, they also disagree in case
8 A certain . . . easier.] This long central section was added in 1535.
9 Frans Titelmans had defended the common reading 'from intercourse one time only.' See *Responsio ad collationes* LB IX 1003D–1004A.
10 For the 'Catalogue of Corruptions' see *Loca manifeste depravata* LB VI *6 verso–*7 recto. After this 'title' Erasmus added a qualification: 'A small

selection taken, in order, from an infinite number.' For Erasmus' version of Titelmans' attack see *Responsio ad collationes* LB IX 1003E.

11 On Erasmus' view, *concubitum* or *cubile* must be taken with *habens* – having intercourse. On Titelmans' view *concubitu* is taken with *uno* – 'one intercourse' – leaving '*habens*' independent and without an object, so that the word 'having' must by itself bear the meaning of 'to be pregnant' (an idiomatic use attested in Greek sources; see ἔχω A II 4 in LSJ).

12 Titelmans would change the Greek from the accusative to the genitive, so that 'bed' or 'intercourse' would modify the genitive 'one,' and so the Greek text would give the Vulgate reading.

13 Though *concubitum* has the support only of the sixth-century Fulda manuscript, Wordsworth and White (II 110 10n) believe that it, rather than *concubitu*, is probably the correct reading.

14 Chrysostom *Hom in Rom* 16.5 PG 60 555; Theophylact *Expos in Rom* 9:10 PG 124 464C

15 Though the differences between the twins described here may be implied in Theophylact, they are mentioned explicitly only in Chrysostom.

16 Origen *Comm in Rom* 7.15 PG 14 1142A

17 The phrase, as in the Vulgate, does appear, however, in Origen's exposition (PG 14 1142C and Merlin fol CXCV verso), where the meaning appears indeed to be 'from one sexual union.'

18 Irenaeus *Adversus haereses* 4.21.2 PG 7 1044B. While in the Latin translation the scriptural text quoted conforms to the Vulgate, it could be gathered from the discussion that Irenaeus understood 'from one father.'

19 Ambrosiaster *Comm in Rom* 9:10. The citation of the text in Vogel's edition (CSEL 81/1 310:14, 311:16) conforms to the Vulgate, but in his exposition of 9:10 Ambrosiaster speaks only of those who are 'from one,' and 'of one race.' But see n22 below.

20 Erasmus refers to Pelagius. See *Expos in Rom* (Souter II 74:12 and 17); for Pseudo-Jerome as Pelagius see the annotation on 5:12 ('in whom [or, in which] all have sinned') n22.

21 For Augustine, see *De spiritu et littera* 24.40 PL 44 224 and *De praedestinatione sanctorum* 4.8 PL 44 966.

22 On this reading, 'Isaac our father,' in the accusative case, becomes the object of 'having.' The reading is cited as an alternative in the critical apparatus of Vogel's edition (CSEL 81/1 311:16ff).

23 Lyra *Postilla* IV fol bb vii recto

24 And yet ... this kind.] Added in *1527*, except that in place of the words 'nothing of this kind' (the reading of *1535*) Erasmus wrote 'a different phrase'

25 On the Greek and Latin editions of Theophylact, see the annotation on 1:4 ('who was predestined') n25. When Erasmus was preparing his response to Titelmans, published in 1529, he did not have the Greek Theophylact at hand (LB IX 1003D–E).

26 genitive absolute] From *1519*. In *1516*, 'accusative,' evidently an inadvertent mistake, since already then he specified by writing the Greek genitive ἐχούσης rather than the accusative ἔχουσαν. Erasmus returns here to the lack of a finite verb in 9:10 (cf n3 above), and proposes to read the sentence as a nominative

absolute (instead of a genitive absolute), with verses 11–12. Smyth offers
no examples of the nominative absolute used for the genitive absolute, but
cf F. Blass and A. Debrunner *A Greek Grammar of the New Testament and
Other Early Christian Literature* trans and rev (from the 9th–10th German
edition, incorporating supplementary notes of A. Debrunner) Robert W. Funk
(Chicago and London 1961) 243 section 466 (2)–(4).

27 St Augustine ... evil.'] Added in *1519*
28 Augustine *Expositio quarundam propositionum ex epistula ad Romanos* 60 PL 35
2078. Erasmus here turns to the first words of the 'parenthesis,' 'for the boys
were not yet born,' which are in a genitive absolute construction in Greek.
Erasmus has turned them appropriately into the corresponding ablative
absolute in Latin, but notes that Augustine quotes them as genitives absolute,
though such a construction is not Latin. For a similar jibe, see the annotation
on 2:15 ('thoughts accusing').
29 I believe ... time.] Added in *1535*

9:12 [ER VG] *maior serviet minori* 'the greater shall serve the lesser.' 'Greater'
and 'lesser' here do not refer specifically to age, but to strength and ex-
cellence: μείζων [greater], ἐλάσσων [lesser]. In Hebrew the first word is רַב
[Rab], which means 'pre-eminent in honour,' whence also the word 'rabbi.'
The second is צָעִיר, which sometimes means 'a mere youth.'

9:15 [ER *miserebor cuiuscumque misereor* 'I will have mercy on whomever I
have mercy']
[VG] *miserebor cui misertus sum* 'I will have mercy on whom I have had
mercy.'[1] It is different in the Greek: ἐλεήσω ὃν ἂν ἐλεῶ, καὶ οἰκτειρήσω ὃν
ἂν οἰκτείρω, that is, 'I will have mercy on whomever I have mercy and
I will have pity on whomever I have pity,'[2] that is, on whomever it has
been determined to have pity. Certainly[3] in the first part of this passage the
Donatian codex supports me, for there it was written: 'I will have mercy on
whom I have mercy.'[4] Here again the Translator strove, as usual, for variety
– somewhat unfortunately;[5] he renders[6] οἰκτειρήσω as 'I will show mercy
to,' οἰκτείρω as 'I have mercy on.'[7] Or rather, the needed variety failed him.
For in[8] Hebrew as also in Greek they are different words,[9] as though you
should say 'I will have mercy,' and 'I will forgive' or 'pardon.'

The expression that follows[10] is strange: 'Scripture says to Pharaoh,'
meaning, 'Scripture reports that it was said to Pharaoh.'

1 The Vulgate printed in 1527 follows the cue phrase here in reading past
tense, found in a minority of Vulgate manuscripts (Wordsworth and White
II 111 15n) though the majority of manuscripts have the present tense.
2 Erasmus and the Vulgate (1527) respectively translated the second part of
this sentence as follows:
ER *et commiserabor quemcumque commiseror* 'and I will have pity on
whomever I have pity'

vG *et misericordiam praestabo cui miserebor* 'and I will show mercy on whom I will have mercy'

3 Certainly . . . I have mercy.'] This sentence was added in *1522*.
4 Valla, too, noted the present tense in the Greek, 'on whom I have mercy'; *Annot in Rom* 9 (I 858).
5 unfortunately] Here, in *1516* only, there followed: 'If anyone asks for the Hebrew, it reads thus: וַחֲנֹתִי אֶת־אֲשֶׁר אָחֹן וְרִחַמְתִּי אֶת־אֲשֶׁר אֲרַחֵם. One can render this literally in this way: I will have mercy on whom I will have mercy and I will be merciful to whom I will be merciful. But in Hebrew there is usually this difference between חָנַן and רָחַם, that the former implies clemency towards someone, and kindness, the latter means to treat with compassion and forgive one who is ill-disposed towards us.'
6 he renders . . . failed him] Added in *1535*
7 While showing the Vulgate's 'variety' of language here ('show mercy,' 'have mercy') Erasmus corrects the Vulgate according to the Greek, which in the second instance requires a present, not (as in the Vulgate) a future tense (cf n2 above). Titelmans objected to Erasmus' criticism of the Vulgate's *copia* (*Responsio ad collationes* LB IX 1004A–B).
8 For in . . . 'pardon.'] Added in *1519*
9 Erasmus refers here to the Translator's version of ἐλέω (verse 15a) and οἰκτείρω (verse 15b), which uses the same word, *misereor*.
10 In 9:17

9:16 [ER *itaque non volentis est neque currentis* 'accordingly it is not of him who wills, or of him who runs']

[VG] *igitur non est volentis neque currentis* 'it is not,[1] then, of him who wills, or of him who runs.' Chrysostom calls this an *antithesis*, [counter-proposition] as if [it were] an objection by an opponent, as is also this: 'Therefore he has mercy on whom he will' [9:18]. Where, then, is the response? – 'O man, who are you' etc [9:20].[2]

1 it is not . . . etc.] The entire annotation was added in *1527*.
2 Chrysostom *Hom in Rom* 16.7 PG 60 558. Chrysostom believed that in 9:14–19 one could find a series of objections (counter-propositions) made by an imaginary opponent and growing out of the doctrine of election in 9:11–13. The opponent claims that God is unjust: God says, 'I will have mercy on whomever I will'; the opponent objects, 'So it is not of our own will or effort, but of God' etc. Other Fathers also saw these verses as conveying objections by an imaginary opponent; see Schelkle 341–3. The imaginary opponent appears in Erasmus' paraphrases on these verses; cf CWE 42 55 and n13. For a discussion of this and other points in Erasmus' exegesis of Rom 9:6–24, see John B. Payne 'Erasmus on Romans 9:6–24,' in *The Bible in the Sixteenth Century* ed David C. Steinmetz (Durham, NC 1990) 119–35.

9:19 [ER *quid adhuc conqueritur* 'why does he still blame']

[VG] *quid adhuc queritur* 'why does he still complain'; τί ἔτι μέμφεται, that is, 'why does he ("God" understood) still blame' or 'accuse?' – though

Lorenzo [Valla] and [Lefèvre] d'Etaples disagree; the latter wants to take *queritur* impersonally, the former as a passive.[1] Yet Valla adds my interpretation, with which all the Greek interpreters agree.[2] First of all, I do not find μέμφεται used in this way (without[3] the person indicated); secondly, my interpretation fits well with the words that follow: 'O man, who are you, who[4] reply to God.' Rufinus,[5] in the third book Περὶ ἀρχῶν [*On First Principles*], renders the thought in different words: 'Why then are we still blamed?'[6] Inexperienced readers should be advised of this only, that *queritur* 'he complains,' comes from the deponent verb *queror*, and not from the active verb *quaero* [I seek].[7] Here,[8] let whoever wishes laugh at a trivial note on grammar; but he should know that the blessed Thomas struck against this little stone, except that he adds a second sense, without rejecting the first.[9]

> 1 Valla *Annot in Rom* 9 (1 858) and Lefèvre *Pauli epistolae* fol 92 recto. Valla prefers the passive ('why is he blamed?') but acknowledges the possibility of the active ('why does God accuse?') Lefèvre says, '[The verb] here is taken "impersonally," ' and explains the meaning of the clause: 'Why is that person accused, blamed, and reproached who sins and is hardened in evil?' *Queritur* was added in *1519*.
> 2 Cf eg Origen *Comm in Rom* 7.16 PG 14 1144C.
> 3 (without ... indicated)] Added in *1519*
> 4 who reply to God] Added in *1519*
> 5 Rufinus ... still blamed?'] Added in *1527*
> 6 Cf Origen *De principiis* 3.1.7 PG 11 259C, where, however, the reading Erasmus cites is listed in a footnote as an alternative reading.
> 7 Similarly Lefèvre *Pauli epistolae* fol 92 recto. *Quaeritur* as the Vulgate reading has the support of numerous witnesses; cf Wordsworth and White II 112 19n.
> 8 Here ... the first.] Added in *1535*
> 9 Thomas Aquinas *Super Rom lect* cap 9 lectio 4.787. Aquinas explains the text in the sense both of seek (*quaero*) and complain (*queror*): 1/ *quaeritur*: why should one seek further (concerning the question of good and evil)? or why does one seek further to do good and avoid evil – since these are not in our power? 2/ *queritur*: why does God complain?

9:20 [ER *atqui O homo tu quis es qui* 'well but, O man, who are you']

[VG] *O homo tu quis es qui* etc 'O man, who are you who etc'; μενοῦνγε ὦ ἄνθρωπε 'Well but, O man who are you?'[1] Besides, the Translator renders μενοῦν below[2] as 'and indeed,' but here he suppresses the word. There is[3] an implied ἐναντίωσις [opposition] in the words 'man' and 'God.' The *emphasis*,[4] moreover, is not without point, for man[5] is nothing when compared to God.

> 1 who are you?] *1516* adds at this point: ' "who reply" – not "that you should reply," for he had already presented him as replying.' In *1519* this was absorbed into the subsequent annotation, 'that you should reply to God.' To

the Greek citation LB adds the words σὺ τίς εἶ 'who are you,' but without
warrant from the editions 1516–1535.
2 In 10:18
3 There is ... point] Added in 1527
4 For ἐναντίωσις see the annotation on 2:8 ('do not give assent to') n2; for
   emphasis, see the annotation on 1:1 ('set apart for the gospel of God') n3.
5 for man ... God] Added in 1535

9:20 [ER *qui ex adverso respondes deo* 'who reply against God']
[VG] *qui respondeas deo* 'that you should reply to God';[1] ὁ ἀνταποκρινόμενος,
that is, 'replying in opposition' – so at least[2] it is cited by Origen in his fourth
homily on Exodus;[3] or, 'who reply against God,' for he had said: 'What reason then does he [God] have to complain, if he does what he wants?' But[4]
in my opinion, indeed, 'who reply,' would be more correct than 'that you
should reply,' for he had already presented him as replying. And [Paul] is
not indignant because he is replying, but because he replies in an irreverent
way;[5] nor[6] is he deterring him from replying, but he is rebuking him because
he dared to reply in such a manner. Origen's translation has, it is true, 'that
you should reply,' but his interpretation makes clear that he read 'you who
reply,' indicating that silence is being imposed on the person for the reason
that he had shamelessly murmured against God.[7] (Likewise the Lord in the
Gospel, in regard to those who were insolently asking with what authority
he was doing what he did, or whence he had received that power, did not
even deign a reply, but raising a question they did not dare to answer he
shut their mouths.[8] But to those who sought reverently to know, [the Lord]
everywhere replied gently.) There is not much difference in the meaning,
but the Greek hardly allows the turn of phrase 'that you should reply.' Just
as earlier πᾶς ὁ κρίνων was not translated 'that you all should judge';[9] likewise in the fourteenth chapter of this Epistle, the Translator renders σὺ τίς εἶ
ὁ κρίνων ἀλλότριον οἰκέτην 'you, whoever you are who judge another's servant' [14:4]. The interpretation of neither Chrysostom, nor Theophylact, nor
Ambrose, nor Augustine indicates that we should read 'should reply' here
rather than 'who reply.'[10] To one who is preparing to make a rather petu-
lant answer, one would appropriately say, 'Who are you that you should
reply?'; but for one who is chiding a person who has already replied rudely,
it fits better [to say], 'Who are you who reply?' The metaphor is taken from
evil servants, who when they murmur against the orders of their masters
are said to 'talk back.' And so in this passage, the intent is: 'What are you
doing, man, talking back to God?' Augustine[11] treats this passage in the
sixty-eighth of the *Eighty-three Questions*. He refutes the slanderous accusations of the heretics who concluded that Paul here had suddenly resorted
to reproach because he could not unravel the knot of the question.[12]

1 In *1516* only, the position of this and the following annotation was reversed.

2 so at least ... Exodus] Added in *1519*

3 Cf Origen *In Exodum homiliae* 4.2 PG 12 318C–D. In Migne, the citations of Rom 9:20a conform to the Vulgate.

4 But ... as replying.] Added in *1519*. Titelmans was to argue that either construction is possible. Cf *Responsio ad collationes* LB IX 1004C.

5 way] From *1519* to *1527* the annotation concluded with the following words: 'And yet the interpretation of Origen is close to the Vulgate reading, and even more clearly Augustine followed it in the sixty-eighth of the *Eighty-three Questions*. He refutes the slanderous accusations of the heretics who concluded that Paul here had suddenly resorted to reproach because he could not unravel the knot of the question.' The allusion to Augustine's refutation of the heretics was included in *1535*; cf n12 below.

6 nor ... talking back to God?] The rest of the annotation from this point was added in *1535*, except for the brief discussion of Augustine at the end (cf n12 below).

7 Origen *Comm in Rom* 7.16 PG 14 1144A–B; and 7.17 PG 14 1148B–C. In the former passage Origen identifies the respondent referred to in 9:20 with the impertinent questioner of 9:19, who there responds to the assertions of 9:14–18; thus in 9:20 he has already 'shamelessly murmured against God.' In the latter passage Origen cites the verb as Erasmus wishes – 'you therefore who insolently reply to God ...' – though elsewhere in his discussion of 9:20 he cites the verse as the Vulgate has it, 'that you should reply.'

8 Matt 21:23–7

9 Rom 2:1, on which see the annotation 'every one of you who judge'

10 Cf Chrysostom *Hom in Rom* 16.7 PG 60 558–9; Theophylact *Expos in Rom* 9:20 PG 124 468D; Ambrosiaster *Comm in Rom* 9:20 (1); Augustine *Expositio quarundam propositionum ex epistula ad Romanos* 62 PL 35 2081. Erasmus argues from silence: nothing in the actual commentary of these Fathers suggests that we ought to follow the Vulgate reading. But Augustine's comments here indicate that he did indeed read 'that you should reply.'

11 Augustine ... question.] Cf n5 above for the *1519* version of this portion of the annotation.

12 Augustine *De diversis quaestionibus* LXXXIII 68.1 PL 40 70: the 'heretics' said that since Paul found himself unable to answer the questions raised in 9:19, he replied with these words, 'Who are you ...?' as a reproach to the curious who raised the questions. These 'heretics' may be the Manichees; see *Saint Augustine: Eighty-Three Different Questions* trans David L. Mosher, Fathers of the Church 70 (Washington 1982) 157 n46 and 158 n2.

9:20 [ER *ei qui finxit* 'to him who formed[1] (it)']

[VG] *ei qui se finxit* 'to him who formed itself.'[2] The Greek is τῷ πλάσαντι '[to him] who formed,' and that was enough; the pronoun *se* [itself] is superfluous.[3]

1 formed] In *1516* Erasmus' translation was identical with the Vulgate here. He omitted the *se* 'itself' from *1519*.

2 For the order of this annotation, see the previous annotation, n1.

3 So Valla *Annot in Rom* 9 (1 858). Valla adds that if a pronoun is to be used, it should not be the reflexive pronoun.

9:21 [ER VG] *ex eadem massa* 'from[1] the same lump'; ἐκ τοῦ αὐτοῦ φυράματος, which Augustine cites as 'from the same dough.'[2] For he means clay that has been softened by moisture and tempered.

1 from ... tempered.] The annotation was added in 1519.
2 Cf Augustine *Expositio quarundam propositionum ex epistula ad Romanos* 62 PL 35 2081; *De diversis quaestionibus* LXXXIII 68.3 PL 40 71–2, and *Contra duas epistulas Pelagianorum* 2.7.15 PL 44 581. 'Dough' here renders the Latin *conspersio*, which implies a paste.

9:21 [ER VG] *aliud in honorem* 'one to honour';[1] τιμὴν καὶ ἀτιμίαν [honour and dishonour]. Lorenzo [Valla] thinks [these words][2] can be more correctly translated *decus* and *dedecus*,[3] especially because vessels are not subject to insult. And yet, since 'insult' comes from 'despising,'[4] what prevents an insult from being applicable to an inanimate object, when it is both coveted and despised? Even if it were less appropriate, the metaphor still adds a fine effect, as though[5] someone should say that when Bassus, in Martial, empties his bowels into a golden chamber pot, he insults the gold.[6] This much is true, that in 'dignity' and 'indignity' we have the pleasure of a studied contrast, which is lost in 'honour' and 'insult.'

1 The arrangement found here of this and the next six annotations was established first in 1519. In 1516 five annotations appeared in the sequence: 'fit for destruction,' 'prepared for glory,' 'whom also he called,' 'but if God wishing,' 'one to honour.' Two annotations, 'endured in much patience' and 'vessels of mercy,' appeared first in 1519.
2 Erasmus' discussion here extends beyond the cue phrase:
   ER *ut ... fingat aliud quidem vas in honorem, aliud vero in ignominiam* 'to form one vessel for honour, but another for shame'
   VG *facere aliud quidem vas in honorem, aliud vero in contumeliam* 'to make one vessel for honour, but another for insult'
3 Valla *Annot in Rom* 9 (1 858). *Decus* and *dedecus* preserve a contrast in sound and meaning characteristic of the Greek *timēn-atimian*. The words *decus* and *dedecus* refer to what is 'becoming' and 'unbecoming' and may be translated here as 'dignity' and 'indignity.'
4 The relationship is more apparent in the Latin, for Erasmus says that *contumelia* comes from *contemnere*. But for the relationship of the two words see *contumelia* in L&s and OLD.
5 as though ... gold] Added in 1519
6 Martial *Epigrams* 1.37

9:22 [ER VG] *quod si deus volens* 'but if God wishing.'[1] Nothing follows which responds to this clause in the sentence, so that we have to refer back to the words above: either to 'Who are you, man, who reply to God?' or to 'Does he not have power?'[2] Origen[3] thinks that the passage, which is in any case quite irregular, can be put together in this way: 'God, wishing to show his wrath and to make known his power, endures with much patience the vessels of his wrath suited for destruction, so that he may make known the riches of his glory towards the vessels of mercy.'[4] But if we should like to supply something [of our own] (for it is clear that the passage is incomplete) we can understand: 'They have no reason to accuse God or dispute with him.'[5] Some[6] Latin codices had 'What if God,' but the Greek is εἰ δέ [but if].[7]

1 For the sequence of this annotation in *1516* see the annotation on 9:21 ('one to honour') n1.
2 At 9:22 a long sentence begins with a subordinate clause ('If God, willing . . .') for which there is apparently no corresponding main clause. Erasmus proposes to take this subordinate clause with verse 20 or 21, giving either the sense 'Who are you who reply to God, if God, willing to show his anger, endured . . . ?' or the sense 'If God, willing to show his anger, endured . . . does he [as potter] not have power over the clay?' For other passages where Erasmus notes the apparently incomplete sentence in the Greek, see the annotation on 5:12 ('therefore just as through one man') n4.
3 Origen . . . dispute with him] Added in *1519*
4 Origen *Comm in Rom* 7.18 PG 14 1149C–1150A
5 The passage would then construe: 'But if God, willing to show his wrath . . . endured . . . the vessels of wrath . . . , they have no reason to accuse him or dispute with him.' It is this reading that underlies the paraphrase on the verse; cf CWE 42 57 ('But what cause . . .').
6 Some . . . δέ.] Added in *1527*
7 Wordsworth and White II 112 22n cite the Froben edition of 1502 as the sole witness to the reading 'what if.'

9:22 [ER *tulit multa animi lenitate* 'bore with much leniency'[1]]

[VG] *sustinuit in multa patientia* 'endured[2] in much patience.' ἤνεγκεν in Greek is an ambiguous word, which Augustine in *Questions on Exodus* reads as 'he brought forward[3] in much patience the vessels of wrath,'[4] and again[5] in the twenty-first book *Against Faustus*, the second chapter.[6] For the Greek is not ἔφερεν, which means 'to bear,' but ἤνεγκεν, which means rather 'to lead forward' or 'to bring forth.'[7] And – lest we plead that in this passage the text has been accidentally corrupted – he cites it again in the same way in the second book to Boniface *Against the Two Epistles of the Pelagians*,[8] and elsewhere as well.[9] But if this is the true reading the sense will be: These vessels, prepared for destruction, were long awaited,[10] and were finally brought forth for their own punishment. And yet Origen clearly interpreted 'endured and bore,'[11] as did Ambrose,[12] who was usually quite happy to follow Origen. Chrysostom[13] agrees with them; and Theophylact accords with him.[14]

1 leniency] First in *1519*; in *1516*, *longanimitate*, long-suffering, a word that appears in the commentary of Ambrosiaster on this verse; see n10 below.

2 endured ... Origen.] With the exceptions noted below (nn5 and 13), this annotation was added in *1519*. The cue phrase began with *sustinuit* first in *1535*, previously with *tulit* 'bore.'

3 Augustine, in all passages identified here, cites the word as *attulit*.

4 Augustine *Quaestiones in Heptateuchum* 2.32 CSEL 28/2 109:13

5 and again ... second chapter] Added in *1522*

6 Augustine *Contra Faustum Manichaeum* 21.2 PL 42 389

7 Erasmus distinguishes between the imperfect and aorist tenses of the Greek verb φέρω. Though the aorist of this verb is used in the New Testament to mean both 'to lead to' and 'to produce,' 'bring forward,' the evidence does not support the distinction Erasmus makes here; see φέρω 4 a and b in BAG.

8 Augustine *Contra duas epistulas Pelagianorum* 2.7.15 PL 44 581

9 Eg *Enarrationes in psalmos* 58.20 PL 36 704

10 The phrase finds clarification in the text of Ambrosiaster, from which it was perhaps cited: 'The sense is that by the will and long-suffering [*longanimitate*] (which is the endurance) of God the unbelieving were prepared for punishment. For though they had been "waited for" a long time, they refused to repent. Thus, because they were "waited for," they perished without excuse: God knew they would not believe' (*Comm in Rom* 9:22).

11 Origen *Comm in Rom* 7.18 PG 14 1150A; Erasmus follows this interpretation in his *Paraphrase* as well (CWE 42 57).

12 Ambrosiaster twice uses the word 'endure' (*sustinere*) in his comments on verse 23 (cf *Comm in Rom* 9:23 (1–2).

13 Chrysostom ... him.] Added in *1527*

14 Chrysostom *Hom in Rom* 16.8 PG 60 560; Theophylact *Expos in Rom* 9:22 PG 124 469B–C

9:22 [ER *apparata in interitum* 'prepared for destruction']
[VG] *apta in interitum* 'fit for destruction';[1] κατηρτισμένα, that is, 'fitted' or 'prepared.'[2]

1 For the sequence of this annotation in *1516* see the annotation on 9:21 ('one to honour') n1.

2 Valla suggested 'fitted' (*Annot in Rom* 9 [I 858]). Titelmans defended *apta* as having the sense of *praeparata* 'prepared' (*Responsio ad collationes* LB IX 1004C–D).

9:23 [ER VG] *vasa misericordiae* 'vessels[1] of mercy'; σκεύη ἐλέους. Augustine rightly observes that σκεῦος in Greek means, not specifically a vessel made to hold liquid, but anything that relates to domestic use.[2] Accordingly, in Livy, in the supposed speeches of the legates, their entire goods are signified by the designation 'slaves and vessels.'[3] The Greeks call a vessel that holds liquid ἀγγεῖον.

1 vessels ... ἀγγεῖον.] The entire annotation was added in 1519.
2 The observation does not arise in Augustine's discussion of this text or, indeed, of other texts of the New Testament where the word σκεῦος occurs. Cf, however, *Enarrationes in psalmos* 57.16 PL 36 821–2, where the 'vessels' in the 'strong man' passage of Matt 12:29 become the apostles, pastors, and teachers whose function is the general ministry in the house of the Lord.
3 Cf Livy 1.24.5.

9:23 [ER *praeparaverat in gloriam* 'had prepared for glory']
[VG] *praeparavit in gloriam* 'prepared for glory.'[1] In some codices,[2] the Greek adds αὐτοῦ, that is, 'his.'[3] I prefer[4] the other reading, so that [Paul] does not appear to say the same thing twice. For here he calls 'glory' what he previously called τιμή [honour].[5]

1 For the sequence of this annotation in 1516 see the annotation on 9:21 ('one to honour') n1.
2 In some codices] Added in 1519
3 Tischendorf II 415 23n lists no manuscript that adds αὐτοῦ.
4 I prefer ... τιμή.] Added in 1519
5 If we read here 'prepared for *his* glory,' we refer to the glory of God, exactly as in the previous clause, 'that he might make known the riches of his glory,' so that the two clauses say much the same thing. But if we read 'prepared for glory,' we refer to the glory of the vessel, just as in 9:21 ('form one vessel to honour') we refer to the honour of the vessel.

9:24 [ER *quos et vocavit nimirum nos* 'whom also he called, namely,[1] "us"']
[VG] *quos et vocavit* 'whom also he called'; οὓς καὶ ἐκάλεσεν ἡμᾶς, that is, 'us whom also he called.' But ἡμᾶς [us] is not added in some Greek codices;[2] it was added by way of explanation: 'whom he also called – namely, us.' And again, so that 'us' should not seem to refer to the Jews alone, he adds, 'not only from the Jews, but also from the gentiles.'

1 namely] Added in 1519. For the sequence of this annotation in 1516 see the annotation on 9:21 ('one to honour') n1.
2 Though 'us' is absent in many Latin manuscripts, Tischendorf II 415 lists no variant reading that omits the word in the Greek. For the Latin manuscripts, see Wordsworth and White II 113 24n.

9:25 [ER omitted]
[VG] *et non misericordiam consecutam, misericordiam consecutam* 'and her that has not obtained mercy, her that has obtained mercy.'[1] These words are not found in the Greek codices,[2] nor[3] are they added by Augustine, who quotes this text in the twenty-second book *Against Faustus*, chapter 89.[4]

Moreover Ambrose does not read this part [in his text], nor does he discuss it in his interpretation.[5] Origen in his commentary recounts this passage of Paul with these words: 'Us who before were not his people he now calls his people, and the not beloved [he calls] beloved'[6] etc, whence it appears that he read only the one part [about the] ἠγαπημένη [beloved]. Moreover, the interpretation of[7] Chrysostom and likewise of Theophylact clearly indicates that they read the passage in the same way as Origen and Ambrose.[8]

Now in the second[9] chapter of Hosea, from which Paul took this text, neither the words 'having obtained mercy' nor 'beloved' are found, but only 'And it will be [that] in the place where it will be said to them, you are not a people, it will be said to them, sons of the living God'[10] – except[11] that there preceded 'And I will have mercy on her who was without mercy.'[12] (For the Apostle rendered the meaning, rather than the words, of the prophet.) But St Jerome, discussing[13] the first chapter of this prophet, on which this passage[14] depends, points out that there were two readings; in some sources was written our reading,[15] οὐκ ἠγαπημένην, ἠγαπημένην [her who was not beloved, her who was beloved]; in others, οὐκ ἠλεημένην [her who has not obtained mercy]. But he prefers the second reading as the truer, because it is so read in the better copies, and because it answers more appropriately to 'Israel not having obtained mercy,'[16] while[17] the converse follows: 'And on the house of Judah I will have mercy' [Hos 1:7]. It also fits better with what we read at the end of the second chapter: 'And I will have mercy on her who was without mercy' [Hos 2:23]. But since this passage depends on the earlier passage, where it is said: 'Call her name "without mercy,"' [Hos 1:6] it is probable that here, too,[18] there was a variant of the scriptural text. Accordingly, some reader, coming upon the discrepant reading, thought that in each text[19] a clause had been omitted, and added what he thought was lacking. Augustine[20] thinks that the apostle Peter was quoting from the same passage of the prophet when he wrote in the second chapter of the first Epistle: '[You] who once were not a people but now are the people of God; you on whom once he did not have mercy but now has mercy' [1 Pet 2:10].[21] Peter appears to differ from Paul here in reading 'had mercy' instead of 'beloved'; but his word order equally differs from the prophet, where the daughter is first, whose name is 'without mercy'; then comes the son, whose name is 'not my people.'[22] The order is the same at the end of the second chapter, where their former names are changed: 'And I will have mercy on her who was "without mercy," and I will say to "not my people," you are my people' [2:23].

What follows in Paul has been taken from the first chapter: 'And it will be [that] in the place where it was said to them, you [are] not my people, there they shall be called the sons of the living God' [1:10]. But what was said in the prophet about the people of Israel, Paul applies by analogy to the gentiles.[23] In the very old Donatian codex I found the second pair of clauses omitted. It reads: 'I will call Not my people, My people; and Her that has not obtained mercy, Her that has obtained mercy.'[24]

1 Though this appears as a separate annotation in all editions published during Erasmus' life, it is conflated in LB with the previous annotation.

2 The witness of the Greek manuscripts supports the omission of these words from 9:25 (Tischendorf II 415 25n). The Latin witnesses offer three major variants: 1/ a few read, with the Greek, 'her that was not beloved, beloved' (cf AV, RSV); 2/ the majority read instead, 'her that had not obtained mercy, one that has obtained mercy'; 3/ some include both readings, ' "and her that was not beloved, beloved, and her that had not obtained mercy, one that hath obtained mercy" ' (DV); cf Wordsworth and White II 113 25n. The third cited is the reading of the Vulgate in 1527; also of the Vulgate printed in Lefèvre's 1512 edition (fol 7 recto). Like Erasmus, Lefèvre chose to read the first; cf *Pauli epistolae* fols 7 recto and 92 recto. Erasmus paraphrased the third; cf CWE 42 57, 'Their own prophets ...'

3 nor ... Origen and Ambrose] Added in 1522, with the exception of the reference to Chrysostom (cf n7 below)

4 Augustine *Contra Faustum Manichaeum* 22.89 PL 42 460

5 Ambrosiaster *Comm in Rom* 9:25–6

6 Origen *Comm in Rom* 7.18 PG 14 1152A–B

7 of ... likewise] Added in 1527

8 Cf Chrysostom *Hom in Rom* 16.9 PG 60 562 and Theophylact *Expos in Rom* 9:25 PG 124 472A.

9 second] From 1522; in the first two editions, 'the first chapter.' The change was made in response to the charge by Zúñiga that Erasmus did not know his Bible well. On Zúñiga's comment and Erasmus' response see ASD IX-2 171–2 and the notes by H.J. de Jonge, especially on lines 120–8, where it is pointed out that the citation in Rom 9:25–6 consists of elements taken from Hos 1:9, 1:10, and 2:23b (2:24 Vulgate).

10 These words are from Hos 1:10. Erasmus evidently did not notice the discrepancy when he changed the chapter number. (While in the Septuagint text these words belong to verse 1 of chapter 2, it is evident that Erasmus was citing from a Vulgate text divided like modern Bibles; see n12.)

11 except ... mercy'] This brief comment was added in 1522.

12 Erasmus quotes here from the Vulgate of Hos 2:23a. These words do not precede Hos 1:10 just quoted (cf n10). It may be noted, however, that 2:23a echoes 1:6–7 and 2:23b echoes 1:10, perhaps facilitating the conclusion that these words from 2:23a preceded 1:10.

13 discussing ... two readings] First in 1522. In the previous two editions, Erasmus wrote, 'discussing this passage, points out that there were two readings for this text.'

14 By 'this passage' Erasmus means Hos 2:23. At the end of his discussion on Hos 1:10 Jerome comments briefly on the two readings of 1:6. Hos 2:23 refers back to (depends on) 1:6–7; cf n16 below.

15 Erasmus quotes 'his reading,' ie of Rom 9:25, where the antithesis 'not beloved, beloved' appears.
16 Jerome *Commentarii in Osee* 1 (on 1:10) PL 25 (1845) 829C. The quotation is from Hos 1:6.
17 while ... scriptural text] Added in *1522*
18 Ie in Hos 2:23
19 Ie the text of Hos 1:6 and of Rom 9:25, since in *1516*, when the sentence was written, Hos 2:23 had not yet become an issue
20 Augustine ... obtained mercy.'] This remaining portion of the annotation was added in *1522*.
21 Augustine *Contra Faustum Manichaeum* 22.89 PL 42 460
22 Cf Hos 1:6 and 9.
23 Cf Jerome, who attempts to show the analogy in *Commentarii in Osee* 1 (on 1:10) PL 25 (1845) 829C.
24 This reading omits the 'not loved-loved' pair printed in the Vulgate of *1527*.

9:26 [ER VG] *ibi vocabuntur* **'there they shall be called.'** ἐκεῖ [there] is not in the prophet, but was added by the Apostle – no doubt to make his meaning clearer.[1]

1 clearer] In *1516* only, the Hebrew of Hos 1:10 followed.

9:26 [ER *dei viventis* **'of the living God'**]
[VG] *dei vivi* **'of the God who is alive.'** The Greek is ζῶντος 'of the living [God].'

9:27 [ER *super Israel* **'over Israel'**]
[VG] *pro Israel* **'for Israel';** 'over Israel' or 'concerning Israel' – ὑπέρ, although this preposition is ambiguous.[1]

1 The senses both of 'concerning,' 'over,' 'about' on the one hand and 'for, on behalf of' on the other, are attested in LSJ.

9:27 [ER VG] *si fuerit numerus* **'if the number be.'** The text is from Isaiah, chapter 10,[1] where the Septuagint version agrees with the Hebrew original; but Paul differs somewhat, though in words rather than meaning. For the LXX translated τὸ ὑπόλειμμα ὑποστρέψει, that is, 'a remainder shall return.'[2] But Jerome translates in this way:[3] 'For if your people Israel be as the sand of the sea, [only] the remnants of it shall return.'[4]

1 Isa 10:22–3
2 Erasmus is evidently quoting the Greek from Jerome (*Commentarii in Isaiam* 4 [on 10:22]). The text quoted in Paul parallels closely that of the Septuagint in Isa 10:22.
3 Cf Jerome ibidem 4 (on 10:22) PL 24 139A–D.
4 return] In *1516* only, the Hebrew followed.

9:28 [ER *sermonem enim perficiens* 'executing his word']

[VG] *verbum enim consummans* 'bringing to completion the word.' 'Word' is in the accusative case; 'bringing to completion' and 'cutting short' are in the masculine gender, with 'is' understood – meaning 'God' [is].[1] λόγου[2] γὰρ συντελῶν, that is, 'bringing his word[3] to completion.' Chrysostom[4] and Theophylact[5] reveal this clearly in their exposition of this passage.[6] What Origen and Ambrose say about 'the word cut short' offers no impediment to this observation, since in this passage one finds expressed two concepts: it is the Father who brings to completion and cuts short; it is either Christ or his doctrine that is brought to completion.[7] But these words, too, differ somewhat from the original Hebrew, for[8] we read in Jerome's version:[9] 'For the Lord God will make a consummation and a cutting short of armies in the midst of every land.'[10] There is a passage with a similar thought in the eighth chapter of the same prophet: 'For I have heard the consummation and the cutting short of armies by the Lord God over the whole earth.'[11]

With[12] respect to the words 'Isaiah said before,' it is not [a matter] of prophesying about the future, but that this text preceded the one he had just cited;[13] hence it would be better rendered 'as Isaiah said above.'[14] Further, the Apostle has retained the Hebrew word צְבָאוֹת 'Sabaoth,' which the Septuagint customarily renders in two ways: sometimes παντοκράτωρ,[15] that is, 'omnipotent,' at other times τῶν δυνάμενων, that is, 'of powers.' Aquila alone renders τῶν στρατευμάτων, that is, 'of armies.'[16] Jerome[17] points this out in his exposition of the first chapter of Isaiah.[18] Paul, as I have said, did not think the Hebrew word should be changed, I believe because [he thought] some mystery lay hidden in it that could not be rendered into another language.[19]

1 So Valla *Annot in Rom* 9 (1 858)
2 λόγου ... that is] Added in 1519
3 Erasmus renders λόγος here by *sermo*, which he prefers to the Vulgate *verbum*. See the annotation on 9:9 ('for the word of promise') and n1. In this case, however, *sermonem* had an added advantage, since as a masculine, its form showed clearly that it was in the accusative case, object of the participles (of which 'God' is subject), whereas the Vulgate *verbum*, a neuter, could be read either as subject ('the word bringing to completion') or object.
4 Chrysostom and] Added in 1527
5 Theophylact ... brought to completion] Added in 1519
6 See Chrysostom *Hom in Rom* 16.9 PG 60 562 and Theophylact *Expos in Rom* 9:28 PG 124 472C.
7 Cf Origen *Comm in Rom* 7.19 PG 14 1153C–1154A and Ambrosiaster *Comm in Rom* 9:28. Origen gives three possible meanings for the 'abridged word': 1/ the fulfilment of the prophecy of the remnant (9:27): many are called but few are chosen; 2/ Jesus' teaching that the Law is summed up in the commandments to love God and neighbour (Deut 6:5; Matt 22:37, 39, 40); or 3/ the creed in which the faith of believers is summarized in a few

words (Origen *Comm in Rom* 7.29 PG 14 1153C–1154A). Ambrosiaster's understanding of the 'abridged word' is that it is by faith alone rather than by the ceremonial works of the Law that salvation is reached (Ambrosiaster *Comm in Rom* 9:28). Neither writer says explicitly that it is the Father who 'completes and abridges,' but both refer the 'abridged word' to the doctrine of Christ. For a similar interpretation of the passage see Colet *Enarratio* (English 49–50, Latin 169).

8 for ... Jerome's version] Added in *1519*

9 Jerome *Commentarii in Isaiam* 4 (on 10:20) PL 24 139A

10 land'] In *1516* only, the Hebrew was inserted at this point.

11 These words are found in Isa 28:22 (Vulgate) rather than in the eighth chapter.

12 With ... language.] In *1516* this paragraph (with exceptions; see nn15 and 17 below) appeared as part of the subsequent annotation ('had left us'), where, however, what is here the first sentence concluded the annotation. It became part of the present annotation in *1519*.

Erasmus discusses here the first part of Rom 9:29:

ER *quemadmodum prius dixit Esaias, nisi dominus Sabaoth reliquisset nobis* 'as Isaiah said before, unless the Lord Sabaoth had left for us'

VG *sicut praedixit Esaias, nisi dominus Sabaoth reliquisset nobis* 'just as Isaiah foretold, unless the Lord of Sabaoth had left for us'

In *1516* Erasmus had accepted the Vulgate's *praedixit* but apparently in the sense of 'said formerly,' not 'predicted.' He changed the translation to *prius dixit* 'said before,' in *1519*.

13 Ie Isa 1:9 preceding Isa 10:22, just cited in Rom 9:27

14 But the term here evidently means 'foretold.' See προεῖπον in BAG and Cranfield II 502.

15 παντοκράτωρ] Until *1535*, this word and the two Greek phrases that follow were preceded by the Greek words ὁ κύριος and rendered 'Lord,' thus reading, respectively, 'Lord omnipotent,' 'Lord of powers,' 'Lord of armies.'

16 Aquila, a Jewish proselyte of the early second century AD, made a very literal rendering of the Hebrew Bible into Greek. His version was included in the *Hexapla* of Origen (cf the annotation on 1:4 ['who was predestined'] n6).

17 Jerome ... Isaiah.] Added in *1535*

18 Jerome *Commentarii in Isaiam* 1 (on 1:9) PL 24 32A

19 For the term Sabaoth see B.W. Anderson 'Hosts of Heaven' in IDB II 654–6.

9:29 [ER VG] *reliquisset nobis* **'had left us';**[1] ἐγκατέλιπεν,[2] that is, 'had left among us.' The text is taken from the first chapter of Isaiah.[3]

1 For the form of this annotation in *1516* see the previous annotation, n12.

2 Here LB adds ἡμῖν 'among us,' but without warrant from the editions published in Erasmus' lifetime.

3 Isa 1:9

9:30 [ER *quid igitur dicemus* **'what then shall we say'**]

[VG] *quid ergo dicemus* **'what therefore shall we say.'** What follows [this question] is to be read as a statement, not a question:[1] 'What therefore shall we say?' – obviously, we shall say this: 'The gentiles having obtained righteousness from faith' etc. Augustine also has annotated this passage in the third book *On Christian Doctrine*.[2] Theophylact's[3] discussion follows in the same vein.[4]

1 The Vulgate printed in 1527 read the sentence as a question: 'What therefore shall we say – that the gentiles obtained righteousness ... ?'
2 Augustine *De doctrina christiana* 3.3.6 PL 34 67. Like Erasmus, Augustine insists that the words in question are a statement in response to the question 'What then shall we say?'
3 Theophylact's ... vein.] Added in 1519
4 Cf Theophylact *Expos in Rom* 9:30 PG 124 473A.

9:31 [ER VG] *non pervenit* **'has not attained'**; οὐκ ἔφθασε. This word is translated in various ways, but it is especially appropriate to one who hastens to gain possession of something, so that you understand that the Israelites pressed thither through the works of the Law, but that the gentiles gained possession, while those were excluded.

9:32 [ER *tamquam ex operibus* **'as though**[1] **from works']**
[VG] *quasi ex operibus* **'as if from works'**; ὡς ἐξ ἔργων, that is, 'as though from works,' and the Greek adds νόμου, that is, 'of the Law,' so that you understand works[2] that are devoid of faith and love; it is[3] not added in the Latin sources.[4] Chrysostom[5] and, following him, Theophylact[6] have noted the word ὡς, as if it indicates that the works of the Jews had not been truly the works of the Law.[7] I think that the word can also suggest 'accounting.' For the Jews gave the credit for salvation to their works, excluding the grace of God.[8]

1 as though] Added in 1519
2 works ... love] First in 1527. Previously, 'ceremonies'
3 it is ... sources] Added in 1535
4 Most, but not quite all, Latin manuscripts omit 'of the Law' (Wordsworth and White II 114 32n), which is also the better reading of the Greek (Metzger 523).
5 Chrysostom ... him] Added in 1535
6 Theophylact ... God] Added in 1527
7 Cf Chrysostom *Hom in Rom* 16.10 PG 60 564; Theophylact *Expos in Rom* 9:32 PG 124 473B.
8 For ὡς used in 9:32 to suggest an 'illusory quest,' see Cranfield II 510; for its use to introduce 'a quality wrongly claimed' or 'objectively wrong' see ὡς III 3 in BAG.

9:33 [ER *petram offensionis* **'rock of offence']**
[VG] *petram* σκανδάλου **'rock of scandal.'** Translators make use of the Greek word [*skandalon*][1] freely, although they could say [a rock of] 'offence' or

'stumbling' or 'hindrance.' Yet[2] I am aware that a Hebrew idiom is retained here: 'a stone of stumbling' for a 'stumbling-stone' or a stone against which they strike. I do not see why some should stumble over προσκόπτω, which without doubt means 'hit against' or 'strike against.'[3]

This text is woven together from two passages of Isaiah. The beginning, namely, 'I lay in Zion a rock' and the end, that is, 'and everyone who believes in him will not be confounded,' are taken from the twenty-eighth chapter of Isaiah; what is inserted in the middle, 'and a stone of offence and a rock of scandal,' is taken from the eighth chapter of the same [book].[4] But in this passage as well, Paul has striven to convey the sense rather than the words. For although the Hebrew original reads 'Who has believed, let him not hasten,'[5] Paul, following the Septuagint edition, said[6] 'will not be confounded.'[7]

1 Though the word appeared in Greek in the cue phrase, the Vulgate printed in 1527 transliterated the word and gave it the Latin case ending: *petram scandali*; cf Wordsworth and White II 114.
2 Yet ... strike.] Added in 1519
3 Possibly a reference to Lefèvre, who translated '*repulerunt*' and interpreted the word in the sense of 'repel, reject,' referring to those who reject Christ, who do not believe. Cf *Pauli epistolae* fols 7 verso and 92 recto. For a similar discussion of the Greek προσκόπτω see the annotation on 14:21 ('in which your brother is offended').
4 Isa 28:16 and 8:14
5 Erasmus refers here to the last half of the quotation (in 9:33), which the final annotation on this chapter addresses.
6 So Jerome in citing the passage from the Septuagint translated into Latin; cf *Commentarii in Isaiam* 9 (on 28:16) PL 24 322A–B.
7 confounded] 1516 adds the Hebrew, with the words 'The Hebrew reads thus.'

9:33 [ER *non pudefiet* 'shall not be made ashamed']
[VG] *non confundetur* 'shall not be confounded'; οὐ καταισχυνθήσεται, that is, 'will not be made ashamed.'

CHAPTER 10

10:1 [ER *propensa quidem voluntas cordis* 'the ready will indeed of (my) heart']

[VG] *voluntas quidem cordis* 'the will indeed of [my] heart'; ἡ μὲν εὐδοκία, which signifies something pleasing to the mind and welcome. Aurelius[1] Augustine, in explicating some selected questions on this Epistle, for εὐδοκία reads *bona voluntas*[2] [good will], as[3] the Translator had rendered the word in Luke.[4] Roman[5] speech has nothing to correspond exactly to the Greek expression, which is modelled on the Hebrew. For no one, I believe, would tolerate somebody saying *delicium cordis mei*[6] [the delight of my heart]. The expression[7] signifies the eager benevolence and the disinterested partiality that one bears towards another, like that of God towards us. Likewise the words that follow[8] [in the Vulgate] do not square exactly [with the Greek]; for the Greek is καὶ ἡ δέησις ἡ πρὸς τὸν θεὸν ὑπὲρ τοῦ Ἰσραήλ ἐστιν εἰς σωτηρίαν, that is, 'and the intercession which is made to God is on behalf of Israel, for their salvation.'[9] He means that he is offering the Jews what he can: a ready will, and intercessions[10] before God.

1 Aurelius ... *voluntas*] Added in 1519

2 Augustine *Expositio quarundam propositionum ex epistula ad Romanos* 66 PL 35 2082

3 as ... Luke] Added in 1527

4 See the annotation on Luke 2:14 (*hominibus bonae voluntatis*), where Erasmus writes at length on the meaning of the Greek word.

5 Roman ... *mei*.] Added in 1519

6 For the difficulty of translating into Latin those expressions in the New Testament Greek that are based on Hebrew idioms see the annotation on 9:33 ('rock of scandal'). *Delicium* is attested in classical Latin frequently with the sense of 'pet,' 'darling'; cf OLD.

7 The expression ... towards us.] Added in 1535

8 After the words of the cue phrase, 10:1 continues:
ER *et deprecatio quae fit ad Deum, pro Israel est ad salutem* 'and the intercession which is made to God is on behalf of Israel for their salvation'
VG *et obsecratio ad deum fit pro illis in salutem* 'and supplication to God is made on behalf of them unto salvation'

9 In the preferred reading, however, 'them' is found in place of 'Israel,' and 'is,' omitted in the text, must be supplied: 'my prayer to God for them [is] for their salvation' (cf RSV); cf Tischendorf II 417 1n.

10 intercessions] First in 1519; in 1516, 'prayers'

10:2 [ER *quod studium* 'that a zeal']

[VG] *quod aemulationem quidem* 'that an emulation indeed'; ὅτι ζῆλον θεοῦ, that is, 'an emulation of God,' without 'indeed.' If one[1] knows nothing but

Latin, what sense will he derive from these words: 'they have an emulation of God?' 'Emulation' in a good sense means imitation; in a bad sense,
jealousy.[2] Neither fits here. Accordingly, I have translated *studium* [zeal];
this Latin word signifies strong devotion. And *scientia* means, rather, dis-
cernment: κατ᾽ ἐπίγνωσιν. They had zeal, but without judgment; 'devotion
becomes a burden to the one who is foolishly loved.'[3]

1 If one ... strong devotion.] Added in *1535*
2 In *Responsio ad collationes* Erasmus extends further the multiple meanings of
  the word (LB IX 1004D).
3 Horace *Epistles* 2.1.260. Modern editors punctuate the line to give the sense:
  'Devotion foolishly becomes a burden to the one who is loved'; see the note
  on line 260 in *The Epistles of Horace* ed A. Wilkins (London 1892; repr 1965).

10:3 [ER *et propriam iustitiam quaerentes constituere* 'and seeking to establish
their own righteousness']
[VG] *et suam quaerentes statuere* 'and seeking to set up their [righteous-
ness].' Here the Greek repeats the word 'righteousness.'[1] The[2] repetition of
the same word makes the language more lively.[3] There is[4] also an underlying ἐναντίωσις [opposition][5] between 'their own' [righteousness] and [the
righteousness] 'of God'; also between 'to set up' and 'have not been subject
to.' The opposition here lies in the sense more than in the words. But ἰδίαν,
that is, *propriam* [their particular], signifies more than *suam* [their].

1 The word is used three times in 10:3: 'Not knowing the righteousness of God,
  and seeking to establish their own righteousness, they were not subject to
  the righteousness of God.' (For variants, however, see Tischendorf II 417 3n.)
2 The ... word] First in *1527*; previously, 'The reduplication'
3 For 'reduplication' (*conduplicatio*) and repetition (*traductio*) see the annotations
  on 8:15 ('Abba, Father') n5, and 8:35 ('who therefore will separate us') n13.
4 There is ... in the words.] Added in *1527*
5 For ἐναντίωσις see the annotation on 2:8 ('do not give assent to').

10:4 [ER *nam perfectio legis Christus* 'for the perfection[1] of the Law is
Christ']
[VG] *finis enim legis Christus* 'for[2] the end of the Law is Christ.' τέλος in
this passage means 'consummation' and 'perfection,' not 'destruction,' as
Augustine also pointed out in elucidating the fifth Psalm,[3] [and] again[4] in
Against the Priscillianists and Origenists, chapter 7.[5] For what has been completed and perfected with all the things usually required, this the Greeks
call τέλειον. Christ is the culmination, therefore, of the Law. And in the
case of the psalms that bear the title *In finem* [to the end], they suppose that
something quite hidden, quite secret must be tracked down.[6] What he here
calls τέλος, he elsewhere calls πλήρωμα [fulfilment].[7]

1 perfection] First in *1519*; in *1516, finis* 'end'
2 for ... πλήρωμα.] With the exception of an addition in *1535* (n4 below) this
   entire annotation was added in *1519*.
3 Augustine *Enarrationes in psalmos* 4.1 PL 36 78
4 again ... chapter 7] Added in *1535*
5 Augustine *Ad Orosium contra Priscillianistas et Origenistas* 7.8 PL 42 674
6 In the Septuagint many of the psalms received titles. One such title, which
   frequently recurs, is εἰς τὸ τέλος (Latin *in finem*). These titles received a
   mystical interpretation by some of the Fathers. Augustine, too, begins his
   interpretation of each psalm with an exposition of the meaning of the title,
   as in the case of Ps 4, where he interprets *in finem* to refer to Christ, citing
   Rom 10:4 (cf n3 above). The same interpretation is found in his exposition
   of other psalms, eg 12, 13, 17 (PL 36 140, 141, 154). On these titles and their
   mystical interpretation by Christians see H.B. Swete *An Introduction to the Old
   Testament in Greek* (Cambridge 1902) 250–1.
7 Erasmus may have in mind such a passage as Rom 13:10, where he translated
   πλήρωμα by *consummatio*, a meaning he gives τέλος here. Erasmus followed
   a strong patristic tradition in understanding τέλος as 'fulfilment' rather than
   'termination'; see Schelkle 365–8. Modern critics are divided on the issue: cf
   Michel 255; Cranfield II 516–22.

10:5 [ER *Moses enim scribit* 'for Moses writes']
[VG] *Moses enim scripsit* **'for Moses wrote.'** The[1] Greek is 'writes.' The Latin
version is corrupt here, but the Greek reads correctly:[2] Μωσῆς γὰρ γράφει,
τὴν δικαιοσύνην τὴν ἐκ τοῦ νόμου, ὅτι ὁ ποιήσας αὐτὰ ὁ ἄνθρωπος, ζήσεται ἐν
αὐτοῖς, that is, 'for Moses writes the righteousness which is from the Law,
that the man who does these things shall live in them.' Lorenzo [Valla]
comments on the passage shrewdly, if somewhat obscurely;[3] he means this,
that the statement as a whole should not be assigned to Moses, namely, 'that
the righteousness which is from the Law, in it shall a man live' – as though
Moses had written this entire thing – but only the latter part, 'the man who
does these things shall live in them.'[4] For [Paul] recalled the words found in
the eighteenth chapter of Leviticus: 'Keep my laws and judgments, which if
a man does, he shall live in them' [18:5]. Likewise you read in the twentieth
[chapter] of Ezekiel: 'They have rejected my judgments; these, if a man will
do, he shall live in them' [20:13].

   Now Paul, for[5] the purposes of teaching, makes righteousness twofold:
that of Moses, which requires the works of the Law, and that of the gospel,
which requires faith in Christ. About[6] the first Moses says (or if you prefer, righteousness itself speaks): 'Whoever does these things shall live in
them.' The second, which is from faith, speaks thus: 'Do not say in your
heart.'[7] Chrysostom interprets in this way. He says: 'Moses shows us the
righteousness that is from the Law, of what sort it is and of what significance. What, then, is its nature, and whence is it commended? From the

fact that it fulfils the precepts – "Who has done these things," says [Paul], "shall live in them." ' Then shortly after: 'But tell us also, Paul, of that other righteousness, which is from grace' etc.[8] The reading of Theophylact agrees with that of Chrysostom, and so does his exposition.[9] Ambrose reads and interprets according to the Greek codices: 'For Moses wrote the righteousness which is from the Law, that the man who has done these things shall live in them.'[10] The translator of Origen reads and interprets what our Vulgate edition reads. But his freedom makes it impossible to determine clearly from the [translation] what [Origen] read.[11]

A reader took offence at the incongruous form of the syntax here, and transposed the conjunction ὅτι [that], eliminated the pronoun *ea* [these things], and put *ea* [it] in place of 'them' at the end: 'For Moses wrote that the man who has done the righteousness that is from the Law shall live in it.' To start with, *scribit iustitiam* [he writes the righteousness], meaning 'describes the righteousness' or 'writes about the righteousness,' seemed harsh. Then, 'who has done these things shall live in them' seemed even harsher to the reader, who did not notice that [these] words of Scripture are reported under the persona of Moses, or of righteousness, so that ὅτι [that] is understood εἰδικῶς [that is, to specify]:[12] 'Moses described the righteousness that is from the Law'; then, as though someone asked what sort of righteousness it was, he replies to the questioner with the words of Leviticus, 'He who has done these things shall live in them.' This can be taken in two ways: he shall have that life which the works of the Law offer for a time;[13] or, he shall not have life, because no one carries out the works of the Law without the gift of faith. Certainly in our [Vulgate] reading, the very manner of expression, so disordered, proves that the passage was corrupted by a scribe: 'For Moses wrote that the righteousness which is from the Law, who has done shall live in it.' I say nothing of the fact that ὅτι is translated as *quoniam*.[14]

1 The ... 'writes.'] Added in 1535
2 Titelmans evidently thought Erasmus challenged the authority of the Translator here. In reply, Erasmus offered the alternative – to fault either the Greek manuscripts or the copyists – and noted that in choosing the latter Titelmans merely followed Erasmus (*Responsio ad collationes* LB IX 1004E).
   In fact, the Greek readings here are varied. The preferred reading is that of the Vulgate (cf Tischendorf II 418 5n; Metzger 524–5; and Cranfield II 520–1). For the text in the versions of Erasmus and the Vulgate, cf n4 below.
3 Valla *Annot in Rom* 10 (I 858)
4 Erasmus followed a Greek text that in general supported Valla's reading, and he translated accordingly:
   ER *Moses enim scribit de iustitia quae est ex lege, quod qui fecerit ea homo, vivet per illa* 'for Moses writes concerning the righteousness which is from the

Law that the person who does these things shall live by them'

VG *Moses enim scripsit quoniam iustitiam quae ex lege est qui fecerit homo vivet in ea* 'for Moses wrote that the one who does the righteousness which is from the Law shall live in it.'

In *1516* only, Erasmus translated, in place of *scribit de iustitia* 'writes concerning the righteousness,' *scribit iustitiam* 'writes with respect to [or, describes] the righteousness'; and in place of *per illa* 'by them,' *in illis* 'in them.'

Among biblical translations AV represents Erasmus' reading, RSV the (preferred) reading of the Vulgate (cf DV).

5 for ... teaching] Added in *1527*
6 About ... *quoniam.*] This remaining portion of the annotation was added in *1535*.
7 Cf 10:6.
8 Chrysostom *Hom in Rom* 17.1–2 PG 60 565–6
9 Theophylact *Expos in Rom* 10:5 PG 124 476C
10 Ambrosiaster *Comm in Rom* 10:5
11 Origen *Comm in Rom* 8.2 PG 14 1160A–C
12 ὅτι may mean either 'that' (as in reporting the words of another) or 'because'; cf the annotation on 8:36 ('as sheep of the slaughter') n6. On εἰδικῶς see the annotation on 4:21 ('whatever God has promised') n1.
13 Cf Pelagius: 'From this passage some think that the Jews have merited from the works of the Law their present life only' (*Expos in Rom* [Souter II 82:4–6]).
14 The Greek ὅτι, here meaning 'that' (but cf n12 above), is translated by *quoniam.* Though in the Vulgate *quoniam* is used for both 'that' and 'since,' in classical Latin it is used only in the sense of 'since,' 'whereas.'

10:11 [ER *omnis qui fidit illi non pudefiet* 'everyone who trusts[1] in him will not be made ashamed']

[VG] *omnis qui credit in illum non confundetur* 'everyone[2] who believes upon him will not be confounded'; οὐ καταισχυνθήσεται. He frequently renders it this way, and it appears that people commonly spoke that way then, though *confundi* is, properly, to be mixed together, or thrown into confusion. *Suffundi* [to be embarrassed] is said of one who comes to feel shame.[3] But sometimes an extraordinary sense of shame is so disturbing that one becomes like a deranged person. With respect to the phrase in Acts, 'and he confounded the Jews,' the word is different – κατέχυννεν – that is, made them disturbed and perplexed, so that they did not know which way to turn.[4] The translator of Origen rendered καταισχυνθήσεται by *erubescet* [blush, feel ashamed], citing the example of Adam, who after his sin felt ashamed and hid himself.[5] But those also feel ashamed who have been defrauded of their hope; for a sense of shame belongs to a righteous person, fear to an evil one. Thus the Jews taunted Christ as though he had lost all hope: 'If he is the Son of God, let him now come down from the cross.'[6]

1 trusts in him] First in 1519; in 1516, *credit in illo* 'believes in him.' In his response to Titelmans, Erasmus defended his translation on the grounds that the Vulgate was not Latin, and that while the devils believe, they do not trust. It was the sense of 'confidence towards God' that Erasmus wished to express in his translation (*Responsio ad collationes* LB IX 1005A–B).

2 everyone ... cross.'] The entire annotation, placed out of sequence with the biblical text, was added in 1535. In LB this annotation follows the annotation on 10:8 ('the word is near').

3 *Suffundere* – 'to pour from below,' 'to suffuse,' hence, 'to blush,' and so, here, 'to be embarrassed' – represents the Greek better than *confundere*, though Erasmus goes on to admit that one can imagine a shame so great that one is genuinely confounded. For other attempts to define the language of 'shame' see the annotations on 1:16 ('for I do not feel ashamed of the gospel') and 5:5 ('does not confound') and nn2 and 3.

4 Cf the annotation on Acts 9:22 (*et confundebat*); also the annotation on 5:5 (cf n3 above).

5 Origen *Comm in Rom* 8.2 PG 14 1164A–B

6 Cf Matt 27:40.

10:6 [ER *ex alto deducere* 'to bring down from on high']

[VG] *deducere* 'to bring down'; καταγαγεῖν, to bring down as though from on high. To this[1] corresponds ἀναγαγεῖν,[2] which the Translator has rendered 'to call back,' though[3] it means more precisely to bring back from the depths below to the height above. It seems to me that especially the Latin interpreters labour mightily over this passage,[4] although its sense is perfectly clear. For [Paul] had said that the gospel asks only for faith. Moreover, faith does not demand the testing of evidence, it perceives with the mind; and the one who believes sees with his own sort of eyes. But the one who doubts requires the testimony even of the senses, saying to himself what we read in the thirtieth chapter of Deuteronomy: 'Who ascends into heaven?' [30:12]. This was[5] said in reference to the Law, but in interpreting, Paul applies it to Christ. 'For that,' he says, 'is to bring Christ down from heaven,' inasmuch as he either is not believed to be there, or is compelled to return hither to display himself a second time to our senses. 'Or who descends into the abyss?' That is, who would believe what is said about hell unless he has seen it? 'That is,' he says, 'to bring Christ back from the dead,' as though either he did not descend to hell, or they are demanding that he descend a second time before their eyes. But evidence would not have to be sought so far away if faith were present in the heart.[6] Now with respect to the phrase 'but what says [he, or it]?' [10:8], it can seem ambiguous whether[7] the subject of 'says' is Moses or the righteousness of faith, which is Christ, and which at this point he has represented as speaking – as Origen and also Chrysostom[8] believe.[9] And yet elsewhere, too, Paul

has used 'says' in this same way, with 'Scripture' understood [as subject].[10]
Accordingly the Translator quite fittingly added this word on his own by
way of clarification.[11]

1 To this ... ἀναγαγεῖν] Added in 1535

2 This annotation carries a discussion of verses 6 and 7; these verses (including
punctuation) appear as follows in the texts of Erasmus and the text of the
Vulgate in 1527:
  ER *quis ascendet in coelum? Hoc est Christum ex alto deducere. Aut, quis
  descendet in abyssum? Hoc est Christum ex mortuis reducere. Sed quid dicit?*
  'Who will ascend into heaven? That is to bring Christ down from on high.
  Or who will descend into hell? That is to bring Christ back from the dead.
  But what does it say?'
  VG *quis ascendet in coelum, id est Christum deducere: aut quis descendet in
  abyssum, hoc est Christum a mortuis revocare. Sed quid scriptura dicit?* 'Who
  will ascend into heaven, that is to bring Christ down; or who will descend
  into hell, that is to call Christ back from the dead. But what does Scripture
  say?'

3 though ... above] In 1535 only; previously, 'as though eager to explain what
had been too obscurely said.' This change and the addition above (cf n1)
were evidently an attempt to respond to Titelmans, who had observed that
revocare translated ἀναγαγεῖν, not καταγαγεῖν, as the annotation before 1535
suggested. See *Responsio ad collationes* LB IX 1004E–F.

4 Rom 10:6–7 inspired a rich variety of comment in Christian antiquity and the
Middle Ages. Origen thought the passage spoke of the immediate presence
of Christ and the availability of the Christian gospel to everyone (*Comm in
Rom* 8.2 PG 14 1160A–1164B); Chrysostom (*Hom in Rom* 17.2 PG 60 566–7)
taught that the passage affirmed the need for faith, an interpretation shared
by Hilary (*De Trinitate* 10.68–9 PL 10 595E–597A) and Ambrosiaster (*Comm
in Rom* 10:7 [1–2]). Augustine struggled with the differences between the
text of Deuteronomy and the text of Romans (*Quaestiones in Heptateuchum*
5.54 CSEL 28/3 413). Thomas Aquinas offered two interpretations: 1/ When
one asks 'Who ascends into the sky?' thinking it impossible, by implication
he asserts that Christ is not there; when one asks 'Who descends into hell?'
thinking this impossible, by implication he denies the death of Christ. 2/ To
ask these questions is to imply that Christ needed no help in his descent and
ascent (Who ascends to bring Christ down?), since he was the Word of God
(*Super Rom lect* cap 10 lectio 1.824–5). On the passage in antiquity cf Schelkle
369–71.

5 was ... Law, but] Added in 1535

6 In *De libero arbitrio* LB IX 1217B Erasmus understands this passage of the word
of God which, he explains, is not to be sought far above in the heavens, nor
far off across the sea, but is at hand, in our mouth and heart.

7 whether] Latin *utro*, in the phrase *utro referatur dicit*, literally 'to which of the
two "says" refers'; first in 1522; previously, *quo* 'to whom'

8 and also Chrysostom] Added in 1535

9 Cf Origen *Comm in Rom* 8.2 PG 14 1161A–C and Chrysostom *Hom in Rom* 17.2
PG 60 566. Origen ascribes the words to Christ speaking in Deuteronomy;

Chrysostom makes 'righteousness' the subject of 'says' when he quotes the
text of 10:6–7: 'But the righteousness which is from faith thus says: "Do not
say …"'

10 Cf such passages as Rom 15:9–10, 1 Cor 15:27, and Eph 4:8, where Scripture
is understood as the subject (and so translated in NEB).

11 The Vulgate of 1527 read, in 10:8, 'But what says Scripture?' Though many
manuscripts so read, the preferred reading of the Vulgate is 'But what does
it say?' Cf Wordsworth and White II 116 8n.

10:8 [ER *prope te verbum est* 'the word is near you']

[VG] *prope est verbum* **'the word is near';** ἐγγύς σου τὸ ῥῆμα 'the word is
near you,' that is, there is no need to seek so far away, from heaven or
from hell, since it is within you. But[1] the text, as I have just said,[2] has been
taken from the thirtieth chapter of Deuteronomy.[3] This Origen first, then
Augustine, has pointed out,[4] except that Augustine adds 'very': 'This word
is very near, in your mouth,' as one reads in our Vulgate edition also.[5]
And yet there are other discrepancies also between Paul's words and the
Hebrew, or our edition rather, which reads as follows: 'This commandment
which I enjoin upon you today is not above you, neither placed far off, nor
set in heaven, so that you can say, "Who of us is able to mount up to heaven
to bring it down to us, so that we may hear it and fulfil it by work?" Nor is
it placed across the sea, so that you might plead excuse and say, "Who of
us can cross the sea and bring it all the way back to us, so that we can hear
and do what has been commanded?" But the word is within you, right in
your mouth and in your heart, that you might do it.'[6] In the first place,
the phrase found there, 'who of us can cross the sea,' Paul has rendered
'who will descend into hell?' But with respect to Augustine's reading in
Questions on Deuteronomy – 'This word is very near, in your mouth and
in your heart and in your hands, to do it' – he thinks Paul omitted the
phrase 'in your hands,' but certainly our Vulgate edition does not have it.
Whether it is in the Hebrew, I leave to those more skilled in that language.[7]
Perhaps[8] someone has corrected the passage in Paul. The phrase is found
in the Septuagint at least, καὶ ἐν χερσί σου ποιεῖν αὐτό.[9]

1 But … language.] The remainder of the annotation, with the exception of the
final two sentences, was added in 1519.

2 Cf the annotation immediately above.

3 See Deut 30:14 for the passage to which the cue phrase refers. In the
annotation Erasmus reviews Deut 30:11–14.

4 Cf Origen *Comm in Rom* 8.2 PG 14 1161B–C; Augustine *Quaestiones in
Heptateuchum* 5.54 CSEL 28/2 413.

5 The Vulgate of 10:8 printed in 1527 reads 'The word is near, in your mouth'
(so Weber II 1761); the Vulgate of Deut 30:14 reads 'The word is very close
to you, in your mouth' (Weber I 277).

6 The Vulgate of Deut 30:14 quoted here is virtually identical to the text in Weber (I 277). Erasmus, however, reads *intra te* 'within you' for Weber's *iuxta te* 'close to you.' Erasmus' reference to 'the Hebrew, or our edition rather' implicitly acknowledged that his Vulgate text of Deuteronomy derived from Jerome's translation from the Hebrew.

7 On Erasmus' knowledge of Hebrew cf Epp 181:42–4, 334:133–7, 373:72–83, 396:292–7. See also Shimon Markish *Erasmus and the Jews* (Chicago 1986) 112–41.

8 Perhaps ... αὐτό.] Added in 1522

9 Deut 30:14 (LXX)

10:12 [ER *vel Iudaei vel Graeci* 'whether of the Jew or of the Greek']
[VG] *Iudaei et Graeci* 'of the Jew and the Greek'; Ἰουδαίου τε καὶ Ἕλληνος. Again the double conjunction[1] makes a more forceful statement.[2] I have translated it by *vel*, a conjunction which conveys the same force.[3]

1 Ie τε καί 'both ... and'
2 On the 'double conjunction' see the annotation on 2:9 ('of the Jew first and of the Greek').
3 *vel ... vel* 'either ... or' (cf Erasmus' translation of 10:12) can suggest alternatives not necessary and exclusive, sometimes with a force similar to that of 'both ... and.'

10:12 [ER VG] *dives in omnes* 'rich unto all.' In Greek this is a participle, πλουτῶν, that is, 'abounding in,' or 'over-flowing with riches.'

10:14 [ER *de quo non audiverunt* 'about whom they have not heard']
[VG] *quem non audierunt* 'whom they have not heard.' It could have been translated 'about whom they have not heard,' for the Greek is οὗ οὐκ ἤκουσαν.[1]

1 The Greek verb ἀκούειν with the genitive is common in the New Testament, but usually with the meaning 'to hear' or 'to heed,' rather than 'to hear about,' as Erasmus translates here; see ἀκούω in BAG and LSJ.

10:15 [ER VG] *quam speciosi pedes* 'how beautiful are the feet.' Paul has quoted this text following the original Hebrew, according to which you read in the fifty-second chapter of Isaiah,[1] in[2] Jerome's version, 'How beautiful upon the mountains are the feet of the one who announces and preaches peace, who announces good, who preaches salvation' [52:7]. The LXX translated ὡς ὥρα [*hōs hōra*]. If this word [ὥρα] is written with an aspirate it signifies either time, as,[3] 'there are twelve hours [*horae*] of the day';[4] or a part of the year: 'And he regulates the world with the changing seasons [*horis*]'[5] (whence also those who have passed the flower of youth are called ἔξωροι [*exōroi*]);[6] or 'beauty' [*pulchritudo*] (and thus[7] ὡραῖος means 'beautiful'). ὥρα [*ōra*] without the aspirate expresses[8] care and concern. According to the Septuagint, then, we read thus: 'As[9] the hour [or, season] upon the mountains, so are the feet of the one who preaches.' But St Jerome prefers 'how beautiful';[10] yet this reading is not much different from the Septuagint, if you take ὥρα as *pulchritudo* [beauty]. Thus one reads, 'As the loveliness upon the mountains, so are the feet' etc.

1 Isaiah] In *1516* only, there followed here the citation in Hebrew.
2 in Jerome's version] Added in *1519*
3 as ... ἔξωροι] Added in *1527*
4 Cf John 11:9.
5 Horace *Odes* 1.12.15–16; cf the annotation on 13:11 ('and knowing this time') n6.
6 As in Lucian *Hermotimus* 78
7 and thus ... 'beautiful'] Added in *1519*
8 expresses] Added in *1535*
9 ὡς [*hōs*] may be taken in the sense of either 'as' or 'how.' Erasmus follows here Jerome's translation of this Septuagint clause; cf Jerome *Commentarii in Isaiam* 14 (on 52:7). In his analysis of the meanings of ὥρα Erasmus also follows closely Jerome's commentary. Jerome explains that if *hora* is taken in the sense of time, the reference will be to the opportune time for salvation.
10 Jerome ibidem PL 24 499D, 500D–501A

10:16 [ER *obedierunt evangelio* 'have obeyed the gospel']

[VG] *obediunt evangelio* 'obey the gospel.' The Greek is 'have obeyed,' ὑπήκουσαν, a verb in the past tense;[1] unless[2] perhaps this verb is one of those which signify an 'abiding action,'[3] like γέγηθα [I rejoice] and δέδια [I fear], where the past is used for the present. One who has written a book is no longer writing; but those who are said to have hoped in the Lord have not, according to Greek idiom, ceased to hope. In any case the present tense is frequently suited to any time.

1 So Valla *Annot in Rom* 10 (I 858). The verb is in the past tense in the preferred reading of the Vulgate, but many Latin manuscripts, and the Vulgate of *1527*, have the verb in the present tense; cf Wordsworth and White II 117 16n.
2 unless ... any time] Added in *1535*
3 In the *Responsio ad collationes* Erasmus refers to the type of verb which in the past tense signifies 'a continuing action, or, rather, state' (LB IX 1005B).

10:16 [ER *domine quis credidit sermonibus nostris* 'Lord, who has believed our words']

[VG] *domine quis credidit auditui nostro* 'Lord, who has believed our hearing.'[2] [Paul] has taken this text from the fifty-third chapter of Isaiah.[3] He has followed the edition of the LXX, who added this word 'Lord' to indicate the person addressed, for it is not found in the Hebrew, but only, 'Who has believed our hearing?' Origen[4] also observed this.[5]

The reader should be advised that in this passage *auditus* [hearing] stands for the actual speech which is heard; accordingly, it would have been clearer to say: 'Who has believed our words?' or 'Who has believed the things heard from us?' For[6] the noun *auditus* in Latin can only signify the power and sense of hearing. But if ἀκοή means the same as our *auditus,* why in this case did the Translator render the same thing differently in the third chapter of Matthew,[7] καὶ ἀκοὰς πολέμων, that is, 'and rumours of wars,'[8] rather than 'the hearings of wars?' And in the last chapter of Acts, why did he venture to translate ἀκοῇ ἀκούσετε 'you will hear with the ear'?[9] I have listed this passage among the obvious solecisms, adding these words: 'What speaker of Latin ever used *auditus* to mean the words of a speaker?'[10] A certain wrangler was infuriated at this and boasted that he could prove that what I had said was a pure falsehood, and that there was no fault in the language here. He said: 'Jerome, Augustine, and Ambrose knew Latin and nevertheless they speak in this way.'[11] First of all, I do not include these authors among those whose authority can excuse a solecism. For in part they lowered the level of language to the ears of the ignorant crowd for whom at that time they were both writing and speaking; and in part the Roman language itself had at this time degenerated from its pristine purity. In the second place, what wonder if in using the texts of Scripture, they use its words? But who of these speaking on his own account wrote, 'One day you shall repent that you did not heed my hearing,' meaning 'that you did not heed my words?' I did not deny that anyone who spoke that way was Latin, but I did say that no one who spoke Latin spoke that way. If that was a pure falsehood, at least a single passage from approved authors ought to have been adduced. Hasn't the Translator been beautifully defended from the charge of solecism, and haven't I been splendidly shown to have spoken pure falsehood? Those who publish such silly jingles in their books, who scold me with amazing arrogance, taunt me with incredible disdain, and are so far from gaining their triumph, would do better meanwhile to learn the rudiments of Greek and Latin grammar.

1 our words] From *1519*; in *1516*, *auditis nobis,* apparently intended to mean 'what they have heard us say'

2 In *1516* only, the position of this annotation and the next was reversed.

3 Isa 53:1

4 Origen ... observed this.] Added in *1519*

5 Origen *Comm in Rom* 8.6 PG 14 1171A

6 For ... grammar.] This remaining portion of the annotation was added in *1535.*

7 The reference is to Matt 24:6.

8 Latin *opiniones bellorum*. The Vulgate text printed in 1527 read *opiniones proeliorum*; so also Weber II 1563.
9 Acts 28:26
10 Cf *Soloecismi* LB VI *5 verso. Zúñiga (*Assertio* [Rome 1524] fol 4d recto) had observed that if the expression is bad Latin, it is also bad in Greek. Erasmus admitted the expression was based on Hebrew idiom and was a solecism in Greek as in Latin (*Epistola apologetica adversus Stunicam* LB IX 398D); for the controversy, cf Erika Rummel *Erasmus and His Catholic Critics* I (Nieuwkoop 1989) 173–6.
11 A reference to Frans Titelmans, to whom Erasmus had already in 1529 made a response similar to the one here. See *Responsio ad collationes* LB IX 1005B–1006A.

10:17   [ER *per verbum dei* 'through the word of God']
         [VG] *per verbum Christi* 'through the word of Christ';[1] θεοῦ, 'of God,' not 'of Christ.'[2] It is[3] certain that Chrysostom reads θεοῦ; he expounds this passage in such a way that [the word of God] refers also to the words of the prophets.[4] Theophylact agrees with him (though his translator has rendered something other than he read[5]), and each of them points out that [the phrase] 'word of God' was used in relation to the difference between it and human speech, which could be rejected. It is not clear from his commentary what Ambrose read.[6] The translator of Origen seems to have read 'of Christ' rather than 'of God.'[7] It does not make much difference to the sense, except that the word 'God' increases more the dignity of the Apostle's language, and a wider range of meaning is exposed. For the prophet seems to make this complaint in relation to himself; Paul applies it, as though it were a prophecy, to the preachers of the gospel.

         1 For the position of this annotation, see the previous annotation, n2.
         2 'Of Christ,' the preferred reading of the Vulgate (Wordsworth and White II 117 17n), is also the reading better attested by the Greek witnesses, but Erasmus here follows the Alexandrian texts and the majority of the Fathers (Schelkle 375–6); cf Tischendorf II 421 17n and Metzger 525.
         3 It is ... gospel.] This remaining portion of the annotation was added in 1535.
         4 Chrysostom *Hom in Rom* 18.1–2 PG 60 573–4
         5 Theophylact *Expos in Rom* 10:17 PG 124 480C–D. Porsena (see annotation on 1:4 ['who was predestined'] n25) translated the biblical text quoted in Theophylact as 'through the word of Christ.' As Erasmus goes on to say, however, Theophylact, like Chrysostom, making in his commentary the contrast with human speech, speaks of the 'word of God.'
         6 Cf Ambrosiaster *Comm in Rom* 10:17. In his brief comment, Ambrosiaster omits reference to either God or Christ. His text reads simply 'through the word'; Metzger 525 attributes the omission of 'Christ' or 'God' to carelessness in an ancestor of the witness he used.
         7 Origen *Comm in Rom* 8.6 PG 14 1170B, 1171B–C

10:19 [ER VG] *primus Moses* 'first Moses'; πρῶτος Μωσῆς. The Greeks frequently
use this word [first] in place of the comparative, 'Moses before' [Isaiah]. For
there is an allusion to Isaiah, whom he cites immediately below. Thomas
Aquinas, however, put a different construction upon it, that[1] he was called
'first' because foremost, or 'first' because he said this first among others;[2]
and yet his[3] second alternative does not differ much from my view.

> 1 that ... view] Added in *1519*
> 2 Thomas Aquinas, *Super Rom lect* cap 10 lectio 3.850. Thomas offers these
>   alternatives to avoid the reading 'the first Moses,' as though a second were
>   implied.
> 3 his] *illius* for LB *illis; illius* in all editions from *1519* to *1535*

10:19 [ER *ego ad aemulationem provocabo vos* 'I will provoke you to jealousy']
[VG] *ad aemulationem vos adducam* 'I will move you to jealousy'; παραζηλώσω, that is, 'I will provoke you to emulate' and, as it were, goad[1] you
with jealousy and grief.[2] So[3] Ambrose.

> 1 goad] *stimulabo*, in all editions from *1516* to *1535*, for LB's *simulabo*
> 2 Erasmus plays on the double meaning of παραζηλόω in his paraphrase on
>   this verse. See CWE 42 64–5 nn3 and 4. See also the annotation on 11:11 ('that
>   they may emulate them'), especially n7. Here, too, Titelmans objected to
>   Erasmus' annotation because it spoke of jealousy and grief, referring to the
>   Jews (*Responsio ad collationes* LB IX 1006B).
> 3 So Ambrose.] Added in *1535*; cf Ambrosiaster *Comm in Rom* 10:19 (2).

10:19 [ER *per gentem quae non est gens* 'through a nation which is not a nation'[1]]
[VG] *in non gentem* 'unto a not nation'; ἐπ' οὐκ ἔθνει, that is, 'in a not
nation'; for in Greek it is in the dative. Likewise immediately after, 'in a
senseless nation.'[2] By a[3] 'nation which is not a nation' he meant an extremely
contemptible nation, one unworthy of any honour; by way of clarification
he adds 'unto a senseless nation.'[4] Similarly elsewhere things that are of no
value he calls 'things that are not.'[5]

> 1 nation] First in *1519*; in *1516, in non gente* 'in a not nation' – as Valla had
>   advised (*Annot in Rom* 10 [I 858])
> 2 After the words of the cue phrase, Erasmus and the Vulgate continued:
>   ER *per gentem stultam ad iram commovebo vos* 'through a foolish nation I
>   shall move you to anger'
>   VG *in gentem insipientem in iram vos mittam* 'unto a senseless nation I shall
>   send you to anger'
>   In *1516* only, Erasmus had translated *in gente stulta* 'in a foolish nation.'
> 3 By a ... are not.'] Added in *1535*
> 4 Erasmus had already made this point to Titelmans, who had objected to the
>   contradiction in the phrase 'a nation which is not a nation' (*Responsio ad
>   collationes* LB IX 1006B–C).
> 5 Cf 4:17; on which verse, see the annotation 'as those which are.'

10:20 [ER *Esaias autem post hunc audet* 'and after him Isaiah makes bold']

[VG] *Esaias autem audet* 'but Isaiah makes bold.' The connective δέ links this clause to Moses, who preceded, as I have shown.[1] And it is not simply τολμᾷ [dares] but ἀποτολμᾷ [makes bold], as though he has taken confidence from him who said this first.[2]

1 Cf the annotation on 10:19 ('first Moses').
2 For the slight distinction between τολμάω and ἀποτολμάω see G. Fitzer in *Theological Dictionary of the New Testament* trans G. Bromiley, 10 vols (Grand Rapids, MI 1972) VIII 184–5. In the case of ἀποτολμάω Erasmus evidently interprets the prefix ἀπο- as adding its full force of 'from' (origin or source) to the verb ἀποτολμάω.

10:20 [ER *inventus fui his qui me non quaerebant* 'I was found by those who did not seek me']

[VG] *inventus sum a non quaerentibus* 'I have[1] been found by those not seeking.' This passage is in the sixty-fifth chapter of Isaiah, where the sense is virtually the same in the Hebrew and the Septuagint. The original Hebrew reads: 'They have sought me, who before did not ask for me. They have found, who did not seek me' [65:1]. According to the Septuagint we read: 'I appeared to them who did not seek me, I was found by those who did not ask for me.'[2] Paul does not seem to have followed with particular care either the Hebrew original or the Septuagint; he is content to render the sense.[3]

1 I have ... sense.] The entire annotation was added in 1519.
The Vulgate reading here is that represented in 1527. The preferred reading of the Vulgate is *inventus sum non quaerentibus* 'I have been found by those not seeking'; this reading appears to represent the Greek dative τοῖς by a Latin dative, not the Latin ablative (cf Wordsworth and White II 118 20n).
2 Erasmus' version of both the Hebrew and the Septuagint is identical with that of Jerome, whom he evidently followed; cf Jerome *Commentarii in Isaiam* 18 (on 65:1) PL 24 629B. The Hebrew is rendered somewhat differently, however, in such versions as the RSV and NEB. For the sense of the Hebrew here, see Cranfield II 540 n5.
3 Apart from one minor variation in the language (the form of γίνομαι) Paul follows the reading of the Septuagint, with the order, however, of the two clauses reversed.

10:21 [ER *adversus Israel autem* 'but against Israel'[1]]

[VG] *ad Israel autem* 'but to Israel'; πρὸς δὲ τὸν Ἰσραήλ. It can be taken also as 'against Israel,' for he is not addressing Israel, but[2] what is said tells against the Jews. For the preposition πρός is ambiguous in Greek. Thomas Aquinas also has noted this.[3]

The text that Paul quotes is from Isaiah, the sixty-fifth chapter.[4] Origen
points out that in the Hebrew manuscripts the phrase 'and contradicts me'
is not added, but it was added by the seventy elders.[5] Jerome's version of
the Hebrew shows the truth of this: 'I have extended my hands all day to
an unbelieving people.' The Septuagint edition reads: 'I have stretched out
my hands all day to a people not believing and contradicting.'[6]

1 against Israel] First in *1519*; in *1516*, 'to Israel'
2 but ... contradicting'] Added in *1519*
3 Thomas Aquinas *Super Rom lect* cap 10 lectio 3.855. Thomas understands
  'against Israel.'
4 Isa 65:2
5 Origen *Comm in Rom* 8.6 PG 14 1175A
6 Erasmus adopts the translation of Jerome here for both the Hebrew and the
  Greek, with one exception: Jerome begins the translation of both the Hebrew
  and the Septuagint with *expandi* 'I have stretched out'; Erasmus reads *extendi*
  ... *expandi* 'I have extended ... I have stretched out.' Cf Jerome *Commentarii
  in Isaiam* 18 (on 65:2) PL 24 630B.

10:21 [ER *et contradicentem* 'and contradicting']
[VG] *et contradicentem mihi* 'and contradicting me'; ἀντιλέγοντα. 'Me' is
added in our version. 'Contradicting' – that is, rebellious and uncompliant
– was enough, as the Greek reads. And[1] I have not found it added in the
Donatian codex.

1 And ... codex.] Added in *1522*

CHAPTER 11

11:1 [ER *dico igitur num ... deus* 'I say then, has God']
[VG] *dico ergo numquid deus* 'I say[1] therefore, can it be that God has.'
The Greek has only μή, *num*.[2] He puts the question to himself, and to himself he replies. All of Paul's discourse is filled with this kind of figure. It brings much clarity and vigour, particularly in argumentation. Some call it *ratiocinatio*.[3]

> 1 I say ... *ratiocinatio*.] This entire annotation was added in 1527.
> 2 *Num* introduces a question expecting a negative response.
> 3 *Ratiocinatio*, a form of inferential reasoning in which an inherent probability once exposed is thought to be convincing in itself. The inference may be explicated, as here, through questions posed and answered by the speaker. See Cicero *De inventione* 1.34.59; *Rhetorica ad Herennium* 4.16.23; Lausberg I 367–72; for Erasmus' description see *Ecclesiastes* III LB V 973D–974C.

11:2 [ER *quem ante agnoverat* 'whom he had acknowledged before'[1]]
[VG] *quam praescivit* 'whom he foreknew'; προέγνω. It is to be observed at this point that the Greek word γνῶναι [*gnōnai*] does not always mean *scire* [to know] or *cognoscere* [to come to know], but sometimes 'to determine' or 'to judge'; hence also the term γνῶμαι [*gnōmai*].[2] And in Latin we find the expression *populus scivit* [the people have ordained] and *scita populi* [ordinances of the people, 'plebiscite'] (though προορίζειν seems to suggest something more than προγνῶναι, for the latter applies to a mental resolve which anyone is free to change, the former to the fixed pronouncement of a formal decision which there is no power to revoke).[3] Hence Lyra is not afraid to explain 'foreknew' here as 'predestined.'[4] And so,[5] too, clearly Augustine interprets in the eighteenth chapter of the second book *On the Good of Perseverance*. I have preferred to translate *quos ante cognovit* [whom he knew beforehand][6] according to an idiom of Holy Scripture, by which God is said to 'know' those in whom he delights and whom he embraces, as I pointed out above, following the opinion of Origen.[7] For it is not reasonable that God rejected a people whom he formerly loved so much and embraced as his own. Chrysostom[8] thinks ὃν προέγνω [whom he foreknew] was added because of those chosen from the Jews. Paul includes himself among these, and, in order not to seem the only one, he adds the reference to seven thousand men. For he[9] did not say simply 'his people,' but 'his people whom he knew before.' Now the preposition πρό [before] can refer to that eternal predestination which existed before the Jewish people came into being; or to the gentiles who

were afterwards summoned to the grace of the gospel, in accordance with that [saying] from the Gospel: 'The last shall be first, and the first shall be last.'[10]

1 acknowledged before] First in *1519*; in *1516*, *quem ante cognoverat* 'whom he had come to know before.' This *1516* translation served as the cue phrase for the annotation until *1535*, when Erasmus changed it to *quam praescivit*, following his usual practice of citing a Vulgate reading for the lemma.

2 The term is used of practical maxims, the judgments of the wise; see LSJ.

3 On the distinction between προορίζειν and προγνῶναι see the annotation on Rom 8:29 ('whom he foreknew') and n4.

4 Lyra *Postilla* IV fol cc verso. Thomas Aquinas had also interpreted the Vulgate's *praescivit* here as *praedestinavit* (*Super Rom lect* cap 11 lectio 1.863).

5 And so ... Perseverance.] Added in *1519*. See Augustine *De dono perseverantiae* 18.47 PL 45 1022–3. In all editions Erasmus quotes the title as *De bono perseverantiae*. In the manuscript tradition, both titles are found; see M.A. Lesousky *The 'De dono perseverantiae' of Saint Augustine* Catholic University of America Patristic Studies 91 (Washington 1956) 95–6.

6 The annotation at this point written for the 1516 edition (see n1 above) was never modified to reflect the translation of *1519* and subsequent editions.

7 See the annotation on Rom 8:29 ('whom he foreknew') and Origen *Comm in Rom* 7.8 PG 14 1125B–C. Origen illustrates the idiom by reference to Gen 4:1; 24:16; Deut 33:9; and 2 Tim 2:19. Erasmus affirms the explanation given here in the *Responsio ad collationes* LB IX 1006D. For a comparison of Erasmus and Origen on foreknowledge and predestination see John B. Payne 'Erasmus on Romans 9:6–24' in *The Bible in the Sixteenth Century* ed David C. Steinmetz (Durham, NC 1990) 119–35.

8 Chrysostom ... men.] Added in *1527*. See Chrysostom *Hom in Rom* 18.3 PG 60 576–7.

9 For he ... shall be last.'] Added in *1535*

10 Mark 10:31

11:2 [ER *quomodo interpellat* 'how he appeals']

[VG] *quemadmodum interpellat* 'in what way he appeals to.' Ambrose reads *postulat* [calls on].[1] The Greek is[2] ὡς ἐντυγχάνει.

1 Ambrosiaster *Comm in Rom* 11:2

2 The Greek is] Added in *1522*. On the Greek word, see the annotation on 8:26 ('the Spirit makes request').

11:3 [ER *subruerunt* 'they have broken down']

[VG] *suffoderunt* 'they have undermined'; κατέσκαψαν, which sometimes means 'broken down' or 'overturned.'

11:4 [ER VG] *divinum responsum* 'the divine response'; χρηματισμός, that is, 'oracle,' which the Translator has explicated by a περίφρασις [*periphrasis*].

11:4 [ER *inflexerunt genu* 'have bent the knee']

[VG] *curvaverunt genua* 'have bowed the knees.' The Greek is 'knee.' Also, 'Baal' is a dative, without the preposition 'before,'[1] which the Latin [manuscripts] add;[2] also τῇ Βάαλ [to the Baal] – so that you understand an image, not a man himself.[3] For in Hebrew בַּעַל signifies 'one in command' and 'idol';[4] hence Beelphegor, 'idol[5] of a corpse,' and Beelzebub, 'idol of the flies.'

    1 After the cue phrase, the passage continues:
        ER *imagini Baal* 'to the image of Baal'
        VG *ante Baal* 'before Baal'
    2 add] First in *1519*; in *1516*, 'render.' Though the preposition *ante* 'before' is attested in some manuscripts, it is not printed in the text by Wordsworth and White (cf II 119 and 4n).
    3 The feminine article precludes reference to a man. On the feminine article with Baal see Cranfield II 547.
    4 Erasmus' definition of 'Baal' is supported in general by modern scholarship; cf J. Gray in IDB I 328: 'The [term] ... applied to men as well as to gods, signifies ownership and may denote locality.' In stressing here that the word is the name of an idol, Erasmus is perhaps following Origen, who had so remarked in his commentary on the passage (*Comm in Rom* 8.7 PG 14 1176B). However, for the designation Beelphegor and Beelzebub (where Erasmus follows the Vulgate spelling), see, in IDB, the articles 'Baal-peor,' 'Baalzebub,' and 'Beelzebul.' On Erasmus' etymology see H.J. de Jonge in ASD IX-2 173 156n. See also *Anchor Bible Dictionary* ed David Noel Freedman et al, 6 vols (New York 1992) I 545–50, 554.
    5 idol] Added in *1519*

11:5 [ER *fuerunt* 'has been']

[VG] *salvae factae sunt* 'has become saved'; γέγονεν, that is, 'has become.' 'Saved' is redundant, just as 'of God' is superfluous.[1] There is[2] only οὕτως οὖν καὶ ἐν τῷ νῦν καιρῷ, λεῖμμα κατ᾿ ἐκλογὴν χάριτος γέγονεν, that is, 'so also in this time there is[3] a remnant according to the election of grace.' For in this passage Paul is not concerned about whose grace it is, but he is opposing grace to the works of the Law, and opposing election to racial affinity. And yet I do not know how it happened that one reads in Origen's exposition 'has become saved,' though indeed 'of God' is not added.[4] Nevertheless[5] I have pointed out that his translator took great liberties with those commentaries.[6] Certainly the words are not added in Chrysostom or Theophylact.[7] Nor is it[8] surprising if some, in the midst of exposition, speak of those who have been saved,[9] since Paul here designates by 'a remnant according to the election of grace' those of the Jewish people who had been predestined for salvation. Thus it is probable that the words I called superfluous were added by some scholar to make the language clearer. Finally, while I was carefully sifting Origen's commentary I discovered that he read as Chrysostom does. For in reporting the passage of Paul he says: 'But with respect to [Paul's] words that there has become a remnant according to grace, the addition here of "election" seems to me superfluous.' Here the true reading resides, no matter how the reader may change the rest. For at first in quoting the text he added 'of God' as well, but in expounding it [the words] are not added.[10] The assiduity of those who have emended, according to the Vulgate edition, texts quoted from Scripture has corrupted many passages in the ancient authors.

1 The discussion here extends beyond the cue phrase:
    ER *reliquiae secundum electionem gratiae fuerunt* 'there has been a remnant according to the election of grace'
    VG *reliquiae secundum electionem gratiae dei salvae factae sunt* 'the remnant according to the grace of God has become saved'
    Tischendorf cites no Greek witnesses with the words 'of God' or 'saved' in this place (II 422 5n).
2 There is ... not added.] Added in 1519
3 'There is,' Latin *sunt*; present tense here, though in his translation Erasmus rendered the Greek perfect tense by a Latin perfect.
4 Cf Origen *Comm in Rom* 8.7 PG 14 1177B–C and n10 below.
5 Nevertheless ... Theophylact.] Added in 1527
6 Cf eg the annotation on 1:4 ('who was predestined') and n5.
7 Cf Chrysostom *Hom in Rom* 18.4 PG 60 577; Theophylact *Expos in Rom* 11:5 PG 124 484D.
8 Nor is it ... authors.] This remaining portion of the annotation was added in 1535.
9 Frans Titelmans had argued that Origen's discussion of those who are 'saved,' whether with or without election (PG 14 1177C), demonstrated that *salvae* was an integral part of the text (*Responsio ad collationes* LB IX 1006D–E).
10 Origen *Comm in Rom* 8.7 PG 14 1176B–1177C. In Migne's text here *dei* is nowhere added, and *salvae* is everywhere found. In the Merlin edition, the 'superfluous' words *dei* 'of God' and *salvae* 'saved' both appear in the citation of the text that Origen quoted to introduce the discussion. In the exposition, where the verse is quoted several times, the word *salvae* is unambiguously omitted only in the passage Erasmus has quoted (in some citations the verb *salvari* seems to have been substituted for the adjective *salvae*), but nowhere does the word *dei* appear (cf fol CCII recto–verso).

11:6 [ER *quod si per gratiam* 'but if through grace']
[VG] *si autem gratia* 'if however grace'; εἰ δὲ χάριτι. 'Grace' is ablative, not nominative.[1]

1 The Vulgate allowed an ambiguous reading of *gratia*, either as a subject nominative or as an ablative signifying means.

11:6 [ER *quandoquidem gratia* 'inasmuch as grace']

[VG] *alioqui gratia* 'otherwise grace'; ἐπεί, that is, 'since' or 'inasmuch as.'
And yet[1] the translator's version is correct and clear, for in the Greek εἰ δὲ
μή [otherwise] is understood, as I shall soon show.[2]

> 1 And yet... soon show.] Added in 1535
> 2 See the next annotation, where ἐπεί is understood to imply an exception, in
> the sense of εἰ δὲ μή 'otherwise.' Cf also the annotation on 11:22 ('otherwise').

11:6 [ER *quandoquidem gratia iam non est gratia* 'inasmuch as grace is no
longer grace']

[VG] *alioqui gratia iam non est gratia* 'otherwise grace is no longer grace.'[1]
The Greek[2] codices have somewhat more here than do the Latin. For they
provide a repetition in the 'works that are not works' expression in the
following manner – for the Latin expresses the form only in relation to
grace: εἰ δὲ χάριτι, οὐκέτι ἐξ ἔργων, ἐπεὶ ἡ χάρις οὐκέτι γίνεται χάρις. εἰ δὲ
ἐξ ἔργων, οὐκέτι ἐστὶ χάρις, ἐπεὶ τὸ ἔργον οὐκέτι ἐστὶν ἔργον, that is, 'but
if through grace, no longer from works, inasmuch as grace is no longer
grace; but if from works, it is no longer grace, inasmuch as work is no
longer work.' And this is how Theophylact reads and also interprets.[3] But
since I do not find this addition in Origen,[4] I am somewhat doubtful that it is
the true reading, especially[5] since Chrysostom in expounding this passage
reads only εἰ δὲ χάριτι, οὐκέτι ἐξ ἔργων, ἐπεὶ ἡ χάρις οὐκέτι γίνεται χάρις.
He adds nothing to these words. Moreover,[6] the parts of the sentence seem
inverted, and should be arranged rather in this order: 'But if through grace,
no longer from works, inasmuch as work is no longer work; but if from
works, no longer from grace, inasmuch as grace is no longer grace' – unless
in ἐπεί there is latent an implied exception, as elsewhere in Paul's use of the
word.[7] Then the sense would be 'if by grace, no longer from works; if this
were not so, grace would not be grace,' that is, it would be falsely called
grace. I incline to the Latin reading,[8] in view of the fact that Paul is not
discussing here whether a work is a work, but is supporting grace, which
the Jews were trying to drive out. And yet[9] the Aldine edition, and even
the Spanish edition,[10] agree with what I have found in the Greek copies.

> 1 All the editions published in Erasmus' lifetime begin a new annotation at
> this point, though LB coalesces this note with the preceding one. In 1516 the
> words *alioqui ... gratia* were preceded by a cue phrase *post ea verba* 'after
> these words.' In all subsequent editions, the original cue phrase dropped out
> and was replaced by *alioqui ... gratia*.
> 2 The Greek ... the true reading] With a small exception (cf n3 below), this
> passage is a 1519 development of the 1516 edition, which read: 'After the
> words "otherwise grace is no longer grace" our codices lack the following:

εἰ δὲ ἐξ ἔργων οὐκέτι χάρις, ἐπεὶ τὸ ἔργον οὐκέτι ἐστὶν ἔργον, that is, "if, then, from works, it is no longer grace, inasmuch as work is no longer work." '

3 and also interprets] Added in 1527. Cf Theophylact *Expos in Rom* 11:6 PG 124 485A–B.

4 See Origen *Comm in Rom* 8.7 PG 14 1175B.

5 especially ... to these words.] Added in 1527. See Chrysostom *Hom in Rom* 18.5 PG 60 578. In Migne's text, though the additional words are present when the biblical text is initially cited, there is no explicit exposition of them in the commentary.

6 Moreover ... drive out.] Except for the last sentence, the remainder of this annotation was added in 1519.

7 Cf eg 3:6 and the annotation on 11:22 ('otherwise'). For the sense here of 'otherwise,' see Cranfield II 548 and 570.

8 In his *Responsio ad annotationes Lei* LB IX 216D–E Erasmus admitted that Lee deserved some credit for this (1519) statement of preference for the 'Latin' reading. Even so, in his text and translation Erasmus followed the Greek rather than the Latin copies. Frans Titelmans complained that Erasmus seldom preferred the Latin readings and he urged that Greek texts should be corrected by the Latin. Erasmus countered that he did not take on the duty of correcting the Greek texts unless there was an obvious mistake made by the copyists (*Responsio ad collationes* LB IX 1006E–F). Modern scholars, on the basis of the manuscript evidence, regard the line as a gloss; see Metzger 526 and Cranfield II 547 n5.

9 And yet ... copies.] Added in 1522, except that the words 'and even the Spanish edition' were added in 1527

10 In the *Apologia* that appeared in the 1527 edition of the *Novum Testamentum* Erasmus says that he used the 'Aldine' Greek New Testament in his third edition, the Spanish in his fourth (see Holborn 166). The Aldine edition, begun in 1501 by the famous printer Aldo Manuzio (Aldus) was not completed until February 1518. According to Allen (I 64:280n) it embodies the Erasmian text of the New Testament, so that the reading here from the Aldine edition is scarcely an independent one. 'The Spanish edition' refers to the New Testament volume of the Complutensian Polyglot Bible which was edited under the leadership of Cardinal Jiménez at Alcalá. Although the New Testament volume was printed by 1514, the Spanish editors did not receive a licence to bind and distribute until 1520. For a description and assessment of this edition see Bentley *Humanists* 70–111.

11:8 [ER *quemadmodum scriptum est* 'as it is written']

[VG] *sicut scriptum est* 'just as¹ it is written.' It is uncertain whether this clause refers to what precedes or to what follows. Origen acknowledges that he, for his part, had never read in the divine books [the words] 'He gave them the spirit of compunction.'² But he pleads in excuse that we understand Paul to be explicating with these words the thought of Isaiah, and adding something on his own. What [Paul] adds at the end – 'right to this present day' – makes this more probable.³ For the substance of the thought is found in Isaiah, chapter 6: 'Hear by hearing, and do not understand; and see by seeing, and do not perceive; blind the heart of this people, and weigh down its ears, and close its eyes, lest perchance it see with its eyes and hear with its ears and understand with the heart and convert and be healed' [6:9–10]. This passage is cited also in the Acts of the Apostles, chapter 28, but from the LXX translation, which interpreted it in such a way that the Lord predicts their blindness but does not order it: 'You will hear with the ears and not understand, and seeing, you will see and not perceive; for the heart of this people has become thick; with their ears they have become hard of hearing; they have shut their eyes lest perchance they should see with their eyes and hear with their ears and understand with their heart and should be converted and I should heal them' [28:26–7]. Indeed, in this passage Jerome, in commenting on Isaiah, excuses Luke – who represents Paul, in discussion with Hebrews, quoting Scripture not from the Hebrew, which he knew to be correct, but from the Septuagint – on the grounds that [Luke] knew Greek better than Hebrew; hence also his language is more polished and is redolent of secular eloquence.[4]

1 just as ... eloquence.] This entire note was added in *1519*.
2 Origen *Comm in Rom* 8.8 PG 14 1179C–1180B
3 In this annotation Erasmus appears to follow Origen in thinking that the Apostle conveys the sense of Isa 6:9–10, adding explanatory words of his own. In fact, the passage quoted is a somewhat free citation from Isa 29:10 and Deut 29:4, the latter including the clause 'right to this present day.'
4 Jerome *Commentarii in Isaiam* 3 (on 6:9–10) PL 24 (1845) 98C–D

11:8 [ER VG] *spiritum compunctionis* **'the spirit of compunction'**; κατανύξεως, [a word] that is used when one is bitten and stung by grief. Hence above he said παραζηλώσω [I will provoke you to jealousy].[1]

1 The allusion here to 10:19 suggests that Erasmus has understood κατάνυξις as the sting of a grief that goads one on; see the annotation on 10:19 ('I will move you to jealousy'). For the word (rarely found in Greek) as the sting that creates numbness, hence here the 'spirit of torpor' that numbs the senses, see Cranfield II 550.
In *1516* only, the annotations on 11:8–9 were arranged in the sequence: 1/ 'into a trap'; 2/ 'before them'; 3/ 'the spirit of compunction.'

11:9 [ER *vertatur mensa illorum in laqueum* **'let their table be turned**[1] **into a snare'**]
[VG] *fiat mensa eorum in laqueum* **'let**[2] **their table be made into a snare.'** The passage he cites is found in the sixty-eighth Psalm [69:22–3]. Not even here does Paul take care to cite the prophetic text exactly. For first he omitted 'before them';[3] then he added 'and into a trap,' which is present

neither in the Hebrew nor in the Septuagint, as Origen pointed out before me.[4]

1 be turned] First in *1519*; in *1516*, with the Vulgate, *fiat* 'be made'

2 Let ... before me.] This annotation appeared first in *1519*, incorporating, however, in abbreviated form, a short annotation in *1516* that read:
   [ER omitted]
   [VG] *coram ipsis* 'before them.' I do not find this in the Greek codices though it is added in the Psalms.
   See next note.

3 Some Latin manuscripts added the phrase that appears in the Latin version of the Psalms based on the Septuagint (Weber I 852); the phrase is found in the Vulgate printed in *1527*: *fiat mensa coram ipsis in laqueum* 'let their table before them be made into a snare.' See Wordsworth and White II 120 9n.

4 Origen *Comm in Rom* 8.8 PG 14 1180B

11:9 [ER VG] *in captionem* 'into a trap.' *Captio*[1] here is not strictly speaking a 'trap' (whence the word *captiosi* [the deceptive]); but it refers to the hunt in which we capture wild animals. It is as though you should say 'let them be taken at their table,' where they ought to relax; for we do not fear an enemy while we are feasting. The Greek is θήρα.

1 *Captio ... θήρα.*] This annotation appeared in this form in *1519*. In *1516* the annotation read: '*Captio* should not be understood here as a trap (whence the word *captiosi* [the deceptive]) but as the hunt in which we capture wild animals – θήρα [the chase].' Erasmus thus continued to adhere to the sense of his *1516* annotation in spite of the criticism of Edward Lee, who insisted that the word should be understood as 'trap,' 'deception' (*Responsio ad annotationes Lei* LB IX 216C–D).

11:11 [ER *num ideo impegerunt ut conciderent* 'have[1] they tripped on this account that they should utterly fall']
[VG] *numquid sic offenderunt ut caderent* 'can it be that they have so stumbled that they fell'; μὴ[2] ἔπταισαν ἵνα πέσωσι, that is, 'can it be that they have slipped in order to fall utterly,' or 'in order to fall' – obviously, to the ground. For πταίειν properly is to strike against [*impingere*] something; and to slip is less serious than to fall, just as it is possible to trip without completely falling down.

The Translator has added *sic* [so] on his own: 'Can it be that they have so stumbled that they fell?'[3] I would approve the addition if in this case the adverb 'so' was used in the sense of 'to such an extent,' as when we say 'he so hates me that he does not even greet me; he is so afraid that he cannot speak.' But the Greek word ἵνα indicates purpose rather; it is different from ὡς and ὥστε, which[4] have a varied force, like *ut* [that] in Latin.[5] Theodorus Gaza includes ἵνα among the causal conjunctions;[6] and he does not suggest that it is understood in any other way, though he carefully indicates its use. (At this point it is not relevant that ἵνα is sometimes an adverb of place.) Here,[7] then, we cannot accept the sense: 'Did they trip (or, stumble) to such an extent that they fell?' It seems,[8] then, that ἵνα must invite a reference to God: 'Did God on this account allow the Jews to slip, that they should fall and perish?' No; but that for a time they might make a place for the gentiles, and in turn they themselves, challenged by the piety of the gentiles, should come to their senses and be saved.

What follows[9] agrees very well with this sense: 'God forbid! but through their trespass, salvation is come to the gentiles'; and the whole passage that follows does not talk about the magnitude of the fall, but about the outcome. Chrysostom expounds [the passage] similarly. He notes that Paul had, through the testimony of the prophets, magnified the wickedness of the Jews who resist the gospel, but had, in his own name, offered consolation. There can be, therefore, no doubt that they have most gravely stumbled, but he consoles them with the outcome. 'What then,' says [Chrysostom] 'is the consolation? "When the fullness of the gentiles has entered," [Paul] says, "then all Israel shall be saved."' So far Chrysostom.[10] And so God has turned the fall of the Jews into good for the gentiles, by envy of whom the Jews are some day to be moved to salvation. Theophylact brings forward nothing else,[11] nor does Origen (except that *sic* [so] has been added by little-skilled scribes),[12] or Ambrose.[13] They all speak about the outcome, not the magnitude of the fall, except that the translator of Origen adds a few words on lesser sins,[14] since here in the whole Epistle Paul magnifies the sin of unbelief. Hence they interpret [the word] πέσωσι [fall] as 'sin incurably' or 'fall without hope of restoration,' just as Lucifer fell utterly.[15] Since, however, the words of the prophets seemed to suggest an irremediable evil, Paul softens this harshness, showing that the sin is indeed most serious; nevertheless, the hope of the entire people has not on this account been taken away: λέγω οὖν [I say, then].

Origen shows clearly in the turn of his sentence the true reading when he says: 'The lapse of Israel, [Paul] says, was such, not that they fell, but that by their trespass they gave salvation to the gentiles.'[16] Likewise Augustine, in his remarks on this Epistle, acknowledges the magnitude of the sin, but points to the good outcome of something terribly bad. These are his words: 'Can it be therefore, that they have trespassed in order to fall? God forbid! but through their trespass salvation has come to the gentiles. [Paul] does not say [this] because [he wished to suggest that] they did not fall, but because their fall was not in vain, since it led to the salvation of the gentiles. Therefore, they did not so trespass that they fell, that is, merely fell, as though solely for their punishment, but so that the very fact of their fall

might contribute to the salvation of the gentiles.'[17] So far Augustine. From
these words it is clear that he did not add *sic* [so], which would nevertheless
be tolerable if it is understood [to imply] not the severity of the fall, but
its manner and its outcome. I have pointed out more than once, on the
authority of ancient writers, that final conjunctions of this kind sometimes
pertain to the outcome, rather than to the purpose or the end.[18]

The[19] Translator has used the word *offenderunt* [they stumbled] with
elegance, certainly, but *offendere* is said also of one who does an injury. Augustine, in explicating some questions on this Epistle, reads *deliquerunt* [they
trespassed] instead of *offenderunt*.[20] For πταῖσμα you might quite rightly use
lapsus [fall] or *delictum* [trespass]; but not likewise *delinquere* [to trespass]
for *impingere* [to trip].

1 have ... account] First in *1519*; in *1516*, *sic lapsi sunt* 'have they so slipped'
2 μὴ ... ὥστε] First in *1519* in its present form. In *1516* the entire note
  consisted of a variation of the first sentence of the *1519* edition. The note was
  introduced with a shorter lemma, *numquid sic offenderunt* 'can it be that they
  have so stumbled,' and read: '*sic* [so] is redundant: μὴ ἔπταισαν ἵνα πέσωσιν,
  that is, can it be that they have slipped in order to fall – obviously to the
  ground.'
3 Erasmus objects to the Vulgate reading *sic* because it suggests a result clause
  – they have so stumbled that they fell – whereas, he believes, the clause is
  final, pointing to the end and purpose. In *1535*, however, he concedes that
  sic would be tolerable if it is understood to indicate not extent, but manner
  and outcome. The significance of ἵνα here was disputed among the Fathers
  (see Schelkle 390 n1) and has been debated in modern times (see Cranfield II
  554–5).
4 which ... adverb of place)] Added in *1535*
5 ὡς and ὥστε, like the Latin *ut*, serve as both adverbs and conjunctions. As a
  conjunction ὡς, like *ut*, can introduce both purpose and result clauses, ὥστε
  normally a result clause.
6 Theodorus Gaza (1400–c 1476), a native of Salonike, came to Italy for the
  Council of Ferrara-Florence in 1438 and remained permanently in Italy. He
  lectured in Ferrara and went to Rome in the service of Pope Nicholas V.
  He produced numerous Latin translations of Greek classics, and wrote a
  Greek Grammar, which Erasmus translated (LB I 117–164), and in which
  the 'causal' conjunctions are listed as: 'so that' (ἵνα), 'in order that,' 'for,'
  'because,' 'wherefore'; see the *Institutio grammatica* I LB I 132E. For Gaza see
  Contemporaries II 81, and for his *Grammar*, Epp 428:15–21, 575:1–8, and 771
  introduction.
7 Here ... they fell?'] Added in *1519*
8 It seems ... and be saved.] Added in *1527*
9 What follows ... the purpose or the end.] Except for the last paragraph, the
  remaining portion of the annotation was added in *1535*. The addition greatly
  enlarges Erasmus' earlier brief response to Frans Titelmans in the *Responsio
  ad collationes* LB IX 1007A.

10 Chrysostom *Hom in Rom* 19.2 PG 60 585–6
11 Theophylact *Expos in Rom* 11:11 PG 124 488A–B
12 Origen *Comm in Rom* 8.9 PG 14 1184–7; cf the quotation cited in the next paragraph.
13 Ambrosiaster *Comm in Rom* 11:11. *Sic* is found in Ambrosiaster as well as in the Latin Origen; but, like Origen, Ambrosiaster shows (11:11 [1–2]) that the outcome of Israel's fall is the salvation of the gentiles.
14 Origen *Comm in Rom* 8.9 PG 14 1185B–C
15 In the citations above Theophylact speaks of Israel as 'not having "sinned incurably,"' Chrysostom speaks of Israel's fall as not 'incurable,' and Origen says that Israel's fall is not like that of Lucifer but also argues that Israel has not been blinded so that she cannot be healed.
16 Origen *Comm in Rom* 8.9 PG 14 1184B
17 Augustine *Expositio quarundam propositionum ex epistula ad Romanos* 70 PL 35 2083. But in Migne the biblical text is cited with *sic*, suggesting a result clause: 'Can it be therefore that they have so trespassed that they fell?'
18 See, as an example, below, the annotation on 11:31 ('unto your mercy') n10.
19 The ... *impingere*.] Added in *1519*
20 Augustine *Expositio quarundam propositionum ex epistula ad Romanos* 70 PL 35 2083, quoted above (see note 17)

11:11 [ER *per lapsum illorum* 'through their fall']¹

[VG] *illorum delicto* 'by their trespass'; τῷ² αὐτῶν παραπτώματι, that is, 'through their fall' rather than 'trespass.' For he has in mind what he had just said, that the Jews tripped. παράπτωμα is³ properly used of one who falls through negligence – from πίπτω, that is 'I fall.'

> 1 fall] First in *1519*; in *1516*, 'trespass'
> 2 τῷ ... παράπτωμα] In this form, first in *1519*, when the second sentence continued (after 'tripped'), 'and from the same [Greek] word is derived παράπτωμα.' (The words 'and ... derived' were removed in *1535*.) In *1516* the annotation consisted of only the cue phrase followed by the words 'through their trespass, τῷ αὐτῶν παραπτώματι.'
> 3 is ... 'I fall'] Added in *1535*. In his *Responsio ad collationes* LB IX 1007B Erasmus expresses some surprise that the Apostle uses here the word παράπτωμα, which he concedes is equivalent to the Latin *delictum* – a word appropriate to a minor offence resulting from ignorance or carelessness, but not appropriate to the serious sin of stubbornly rejecting the gospel.

11:11 [ER *ut eos ad aemulandum provocaret* 'that he should provoke them to emulation']

[VG] *ut illos aemulentur* 'that they may emulate them'; εἰς τὸ παραζηλῶσαι αὐτούς. This could have been translated more correctly 'for provoking them,' so that the action of the verb would refer to God,¹ who wished in this way to goad the Jews with a kind of envy and jealousy, when they saw that what had been promised to them was transferred to the gentiles. Hence to avoid

ambiguity I have translated 'that he should provoke them to emulation,' εἰς
τὸ παραζηλῶσαι αὐτούς. There was no need for the fourfold interpretation
that Thomas Aquinas[2] imposed on this passage; even so, he missed the
true meaning. For this we must in no way blame him, but the Translator.
For who,[3] without knowing Greek, would perceive from these words what
Paul meant? So also,[4] just below,[5] Paul used this word: εἴ πως παραζηλώσω
μου τὴν σάρκα [if I might provoke my own flesh to emulation]; and in the
previous chapter: ἐγὼ παραζηλώσω ὑμᾶς ἐπ᾽ οὐκ ἔθνει [I will provoke you
to emulate a 'not-nation'].[6] Yet translators have used this same word elsewhere in an unfavourable sense, as in Psalm 77: καὶ ἐν τοῖς γλυπτοῖς αὐτῶν
παρεζήλωσαν αὐτόν [and they provoked him to jealousy with their graven
images] [78:58]. Moreover a certain person applies the verb παραζηλῶσαι to
the Jews, so that αὐτούς [them] refers to the gentiles.[7] No interpreter has
this idea, nor will the Greek allow it, but he has preferred to wrench out
this sense, rather than to stop tearing at my annotation. And yet[8] there are
some who twist the words of the commentators in this direction,[9] though
wrongly. These commentators do indeed speak of the Jews who are about to
emulate the faith of the gentiles, but this is not surprising, since παραζηλόω
signifies 'to provoke to envy and zeal of emulation.' I have shown several
passages in which παραζηλόω means 'provoke,' either to anger or to zeal
of emulation; let them produce for us one where it is used in the sense of
aemulari [to emulate].

1 So Valla; see *Annot in Rom* 11 (I 859). On this and other points of comparison
between the exegesis of Valla and Erasmus on Rom 11, see Jean-Claude
Margolin 'The Epistle to the Romans (chapter 11) according to the Versions
and/or Commentaries of Valla, Colet, Lefèvre and Erasmus' in *The Bible in
the Sixteenth Century* ed David C. Steinmetz (Durham, NC 1990) 142–50.

2 Thomas Aquinas] First in 1522; previously, 'St Thomas Aquinas.' See *Super
Rom lect* cap 11 lectio 2.882. The four alternative interpretations Aquinas
gives are: the gentiles might 1/ imitate the Jews and convert to the worship
of one God or 2/ become angry at the Jews because of Jewish unbelief; the
Jews might 3/ imitate the gentiles and convert to Christ or 4/ become angry
at the gentiles because the glory of the Jews has been transferred to them.

3 For who ... meant?] Added in 1519

4 So also ... my annotation.] Added in 1522

5 In 11:14

6 Cf 10:19 and the annotations on that verse. Erasmus' translation had
represented the Greek in this sense: 'I will provoke you to jealousy through
a nation which is not a nation.'

7 The critic is Zúñiga. In defending the Vulgate's *aemulentur* for παραζηλῶσαι
Zúñiga had proposed the interpretation 'that the Jews might "emulate"
the gentiles.' But παραζηλῶσαι here means 'to provoke to envy,' a meaning
unattested for *aemulor*, which is used rather in the sense of 'to be jealous
of,' or 'to strive to imitate.' Moreover, when the Greek verb is understood

correctly it makes no sense in this context to make αὐτούς (the gentiles) its
object, ie 'that the Jews might provoke to envy the gentiles.' See *Apologia ad
annotationes Stunicae* ASD IX-2 172–4 and 173n.
8 And yet ... *aemulari.*] Added in *1535*
9 Apparently a reference to Zúñiga, who defended his explanation of the Greek
by appealing to Origen, *Comm in Rom* 8.9 PG 14 1184B–C and Theophylact
Expos in Rom 11:11 PG 124 488B–C. See the reference in n7 above.

11:13 [ER *quatenus ego quidem sum apostolus gentium* 'inasmuch as I am indeed
the apostle of the gentiles']
[VG] *quamdiu quidem ego sum gentium apostolus* 'as long indeed as I am
the apostle of the gentiles'; ἐφ' ὅσον μέν εἰμι. Origen seems to take ἐφ' ὅσον
to mean 'as long as,' supplying χρόνον [time].[1] He hesitates[2] whether it is
to be understood 'as long as I am in this life' and is thus directed towards
bringing out the strength of his affection, as when we say 'I will not desert
you as long as I live,' or whether Paul even after his death will be an apostle
to the invisible beings.[3] But since this is rather harsh, I prefer to take ἐφ' ὅσον
as 'inasmuch as' or 'to the extent that.' Theophylact[4] seems to have thought
thus, so far as we may conjecture from his interpretation. The Greek[5] [of
Theophylact] says the same as Chrysostom, who clearly interprets that Paul
is compelled by the responsibility delegated [to him] to provoke some Jews
and so save them.[6] For thus will he save those provoked, if he entices as
many gentiles as possible to the gospel. He does not speak of a period
of time, as though he were soon about to resign his apostolic duties; but
since he was called as an apostle to the gentiles, he is striving diligently
to discharge the office committed to him, to adorn and embellish it. Nor[7]
does Ambrose make any mention of the time; he talks only about the task.[8]
Likewise in the twenty-fifth [chapter] of Matthew – 'as long as you did it
to one of the least of these' [25:40] – [the Translator] would have rendered
ἐφ' ὅσον more correctly, in my opinion, by 'inasmuch as' or 'to the extent
that.'[9]

1 Thus yielding the phrase ἐφ' ὅσον χρόνον 'for so much time as'
2 He hesitates ... to the invisible beings.] Added in *1519*
3 Origen *Comm in Rom* 8.10 PG 14 1187C–1188B. Origen states (but rejects) the
view that Paul knew that after his death he would be an apostle not only of
the gentiles, but also of the Jews, and perhaps of the 'other invisible beings'
where the souls of the just bless the Lord PG 14 1188B. Ambrosiaster sees in
the clause a reflection of Paul's affection (see n8 below).
4 Theophylact ... interpretation.] Added in *1519*. Cf Theophylact *Expos in Rom*
11:13–14 PG 124 488D–489A.
5 The Greek ... the gospel.] Added in *1527*, except that the words 'The Greek
says the same as ... who' were added in *1535*, so that in *1527* the sentence
began: 'Chrysostom clearly interprets that ...' Theophylact, in words similar

to those of Chrysostom, paraphrases the first part of 11:13: 'I praise you, gentiles, for two reasons, first, because I am compelled [to glorify my ministry to you], inasmuch as I have been entrusted with your instruction; second ...' On the Greek and the Latin Theophylact see the annotation on 1:4 ('who was predestined') and n25.

6 Chrysostom *Hom in Rom* 19.3 PG 60 587
7 Nor ... 'to the extent that.'] Added in *1535*
8 Ambrosiaster *Comm in Rom* 11:13–14 takes the clause causally: Since Paul was an apostle to the gentiles, he adorned his office in the first place by fulfilling his task to the gentiles, but even more if, because of his great affection for his race, he brought to the faith the Jews, to whom he had not been sent.
9 For his own translation of Matt 25:40 Erasmus replaced the Vulgate's *quamdiu* with *quatenus*.

11:13 [ER *illustro* 'I embellish'[1]]

[VG] *honorificabo* 'I will honour'; δοξάζω, that is, *glorifico* [I glorify]. So Augustine[2] cites the passage in quite a few places, and specifically[3] in the ninth book *Against Faustus*, chapter 2. Lefèvre d'Etaples prefers *existimo* [I think, I judge].[4] But I do[5] not know whether δοξάζω is found in Greek in the sense of *existimo*, and the sense fits well if you understand that Paul makes his ministry in the gospel of the gentiles the more celebrated in order to move the Jews, if only by emulation, to Christ. The translator of Origen renders δοξάζω as *illustro et exorno* [I embellish and adorn], discoursing at length on this sense.[6]

1 embellish] First in *1519*; in *1516*, *glorifico* 'I glorify.' There was a change also in the cue phrase: from *1516* to *1527*, *glorificabo*; *honorificabo* first in *1535*. *Honorificabo* is the preferred Vulgate reading, and the reading of the Vulgate in *1527*, but some manuscripts have *glorificabo*; cf Wordsworth and White II 121 13n.
2 So Augustine ... places] Added in *1519*
3 and specifically ... chapter 2] Added in *1522*. For the citation of Rom 11:13 see Augustine *Contra Faustum Manichaeum* 9.2 PL 42 241; see also *De baptismo contra Donatistas* 5.14.16 PL 43 184, where, however, the word *ministerium*, not *glorifico*, is cited. Augustine occasionally cites Rom 11:14, which follows immediately upon the *glorifico* of 11:13 and amplifies its meaning (eg *De doctrina christiana* 2.12.17 PL 34 43, *Enarrationes in psalmos* 87.10 PL 37 1116), but Erasmus apparently exaggerates the frequency with which Augustine cites this word from 11:13.
4 Lefèvre (*Pauli epistolae* fol 96 recto) understands Paul to say: 'I judge it to be my duty somehow to provoke my race to jealousy.' Though δοξάζω is found in Greek authors in the sense of 'suppose,' 'judge' (cf LSJ), prevailing interpretations of Rom 11:13 understand the word here generally in the sense of 'glorify,' 'esteem.' The specific intent of the word in its context, however, is widely debated; cf Cranfield II 560.
5 I do ... *existimo*, and] Added in *1519*
6 Origen *Comm in Rom* 8.10 PG 14 1188C–1190A

11:15 [ER *reiectio illorum* 'their rejection']

[VG] *amissio eorum* 'their loss'; ἀποβολή, that is, 'a casting away' or 'rejection.' He[1] contrasts this word with 'adoption.' Augustine[2] in the ninth book *Against Faustus*, chapter 2, cites *reiectio* instead of *amissio*, according to the witness of an ancient volume in manuscript.

> 1 He ... 'adoption.'] Added in *1519*
> 2 Augustine ... manuscript.] Added in *1522*. For the reference see Augustine *Contra Faustum Manichaeum* 9.2 PL 42 241.

11:15 [ER VG] *quae assumptio* '**what the adoption**'; τίς ἡ πρόσληψις, that is, 'the union,' in which we receive, that is, attach someone to ourselves as a companion. He has contrasted 'adoption' with 'rejection,' as[1] I said.

> 1 as I said] Added in *1519*; cf the immediately previous annotation, n1.

11:16 [ER *quod si primitiae* '**but if the first-fruits**']

[VG] *quod si delibatio* '**but if the first portion**'; ἀπαρχή, that is, 'first-fruits.' Theophylact interprets ἀπαρχή as ἡ ζύμη , that is, 'leaven,' so that lump corresponds to tree, leaven, to root.[1] I should prefer that we understand it to be the grain itself, whence comes the dough [*conspersio*]. Now from spoiled wheat you cannot make good dough. Accordingly, he has spoken of the 'first-fruits' because the most praiseworthy are usually consecrated to the divine power, and hence are also called ἀκροθίνια as being *praecipua* [what is taken first, reserved portion]. I think, moreover, that *conspersio* refers not to the flour mixed with water,[2] but rather to the sacrificial meal [*molae*] or cakes: this was the flour sprinkled [*conspersa*] with oil, which was once sacrificed [*immolabantur*] according to the ritual of the Mosaic law; hence also it is called 'holy.' Chrysostom[3] interprets ἀπαρχαί [first-fruits] and ῥίζα [root] as Abraham and the other patriarchs; dough [φύραμα] and branches [κλάδοι] as their descendants.[4] 'Oleaster'[5] in Greek is ἀγριέλαος, which means 'wild or woodland olive.' Its counterpart is καλλιέλαιος, which is a fruit-bearing olive.

> 1 Theophylact *Expos in Rom* 11:16 PG 124 489B. The references here to Theophylact and that to Chrysostom below extend the discussion to the entire verse:
>> ER *quod si primitiae sanctae sancta est et conspersio. Et si radix sancta sancti erunt et rami* 'but if the first-fruits [are] holy, the dough is holy; and if the root [is] holy the branches also will be holy'
>> VG *quod si delibatio sancta est et massa. Et si radix sancta et rami* 'but if the first portion is holy so also the lump; and if the root [is] holy so also the branches'
> Theophylact's interpretation of 'first portion' as 'leaven' assumes a double set of parallel images: leaven-lump, root-branches (= tree).

2 water] Here was added, from 1516 to 1522, the words 'to be beaten.' Erasmus
disagrees with Valla, who thought the Greek word did indeed refer to flour
mixed with water (*Annot in Rom* 11 [I 859]).
3 Chrysostom ... descendants.] Added in 1535
4 See Chrysostom *Hom in Rom* 19.4 PG 60 588. For the exegesis of the passage
in patristic literature see CWE 42 65 n6.
5 'Oleaster' ... fruit-bearing olive.] These words appeared first in 1516 in the
annotation on 11:17 ('you have been inserted in them') (cf n2), and were
placed here in 1519.

11:17 [ER *insitus fuisti* 'you were grafted on']

[VG] *insertus es* 'you have been inserted'; ἐνεκεντρίσθης, that is, 'you have
been grafted on[1] – whenever a shoot is inserted into a slit made in the
branch of a tree. This is one type of grafting. Yet here[2] it seems rather to
signify 'inoculation,' when the bark is perforated where the bud grew, and
a sprout inserted.

1 Valla had already argued that the proper translation of the Greek here was
insitus, not *insertus*; see *Annot in Rom* 11 (I 859).
2 Yet here ... inserted.] Added in 1527

11:17 [ER *insitus fuisti illis* 'you were grafted on them']

[VG] *insertus es in illis* 'you have been inserted in them';[1] ἐν αὐτοῖς 'among
them' would be clearer. That is, the grafting has given you what nature gave
them.[2] But[3] it is ridiculous that a certain person should interpret 'in them' to
mean 'in their place.'[4] Since by 'olive tree' [Paul] understands the people of
the Jews, the change in number and gender causes no difficulty.[5] In accordance with Hebrew idiom, the preposition is often added superfluously, as
confitetur in me [(who) acknowledges me], *confitebor in illo* [I will acknowledge him], and *percussit in gladio* [he struck with the sword].[6]

1 In LB this annotation is included as part of the previous annotation, but in all
editions from 1516 to 1535 it appears as a separate annotation.
2 them] In 1516, after this sentence the annotation concluded with the words
'Oleaster' ... fruit-bearing olive,' placed in 1519 at the end of the annotation
on 11:16 ('but if the first portion'); cf n5 there.
3 But ... *gladio*.] Added in 1535
4 Frans Titelmans had argued that gentiles could not be grafted onto branches
already broken off; *in illis* must therefore be understood as *pro illis* 'in their
place.' Erasmus replied that the gentiles were grafted on the part of the
branch still attached to the tree. See *Responsio ad collationes* LB IX 1007B–C.
5 The word for 'olive-tree' in Greek (ἡ ἐλαία), as in Latin (*oliva*, or, as used in
the annotation here, *olea*), is feminine singular, while the pronoun 'them' in
the Greek text of 11:17 is masculine plural.
6 For the citations see Luke 12:8, 22:49. The Vulgate had followed the Greek
in repeating the preposition *in*: *insertus ... in*, following, Erasmus argues,
Hebrew idiom.

11:17 [ER *consors radicis* 'partner of the root']

[VG] *socius radicis* 'associate of the root'; συνκοινωνός, that is, 'a sharer' or 'joint-sharer' or 'partner,' that is, along with the other branches on which you were grafted.

11:20 [ER *bene dicis* 'well said']

[VG] *bene* 'well.' This must be punctuated so that it is a response – καλῶς [well (said)!] – to the preceding words, [the response] of [Paul] assenting to what had [just] been said in the persona of a gentile, and is to be read as an affirmative statement. So,[1] clearly, Augustine punctuates in his *Letters* when he cites this passage.

> 1 So ... passage.] Added in 1519. Cf Augustine *Epistulae* 140.20.51 CSEL 44
> 198.5.

11:20 [ER *ne efferaris animo* 'do not be haughty']

[VG] *noli altum sapere* 'be not high-minded'; μὴ ὑψηλοφρόνει, that is, 'do not be arrogant,'[1] 'do not be self-satisfied,' 'do not be haughty.' He uses[2] *sapere* [to be minded] here of an attitude of mind, φρονεῖν,[3] which elsewhere[4] is called μέγα πνέειν [to give oneself airs]. For it is not a question here of wisdom or stupidity, but of presumption and modesty.

> 1 do not be arrogant] First in 1527; in 1516, 'arrogantly'; from 1519 to 1522,
> 'not with arrogance.' For a similar explanation of the Greek see Valla *Annot
> in Rom* 11 (I 859).
> 2 He uses ... mind] Added in 1519
> 3 φρονεῖν ... modesty.] Added in 1527
> 4 Cf eg Euripides *Andromache* 189.

11:21 [ER *vide ne qua fiat ut nec tibi* 'take care lest it should somehow happen that neither you']

[VG] *ne forte nec tibi* 'lest perhaps neither you'; μήπως. The adverb should either have been omitted or translated 'lest "somehow," "in some way,"' for 'perhaps' is not compatible with the thought here.[1]

> 1 Frans Titelmans evidently wished to read 'lest' with the preceding 'fear'
> of 11:20, taking the intervening clause as a parenthesis: fear (if indeed
> God did not spare the natural branches) lest perhaps he will not spare
> you. But Erasmus objects that the parenthesis makes the construction too
> harsh. Hence he read: 'Do not be haughty, but have fear. For if God
> did not spare the natural branches, take care lest it should somehow
> happen that neither should he spare you.' See *Responsio ad collationes* LB IX
> 1007C.
> Tischendorf omits μήπως (II 425–6), and Cranfield regards the word as a
> secondary variant (II 569 n6); reasons for its retention in the text are given
> by Metzger (526–7).

11:22 [ER *vide igitur bonitatem* 'see[1] then the goodness']
[VG] *vide ergo bonitatem* 'see[2] therefore the goodness'; ἴδε, that is, *vide* [see], was the reading of most of the Greek codices, but this does not bear on the sense.[3]

> 1 see] First in *1527*; in the first three editions, *ecce* 'behold'
> 2 see ... sense] Added in *1522*. Though in LB this annotation is coalesced with the subsequent annotation, it remained a separate annotation in the editions from *1522* published during Erasmus' lifetime.
> 3 For the explanation of this brief note see the *Apologia ad annotationes Stunicae*, where Erasmus notes that if ἴδε is read, then the proper translation is *vide*, but if ἰδέ, then one should translate *ecce* (cf ASD IX-2 174:190–3 and 190n).

11:22 [ER VG] *bonitatem et severitatem* 'goodness and severity'; τὴν χρηστότητα, καὶ τὴν ἀποτομίαν. *Bonitas* is that which I previously translated as *benignitas* [kindness] following the opinion of St Jerome.[1] It is a certain inclination to treat another with consideration, which [the Translator] might have rendered, not inappropriately, *indulgentia* [indulgence]. To this, [Paul] opposes ἀποτομία, which means, literally, 'a cutting back' – whenever, that is, something is exacted *ad vivum* [to the quick, to the point of blood]. You could[2] also call this *rigor* [harsh inflexibility].

> 1 Jerome *Commentarius in epistulam ad Galatas* 3.5 (on 5:22) PL 26 (1883) 448B. In Gal 5:22, 2 Cor 6:6, and Eph 2:7 Erasmus translates χρηστότης by 'benignitas'; in Romans he consistently translates 'bonitas'; but in his annotations on 2:4 ('the riches of his goodness') and 15:14 ('you are full of love') he argues that the Latin equivalent of χρηστότης is *benignitas*.
> 2 You could ... rigor.] Added in *1519*

11:22 [ER VG] *alioqui* 'otherwise.'[1] Again the word is ἐπεί, that is, 'inasmuch as.'[2] But[3] the Translator's version is correct.

> 1 otherwise] Erasmus rendered ἐπεί here as *quoniam* 'since' from *1516* to *1527*, but returned to the Vulgate *alioqui* in *1535*.
> 2 Cf the annotation on 11:6 ('otherwise grace').
> 3 But ... correct.] Added in *1535*

11:24 [ER *in veram oleam* 'into the true olive']
[VG] *in bonam olivam* 'into the good olive tree'; καλλιέλαιον, which is the opposite of ἀγριέλαιος, that is, 'the wild olive,' as was just said.[1]

> 1 Cf the annotation on 11:16 ('but if the first portion').

11:25 [ER VG] *fratres mysterium hoc* 'brothers this mystery'; μυστήριον. In this passage 'mystery' means something hidden, and known to few, and which is to be shared only with initiates.

11:25 [ER *apud vosmetipsos elati animo* 'of a mind exalted[1] in your own sight']
[VG] *vobisipsis[2] sapientes* 'minded towards yourselves'; παρ᾽ ἑαυτοῖς, that
is, 'wise in your own sight.'[3] φρόνιμος refers to an attitude rather than to
wisdom. 'Do not[4] be insolent, and of a too exalted mind';[5] in any case,[6] he
is 'minded towards himself' who looks[7] to his own advantage.

1 of a mind exalted] First in *1519*; in *1516*, *prudentes* 'wise'
2 The Vulgate printed in *1527* reads *vobismetipsis*.
3 So Valla; see *Annot in Rom* 11 (I 859). To παρ᾽ ἑαυτοῖς LB adds φρόνιμοι,
  without warrant, however, from the editions *1516–1535*.
4 'Do not ... mind'] Added in *1519*
5 Cf the annotation on 8:7 ('because the wisdom of the flesh').
6 in any case ... himself] Added in *1527*
7 who looks ... advantage]. The reading of *1535*. In place of this, *1527* had
  added 'who is of a too exalted mind.'

11:26 [ER *liberat et avertet impietates* 'who liberates, and will turn away
impieties']
[VG] *eripiat et avertat impietatem* 'who is to deliver, and turn away impiety';[1] ἀσεβείας, that is, 'impieties.' Also: 'who is to deliver' – ὁ ῥυόμενος,
that is, 'the one who liberates,' as though you said 'the liberator.'[2] And
'will turn away,' not 'to turn away' – ἀποστρέψει, a verb[3] in the future
tense. The text is taken from the fifty-ninth chapter of Isaiah, where we
read, according to the Hebrew original, 'And those from the west shall
fear the name of the Lord, and those from the rising of the sun his glory,
when he comes like a violent river which the breath of the Lord drives;
and a redeemer shall come [near] Zion, and [to those] who return from
the iniquity [in] Jacob, says the Lord: this is my treaty with them, says the
Lord' [59:19–21]. In the Septuagint we read as follows: καὶ[4] φοβηθήσονται
οἱ ἀπὸ δυσμῶν τὸ ὄνομα κυρίου, καὶ οἱ ἀπ᾽ ἀνατολῶν τὸ ὄνομα τὸ ἔνδοξον·
ἥξει γὰρ ὡς ποταμὸς βίαιος ἡ ὀργὴ παρὰ κυρίου. ἥξει μετὰ θυμοῦ, καὶ ἥξει
ἕνεκα Σιὼν ὁ ῥυόμενος, καὶ ἀποστρέψει ἀσεβείας ἀπὸ Ἰακώβ, καὶ αὕτη αὐτοῖς
ἡ παρ᾽ ἐμοῦ διαθήκη, εἶπε κύριος, that is, 'And those[5] from the west shall fear
the name of the Lord, and those from the rising of the sun the illustrious
name; for the wrath of the Lord shall come like a violent river, it shall come
with fury, and he shall come from Zion who is to liberate, and will turn
away the impieties from Jacob, and this shall be my covenant with them,
says the Lord.' From this it is clear that Paul has quoted according to the
Septuagint edition, except that he added on his own 'when I shall take away
their sins,' which is found neither in the Hebrew nor in the Septuagint, but
[Paul] added it as though in explication of the Prophet's meaning.[6] For [the
Septuagint] διαθήκη 'covenant' is in the Hebrew [a word that translates as]
'treaty'; and what the Septuagint rendered as 'from Zion' is 'near Zion' in

the Hebrew. Origen points out that in the Hebrew it is 'on account of Zion.'[7] And thus[8] clearly the Septuagint edition reads, but[9] I suspect that this is a corruption due to the copyist, when the reading had been 'near Zion.'[10] Jerome interprets it as ἀγχιστεύς in Greek, that is, *propinquus* [near relative, close relation];[11] unless someone demonstrates that *propter* [on account of] is used for *prope* [near]. What[12] Jerome quotes as 'the wrath of the Lord' is in the Greek ὀργὴ παρὰ κυρίου [wrath from the Lord].

1 The lemma represents the reading of LB. In all the editions published during Erasmus' lifetime, this annotation was introduced by a lemma consisting of a single word, from 1516 to 1527 *iniquitatem* 'iniquity,' and in 1535 *impietatem* 'impiety.'
2 Erasmus reflected this interpretation in his own translation. Where the Vulgate read, 'One will come from Zion who is to deliver,' Erasmus' translation reads, 'He who liberates will come from Zion.'
3 a verb ... read as follows] Added in 1519
4 καί ... κύριος, that is,] Added in 1522. The text written in the annotation differs in some minor points from the text of Isa 59:19–21 in Rahlf's edition. Cf n8 below.
5 'And those ... 'on account of Zion.'] Added in 1519
6 These words, which form the concluding clause of 11:27, are quoted, with slight modifications, from the Septuagint of Isa 27:9. In asserting that they are to be found neither in the Hebrew nor the Septuagint, Erasmus may have been influenced by Origen *Comm in Rom* 8.12 PG 14 1197A.
7 Origen *Comm in Rom* 8.12 PG 14 1197A
8 And thus ... edition reads] Added in 1522. It was not until 1522 that Erasmus added the Greek text of the Septuagint (see n4 above); in giving the Latin for the 'original Hebrew' and the Septuagint in 1519 he seems not to have made his own translation, but to have followed the versions already prepared by Jerome (see Jerome *Commentarii in Isaiam* 16 [on 59:20] PL 24 582D–583A). Now Jerome's version reads 'from Zion,' and though, in 1522, Erasmus printed here a Septuagint Greek text reading 'on account of Zion,' he left Jerome's version unchanged, so that the Latin translation added in 1519 no longer corresponded exactly to the Greek text he printed in 1522. The brief addition here interrupts the exposition of 1519 to acknowledge the correct reading of the Septuagint, but cf n10 below. On the relation between the Septuagint reading ('on account of') and its citation (as 'from') here in 11:27 see Cranfield II 577.
9 But ... *prope*] Added in 1519
10 The brief addition of 1522 (cf n8 above) interrupts the course of the argument of 1519, which attempted to show that a corruption had occurred in the text of Origen (not in the Septuagint). The Latin Origen reads: 'One must recognize that in Isaiah, from whom Paul takes this text, what the Apostle quotes as "he shall come from Zion" was written "he shall come on account of [*propter*] Zion"' (for the reference, see n6 above). The similarity between *propter* 'on account of' and *prope* 'near' had evidently suggested to Erasmus that Origen wrote *prope*, which was corrupted to *propter* by a copyist.

11 Jerome *Commentarii in Isaiam* 16 (on 59:20) PL 24 584B explains the *propinquus Zion* as 'a descendant from the race of Israel.'

12 What ... κυρίου.] Added in 1522

11:27 [ER VG] *et hoc illis a me testamentum* 'and this[1] [is] the covenant[2] from me to them.' The Greek word is indeed διαθήκη [testament, covenant]. But even Augustine has pointed out in the first book [of his work] *On Expressions in Genesis*, that frequently in the sacred books *testamentum* [covenant, testament] is used in place of *pactum* [compact, agreement],[3] although in Greek διαθήκη derives not from [a word of] 'testifying,' but of arranging and disposing.

1 and this ... disposing.] The entire annotation was added in 1519.

2 covenant] From 1519 Erasmus translated, like the Vulgate, 'covenant'; in 1516, however, he had written *perfectum testamentum*, by which he appears to mean 'perfect covenant'; cf Origen *Comm in Rom* 8.12 PG 14 1197A–B and Jerome *Commentarii in Isaiam* 16 (on 59:19–20) PL 24 584C.

3 Augustine *Locutiones in Heptateuchum* 1.68 CSEL 28/1 518:7

11:28 [ER *secundum electionem autem dilecti* 'but according to the election beloved']

[VG] *secundum electionem autem charissimi* 'but according to the election most dear'; ἀγαπητοί, that is, 'beloved,' though he often translates the word thus [as *charissimi*].[1] The two[2] nominatives, 'enemies' and 'most dear,' grammatically do not have [a verb] on which to depend, unless you supply 'are.' But it is more likely that Paul has been careless about agreement of case; otherwise[3] he would have said 'most dear' and 'enemies' [in the genitive case].[4]

1 Cf eg 1 Cor 4:14, 17; Eph 5:1; Philem 16; and the annotation on 12:19 ('most dear'). Jacques Lefèvre d'Etaples also preferred *dilecti* 'beloved' here (*Pauli epistolae* fol 90 recto).

2 The two ... agreement of case] Added in 1519

3 otherwise ... 'enemies'] Added in 1527

4 11:28 has no verb: 'According to the gospel, enemies because of you, but according to the election, beloved because of the fathers'; grammatically, then, 'enemies' and 'most dear' might have been put in the genitive case, in agreement with αὐτῶν = *eorum* (Vulgate) in the previous verse: I will forgive the sins of them, enemies ... most dear.

11:29 [ER *ut eorum illum poenitere non possit* 'that he cannot repent of them']

[VG] *sine poenitentia* 'without repentance'; ἀμεταμέλητα, that is, he who gave or promised 'cannot repent of these,' as though you were to say *impoenitibilia* [things not able to be repented of]. Augustine[1] somewhere reads

impoenitenda [not to be repented of].[2] Ambrose[3] twists [the words] to say
that sin is freely remitted in baptism, and that weeping or wailing is not
required, or any other good work, but only a heartfelt profession.[4] This
interpretation seems to me rather forced, and is not mentioned by Origen.[5]
Thomas finally mentions this meaning at the very end of his interpretation,
as though he did not fully approve.[6]

1 Augustine ... *impoenitenda*.] Added in 1535
2 In citing this verse Augustine consistently reads *sine poenitentia* 'without
  repentance'; cf *De correptione et gratia* 12.34 PL 44 937, *De praedestinatione
  sanctorum* 16.33 and 19.38 PL 44 985, 988, and *De dono perseverantiae* 13.36 and
  14.36 PL 45 1012, 1015.
3 Ambrose ... approve.] Added in 1519
4 Ambrosiaster *Comm in Rom* 11:29. Ambrosiaster understands 'without
  repentance,' ie without doing penance, for the believer need only profess
  faith.
5 Cf Origen *Comm in Rom* 8.13 PG 14 1199B.
6 Thomas Aquinas *Super Rom lect* cap 11 lectio 4.927

11:30 [ER *per illorum incredulitatem* 'through their unbelief']
[VG] *propter incredulitatem illorum* 'on account of their unbelief'; τῇ
τούτων ἀπειθείᾳ, that is, 'through [*per*] the unbelief of these,' not 'on account of'[1] [*propter*]. For *propter*[2] signifies cause, *per* indicates the instrument
or means; but this makes little difference as far as the meaning is concerned.

1 not 'on account of'] Added in 1519
2 For *propter* ... concerned.] Added in 1535. Erasmus reports that Frans
  Titelmans had preferred *propter* in order to suggest the opportunity or
  occasion from which the gentiles received mercy, while *per* signified the
  cause, or reason (*Responsio ad collationes* LB IX 1007D); cf the following
  annotation.

11:31 [ER *ex eo quod vos misericordiam estis adepti* 'from[1] this, that you have
gained mercy']
[VG] *in vestram misericordiam* 'unto your mercy';[2] τῷ ὑμετέρῳ ἐλέει
'through the mercy shown to you' – for the dative is similar to the preceding one, τῇ τούτων ἀπειθείᾳ [through their unbelief]. The sense is: just
as their falling away made for you an access to faith, so your faith, which
you have obtained by God's mercy, will challenge them to repent, and to
show themselves worthy to be received by God.

Ambrose[3] reads '*in the compassion shown to you*,'[4] as though the
Greek had read ἐν τῷ ὑμῶν ἐλέει. If this reading were acceptable there
would be no difficulty. For the sense would be: 'When the gentiles had
been called to life by the mercy of God, the Jews persisted in unbelief.'
And perhaps the Translator followed the same reading as did Ambrose.

I know that some interpret 'unto your mercy' to mean 'Christ.' Thomas Aquinas expounds the passage in three ways: 'unto your mercy,' that is, 'on the grace of Christ'; or, they did not believe, so that through this they might enter into your mercy; or, they did not believe, which, as it happened, accrued to your mercy.⁵ However, to devise constructions of this sort without consulting the Greek – what else is it but to guess? Chrysostom takes no explicit notice of this phrase, 'in your mercy.'⁶ Theophylact brings forward a new interpretation as though he construes thus: οὕτως καὶ οὗτοι ἠπείθησαν, τῷ ὑμῶν ἐλέει ἵνα καὶ αὐτοὶ ἐλεηθῶσι, that is, 'Thus they too did not believe, so that by the mercy you have received they too might gain mercy.' For he makes the comment: 'But the mercy you have received will be theirs, too, for they will emulate you.'⁷ Chrysostom's interpretation is not unlike this, showing that each people had in turn been unbelieving, and each in turn was called to grace. For when the gentiles persisted in their unbelief, the Jews were called to the Law; afterwards, when the gentiles were called to the gospel, the Jews fell away, persevering in unbelief; but they were once more, through the example of the gentiles, to be recalled to faith. Thus, in a sort of reciprocal succession, each was saved through the other.⁸ Commentators seem to have shrunk from this interpretation, fearing they should say that the Jews' persistence in their unbelief was caused by the opportunity of the gentiles, when, on the contrary, the unbelief of the Jews offered the occasion for the gospel to pass to the gentiles.⁹ But if we remember that ἵνα [so that] here does not signify a purpose or intention, but rather a consequence or outcome,¹⁰ and that it is in other respects more reasonable to understand 'occasion' than 'cause,' then I do not see why we should be alarmed at this interpretation, which, taken in its simplest sense, the Greek expresses in a passage developed on the basis of mutually related contraries. [Paul] calls the faith of the gentiles 'mercy,' so that they would not pride themselves on being preferred to Jews. For the grace of the gospel seemed somehow owed to the Jews, either because it was promised especially to them, or because they had observed the Law and worshipped the one God.¹¹ And so he says: ὥσπερ γὰρ ὑμεῖς ποτε ἠπειθήσατε τῷ θεῷ, νῦν δὲ ἠλεήθητε τῇ τούτων ἀπειθείᾳ, οὕτως καὶ οὗτοι ἠπείθησαν, τῷ ὑμῶν ἐλέει, ἵνα καὶ αὐτοὶ ἐλεηθῶσι, that is, 'For just as you once did not believe in God, but now you have believed because of their unbelief, so also these do not believe because of your belief, so that they too may be called back to belief.'¹²

The construction that Theophylact seems to follow is somewhat forced; it is not less difficult that in the first part the Greek dative expresses occasion: ἐλεήθητε τῇ τούτων ἀπειθείᾳ [you (gentiles) have obtained mercy through the occasion of their unbelief], but in the second it conveys the idea of gain: ἠπείθησαν τῷ ὑμῶν ἐλέει [they (the Jews) did not believe for your mercy], as when we say, 'he has become rich "for you,"' that is, he has become rich to your advantage, because he shares his wealth with you.[13] Those who read 'unto your mercy' seem to have had this in mind, since 'to your mercy' seemed obscure. This sudden change in the figuration of the contrast is rather harsh. In addition, there is another difficulty, that according to their interpretation the same thing is said twice, which the terms 'just as' and 'so' do not allow: he says, ὑμεῖς δὲ ἐλεήθητε τῇ τούτων ἀπειθείᾳ [you have received mercy through their unbelief], then repeats this in a contrasting form, οὕτως καὶ οὗτοι ἠπείθησαν τῷ ὑμῶν ἐλέει [so also they have not believed to your mercy], as though one were to say, 'Just as princes grow rich by the poverty of the people, so the poverty of the people adds riches to princes.'

Moreover, since the discussion here is about the evil Jews, who cried 'Crucify him!,'[14] who persecuted the apostles, who boasted in the works of the Law, who were puffed up because of their kinship with the patriarchs and thus spurned the other nations as though they were dogs, there would be nothing absurd in saying that the belief of the gentiles was a stumbling-block to the Jews so that they became strangers to the gospel.[15] Peter, the prince of apostles, was compelled to justify himself before the brethren because he had baptized Cornelius along with his whole family;[16] in a banquet when Paul was present he withdrew from the table to avoid scandalizing the Jews by eating common food.[17] And in Acts the Jews murmur against the gentiles because their women were received into the ministration of the apostles.[18] Paul obtained with great difficulty the freedom of the gentiles from the burden of the Law.[19] If such things occurred among those who had embraced the faith of the gospel, is it not likely that a great many Jews either held back or recoiled from the gospel? What Paul had said just above supports this sense: 'According to the gospel enemies on account of you' [11:28]. In his interpretation of this passage, Origen says: 'He says "on account of you," whose salvation they envy, [preventing] the apostles from speaking to the people and persecuting those who proclaim Christ.'[20] Does he not mean that envy was the reason for their failure to believe in the gospel? This passage is supported by the parable of the Gospel in which the elder son refused to enter the house when he had heard that the prodigal was received with such joy among the household.[21] And so I have followed this interpretation because it seemed to me simpler, although none of the others strays from [the path of] piety.[22]

1 from ... mercy] First in 1519; in 1516, *per vestri misericordiam* 'through the mercy towards you.'
2 unto your mercy ... received by God] First in 1519; in 1516 the annotation appeared in a different form immediately following the annotation on 12:3 ('for I say through the grace'), where see n4.

3 Ambrose ... piety.] This remaining portion of the annotation was added in
  1535.
4 Ambrosiaster *Comm in Rom* 11:31. As the next sentences show, Erasmus
  evidently takes Ambrosiaster's *in* to indicate circumstance or time.
5 Cf Thomas Aquinas *Super Rom lect* cap 11 lectio 4.931. Erasmus abbreviates
  Thomas, who explicates: They have not believed, that is, in Christ ... Hence
  he adds 'unto your mercy,' that is, on the grace of Christ through which
  you gained mercy ... Or, they did not believe so that through this they
  might enter into your mercy. Or, they did not believe, which as it happened,
  accrued to your mercy, so that they themselves might some day find mercy.
6 Chrysostom *Hom in Rom* 19.7 PG 60 592. Though Chrysostom offers no
  explicit explanation of this particular phrase, his interpretation of this
  sentence anticipates the view of Theophylact.
  A few Latin witnesses read, as Erasmus quotes here, 'in your mercy'; cf
  Wordsworth and White II 124 31n.
7 Theophylact *Expos in Rom* 11:31 PG 124 493C–D. Theophylact continues: '...
  and they will themselves believe; and in this way they will gain mercy by
  the mercy you have received.'
8 For the reference, see n6 above.
9 So, explicitly, Frans Titelmans; see *Responsio ad collationes* LB IX 1007D–E. Cf
  the preceding annotation, n2.
10 Cf the annotation on 11:11 ('can it be that they have so stumbled that they
   fell') and n3.
11 For a variation on this theme see the paraphrase on 3:1–2 CWE 42 23 and n2.
12 Erasmus' Latin here is a free translation of the Greek designed to sharpen
   the contrasts in the 'reciprocal succession' of Jewish and gentile belief.
13 As his translation of the citation from Theophylact (see n7 above) suggests,
   Erasmus understood Theophylact to take the phrase 'by the mercy you have
   received' with the purpose clause that follows, to read 'so that by the mercy
   ...,' though it would seem less forced to take it with the verb that precedes:
   'they have not believed ... as a consequence you gentiles have received
   mercy.'
14 See Mark 15:13 and parallels; so also Origen, who alludes specifically to John
   19:15 (*Comm in Rom* 8.13 PG 14 1199B).
15 Erasmus has returned here to the defence of his own translation: Just as once
   you were unbelievers, but now have gained mercy through their unbelief, so
   also now they have become unbelievers through (ie as a consequence of) the
   mercy shown to you so that they too might gain mercy.
16 Acts 10:1–11:18
17 Gal 2:11–14
18 An allusion apparently to Acts 6:1. In that account, it is the 'Hellenists' who
   murmur against the 'Hebrews,' because their widows were being neglected
   in the daily ministration. In his annotation on Acts 6:1 (*murmur Graecorum*),
   as in his paraphrase on that verse, Erasmus identifies the Hellenists as
   Greek-speaking Jews born among the gentiles.
19 See Acts 15:1–35; Gal 2:1–8.
20 Origen *Comm in Rom* 8.13 PG 14 1199B. Erasmus has omitted from his
   quotation the word *prohibentes* 'preventing,' which is essential to Origen's
   meaning.

21 Luke 15:11–32
22 For the various ways, including those outlined here by Erasmus, in which
11:31–2 have been construed see Cranfield II 582–6.

11:32 [ER *conclusit enim deus omnes* 'for God has shut all people']
[VG] *conclusit enim deus omnia* 'for God has shut all things';[1] τοὺς πάντας,
that is, 'all people' not 'all things.'[2] The sense[3] is the same, except that 'all
things' is a stronger expression. Further, the word that follows, [translated]
'by unbelief,' can also be understood as 'disobedience,' for it[4] is ἀπείθεια.
And in Greek it is 'into unbelief,'[5] as we say 'I will shut myself into a
corner.'

   1 This annotation was placed here in 1519. In 1516 it followed, in its original
     form, the annotation on 11:33 ('of the riches of wisdom').
   2 So Valla *Annot in Rom* 11 (I 859)
   3 The sense ... expression.] Added in 1535
   4 for it ... corner'] Added in 1527
   5 In 1516 Erasmus kept the Vulgate reading *in incredulitate* 'in unbelief,' but
     changed his translation in 1519 to read *sub incredulitatem* 'under unbelief.'

11:33 [ER *O profunditatem* 'Oh, the depth']
[VG] *O altitudo* 'Oh, the extent'; ὦ βάθος, that is, 'Oh, the depth.' I am
surprised that the Translator has chosen an ambiguous word.[1]

   1 *Altitudo* can refer to either height or depth. Jacques Lefèvre d'Etaples also
     preferred *profunditas* to *altitudo*; cf *Pauli epistolae* fol 8 verso and fol 96
     verso.

11:33 [ER *divitiarum et sapientiae* 'of the riches and the wisdom']
[VG] *divitiarum sapientiae* 'of the riches of wisdom.' The Greek divides
these two words by an intervening conjunction, πλούτου καὶ σοφίας [of the
riches *and* of the wisdom]; all the copies I have seen agree with this,[1] as
does[2] Chrysostom also. Thus you understand that Paul is marvelling at
three things in God:[3] 'riches,' because he was so generous towards the
gentiles; 'wisdom,' because he has imparted to them such great wisdom;
'understanding,' because he so wisely discerns what is best for each. It is in
this way that Theophylact expounds [the passage].[4] But Chrysostom[5] seems
to read somewhat differently, joining the two words βάθος πλούτου [depth
of riches], so that the genitives that follow do not depend on βάθος, but on
the two words combined, as though you said, 'Oh, the deep riches of the
wisdom and of the knowledge of God.' One gathers this was his opinion
from his observation that to magnify the wisdom of God Paul had used two
words that lend intensity, βάθος and πλοῦτος.[6] For *profundum* [deep] possesses in itself a sense of augmentation, and 'riches' suggests abundance.[7]

The amplification is doubled if you say 'deep riches of wisdom.' I prefer rather that it should refer to the whole dispensation of this plan, by which it came about that the gentiles, who previously served the demons, should suddenly be called to the grace of the gospel; and the Jews, to whom this grace seemed to have been specially promised, fell away from it.[8]

1 'Riches and wisdom' is the preferred reading; it was also the reading adopted by Jacques Lefèvre d'Etaples (cf *Pauli epistolae* fol 8 verso and fol 96 verso). For the evidence of the witnesses, see Tischendorf II 428 33n.
2 as does Chrysostom also] Added in 1527. See *Hom in Rom* 19.7 PG 60 592.
3 The Vulgate reading offered only two attributes for wonder: 'Oh the extent of the riches of the wisdom and of the knowledge of God;' Erasmus' rendering offered three: 'Oh the depth of the riches and of the wisdom and of the understanding of God.'
Paul] In this sentence the Apostle's name was not specified until 1522.
4 Theophylact *Expos in Rom* 11:33 PG 124 496B
5 But Chrysostom ... 'deep riches of wisdom.'] Added in 1535
6 Chrysostom *Hom in Rom* 19.7 PG 60 592–3
7 Cf the annotation on 2:4 ('the riches of his goodness').
8 It is in relation to Theophylact's explicit exegesis of the three words that Erasmus expresses his preference for a more general allusion to the divine dispensation.

11:33 [ER *inscrutabilia* 'inscrutable']

[VG] *incomprehensibilia* 'incomprehensible'; ἀνεξερεύνητα, that is, 'inscrutable.'[1] And thus Jerome cites it repeatedly.[2]

1 See the annotation on 3:5 ('is God unfair who inflicts wrath') and n9.
2 See Jerome *Commentarii in Isaiam* 2 (on 5:16); 3 (on 6:9–10); 15 (on 54:12); 15 (on 55:8–9) PL 24 84C, 99C, 522B, 535A.

11:33 [ER *impervestigabiles* 'thoroughly untraceable']

[VG] *investigabiles* 'untraceable'; ἀνεξιχνίαστοι, that is, *ininvestigabiles*, as St Hilary[1] reads in the eighth book *On the Trinity* – according to the witness of the oldest manuscripts; that is, *non vestigabiles* [not to be traced out] or *impervestigabiles* [not to be traced through at all]. For Chrysostom,[2] followed by Theophylact, has noted the implication of this word. [Paul] did not say δυσνόητα [hard to perceive] or ἀκατάληπτα [not to be grasped] but 'unsearchable' and 'thoroughly untraceable.' So great is the depth that it is not permitted to search it out. Now,[3] one ought to consider whether in Greek there is the same difference between ἐρευνᾶν and ἐξερευνᾶν as there is in Latin between *vestigare* [to trace] and *investigare* [to trace out] and *pervestigare* [to trace through]. Further: St Jerome thinks that Paul was referring to the passage in the eleventh chapter of Isaiah: 'And there is no tracing out his way.'[4]

1 as St Hilary ... manuscripts] Added in 1527. Cf Hilary *De Trinitate* 8.38 PL 10 266A.
2 For Chrysostom ... to search it out.] Added in 1527, except that the words 'followed by Theophylact' were added in 1535. Though in 1527 Erasmus claims to be reporting the comment of Chrysostom, his words approximate more closely those of Theophylact. For the allusion to Chrysostom see *Hom in Rom* 19.7 PG 60 593; for Theophylact *Expos in Rom* 11:33 PG 124 496B. In fact Valla, too, had attempted to work out the implication of the word, stressing the propriety of the image: the paths of God cannot be traced out (*Annot in Rom* 11 [I 859]).
3 Now ... *pervestigare*.] Added in 1535
4 The citation is incorrectly quoted from Isa 40:28, 'there is no tracing out his wisdom.' See Jerome *Commentarii in Isaiam* 12 (on 40:28) PL 24 411C–D.

11:34 [ER *mentem Domini* 'the mind of the Lord']
[VG] *sensum Domini* 'the understanding of the Lord'; νοῦν, that is, 'the mind'[1] or 'the design.'

> 1 So Valla *Annot in Rom* 11 (I 859) and Jacques Lefèvre d'Etaples *Pauli epistolae* fol 9 recto and fol 96 verso; cf the annotation on 1:28 ('to a reprobate sense').

11:36 [ER *quoniam ex illo et per illum* 'since from him and through him']
[VG] *quoniam ex ipso et per ipsum* 'since[1] from him and through him.' The old theologians philosophize about these three prepositions.[2] Thomas interprets 'from him' as 'from the first cause of all things'; 'through him,' as 'the one working and administering'; 'in him' as 'in the end' – though it has not escaped my notice that he discusses these terms in various ways.[3] He is not, however, far from the opinion of Origen, who explicates in this way: 'In the phrase "from him," he points to the very fact that we exist; "through him," however, to the fact that our lives are ordered through his providence; and "in him," to the fact that the perfection and end of all will be in him, at the time when God will be all in all.'[4] Thomas points out that the preposition *de* has nearly the same meaning as *ex*, except that it adds [the notion of] participation in the substance.[5] We may conjecture that he followed Augustine, who expresses virtually the same opinion in chapter 26 of the book he wrote against the Manichaeans, *On the Nature of the Good*.[6] Others may decide whether this is true in Latin, but certainly in Greek the preposition is the same.[7] And when we say 'he speaks *de illo* [about him],' there is no suggestion of common essence. Ambrose[8] seems to have read 'unto him,' since he says that all things look to the end.

> 1 since ... essence.] Except for the last sentence, this annotation was added in 1519.
> 2 Erasmus' discussion goes beyond the cue phrase:
> ER *quoniam ex illo et per illum et in illum omnia* 'since from him and through him and unto him, [are] all things'

VG *quoniam ex ipso et per ipsum et in ipso sunt omnia* 'since from him and
through him and in him are all things'

3 Thomas Aquinas *Super Rom lect* cap 11 lectio 5.942–9. In his lengthy
discussion of these words, Thomas explores various ways in which the
prepositions may be understood. Erasmus gives only a general summary
of Thomas' interpretation. 'In the end' refers to Thomas' explication of the
'final' sense implied by the preposition *in*: we find our true goal – our end –
in God.

4 Origen *Comm in Rom* 8.13 PG 14 1202B

5 Thomas Aquinas *Super Rom lect* cap 11 lectio 5.942–4. Thomas distinguishes
between *ex* and *de* in terms of originating and consubstantial cause applied
to God. The universe of creatures has been brought into being out of nothing
ex deo as the originating agent. The Son, however, proceeds *de patre* (from
the Father) as consubstantial with him.

6 Augustine *De natura boni* 26 PL 42 559–60

7 ἐκ for both *ex* and *de* in Latin

8 Ambrose ... end.] Added in 1535. See Ambrosiaster *Comm in Rom* 11:36 (1–3).
In his commentary on this verse, Ambrosiaster reads 'in him'; and he does
not give the interpretation 'all things look to the end.' This does, however,
approximate the interpretation of Valla, who seems to have understood:
'unto him ... as the end of all things' (*Annot in Rom* 11 [I 859]).

11:36 [ER *gloria* 'glory']
[VG] *honor et gloria* 'honour and glory.' In the Greek, only 'glory' is written,
ἡ δόξα; 'honour' is not added.

11:36 [ER *in saecula* 'forever'[1]]
[VG] *in saecula saeculorum* 'forever and ever.'[2] *Saeculorum* [of ages] has
been added in the Latin. For[3] the Greek reads only εἰς τοὺς αἰῶνας. It is[4] not
added in Origen, or[5] in Theophylact, or in Chrysostom.

1 forever] First in 1519; in 1516, with the Vulgate, 'forever and ever.'

2 forever and ever] The cue phrase first in 1519. In 1516 the entire annotation
read:
[VG] *et saeculorum* 'and ever'; [this] likewise has been added in the Latin:
εἰς τοὺς αἰῶνας [forever].
'Forever and ever' is English idiom for the more literal translation, 'to the
ages of ages.' The preferred reading of both the Greek and Latin manuscripts
is 'to the ages' (omitting 'of ages'); cf Tischendorf II 428 36n and Wordsworth
and White II 126 36n.
In LB this annotation is included in the preceding one but it appears as a
separate annotation in all the editions published during Erasmus' lifetime.

3 For ... only] Added in 1519

4 It is ... in Origen] Added in 1519. See Origen *Comm in Rom* 8.13 PG 14 1202B.
Saeculorum is present in the Migne text, but not in the text of Merlin (cf fol
CCVII recto).

5 nor ... Chrysostom] Added in 1527. See Theophylact *Expos in Rom* 11:36 PG
124 496D and Chrysostom *Hom in Rom* PG 19.7 60 593.

12:1 [ER VG] *obsecro vos* 'I beseech[1] you'; παρακαλῶ, which[2] could also be taken as 'I urge' or 'I exhort,' for the Greek word is ambiguous; but what immediately follows, 'by the mercy,' seems more appropriate to one beseeching or imploring than to one exhorting.[3]

> 1 beseech] From 1519 Erasmus followed the Vulgate; in 1516 he had translated *adhortor* 'exhort.'
> 2 which ... exhorting] In 1516 the annotation read: 'παρακαλῶ, that is, "I urge," or "I exhort." ' All additions were made in 1519.
> 3 Cf the annotation on Rom 15:30 ('I beseech you therefore').

12:1 [ER *ut praebeatis corpora vestra* 'that you furnish your bodies']
[VG] *ut exhibeatis corpora vestra* 'that[1] you present your bodies'; παραστή-σατε τὰ σώματα ὑμῶν. [We use the word] *exhibetur* when something once promised is in fact made good, or something before concealed is produced, as promissory notes are 'presented'; frequently in a bad sense, as *exhibere negotium* is said of one who causes trouble. [We use] *praebetur* of that which is provided for use, as when we 'give' ear to one speaking, or 'furnish' the expenses for a wedding. Chrysostom and Theophylact point out that παραστῆναι is properly used of those who furnish war-horses to a general.[2] Thus I have translated it *praebere* [to furnish].

If you reflect that in baptism we have renounced the desires of the flesh and dedicated ourselves to Christ, the word *exhibere* is appropriate, for it admonishes us to make good our profession. Or again, if we have in mind that there is an allusion to the ancient custom of burnt offerings, in which the priest placed the victim on the altar while God consumed it with fire from heaven, the word 'present' fits well. What has once been devoted to God should not be used for any other purpose; just as he who has furnished horses for a commander in war has nothing to do with them in the future; he cannot recall for his personal use what he has once handed over.

Chrysostom has also observed that [Paul] did not say ποιήσατε, that is, 'make your bodies a sacrifice,' but παραστήσατε, that is, *tradite* [hand (them) over], so that they no longer belong to you but come under the control of God.[3] And it would be sacrilege to appropriate anew to the service of the devil what you once furnished to your commander, God, for fighting the devil. At the same time we are admonished to take care to treat our bodies in such a way that they are instruments suitable for the divine will[4] and worthy to be presented before his eyes.

1 that ... eyes.] This entire annotation was added in *1535*, when it followed
immediately after the first annotation ('I beseech you'), not, as in LB, after the
annotation 'through the mercy.'

Erasmus cites the Greek verb twice as a first aorist imperative (παραστήσατε;
LB's παραστήσετε, future, is evidently a mistake), and once as a second
aorist infinitive (παραστῆναι); for his own Greek text (all editions) he read
παραστῆσαι (first aorist infinitive). He had already outlined in his response
to Frans Titelmans the distinction he makes here between the Vulgate's
exhibeatis and his own *praebeatis* (*Responsio ad collationes* LB IX 1007E–1008A).
Cf also the annotation on 6:13 ('but do not present').

2 Chrysostom *Hom in Rom* 20.1 PG 60 596; Theophylact *Expos in Rom* 12:1
PG 124 497B. Chrysostom speaks of furnishing horses for war; Theophylact
evokes the image of a general offering his troops to battle. The chief point
of both Chrysostom and Theophylact is to show that the word παρίστημι is
used in contexts expressing the total dedication of what is furnished for war.

3 Chrysostom *Hom in Rom* 20.1 PG 60 596

4 Here, too, Erasmus appears to follow Chrysostom; cf *Hom in Rom* 20.1 PG 60
595–6.

12:1 [ER *per miserationes* 'through the compassion'[1]]

[VG] *per misericordiam* 'through the mercy'; διὰ τῶν οἰκτιρμῶν [plural], that
is, 'through the "compassions."' Chrysostom[2] and Theophylact agree on
this reading.[3] Origen[4] also has remarked the point of the plural, thinking
that it implies a sense of the immense mercy of God.[5]

1 compassion] First in *1519*; in *1516*, *misericordias* 'mercies'

2 Chrysostom ... reading.] Added in *1527*

3 Chrysostom *Hom in Rom* 20.1 PG 60 595 and Theophylact *Expos in Rom* 12:1
PG 124 497A

4 Origen ... God.] Added in *1519*

5 Origen *Comm in Rom* 9.1 PG 14 1204C; Origen notes that as God is the Father
of Christ and the father of mercies, so Christ, as he is all other things, is also
himself 'mercies' – many mercies, not one.

12:1 [ER *rationalem cultum* 'rational worship']

[VG] *rationabile obsequium* 'reasonable service'; τὴν λογικὴν λατρείαν ὑμῶν,
that is, 'your rational worship,' so as to join in apposition with the preceding
words, as[1] the Greek article τήν indicates: 'which[2] is your rational and
spiritual worship.' [It is] as though Paul said, 'If you slay and sacrifice to
God your bodies, that is, the affections of the body – not shedding the blood
of irrational and dead animals, as the Jews have hitherto done – only so will
you present to him an acceptable sacrifice.' He calls [the worship] 'rational,'
not that you should understand a moderate worship, that is a moderate
maceration of the body, as the common run of preachers[3] are everywhere
proclaiming today (with erudition, as they think, but to those who know

Greek, with absurdity enough); but a victim[4] living and possessing reason. For[5] they suppose 'reasonable' is meant – what is in accord with reason and governed by reason. But Paul here calls worship 'rational' in precisely the same way that milk is said to be 'spiritual' in the First Epistle of Peter: λογικὸν γάλα [1 Peter 2:2], that is, 'the milk of the mind and the spirit.' But what are they to do when the point of the phrase depends on a Greek idiom, and the interpreter is utterly ignorant of that language?[6]

[Paul] has used the word 'service' [obsequium][7] here, in his customary manner, for sacrifice or worship.[8] But to show that Christian worship is different from Jewish ceremonies, in which dumb animals were sacrificed, [Paul] adds the word rationale, obviously thinking of human beings who are victims 'possessing reason' and on this account more acceptable to God, for in Isaiah[9] God loathes the beasts of the Jews. St Jerome clearly cites it in this sense in the letter to Pammachius that begins 'To a wound that has been healed,' and in several other places as well.[10] Origen[11] interprets similarly, when he says: 'Whereas formerly this worship consisted in the bodies of dumb animals, it is now offered in the body of a rational person, and your bodies, rather than beasts, become a sacrifice to God' etc.[12] Chrysostom[13] expounds in the same way, pointing out that the word λογικός is used because it is a matter of the mind and the spirit: in place of a temple, there is a human breast; in place of a beast, a human body, that is, the affections of the flesh; in place of fire, there is the love of God. And to this extent it belongs to Christian piety to imitate Christ, who offered himself as a sacrifice for us.[14] Origen, as usual, mentions still another interpretation: that worship is rational of which a sufficient explanation [ratio] can be given, as though no good reason could be found for the victims of the Jews.[15] Theophylact mentions something similar, namely, that we should conduct our whole life with reason.[16] I admit that this has been well said; still it seems to depart from the simplicity of apostolic speech.

1 as ... acceptable sacrifice'] Added in 1519, except for the clause cited in n2 below. Erasmus explicates images evidently implied by the phrase 'slay ... the affections' in his paraphrase on 12:1 (CWE 42 69).
2 'which ... worship'] Added in 1535
3 common run of preachers] So first in 1522; in 1516 and 1519, 'common theologians'
4 but a victim ... possessing reason] Added in 1527
5 For ... and the spirit.'] In 1535 this passage was substituted for a sentence that appeared virtually unchanged from 1516 to 1527: 'And yet I think that these, too, must be forgiven, since they have interpreted it in the same way as – to say nothing of the others – Thomas Aquinas [in 1516 and 1519, 'St Thomas'], who as a rule did not easily slip, and Lyra.' Frans Titelmans had

attacked Erasmus for this 'injury' to Thomas, and in a lengthy reply, Erasmus
introduced the comparison with 1 Pet 2:2 found here in the 1535 substitution.
See *Responsio ad collationes* LB IX 1009C–E.

Among the three ways one may present his body as a sacrifice to God,
Thomas mentions 'macerating it with fasts and vigils.' He goes on to explain
the phrase *rationabile obsequium*: 'Present your bodies as a sacrifice with the
discretion [of good judgment], whether through martyrdom or abstinence or
any other work of righteousness' (*Super Rom lect* cap 12 lectio 1.959–63). Lyra
too refers to a 'moderate maceration' of the flesh; cf *Postilla* IV fol cc iii recto.

 6 language] After 'language' Erasmus inserted, in 1527 only, the sentence:
   'And so he interprets whose scholia on this Epistle appear under the name
   of Jerome.' Cf Pelagius *Expos in Rom* 12:1 (Souter II 94).
 7 service] So first in 1522, following the Vulgate *obsequium*. In 1516 and 1519,
   cultum 'worship.' On *cultus* see the annotation on 1:9 ('whom I serve'). Cf
   also Valla *Annot in Rom* 12 (I 859).
 8 or worship] Added in 1535
 9 for in Isaiah ... Jews] Added in 1535. Cf Isa 1:11
10 Jerome *Epistulae* 66.12 CSEL 54 662:14. Cf also *Adversus Jovinianum* 1.37 PL 23
   (1883) 274C–275A.
11 Origen ... etc.] Added in 1519
12 Cf Origen *Comm in Rom* 9.1 PG 14 1203B–C.
13 Chrysostom ... apostolic speech.] Added in 1535
14 Erasmus evidently offers here a somewhat free interpretation of Chrysostom
   Hom in Rom 20.1–2 PG 60 596–7.
15 Origen *Comm in Rom* 9.1 PG 14 1204B
16 Theophylact *Expos in Rom* 12:1 PG 124 497C

12:2 [ER *sed transformemini* 'but be transformed']
[VG] *sed reformamini* 'but you are reformed'; μεταμορφοῦσθε, that is, 'you
are transformed,' or[1] 'be transformed.' It can be taken in either way – as an
indicative or an imperative.[2]

>   1 or ... imperative] Added in 1519
>   2 For the Greek word, as for the Latin, the indicative and imperative have the
>   same form in the passive, second person plural.

12:2 [ER *per renovationem mentis* 'through the renewal of the mind']
[VG] *in novitate sensus* 'in the newness of the understanding'; τῇ ἀνα-
καινώσει τοῦ νοός, that is, 'by the renewal of the mind,'[1] that is, 'through
the restoration of the mind.' No doubt he is alluding to that debased mind
to which they had been handed over before, when they gave honour to
images instead of to God.

>   1 Cf Valla *Annot in Rom* 12 (I 859): 'I should have preferred to say "of our mind
>   – νοός" '; cf also the annotation on 11:34 ('the understanding of the Lord').

12:2 [ER *quae sit voluntas dei, quod bonum est acceptumque et perfectum* 'what[1] the will of God is – (something) which is good and acceptable and perfect']

[VG] *quae sit voluntas dei bona et beneplacens et perfecta* 'what[2] is the good and the well-pleasing and the perfect will of God.' It is hard to know what copy Augustine was following when he read as follows in the tenth book of the *City of God* (and again in Letter 86): 'To prove what is the will of God – which is good, well-pleasing, and perfect';[3] as though these three epithets did not refer to the will of God, but to the whole complex of preceding words, 'Let us present our bodies' etc, 'and not be conformed to this world, but be reformed' etc, so that we obey not our own desires, as the heathens do, but the divine will. If we do this, I say the sacrifice will be good, pleasing, and appropriate to God. The addition of the article τὸ ἀγαθὸν καὶ εὐάρεστον καὶ τέλειον [a thing good and acceptable and perfect] makes it possible to be understood in this sense. For those things are properly called τέλεια [perfect] from which nothing is lacking that belongs to sacred procedure and religious ritual; and, just before, he had begun with the metaphor of sacrifice. The translator of Origen points out that the Latin text varies here somewhat from the Greek, but I really do not know what he had in mind, for the Greek text admits of either sense.[4] Certainly Ambrose agrees with Augustine. He interprets[5] his reading in these words, as he concludes his commentary: 'This will be [what it is] to be conformed to the spiritual, renewed in spirit and in faith; this will be to know what pleases God, and that nothing else is good and perfect.'[6]

The addition of the article brings an ambiguity to the passage; there would be no ambiguity if he had removed the article and said τί τὸ θέλημα τοῦ θεοῦ ἀγαθὸν καὶ εὐάρεστον [what is the will of God, good and well-pleasing] etc. Now since he said τὸ ἀγαθόν, the article can be taken in two ways: either to distinguish [one] will from [another] will, or to refer to the preceding words, 'to know what is the will of God.' The interpreters touch on both senses. According to the former interpretation, not only is the will of God distinguished from our will, but a distinction is made even in the will of God itself. For that ancient worship of the Jews and their practises were, to be sure, the will of God, but not that good or well-pleasing or perfect [will]. The will of God was indulgent to them because of their weakness, when, for example, he granted a king at the demand of the people.[7] But the New Testament was this perfect will of God. So Chrysostom and Origen.[8] Ambrose treats this clause in such a way that the article τό [the] refers not only to the immediately preceding words, 'that you may know what is the will of God,' but to the entire passage taken as a unit, and covers its entire scope: 'That you present your bodies as a living sacrifice, holy, pleasing to God, your rational service;

and do not be conformed to this world, but be reformed in the newness of your understanding, that you may prove what is the will of God – to do which is good, acceptable to God, and perfect.'[9] Thus we should understand that [these] are the same: to offer a living sacrifice, holy, pleasing to God; not to be conformed to this world, which does not know the will of God but still clings to the rites of idolatry or the ceremonies of Moses and lives its life by the will of the affections; but to be reformed in a newness of understanding, so that, denying the will of the flesh, we are able to know the will of God – all this is a worship good, well-pleasing, and perfect before God.

Now μεταμορφοῦσθε [are, or be, transformed], as I said before, can be either imperative or indicative.[10] If imperative, it answers to the preceding μὴ συσχηματίζεσθε [do not be conformed]. If indicative, you are to understand that we are transformed through the things said about 'rational worship,' so that when we are transformed we may be able to know the will of God. For unless we sacrifice the desires of our flesh, we cannot be capable of discerning what the will of God is in our actions, but we interpret as the will of God whatever we especially want to think. [Paul] teaches something similar in the fifth [chapter] of Ephesians, δοκιμάζοντες τί ἐστιν εὐάρεστον τῷ κυρίῳ, that is, 'proving what is well-pleasing to the Lord' [5:10]. Similarly in the second chapter of this Epistle Paul writes: καὶ γινώσκεις τὸ θέλημα, καὶ δοκιμάζεις τὰ διαφέροντα 'and know [his] will and prove what are the better things' [2:18].

1 what ... perfect] First in 1519; in 1516, *quae sit voluntas dei et accepta et perfecta* 'what is the acceptable and perfect will of God.' Erasmus refused to give Edward Lee credit for the change (*Responsio ad annotationes Lei* LB IX 217A–B).
2 What ... agrees with Augustine.] This was the full extent of the annotation when it was introduced in 1519.
3 Augustine *De civitate dei* 10.6 CCL 47 279:3–4. In the *Epistulae* Rom 12:2 appears not in Ep 86 (36 in Migne) but in Ep 120.3.20 PL 33 462.
4 For the Greek text, the 'Latin Origen' cites a Latin translation virtually identical with that of the cue phrase and with the Vulgate of 1527. What the Latin cites as the 'Latin reading' is equivalent to the one just cited from Augustine and similar to the 1519 translation of Erasmus. In fact, the witnesses support the latter (= Erasmus' 1519 translation) as the reading of the Greek text, while the former (= the Vulgate cue phrase) represents the preferred Latin reading; cf Tischendorf II 429–30 2n, and Wordsworth and White II 126–7 2n.
   According to 'Origen' the 'Latin reading' (eg the translation in Augustine) would mean that God wills only what is good, the 'Greek reading' (= the cue phrase) that God's entire will is good; cf Origen *Comm in Rom* 9.1 PG 14 1205C, 1207A–C and Merlin fol CCVIII recto.
5 He interprets ... better things.'] This remaining portion of the annotation was added in 1535.
6 Ambrosiaster *Comm in Rom* 12:1–2 (1b) (recensions β and γ)

7 Cf 1 Sam 8:4–22.
8 Chrysostom *Hom in Rom* 20.3 PG 60 598–9; Origen *Comm in Rom* 9.1 PG 14 1207C. In commenting on this passage Chrysostom and Origen follow distinct lines. Chrysostom contrasts the 'old πολιτεία' (life under the Law) with the new: the old represents the will, but not the preferred will, of God; the latter the perfect will of God. Origen observes that the will of God is always good, but we do not always deserve God's perfect will, and he cites the example of the Israelites' demand for a king.
9 Cf n6 above. *Facere* 'to do' is not present in Ambrosiaster's text of 12:2, where the last clause reads, 'which is good, well-pleasing and perfect.'
10 See the annotation on 12:2 ('but you are reformed').

12:3 [ER VG] *dico enim per gratiam* 'for[1] I say through the grace'; λέγω. He has said 'I say' for 'I bid' or 'I admonish,' as also in Latin one 'bids'[another] be well and 'says' greetings; similarly in Greek[2] οἰμώζειν λέγω [I say, or I bid you to, lament, that is, 'A curse on you!']. For this reason,[3] he adds 'through the grace which has been given to me,' so that he will not seem to instruct them with arrogance or to admonish them without authority. He instructs as an apostle, and as one who understands what is pleasing to God; but this itself he credits to the divine beneficence. Perhaps, however, you would prefer to interpret the words in this way, that Paul is clarifying and illustrating what he had said above, about offering the body, about fleeing the desires of this world; for he makes the point more obvious by adding examples. Arrogance above all must be sacrificed to God.[4]

1 for ... grace] For the Vulgate cue phrase, first in 1535; from 1516 to 1527, 'for I say to you,' perhaps an inadvertent mistake, though a minor variant so reads (cf Wordsworth and White II 127 3n). In his own text Erasmus read consistently 'for I say through the grace,' though, in 1516 only, he translated the Greek γάρ by *autem* 'but,' 'now' rather than by 'for.'
2 similarly in Greek] Added in 1519. For the Greek expression cited see eg Aristophanes *Plutus* 58.
3 For this reason ... to God.] This remaining portion of the annotation was added in 1519.
4 In 1516 this annotation was immediately followed, apparently through a mistake, by an annotation with the lemma 'unto your mercy,' which was clearly intended for Rom 11:31. It read:
τῷ ὑμετέρῳ ἐλέει, that is, 'by your mercy, or, through your mercy,' that is, 'through this, that you gained mercy' [*per hoc quod vos misericordiam estis consecuti*]. Hence I have rendered *per vestri misericordiam* [through the mercy (shown to) you], so that you understand 'mercy' in a passive sense.
Erasmus caught the mistake in 1519, when the annotation appeared in a different form in its proper place. See the annotation on 11:31 ('unto your mercy') and n2.

12:3 [ER *cuilibet versanti inter vos* 'to whomever it may be who lives among
     you']
     [VG] *omnibus qui sunt inter vos* 'to all[1] who are among you'; παντὶ τῷ ὄντι
     ἐν ὑμῖν. The translator of Origen thought it should be noted that in the Greek
     it is not 'to all who are among you,' but 'to everyone who is among you.'[2]
     I wonder why he thought he should point this out, since it is clear that it
     makes no difference to the sense. I preferred to translate 'to anyone at all'
     [*cuicumque*] or 'to whomever it may be' [*cuilibet*]. For it appeared that a
     kind of arrogance was to be attributed to those who excelled in fortune or
     in talent. Paul completely eliminates this distinction of persons and serves
     notice to whoever he may be – if only he lives among Christians – that he
     should not esteem himself more highly than another, but that each should
     apply the gift received from God to the advantage of his neighbour.

     1 to all ... his neighbour.] This entire annotation was added in 1519.
     2 Origen *Comm in Rom* 9.2 PG 14 1208A

12:3 [ER *ita sentiat ut modestus sit et sobrius* 'should regard (himself) in a
     modest and sensible way']
     [VG] *sapere ad sobrietatem* 'to be wise unto sobriety'; εἰς τὸ σωφρονεῖν. St[1]
     Jerome, contending against Jovinian (in the first book), because of his zeal to
     uphold virginity thinks that we must read 'unto chastity'; and he condemns
     what the church now reads, 'to be wise unto sobriety.'[2] But σωφρονεῖν means
     'to be temperate, modest, and sensible.' Sometimes it refers also to chastity,
     but not indeed in this passage. Now[3] the translator of Origen on the Epistle to
     the Romans prefers 'temperance,' rather than 'sobriety,' because the virtue
     that the Greeks call σωφροσύνη educated Latin-speakers term *temperantia*
     [temperance], which is the restraint and control of desires and actions.[4] And
     in fact Augustine so cites this passage in his forty-seventh letter.[5]
          Hilary,[6] in the tenth book *On the Trinity*, renders the Greek word
     ὑπερφρονεῖν by *supersapere* [to be overly clever].[7] It is true that elsewhere
     Paul writes, 'Knowledge – unaccompanied by love – puffs up,'[8] but here the
     discussion is not really about knowledge. There is a pleasant play on words
     in the Greek, which the Latin Translator was unable to convey: ὑπερφρονεῖν,
     φρονεῖν, εἰς τὸ σωφρονεῖν [hyperphronein, phronein, eis to sōphronein]. In this
     passage φρονεῖν, that is, *sapere* [be of a mind][9] does not refer to learning, but
     to thinking and to opinion, when, for example, someone is haughty and has
     a high opinion of himself, as I suggested above.[10] Origen[11] shows clearly
     enough that this is so, for he points out at once that this passage refers to
     those from the wild olive tree who have been grafted onto the olive, and are
     harsh and insolent towards the branches that have been broken off the olive;

and that [Paul's] words here have almost the same force as elsewhere, when
he said, 'Do not be of an insolent mind.'[12] Now the fact that Origen cites from
philosophical sources concerning the state of virtue produced from the mean
between two extremes[13] suggests that he has offered an interpretation following the opinion of another rather than his own.[14] Chrysostom[15] likewise
points out that here is disclosed the mother of all good things – *modestia*, that
is, ταπεινοφροσύνη [humility, the unassuming mind].[16] Theophylact agrees
with him.[17] Ambrose reads as we [Latins] do, 'unto sobriety'; and his exposition makes no mention of 'chastity.'[18] But in his dispute, the blessed Jerome
has allowed himself to reject here what elsewhere he approves. For he cites
this passage thus: 'Not to be wiser than is right, but to be wise unto chastity
– not "unto sobriety," as one reads in the Latin codices (wrongly); [Paul]
says "to be wise unto chastity." '[19]

1 St ... unto sobriety.'] This sentence, much shorter in *1516*, appeared in this
form first in *1535*; 'contending' was added in *1519*; and '(in the first book)'
as well as the final clause, 'and he condemns ... sobriety,' in *1535*.

2 Jerome *Adversus Jovinianum* 1.37 PL 23 (1883) 274C. Valla had pointed to
Jerome's reading, but had argued from the use of the word in Acts 26:25
that its normal sense was 'modest,' 'temperate' (*Annot in Rom* 12 [I 859]).
Likewise, Jacques Lefèvre d'Etaples interpreted the word as 'modesty' and
thought Jerome's interpretation unsuitable (*Pauli epistolae* fol 97 verso).

3 Now ... forty-seventh letter.] Added in *1519*, except that from *1519* to *1527*,
instead of *at* 'now' Erasmus wrote *idem* 'the same,' meaning 'Jerome also as
translator of Origen.' On Erasmus' views concerning the translator of Origen,
see the annotation on 3:5 ('is God unfair who inflicts wrath') and n11.

4 Origen *Comm in Rom* 9.2 PG 14 1210C–1211A

5 Augustine *Epistulae* 215.4 CSEL 57 391:8

6 Hilary ... about knowledge.] Added in *1527*

7 Hilary *De Trinitate* 10.53 PL 10 385C

8 Cf 1 Cor 8:1.

9 that is, *sapere*] Added in *1519*

10 Cf the annotation on Rom 8:7 ('because the wisdom of the flesh').

11 Origen ... his own.] Added in *1519*

12 Cf 11:20.

13 Cf Aristotle *Nichomachean Ethics* 1104a.

14 In this passage Erasmus summarizes Origen *Comm in Rom* 9.2 PG 14
1209C–1211A. Origen himself says that 'other scholars' interpret this
expression from Rom 12:3 in the light of the Aristotelian doctrine of the
mean, though he adds examples apparently of his own (eg the serpent in
Eden, who was not imprudent but malicious – imprudence and malice being
the two extremes of which the mean is prudence). The Latin Origen also
credits to 'other scholars' the view that *temperantia* 'moderation' is a better
translation of the Greek here than *sobrietas* (see n4 above).

15 Chrysostom ... "to be wise unto chastity." '] The remainder of the annotation
was added in *1535*.

16 Chrysostom *Hom in Rom* 20.3 PG 60 599
17 Theophylact *Expos in Rom* 12:3 PG 124 501A–B. Theophylact agrees with
   Chrysostom in understanding the expression here as a call to humility, but
   he does not evoke the latter's striking image of modesty as the mother of all
   good things.
18 Ambrosiaster *Comm in Rom* 12:3. *Prudentia* is the better attested reading,
   though some manuscripts have either *sobrietas* or *temperantia* (see CSEL 81/1
   394:26 and 395:17 with 17n).
19 Cf n2 above. In Acts 26:25 the Vulgate ('Jerome') had rendered the Greek
   σωφροσύνη by *sobrietas* 'sobriety.'

12:3 [ER *ut cuique deus partitus est* 'as[1] God has apportioned to each']
[VG] *et unicuique sicut deus divisit* 'and[2] to each one as God has divided.'
So too, indeed, the Greek reads, but 'each one' does not have an antecedent
point of reference. Hence one must admit that here also Paul has had regard
more to the sense than to correct expression – unless we prefer to construe
thus: 'Let each esteem himself as God has distributed to each the measure
of faith.'[3] Origen implies that something must be understood, when he says:
'So as to keep the measure of faith as God has divided to each.'[4]

    1 as ... each] First in 1519; in 1516, 'to each one as God has apportioned'
    2 and ... to each.'] This entire annotation was added in 1519.
    3 The construction assumed in Erasmus' 1519 translation. On the construction
      here see Cranfield II 613.
    4 Origen *Comm in Rom* 9.2 PG 14 1211B. Origen says that each one is given
      the gift, or the good work, he has deserved through faith. Anyone who
      assumes he possesses a gift, or a work, not given to him 'is not wise unto
      moderation so as to keep, "as God has divided to each, the measure of
      faith." '

12:5 [ER *singulatim autem alii aliorum membra* 'individually,[1] however,
members of one another']
[VG] *singuli autem alter alterius membra* 'as individuals, however, members each of the other'; ὁ δὲ καθεῖς ἀλλήλων μέλη, that is, 'as individuals,
however, members one of another,'[2] or, as I have translated, 'as individuals,[3]
however, members of one another.' He refers to the mutual participation of
the members in one another.

    1 individually] First in 1519; in 1516, with the Vulgate, *singuli*
    2 Valla, too, had objected to the Vulgate's *alter alterius*, and had proposed as a
      'more elegant' translation, *alius alterius* 'one of the other' (*Annot in Rom* 12 [I
      859]).
    3 For the translation in 1516 and 1519 see n1 above. The annotation, written in
      1516, was never corrected to correspond with the change in translation made
      in 1519.

12:6 [ER *sed tamen habentes dona* 'but nevertheless having gifts']

[VG] *habentes donationes* 'having gifts.' The Translator, or, as I rather think, a scribe, omitted the conjunction [but], which most effectively joined this clause with the former: ἔχοντες δὲ χαρίσματα. For since [Paul] had said, 'As individuals we are members one of another,' lest [from this] we should imagine an undistinguishable fusion, he made an addition, 'we are[1] indeed members of the same body, "but having gifts" ';[2] otherwise the passage would have been incomplete. Wherefore, someone, taking offence and thinking[3] this clause was not connected to the preceding, removed the conjunction [but]. Certainly[4] 'however' is added in Ambrose[5] and in the manuscript in St Paul's, though 'but' would be clearer and more suitable than 'however.'[6] Similarly[7] he had said immediately above: 'For just as in one body we have many members, all members, however, have not the same function'; ' "but" not all members' [would have been better].[8]

1 'we are ... same body'] Added in 1527
2 "having gifts"] First in 1522; previously, "having various gifts." Erasmus argues for a connection between 12:5 and 12:6: unless the clause beginning 'having gifts' is connected to the preceding clause, it introduces an incomplete sentence, having no main verb.
3 and thinking ... preceding] Added in 1519
4 Certainly ... than 'however.'] Added in 1519
5 Ambrosiaster *Comm in Rom* 12:6
6 Though the conjunction is absent from some Vulgate manuscripts, it is present as *autem* in the Vulgate printed in 1527. There are variants in both the Greek and Latin texts at this point, but the preferred reading of the Greek is δέ, of the Latin *autem*; cf Tischendorf II 430 6n and Wordsworth and White II 127 6n. For the 'manuscript in St Paul's' see the annotation on 4:5 ('according to the purpose of the grace of God') n5.
7 Similarly ... not all members.'] Added in 1527
8 Cf 12:4, where the Vulgate translated *autem* 'however,' Erasmus, *vero* 'but.'

12:6 [ER *dona* 'gifts']

[VG] *donationes* 'gifts';[1] *donationes* [gifts] χαρίσματα. [The Translator] seeks to achieve variety when there is no need, especially[2] since *donationes* in this passage is really not the Latin term.[3]

1 In all editions this appeared as a separate annotation, though LB includes it with the preceding.
2 especially ... term] Added in 1522
3 Just above, in 11:29, the Vulgate renders the same Greek word by the Latin *dona*. Erasmus' comment here on the Translator was badly received. Zúñiga charged that this note demonstrated Erasmus' 'thirst for glory,' not his charity (*Apologia ad annotationes Stunicae* ASD IX-2 174–5), and Frans Titelmans accused him of 'bitter irony' (*Responsio ad collationes* LB IX 1010A–B). On the word *donationes* see H.J. de Jonge in ASD IX-2 175:196n.

12:6 [ER *varia* 'varied']

[VG] *differentes* 'different';[1] διάφορα, that is *diversas* [*donationes*], or rather *diversa dona* [diverse gifts].

  1 This appeared as a separate annotation first in 1522.

12:6 [ER *iuxta portionem fidei* 'according to the portion of faith']

[VG] *secundum rationem fidei* 'in accordance with the rule[1] of faith'; κατὰ τὴν ἀναλογίαν, that is, 'in proportion,'[2] so that you understand that the gifts are greater in the degree to which your faith is the more complete. The translator[3] of Origen points out that *ratio* [rule] is not a very apt translation of ἀναλογία [*analogia*], which is a 'corresponding measure' rather than a 'rule.'[4] Certainly[5] Paul has spoken here of the ἀναλογία [proportion (of faith)] in the same sense as he spoke just above of μέτρον [measure (of faith)].[6] Here ' "in proportion to" ' or ' "according to" the portion of faith' would be clearer. For an *analogia* [analogy] is a congruity of one thing in relation to another, as when we say 'the locust has large wings in proportion to its body,' for its wings are small when compared to the wings of butterflies.[7]

  1 It is unclear precisely what meaning Erasmus gave to the Vulgate's *ratio* here. Our translation follows DV.
  2 So Valla *Annot in Rom* 12 (I 859)
  3 The translator ... a 'rule.'] Added in 1519
  4 Origen *Comm in Rom* 9.3 PG 14 1213A–B
  5 Certainly ... butterflies.] Added in 1527
  6 Cf 12:3
  7 For the analogy see Pliny *Naturalis historia* 11.32.95. The connection between the Greek ἀναλογία and the Latin *proportio* is standard; cf Quintilian 1.16.3 and Aulus Gellius 15.9.4.

12:7 [ER *in administratione ... in exhortatione* 'in ministration[1] ... in exhortation']

[VG] *in ministrando et in exhortando* 'in ministering and exhorting.' These are nouns: ἐν τῇ διακονίᾳ, ἐν τῇ παρακλήσει, that is, 'in ministration and in exhortation.' But this point in no way changes the Apostle's meaning. Origen[2] thinks that the clauses [in 12:6–8] can each be referred individually to what preceded [in 12:3], [for example] 'if one has prophecy according to the measure of faith' [12:6], one should not 'think more highly than he ought but in this [be] modest' [12:3], and likewise for the others.[3]

  1 ministration] First in 1519; in 1516, *ministerio* 'ministry'
  2 Origen ... the others.] Added in 1519
  3 Origen *Comm in Rom* 9.3 PG 14 1216C–1217A. Origen refers the other gifts defined in 12:6–8 to the same preceding verse (12:3), so that whatever the gift, 'one should not think more highly than he ought.'

12:9 [ER *sitis odio prosequentes quod malum est* 'turn[1] with hatred upon what is evil']

[VG] *odientes malum* 'hating the evil'; ἀποστυγοῦντες, that is, 'regarding with hatred,' though here it would be neatly [rendered] to say 'shrinking from evil,'[2] to correspond to 'clinging,' which follows.[3] 'Good'[4] and 'evil' here cannot refer to people; since it is τὸ ἀγαθόν [the good, neuter], it must refer to a thing. By 'the good' he meant moral integrity, by 'evil' the morally shameful.

> 1 turn] First in *1519*; in *1516*, without *sitis* 'turning'
> 2 from evil] Added in *1519*
> 3 12:9 continues:
>> ER *adhaerentes ei quod bonum est* 'clinging to that which is good'
>> VG *adhaerentes bono* 'clinging to the good'
> 4 'Good' ... shameful.] Added in *1519*

12:10 [ER *per fraternam charitatem ad mutuo vos diligendos propensi* 'through fraternal charity eager to love each other']

[VG] *charitatem fraternitatis invicem diligentes* 'loving in turn the charity of brotherhood.' The Greek has a different meaning, τῇ φιλαδελφίᾳ εἰς ἀλλήλους φιλόστοργοι, that is, 'with fraternal charity, eager to love each other.' Plutarch wrote an essay entitled Περὶ τῆς ἀδελφίας, that is, 'On Charity among Brothers.'[1] The apostles frequently use this word for the mutual devotion and love among Christians;[2] whence also[3] the Greek compound [φιλαδελφία, *philadelphia*] is formed. Ambrose reads, 'by the love of the brotherhood, kindly disposed to each other.'[4] For in Greek one is said to be φιλόστοργος [*philostorgos*] who has an eager affection for his family and relatives. Conversely, those who are not touched by a feeling of devotion are said to be ἄστοργοι [*astorgoi*]. For by this one word Paul wishes to say that a Christian is dear to a Christian because he is a Christian. Chrysostom[5] thinks that στέργειν [to love] is something more than φιλεῖν [to love],[6] for we love our relatives spontaneously even if they have not obliged us by any service, and though they are disagreeable we still endure and cherish them simply because they are relatives.

I plainly[7] detect a copyist's mistake in a change from *charitate* to *charitatem*: *charitate fraternitatis* [with the charity of brotherhood],[8] that is, loving one another like brothers. The ablative, 'in charity,' corresponds to what follows, 'in honour [*honore*, ablative] anticipating one another,' for the one grows out of the other – kindness out of love.

> 1 See Plutarch *Moralia* 478A–492D, 'On Brotherly Love' in Plutarch's *Moralia* VI trans F.C. Babbitt, Loeb Classical Library (London 1939) 247–325. Though Erasmus translated a number of Plutarch's treatises from Greek into Latin, this was not among them. On Erasmus' translations of Plutarch's *Moral Essays* see Erika Rummel *Erasmus as a Translator of the Classics* (Toronto 1985) 71–81.

2 φιλαδελφία occurs six times in the New Testament Epistles; in those of Paul only here and in 1 Thess 4:9.

3 whence also ... because he is a Christian] Added in *1519*. *Philadelphia* is a compound from *philia* 'love,' 'affection' and *adelphos* 'brother.'

4 Ambrosiaster *Comm in Rom* 12:10

5 Chrysostom ... relatives.] Added in *1535*

6 Cf Chrysostom *Hom in Rom* 21.2 PG 60 605: 'Paul asks ... not merely that we love (φιλεῖν), but that we embrace with affection (στέργειν).'

7 I plainly ... love.] Added in *1527*

8 The Vulgate *charitatem*, accusative, becomes the object of *diligentes*, as in the cue phrase above. The ablative, *charitate*, gives an adverbial phrase: loving one another in the charity of brotherhood.

12:10 [ER *honore alius alium praevenientes* 'in honour anticipating[1] one another']
[VG] *honore invicem praevenientes* 'in honour mutually anticipating'; the sense of the Greek is quite ambiguous, τῇ τιμῇ ἀλλήλους προηγούμενοι. For one[2] προηγεῖται τῇ τιμῇ who excels in honour. And yet the Greeks interpret προηγεῖσθαι here as προλαμβάνειν, that is, 'to anticipate,' or 'to take the lead.'[3] If the text is free from error, it has followed the participle with the accusative case, which is unusual – the genitive would be more suitable because[4] of the preposition πρό. He uses[5] *honor*, meaning *subsidium* [aid]. For[6] it is appropriate to fraternal charity to hasten to be first in a competition with one another in performing services. All the same, the other sense is not unreasonable if we understand 'honour bestowed.' For where there is brotherly love, no one seizes honour for himself, but each rather gives place to the other, in modesty judging another more worthy than himself; and προηγεῖσθαι does not militate against this sense. For ἡγεῖσθαι [to lead] sometimes means 'to judge.' The Latins imitate this in their use of *ducere* [to lead], as in *dignum ducere* [to consider worthy]. Hence one προηγεῖται [judges as preferable] who has a better opinion of another than of himself. Sometimes ἡγεῖσθαι [*hēgeisthai*] means 'to be leader' (hence ἡγεμών [*hēgemōn*] 'prince' [*princeps* 'first one'], or 'governor' [*praeses* 'one set before']); in accordance with this, the Translator has rendered *praevenientes* [going before]. So also Theophylact, who explains προηγεῖσθαι as προφθάνειν, προλαμβάνειν, that is, 'to anticipate.'[7]

1 anticipating] First in *1527*; in the first three editions, *praecedentes* 'preceding.' In his response to Frans Titelmans, who had remarked on the change in the fourth edition, Erasmus said it made little difference which word one used (*Responsio ad collationes* LB IX 1010E).

2 For one ... 'to take the lead.'] Added in *1527*

3 So Theophylact: τὸ προηγεῖσθαι 'is to anticipate one another in bestowing honour' (cf n7 below); but not Chrysostom, who understands the expression to mean 'excelling your neighbour in [bestowing] honour' (*Hom in Rom* 21.3 PG 60 605).

4 because ... πρό] Added in 1535. πρό is a preposition with the genitive, and προηγεῖσθαι is followed by the genitive, though in 'later Greek' by the accusative; cf LSJ.

5 He uses ... *subsidium*.] Added in 1519

6 For ... 'to anticipate.'] This remaining portion of the annotation was added in 1535. These comments of 1535 were already anticipated in Erasmus' response to Titelmans (cf n1 above).

7 Theophylact *Expos in Rom* 12:10 PG 124 508A

12:11 [ER *studio non pigri* 'in zeal[1] not sluggish']

[VG] *sollicitudine non pigri* 'in solicitude not sluggish'; σπουδῇ[2] μὴ ὀκνηροί. By σπουδή he means earnestness and zeal in performing service. One is said to be ὀκνηρός who does something reluctantly. Thus he bids us not only to love and honour one another, but also to hasten promptly and eagerly with mutual aid.

1 First in 1519; in 1516, *diligentia* 'in care'
2 LB adds the article, τῇ σπουδῇ, without warrant, however, from the editions 1516–1527.

12:11 [ER *tempori servientes* 'serving the time'[1]]

[VG] *domino servientes* 'serving[2] the Lord'; Origen, or at least his translator, points out that in some manuscripts 'serving the time' was written and that it could be understood [in the sense that] we must make careful use of the opportunity provided by the time, inasmuch as the time is brief.[3] I think the correct meaning is that we should take it in good part if we meet with some detriment arising from the circumstances of the moment, for that, in my opinion, is 'to serve the time.' What follows – 'rejoicing in hope' – agrees with this: if someone demands a tribute, render it, if someone a tax, pay it; if someone demands an honour, give it; if someone injures you, suffer it – and do not let this make you sad, but let hope give you heart in the midst of troubles. So also[4] 'fervent in spirit,' which precedes. For fervour of spirit despises obstacles and seizes every opportunity for doing good to a neighbour. Ambrose[5] also testifies that he was told the Greek codices read τῷ καιρῷ δουλεύοντες 'serving the time.'[6] And, in passing, I wonder why, when he knew Greek, he did not himself consult the Greek copies.[7] Further,[8] the *Gloss* which is called 'ordinary' points to a double reading, on Bede's authority, I think.[9] St Jerome in one of his letters to Marcella prefers the reading we commonly use, but does not give a single reason for his preference.[10] Each[11] should be free to follow whichever reading he wishes; I favour 'serving the time.'[12] But since this maxim was commonly circulated under the name of a pagan philosopher[13] and seemed to teach a certain cunning, someone took offence and changed it to 'serving the Lord,' not noting carefully enough that 'serving the Lord' does not particularly suit the complete text of this passage. Now although there is no resemblance in the Latin between the words *tempori* and *domino*, there is in the Greek καιρῷ [*kairō* 'time'] and κυρίῳ [*kuriō* 'Lord'] especially[14] since scribes are accustomed to cut syllables short when writing. Chrysostom and Theophylact read and interpret 'serving the Lord' and make the following connection: by loving, honouring, and loving deeply in return, you will offer to the Lord a worship most pleasing; any service[15] rendered to a neighbour reaches the Lord himself.[16]

Chrysostom[17] notes the richness of meaning, or rather the intensification of thought conveyed by the individual words that Paul used here. For he did not say merely μεταδίδοτε, that is, 'share,' but μετὰ δαψιλείας, that is, 'bountifully and eagerly'; nor did he say προίστασθε, that is, 'care for,' but added μετὰ σπουδῆς, that is, 'zealously.' He did not say ἐλεεῖτε, that is, 'show mercy,' but ἀγαπᾶτε 'love,' and that 'without hypocrisy';[18] nor did he say ἀπέχεσθε τῶν κακῶν 'abstain from evil,' but μισεῖτε 'regard with hatred.' It is not ἔχεσθε τῶν ἀγαθῶν 'cling to the good,' but κολλᾶσθε 'stick fast,' nor did he merely say φιλεῖτε [love], but added φιλοστόργως, that is, 'with devoted affection.' He did not say simply σπουδάζετε, that is, 'be attentive,' but also μὴ ὀκνηρῶς, that is, 'not sluggishly,' nor did he say πνεῦμα ἔχοντες, that is, 'having the Spirit,' but πνεύματι ζέοντες, that is, 'fervent in the Spirit.'[19]

1 the time] First in 1519; in 1516, *domino* 'the Lord'
2 serving ... troubles.] Added in 1519, when the annotation was introduced. In 1516 Erasmus' translation had followed the Vulgate. He tells us that 'when he discovered the variant reading, he did not conceal it from the reader.' He apparently thought that Edward Lee wished to take credit for the discovery (cf *Responsio ad annotationes Lei* LB IX 216E–F). For the expression elsewhere in Erasmus see CWE 42 2 n5.
3 Origen *Comm in Rom* 9.10 PG 14 1220A
4 So also ... neighbour.] Added in 1527
5 Ambrose ... Greek copies.] Added in 1519
6 Erasmus is in error here. Ambrosiaster reports that the Greek codices read 'serving the Lord,' but argues, like Erasmus, that this Greek reading does not fit the context. See Ambrosiaster *Comm in Rom* 12:11 (1b).
7 Erasmus seems not to have questioned the Ambrosian authorship of these commentaries until well after 1519, when this addition was inserted (see CWE 42 7 n13). There could be no doubt that Ambrose, bishop of Milan (AD 339–97) knew Greek well. Modern scholarship has wavered on whether Ambrosiaster also knew Greek. He seems to have followed a Latin text of the New Testament, however, and was deeply suspicious of Greek texts (cf *Comm in Rom* 5:14 [4e–5a]). See A. Souter *A Study of Ambrosiaster* (Cambridge 1905) 200, and *The Earliest Latin Commentaries on the Epistles of St Paul* (Oxford 1927) especially 49, 61, 63–6, 84.
8 Further ... preference.] Added in 1522

9 Cf *Biblia cum Glossa ordinaria et expositione Lyre literali et morali nec non Pauli Burgensis additionibus ac Matthiae Thoringi replicis* (Basel 1498) VI fol 27 verso. Originally known in the early Middle Ages simply as the *Glossa*, but later as the *Glossa ordinaria* (no doubt because it had become a standard textbook for biblical exegesis), this work consisted of marginal and interlinear notes, extracted from the Fathers and early medieval writers, on the biblical text. Compiled in the early twelfth century, it was the product of several collaborators, but the central figure was Anselm of Laon, who was principally responsible for the glosses on the Pauline letters. See Beryl Smalley *The Study of the Bible in the Middle Ages* (Oxford 1952) 46–66. In the late fifteenth century the *Gloss* was printed in six volumes along with the *Postilla* of Nicholas of Lyra and the additions by Paul of Burgos and Matthias Doring. For Bede in the *Gloss* and for Erasmus' attitude to the *Gloss* see nn28 and 29 to the Translator's Note by John Bateman in CWE 44. Cf H.J. de Jonge 'Erasmus und die Glossa Ordinaria zum Neuen Testament' *Nederlands Archief voor Kerkgeschiedenis* 56 (1975) 51–77.

10 Jerome *Epistulae* 27.3 CSEL 54 225:17–18

11 Each ... κυρίῳ] Added in *1519*

12 For his Greek text and Latin translation, Erasmus adopted the reading 'supported chiefly by Western witnesses' (Metzger 528) and followed it unambiguously in his paraphrase on the verse (CWE 42 72). Modern interpreters are divided on the more probable correct reading: cf Tischendorf II 431–2 11n; Michel 304; and Cranfield II 634–6.

13 See Cicero *Tusculan Disputations* 3.27.66: 'It is therefore in one's power to cast aside grief, whenever one wishes, "serving the time." Or is there any "time" we should not "serve" for the sake of putting aside our care and concern – since it is in our power?' For a Greek equivalent see the *Greek Anthology* 9.441.6.

14 especially ... pleasing] Added in *1527*

15 any service ... Lord himself] Added in *1535*

16 Chrysostom *Hom in Rom* 21.3 PG 60 605; Theophylact *Expos in Rom* 12:11 PG 124 508B

17 Chrysostom ... Spirit.'] This remaining portion of the annotation was added in *1527*.

18 In these comments on 12:8–11, Erasmus follows Chrysostom closely, but omits at this point what is a full line in the Migne text, which, when inserted, gives here the reading: 'He did not say "show mercy" but "with cheerfulness," he did not say "honour," but "prefer one another," he did not say "love," but "without hypocrisy." '

19 Cf Chrysostom *Hom in Rom* 21.3 PG 60 605.

12:12 [ER *precationi instantes* 'importunate in supplication'[1]]

[VG] *orationi instantes* 'importunate in prayer'; τῇ προσευχῇ προσκαρτεροῦντες, which signifies an unremitting importunity.

1 supplication] First in *1519*; in *1516*, with the Vulgate, 'prayer'

12:13 [ER VG] *necessitatibus sanctorum communicantes* 'sharing[1] in the needs of the saints.'** Ambrose reads 'sharing in the memories of the saints,'[2]

and the translator of Origen acknowledges that so it is found in the Latin manuscripts.[3] It is not entirely improbable that some scribe who had a little education changed [the original] μνείαις [memories] into χρείαις [needs], especially since with 'memories' the expression seemed almost absurd. However, Paul seems to be concerned that those present should not only bestow mutual charity on the others who were present, but should also be mindful of those who were absent – following Paul's action when, in the Epistle to the Galatians, he was admonished by Peter to remember the poor and to collect donations of money.[4] Chrysostom[5] and Theophylact both read and interpret χρείαις, that is, 'needs.'[6] Now [Paul] said 'needs,' not 'luxuries,' and he spoke of 'sharing,' not 'coming to aid,' because there is an exchange between the one who gives and the one who receives, and he who bestows a benefit gains more than the one who receives.[7] Nor yet is it ἀνάγκαις [necessities], but χρείαις, which signifies rather 'to have use for' or 'need of.' I have pointed this out because some think we should not come to the aid of our neighbour except in extreme necessity.

1 sharing ... donations of money.] Added in 1519. In 1516 Erasmus was unaware of the reading 'memory,' which Edward Lee claimed to have pointed out to him (*Responsio ad annotationes Lei* LB IX 216F–217A).

2 Ambrosiaster *Comm in Rom* 12:13. For Ambrosiaster, 'to share in the memory of the saints' is to remember to imitate them, and so, like Paul in Galatians, to be mindful of the poor, that is, to share one's goods with the needy (cf 12:13 [1]). This is a Western reading which, once again, Erasmus refuses to discount; see above, annotation on 12:11 ('serving the Lord') n12. Cf Tischendorf II 432 13n and Cranfield II 638.

3 Origen *Comm in Rom* 9.12 PG 14 1220B

4 Gal 2:10, to which Ambrosiaster also had alluded; cf *Comm in Rom* 12:13 (1a).

5 Chrysostom ... necessity.] Added in 1527

6 Chrysostom, *Hom in Rom* 21.3 PG 60 606; Theophylact *Expos in Rom* 12:13 PG 124 508D

7 Erasmus follows both Chrysostom and Theophylact (cf n6) in thus interpreting κοινωνοῦντες 'sharing in.'

12:14 [ER] *bene loquamini de iis qui vos insectantur* 'speak well of those who assail you']

[VG] *benedicite persequentibus vos* 'bless those[1] who persecute you.' The Greek indeed is εὐλογεῖτε 'bless,' that is, 'speak well of.' The translator of Origen interprets this as 'invoke good upon,'[2] in my opinion because it is followed by μὴ καταρᾶσθε, that is, 'do not call down curses upon.' For those who cannot avenge an injury commonly call down horrible curses on those who have harmed them. In some instances εὐλογεῖν means 'to praise;' here clearly it cannot be taken in that way.[3] For [Paul] does not ask that the assailant be praised, but that we invoke good upon him or warn him of his error with kindly words. Chrysostom[4] appears to

interpret [it] of reproaches, saying μὴ λοιδορήσητε [do not cast reproaches].⁵
I have translated 'speak well of' those who persecute you, to include this
sense as well. Among unbelievers the disciples were ill spoken of, and
he who is disparaged is ill spoken of, and he on whom people invoke
ill. Likewise he who does not disparage 'speaks well' of another, and
he who prays for his enemies 'invokes good upon [them]'; one 'speaks
well' who instructs⁶ without casting reproaches, but from a feeling of
love.

1 bless those ... kindly words.] Added in *1519*, when the annotation was
introduced
2 Origen *Comm in Rom* 9.14 PG 14 1221A
3 Origen says that when one speaks of human beings 'blessing' God, one
means that we 'praise' him. Cf the passage in n2 above.
4 Chrysostom ... love] Added in *1535*
5 Chrysostom *Hom in Rom* 22.1 PG 60 609, where the singular, μὴ λοιδορήσῃς,
rather than the plural, is found. Chrysostom is commenting on the words
'bless and do not curse,' which follow the cue phrase.
6 Latin *docere*, perhaps in the sense of 'correcting'

12:14 [ER *ne male precemini* 'do not invoke evil upon']
[VG] *nolite maledicere* 'do not curse'; μὴ καταρᾶσθε, that is, 'do not invoke
evil upon,' 'do not call down curses upon anyone.' If Paul¹ so pointedly
insists that we do not invoke evil on anyone, where are those who think it
holy to shed the blood of an enemy, or [someone] not even an enemy?

1 If Paul ... enemy?] Added in *1519*

12:15 [ER *gaudete* 'rejoice']
[VG] *gaudere* 'to rejoice'; χαίρειν. In Greek it is customary to use an infinitive
in place of an imperative: 'to rejoice' for 'rejoice,' and 'to weep' for 'weep';
I think¹ because they understand 'it is necessary.' A similar² figure is found
in Latin, especially among the historians: 'to hunt' for 'he was hunting,'
in which one understands 'he is accustomed' or 'he begins.'³ But no Latin
has imitated this [Greek] figure. Chrysostom has observed the order of the
words, holding that 'to rejoice with those who rejoice' is something more
than 'to weep with those who weep,' because calamity wrings pity even from
the unwilling, while good fortune arouses jealousy. Here, too, Chrysostom
speaks as though the superior is customarily placed first.⁴

1 I think ... is necessary'] Added in *1519*
2 A similar ... placed first.] Added in *1527*
3 On the infinitive used as an imperative see Smyth 2013; on the 'historical'
infinitive in Latin see Allen and Greenough 463.
4 Chrysostom *Hom in Rom* 22.1 PG 60 610

12:16 [ER *eodem animo alii in alios affecti* 'having the same mind one towards another']

[VG] *idipsum invicem* [*sentientes*] '[feeling] the same thing in turn'; τὸ αὐτὸ εἰς ἀλλήλους φρονοῦντες, that is, 'holding one another in the same regard,' or 'having the same regard for one another.' This too refers to the attitude of a modest mind, where no one thinks another less than himself, but accommodates himself to all, regards all equally well. For Paul wishes [to say] that among Christians there is a common feeling, so that we measure all not by wealth or birth or learning or honours but by Christ, who is equally common to all. Now the high-born scorns the humble, the rich regards the poor scarcely as human, the educated despises the ignorant, the priest abhors the layman, the monk considers the laity hardly Christian, the Italian spurns and loathes all others as barbarians and almost animals, the German hates the French, the Englishman hates the Scot; and out of these utterly stupid attitudes, and others of the same kind, arise wars and disputes and the widespread turmoil that we have seen for some years now.[1] But Paul wished every Christian to be disposed towards the others in the same way that the individual members of the body are disposed towards the others, as he explains more clearly elsewhere;[2] and this is what he means by τὸ αὐτὸ φρονεῖν [to have the same mind]. Chrysostom and[3] Theophylact[4] speak to the same effect,[5] if anyone is more impressed by authority than by reason.

> 1 On rivalries between nations see *Querela Pacis* CWE 27 305–10. In her brief Introductory Note, Betty Radice sets the *Complaint of Peace* (written in 1516) in the context of Erasmus' major anti-war writings (cf 290–1).
> 2 Cf 1 Cor 12:12–31; Eph 4:15–16; Phil 2:2–5.
> 3 Chrysostom and] Added in *1527*
> 4 Theophylact ... reason] Added in *1519*
> 5 Chrysostom *Hom in Rom* 22.2 PG 60 610; Theophylact *Expos in Rom* 12:16 PG 124 509C

12:16 [ER *arroganter de vobisipsis sentientes* 'having a haughty opinion about yourselves']

[VG] *alta sapientes* 'minding high things.'[1] It is the same participle as before, φρονοῦντες, that is, 'feeling,' or 'thinking'; so that it refers to an attitude of mind.[2] And this clause should be connected with the preceding words, which the Translator has wrongly isolated. For Paul added this as though explaining the words 'feeling the same thing in turn':[3] when someone has a proud opinion of himself and his friends, he may be expected to look down on others.

> 1 In *1516* this annotation followed the annotation below on 12:16 ('do not be prudent'). It was placed in its present position, which reflects the biblical order of clauses, in *1519*.

2 For the definition see the preceding annotation and the annotation on 12:3 ('to be wise unto sobriety') nn9 and 10.

3 Where Erasmus' translation brings the first three clauses of 12:16 into a close relationship, the Vulgate of 1527 had placed a full stop after the first clause. Erasmus' translation reads: 'Having the same mind one towards another, not having a haughty opinion about yourselves, but accommodating yourselves to the humble.' The Vulgate reads: 'Feeling the same thing in turn. Not minding high things, but agreeing with the humble.'

12:16 [ER *sed humilibus vos accomodantes* 'but accommodating yourselves to the humble']

[VG] *sed humilibus consentientes* 'but agreeing with the humble'; τοῖς ταπεινοῖς συναπαγόμενοι. It is not the modest here whom he calls 'the humble,' but persons of lowly station such as the poor, the lowly born, the uneducated, and the common people. And it is not 'agreeing with' but 'complying with' and 'accommodating yourselves to,' so that each one forgets his own proud rank and stoops to the feelings of those below him. This Paul drives home with remarkable assiduity in many passages,[1] well aware that from this source spring life's worst plagues. Paulinus,[2] in his letter to Augustine, reads *humilibus congruere* [to adapt to the humble].[3]

1 See CWE 42 72 n9.
2 Paulinus ... *congruere*.] Added in 1535
3 Paulinus *Epistulae* 4.5 CSEL 29 23:10

12:16 [ER *ne sitis arrogantes* 'do not be haughty']

[VG] *nolite esse prudentes* 'do not be prudent'; φρόνιμοι. By φρόνιμος he means not someone who is wise, but someone with a rather extravagant opinion of himself, as I noted before;[1] and in this way the Greek commentaries interpret.[2] In any case what connection is there between prudence and revenge?[3] But it is arrogance that seeks revenge, when each one thinks he is too good to have[4] to yield to anyone else.

1 Cf the annotation on 12:16 ('minding high things').
2 Chrysostom *Hom in Rom* 22.2 PG 60 610; Theophylact *Expos in Rom* 12:16 PG 124 509D
3 The theme of revenge follows immediately in 12:17-21.
4 to have] Added in 1519

12:17 [ER *provide parantes honesta* 'with forethought furnishing what is honourable']

[VG] *providentes bona* 'providing good things.' The words 'not only before God, but also' are not in the Greek, but only ἐνώπιον πάντων ἀνθρώπων, that is, 'before all people.'[1] Likewise[2] they are not added in Origen, or in Chrysostom or Theophylact;[3] it appears they were added by someone explicating Paul's thought. For Paul here is not setting in contrast human beings and God, but putting together those who are perfect and those who are imperfect, the good and the bad, to all of whom, nevertheless, he wishes us to make ourselves acceptable if possible. And the phrase which follows, εἰ δυνατόν [if it is possible], in my opinion would be more correctly taken with what precedes,[4] since the next clause has its own phrase, τὸ ἐν ὑμῖν [as far as it lies in you], with the same meaning, though[5] others punctuate differently.[6] Whoever added 'not only before God' wanted to fill out the thought, so that Paul would not seem to be content with human praise. I indeed[7] do not criticize this, though we would better leave Scripture with its own integrity, unless pressed by some necessity, of which I see nothing here. For he does not say 'before people,' but 'before all people,' that is, Jews and gentiles, strong and weak. 'Not only before God' is patched on to this thought rather roughly.

1 Erasmus' discussion goes beyond the cue phrase:
  ER *provide parantes honesta in conspectu omnium hominum* 'with forethought furnishing what is honourable in the sight of all'
  VG *providentes bona non tantum coram deo sed etiam coram omnibus hominibus* 'providing the good not only before God but also before all'
2 Likewise ... same meaning] Added in 1519, except for the allusion to Chrysostom, which appeared in 1527
3 Cf Origen *Comm in Rom* 9.20 PG 14 1223A; Chrysostom *Hom in Rom* 22.2 PG 60 611; Theophylact *Expos in Rom* 12:17 PG 124 512A. Though the witnesses differ on the reading here, scholars have generally adopted the reading of Erasmus; cf Tischendorf II 433 17n and Metzger 528.
4 Ie 'with forethought furnishing what is honourable in the sight of all people, if it is possible' – the reading of Jacques Lefèvre d'Etaples (*Pauli epistolae* fol 9 recto). Nevertheless, in all editions of his translation Erasmus follows the Vulgate in taking this phrase with what follows. In his paraphrase, however, the phrase is taken with what precedes; see CWE 42 72–3.
5 though ... human praise] Added in 1527
6 Cf eg Ambrosiaster *Comm in Rom* 12:18 (2) and Chrysostom *Hom in Rom* 22.2 PG 60 611. The Greek τὸ ἐν ὑμῖν is evidently a slip for τὸ ἐξ ὑμῶν, the correct reading, and the reading of the Greek text in all the lifetime editions.
7 I indeed ... roughly] Added in 1535

12:19 [ER *ulciscentes* 'taking revenge']

[VG] *defendentes* 'defending'; ἐκδικοῦντες, that is, 'avenging.'[1] It is the participle of the verb whose noun analogue is ἐκδίκησις, which [the Translator] has rendered *vindicta* [vengeance]. However,[2] *defendere* is frequently used among churchmen for *ulcisci*. In any case defence is permitted to Christians, if 'to defend' is to avert injury, with the restriction that the defence made is without blame.

1 Latin *vindicantes*. In the next sentence, Erasmus follows Valla, who preferred *vindicantes* to the Vulgate's *defendentes* because it retained the same relation in Latin between noun and participle as in the Greek (see *Annot in Rom* 12 [I 859]). Jacques Lefèvre d'Etaples also preferred *vindicantes* and so translated (*Pauli epistolae* fol 9 verso and fol 98 recto).
2 However ... without blame.] Added in *1535*

12:19 [ER *dilecti* 'beloved']

[VG] *charissimi* 'most dear';[1] ἀγαπητοί, that is, 'beloved.'[2] He added this, wishing to persuade as though with flattery, since otherwise it would be hard for one[3] who has been provoked by an injury to forego vengeance.

1 In all editions from *1516* to *1535*, a new annotation begins at this point, though LB includes it in the previous annotation ('defending').
2 Cf the annotation on 11:28 ('but according to the election most dear') and n1. Here, too, Lefèvre preferred *dilecti* 'beloved' (*Pauli epistolae* fol 98 recto).
3 for one ... vengeance] Added in *1535*

12:19 [ER *mihi ultio* 'vengeance is mine']

[VG] *mihi vindictam* 'revenge is mine'; ἐμοὶ ἐκδίκησις, that is, 'revenge (or, vengeance) is mine,' in the nominative case.[1] It is so cited by Jerome in the letter against Rufinus that begins 'Having read the letter of your wisdom.'[2] In the thirty-second chapter of Deuteronomy, from which this passage is taken, it is explicated with greater clarity: 'Vengeance is mine,' that is, 'It is mine to exact retribution' – for I am judge.[3] The Greek codices do not add ['and'] – 'and I will repay' – but [read] 'I will repay,' without the conjunction,[4] as[5] it was written in the very old codex at Constance.

1 So Valla *Annot in Rom* 12 (I 859). The Vulgate's accusative case has no support in the Greek manuscript tradition, though it is found in most of the Latin manuscripts; cf Tischendorf II 433 19n and Wordsworth and White II 130 19n.
2 For *vindicta*, cited in the nominative, see *Apologia adversus libros Rufini* 3.1 PL 23 (1883) 479A. The third book *Against Rufinus* begins with the words 'Having read the letter of your wisdom' (ie 'your Grace's letter').
3 Deut 32:35–41
4 Valla, too, had noted the absence in the Greek of any conjunction (*Annot in Rom* 12 [I 859]). The conjunction appears, however, in the Vulgate of Deut 32:35. The evidence for the conjunction here in 12:19 is weak in both the Greek and Latin manuscript tradition; cf Tischendorf II 433 19n and Wordsworth and White II 130 19n.
5 as ... Constance] Added in *1527*

12:20 [ER *pasce illum* 'feed him']

[VG] *ciba illum* 'give him to eat'; ψώμιζε. The word does indeed have a special significance. For ψωμίζειν is not simply 'to feed,' but 'to feed indulgently,'

as though with bread in delicate bits, or with food in refined morsels. Some
do this for favoured guests, allowing others, meanwhile, to go hungry.[1]

> 1 A complaint common in classical antiquity; cf Juvenal *Satires* 5; Pliny *Letters*
> 2.6; Martial *Epigrams* 3.60, 6.11; and Lucian *De mercede conductis* 26.

12:20 [ER *si sitit da illi potum* 'if he thirst, give him a drink']

[VG] *si sitit potum da illi* 'if[1] he thirst, give a drink to him.' This was not
added in some of the Greek manuscripts.[2] It is not sufficiently clear from
Origen what he read;[3] it is added in Ambrose,[4] and likewise in the old
manuscripts; also[5] in Theophylact and Chrysostom.[6] But in the word 'food'
drink, too, is included.

> 1 if ... old manuscripts.] Added in *1519*
> 2 Only a few Greek manuscripts omit these words; cf Tischendorf II 433 20n.
> 3 Origen *Comm in Rom* 9.23 PG 14 1224B–C. Though the passage is cited in the
> Latin text that introduces Origen's comments here, the words do not appear
> in his commentary on 12:20.
> 4 Ambrosiaster *Comm in Rom* 12:20
> 5 also ... included] Added in *1527*
> 6 Theophylact *Expos in Rom* 12:20 PG 124 512C; Chrysostom *Hom in Rom* 22.3
> PG 60 612

12:20 [ER *coacervabis in caput* 'you will heap upon the head']

[VG] *congeres super caput* 'you will bring together[1] above the head'; σω-
ρεύσεις, that is, 'you will load up' or 'heap.' And 'coals of fire' is a Hebrew
figure meaning 'burning coals,'[2] which[3] Theophylact interprets thus: 'Do
you want a glorious revenge upon your enemy? Load kindness upon him,
for so God will punish him the more terribly.'[4] It seems to me more suitable
to Christian teaching if we understand that an enemy is to be overcome by
acts of kindness, so that at length he will repent; won by our favours and
our gentleness, the enemy will become a friend.[5]

> 1 The Latin *congero* 'carry or bring together' is also used in the sense of
> 'construct,' 'build up,' 'heap up.' Erasmus' *coacervo* conveys more definitively
> the image of the 'heap.'
> 2 For the 'Hebrew figure' see the annotation on 1:4 ('through the spirit of
> sanctification') and n3.
> 3 which ... friend] Added in *1519*
> 4 Theophylact *Expos in Rom* 12:20 PG 124 512D
> 5 So Origen *Comm in Rom* 1.23 PG 14 1225A; cf the paraphrase on 12:20 CWE 42
> 73.

12:21 [ER *ne vincaris a malo* 'be not overcome by evil']

[VG] *noli vinci a malo* 'do not be overcome by evil.' 'Good' and 'evil' do not
refer here to a wicked or an upright person but indicate kindness itself or

injury. Thus one is overcome by evil who does not restrain his spirit when provoked by injury but is driven to retaliate. One overcomes evil with good who repays evil deeds with good deeds, causing his enemy to repent and become his friend.

This precept, since the human disposition would find it difficult, Paul added with the authority of the Lord – 'says the Lord.'[1] Christ, too, enjoined the same in the Gospel.[2] And yet somehow those who very much think themselves Christians not only neglect this teaching but even laugh at it openly; and those whose ears – pious, no doubt – do not bear to hear censured even the superstitious cult of Christopher, Barbara, or Erasmus do not scruple to raise a laugh at these most holy precepts of Christ.[3] And what Socrates taught the heathen before Christ,[4] which was handed down by Christ himself and inculcated so many times by the apostles, Christians laugh at, although Christ distinguished his own from the world chiefly by this mark of identity. But this is not the place for such a lament.

From[5] this chapter St Augustine offers an example of the middle style as well as of measured diction.[6] Certainly there is scarcely another passage in Paul better ordered and, so to speak, more patterned. To point out only the more outstanding examples, how much dignity that *distributio* has – for so the rhetoricians designate [the figure] wherein each [in a series] is given its appropriate correspondent:[7] 'Having gifts that differ according to the grace given to us: whether prophecy, according to the measure of faith; or ministry, in ministering; one who teaches, in teaching; one who exhorts, in exhorting; one who contributes, in simplicity; one who presides, in solicitude; one who has pity, in cheerfulness.' The rest follows with the same pleasant measures, continuing until the period in two parts, 'not minding high things, but agreeing with the humble.' Meanwhile, there is much charm in the repetition of the same words in different forms, or of similar words of like sound,[8] likewise by the juxtaposition of opposites. Examples of the former are: 'rejoice with those who rejoice,' and 'evil for evil.' There is ἐναντίωσις [juxtaposition of opposites][9] in 'weep with those who weep, rejoice with those who rejoice,' and likewise in 'bless and do not curse' and 'do not be overcome by evil, but overcome evil with good' and 'minding high things, agreeing with the humble.' The passage is so modulated by clauses and phrases of equal length, by similar end-rhythms and word-endings, that no song could be more pleasant. But I do not intend to delay by pursuing this further, lest I wear out the reader and at the same time seem to digress from the matter in hand.

1 'says the Lord'] Added in 1527. The words are found in 12:19.
2 Cf Luke 6:27–35.
3 Christopher, Barbara, and Erasmus are three of the fourteen 'auxiliary'

saints (also known as the Holy Helpers) who enjoyed widespread popular veneration throughout the Middle Ages for the efficacy of their prayers on behalf of human necessities. There is considerable confusion between Erasmus (St Elmo), patron saint of those suffering from intestinal ailments, of women in labour, and of seamen, whose legend derives from a fourth-century martyr, and St Elmo (thirteenth century), patron of seamen. Barbara is the patron saint of those engaged in trades involving liability to sudden death, especially therefore of soldiers, and is protectress against thunderstorms, lightning, and fire. Christopher is the patron of travellers.

Erasmus repeatedly criticized the cult of saints in his day. Barbara and Christopher appear in his critique in rule 4 of the *Enchiridion* (see CWE 66 63) and again in the *Colloquia*, where the veneration of saints is satirized (see Thompson *Colloquies* 14–15, 141–2, 355). In the *Moria* Erasmus attacked the popular veneration of Christopher, Barbara, and Erasmus, where the latter, however, appears (possibly as a personal joke) as the helper of those who pray for riches (see CWE 27 114, 118). Erasmus explained and defended his criticisms of the veneration of saints in *Apologia adversus rhapsodias Alberti Pii* LB IX 1162B–3D.

4 Cf Plato *Crito* 49C–E; *Republic* 1 335B–E.

5 From ... hand.] This entire remaining portion of the annotation was added in *1527*.

6 Augustine *De doctrina christiana* 4.20.40 PL 34 107–8

7 For the *distributio*, see *Ecclesiastes* III LB V 1003F–1004B; also *Rhetorica ad Herennium* 4.35.47; Lausberg I 675.

8 Cf the annotation on 8:35 ('who therefore will separate us') and n13. The examples Erasmus gives here are more obvious in Latin than in English: *gaudere cum gaudentibus, malum pro malo* 'rejoice with those who rejoice,' 'evil for evil.' Though Erasmus illustrates the figures from the Vulgate from which he quotes, they are present also in the Greek text.

9 For this figure see the annotation on 2:8 ('do not give assent to') n2. For the significance of Erasmus' stylistic analysis of this passage see Robert D. Sider 'Erasmus on the Epistle to the Romans: A Literary Reading' in *Acta Conventus Neo-Latini Torontonensis* Medieval and Renaissance Texts and Studies (Binghamton 1991) 132–5.

CHAPTER 13

13:1 [ER VG] *omnis anima* 'every¹ soul.' He said 'every soul,' meaning every person. Origen's philosophizing here seems to me more clever than true: a person is called 'soul' with reference to the part inferior to the spirit, just as he is called 'flesh' with reference to his worse part;² consequently the 'soul' is understood to be the person who is not entirely free from the things of the world, and for this reason rightly ought to obey those who administer the affairs of the world.³ It is perhaps through the error of the copyists that the reading of Ambrose is different from ours: 'Be subject to all the higher powers.'⁴

> 1 every ... powers.'] The entire annotation was added in 1519.
> 2 For this Origenistic anthropological trichotomy elsewhere see the *Enchiridion* CWE 66 51
> 3 Origen *Comm in Rom* 9.25 PG 14 1226A–C
> 4 Ambrosiaster *Comm in Rom* 13:1. Compare the three versions:
> ER *omnis anima potestatibus supereminentibus subdita sit* 'let every soul be subject to the powers that stand over us'
> VG *omnis anima potestatibus sublimioribus subdita sit* 'let every soul be subject to the higher powers'
> Ambrosiaster *omnibus potestatibus sublimioribus subditi estote* 'be subject to all the higher powers'

13:1 [ER *supereminentibus* 'that stand over¹ (us)']
[VG] *sublimioribus* 'higher'; ὑπερεχούσαις, that is, 'are pre-eminent.' It is a positive, not a comparative.² For³ he is thinking of those who are granted the public authority, like that of kings, governors, and magistrates. The comparative, which the Latin Translator has used, makes it possible for someone to take this sense also: kings and governors must be obeyed, but not the lower magistrates. The word that he here translated by *sublimior* [higher] he rendered by *praecellens* [pre-eminent] in the second chapter of First Peter: εἴτε βασιλεῖ ὡς ὑπερέχοντι 'whether to a king as standing over' [2:13].

> 1 that stand over] The translation from 1522; in 1516 and 1519, *excellentibus* 'that are elevated above [us].' For the full text see the preceding annotation, n4.
> 2 In 1529 Erasmus acknowledged to Titelmans that the prefix ὑπερ- gave the Greek word the force of a comparative, a force caught in a word like 'pre-eminent.' Paul wants us to obey magistrates because they are pre-eminent in their public authority (*Responsio ad collationes* LB IX 1011A–B).
> 3 For ... standing over.'] Added in 1535

13:1 [ER *quae vero sunt potestates a deo* 'but the powers which are, by God'[1]]
[VG] *quae autem sunt a deo* 'those, however, which are from God.'[2] The
Greek punctuates differently: αἱ δὲ οὖσαι ἐξουσίαι, ὑπὸ θεοῦ τεταγμέναι εἰσίν,
that is, 'but the powers which are, have been ordained by God,' putting the
comma after *potestates.*[3] For he reiterates what he had said just before, 'there
is no power except from God.' Ambrose[4] so reads and interprets: 'But those
which are, have been ordained [*ordinatae*] by God.'[5] Again,[6] [commenting]
on the third chapter of Luke: ' "But," says he, "those which are, have been
ordained [*ordinatae*] by God; not given, but ordained." '[7] So[8] also do the
very oldest manuscripts punctuate, specifically[9] the one supplied by the
college of the church of Constance.[10] Again, in my copy, in old type,[11] and
in the codex of Constance, the reading is *ordinatae*, not *ordinata*, so that the
latter appears to be a corruption of the copyists.[12] Augustine[13] construes
similarly when he cites this text in Letter 54, to Macedonius, except that he
does not repeat the word 'powers.' He reads: 'For there is no power except
from God, but those which are, have been ordained by God,' so that a
comma follows the word 'are.'[14] Theophylact does not repeat 'powers' ('[the
powers] which are from God, have been ordained'); but [he writes] in such
a way that he intends it to be understood.[15] It[16] is repeated in Chrysostom.[17]
And yet[18] in Origen I find nothing of these two short clauses; not even in
his interpretation is there any mention of the matter.[19] One might think that
it was added by some interpreter who, wishing to establish firmly that all
power is from God, expressed the same idea again, achieving emphasis in
a progressive sequence – 'Accordingly, those who resist, resist the ordering
of God'[20] – [and so] leading to what will then follow; though Chrysostom
and[21] Theophylact, as I[22] have just said, construe in my way.

Paul was aware that some Christians, under the pretext of religion,
were refusing the orders of their rulers, and that as a result the established
order would be upset and all things thrown into disarray. Therefore he
taught that they should obey any one at all entrusted with public authority
– making exception for the interests of faith and piety. True, these very
rulers are pagan and evil; but order is still good, and for the sake of this,
the godly[23] must sometimes bear even bad rulers.[24]

Chrysostom[25] noted ὑποτασσέσθω [be subject to]: 'For he did not say,
πειθέσθω, which is simply "obey," but "be subject to." '[26] For[27] πείθεσθαι is
used of those who obey when persuaded, that is, who heed what is said ([a
sense] the Greeks convey by a single word, πειθαρχεῖν); but ὑποτάσσονται
[are subject] is used of slaves as well. The Apostle then, requires of Christians that they should comply even with tyrants and bear them: when, for
example, a tyrant says 'Go to prison,' they should go; [if he says] 'Submit
your neck,' they should do so.

The word[28] 'soul'[29] is more expressive than the word 'person' – let no one at all think himself exempt from obedience to rulers, whether he is an apostle or a prophet. [Chrysostom] has also observed that he said, not 'all rulers,' but '[all] power' has been ordained by God, just as marriage is from God, but God does not join all partners in marriage.[30]

1 In Erasmus' translation the sentence concludes with the words *ordinatae sunt* 'have been ordained.'
2 The Vulgate printed in 1527 concluded *ordinata sunt* 'have been ordained.' For *ordinata* instead of *ordinatae*, see n12 below.
3 The annotation presupposes a Vulgate reading that placed the comma after 'God': *quae autem sunt a deo, ordinata sunt* 'those, however, which are from God, have been ordained.' However, the Vulgate of 1527 punctuates as Erasmus wishes: 'those, however, which are, have been ordained by God.' Wordsworth and White cite three early editions of the Vulgate (published in 1476, 1481, and 1502) with the former punctuation, and three editions (published in 1531, 1534, and 1534) with the latter; cf II 130–1 1n.
4 Ambrose ... God.'] This sentence was added in 1519.
5 Ambrosiaster *Comm in Rom* 13:1 (1)
6 Again ... but ordained." '] Added in 1527
7 The reference is to the commentary by Ambrose of Milan (on Luke 4:6, not Luke 3), *Expositio evangelii secundum Lucam* 4.29 *Sources chrétiennes* 45 161. For the false identification of Ambrosiaster, the author of the *Commentary on Romans*, with Ambrose of Milan see the annotation on 12:11 ('serving the Lord') and n7.
8 So ... punctuate] Added in 1519
9 specifically ... copyists] Added in 1527
10 In September 1522, Erasmus visited Constance on the invitation of his friend, John Botzheim, canon of the cathedral (Allen Ep 1315 introduction), and presumably had an opportunity then to view the New Testament manuscripts housed in the chapter library. Later, in 1526, when he was preparing the fourth edition of his New Testament (1527), Botzheim sent to him from Constance two manuscripts (now lost) of the Epistles (cf Allen Epp 373 introduction and 1761:12–13 and 10n). See John Wordsworth *Old Latin Biblical Texts* 5 vols (Oxford 1883–1907) 1 (1883) 52–3.
11 See the annotation 5:8 ('since if') and n6 for an allusion to what is apparently the same copy.
12 The 1527 addition that concludes here raises, beyond the question of punctuation, a further problem: are we to read *ordinata*, with the Vulgate, or *ordinatae*? As it stands in the Vulgate printed in 1527, *ordinata* can be read as a neuter participle in agreement with the neuter pronoun *quae*: those (things) which are, have been ordained by God. If we read *ordinatae*, *quae* will be feminine, referring to 'powers': 'Those (powers) which are, have been ordained by God.'
Ambrosiaster had been cited in 1519 as a witness to the proper punctuation of this sentence (n5 above). Erasmus had at that time quoted Ambrosiaster as reading *ordinatae* '[those powers which] have been ordained.' In fact, however, Ambrosiaster reads with the Vulgate *ordinata* 'those [things] which

have been ordained.' But Erasmus never corrected in subsequent editions his *1519* quotation of *ordinatae*. Instead, in *1527* he inserted a citation from 'Ambrose' on Luke which verified, both in respect to punctuation and to the feminine *ordinatae*, the reading from Ambrosiaster as cited, and so he argued that *ordinata* was a copyist's mistake.

Though a minority of Latin manuscripts support *ordinata*, the preferred reading is, as Erasmus wishes, *ordinatae* (cf Wordsworth and White II 130–1 1n).

13 Augustine ... understood.] Added in *1519*
14 Augustine *Epistulae* 153.6.19 CSEL 44 417
15 Theophylact *Expos in Rom* 13:1 PG 124 513B–C. Erasmus cites Theophylact here on yet another textual problem, whether *potestates* is to be repeated, making no comment in *1519* on the punctuation. The punctuation, as Erasmus cites Theophylact (from *1519* to *1535*), supports the Vulgate presupposed by the annotation. It is clear, however, from the commentary, that Theophylact construed the passage (as did Chrysostom, from whom he took much), with the punctuation adopted by Erasmus: 'Any power you might consider,' writes Theophylact, 'has been ordained by God' (513C).
In both Greek text and Latin translation Erasmus repeated the word 'powers' in 13:1C. The preferred reading, however, does not repeat the word; cf Tischendorf II 434 1n.
16 It ... Chrysostom.] Added in *1527*
17 Chrysostom *Hom in Rom* 23.1 PG 60 615
18 And yet ... then follow] Added in *1519*
19 Cf Origen *Comm in Rom* 9.26–7 PG 14 1226C–1227B
20 Rom 13:2. This quotation becomes the third step in the progression Erasmus envisions: 1/ there is no power except from God; 2/ the powers which are, have been ordained by God; 3/ accordingly those who resist, resist the ordering of God. It is the two clauses of the second that Origen's text omits, leading Erasmus to suggest that they were added to give a more emphatic sequence.
21 Chrysostom and] Added in *1527*
22 as I have just said] Added in *1535*
23 the godly] Added in *1519*. In the Latin, the construction is in the passive, 'bad rulers must be borne by the godly.'
24 The point of view found in this paragraph is expressed in the paraphrase on this verse; cf CWE 42 73–4 and (for Erasmus' attitude to governmental authority generally) nn1 and 2.
25 Chrysostom ... "be subject to." '] Added in *1527*
26 Chrysostom *Hom in Rom* 23.1 PG 60 615
27 For ... should do so.] Added in *1535*
28 The word ... marriage.] Added in *1527*
29 Erasmus returns here to the word 'soul' already discussed in the first annotation on 13:1 ('every soul').
30 Chrysostom *Hom in Rom* 23.1 PG 60 615. Chrysostom explains that God ordains all power, though he has not necessarily ordained all rulers (eg bad rulers); marriage, like power, is a divine institution, but one ought not to blame God for bad marriages.

In his annotation on 1 Cor 7:39 (*liberata est a lege, cui autem vult, nubat*) LB VI 698D–E Erasmus argued that some marriages were joined not by God but by the devil, and so for bad marriages the church should permit divorce.

13:2 [ER *iudicium accipient* 'will receive judgment']
[VG] *damnationem acquirunt* '**get damnation**'; λήψονται, that is, 'will receive,' in the future tense.[1] But κρῖμα, that is, 'judgment,' is well rendered by *damnatio* [damnation].[2]

> 1 So Valla *Annot in Rom* 13 (1 859), though Lee objected (*Responsio ad annotationes Lei* LB IX 217B)
> 2 For his own translation, however, Erasmus adopted an idiom already recommended by Lefèvre: *iudicium accipient* (*Pauli epistolae* fol 100 recto).

13:3 [ER *non terrori sunt bene agentibus* '**are not for inspiring terror in those who do well**']
[VG] *non sunt timori boni operis* '**are not for the fear of good work**'; οὐκ εἰσὶ φόβος τῶν ἀγαθῶν ἔργων, that is, 'are not the terror' or 'the fear of good works,'[1] that is, they are not to be feared by those who behave well. For[2] [rulers] restrain not from good but from evil deeds.

> 1 Valla offered a similarly literal translation (*Annot in Rom* 13 [1 859]); however, the preferred reading is not a genitive plural 'of good works,' but a dative singular 'to good work' (cf Tischendorf II 434 and 3n and RSV).
> 2 For ... evil deeds.] Added in 1519

13:4 [ER VG] *dei enim minister est* '**for he is God's minister**'; διάκονος, that is, 'agent' – for he is talking about power. And yet, just as the one who acts as a magistrate sometimes goes by the name of his magistracy, so one who is entrusted with power goes by the name of the 'power.'[1] And[2] the Greek adds the pronoun σοί [for you]. 'He is God's minister, but for your good,' so there is little reason why you should fear or hate.

> 1 A reference to the term 'power' ('authority' RSV) in 13:3
> 2 And ... hate.] Added in 1527

13:5 [ER *quapropter oportet esse subditos* '**wherefore you**[1] **ought to be subject**']
[VG] *ideoque necessitati subditi estote* '**and on this account be subject to**[2] **necessity.**' The sense of the Greek is different: διὸ ἀνάγκη ὑποτάσσεσθαι 'hence it is necessary to be subject.' The Translator seems to have read ὑποτάσσεσθε [imperative form, 'be subject'] (with an epsilon, not the diphthong αι [infinitive form]). However, if ὑποτάσσεσθε is ὁριστικόν [indicative], it will give the same sense as the infinitive,[3] since[4] the infinitive is used instead of the indicative. Indeed in Ambrose one finds no word at all

for 'necessity.'[5] Origen, in his usual way, twists this necessity to apply only to those who are not yet entirely spiritual.[6] In my opinion, however, rulers should be borne by the rest also so that [the rulers] are not provoked, at the risk of the calamitous ruin of the commonwealth – and this, if I am not mistaken, he calls 'necessity.' By 'wrath'[7] he means (following Hebrew idiom) the vengeance and punishment by which crimes are chastised. 'Conscience' can be taken in two ways, [the conscience] either of the person who does not obey the one God wants him to obey, or of the person who through your example thinks he ought to disregard a magistrate to whom he finds you heedless, and wrongly imitates you who (rightly) do not pay heed. Augustine interprets 'necessity' as the authority which rulers exercise in seizing the property[8] of their subjects.[9]

This,[10] too, I shall not conceal, that in Theophylact and Chrysostom the words διὸ ἀνάγκη ὑποτάσσεσθαι [therefore it is necessary to be subject] have been inserted to connect the text above with that below: he is the minister of God [13:4]; therefore one should obey him [13:5a] – as I [Paul] had at the first [13:1] begun to say.[11] Since, however, these words, 'not only because of wrath' [13:5b] etc, seemed because of the length of the intervening passage [13:1b–4] to join rather roughly with what had preceded – 'let every soul be subject' [13:1a] – someone repeated the earlier clause[12] to give a smoother sequence of thought. Anyone will see the truth of this who inspects the very old and carefully written codex supplied to me by the Dominican college of Basel[13] and the codex of Chrysostom, which has aided me in writing this.[14] Nevertheless I do not find fault, but praise what was done.

1 you] First in 1519; in 1516, oportet esse subditum 'one ought to be subject'
2 to] First in 1519; in 1516, in place of necessitati, the cue phrase read necessitate 'by necessity,' the reading of the Vulgate printed in 1527. On the two readings, the Latin witnesses are divided; cf Wordsworth and White II 131 n5.
3 If the verb is read as an infinitive, ὑποτάσσεσθαι, the sense must be 'it is necessary to be subject.' However, by changing the final αι to ε we have the form ὑποτάσσεσθε, which can represent either the imperative or the indicative. The Translator understood the verb as an imperative, reading 'be subject to [1516 cue phrase, 'by'] necessity'; however, if the same form is read as an indicative, the meaning will be 'you are, by necessity, subject,' and this yields the same sense as the infinitive.
4 since ... their subjects] Added in 1519
5 Ambrosiaster Comm in Rom 13:5. But Ambrosiaster's text is, in fact, ambiguous; see CSEL 81/1 420:12 and 421:9n and 11.
Some witnesses support the omission of ἀνάγκη, but the preferred reading includes this word. See Metzger 529 and Wordsworth and White II 131 5n.
6 Origen Comm in Rom 9.30: 'Those who are still of the world ... who seek the things of the flesh, are of necessity subject to the ministers of the world' (PG 14 1230A)

7 Erasmus turns here to the second part of 13:5, 'not only on account of wrath, but also on account of conscience.' His translation follows, substantially, that of the Vulgate: *non solum propter iram, sed* [ER *verum*] *etiam propter conscientiam.*

8 Augustine *Expositio quarundam propositionum ex epistula ad Romanos* 74 PL 35 2084. Augustine urges us not to resist those with authority to take our 'temporal goods' because our 'subjection stands not in goods that last, but in things "necessary" for our present life.'

9 their subjects] In *1535* only; until then, *suorum* 'their people'

10 This ... done.] This remaining portion of the annotation was added in *1527*.

11 Chrysostom does not comment specifically on 13:5a, but only on the phrase 'not only on account of anger' (13:5b); he introduces his exposition of this phrase by a summary reference to 13:1–4. Theophylact's commentary, however, clearly presupposes the presence of the clause in question (13:5a). See Chrysostom *Hom in Rom* 23.2 PG 60 617; Theophylact *Expos in Rom* 13:5 PG 124 516C.

12 Ie someone added the clause 'wherefore it is necessary to be subject' [13:5a] to recall the earlier clause 'let every soul be subject' [13:1a]

13 On this manuscript, see the annotation on 5:11 ('but we boast also') n1.

14 By August 1526 Erasmus had acquired a manuscript of Chrysostom's *Homilies on Romans* (Allen Ep 1736:22–4) which he used for the 1527 edition of his New Testament. According to Allen the manuscript was a copy made for Erasmus from a manuscript found at Ladenburg, apparently from the library of Johann von Dalberg (Ep 2258:6n). For Dalberg's library see *Contemporaries* I 374.

13:6 [ER *in hoc ipsum incumbentes* '**devoting themselves to this very end**']
[VG] *in hoc ipsum servientes* '**serving to this very end**'; προσκαρτεροῦντες. A little before, he had translated this word by *instantes* [pressing],[1] now he renders it 'serving.' I have translated it by *incumbentes*, that is, paying close attention and striving. Augustine[2] supports me when he cites this passage in the fourth book *On Christian Doctrine*, chapter 20, where he reads *in hoc ipso perseverantes* [persevering in this very thing].[3]

    1 Cf Rom 12:12 and the annotation there ('importunate in prayer').
    2 Augustine ... *perseverantes.*] Added in *1519*
    3 Augustine *De doctrina christiana* 4.20.40 PL 34 108

13:8 [ER VG] *nemini quicquam debeatis* '**owe no one anything**'; ὀφείλετε. It is unclear whether this is indicative, 'you owe,' or imperative, 'owe.'[1] The sense of the passage is ambiguous in the Greek, for it can be taken thus: 'Pay to each person what you owe, and after you have paid it, you cease to owe. On the other hand love would not cease to be owed, but would always be paid, and nonetheless always owed, so that there might be no end of doing good.' Origen, Chrysostom,[2] and Theophylact expound [the passage] in this way.[3] It can also be understood in such a way that the previous words refer to magistrates who were pagan, as they all were at that time; what follows[4] – [owe] no one anything etc – refers to Christians: 'Pay them [the magistrates] what you owe, but a Christian owes a Christian nothing except mutual love.' Ambrose[5] adopted this sense in the explication: 'He wishes us to have peace, if possible, with all; but with our brothers, love [as well].'[6]

Augustine has observed the pleasing effect of the phrasing, the order of ideas, the neat correspondence of pairs, the measured course of the language: tribute to whom tribute; tax to whom tax; fear to whom fear; honour to whom honour [13:7]. 'And these words distributed into separate pairs,' [Augustine] says, 'are concluded also by a period[7] which itself has two parts: ' "owe no one anything, except to love one another." '[8] In this,[9] too, there is much that is pleasant: in the equal length of clauses, in the asyndeton,[10] and the transposition of the same noun;[11] also, finally, from the repetition[12] of the initial pronoun, 'to whom, to whom, to whom.'

1 In the second person plural, as here, the Greek imperative and indicative (in the active voice) have the same forms, and are distinguished by the context. Erasmus has noted the same ambiguity in the passive voice; cf eg the annotations on 12:2.

2 Chrysostom] Added in *1527*

3 Cf Origen *Comm in Rom* 9.30 PG 14 1231A; Chrysostom *Hom in Rom* 23.3 PG 60 618; Theophylact *Expos in Rom* 13:8 PG 124 517B–C. The 'passage' under discussion is Rom 13:7–8.

4 The 'previous words' refer to 13:7: 'Pay to everyone what is owed: tribute to whom tribute is owed, tax to whom tax, fear to whom fear, honour to whom honour'; 'what follows,' to 13:8: 'Owe no one anything except to love one another, for the one who loves another has fulfilled the Law.'

5 Ambrose ... love one another,'] Added in *1519*

6 Ambrosiaster *Comm in Rom* 13:8 (1)

7 Quintilian distinguishes the period (*circuitus*) from the *comma* and the *colon*, both of which were parts of a sentence. The period consisted either of a single thought rounded out to a close, or (as here) of several thoughts expressed in a balanced way and brought to a conclusion (Quintilian 9.4.122–4); cf Cicero *Orator* 61.204 and Lausberg I 923.

8 Augustine *De doctrina christiana* 4.20.40 PL 34 108

9 In this ... to whom.'] Added in *1527*

10 For asyndeton see eg the annotation on 1:31 ('apart from contract').

11 *traductio*, for which see the annotation on 10:3 ('and seeking to set up their [righteousness']) n3. In the sequence of 13:7 the same noun is 'transposed' from the first to the second clause in each pair – 'tribute to whom tribute' etc.

12 Roman rhetoricians regarded *repetitio* as a figure capable of conveying important effects. See *Rhetorica ad Herennium* 4.13.19 and Quintilian 9.1.33, and, for a noteworthy example, Cicero *Pro Caecina* 9.24. Cf also *Ecclesiastes* III LB V 990F–991A.

13:8 [ER *nam qui diligit alterum* 'for one who loves the other']

[VG] *qui enim diligit proximum* 'for one who loves his neighbour'; ὁ γὰρ ἀγαπῶν τὸν ἕτερον, that is, 'for one who loves the other.' The Translator seems to have read τὸν πλησίον [his neighbour]. But[1] this is of small importance to the sense.

1 But ... sense.] Added in 1519

13:9 [ER *siquidem illa, non moechaberis* 'for with respect to those (commandments): you shall not commit adultery'[1]]

[VG] *nam non adulterabis* 'for you shall not commit adultery.' As just above so here he has not conveyed the force of the Greek article: εἰ μὴ τὸ ἀγαπᾶν, which I expressed by 'except this, that you love one another,'[2] and: τὸ γὰρ οὐ μοιχεύσεις 'for with respect to those [commandments], you shall not commit adultery'[3] etc.

1 commit adultery] From 1516 to 1522 Erasmus printed *adulteraberis. Adulterare* is the standard word in classical prose for 'to commit adultery.' *Moechor*, also 'to commit adultery,' appears in poets and later Latin; cf the annotation on Matt 5:27 (*moechatus est eam*) – on which see Rummel *Erasmus' 'Annotations'* 45.
2 The reference is to 13:8:
      ER *nisi hoc ut invicem diligatis* 'except this, that you love one another'
      VG *nisi ut invicem diligatis* 'except that you love one another'
   Cf also 11:11, where Erasmus has rendered the article with the infinitive (εἰς τὸ παραζηλῶσαι) by *in hoc ut eos aemulandum provocaret* 'for this, that he should provoke them to emulation,' the Vulgate simply by *ut illos aemulentur* 'that they may emulate.'
3 commit adultery] Latin *adulterabis*, first in 1527; previously, *adorabis* 'worship,' apparently by mistake

13:9 [ER *in hoc sermone summatim comprehenditur* 'it is summarily embraced in this saying']

[VG] *in hoc verbo instauratur* 'it is restored in this word'; ἀνακεφαλαιοῦται, that is, 'it is recapitulated,' that is, 'is summarily contained in this word.'[1] In one of his letters Augustine translates *recapitulatur* [is recapitulated].[2] The phrase is taken from the epilogues of the orators, in which a case is repeated in summary; those[3] call this the ἀνακεφαλαίωσις.[4] For[5] something is 'restored' when it is renewed in its former likeness; we speak of restoring a collapsed building.[6] Ambrose[7] reads *consummatur* [is summed up].[8] I[9] have translated 'is summarily embraced.' I am not sure whether *recapitulari* is found in Latin authors – I should certainly wish it were.[10] Chrysostom has observed the propriety of this word: [Paul] did not say, πληροῦται 'is fulfilled,'[11] but ἀνακεφαλαιοῦται, to express brevity and compendiousness.[12]

1 Cf Lefèvre d'Etaples: 'In Greek [the word means], "is recapitulated," that is, is summarily contained' (*Pauli epistolae* fol 100 recto).
2 Augustine *Epistulae* 196.4.16 CSEL 57 230
3 those] In *1516* only, 'they'
4 See Quintilian 6.1.1 and Lausberg I 434.
5 For ... building.] Added in *1519*
6 Erasmus acknowledged to Titelmans that *instauratur* is acceptable here in the sense of *renovatur* (is renewed): the New Law 'renews,' as it were, the Old Law, in renewal making it compendious; for the force of the prefix *re-* is clearly in the Greek (*Responsio ad collationes* LB IX 1011B). But Valla, before Erasmus, had found *instauratur* inadequate to express the Greek (*Annot in Rom* 13 [I 860]).
7 Ambrose ... compendiousness.] Except for the next sentence (see n9 below), this remaining portion of the annotation was added in *1535*.
8 Ambrosiaster *Comm in Rom* 13:9 (1)
9 I ... embraced.'] Added in *1527*, when, however, the sentence read: 'I have translated *consummatio* [summing up, completion].' In *1535*, *consummatio*, drawn evidently by mistake from Erasmus' translation of 13:10, was corrected to *summatim comprehenditur*.
10 The word is found only in late Latin, and primarily in Christian authors. Pelagius uses the word in his exposition of this verse: 'All righteousness is recapitulated in the love of one's neighbour' (*Expos in Rom* 13:9 [Souter II 103:20]).
11 As in Rom 8:4
12 Chrysostom *Hom in Rom* 23.3 PG 60 618–19

13:10 [ER *dilectio proximo* 'love to a neighbour']

[VG] *dilectio proximi* 'love of a neighbour';[1] τῷ πλησίον, that is, 'to a neighbour,' in the dative case[2] following the verb 'works,' for it strengthens with an explanation the 'epilogue'[3] he had just spoken, that in charity lies the sum of the whole Law. The Law, by various commandments, restrains us from harming our neighbour: You shall not swear falsely, you shall not steal, you shall not commit adultery, you shall not bear false witness, you shall not kill, and others. But when one is endowed with Christian charity he harms no mortal at all, he helps everyone he can, both good and bad. And yet[4] the other reading, τοῦ πλησίον [(love) of a neighbour], makes good sense. Chrysostom[5] reads τῷ πλησίον [to a neighbour] and also Theophylact,[6] however his translator treated it.[7]

1 Both Erasmus and the Vulgate completed the clause with *malum non operatur* 'works no ill.'
2 So Lefèvre d'Etaples, who, like Erasmus, took the dative with the verb: 'works no ill to a neighbour' (*Pauli epistolae* fol 100 recto). The majority of Latin manuscripts read the genitive, though some read the dative. The Greek manuscripts read the dative. See Tischendorf II 436 10n and Wordsworth and White II 133 10n. Weber, however, prints

the dative, though the genitive is recorded as a variant (II 1765 and
10n).
3 For the meaning of the word in this context see the previous annotation.
4 And yet ... sense.] Added in 1519
5 Chrysostom ... it.] Added in 1535
6 Chrysostom *Hom in Rom* 23.4 PG 60 619; Theophylact *Expos in Rom* 13:10
PG 124 517D
7 Porsena translated with the genitive, *proximi* (fol XXI verso). For the
1529 edition of Porsena's translation cf the annotation on 1:4 ('who was
predestined') n25.

13:11 [ER *praesertim cum sciamus tempus* 'especially[1] since we know the time']
[VG] *et hoc scientes tempus* 'and knowing this time.' In Greek the pronoun
'this' does not modify 'time,' since in Greek 'time' is masculine. But he is
speaking in this manner: 'And this' or 'and that, since we know – to be
sure – the time,' καὶ τοῦτο εἰδότες τὸν καιρόν – so that 'and this' has the
effect of intensifying, as when we say, 'You go to the brothel,[2] and this
during Lent!' Thus we understand that his precepts must be pre-eminently
practised now, under the evangelical law, which requires something beyond
the law of Moses or of nature.

'Time' in this passage signifies opportunity or occasion – καιρός,[3] for
which [the Greeks] also use ὥρα [*hōra*]. *Hora*[4] is a part of the day, as in the
phrase 'and changes every hour.'[5] *Hora* is a part of the year, like winter,
spring, summer, autumn, each of which acts in its own way – as in the
same poet: 'He regulates the world with changing seasons.'[6] Hence ὡραῖον
[*hōraion*] means 'seasonable'[7] or 'beautiful.' That which has already with-
ered is ἔξωρον [*exōron*].[8] So all time is divided into various *horae* [periods]:
there was a period before the Law; under the Law; under the gospel.[9] The
gentiles lived in darkness, the Jews in shadows, unaware that they were
asleep. But now that the clear light of the gospel has shone forth, it is
shameful for anyone still to sleep.

1 especially ... time] First in 1519; in 1516, *et hoc cum sciatis tempus* 'and this
since you know the time.' While the Vulgate, too, could be understood in the
sense 'and this, knowing the time,' Erasmus' discussion assumes the reading
'and knowing this time.'
2 'You go to the brothel] First in 1519; in 1516, 'You fornicate'
3 καιρός] Added in 1519
4 *Hora* ... to sleep.] Added in 1535
5 For the phrase see Horace *Ars poetica* 160.
6 Horace *Odes* 1.12.15–16
7 Latin *tempestivum* 'seasonable,' 'timely.' In the discussion of *hora* here
Erasmus has evidently proceeded to the next clause of 13:11, where the Greek
reads ὅτι ὥρα [*hoti hōra*]:

ER *quod tempestivum sit* [1516, *est*] 'that it is high time [ie timely]'
  VG *quia hora est* 'that it is the hour'
For Titelmans, Erasmus justified his translation on the grounds that he did
not think *hora* could be used with this sense in Latin (*Responsio ad collationes*
LB IX 1011D).
8 With the definition of *hora* here, compare the annotation on 10:15 ('how
  beautiful are the feet').
9 For a disquisition on the 'division of time' see the *Ratio* (Holborn
  198:33–201:33), where, however, Erasmus describes five periods in the history
  of salvation.

13:11 [ER *a somno expergisci* 'to waken from sleep']

[VG] *de somno surgere* 'to rise¹ from sleep'; ἐξ ὕπνου ἐγερθῆναι. One² who
has been lying down or seated ἐγείρεται [rises]; a structure that rises aloft
ἐγείρεται; one who wakens [*expergiscitur*] ἐγείρεται [is roused]. Genesis 41:
ἠγέρθη δὲ Φαραώ 'and Pharaoh awoke' [*experrectus*] [41:4]. The Lord says of
the temple of his body in John: ἐγερῶ, *excitabo* [I shall raise] [2:19], and in
Isaiah, the twenty-sixth chapter: 'Awake [*expergiscimini*] and praise' [26:19].
The LXX translated this ἐγερθήσονται, with tense and person changed.³
In Ephesians 5: 'Rise [*exsurge*] sleeper' [5:14] – ἔγειραι ὁ καθεύδων – and
'rise [*exsurge*] from the dead' [Eph 5:14] – ἀνάστα – an ambiguous word,
like ἐγείρεσθαι.⁴ Now the proper words to signify waking from sleep are
ἐκνήφειν and ἐξυπνιάζεσθαι. But in the First Epistle to the Thessalonians,
chapter 5, the Apostle calls a life lived in sin 'sleep,' expressing a thought
similar to the one here: 'You are all sons of the light and sons of the day;
we are not of the night or of the shadows. And so let us not sleep like
the others, but be wakeful and sober. For those who sleep, sleep at night'
[5:5–7]. With this in mind I have translated *expergisci* [to awake] instead
of *surgere* [to rise], and if there is some special significance⁵ in *surgere*, the
same remains in *expergisci*. For it seems that *expergisci* [to awaken, rouse]
is used of one who has, as it were, proceeded [*pergere*] from [*ex*] sleep.⁶
But if someone believes that this passage pertains to the resurrection of the
dead, who, the Apostle says, 'sleep,'⁷ the word *expergisci* is well suited. It
is frivolous to talk, as some do, about rising [*surgere*] to good works, and
to allege that those who have wakened [*expergisci*] go back to sleep again.⁸
But also those who have risen [*surgere*] go back to bed again; some rise
[*surgere*] when they are still asleep. We are aroused [*excitare*] from sleep in
order to rise [*surgere*].

1 to rise ... to rise.] The entire annotation was added in 1535.
2 For the analysis here of the usage of the Greek word, see the similar
  illustrations in *Responsio ad collationes* LB IX 1011C.

3 Compare the Vulgate and the LXX of Isa 26:19:

> VG Your dead shall live, my slain shall rise [*resurgent*]. Awake [*expergisci-mini*] and praise, you who dwell in the dust.
>
> LXX The dead shall rise. Those in the tombs shall arise [or, awake (ἐγερθήσονται)]. And those in the earth shall be glad.

Erasmus identifies the verb in the second clause of the LXX (shall arise, awake – future, third person) with that in the third clause of the Vulgate (*expergiscimini* – present, second person); cf Jerome *Commentarii in Isaiam* 8 (on 26:19) PL 24 303B: 'Since their death is sleep, they are not said, as in the LXX, to rise, but to awake and be vigilant.'

4 In Greek these two clauses of Eph 5:14 have entirely different verbs: ἐγείρομαι 'rouse,' 'awaken' and ἀνίσταμαι 'rise,' 'stand up.' The Vulgate blurred the distinction by translating, respectively *surgere* and *exsurge* (Weber II 1813), while Erasmus' quotation *exsurge ... exsurge* eliminates the formal distinction altogether. In his own translation, he attempted to convey the distinction found in the Greek verbs: *expergiscere qui dormis et surge a mortuis* 'waken, sleeper, and rise from the dead.'

5 On the 'special significance' (Latin *emphasis*) of the word *surgere*, see the *Responsio ad collationes* LB IX 1011C–D. Titelmans evidently argued that *surgere* necessarily entailed rising, *expergisci* did not: 'He says that many who are roused, do not rise ... But [replied Erasmus] whoever is awakened, is awakened for the purpose of rising.'

6 Cf the *Responsio ad collationes* LB IX 1011D, where Erasmus derives *expergisci* from *pererigo* (*per* + *erigo*: to make erect). On the relationship between *expergiscor* and *pergo* see A. Ernout and A. Meillet *Dictionnaire étymologique de la langue latine* 4th ed rev Jacques André (Paris 1979) 206.

7 Cf 1 Cor 15:51 and 1 Thess 4:14.

8 In these last few lines Erasmus has Titelmans in mind; cf n5 above. As the Latin in square brackets indicates, Erasmus responds here to complaints about the inadequacy of the word *expergisci* in comparison with *surgere*, with its 'special significance.'

13:11 [ER *nunc enim propius adest* 'for now there is more nearly at hand']
[VG] *nunc enim propior est* 'for now is nearer';[1] ἐγγύτερον ἡμῶν, that is, *propius nos est* [is nearer us] or 'is nearer to us,' so that 'nearer' is an adverb,[2] and takes the same case as does the preposition from which it derived.[3] For[4] the Greeks say ἐγγύς σου [adverb with genitive case], that is, 'near you.' Accordingly, two genitives go with the comparative ἐγγύτερον, one consequent upon the adverb, the other a genitive of comparison. Here ἡμῶν [us] is not a genitive of comparison, but one consequent upon the adverb. Similarly in Latin if you say *Sum abundantior pecuniis te* [I am more abounding in wealth than you], 'wealth' is an ablative consequent upon the adjective,[5] 'you' an ablative of comparison. In this passage the Translator has joined the genitive ἡμῶν [of us] with σωτηρία [salvation], though it belongs with ἐγγύτερον.[6] For [Paul] means that now salvation through gospel

faith[7] is closer than it was when they relied upon themselves in philosophy and the works of the Law. In any case, if he had meant 'our salvation' he would have said ἡ σωτηρία ἡμῶν or ἡ ἡμῶν σωτηρία.[8] Now it is ἡμῶν ἡ σωτηρία; he is speaking unconditionally of the salvation which comes to all.

1 The chief point of this annotation is to demonstrate the place in this clause of the personal pronoun ἡμῶν 'us,' which lies outside the cue phrase:
ER *nunc enim propius adest nobis salus* 'for now salvation is more nearly at hand for us'
VG *nunc enim propior est nostra salus* 'for now our salvation is nearer'
2 So Valla *Annot in Rom* 13 (I 860)
3 In Greek ἐγγύς is one 'of the adverbial words used as prepositions' (Smyth 1700), and may be followed by the genitive case (or, in poetry and later authors, by the dative). In Latin *prope* serves as both adverb and preposition; as preposition it takes the accusative case, as adverb it may be followed by the dative or by *ad* or *ab* (*prope* A1 in OLD).
4 For ... to all.] This remaining portion of the annotation was added in 1527.
5 Here, and just above, we have rendered *thematis* somewhat freely as 'consequent upon the adjective' and 'upon the adverb.' Modern grammars describe the genitive in the first case as partitive, the ablative in the second as one of specification (see Smyth 1439–40 and Allen and Greenough 418).
6 Reading in the first case (with the Vulgate) 'our salvation,' in the second 'closer to us' (cf n1 above)
7 On the use and connotations of the word 'faith' see the annotation on 1:17 ('from faith unto faith').
8 On the proper position of the pronoun in such phrases see the annotation on 14:16 ('therefore let not our good be blasphemed') and nn10 and 12.

13:11 [ER *quam tum cum credabamus* 'than at the time when we began to believe']

[VG] *quam cum credidimus* 'than when we believed'; ἢ ὅτε ἐπιστεύσαμεν. Certainly it would have been clearer, and not just better Latin, to say 'than at the time when we began to believe.' For in the law of Moses there was a conception of salvation, more than there was salvation, a shadow rather than the reality. Thus he speaks of the night before the sunrise, a night which gradually disappears at the approach of light.

13:12 [ER *nox progressa est* 'the night has advanced']

[VG] *nox praecessit* 'the night has preceded'; προέκοψεν, that is, 'has proceeded,' or 'has advanced' and is coming to a close, that is, the night has largely passed and day presses in, as the light of the gospel gradually dawns. Cyprian[1] in his discourse *On Jealousy and Envy* reads 'the night has passed.'[2] The translator of Origen, in the thirty-fifth homily, reads 'the night has moved forward.'[3] Thus it cannot be doubted that *praecessit* [preceded] arose through an error of the copyists from *processit*[4] [proceeded]. Chrysostom[5] clearly interprets [the expression] of the night advancing: ' "The day," [Paul] says, "is approaching." Accordingly,' says [Chrysostom] 'if the night is ending, while the day is drawing near, let us henceforth do those things which are of the day, not of the night, for this is likewise practised in worldly matters. For when we see the night hastening towards the dawn and hear the swallow singing, we each rouse our neighbour, though it is still night. Then when the night has passed, we make haste to address one another, saying "It is day," and we do all the things that are of the day, clothing ourselves, casting aside our dreams, shaking off sleep, so that the day will find us prepared.'[6] Theophylact is even clearer. He supposes, by way of example, that there are twelve hours in the night and when ten have passed we say ἡ νὺξ προέκοψεν [the night has advanced], that is, πρὸς τέλος ἐστί [is near the end].[7] It is not unreasonable to say that by then the night has passed; but this is not the meaning of προέκοψεν, which word is uniformly in the Greek codices. Finally, the verb 'has preceded' is not suited to the phrase that follows, 'the day approaches' or 'is close at hand.' For when the night has passed, day is no longer imminent – it has already come, and it is too late to rouse people from sleep. I am aware that all interpret this passage of the resurrection.[8] If we approve this interpretation, the night has not completely passed, nor is the day at hand, but we are still in the dim light of hope, awaiting the day of resurrection as though it were almost upon us. Thus there can be no doubt that *praecessit* is a corruption from *processit* by copyists who did not notice that *procedere* is not always 'to go forth into public,' but sometimes 'to go forward' or 'to advance.' They could have learned this from the first chapter of Luke, who writes that Zachariah and Elizabeth *processisse* [were advanced RSV] in their days,[9] meaning that they were already of an advanced age, when life was not yet past, but was near the end.

1 Cyprian ... *processit*.] Added in 1519
2 Cyprian *De zelo et livore* 10 CSEL 3/1 425:23
3 This citation is not found in *In Lucam homiliae* (the only extant work of Origen to contain thirty-five homilies), though Homily 35 does cite Rom 13:7. Elsewhere in Origen the text (13:12) is cited with *praecessit* 'preceded,' eg *Comm in Rom* 9.32 PG 14 1232B, *In Genesim homiliae* 10.1 PG 12 216B, *Libri in Canticum canticorum* 2 PG 13 122A.
4 While *processit* is found in some of the manuscripts of the Vulgate, *praecessit* is the preferred reading; see Wordsworth and White II 133 12n.
5 Chrysostom ... the end.] This remaining portion of the annotation was added in 1535.
6 Chrysostom *Hom in Rom* 24.1 PG 60 623

7 Theophylact *Expos in Rom* 13:12 PG 124 520B
8 Not exactly everyone. Chrysostom (*Hom in Rom* 24.1 PG 60 622–3) and Theophylact (*Expos in Rom* 13:12 PG 124 520B) adopt an eschatological interpretation, but Origen gives a predominantly moral one, though there are eschatological traces (*Comm in Rom* 9.32 PG 14 1232C–1233C). In the case of Ambrosiaster, the manuscript tradition reflects both the moral and eschatological interpretations, the alpha recension giving the eschatological, the beta and gamma the moral (Ambrosiaster *Comm in Rom* 13:12 [1]). In his paraphrase Erasmus gives predominantly the moral interpretation; see CWE 42 76–7.
9 Cf Luke 1:7.

13:12 [ER *appropinquat* 'approaches']

[VG] *appropinquavit* 'has approached';[1] ἤγγικεν. It is, indeed, a past tense, but would be rendered into better Latin by a verb in the present tense – with no harm to the sense: 'approaches'[2] or 'is at hand.' I see that in most manuscripts the word has been corrupted into 'will approach.'[3] He means that the day of the coming of Christ is now impending; the night of their former ignorance is already coming to an end.

1 approached] Except for the words noted below (n2), this annotation was added in 1519.
2 'approaches' ... hand'] Added in 1535
3 The tense of the verb varies in the manuscripts of the Vulgate; see Wordsworth and White II 133 12n.

13:13 [ER *composite ambulemus* 'let us walk in a well-ordered way']

[VG] *honeste ambulemus* 'let us walk honourably'; εὐσχημόνως, that is, 'in a well-ordered way' or 'discreetly.'[1] Cyprian,[2] in the passage I have just cited,[3] translated [the word by the Latin] *decenter* [becomingly]. For when the light has arisen, one conducts himself more modestly from a sense of shame, and[4] orders his behaviour with a view to human judgment; for[5] night is without shame.

1 discreetly] First in 1527; previously, *honeste* 'honourably'
2 Cyprian ... *decenter*.] Added in 1522
3 Cf the annotation on 13:12 ('the night has preceded') n2.
4 and ... judgment] Added in 1527
5 for ... shame] Added in 1519

13:13 [ER *non comessationibus* 'not with revels']

[VG] *non in comessationibus* 'not in revels.' The Greek lacks the preposition 'in'[1] – μὴ κώμοις [*mē kōmois*], that is, 'not with revels' – though[2] I am not entirely displeased by the addition. In Greek Κῶμος [*Kōmos*] is the god of drunkenness,[3] and the same term designates a lively and thoroughly licentious party.[4] Moreover,[5] wanton songs and dances are called κῶμοι [kōmoi] in Greek. Hence also the term 'comedy.'[6] And they are said κωμάζειν [to revel] who, garlanded and quite drunk, would rush into someone else's banquet along with a flute player; so in Plato, when Alcibiades burst into the banquet of Agathon.[7] Athenaeus shows in several passages that this was a custom among the Greeks.[8]

1 So Valla *Annot in Rom* 13 (I 860)
2 though ... addition] Added in *1519*
3 Komos as the god of drunken revelry belongs to later antiquity. With name anglicized as Comus, he is imaginatively portrayed in John Milton's *Comus*, where, for his pedigree, see lines 46–59.
4 On *komos*, see the article in Pauly-Wissowa *Realencyclopädie* XI-2 1286–1304, which traces the connection between *komos* 'revel' and *komazein*, meaning 'to burst into a party,' and shows that in Greek art from later antiquity, Komos is sometimes shown as a figure who personifies merrymaking. Cf Jacques Lefèvre d'Etaples, who explains *komoi* here as the 'lust, wantonness, and all the immodesty' of banquets, and refers to St Athanasius' interpretation of *komoi* as 'wanton songs' that follow upon too much drinking (*Pauli epistolae* fol 100 recto).
5 Moreover ... Greeks.] Added in *1535*
6 'Comedy' (Latin *comoedia*) is derived from the Greek κωμῳδία, itself derived from the compound κωμῳδός, from κῶμος (kōmos) 'revel' and ἀοιδός (aoidos) 'a singer'; see Chantraine *Dictionnaire* I 606.
7 Cf Plato *Symposium* 212C–213E.
8 Athenaeus was the author of *The Sophists at Dinner* (*Deipnosophistae*), written in the late second or early third century AD, a storehouse of anecdotes (in fifteen books) about banqueting and drinking, with thousands of literary allusions. In *Deipnosophistae* 5.180 the author censures Alcibiades for bursting drunk into the banquet that is the setting of Plato's *Symposium* (*Deipnosophistae* II trans C.B. Gulick, Loeb Classical Library [London 1928] 341); cf also *Deipnosophistae* 10.439 (in the same edition IV [London 1930] 489–91).

13:14 [ER *ad concupiscentias* 'unto lusts']
[VG] *in desideriis* 'in desires'; εἰς ἐπιθυμίας, that is, 'unto lusts,'[1] that is, [have regard] to necessity, not[2] to pleasure. He has translated πρόνοια, that is, 'forethought' by *cura* [care, regard];[3] so[4] reads Origen in his ninth homily on Exodus.[5] Likewise Augustine, in citing this passage in the fourth book *On Christian Doctrine*, chapter 20; though he admits that the rest of the discussion is measured and rhythmic, he is nevertheless somehow offended by the final clause, *carnis curam ne feceritis in desideriis*, and would prefer this construction: *carnis providentiam in desideriis ne feceritis.*[6] Come now[7] and let those condemn my μικρολογία [splitting hairs] over sacred literature, when such minutiae were the concern of so great a bishop.[8] And yet[9] I cannot

guess what it is that offended Augustine. Indeed [the phrase] 'in lusts' is placed at the end not only to imitate the order of the Greek, but also because there it strikes the ears more forcefully.[10] For [Paul] does not forbid us to have 'regard for the flesh'; it is on this account that he ἐπιφωνεῖ [subjoins], as it were, 'in lusts.' In Greek the first part, καὶ τῆς σαρκὸς πρόνοιαν, is trochaic dimeter catalectic in its accentual rhythm, a feature that is particularly prominent in prose; the last part is trochaic trimeter brachycatalectic.[11]

This passage,[12] indeed, Augustine cites as an example of the 'middle style,'[13] which he thinks is appropriate to exhortation.[14] And yet there are also many other fine touches in it, like ἐναντίωσις [opposition][15] and ὁμοιοτέλευτον [similar endings][16] in *nox praecessit dies appropinquavit* [night has preceded, day has approached]. Likewise, ἐναντίωσις in 'casting off' and 'putting on,' in 'light' and 'darkness.' In addition metaphor[17] in the single phrase 'armour of light'; further, comparison,[18] 'as in the day.' The sound of the Greek words, however, is more pleasing: ἀποθώμεθα, ἐνδυσώμεθα, σκότους, φωτός [apothōmetha, endysōmetha, skotous, phōtos].[19] In the verbs there is complete ὁμοιοτέλευτον [homoioteleuton], in the nouns, partial ὁμοιόπτωτον [similar cases];[20] in the Latin this is totally lacking. The pleasure of *catachresis* [analogical application] is found in περιπατῶμεν [let us walk] and εὐσχημόνως [orderly]: neither word is used with its literal meaning.[21] This is to say nothing meanwhile of the elegance of neatly fitted clauses, phrases, and of balanced parts. This is even more evident in the lines that follow. And yet we can see that this whole passage is metaphorical: 'The night has preceded, the day has approached, let us cast off the works of darkness, let us walk honourably as in the day' [13:12–13]. None of these words is used in its literal sense. The movement is more measured and rhythmic in *non in comessationibus et ebrietatibus, non in cubilibus et impudicitiis, non in contentione et aemulatione* [not in rioting and drunkenness, not in wantonness and impurity, not in contention and envy] [13:13]. Each clause here consists of a pair of related vices, so that the figure is conveyed even in translation. The repetition of the same word [*non*] at the beginning of the clauses is not without pleasure. Add to this the almost equal rhythm[22] of clauses and phrases; then, too, the ὁμοιόπτωτον [homoioptōton]. Yet these do not always correspond in the Greek, for, while κώμοις [kōmois] and μέθαις [methais] have the same rhythm, the ὁμοιόπτωτον is not complete, as in the Latin.[23] Again, in the Latin *contentione et aemulatione* there is ὁμοιόπτωτον, but not at all in the Greek: ἔριδι καὶ ζήλῳ [in quarrelling and jealousy]. In sum, the rhetorical figures that arise from the form of expression do not always concur in the Latin and Greek texts; but those that arise from the ideas are common to all languages.

1 So Valla *Annot in Rom* 13 (I 860)
2 not] First in *1519*; in *1516* the passage read, apparently by mistake, 'not to necessity but to pleasure.'
3 For the ensuing discussion compare the translations of Erasmus and the Vulgate of 13:14b:
    ER *et carnis curam ne agatis ad concupiscentias* 'and have no regard for the flesh, [looking] unto lusts'
    VG *et carnis curam ne feceritis in desideriis* 'and make no regard of the flesh in its desires'
4 *so ... feceritis*] Added in *1519*
5 Origen *In Exodum homiliae* 9.3 PG 12 366A
6 Ie: 'Make no provision for the flesh in its desires.' Cf Augustine *De doctrina christiana* 4.20.40 PL 34 108. Erasmus may mislead here. Augustine is explicitly concerned with the position of the phrase *in concupiscentiis*, which in his source concludes the sentence, as *in desideriis* concludes the Vulgate sentence. He would have preferred *carnis providentiam in concupiscentiis ne feceritis*, because he thought it would have made for a better concluding rhythm.
7 Come now ... bishop.] Added in *1522*
8 When Erasmus wrote his preface 'To the Reader' for the annotations in his *1516* edition of the New Testament, he anticipated the criticism of those who would find his attention to minutiae irksome; cf Ep 373:84–118. He returned to the criticism again in the *Contra morosos quosdam ac indoctos*, where he cites not only Augustine but also Origen and Jerome as exegetes who understand the importance of minutiae; cf LB VI ***2 recto–verso.
9 And yet ... all languages.] This remaining portion of the annotation was added in *1527*.
10 For Augustine's opinion see n6 above.
11 The trochaic metron scans as - ˇ - ˇ . A trochaic dimeter has two such metra; but catalectic means that the line will lack the final syllable. A trochaic trimeter has three metra, but brachycatalectic means that the line will lack two syllables. It is not clear how Erasmus scanned the two Greek phrases in question. He seems to have in mind accentual, not quantitative, rhythms. In Erasmus' time Greek words were heavily accented, to the neglect and distortion of the classical quantities; cf *De recta pronuntiatione* CWE 26 422 and nn261–6 and 304.
12 Erasmus refers to all of 13:12–14.
13 Classical rhetoricians distinguished three styles of speaking: the plain (*subtile*), the middle (*modicum*), and the grand (*vehemens*). According to Quintilian, the plain was best adapted to teaching, the middle to giving pleasure, the grand to 'moving' the audience (*docere, delectare, movere*); see *Rhetorica ad Herennium* 4.8.11–11.16; Cicero *Orator* 21.69; Quintilian 12.10.58–9. See also Lausberg I 1078–9 and George Kennedy *Classical Rhetoric and Its Christian and Secular Tradition from Ancient to Modern Times* (Chapel Hill 1980) 99–104.
14 For Augustine's revision of the classical theory of the three styles for the purposes of Christian preaching and teaching see *De doctrina christiana* 4.18.35–4.30.63 PL 34 105–20.
15 For ἐναντίωσις see the annotation on 2:8 ('do not give assent to') n2.

16 In the rhetorical figure 'homoeoteleuton,' words, usually in a sequence of clauses, end with the same sound – in this case praecess*it* ... appropinqua*vit*. See Quintilian 9.3.77 and Lausberg I 725–8.

17 Quintilian 8.6.4 characterizes 'metaphor' as 'the most beautiful of tropes'; Erasmus says that 'nothing moves the emotions so forcefully, nothing brings so much distinction, beauty, and pleasure' as metaphor (*Ecclesiastes* III LB V 1008B).

18 *Collatio*, a comparison of resemblances (which may be taken somewhat broadly). Cicero and Quintilian both distinguish *collatio* from *imago* (a comparison of physical or natural features) and *exemplum* (precedents or similar experiences). Quintilian regards *collatio* as equivalent to παραβολή; cf Cicero *De inventione* 1.30.49; Quintilian 5.11.22–4.

19 In translation, 'let us cast off, let us put on, darkness, light' (from 13:12)

20 According to Quintilian (9.3.78–9), *homoioptōton* requires only similarity of cases, though similarity of sound is desirable. In both Greek and Latin, the nouns here ('darkness' and 'light') have the same case (genitive); in Greek there is a 'partial' similarity of sound in the endings, but none at all in Latin. See Lausberg I 729–31. Erasmus criticized the unrestrained use of this figure (cf *Ecclesiastes* III LB V 1000C–F).

21 Quintilian 8.6.34–6 believes the correct Latin translation of the Greek *catachresis* is *abusio*, where a word is used in a sense not, strictly speaking, correct, as when the word 'parricide' is adapted, by analogy, to include not only the slayer of a father but of a brother too, or as when some use the word 'liberality' to denote 'prodigality.' Cf Cicero *De oratore* 3.38.155 and Lausberg I 562. Erasmus regards *catachresis* as 'very like' metaphor (*Ecclesiastes* III LB V 1010B).

22 rhythm] *numerum*, accusative, in both 1527 and 1535. LB's *numerorum*, genitive, appears to be a misprint.

23 See n20 above. Here, the case endings, all in the ablative, have similar sounds in the first and third pairs. Thus in the first pair in Latin (*comessationibus et ebrietatibus*) the *homoioptōton* is complete, whereas it is not quite perfect in the corresponding Greek: *kōmois* ... *methais*; in the final pair the Greek (*eridi* ... *zelō*) has no similarity of sound at all.

CHAPTER 14

14:1 [ER *porro eum qui infirmatur* 'moreover, him who is weak']

[VG] *infirmum autem* 'the weak however'; τὸν δὲ ἀσθενοῦντα, that is, 'him who is weak.' It is not 'in faith'[1] but 'in respect to faith'; [the word 'faith'] belongs[2] with the participle ἀσθενοῦντα, not with the following verb 're-ceive':[3] you[4] who are stronger, receive him who is not yet strong in faith. By 'the weak'[5] he means the Jews,[6] who were not yet able to disregard the choice of foods; and yet he directs his speech to the strong, the more easily to bring health and strength to the feeble. So Chrysostom.[7]

> 1 Valla, too, had noted the absence of the preposition 'in' (*Annot in Rom* 14 [I 860]).
> 2 belongs ... 'receive'] Added in 1519
> 3 Compare the translations of Erasmus and the Vulgate:
>> ER *porro eum qui infirmatur fide assumite* 'moreover, him who is weak in faith, receive'
>> VG *infirmum autem in fide assumite* 'the weak, however, in faith receive'
> 4 you ... faith] Added in 1527
> 5 By 'the weak' ... Chrysostom.] Added in 1535
> 6 In his paraphrase on this verse, it is the Christian convert from Judaism who is represented as 'the weak'; cf CWE 42 77.
> 7 Chrysostom *Hom in Rom* 25.1 PG 60 627–9

14:1 [ER VG] *assumite* 'receive.' προσλαμβάνεσθε; that is, 'join[1] him to your-selves,' and 'take[2] him into your fellowship.' One whose faith is not yet perfectly developed should not be cast out, lest the smouldering wick be extinguished,[3] but should be tolerated and nourished until he advances to better things.

We must note in passing that Paul attributes abstinence from foods to weakness of faith: he is not speaking of those who abstain from the more luxurious foods the more to bring their body under control, but of those who in the manner of the Jews avoid certain foods. And yet he wants such people to be tolerated, in the hope that they may progress in faith and disregard ceremonies of this kind. But today we see among Christians almost more supersitition in the choice of foods than there ever was among the Jews.[4] These things are no longer [merely] tolerated, but in these some people find perfect piety, for these we fight with every weapon at our disposal, on the basis of these we judge, we shun, we abhor our neighbour as though he were very little a Christian; as[5] a result of these we take pride in ourselves – most foolishly, when[6] in other respects we are infected with the most horrible diseases of the soul: pride, anger, envy, self-love.

1 Lee had pointed out to Erasmus that Jerome had used 'receive' rather than 'join.' Erasmus responded that 'receive' is acceptable, but in the context here 'join' is better. With this Erasmus concluded his response to Lee's criticisms of the annotations on Romans (*Responsio ad annotationes Lei* LB IX 217C), because the rest, he said, are mere chaff, like this one!

2 and 'take ... fellowship'] Added in *1519*

3 Cf Isa 42:3; Matt 12:20.

4 Elsewhere, too, Erasmus severely criticized dietary laws. See his letter to Udalricus (Ulrich) Zasius, where he says that nothing is nearer Judaism than the choice of foods, and questions whether it is Christian to force anyone to risk epilepsy, paralysis, and apoplexy by eating fish (Ep 1353:40–63). In 1522 he submitted to the bishop of Basel an 'Apologetic Epistle' urging that the laws concerning fasting be relaxed to take into account matters of health and old age (*De interdicto esu carnium* LB IX 1197–1214). See also 'A Fish Diet' in Thompson *Colloquies* 312–57.

5 as ... foolishly] Added in *1519*

6 when ... self-love] Added in *1522*

14:1 [ER *non ad diiudicationes* 'not for the judgments of disputes']

[VG] *non in disceptationibus cogitationum* 'not in disputes of thoughts'; μὴ εἰς διακρίσεις διαλογισμῶν, that is, 'not for judgments of disputes,' that is, 'not in troublesome disputes' through which one will be alienated who[1] ought rather to be fostered by kindness until he progresses to the more perfect things. Most [commentators] refer this to the gentiles,[2] but I think that it applies to both [Jews and gentiles], so that we understand [here] a reference to the disputations that arise between them from the distinctions among foods.[3] For, as he shows elsewhere,[4] each was judging the other. Those who ate called the abstinence of the others 'superstition'; those who did not eat passed judgment on those who ate on the grounds that they were taking prohibited foods. [Paul] does not want disputes among Christians to arise from trivialities of this sort, but wants each to make concessions to the other to preserve harmony.

I find it strange that the Translator preferred to say 'of thoughts' rather than 'of disputes.' Perhaps he did not read διαλογισμῶν but λογισμῶν. In Greek, διαλογισμός sometimes means an empty battle of words over matters of no importance.[5] 'Thinking' requires one person, 'disputation' several. They were judging one another; it makes no difference whether they did so in silent thought or in open speech. I should add that *diiudicationes cogitationum* is an expression you should understand not as 'thoughts that have been judged' but appositively as 'judgments that are thoughts,' as though he had said 'unspoken judgments.'

1 who ... judgments] This remaining portion of the annotation was added in *1535*.

2 So eg Origen *Comm in Rom* 9.35 PG 14 1234C
3 So Ambrosiaster *Comm in Rom* 14:1; also Thomas Aquinas *Super Rom lect* cap 14 lectio 1.1082
4 Cf 14:10–13, 22–3; also 1 Cor 8.
5 But for διαλογισμός as 'thought,' see the word in BAG.

14:2 [ER *vescendum esse quibuslibet* 'that he ought to take any kind of food he likes']

[VG] *manducare omnia* 'that he consumes all things'; φαγεῖν καὶ ἐσθίειν. [This verb], which is the equivalent of *edere* [to eat] or *vesci* [to take food, feed on][1] here he constantly translates as *manducare*, though *mandere* or *manducare* is, properly, to crush food with the teeth. Furthermore, he would have translated πάντα more precisely by *quaevis* [any at all] that is, any food at all, without distinction; for πᾶν has this meaning also. What one person, however, would be able to eat 'all' things?[2] I should also briefly note that 'believes that he consumes'[3] is a strange figure of speech both in the Greek and in the Latin – for the Greek says 'one thinks that he consumes everything,' although the meaning is that one thinks he is allowed to take any food he likes, without distinction. Hence [the Translator] would more correctly have rendered the infinitive by a gerundive: 'one believes he ought to take any kind of food he likes.'[4]

  1 Cf the annotation on 14:6 ('and he who does not eat, to the Lord he does not eat') where Erasmus notes that in speaking of kinds of food *vescor* is more appropriate (*elegantius*) than *edo*.
  2 Titelmans evidently took this comment as carping, but Erasmus reiterated the point that the Latin *quaevis* can translate the Greek πᾶν (*Responsio ad collationes* LB IX 1011D–E).
  3 Both Erasmus and the Vulgate translated the Greek verb πιστεύει here by *credit*: one believes that ...
  4 In Latin, the gerundive with the verb 'to be' 'denotes obligation, necessity, or propriety' (Allen and Greenough 194b).

14:2 [ER *alius autem qui infirmus est* 'but another who is weak']

[VG] *qui autem infirmus est* 'but he who is weak'; ὁ δὲ ἀσθενῶν λάχανα ἐσθίει, that is, 'but one who is weak, eats vegetables' – indicative, not imperative.[1] With[2] the same words, Jerome cites the passage in his commentary on the second chapter of Ecclesiastes.[3] For [Paul] is not demanding that [the weaker] eat vegetables, whom he would prefer to become stronger and eat anything he liked; rather, he is showing what the weak person does, giving way to his superstition. The word 'weak' should be taken to refer not to infirmity of the body, but to superstition of the mind. And in Latin also we speak of *infirmitas* [in this sense]; Horace in the *Satires* writes, 'But for myself I am somewhat weaker,'[4] that is,[5] 'more superstitious.'[6] Chrysostom reads ἐσθίει, that is, 'eats' [indicative] and he interprets likewise, saying that from this circumstance[7] it happened that then they abstained totally from meat – in order that it might appear as νηστεία, that is, 'as fasting,' not as observance of the Mosaic law.[8] There is not a single word in [Chrysostom's] commentaries that indicates that Paul is enjoining this. Theophylact agrees with Chrysostom in every respect, expressing the same opinion in almost the same words.[9] Origen suggests nothing else;[10] and Ambrose seems to have read the same, except that his interpretation appears to have been corrupted. Says he: ' "But he who is weak, let him eat vegetables." Therefore because he thinks that the [weak] one should eat vegetables, he should not be persuaded to eat meats.' I think we should read: 'Because the [weak] one thinks he should eat vegetables, he should not be persuaded to eat meat.'[11] It is indeed true that 'let him eat' can be taken as an expression of permission, not a command, but both the reading and the interpretation of the Greek codices agree in opposing this.[12] Hence, it is probable that wherever manducet [let him eat] is read, the reading has been corrupted, or whoever so interprets has not consulted the Greek. A comment of this sort is added in the Latin scholia;[13] but it had made clear earlier that [the verb] must be read as an indicative.

In some[14] of the Greek copies the reading was ὃς δὲ ἀσθενῶν [but who being weak]. But Paul often uses the relative pronoun for the article in such passages.[15] Therefore it should be translated 'one believes that he should eat everything (or, anything); on the other hand, another who is weak eats vegetables.' Otherwise 'one,' which comes in the first part of the sentence, has no word to correspond with it.[16]

1 The Vulgate had translated with a jussive subjunctive:
  ER oleribus vescitur 'eats vegetables'
  VG olus manducet 'let him consume vegetable food'
2 With ... his superstititon.] Added in 1519
3 Jerome Commentarius in Ecclesiasten (on 2:5) PL 23 (1883) 1078C. Jerome cites the passage as qui infirmus est, oleribus vescitur.
4 weaker] In 1516 only, the annotation continued (and concluded) with the following: 'I must not conceal what Valla rightly notes, that the Translator failed to reproduce the balanced structure [of the clauses]: this person thinks he can eat anything at all, that one, on the other hand, who is weak, eats vegetables.' For the clauses in question see n15 below. For Valla, see Annot in Rom 14 (I 860).
5 that is ... indicative] Added in 1535
6 Cf Horace Satires 1.9.71. The editions from 1516 to 1527 included the word unus: 'But for myself I am one somewhat weaker.' Even so, the quotation is not quite accurate.
7 The circumstance that many Jewish believers, as Jews, were afraid not to practise the Law but, as Christians, did not want to seem to practise it –

as they would seem to do if they refused only pork. Thus they rejected all meats, as though practising Christian fasting, rather than following the Jewish law.

8 Chrysostom *Hom in Rom* 25.1 PG 60 627
9 Theophylact *Expos in Rom* 14:1 PG 124 521D
10 Cf Origen *Comm in Rom* 9.35 PG 14 1234C
11 Cf Ambrosiaster *Comm in Rom* 14:2 (1–2) CSEL 81/1 435:8–10. Erasmus quotes Ambrosiaster evidently from a representative of those manuscripts of the gamma recension whose reading is cited in CSEL only in a footnote (cf 435:8n). The text CSEL adopts translates: ' "But he who is weak let him eat vegetables." Therefore so that he might eat vegetables, since he thinks this useful, he should not be persuaded to eat meat.' Erasmus believed that Ambrosiaster's commentary, as he had cited and corrected it, was evidence that Ambrosiaster had read the indicative, so that the biblical citation in Ambrosiaster's text, reading *manducet* 'let him eat,' must have been corrupted as an accommodation to the Vulgate text. But in his response to Titelmans, Erasmus noted that the reading of Ambrosiaster, Jerome, and others was irrelevant since these had made the words of Paul fit their own opinion (*Responsio ad collationes* LB IX 1011F).
12 The best Greek reading gives the verb in the indicative, though some manuscripts read a jussive subjunctive here. See Tischendorf II 437 2n and Cranfield II 701 3n; on the Latin reading, see Wordsworth and White II 134 2n.
13 A reference evidently to the commentaries of Pelagius and Pseudo-Jerome, whom elsewhere Erasmus calls the Latin scholiast; cf the annotations on 5:12 ('in whom [or, in which] all have sinned') n22, and 9:10 ('from intercourse one time only') n20. For the reference, see Souter II 106 and III 24–5.
14 In some ... with it.] Added in *1519*
15 The discussion here extends the reference beyond the cue phrase:
     ER *alius quidem credit vescendum esse quibus libet; alius autem qui infirmus est oleribus vescitur* 'one indeed believes that he ought to eat anything he likes; another, however, who is weak, eats vegetables'
     VG *alius enim credit se manducare omnia. Qui autem infirmus est, olus manducet* 'for one believes that he eats all things; who, however, is weak, let him eat vegetables'
     For the use of the relative pronoun ὅς (*hos*) 'who' with the force of the article ὁ (*ho*) in the sense of 'one,' see 14:5: 'one [ὃς μέν] judges ... another [ὁ δέ] judges' and the annotation on this verse ('for one judges') below.
     In *1516* Erasmus printed the Greek text of 14:2 with the pronoun in the first clause, the article in the second (ὃς μέν ... ὁ δέ), but from *1519* followed the inferior reading in printing the pronoun in both clauses (ὃς μέν ... ὃς δέ), which gave a neat parallelism in the Greek as in his translation: *alius ... alius*. The Vulgate translation *alius ... qui* failed to observe the parallelism. For ὃς as the inferior reading in the second clause, see Tischendorf II 437 2n; for *qui* as the preferred Latin reading, Wordsworth and White II 134 2n.
16 For the concluding sentence of *1516*, small parts of which were incorporated into this *1519* addition, see n4 above.

14:3 [ER *ne despiciat* 'should not despise']

[VG] *non spernat* 'let him not spurn'; ἐξουθενείτω, as though to say 'judge [him] worth nothing' and 'count as nothing' (as the Greek word shows, in its derivation from[1] [the word for] 'nothing').

> 1 from 'nothing'] Added in 1519. The Greek verb is compounded from the preposition ἐξ 'from,' 'out of' and οὐθέν = οὐδέν 'nothing,' plus verbal suffix.

14:4 [ER *proprio domino stat aut cadit* 'to his own Lord he stands or falls']

[VG] *domino suo stat aut cadit* 'to his[1] Lord he stands or falls'; 'but he shall stand,'[2] σταθήσεται δέ. Cyprian cites this passage in the second letter of the fourth book, and not unskilfully translates the subsequent verb στῆσαι[3] by *stabilire* [to make firm, to establish], though indeed the [Greek] verb is the same as the previous one: 'God is able to make him firm.'[4]

> 1 to his ... firm.'] The annotation was added in 1519.
> 2 After the cue phrase 14:4 continues:
> > ER *imo fulcietur autem ut stet* 'rather, he shall be given the support to stand'
> > VG *stabit autem* 'but he shall stand'
> 3 Ie in the next clause of 14:4, where Erasmus translated *efficere ut stet* '[for God is able] to cause him to stand'; the Vulgate, *statuere illum* '[for God is able] to make him stand'
> 4 Cyprian *Epistulae* 55.18 CSEL 3/2 637:6

14:5 [ER *hic quidem iudicat* 'this person judges']

[VG] *nam alius iudicat* 'for one judges'; ὃς μὲν κρίνει ἡμέραν παρ᾽ ἡμέραν. ὃς δὲ κρίνει πᾶσαν ἡμέραν. ἕκαστος etc, that is, 'this person judges the day according to the day, while that one judges every day; [let] each one' etc. But[1] if, as is right, one is permitted to render faithfully the thought, disregarding superstitious adherence to the words, it could be translated in this way: 'This person thinks that there is some difference between one day and another, while that person feels the same about any day at all.'[2] Augustine in his questions on this Epistle reads: 'One judges different days; but another judges every day.'[3] But I am embarrassed by his note on[4] this same passage, which he would by no means have written if he had consulted the Greek or if a better interpretation had been available to him. I will add his own words, lest any one should mistrust me: 'In want of a better idea, I think that this speaks not of two persons, but of man and God. He who judges different days is man. For he can judge one thing today, and another tomorrow, that is, someone he has today condemned as evil – convicted and confessed – tomorrow he will find good [...][5] corrupt. But he who judges every day is God, for he knows the nature of every man.[6] Each one, [Paul] says, abounds[7] in his own understanding, that is, let each venture to judge in so far as it is granted to human understanding, or to each one. He who discerns the day, says [Paul],[8] discerns it to the Lord; that is, he discerns it to the Lord, because in this very respect, he judges well in relation to the present day. But "to judge well" in relation to the day is this, that you know you must not despair of the future correction of one concerning whose evident fault you have judged for the present.' So far Augustine. I ask you, reader, does he not seem to be living in some other world when he writes this? I should not want anyone to seize upon what I have said as an insult against the words of Augustine, whose learning I esteem and whose holiness I revere. But this error on the part of so great a man should convince us that we must not neglect to consult the Greek volumes.

St Jerome, in the second book *Against Jovinian*, translates in this manner: 'One man judges [one] day more than [another] day,'[9] taking παρά as 'above' or 'beyond,'[10] as it is sometimes found in Greek. But in Greek, παρά sometimes implies a basis of comparison, as in their proverb τὴν πορφύραν παρὰ πορφύραν, that is, 'purple against purple.'[11] And indeed he who compares thinks one is better than another. To the Jews, one day was profane and another holy. To Christians, however, every day is equally holy: not that the feast days should not be observed which the holy Fathers then established so that Christian people might more conveniently assemble for the preaching in church and for the divine liturgy, but these are very few, namely the Lord's day, Easter, Pentecost, and a few others of this sort which Jerome recounts.[12] But I am not sure that it is advantageous to heap feast day on feast day for any reason whatever, especially when we see that Christian behaviour has reached such a point that just as it was once conducive to godliness to institute these days, so now it would seem expedient to let the same pass out of use.

1 But ... Greek volumes.] The remainder of this paragraph was added in 1519.
2 Compare the translations of Erasmus and the Vulgate:
    ER [1516] *alius quidem iudicat diem ad diem, alius autem iudicat omnem diem* 'for one judges the day in relation to the day, but another judges every day'
    ER [1519–1535] *hic quidem iudicat diem ad diem conferens, ille autem idem iudicat de quovis die* 'this one judges, comparing day in relation to day; but that one makes the same judgment about any day at all'
    VG *nam alius iudicat diem inter diem, alius autem iudicat omnem diem* 'for one judges day among day; but another judges every day'
3 Augustine *Expositio quarundam propositionum ex epistula ad Romanos* 80 PL 35 2086
4 note on] Until 1535, 'interpretation of'
5 Erasmus omitted a line from Augustine's text. Augustine reads: '... will find good, when he has corrected himself; on the other hand, someone whom he has today praised as just, tomorrow he will find corrupt. But he who judges ...'

6 Erasmus has abbreviated. Augustine says here: '... for he not only knows what the nature of each person is, but what each will be like on every day.'

7 In Migne 'let each one abound'

8 Augustine goes on here to comment on 14:6.

9 Jerome *Adversus Jovinianum* 2.16 PL 23 (1883) 324B

10 The παρά is represented in Erasmus' translation (*1516* to *1535*) by *ad* 'in relation to'; in the Vulgate by *inter* 'among' (cf n2 above).

11 For the proverb, see *Adagia* II i 74.

12 Cf Jerome *Commentarius in epistulam ad Galatas* 2.3 (on 4:10–11) PL 26 (1883) 404B–405B. For Jerome's homilies on the great feast days see Quasten *Patrology* IV 236.

14:5 [ER *sua mens* 'his mind']

[VG] *in suo sensu* '**in his understanding**'[1]; ἰδίῳ νοΐ πληροφορείσθω, that is, 'let him be sure in his own mind or heart,' or 'let him hold a clear conviction,' that is, let him be at rest in his opinion. Ambrose[2] interprets, 'let each one be confident in his judgment.'[3] I have just pointed out Augustine's interpretation.[4] In any case [the expression] *abundare in suo sensu* describes a person of inflexible mind and obstinate will.[5]

1 For the context of the phrase compare the translations of Erasmus and the Vulgate:
ER *unicuique sua mens satisfaciat* 'let his mind satisfy each'
VG *unusquisque in suo sensu abundet* 'let each abound in his understanding'

2 Ambrose ... will.] Added in *1519*

3 Ambrosiaster *Comm in Rom* 14:5 (3)

4 Cf the previous annotation, nn7 and 3.

5 Lefèvre also substituted *mens* for the Vulgate *sensus* (*Pauli epistolae* fol 10 recto). For *mens* in place of the Vulgate *sensus* see the annotation on 12:2 ('in the newness of the understanding').

14:6 [ER *et qui non vescitur, domino non vescitur* '**and he who does not take food, to his Lord he does not take food**']

[VG] *et qui non manducat, domino non manducat* '**and he who does not eat, to the Lord he does not eat.**' The Greek [codices] add καὶ ὁ μὴ φρονῶν τὴν ἡμέραν, κυρίῳ οὐ φρονεῖ, that is, 'and he who does not discern the day, to the Lord he does not discern it'; then follows 'and he who eats, to the Lord he eats, for he gives thanks' etc.[1] Otherwise[2] there will be no corresponding negative to contrast with the first proposition, 'he who discerns the day, to the Lord he discerns it.' This[3] statement is certainly added in Theophylact.[4] But since there is a general agreement in the Latin codices, and it is not found in Ambrose or Origen,[5] it may be that someone supplied on his own what was lacking in Paul. I doubt that 'gives thanks' can be referred to the one who distinguishes the day.[6] For the one who takes food and the one who does not take food, each nevertheless eats and gives thanks alike for his food, different though it may be.

This, too, should be noted, that Paul puts forward the statements on the 'strong' and the 'weak' in a varied order. When first he said, 'One believes he can eat anything, while he who is weak takes vegetables,' he put the case of the strong first and made that of the weak second. Then he repeats it in the same order: 'And so he who eats should not spurn the one who does not eat. The one who does not eat should not judge the one who does.' Then just below, he reverses the order: 'For one judges among days, while another judges every day.' Here he has put the case of the weak in the earlier position. In the [sequence] that follows there is another reversal in the order,[7] for when he says, 'He who discerns the day, discerns it to the Lord,' he has put the case of the weak first. For 'to discern' in this passage is to have an anxious concern for and to be aware of the distinction between one day and another, which is characteristic of Jewish superstition. And not to discern is not to be concerned about the distinction between days. Then soon: 'He who eats, eats to the Lord, and he who does not eat, does not eat to the Lord.' Here he has put the case of the stronger first, that of the weaker second; unless someone prefers to interpret 'discern the day' in a different sense.

Certainly, Thomas Aquinas explains it in such a way that one is said to 'discern the day' who distinguishes between one day and another, but [Aquinas] twists this to apply to our feast days and fast days, which he regards as praiseworthy.[8] If this interpretation is true, it will not be a matter of weakness to judge between days, but of perfect godliness; and to judge every day [alike] will not be a matter of firm faith, but of ungodliness. Even Ambrose himself somehow twists this passage, adding this by way of commentary: 'It is true that he who always abstains thinks he is pleasing God.'[9] (Always to abstain is more perfect than sometimes to abstain, sometimes not to abstain.) But if 'he who judges every day alike always abstains,'[10] how – since earlier [Paul] made the one not eating the weaker – is he here, conversely, the stronger who previously was considered the weaker? But what Paul said about the choice of foods according to the custom of the Jews, likewise about the distinction of days according to the rites of these same people, Ambrose and Thomas apply to later times,[11] in which the bishops proclaimed both feast days, though fewer than we have, and specific fasts, of which I think there were as yet none in Paul's time – I[12] am speaking of those established by decree.

Origen explains that one 'discerns the day' who does *not* distinguish one day from another, and he couples the one who eats anything with the one who discerns every day.[13] Hence it has occurred to me that this clause can refer to both, the one who distinguishes and the one who does not distinguish. For since one who feels the same about any day at all 'discerns the day,' and one who feels differently about different days 'discerns the day,' [Paul] has included both parties in a general statement. The one who discerns the day – whether he does so in one way or another – discerns it to his Lord, not to you, to whom it is no concern. And this appears to be the reason why this statement has no contrasting negative,[14] although the one not eating is contrasted with the one who eats. Chrysostom,[15] to be sure, does not touch upon this statement in his exposition.[16]

Here I have preferred to translate *vescitur* [takes food] and *non*[17] *vescitur*, because it is not a question simply of eating or not eating, but of the kind of food, [a question], that is, of pork, or[18] meat offered to idols. Moreover, whenever we speak of kinds of food, *vesci* is more appropriate than *edere*.[19] Further instead of *sapit* [discerns] I have preferred *curat* [has regard for]. The Greek word φρονεῖν is πολύσημος [of many meanings]; at one time it means 'to feel,' at another 'to discern,' or again 'to think,' occasionally 'to have a particular attitude'; sometimes the Latin language is scarcely able to render its meaning.[20]

1 Erasmus believed the Greek manuscripts demonstrated that a pair of clauses (italicized in what follows) had been lost in the Vulgate translation of 14:6. According to Erasmus this verse should be read (as in his own translation):
    [6a] One who has concern for the day [*curat diem*] has concern to the Lord, *and one who does not have regard for the day does not have regard to the Lord.*
    [6b] One who takes food takes food to the Lord, for he gives thanks to God; and one who does not take food does not take food to the Lord, and gives thanks to God.
    In his annotation, Erasmus generally quotes the Vulgate text, where, in place of his phrase *curat diem*, the Vulgate reads *sapere diem* 'discerns the day,' and in place of 'takes food,' 'eats.' The sentence Erasmus adds is found in the later witnesses and was adopted by Lefèvre (*Pauli epistolae* fol 10 recto). It is, however, regarded as a gloss. See Tischendorf II 438 6n and Metzger 531. the day] In the clause 'and he who does not discern the day,' 'the day' was added in *1522*.
2 Otherwise ... contrasted with the one who eats.] This lengthy central section was added in *1519*, with the exceptions noted below (cf nn3 and 12).
3 This ... Theophylact.] Added in *1527*
4 Theophylact *Expos in Rom* 14:6 PG 124 525B
5 Cf Ambrosiaster *Comm in Rom* 14:6 (1–2) and Origen *Comm in Rom* 9.38 PG 14 1237C.
6 Erasmus' point appears to be that the phrase 'gives thanks,' repeated as it is in 14:6b, invites us to see a structured unity in the contrast between one who does and one who does not take food. This suggests that a similar contrast should be available in 14:6a between one who discerns the day and one who does not. If, however, the phrase 'gives thanks' of 14:6b could refer also to

14:6a, then 6a is tied more closely to 6b, the structure envisioned begins to break down, and there remains no compelling reason to include the 'omitted' words of 6a. Erasmus prefers, therefore, to confine the field of reference of 'gives thanks' to 6b and supply the omitted clauses in 6a, which will then yield a set of contrasts parallel to those of 6b.

7 Erasmus sees a pattern of inversions in two sequences, the first in verses 2–5, the second in verse 6; for the pattern in verse 6 to be complete the two clauses generally regarded as a gloss (cf n1 above) are required.

8 Thomas Aquinas *Super Rom lect* cap 14 lectio 1.1100: 'Hence he says "who discerns the day," that is, abstaining on one day and not on another ... just as we distinguish the "watches," in which we fast, from feast days in which we are free from fasting because of our reverence for God.'

9 Ambrosiaster *Comm in Rom* 14:6 (1). In spite of the italics in LB, this sentence alone constitutes the full commentary on 'who discerns the day, discerns it to the Lord.' The sentence that follows (and that we have placed in parenthesis) may be an interpretive gloss on the commentary.

10 Erasmus draws the premise from Ambrosiaster's commentary on 14:5 ('but one judges every day'): 'The one who judges every day is the person who never eats' (*Comm in Rom* 14:5 [2]). Hence the conclusion following from the interpretive gloss (the one who always abstains is the more perfect), that the one who does not eat is the stronger. Cf n9 above.

11 For Thomas Aquinas see n8 above; for Ambrosiaster see *Comm in Rom* 14:5 (1a): 'Some have determined not to eat meat on the third weekday, some on the sabbath; there are, again, some who eat from Easter to Pentecost.'

12 I ... decree] Added in 1527

13 Origen offers both a literal and an allegorical interpretation. On the literal interpretation, the one who judges every day is the one who practises abstinence always, and so does not distinguish one day from another. But Origen equates the one who judges the day (14:5) with the one who discerns the day (14:6). This person is paired with the one who eats all things, since on an allegorical interpretation, both signify the individual who examines the Scriptures continuously and deeply. Cf Origen *Comm in Rom* 9.37–8 PG 14 1237B–1238B.

14 Ie in the Vulgate. Erasmus' translation adds a contrasting negative; cf n1 above.

15 Chrysostom ... exposition.] Added in 1527

16 The sentence appears in Chrysostom's citation of the biblical text, but is not discussed in his exposition; cf *Hom in Rom* 25.2 PG 60 630–1.

17 *non*] Omitted, perhaps inadvertently, until 1527

18 pork, or] Added in 1535

19 Cf Valla, who contrasts *pasco* and *vescor*, the former appropriate to animals, the latter to humans (*Elegantiae* 4.54 [I 141–2]).

20 Cf the annotation on 8:5 ('discern the things that are of the Spirit') and n6.

14:9 [ER *et mortuus est et resurrexit et revixit* 'and he died and rose and lived again']

[VG] *mortuus est et resurrexit* 'he died and rose again.'[1] Here the Greek codices add καὶ ἀνέζησεν, that is, 'and lived again,'[2] though Theophylact reads ἔζησε, that is, 'lived,' not ἀνέζησεν.[3] If we follow this we shall have to take the past tense as a present,[4] which is often the case with such verbs: 'For this he died, for this he rose again, and for this he now lives, so that' etc. Ambrose[5] reads and interprets: 'For this Christ both lived and died and rose again.'[6] In the codex of St Paul's, which to me was worth many when I first published this,[7] [the passage] had been written thus: 'For this, Christ both died and lived again, that' etc. (Certainly it agrees with the Greek copies in this, that it duplicates the conjunction.[8]) That Origen read thus is demonstrated by his interpretation of the passage, which begins: 'He says that Christ died, without doubt through the "economy" of the passion; that he lived, however, through the mystery of the resurrection.'[9] And this reading has a correspondence in what follows, 'that he might be Lord both of the dead and of the living,' for it is read in this order both in the Greek and by Origen, who discusses the passage in these words: 'Someone will, perhaps, be disturbed by the Apostle's words, that [Christ] died and lived for this reason, that he might be Lord over the dead and the living; as though we had been given to understand that if he had not died and lived again after his death, he would not have held dominion over the living.'[10] There is the same order[11] in Ambrose;[12] and also in the very old manuscript that I just cited 'the dead' precedes and 'the living' follows; for dying comes first, living second, especially in the case of Christ, in so far as he took on human nature, which is subject to death. But in the previous lines 'the living' had preceded: 'Whether we live, we live to the Lord, or whether we die, we die to the Lord.'[13]

In Chrysostom[14] there is only ἀπέθανεν, ἔζησεν [he died, he lived].[15] But[16] the Verona edition has the three, ἀπέθανεν, ἀνέστη, ἔζησεν [he died, he rose again, he lived].[17] The middle word, ἀνέστη, seems to be an addition, for near the end of Chrysostom's discussion he says νεκρὸς ὢν ἔζησεν [being dead, he lived].[18] The Aldine edition agrees with the Verona edition.[19] But I am delaying too long on these matters, which have little or nothing to do with the sense.

1 In 1516 only, the order of this annotation and the next was reversed.
2 There is considerable variation here among the Greek witnesses. Some support Erasmus, but the best reading is 'died and lived again.' See Tischendorf II 439 9n; Metzger 531; and Cranfield II 708 n1. Lefèvre read 'both died and rose and lived' (Pauli epistolae fol 10 recto). On 'lived again' see n3 below.
3 Theophylact Expos in Rom 14:9 PG 124 525D. The best reading is ἔζησεν, not ἀνέζησεν, but in biblical Greek the uncompounded ζάω, when used of the dead, means 'live again,' not, as Erasmus suggests, 'live'; see ζάω 1B in BAG.
4 a present] From 1519; in 1516, 'a future'
5 Ambrose ... die to the Lord.'] This long central section was added in 1519, with the exception noted below (n7).

6 Ambrosiaster *Comm in Rom* 14:9

7 first published this] In *1535* only; from *1519* to *1527*, 'when I added this.' For this codex see the annotation on 4:5 ('according to the purpose of the grace of God') n5.

8 In the Latin of 14:9, *et ... et*; in the Greek, καί ... καί 'both died *and* rose again.' The best reading has a single conjunction, 'died and lived again'; cf n2 above. Erasmus printed the Greek text with the conjunction tripled, and so translated.

9 Origen *Comm in Rom* 9.39 PG 14 1239A–B

10 Erasmus omits a clause from the text of Origen, which reads: '... if he had not died, he would not have had the lordship over the dead, and if after death, he had not lived again, he would not have held dominion over the living' (*Comm in Rom* 9.39 PG 14 1239B).

11 Erasmus discusses here both parts of 14:9, in particular the verbs of 9a and the substantives of 9b, since he evidently thinks the order of the substantives in 9b should parallel the order of the verbs in 9a. In the Vulgate printed in *1527*, the order of the words in question is: he died, he rose again ... the living, the dead. Compare the Vulgate and Erasmus' translations of 14:9b:

> ER *ut mortuis ac viventibus dominetur* 'that he might be Lord over the dead and the living'
> VG *ut et vivorum et mortuorum dominetur* 'that he might be Lord of both the living and the dead'

There is strong support in the Latin manuscripts for the order of both the Vulgate and Erasmus' translation; cf Wordsworth and White II 136 and 9n.

12 In fact, Ambrosiaster's commentary follows the same order as his citation of the biblical text: the living and the dead; cf n6 above.

13 Rom 14:8

14 In Chrysostom ... ἔζησεν.] Added in *1527*, with additional words so that the passage read: 'In Chrysostom there is only ἀπέθανεν [he died]; ἔζησεν [he lived] would seem to have been omitted through the carelessness of scribes, except that he does not mention this word in his commentary.' The additional words ('would ... commentary') were omitted in *1535*.

15 Chrysostom *Hom in Rom* 25.3 PG 60 631. In the Migne edition, the passage is cited first with the three verbs, as in the text Erasmus printed, then with one verb only, 'he died,' and finally with the two verbs mentioned here.

16 But ... sense.] Added in *1535*

17 In *1529* the Greek text of Chrysostom's homilies on the Pauline Epistles was published in three folio volumes under the direction of John Matthew Giberti, bishop of Verona (see *Contemporaries* II 95). For the manuscript of Chrysostom's homilies available to Erasmus first for the *1527* edition see the annotation on 13:5 ('and on this account be subject to necessity') n14.

18 Chrysostom *Hom in Rom* 25.3 PG 60 632

19 For the Aldine edition of the New Testament, see the annotation on 11:6 ('otherwise grace is no longer grace') n10.

14:10 [ER *aut etiam tu cur despicis* 'or you, too, why do you despise']
[VG] *aut tu quare spernis* 'or you, why do you spurn';[1] ἢ καὶ σὺ τί ἐξουθενεῖς,

that is, 'or you, too, why do you spurn?' The first 'you'[2] refers to the one who does not eat, the second to the one who eats; so the conjunction καί is not superfluous.[3] For the one who does not eat, because of his superstition, judges him who eats. On the other hand, the one who eats because of his knowledge disdains the weakness of the one who does not eat. Ambrose[4] reads (with a few words added): 'But you, why in not eating do you judge your brother? and you, why in eating do you spurn your brother?'[5] But I think he added 'in not eating' and 'in eating' on his own to explicate the meaning.[6]

1 For the position of this annotation in 1516 see the previous annotation, n1.
2 In 14:10a: But you, why do you judge your brother?
3 The καί is represented in Erasmus' translation by etiam 'too,' but is not represented in most Vulgate texts (cf Wordsworth and White II 136 10n).
4 Ambrose ... meaning.] Added in 1519
5 Ambrosiaster Comm in Rom 14:10
6 For the added words as variants in the textual tradition see Wordsworth and White II 136 10n.

14:10 [ER *omnes enim statuemur* 'for we shall all be made to stand']
[VG] *omnes enim stabimus* 'for we shall all stand'; πάντες γὰρ παραστησό-μεθα,[1] that is, 'for we shall all appear[2] (or, are to appear) at the judgment seat of Christ.' For defendants, or those who are to be tried, are said to appear for trial when they are forced to be present.

1 After παραστησόμεθα, LB adds the words τῷ βήματι τοῦ Χριστοῦ. These words are found in no edition printed in Erasmus' lifetime. They appear in LB to complete the sentence: 'For we shall all be made to stand before the tribunal of Christ.'
2 Latin *sistemur*; as a legal term, the word is regularly used in the sense of 'appear before a court.'

14:11 [ER *mihi sese flectet* 'shall bend[1] to me']
[VG] *mihi flectetur* 'shall be bent to me'; ἐμοὶ κάμψει, that is, 'shall bend to me,' with 'itself' understood. At least,[2] in one or two[3] very old manuscripts I have found *flectet* written, not *flectetur*.[4] This scriptural text is to be found in the forty-fifth chapter of Isaiah, but Paul's citation corresponds word for word with neither the Hebrew original nor the Septuagint edition.[5] For according to the latter, we read: 'By my own self I swear, unless[6] right-eousness go forth from my mouth, my words will not be turned aside, that every knee shall bow to me, and every tongue shall swear and confess, saying' [45:23]. According to the Hebrew, Jerome translates: 'On my own self have I sworn, let the word of righteousness go forth[7] from my mouth,

and it shall not return, that every knee shall bow to me, and every tongue shall swear and confess[8] to God.'[9]

1 shall bend] First in *1519*; in *1516*, like the Vulgate
2 At least ... God.'] This remaining portion of the annotation was added in *1519*, with the one exception noted (cf n3 below).
3 one or two] Added in *1522*
4 *Flectet*, supported by a large number of manuscripts, is the preferred reading, though *flectetur* has the support of some witnesses. See Wordsworth and White II 136 11n.
5 In Paul's quotation the introductory formula is taken from Isa 49:18 (LXX). Thereafter ('that every knee ...') Paul follows the Septuagint of Isa 45:23 closely, though there are variations in the textual tradition of the Septuagint (see Rahlfs II 629 23n). Erasmus himself appears to have relied here on the translation of the Septuagint he found in Jerome's commentary, which offers a text reflecting a minor variation from Paul's citation. See Cranfield II 710.
6 Jerome (cf n9 below) reads *nisi* 'unless,' based on the εἰ μή of a number of manuscripts, which gives, however, an unsatisfactory sense.
7 In Jerome, future tense: 'shall go forth'
8 Jerome omits 'and confess.'
9 Jerome *Commentarii in Isaiam* 13 (on 45:23) PL 24 448A and C

14:13 [ER *verum illud iudicate magis* 'but judge that rather']

[VG] *sed hoc iudicate magis* 'but judge[1] this rather.' Ambrose reads 'and in this (or, in that) judge rather' – what manuscript he was following I do not know.[2] Both the Greek codices and the old Latin codices oppose [his reading]. Jerome, or the translator of Origen, whoever he was, points out in his exposition that *iudicate* is not used here in the sense of 'condemn,' as in the previous clause,[3] but in the sense of 'decide.'[4] It is peculiar to Hebrew to use 'judgment' in the sense of 'condemnation.' The Greek word, κρίνειν, is ambiguous. At one time it means 'to judge,' at another 'to decide' or 'to determine.' But if anyone would rather not take the verb 'to judge' in a sense different from that in the other passages, the meaning might also be this: it is not fitting that any of you should judge another who, whether he is speaking rightly or not, remains to be judged by his Lord; but if it is permitted to judge anyone in any respect, he is to be judged who, on account of food for the body, is unwilling to avoid an offence to his brother, rather than the one who either suspects that the former is taking food with an insecure conscience or is provoked by his example into doing something he believes is wrong.

1 but judge ... wrong.] This entire annotation was added in *1519*.
2 Ambrosiaster *Comm in Rom* 14:13 (1–2). Ambrosiaster is the chief witness to this reading; cf Wordsworth and White II 137 13n.
3 Ie in 14:13a: 'Let us not henceforth judge one another'
4 Origen *Comm in Rom* 9.41 PG 14 1245A

14:14 [ER *novi siquidem et persuasum habeo* 'for I have come to know and
am persuaded']
[vg] *scio et confido* 'I know and am confident'; οἶδα καὶ πέπεισμαι, that is,
'I know and am certain' or 'am persuaded.'[1]

> 1 So, similarly, the annotation on 8:38 ('for I am certain')

14:14 [ER *nihil esse commune per se* 'nothing is common of itself']
[vg] *nihil commune per ipsum* 'nothing[1] is common through himself.'[2] The
Translator seems to have read δι᾽ αὐτοῦ with an unaspirated alpha. And so
reads Ambrose, commenting that through the kind deed of Christ nothing
is common.[3] But the more correct reading is δι᾽ αὑτοῦ with an aspirated
alpha, or δι᾽ ἑαυτοῦ, that is, *per seipsum* or *per se*,[4] because there follows
'but to him who thinks it unclean, it is unclean.'[5] So reads Origen,[6] and
Chrysostom and[7] Theophylact agree with him.[8] They[9] interpret δι᾽ αὐτοῦ to
mean τῇ φύσει, that is, 'by nature.'

> 1 nothing ... with him.] With the exception of the last sentence and the
> reference to Chrysostom (see nn7 and 9 below), this annotation was added
> in 1519.
> 2 *Ipsum* after *per* may be either masculine (himself) or neuter (itself).
> Ambrosiaster (n3 below) understands it as a masculine.
> 3 Ambrosiaster *Comm in Rom* 14:14 (1)
> 4 Though the unaspirated *autou*, standing alone, would normally be read as
> a personal pronoun, it may, in form, be either a personal or an intensive
> pronoun, and either masculine or neuter, 'himself' or 'itself,' ambiguities
> reflected in the Vulgate's *per ipsum* (cf n2 above); the aspirated *hautou* or
> *heautou* is a reflexive pronoun (Latin *sui, se*) and here therefore can only be
> neuter: 'nothing ... through (or, of) itself.'
> 5 Cf 14:14b; Erasmus gives the sense rather than quotes directly either from
> the Vulgate or his own translation.
> 6 Origen *Comm in Rom* 9.42 PG 14 1245B–1247A. Though the biblical citations in
> this passage follow the Vulgate, Origen understands the pronoun as reflexive:
> 'nothing is common of its own nature.'
> 7 Chrysostom and] Added in 1527
> 8 Chrysostom *Hom in Rom* 26.1 PG 60 637; Theophylact *Expos in Rom* 14:14
> PG 124 528C–D. Chrysostom's text, according to Migne, has both readings,
> Theophylact's only the reflexive, but both exegetes interpret, as Erasmus
> says, in a reflexive sense, 'by nature,' ie 'of itself.'
> 9 They ... 'by nature.'] Added in 1535

14:15 [ER vg] *contristatur* 'is saddened'; λυπεῖται, that is, 'grieves' or 'feels distress.'

14:16 [ER *ne vestrum igitur bonum hominum maledicentiae sit obnoxium* 'let not,
then, your good be liable to human slander']
[vg] *non ergo blasphemetur bonum nostrum* 'therefore let not our good be

blasphemed.' The Greek is 'your'[1] – second person – ὑμῶν τὸ ἀγαθόν, that is, 'your good':[2] you must take care that what you do (rightly) should not offer anyone an opportunity for disparagement. Or[3] 'your good' [means] your correct opinion, by which you feel that it is permitted to take any food at all. Theophylact explains [the passage] along these lines.[4] Chrysostom[5] likewise reads ὑμῶν 'your,' interpreting [your good] as Christian concord.[6] This[7] expression seems similar to the previous one, ἡμῶν ἡ σωτηρία [our salvation],[8] though[9] the more usual form of speech is τὸ ὑμῶν ἀγαθόν.[10] What he here calls 'the good' is not that which is without qualification good, but that which is good to him who acts with a good intent, and for this reason he defines it by a pronoun.[11] And yet there is no reason why I should do battle with anyone who would argue that the form of expression is entirely similar.[12]

1 So Valla *Annot in Rom* 14 (1 860) and Lefèvre *Pauli epistolae* fol 102 recto. Among the Greek witnesses the second person has the better support (Tischendorf II 440 16n; Metzger 532; Cranfield II 716 n5); among the Latin witnesses, the first person is the preferred reading (Wordsworth and White II 137 16n).
2 good] Added in 1519
3 Or ... these lines.] Added in 1519
4 Theophylact *Expos in Rom* 14:16 PG 124 529B: 'You have perfect faith – this he calls "the good." Do not abuse this perfection of yours, or cause it to be blasphemed.'
5 Chrysostom ... concord.] Added in 1535
6 Chrysostom *Hom in Rom* 26.1 PG 60 638. For Chrysostom, 'outsiders' blaspheme when Christian concord is disrupted.
7 This ... similar.] This remaining portion of the annotation was added in 1527, with the exception noted below (n9).
8 In 13:11, where, on the Vulgate reading ('our salvation') the pronoun precedes the article
9 though ... ἀγαθόν] Added in 1535
10 In the biblical text here, the pronoun ὑμῶν precedes the article τό rather than follows (as in the 'usual form of speech') between the article and noun. Cf the annotation on 13:11 'for now is nearer.'
11 Ie *your* good
12 Cf the annotation on 13:11 ('for now is nearer'), where Erasmus had argued on the basis of the 'form of expression' that the pronoun should not be taken with the word 'salvation' ('our salvation'), but with the adverb 'nearer' ('salvation is nearer us').

14:17 [ER VG] *iustitia et pax et gaudium in spiritu sancto* 'righteousness[1] and peace and joy in the Holy Spirit.' Here as well[2] the preposition ἐν [in], following Hebrew idiom, stands for διά, that is, 'through' – as Origen makes quite clear in his discussion of this passage.[3]

He sets in contrast the Holy Spirit and contention over foods. The latter brings forth anger, sadness, and unrighteousness, the former peace instead of anger, joy instead of sadness, righteousness instead of offence and injury.

1 righteousness ... injury.] This entire annotation was added in 1519.
2 Cf the annotation on 1:4 ('in power') and n8, and 1:24 ('to the desires of the heart').
3 Origen Comm in Rom 10.1 PG 14 1250C–1251A

14:18 [ER etenim qui per haec servit Christo 'for he who through these[1] things serves Christ']

[VG] qui enim in hoc servit Christo 'for he[2] who in this serves Christ.' The Greek[3] reads 'in these things,'[4] which has the same force as if he had said 'through[5] these things,' ὁ γὰρ ἐν τούτοις δουλεύων. He has represented the [antecedent] feminine nouns by a neuter pronoun[6] so that you think simultaneously of other things also which are of the same kind as justice, peace, and joy. So[7] indeed Theophylact reads and expounds,[8] and Chrysostom[9] reads thus, though in his commentary he does not reveal what he read.[10] Nevertheless[11] Ambrose disagrees;[12] Origen disagrees, and relates 'in this' to the Holy Spirit,[13] which[14] had been mentioned just before:[15] as though[16] to say, those[17] who contend about foods serve Christ in the flesh; but they serve [him] in the spirit who disdain such things and pursue only those things which make for peace and concord.[18] The old Latin copies also disagree.

1 through these] First in 1519; in 1516, in his 'in these things'
2 for he ... Christ] In this form first in 1519. In 1516 the cue phrase read: qui enim in his servit 'for he who in these serves.' The Vulgate printed in 1527 reads in hoc, and many old Vulgate manuscripts support this reading (as Erasmus notes at the end of this annotation), though the reading in his is found in the manuscript tradition; see Wordsworth and White II 137 18n.
3 The Greek ... 'through these things.'] Added in 1519
4 In the Greek manuscript tradition the better reading is ἐν τούτῳ 'in this' (Latin in hoc); cf Tischendorf II 441 18n and Cranfield II 719–20.
5 On ἐν with the force of διά (Latin per) see the previous annotation, n2.
6 The pronoun τούτοις (ER haec) is apparently neuter, its antecedents are the nouns righteousness, peace, and joy (14:17), which are all feminine in Greek. Lefèvre also identifies these nouns as the antecedents of the plural τούτοις (Pauli epistolae fol 102 recto).
7 So ... expounds] Added in 1519
8 Theophylact Expos in Rom 14:18 PG 124 529D
9 and Chrysostom ... he read] Added in 1535
10 Chrysostom Hom in Rom 26.2 PG 60 639. Chrysostom's brief comment does not indicate decisively whether he read the singular or plural: 'No one will

admire you because of your perfection, but because of peace and concord. This good [peace and concord] all will enjoy; that, none.'

11 Nevertheless ... Holy Spirit] Added in *1519*
12 Ambrosiaster *Comm in Rom* 14:18. Ambrosiaster reads the singular.
13 Origen *Comm in Rom* 10.1 PG 14 1251B: ' "In this," that is, "in the Holy Spirit" '
14 which ... before] Added in *1535*
15 In 14:17
16 as though ... disagree] With one exception (see n17 below), this remaining portion of the annotation was added in *1519*.
17 those] *eos*, added in *1535*
18 This constitutes Erasmus' gloss on Origen, drawn evidently from a loose reading of the context of Origen's comment (cf PG 14 1250C–1251B).

14:19 [ER *et quae aedificationis alius erga alium* 'and the things that are of edification one towards another']

[VG] *et quae aedificationis sunt invicem custodiamus* 'and let us guard in turn the things that are of edification'; καὶ τὰ τῆς οἰκοδομῆς τῆς εἰς ἀλλήλους, that is, 'the things that pertain to mutual edification'; and διώκωμεν, that is, 'let us pursue,' is understood.[1] Further, Paul, in his customary way, speaks of 'edifying' when he means 'to help'; while nothing prevents [the phrase] τῆς εἰς ἀλλήλους [mutually] from referring also to peace, so that you would understand [both] mutual peace and mutual aid.

The verb 'let us guard,' which someone has added, is not found in the Greek codices,[2] or[3] in Chrysostom or Theophylact.[4] It[5] is not necessary, since 'let us pursue' has preceded. It[6] was not added in the very old codex of Constance,[7] except that someone with an unskilled hand had written it between the lines.

1 The word is supplied from the preceding clause of 14:19: 'Let us pursue the things that pertain to peace.' So Lefèvre *Pauli epistolae* fols 10 recto and 102 recto.
2 φυλάξωμεν (Vulgate *custodiamus* 'let us guard') is indeed omitted in the preferred reading; cf Tischendorf II 441 19n and Cranfield II 721 3n.
3 or ... Theophylact] Added in *1535*
4 Cf Chrysostom *Hom in Rom* 26.3 PG 60 639 and Theophylact *Expos in Rom* 14:19 PG 124 529D.
5 It ... preceded.] Added in *1519*
6 It ... lines.] Added in *1527*
7 On this manuscript, see the annotation on 13:1 ('those, however, which are from God') and n10.

14:21 [ER *per quod frater tuus impingit* 'through which[1] your brother stumbles']

[VG] *in quo frater tuus offenditur* 'in which[2] your brother is offended.' The Greek reads προσκόπτει, that is, 'stumbles.' And in the Donatian codex[3] it was written *offendit* [offends], not *offenditur* [is offended]. The[4] very old manuscript of Constance[5] was in agreement. It[6] makes little difference to the sense, except that in Latin one 'is offended' who is provoked to anger; for example a king is offended, but he does not stumble. On the other hand one who sees a girl and lusts after her offends; he is not offended. Chrysostom and Theophylact, who spoke Greek, rightly interpret προσκόπτει as σκανδαλίζεται.[7]

1 through which] First in *1519*; in *1516*, 'on which'
2 in which ... *offenditur.*] This annotation was introduced first in *1522* with this short entry. For a similar discussion, see the annotation on 9:33 ('rock of scandal').
3 On this codex see the annotation on 1:22 ('saying that they were wise') n3.
4 The ... agreement] Added in *1527*
5 On the manuscripts from Constance see the annotation on 13:1 ('those, however, which are from God') n10.
6 It ... σκανδαλίζεται.] Added in *1535*
7 Chrysostom *Hom in Rom* 26.2 PG 60 639–40; Theophylact *Expos in Rom* 14:21 PG 124 532B–C. Erasmus accepted the Western reading (found also in the Vulgate) 'stumbles or is offended or becomes weak.' Both Chrysostom and Theophylact in their exposition associate closely the word 'stumbles' (προσκόπτει) with the subsequent words 'is offended' (σκανδαλίζεται) and 'becomes weak' (ἀσθενεῖ). Modern editions, however, regard the last two alternatives as an addition and only the first verb ('stumbles') as original (see Tischendorf II 441 21n; Metzger 532; and Cranfield II 725 1n).

14:22 [ER *tu fidem habes* 'you have faith']
[VG] *tu fidem quam habes* 'you [have] the faith that you have.' The relative 'that' is absent from the Greek: σὺ πίστιν ἔχεις, κατὰ σαυτὸν ἔχε, that is, 'you have faith, have it in yourself,' or 'within yourself alone.'[1] I[2] have found it so written in the codex of St Paul's[3] – if anyone places little value on the Greek, though Ambrose, Chrysostom,[4] and Theophylact[5] agree with the Greek.[6] And the expression is altogether more vivid if 'that' is omitted. He added[7] 'before God'[8] to restrain the empty glory that is generally attendant upon knowledge. Now Chrysostom points out that 'faith' is not to be taken here as faith in dogma, but rather the confidence of one's conscience, which is contrasted with weakness and fear.[9] Some punctuate thus: 'Do you have faith within yourself? Have it before God.'[10] This is more harsh.

1 Compare the Vulgate and the translation of Erasmus for the complete citation:
  ER *tu fidem habes? Apud temetipsum habe coram deo* 'you have faith? Have it within yourself before God'
  VG *tu fidem quam habes penes temetipsum habe coram deo* 'you have the faith that you have with yourself before God'
2 I ... Greek.] Added in *1519*, with the exceptions noted below (nn4 and 5). In *1516*, after the first sentence, the annotation concluded with: 'To these words, the blessed Ambrose adds "before God." '

3 On this codex, see the annotation on 4:5 ('according to the purpose of the grace of God') n5.
4 Chrysostom] Added in 1535
5 and Theophylact] Added in 1527
6 Cf Ambrosiaster *Comm in Rom* 14:22; Chrysostom *Hom in Rom* 26.2 PG 60 640; Theophylact *Expos in Rom* 14:22 PG 124 532C.
7 He added ... harsh.] Added in 1535
8 This 1535 addition returned to the text a discussion of the Vulgate phrase *coram deo*, to which reference was made in 1516 (cf n2 above); the phrase was omitted from the editions between 1519 and 1527.
9 Cf Chrysostom *Hom in Rom* 26.3 PG 60 640: 'By "faith" here he means not that which has to do with dogma ... [Moreover] he directs a point to the weaker brother and shows that the crown of conscience is enough for him.'
10 A number of witnesses punctuate thus, including Origen (PG 14 1254C) and Pelagius (Souter II 111:12–13).

14:23 [ER *at qui diiudicat* 'but one who discriminates']
[VG] *qui autem discernit* 'one, however, who discerns'; ὁ δὲ διακρινόμενος, that is, 'but one who hesitates.' And yet the participle is in the middle voice, so that it can be understood, 'he who is divided in his judgment.'

[14:24] [ER omitted]
[VG] *ei autem qui potens est* 'now to him who is able.'[1] This section, down to 'but we ought,'[2] is not found at all in some codices; some add it at the end of the Epistle.[3] Chrysostom[4] expounds it at the end,[5] Theophylact in this place,[6] though his Latin translator rendered it neither here nor at the end, which I think happened unintentionally. He omitted it here in order to agree with our codices; when he came to the end he forgot to add it.[7] Since it does not seem to belong in this place, I have removed it to the end of this Epistle. Marcion[8] ended the Epistle to the Romans at this point, claiming that the rest is a spurious addition.[9]

1 These words introduce the doxology, normally placed at the end of the Epistle (16:25–7). In the Vulgate printed in 1527 neither these words nor any part of the doxology is found here at the end of chapter 14, but only in chapter 16. In Erasmus' translation the doxology is also reserved for chapter 16. All the lifetime editions, however, have an annotation here, introduced with the cue phrase *ei autem qui potens est*. For the witnesses that add the doxology here, see Tischendorf II 442 23n and Wordsworth and White II 138 23n.
In LB this annotation is conflated with the previous one.
2 Rom 15:1
3 On the textual evidence see the annotation on 16:25 ('now to him who is able') n5.
4 Chrysostom ... add it.] Added in 1527

5 In Migne these verses are found in Chrysostom's exposition of chapter 14, and not at the end; see *Hom in Rom* 27.1 and 32.2–4 PG 60 643–5 and 677–82.
6 Theophylact *Expos in Rom* 14:24–6 PG 124 533A–D
7 On the Latin translation, see above, the annotation on 1:4 ('who was predestined') n25.
8 Marcion ... addition.] Added in *1527*
9 On Marcion and his Bible, see the annotation on 16:25 ('now to him who is able') and n8.

CHAPTER 15

15:1 [ER *nos qui potentes sumus* 'we who are strong']

[VG] *nos firmiores* 'we the more robust'; ἡμεῖς οἱ δυνατοὶ τὰ ἀσθενήματα τῶν ἀδυνάτων βαστάζειν, that is, 'we who are strong [ought] to bear the frailties of the weak.'[1] Lorenzo[2] [Valla] prefers *validi* and *invalidorum* [vigorous ... languishing]. In this[3] way the ἐναντίωσις and the προσονομασία, which are in the Greek words, are reproduced.[4] The [Translator] would have gained this effect if he had rendered *firmi, infirmorum* [robust, frail][5] or *validi, invalidorum* [vigorous, languishing], for here Ambrose reads *invalidorum* instead of *infirmorum*.[6]

    1 Compare the translations of Erasmus and the Vulgate:
        ER *debemus autem nos qui potentes sumus infirmitates impotentium portare* 'we who are strong ought to bear the frailties of the weak'
        VG *debemus autem nos firmiores imbecillitates infirmorum sustinere* 'we who are the more robust ought to endure the feebleness of the frail'
    2 Valla *Annot in Rom* 15 (I 860); Lefèvre adopted Valla's preference (*Pauli epistolae* fols 10 verso and 103 verso).
    3 In this ... *infirmorum*.] Added in 1527
    4 On ἐναντίωσις see the annotation on 2:8 ('do not give assent to') n2; on προσονομασία see the annotation on 1:31 ('apart from contract') n3. The Greek *dynatoi* and *adynaton* ('strong' and 'not-strong') not only reflected opposites, but allowed a play on words as well. Both Erasmus and Valla sought to retain the verbal play in their translations, *potentes ... impotentium, validi ... invalidorum*, as indeed did the Vulgate, *firmiores ... infirmorum*, though the comparative *firmiores* loses the clean contrast of the Greek (see n5). The English in our translation represents the contrast between, but not the play on, the two words in Greek.
    5 The neat effect of 'firm ... infirm' is partially lost in the Vulgate sequence, where the first member is in the comparative degree, the second in the positive, 'more firm ... infirm.'
    6 For the text in Ambrosiaster see CSEL 81/1 453:12–13 and the alternative readings cited for these lines. Vogels prints *debemus autem nos firmiores infirmitates invalidorum portare*, but cites textual evidence for *debemus autem nos firmiores inbecillitates infirmorum sustinere*. In his exposition Ambrosiaster speaks of *infirmi* rather than *invalidi* (*Comm in Rom* 15:1 [1]). For *potens* as a translation of the Greek *dynatos* see the annotation on 1:4 ('in power').

15:2 [ER *nam unusquisque nostrum* 'for every one of us']

[VG] *unusquisque vestrum* 'every one of you.'[1] The readings[2] of both the Greek and Latin manuscripts vary here. [Of the Greek texts] some read ἔκαστος γὰρ ἡμῶν, that is, 'for every one of us.' Some do not add the conjunction γάρ [for]; some read δέ [but] in place of γάρ, which is more tolerable. Of the Latin texts, some have 'of you' for 'of us,'[3] though the Greek is ἡμῶν,

first person.[4] In[5] the Greek 'his own' is not added; there is only τῷ πλησίον
ἀρεσκέτω, 'let him please his neighbour.'[6] Ambrose does not include the
pronoun ['of us,' or 'of you']: 'And let each one please his[7] neighbour.'[8]
'Please'[9] is used here to mean 'comply with' and 'respect the wishes of'
another. For Paul did not please everyone, and yet he says: 'Just as I in
every way please all.'[10] But Paul did in all things accommodate himself to
all so that he might gain them all.[11] In the same way he goes on to say:[12]

1 In 1519 both the sequence and number of annotations on Rom 15:2–6 were
  established for the remaining editions. But the 1519 text made a considerable
  change in both the sequence and the number of annotations from 1516. In
  1516 the sequence was: 1/ 'for whatever things have been written,' 2/ 'every
  one of you,' 3/ 'that being of one accord,' 4/ 'let every one of you please
  his own neighbour,' 5/ 'this itself.' In 1519 the fourth was absorbed into
  the second, the remaining four annotations were rearranged, and three new
  annotations were inserted among them ('Christ did not please himself,' 'but
  just as it is written, the taunts etc,' 'through patience and the comfort') to
  give the sequence and number of annotations found here.
2 The readings ... each one please his neighbour.'] This portion appeared first
  in this form in 1519; but cf below nn3, 5 and 7.
3 'of us' ... first person] In 1516 only, the entire annotation (ie the second in
  the sequence listed in n1 above), consisted only of the cue phrase and the
  words, ' "of us"; the Greek is ἡμῶν, first person.' But cf n5 below.
4 The vast majority of Greek manuscripts read 'us,' but the preferred Latin reading is 'you.' See Tischendorf II 442 2n and Wordsworth and White II 139 2n.
5 In ... 'let him please his neighbour.'] In 1516 only, the point Erasmus made
  here appeared in a separate annotation (fourth in the sequence listed in
  n1 above), which also reiterated, somewhat redundantly, the point of the
  annotation identified in n3 above:
    [ER unusquisque nostrum proximo placeat 'let every one of us please his
    neighbour']
    [VG] unusquisque vestrum proximo suo placeat 'let every one of you please
    his own neighbour.' Suo [his own] is redundant; and it is 'of us,' not 'of
    you': ἔκαστος δὲ ἡμῶν τῷ πλησίον ἀρεσκέτω, that is, 'let every one of us
    please his neighbour.'
6 In Greek the article itself frequently (as here), serves as a weak possessive;
  see Smyth 1121.
7 his] First in 1527; in 1519 and 1522, 'his own'
8 Ambrosiaster Comm in Rom 15:2. In Vogels' edition the pronoun 'us' or 'you'
  is not printed in the text, but see the critical apparatus (gamma recension)
  for the reading unusquisque vestrum 'each one of you' (CSEL 81/1 453:20n).
9 'Please' ... to say:] Added in 1535
10 1 Cor 10:33. The text is cited also by Ambrosiaster in his exposition of this
   verse; cf Comm in Rom 15:2.
11 Cf 1 Cor 9:22.
12 This final clause of the 1535 addition introduced the cue phrase for the next
   annotation.

15:3 [ER *Christus non placuit sibi ipsi* 'Christ did not please his own self']
[VG] *Christus non placuit sibi* 'Christ[1] did not please himself.' What was
there in Christ that he should be displeased with himself? But in this passage one 'pleases' oneself in the sense that he serves his own advantage and
turns everything he does[2] into a profit for himself. In Greek, people of this
sort are called φίλαυτοι [self-lovers], not only because of their arrogance,
but also because of their efforts to secure their personal advantage.[3] From
this vice Christ was far, far removed, who gave his whole self for us. Origen
also has noted that here the vice of φιλαυτία is condemned.[4]

> 1 Christ ... condemned.] The entire annotation was added in *1519*; see the
> preceding annotation n1.
> 2 LB prints *ait* 'he says,' but *agit* 'he does' is the reading of all editions from
> *1519* to *1535*.
> 3 Cf the use of the word in Aristotle *Magna moralia* 1212a29; the word is also
> used in this sense in 2 Tim 3:2. Philautia is praised as one of the blessings of
> Folly in the *Moria* CWE 27 99 and 117; cf also *Adagia* I iii 92.
> 4 Origen *Comm in Rom* 10.6 PG 14 1258B–C

15:3 [ER *sed quemadmodum scriptum est opprobria* etc 'but as it is written,
the reproaches etc']
[VG] *sed sicut scriptum est improperia* etc 'but[1] just as it is written, the
taunts etc.' Here, too, the thought has not been fully expressed, and we
have to supply the antithesis: 'Christ did not please himself – but did what
was not pleasing to himself,' that is, he did not serve his own advantage,
but took thought for our advantage at the cost of his own disadvantage –
'as it is written' etc.

> 1 but ... etc.] The entire annotation was added in *1519*; see the annotation on
> 15:2 ('every one of you') n1.

15:4 [ER *nam quaecumque praescripta sunt* 'for whatever things have been
described[1] before']
[VG] *quaecumque enim scripta sunt* 'for whatever things have been written.'[2] In Greek[3] it is not simply 'written,' but in both[4] instances προεγράφη,
that is, 'described before' [*praescripta*] or 'written previously' [*antescripta*].[5]
Augustine cites the passage in precisely this way in his one hundred and
thirty-seventh letter: 'For whatever things have been written previously
have been written for our instruction.'[6] Likewise[7] in the thirteenth book
Against Faustus, the last chapter.[8] For he means that these events were described before they occurred or before[9] they were brought to light. The
promise precedes, the event follows; the Scriptures promise what will later
be presented to view. Both[10] Chrysostom and Theophylact agree in this
reading.[11] [Paul] used[12] the same word in the Epistle to the Galatians,

chapter 3: 'Before whose eyes Christ was depicted [*praescriptus*]' [3:1].[13] Thus it would not be absurd to take *praescripta* as those things which have been set forth for imitation; hence also we speak of a *praescriptum* – a model[14] set out for imitation.[15]

I do[16] not doubt that Origen and Ambrose read this. The former interprets the preposition πρό in a double sense; first, of the figures of the Old Testament, which, though now they have given way like shadows at the break of day, have nevertheless been handed down for us in the writings of old, through which the mysteries revealed bestow the saving doctrine – even those passages which would seem to be of no import. Examples are: 'You shall not muzzle an ox when it is treading out the grain';[17] that Abraham had two sons, the first by a slave, the second by a free woman;[18] that the people ate manna in the desert and drank water from a rock.[19] Of the same kind are the examples Paul mentions in First Corinthians, the tenth chapter.[20] In fact, even the account of the creation of the world has much to teach us if we interpret it allegorically.[21] All of these passages were written before the mystery was revealed. [Origen] explains [πρό], in the second place, in reference to the prophetic Scriptures; it was foretold to the Jews: 'You will listen with your ears, and you will not hear; seeing, you will see, and will not understand.'[22] Concerning us it was foretold: 'Those who have not been told of him will see him.'[23] Since the gospel has displayed all these things as fulfilled, we acquire confidence that those things also which have been promised to us about the coming age will surely come to pass.[24] Ambrose speaks in the same manner about the promises.[25] Augustine, too, interprets this passage in reference to prophetic scriptures[26] of the kind Paul has just cited: 'The reproaches of those who taunted you have fallen on me.'[27] According to Chrysostom, these are the words of the Father to the Son. For when the Jews cried out: 'If he is the Son of God, let him come down now from the cross,'[28] they insulted, through the Son, the Father as well. And just as Christ reached eternal glory through torture and disgrace, we too should bear with equanimity the injuries and the taunts of evil persons, so that we may be glorified together with Christ.[29]

And so the preposition πρό is not superfluous, for it implies that those things which are written in the Old Testament are now either set forth or disclosed through the gospel, so that the gentiles should not think that such things have no relation to them. They have been written, however, not only that we should believe them, but that we should imitate them as well. Accordingly nothing prevents *praescripta* from being understood as those things that are set out before the eyes, as in Galatians 3, where Paul says that Christ was depicted [*praescriptum*] before their eyes [3:1]. Two very trifling quibbles remain. Many crimes are described in the Old Testament that

were not set forth to be imitated, like the parricide of Cain; likewise many
miracles, like the crossing of the Red Sea.³⁰ I have already remarked that in
the latter there are things that we should imitate, according to the mystical
sense; and the crimes that are recorded remind us to imitate the good.³¹
Thus these stories too give us an example to follow. The second difficulty
is that many things were written about after they occurred. Here, however,
it was a question of the prophetic Scriptures, from which he had just cited
a text. But if someone insists that [Paul's] statement is a general one, since
a mystical sense lies concealed in every passage, rightly are things said to
have been written 'beforehand,' [though] under cover, which afterwards
have been laid open through the gospel. And it is obviously true that there
is nothing in the divine books³² that does not pertain to our instruction.
But Paul seems here to speak specifically about the prophetic Scriptures
that preceded and pointed to the gospel and Christ. Someone might say
that this is a trivial point and that it does not matter if the Translator has
omitted a syllable. But if I should [be the one who] does something of the
sort, then [some insist that] in every single dot there lies a great mystery,
and a sacrilege has been committed.

1 described] First in *1519*; in *1516, ante ... scripta* 'written previously'
2 For the position of this annotation in *1516* see the annotation on 15:2 ('every
  one of you') n1.
3 In Greek ... but] Added in *1519*
4 in both ... *antescripta*] The text, established in this form in *1519*, is a slight
  adaptation of the text of *1516*, when the entire annotation consisted of the
  words: 'In both instances [the Greek] is προεγράφη, that is, "have been
  described before," that is, "written previously."' Valla, too, had noted the
  Greek προεγράφη, and Erasmus' explanation follows exactly that of Valla; cf
  Annot in Rom 15 (i 860).
  The cue phrase gives only the first of the two instances. Erasmus and the
  Vulgate continued:
      ER *in nostram doctrinam praescripta sunt* 'have been described before for
      our learning'
      VG *ad nostram doctrinam scripta sunt* 'have been written for our learning'
  Like Erasmus, Lefèvre had rendered the Greek with the Latin *praescripta sunt*
  in both clauses (*Pauli epistolae* fol 10 verso).
5 In the first instance, scholars generally regard προεγράφη (= ER *praescripta
  sunt*) to be the more probable reading, though some witnesses support
  ἐγράφη (= VG *scripta sunt*); cf Michel 356 n2 and Cranfield II 734 n2. In the
  second instance, however, the preferred reading is ἐγράφη (*scripta sunt*); cf
  Tischendorf II 442–3 4n and Cranfield II 734 n3.
6 Augustine *Epistulae* 78.1 CSEL 34 332:1–2
7 Likewise ... last chapter.] Added in *1522*
8 Augustine *Contra Faustum Manichaeum* 13.18 PL 42 294
9 or before ... light] Added in *1535*

10 Both ... reading.] First in *1527*; in *1519* and *1522* the passage read: 'Theophylact virtually suggests as much.'

11 Cf Chrysostom *Hom in Rom* 27.2 PG 60 646 and Theophylact *Expos in Rom* 15:4 PG 124 536B–C.

12 [Paul] used ... *praescriptum*] Added in *1519*

13 Erasmus quotes the Vulgate of Gal 3:1 reading the variant *praescriptus* rather than the preferred *proscriptus* (see Weber II 1804 1n). For his own translation of Gal 3:1 Erasmus rendered the Greek by the Latin *depictus* 'portrayed,' and in his annotation on the verse noted that the Greek προγράφειν can be used both of writing and of portrayal; cf the annotation on Gal 3:1 (*ante quorum oculos*). In his paraphrases on both Rom 15:4 and Gal 3:1 he represented the Greek likewise by *depictus*; see CWE 42 83 and n2, and 108 and n3.

14 a model ... committed] With the exception noted below (n16), the remaining portion of the annotation was added in *1535*.

15 Frans Titelmans had objected to this sense, evidently on the ground that 'whatever things' included things we should not imitate. Erasmus thought the objection mere sophistry, but it seems to have motivated this long addition of *1535*. See *Responsio ad collationes* LB IX 1012A–B.

16 I do ... this.] From *1519* to *1527* the allusion to Origen and Ambrose, which then concluded the annotation (cf n14 above), appeared thus: 'One cannot deduce from Origen's interpretation what he read. Ambrose read "have been written" [*scripta sunt*]. It does not make much difference to the sense.'

17 Deut 25:4; cf 1 Cor 9:9.

18 Gen 16–17, 21; cf Gal 4:22–31.

19 Exod 16:35, 17:6

20 1 Cor 10:1–13

21 The example of creation comes from Erasmus, not from the text of Origen. On Erasmus' understanding of allegory see J.B. Payne 'Toward the Hermeneutics of Erasmus' in *Scrinium Erasmianum* ed J. Coppens 2 vols (Leiden 1969) II 35–49; Georges Chantraine '*Mystère*' et '*Philosophie du Christ*' *selon Erasme* (Namur 1971) 316–62; Godin *Erasme* 248–413; Chomarat *Grammaire et rhétorique* I 332–6, 568–79, 679–90.

22 Isa 6:9

23 Isa 52:15; cf Rom 15:21.

24 Origen *Comm in Rom* 10.6 PG 14 1260B–1261C. Though Origen expounded the passage along the lines followed by Erasmus, in the translation of Rufinus represented in the Merlin text, one finds in the biblical citation and throughout the entire exposition only *scripta sunt* (cf fol CCXVIII recto).

25 Ambrosiaster *Comm in Rom* 15:4

26 Cf Augustine *De catechizandis rudibus* 3.6 PL 40 313–14.

27 Ps 69:9. In the passage from the *De catechizandis rudibus* just cited, where Rom 15:4 is discussed, Augustine illustrates the prophetic character of the Old Testament by reference first to the birth of Jacob and Esau (Gen 25:26), then to Ps 20:8.

28 Matt 27:40, 42

29 A somewhat selective (but not misleading) summary of Chrysostom's exposition of Rom 15:3–5; cf *Hom in Rom* 27.2 PG 60 646.

30 For Cain see Gen 4:1–16; for the crossing of the Red Sea, Exod 14.

31 Cf above n15 and n21. On the necessity to interpret allegorically crimes
recorded in the Old Testament see *Ecclesiastes* II LB V 869E–870F and
Enchiridion CWE 66 67–9.
32 books] Omitted in LB but present in the 1535 edition

15:4 [ER VG] *per patientiam et consolationem* 'through[1] patience and the comfort.' In place of 'comfort' Ambrose reads 'exhortation.'[2] For [the Greek]
is παράκλησις, a word that can take either meaning. But it makes no great
difference to the sense of this passage whichever is read.

1 through ... read.] The entire annotation was added in *1519*; cf the annotation
on 15:2 ('every one of you') n1.
2 Ambrosiaster *Comm in Rom* 15:4

15:5 [ER *idem* 'the same']
[VG] *idipsum* 'this itself';[1] τὸ αὐτό, that is, 'the same.'[2] In speech,[3] the [two
Greek] words are blended [into one], ταὐτό. For τό is nothing other than the
prepositive article; it is not reproduced in Latin by a double pronoun. And
[again we find the words] ἐν ἀλλήλοις, that is, 'among yourselves mutually'
or 'in turn,'[4] as I have pointed out above.[5] Lorenzo[6] [Valla] fastens upon
the Translator a double solecism here[7] – which a certain man[8] excuses thus:
Ambrose and Augustine spoke in this way, men of excellent Latin; here we
are not poring over Ciceronian speeches, it is a question rather of the truth
of simple Scripture.[9] First of all, [Ambrose and Augustine] may be the most
Latin of writers, but what difference does it make if they speak thus when
quoting the words of Scripture? Cicero himself would have done the same.
Moreover, to plead here the 'simplicity of Scripture' – what else is this but
to acknowledge the solecism?

1 For the order in which this annotation appeared in *1516* see the annotation
on 15:2 ('every one of you') n1.
2 So Valla *Annot in Rom* 15 (I 860)
3 In speech ... pronoun.] Added in *1535*
4 For the context compare the translations of Erasmus and the Vulgate for
15:5b:
    ER *det vobis idem mutuo inter vos sentire* 'that he might grant you to have
    the same feeling mutually among yourselves'
    VG *det vobis idipsum sapere in alterutrum* 'that he might grant you to mind
    the very same thing the one unto the other'
5 Cf eg the annotations on 1:12 ('to be comforted together') and 14:19 ('and let
us guard in turn the things that are of edification').
6 Lorenzo ... solecism?] This remaining portion of the annotation was added
in *1535.*
7 See Valla *Annot in Rom* 15 (I 860). Valla complained of a double solecism
here, first 'because of the preposition' – the retention in Latin of the Greek
preposition ἐν (Latin *in*); second 'because of the meaning,' – the translation

of ἀλλήλοις by *alterutrum* 'one of two' rather than by *invicem* 'reciprocally' or *mutuo* 'mutually.'

8 a certain man] Reading *quidam*, as in the 1535 edition, rather than the *quidem* of LB

9 The 'certain man' is once again Frans Titelmans; cf Titelmans' *Collationes quinque super epistolam ad Romanos* (Antwerp 1529) fol 282 recto: 'If this is so, then twice Augustine, Ambrose, and Jerome are not [speaking] Latin.' Erasmus, in his *Responsio*, does not, in his discussion of Rom 15, make reference specifically to the solecisms here, but Titelmans' 'excuses,' as described here, may be found in the discussion of Rom 10:16, for which see *Responsio ad collationes* LB IX 1005B–F, on the words 'who has believed our hearing' and the annotation on the same words, especially n11.

15:6 [ER *ut unanimiter* 'that with one accord']

[VG] *ut unanimes* 'that being of one accord';[1] ἵνα ὁμοθυμαδόν, that is, 'that with one accord.' The Translator[2] seems to have read ὁμόθυμοι [of one accord],[3] but it makes no great difference to the sense.

    1 For the order in which this annotation appeared in 1516, see the annotation on 15:2 ('everyone of you') n1.
    2 The Translator ... sense.] Added in 1519
    3 Ie the Translator read an adjective rather than the adverb

15:7 [ER *assumite vos invicem* 'receive one another in turn']

[VG] *suscipite invicem* 'take up one another in turn'; προσλαμβάνεσθε ἀλλήλους, that is, 'receive in turn,' that is, let one[1] join another to himself, and help him. This corresponds to that above, 'receive the weak in faith.'[2]

    1 let one ... help him] First in 1519. In 1516 the sentence read 'that is, receive in turn, the one the other.'
    2 Cf the annotation on Rom 14:1 ('receive'), where the same verb, προσλαμβάνεσθε, is translated *assumite* by both Erasmus and the Vulgate.

15:7 [ER *in gloriam* 'unto the glory']

[VG] *in honorem* 'unto the honour'; εἰς δόξαν, that is, 'unto the glory.' The Translator indulges in the affectation of variety.[1] Paul[2] means that one must sustain his brother, so that this redounds to the glory of God, who is praised by the good deeds of those who profess him. So, certainly, do Chrysostom and Theophylact explain [the phrase].[3]

    This[4] phrase, 'unto the honour of God,' may be taken with the immediately preceding phrase: just as Christ has received you, bringing you by adoption into the status of sons of God, who is glorified among the unbelieving by your harmony; or with the previous clause: receive one another to the honour of God; or with both: just as it has contributed to the glory

of God that Christ has mercifully received you, so it will result in the glory
of God if you receive one another.

Further, just as it is true that it sometimes makes no difference whether
you say 'honour' or 'glory,' so it more frequently happens that only one of
the two is suitable. Latin idiom permits us to say 'a parent must be held in
honour' but not 'must be held in glory.' We preface a remark 'with all due
respect' [honour], not 'with glory.' Those who excel in dignity and authority
are [held] 'in honour,' not 'in glory,' and the people entrust to candidates
'public offices' [honores], not 'glories.' Children bestow 'honour,' not 'glory,'
upon their parents. But Jerome is brought to my attention, in his exposition
of the first chapter of Malachi; I will quote his words: 'What I have called
"glory" or "honour" is one word both in Greek (δόξα), and in Hebrew (כָּבוֹד);
but I have used "honour" in accordance with the proper Latin idiom.'[5]
What is [the significance] of 'in accordance with the proper Latin idiom?'
If 'honour' and 'glory' mean the same, what is that idiomatic propriety
which persuaded him to translate δόξα as 'honour' rather than 'glory'?
This demonstrates that in Hebrew there is a word equally appropriate to
δόξα [glory] and τιμή [honour], but in Latin there is a difference between
honor and gloria, just as in Greek there is some difference between δόξα and
τιμή. For example in [the Septuagint of] Exodus 20, 'honour your father and
mother' [20:12], [the word] is not δόξασον but τίμα [honour]; in Leviticus 19,
'honour the face of an old man' [19:32], it is τιμήσεις. In the eighth Psalm the
two words are joined, δόξᾳ καὶ τιμῇ, that is, 'with glory and honour' [8:5;
LXX 8:6], and Jerome distinguishes these two words in his interpretation:
' "Glory" when the lower world was illuminated by his descent, "honour"
when he conquered death, "the crown" when he triumphantly returned
from hell surrounded by a chorus of saints.'[6] 'To honour' and 'to confer
honour' do not have quite the same force; nor do 'to honour' and 'to make
illustrious.' In Greek, δόξα means an exalted reputation; hence those who
are distinguished in authority are called δοκοῦντες [persons of repute].[7] τιμή
means the discharge of a duty owed; it is derived from τίω [I pay honour].
Thus it is said that 'honour nourishes the arts,'[8] not only because of the
glory but because of the reward paid, and 'to honour' one's parents is not
to celebrate their praises, but to discharge the whole duty of filial devotion,
especially assistance in need. There is a similar case in the fifth chapter of
First Timothy: 'The elders who rule well are worthy of a double honour'
[5:17], where it would be inappropriate to put δόξα for τιμή. Finally, while
the word 'honour' is not entirely unsuited to this passage, I think that
'glory' conveys something more majestic. The phrase corresponds to that
in the fifth chapter of Matthew's Gospel: 'That they may see your good

works and glorify your Father' [5:16]. There, the word is δοξάσωσι, and the Translator has rendered 'glorify,' not 'honour.'

1 Once again Titelmans complained of Erasmus' judgment here on the Translator's variety. Erasmus replied (*Responsio ad collationes* LB IX 1012B) that to indulge in *copia* is not a disgrace, but constantly to quarrel with a brother is a sin!

2 Paul ... explain.] Added in *1519*, with the exception of the reference to Chrysostom, which was added in *1527*

3 Chrysostom *Hom in Rom* 27.3 PG 60 647; Theophylact *Expos in Rom* 15:7 PG 124 537A

4 This ... 'honour.'] This remaining portion of the annotation was added in *1535*, in response, evidently, to Titelmans' defence of the Vulgate's translation of δόξα by *honor*; see *Responsio ad collationes* LB IX 1012B–C.

5 Jerome *Commentarii in Malachiam* (on 1:6) PL 25 (1845) 1547A

6 Pseudo-Jerome *Breviarium in psalmos* 8 PL 26 (1884) 888B

7 Cf Euripides *Hecuba* 295. In his annotation on Gal 2:2 (*qui videbantur aliquid*), Erasmus quotes this passage from Euripides to illustrate this use of the word.

8 Cicero *Tusculan Disputations* 1.2.4. Cf Seneca *Epistulae morales* 102.16. See Erasmus *Adagia* I viii 92, where Erasmus traces this proverb to Aristophanes *Plutus* 408.

15:8 [ER VG] *ad confirmandas promissiones patrum* **'for confirming the promises of the fathers.'** The Translator has changed one of the infinitives into a gerund and kept the other;[1] thus he has obscured the point, which is something like this: Paul, as though he had digressed somewhat, returns to the point of departure: 'I say,' he says, 'that is, what I have said thus far is directed to this end, that you should understand that Christ is the author of the New Covenant, which he administered first to the Jews to show that the Father, who had made the promise to them through the prophets, is true. But he wanted it to be shared with the gentiles, not because of a promise (although there had been prophecies about them as well), but out of mercy, and [he wanted] the gift to be the more welcome because it had been bestowed upon those who were not expecting it.' Therefore Paul set in contrast 'mercy' and 'the promises,'[2] for mercy is pure good will, while there appears to be [some obligation] in a promise. For he to whom you have made a promise has a claim unless you do fulfil it; and yet a good that comes beyond all hope brings more pleasure and praise. Accordingly, it could be rendered with clarity in this way: 'But what I am saying is this, that Jesus Christ fulfilled his duty towards the Jews to this end, that he might for the sake of the truthfulness of God confirm the promises made to the fathers; but also that the gentiles, because of his mercy, might glorify God, for to them nothing had been promised, and yet they received the same thing as the Jews.' Chrysostom[3] finds nothing wrong with the language.[4] There are those who think that both infinitives refer back to λέγω [I say];[5] this is tolerable if the 'I say' is understood as introducing in the first part a statement of exposition, in the second, a command.[6] It is possible, however, to take the infinitive δοξάσαι [glorify] as an imperative.[7] But it is of no significance that Theophylact and Origen in their commentaries sharply distinguish the [second] clause, 'but the gentiles [. . .],' for the conjunction δέ [but] joins it closely [to the preceding].[8] It is remarkable how very skilfully[9] Paul directs his words: so that the gentiles might acknowledge God's clemency towards them, he speaks of mercy; again, lest the Jews should not tolerate the admission of the gentiles to a common grace, he adds the witness of the Jewish Scriptures, in which he shows that the promise was to the gentiles, though not so clearly.

1 Erasmus discusses here the syntax of Rom 15:8–9:
ER *illud autem dico, Iesum Christum ministrum fuisse circumcisionis pro veritate dei ad confirmandas promissiones patrum. Ceterum* [1516 *In hoc autem*] *ut gentes pro misericordia glorificent deum* 'this I say, that Jesus Christ was a minister of the circumcision on behalf of the truth of God for confirming the promises of the fathers. But [1516 to this end, however] that the gentiles might glorify God because of mercy'
VG *dico enim Christum Iesum ministrum fuisse circumcisionis propter veritatem dei ad confirmandas promissiones patrum; gentes autem super misericordiam honorare deum* 'for I say that Jesus Christ was a minister of the circumcision on account of the truth of God for confirming the promises of the fathers; that the gentiles, however, honour God over mercy'
In this passage Erasmus and the Vulgate translated the first Greek infinitive, εἰς τὸ βεβαιῶσαι (15:8), by *ad* with the gerundive *confirmandas*; the second, δοξάσαι (15:9), Erasmus translated with a subjunctive expressing purpose, *glorificent*, while the Vulgate carried the Greek infinitive form over into the Latin *honorare*.
2 The contrast is noted also by Ambrosiaster *Comm in Rom* 15:9 (1), and Theophylact *Expos in Rom* 15:9 PG 124 537C–D; likewise Chrysostom, on whom Theophylact depends, *Hom in Rom* 38.1 PG 60 650.
3 Chrysostom . . . closely.] Added in 1535
4 An inference; Chrysostom says nothing about the syntax (cf *Hom in Rom* 38.1 PG 60 649–50).
5 Titelmans' view, evidently; cf *Responsio ad collationes* LB IX 1012D.
6 As Erasmus points out in his reply to Titelmans (cf n5 above) if one reads the infinitive in the second clause as a command dependent on an introductory 'I say,' one will have to understand 'I say' in the sense of 'I order,' or else read into the infinitive an implied imperative, 'I say that the gentiles ought to glorify.'
7 For this construction see the annotation on 12:15 ('to rejoice') and n3.
8 Cf Theophylact *Expos in Rom* 15:9 PG 124 537B–D and Origen *Comm in Rom* 10.8 PG 14 1263B. Both Theophylact and Origen (in the Merlin edition fol

CCXVIII verso) quote and then comment at some length on Rom 15:8 before
quoting Rom 15:9, and so may appear to distinguish sharply the 'second
clause.'
On the difficulties of construing the passage, see Michel 358 n5 and Cranfield
II 742–4.

9 how very skilfully] First in *1519*; in *1516*, 'how skilfully'

15:9 [ER *propter hoc confitebor tibi in gentibus* 'on account of this I will confess
you among the gentiles']

[VG] *propterea confitebor tibi in gentibus domine* 'therefore[1] I will confess you among the gentiles, Lord.' This prophecy is from the eighteenth
Psalm.[2]

> 1 therefore . . . Psalm.] The annotation was added in *1519*. Though the Vulgate
> of *1527* reads both *propterea* and *domine*, the preferred Latin reading has, with
> Erasmus, *propter hoc* and omits *domine*; cf Wordsworth and White II 140 9n.
> 2 Ps 18:49

15:10 [ER *gaudete gentes cum populo eius* 'rejoice, gentiles, with his people']
[VG] *laetamini gentes cum plebe eius* 'be joyful,[1] gentiles, with his folk.'
'His,' αὐτοῦ, refers to God; the implication is that he will be common to
both peoples. For [the writer] has called the Jews the people of God.[2] [Paul's
quotation] is found in as many words in a canticle of Deuteronomy.[3] It is
strange, however, that Thomas[4] cites from the thirty-fifth chapter of Isaiah
– whether from a lapse of memory or because a similar theme is treated
there.[5] It is also strange that our [Vulgate] edition [of Deut 32:43] disagrees
with Paul. The former has: 'Gentiles, praise his people.' The Hebrew has:
'Gentiles, celebrate his people in song.'[6] But[7] here the Apostle is following
the edition of the LXX, who translated εὐφράνθητε ἔθνη μετὰ τοῦ λαοῦ αὐτοῦ
[rejoice, gentiles, with his people].

> 1 be joyful . . . in song.'] This annotation was introduced in *1519*, with this
> passage.
> 2 Cf Rom 11:1–2; also Deut 32:9.
> 3 Deut 32:43
> 4 Thomas] First in *1522*; in *1519*, St Thomas
> 5 Cf Thomas Aquinas *Super Rom lect* cap 15 lectio 1.1159. The quotation with
> the reference to Isa 35 is listed as a variant reading in the Parma edition
> (Paris 1852–72); cf *Opera omnia* XIII 147 n1. In commenting on this verse
> Thomas cites Isa 9:3 and 66:10, which similarly speak of rejoicing.
> 6 For the meanings of this verb – praise, sing joyously, rejoice – in its Old
> Testament contexts, see S.R. Driver *Deuteronomy* International Critical
> Commentary (New York 1895) 380 and A.D.H. Mayes *Deuteronomy* New
> Century Bible (Grand Rapids, MI 1981) 393.
> 7 But . . . αὐτοῦ] Added in *1535*

15:11 [ER *et collaudate eum* 'and greatly praise him']

[VG] *et magnificate eum* 'and magnify him'; καὶ ἐπαινέσατε¹ 'and *adlaudate*'
[praise], in the sense of 'join in the praises' – so similarly ἐπαιάζειν [join in
the lament]. Ambrose² likewise reads 'magnify.'³ But 'magnify' means to
exalt, to lift up with praise. Origen notes that in the psalm *collaudate* [greatly
praise] was written rather than *magnificate* [magnify].⁴ Hence it is clear that
in his codex [the reading] was μεγαλύνατε [magnify], not ἐπαινέσατε [praise],
unless⁵ perhaps the Latin translator added this on his own. Rufinus, who
corrupts everything, seems to have been the translator of this work.⁶

> 1 The preferred reading in Rom 15:11 is ἐπαινεσάτωσαν 'let the peoples praise';
>   cf Tischendorf II 444 11n. In the Septuagint of Ps 116:1 (117:1 AV, RSV),
>   however, Rahlfs prints ἐπαινέσατε 'praise' in the text, but notes the variant
>   ἐπαινεσάτωσαν; cf Rahlfs II 129.
> 2 Ambrose ... ἐπαινέσατε] Added in 1519
> 3 Ambrosiaster *Comm in Rom* 15:11
> 4 Origen *Comm in Rom* 10.8 PG 14 1264B–C
> 5 unless ... work] Added in 1535
> 6 For Erasmus' changing views on the translator of Origen's commentary see
>   the annotation on 3:5 ('is God unfair who inflicts wrath') n11.

15:12 [ER *erit radix Iesse* 'there will be a root of Jesse']

[VG] *erit illa radix Iesse* 'there¹ will be that root² of Jesse.' This text is from
the eleventh chapter of Isaiah,³ but Paul cites it according to the Septuagint
translation, as he usually does. According to the Septuagint we read thus:
'And there will be in that day a root of Jesse, and he who shall rise up
to be ruler of the gentiles; in him the gentiles shall hope, and his rest
will be honour' [Isa 11:10]. According to the Hebrew original [we read] as
follows: 'In that day there will be a root of Jesse; one who shall stand for
a sign of the peoples, him shall the gentiles seek in prayer, and his tomb
shall be glorious.'⁴ Jerome points out that for 'his rest' the Hebrew has
מְנֻחָתוֹ [*menuchatho*], a term on which all interpreters agree, though Jerome
translates it as 'his tomb,' wishing to clarify the meaning, which is otherwise
quite obscure.⁵ For *menucha*⁶ means 'rest' – properly the kind of rest that
we pray for the dead. Thus while the Septuagint and Jerome use different
words, they agree in meaning. Further, what Jerome renders 'stand for
a sign' is in Hebrew עֹמֵד לְנֵס. Now נֵס means 'standard' or 'trophy,' and
also 'a miracle attested in fact.' The sense [of the Hebrew] is nearly the
same [as that in the Septuagint] for the people act under the standard of
a ruler. Moreover, 'shall seek in prayer' is in Hebrew יִדְרֹשׁוּ, which means
'search for'; however, one who 'searches for' directs his course towards,
and those who 'run to someone' hope. I should add that the phrase 'and
his rest will be honour,' though it is in the text in Isaiah and in Origen,⁷

does not appear to have been added by Paul – it is not found in the Greek manuscripts, is not explicated by Origen, and is never added in the Latin copies.

1 there ... copies.] The entire annotation was added in *1519*, but see n6.
2 that root] First in *1535*; from *1519* to *1527* the cue phrase read *erit in illa die radix Iesse* 'there will be in that day a root of Jesse.' The Vulgate printed in *1527* omits *in illa die* 'in that day,' and so is identical here with Erasmus' translation. For this verse neither the word *illa* nor the phrase *in illa die* is found in Wordsworth and White; cf II 140–1 12n.
3 Isa 11:10
4 Erasmus' translation here follows closely that of Jerome both for the LXX and for the Hebrew; cf Jerome *Commentarii in Isaiam* 4 (on 11:10) PL 24 149A.
5 Cf Jerome (ibidem 149A–B), who interprets the 'rest' as the 'rest' of death, specifically of Christ's death, and says that to make the meaning clearer he has translated the Hebrew as 'tomb.'
6 *menucha*] First in *1522*; in *1519*, *menuchatho* 'his rest'
7 Ie in Origen's citation of Isa 11:10. Cf Origen *Comm in Rom* 10.8 PG 14 1264C, who notes that Paul quotes the passage omitting both 'in that day' and 'his rest will be honour.'

15:12 [ER VG] *et qui exsurget* 'and he[1] who shall rise up'; ὁ ἀνιστάμενος 'rising up.' Though this is in the present tense, still the Translator has not without reason changed it to a future, for it is completed by a verb in the future tense, ἔσται, that is, 'will be.'[2] Otherwise,[3] it could also be translated thus: καὶ ὁ ἀνιστάμενος ἀρχεῖν, that is, 'and one who is to rise up to rule.'[4]

1 and he ... 'will be.'] Added in *1519* as a separate annotation; but see n4 below.
2 Ie the 'will be' in the preceding clause: there will be a root of Jesse
3 Otherwise ... thus] Added in *1522*
4 καί ... rule'] These words appeared first as a brief annotation in *1516*, thus: [VG] *et qui exsurget regere gentes* 'and who will rise up to rule the gentiles'; καὶ ὁ ἀνιστάμενος ἀρχεῖν, that is, 'and one who is to rise up to rule.'
In *1519* a second annotation on the same passage was added with its own cue phrase (cf n1 above); in *1522* the annotation of *1516* was added (without its cue phrase) to the annotation of *1519*, with the small addition of *1522* (n3 above).

15:14 [ER *persuasum enim habeo* 'for I am persuaded']
[VG] *certus sum autem* 'however, I am certain'; πέπεισμαι, that is, 'I am persuaded.'[1]

1 Similarly Valla *Annot in Rom* 15 (I 860). Erasmus' translation, perfect participle with *habeo*, nicely catches the nuance of the Greek perfect – completed action with 'continued effect' (Allen and Greenough 497b; cf Smyth 1852b). Cf the annotation on 14:14 ('I know and am confident').

15:14 [ER *pleni estis bonitate* 'you are full of goodness']

[VG] *pleni estis dilectione* '**you are full of love**'; ἀγαθωσύνης, that is, 'of goodness.' The Translator seems to have read ἀγαπωσύνης.[1] Chrysostom[2] reads and interprets ἀγαθωσύνης, and Theophylact accords with him, for they point out that in this word general virtue is implied.[3] But while Origen reads 'goodness' in his commentary, someone has corrupted this to 'love' in his text;[4] as did the translator of Theophylact[5] in his usual way. Here, however, it is the goodness [*bonitas*] which is opposed to evil, not that which corresponds to χρηστότης – 'kindness' [*benignitas*].[6]

1 Some Greek witnesses read ἀγάπης, though ἀγαθωσύνης is the better reading. See Tischendorf II 444 14n, and Cranfield II 753 n1. ἀγαπωσύνης, intended to mean 'of love,' is a formation not attested in LSJ.
2 Chrysostom ... usual way.] Added in *1535*
3 Chrysostom *Hom in Rom* 29.1 PG 60 653 and Theophylact *Expos in Rom* 15:14 PG 124 540C–D. On 'general virtue' see the annotation on 4:9 ('does it remain only') and n16.
4 Origen *Comm in Rom* 10.10 PG 14 1266A. In the citation of the biblical text, Migne reads *bonitate* 'goodness,' but in a footnote gives the variant *dilectione* 'love.' In the Merlin edition, however, the biblical text is cited with *dilectione* (fol CCXIX recto).
5 Porsena; cf the annotation on 1:4 ('who was predestined') and n25.
6 See for a similar definition the annotation on Rom 2:4 ('the riches of his goodness').

15:14 [ER *valentes etiam invicem alius alium (admonere)* 'capable even yourselves of (admonishing) one another'[1]]

[VG] *ita ut possitis alterutrum* [*monere*] '**so that you might be able [to warn] each other**'; δυνάμενοι καὶ ἄλλους νουθετεῖν, that is, 'having the ability to admonish others also.' And so,[2] indeed, Theophylact interprets.[3] From[4] Chrysostom's exposition it is not clear what he read, except that once he has ἄλλους [others], and twice ἀλλήλους [one another].[5] It appears that the Translator read ἀλλήλους rather than ἄλλους; and certainly[6] I prefer ἀλλήλους.[7] For the sense is: you are so strong in knowledge and love that without my admonition you yourselves are able to admonish one another if the need should arise. That Ambrose read in this way is clear from his interpretion. He says: 'He did not say that they should "teach" one another, but that they should "admonish" one another.'[8]

    The pronoun αὐτοί [yourselves] is not superfluous;[9] in Greek it often means 'of one's own accord,' or 'voluntarily,' as in Homer: τί με σπεύδοντα καὶ αὐτὸν[10] ὀτρύνεις,[11] that is, 'Why do you urge me on when I am hastening, even of my own accord?' Nor is the conjunction[12] superfluous in Paul – as it is not in Homer. It implies an allusion to Paul as the one who is

admonishing, so that you understand, 'even if I were not admonishing
you, you yourselves could admonish one another.'

1 yourselves ... one another] From *1519*; in *1516*, *et alios* 'others also'
2 And so ... interprets.] Added in *1519*
3 Theophylact *Expos in Rom* 15:14 PG 124 540C–D
4 From ... twice ἀλλήλους.] Added in *1535*
5 Cf Chrysostom *Hom in Rom* 29.1 PG 60 653. In the text of Migne, only ἄλλους
  appears here.
6 and certainly ... another] This remaining portion of the annotation was
  added in *1519*.
7 In *1516* Erasmus printed ἄλλους in his Greek text, but changed the text to
  ἀλλήλους in *1519*, thus returning to the sense understood by the Vulgate
  (for a corresponding change in his translation, see n1 above). Erasmus notes
  the change in the *Responsio ad collationes* LB IX 1012E. ἀλλήλους is the better
  reading; Tischendorf II 444–5 14n.
8 Ambrosiaster *Comm in Rom* 15:14
9 Erasmus comments on the two words in 15:14 which precede the previous
  cue phrase, 'you are full of love': in the Greek, καὶ αὐτοί; in the translation of
  both Erasmus and the Vulgate, *et ipsi* 'even you yourselves.'
10 αὐτόν] In LB αὐτοί, which is syntactically impossible; but in all editions from
   1519 to *1535*, αὐτόν
11 *Iliad* 8.293–4
12 Erasmus refers to the conjunction καί repeated three times in 15:14 to give
   emphasis: 'I *too* myself, my brothers, am persuaded of you that you *yourselves*
   are full of goodness, filled with all knowledge, able *even* yourselves to
   admonish one another.'

15:15 [ER *sed tamen audacius* 'but[1] nevertheless, the more boldly']
[VG] *audacius autem* 'the more[2] boldly, however.' He said 'the more
boldly,' meaning 'with greater intimacy' or 'more freely.' Its point of reference is the previous sentence: You have no need of my admonition, for
you yourselves can do this for one another; nevertheless, relying upon your
goodness, I was not afraid to write to you – to remind more than to teach. In
order to make this clearer to the reader, I have translated 'but nevertheless
more boldly.' Paul[3] frequently uses this figure, by which we alleviate what
could have given offence.[4]

1 but ... boldly] First in *1519*; in *1516*, like the Vulgate, 'the more boldly,
  however'
2 the more ... nevertheless more boldly.'] The annotation was introduced in
  1519 with this passage.
3 Paul ... offence.] Added in *1527*
4 See eg the annotation on 1:12 ('to be comforted together'), where Erasmus notes that Paul attempted to soften a statement that might give
  offence.

15:15 [ER VG] *ex parte* '**in part**'; ἀπὸ μέρους. He added this to soften what he had said, 'the more boldly.' It has the same force as if you should say 'to some degree.' For he included some things spoken rather freely about foolish wisdom, idols, and perverted desire.[1] Consequently, he says that he has spoken some things rather freely, not because of his disdain for them, but because of his faith in them, inasmuch as [he was] their own apostle. For we are bolder among those we love quite intimately.

   1 perverted desire] From *1519*; in *1516*, 'fornication.' For the allusions see 1:18–32.

15:16 [ER *administrans evangelium dei* '**ministering the gospel of God**']
[VG] *sanctificans evangelium dei* '**sanctifying the gospel of God**'; ἱερουρ-γοῦντα, as of one performing a sacred ritual. It corresponds to the λει-τουργός, who is, properly, a minister of religious rites or[1] of the state. And[2] ἱερουργεῖν means to perform the ministration of sacred rites. Augustine, in the book in which he explicates certain questions on the Epistle to the Romans, reads 'consecrating' rather than 'sanctifying,' expressing more nearly [the meaning of] the Greek word.[3] For Paul wanted the preaching of the gospel to appear as a thing sacred above all, and, as it were, a sacrificial victim, most pleasing to God because it made the gentiles worthy of Christ. And he makes himself the sacrifice, as it were, in this sacred rite. It is the rule, however, to require that victims be pure and holy, and suitable for the divine ritual – what Paul elsewhere calls τέλειος.[4] The translator[5] of Origen has some comments on this matter.[6] But Chrysostom[7] explicates carefully the implication of the Greek word.[8] The Greek[9] word is a compound from ἱερός 'sacred' and ἔργον 'work'; thus ἱερουργεῖν means 'to do the sacred work'; hence there follows προσφορά, that is, 'offering.'[10]

   1 or of the state] Added in *1535*
   2 And ... on this matter.] Added in *1519*
   3 Augustine *Expositio quarundam propositionum ex epistula ad Romanos* 83 PL 35 2087. In citing the text Augustine reads, 'that I might be a minister ... consecrating the gospel of God.' Augustine comments: 'This means that the gentiles might be offered to God as an acceptable sacrifice when they are sanctified by believing in Christ through the gospel.'
   4 Cf 12:2 and the annotation, 'what is the good and the well-pleasing and the perfect will of God.'
   5 The translator] First in *1535*. From *1519* to *1527* the editions all read 'Jerome, the translator.'
   6 Origen *Comm in Rom* 10.11 PG 14 1268B: 'The Greek ... is more eloquent than our [Latin] translation. It would be possible to translate *sacrificans evangelium dei* "offering the sacrifice of the gospel of God," though this does not fully express the meaning.'
   7 But Chrysostom ... Greek word.] Added in *1535*

8 Cf Chrysostom *Hom in Rom* 29.1 PG 60 655: 'He does not say simply λατρεία
  [service] ... but λειτουργία and ἱερουργία. This is my priesthood, to preach
  and proclaim, this the sacrifice I offer.'
  If Erasmus thought the Vulgate *sacrificans* did not express the full meaning
  of the Greek word, Titelmans complained that neither did Erasmus' choice
  of *administrans*; cf *Responsio ad collationes* LB IX 1012F.
9 The Greek ... sacred work'] Added in *1519*
10 The Greek word, translated *oblatio* 'offering' by both Erasmus and the
  Vulgate, appears in the clause that follows the cue phrase, 'ministering the
  gospel of God, so that the offering of the gentiles might be acceptable.'

15:16 [ER *acceptabilis sanctificata* 'acceptable sanctified']
[VG] *accepta et sanctificata* 'accepted and sanctified.' The conjunction 'and'
is unnecessary,[1] and[2] was not added in the codex at Constance. For 'sanctified' relates to what immediately follows, 'in the Holy Spirit,' that is,[3]
'through the Holy Spirit'; thus [Paul] shows that his sacrifice lacks nothing,
for[4] the Holy Spirit himself has consecrated it.

1 So Lefèvre *Pauli epistolae* fol 104 recto. Some Latin manuscripts include
  et 'and,' some omit it; cf Wordsworth and White II 141–2 and 16n. The
  conjunction is not printed or listed as a variant in Tischendorf; cf II 445 16n.
2 and ... Constance] Added in *1527*
3 that is ... Spirit'] Added in *1519*
4 for ... it] Added in *1519*

15:17 [ER *habeo igitur quod glorier* 'I have therefore that[1] in which I might
boast']
[VG] *habeo igitur gloriam* 'I have therefore glory'; καύχησιν, that is, 'boasting,' or 'I have [that] about which I might boast.'[2]

1 that ... boast] First in *1519*; in *1516*, *habeo igitur gloriationem* 'I have therefore
  boasting'
2 In his commentary, Lefèvre equated the Greek with the Latin *gloriatio*
  'boasting' (*Pauli epistolae* fol 104 recto); but he translated *unde glorier* 'whence
  I might boast' (ibidem fol 11 recto) – as Valla had recommended (*Annot in
  Rom* 15 [I 860]).

15:17 [ER *in his quae ad deum pertinent* 'in those things which pertain to God']
[VG] *ad deum* 'towards God'; τὰ πρὸς τὸν θεόν, that is, 'in those things which
pertain to God.'[1] The Translator has omitted the article τά.[2] The[3] addition
or omission of the article does not indeed change the sense, but it does
have the force of distinguishing or excluding, as, for example, the phrase
in the first chapter of this Epistle, τὸ κατ' ἐμέ.[4] Chrysostom, Theophylact,
and Origen, in their interpretation, imply this, for they advise that we must
not make our boast in anything at all, neither in works nor in wisdom, but
only in those things which belong to the divine grace.[5]

1 So Valla *Annot in Rom* 15 (I 860). In his annotation on Heb 2:17 (*ad deum*) Erasmus notes that this Greek expression may be translated either 'in those things which pertain to God' or 'which are done before God.'

2 Represented in Erasmus' translation by the pronouns *in his quae* 'in those things which'

3 The ... divine grace.] Added in *1535*

4 In his annotation on 1:15 ('thus what in me is ready'), Erasmus does not discuss the significance of the article in the phrase τὸ κατ' ἐμέ, but for the sense of limitation conveyed by the article, see his translation there.

5 Cf Chrysostom *Hom in Rom* 29.2 PG 60 655; Theophylact *Expos in Rom* 15:17 PG 124 541C; Origen *Comm in Rom* 10.12 PG 14 1269A–B. Erasmus generalizes from all three: 'Paul says, "I glory not in myself, or in my diligence, but in the grace of God"' (Chrysostom); 'Not in common, but in spiritual things' (Theophylact); 'Not in riches, or worldly honour, or worldly wisdom or the other arts that are outside Christ' (Origen).

15:18 [ER *non enim ausim* 'for I should not dare']

[VG] *non enim audeo* 'for I do not dare'; τολμήσω, that is, 'I will dare' or 'I should dare,' for with this little preface,[1] so to speak, he both excludes the charge of arrogance and at the same time wins the reader's confidence.

1 *prooemiolo*, ie the 'preface' to the brief narrative of the great deeds described in 15:19–20. For the 'preface' in classical rhetoric see the annotation on 1:1 ('called an apostle') n9.

15:18 [ER *eorum quae non effecit (Christus) per me* 'of those things which (Christ) did not effect through me']

[VG] *eorum quae per me non effecit [Christus]* 'of those[1] things which through me [Christ] did[2] not effect.' Ambrose interprets as though Paul is not able to recount anything pertaining to the commendation of preaching that was not, with the help of God, achieved through him. I shall quote [Ambrose's] own words: '[Paul] says that he has "glory before God" through Christ Jesus. For in believing and serving Christ Jesus with a pure conscience he has won merit for himself before God the Father, so much so that he claims there is nothing Christ has not done through him for the exhortation of the gentiles.' Then soon: 'For in serving Christ, he has "glory towards God" to such an extent that, of the divine power of which he has need, there is nothing God has not furnished him; rather, since he was found to be a capable steward, he has obtained everything that would contribute to the conversion of the gentiles through the power of signs.'[3] Origen follows a different interpretation, namely this: I should not wish to claim for myself praise for the deeds of others; I shall speak only of those things Christ has effected through me. I shall quote [Origen's] words too: ' "What I speak," says [Paul], "are not words about the work of another, nor shall I be

made eulogist for the deeds of others. But what I know Christ has wrought
through me, and has fulfilled in me, by word and deed, through the obedience of the gentiles, this I write to you." '[4] I prefer Origen's interpretation,
not only because it is more modest and fits better with what follows ('But
I have so preached the gospel [. . .]'[5] – for he sets this [latter] sentence in
opposition to the one above, because to narrate the deeds of others, and to
preach deliberately where others have not, are [here] mutually exclusive),
but also because I do not see how the sense Ambrose wants can be gathered
from the Greek. The Greek reads like this: οὐ γὰρ τολμήσω λαλεῖν τι ὧν οὐ
κατειργάσατο Χριστὸς δι᾽ ἐμοῦ [for I shall not dare to speak anything of those
Christ has not wrought through me]. This is certain: 'of those' cannot refer
to the other apostles but [must refer] to the actual deeds themselves. A third
sense might also be possible, in this way: I should not dare to say anything
about my own deeds, but only about those which Christ has done through
me. But I give the palm to the interpretation of Origen. For the focus of
meaning in this whole passage is the pronoun 'me,' which excludes the
deeds of others. Chrysostom and[6] Theophylact in their commentaries embrace and combine both interpretations: I do not flaunt what I myself have
not done; rather, what I have done, not I, but Christ has done through me.[7]

'Did[8] effect' is in the past tense, not present, for he has in mind what
he had already done.

1 of those ... through me.] This entire annotation, with the exception of the
  reference to Chrysostom and the final sentence (see nn6 and 8 below), was
  added in 1519.
2 The Vulgate printed in 1527 reads *non efficit* 'does not effect.'
3 Ambrosiaster *Comm in Rom* 15:17–19 (1–1a). Erasmus' text appears to follow
  the γ recension with variants in D and C; see CSEL 81/1 465:28–467:11, and
  the notes to 467:8.
4 Origen *Comm in Rom* 10.11 PG 14 1269B, where, in place of 'nor shall I be
  made' the reading is 'nor am I made.' The Merlin edition also reads the
  present tense of the verb (fol CCXIX verso).
5 Rom 15:20
6 Chrysostom and] Added in 1535
7 Chrysostom *Hom in Rom* 29.2 PG 60 656; Theophylact *Expos in Rom* 15:18
  PG 124 541D
8 'Did effect' ... done.] This sentence originally, in 1516, concluded the
  annotation on 15:19 ('through a circuit') below. It was moved in 1519 to
  become part of this annotation.

15:19 [ER *prodigiorum per potentiam spiritus dei* 'of wonders through[1] the
power of the Spirit of God']
[VG] *prodigiorum in virtute spiritus sancti* 'of wonders[2] in the strength
of the Holy Spirit.' The Greek is 'the Spirit of God,' ἐν δυνάμει πνεύματος

θεοῦ, and so, certainly, reads Origen, also Chrysostom,[3] and Theophylact agrees with him.[4] And yet, Ambrose and the old Latin manuscripts[5] have it otherwise. It is[6] not surprising if Origen in his exposition mentions the Holy Spirit, since the Spirit of God is the Holy Spirit.[7] But the word 'God' expresses better the convincing authority of miracles. And in the comments of Ambrose, there is nothing to suggest he read anything other than 'the Spirit of God.'[8]

In this passage Chrysostom seems covertly to censure certain bishops who claim authority for themselves on the basis of their mitres, staffs, and robes, while Paul proves that he is an apostle by arguments far superior – by the greatness of the miracles and the success of the evangelical doctrine.[9] And yet he does not arrogantly claim any of these for himself, but ascribes all the glory to God, a man boasting with the greatest modesty and modest in his vaunting, proud in Christ, humble in himself.

1 through] First in 1519; in 1516, 'in'
2 of wonders ... otherwise.] This short passage, with the exception noted below (n3) constituted the annotation when it was introduced in 1519. In the editions from 1519 to 1527 the position of this annotation and the next was reversed.
3 and Chrysostom] Added in 1535
4 Origen *Comm in Rom* 10.12 PG 14 1269B; Chrysostom *Hom in Rom* 29.2 PG 60 655; and Theophylact *Expos in Rom* 15:19 PG 124 541C
The Greek witnesses are fairly evenly divided between the two readings, 'Spirit of God' and 'Holy Spirit.' One important manuscript (B [Vaticanus]) has simply 'Spirit.' See Tischendorf II 446 19n; Metzger 537; and Cranfield II 758 n5.
5 old Latin manuscripts] First in 1535; previously, 'old manuscripts.' For Ambrosiaster, see *Comm in Rom* 15:19. Ambrosiaster reads 'Holy Spirit.' The Latin witnesses are divided, though the predominant reading is 'Holy Spirit.' See Wordsworth and White II 142 19n.
6 It is ... himself.] This remaining portion of the annotation was added in 1535.
7 Cf Origen *Comm in Rom* 10.12 PG 14 1269C.
8 In his commentary on this verse Ambrosiaster does not mention 'the Spirit'; he attributes Paul's power either to Christ or to God; see *Comm in Rom* 15:19 (1–2).
9 Chrysostom *Hom in Rom* 29.2 PG 60 656. Chrysostom evidently alludes to the Jewish priesthood: '[Paul says], "There are many symbols of my priesthood; I have many signs of my authority to produce, not the long robes and bells as of old, not turban and tiara, but signs and wonders much more awesome than those." '

15:19 [ER *in circumiacentibus regionibus* 'in the surrounding regions']
[VG] *per circuitum* 'through[1] a circuit'; καὶ κύκλῳ, that is, 'and in a circuit'[2] or 'on all sides.'[3]

1 In the editions from 1519 to 1527 this and the preceding annotation were in reverse order.
2 The reading of some Latin manuscripts and Latin Fathers; cf Wordsworth and White II 142 19n.
3 sides] For the concluding sentence, in 1516 only, of this annotation cf the annotation on 15:18 ('of those things which through me [Christ] did not effect') n8.

15:20 [ER *ita porro annitens praedicare* 'and moreover[1] so striving to preach']
[VG] *sic autem praedicavi* 'but thus have I preached.' The Greek is somewhat different from the Latin: οὕτως δὲ φιλοτιμούμενον εὐαγγελίζεσθαι 'but thus striving to preach the gospel';[2] φιλοτιμεῖσθαι is to attempt something as though for reasons of vainglory.[3] So Paul, from a kind of holy ambition, stayed away from those places where the rest of the apostles had preached, so that he himself might be the father and author of his own people. Chrysostom[4] has pointed out ever so briefly the special significance of the verb φιλοτιμεῖσθαι, saying that the Apostle had acted for the sake of glory in studiously avoiding those who had already heard the gospel.[5] In his exposition Ambrose used the word *nitor* [I strive].[6]

The conjunctive δέ, although it could not be rendered suitably, is by no means without meaning in the Greek; for it indicates that something of great importance is being added, something that greatly increases the force of the statement. We normally convey this by 'besides' or 'moreover,' as if you should say, 'I have nourished them all, and alone besides,' or 'I have nourished them all, and moreover alone.'

1 moreover] Added in 1519. For the position of this annotation in LB, see the next annotation, n1.
2 So Valla *Annot in Rom* 15 (I 860)
3 On the meaning of this verb see Cranfield II 763 n1, where several scholars are cited who concur with Erasmus that the connotation of the word includes a sense of ambition or honour desired; but Cranfield thinks the primary sense in the New Testament is 'eagerly to strive.'
Lefèvre had taken this verb to imply a commendable ambition and a proper desire for honour, and wished to see many in his own day with this kind of holy ambition (*Pauli epistolae* fol 104 recto); cf Erasmus' criticism of bishops in the annotation on 15:19 ('of wonders in the strength of the Holy Spirit').
4 Chrysostom ... *nitor.*] Added in 1535
5 Chrysostom *Hom in Rom* 29.3 PG 60 656–7. Chrysostom stresses, however, that Paul did not act from motives of glory, and he appears to understand the verb φιλοτιμέομαι here primarily in the sense of 'to be eager.'
6 Cf Ambrosiaster *Comm in Rom* 15:20 (1): 'With good reason he said that he "strove" to preach where Christ was not named.'

15:19 [ER *impleverim evangelium Christi* 'I have fulfilled the gospel of Christ']
[VG] *repleverim evangelium Christi* 'I have[1] replenished the gospel of
Christ.' Here the Translator has not rendered the pronoun ἐμέ [me];[2] but
elsewhere he has added ὑμεῖς [you],[3] rather harshly.

By 'gospel' he means here the preaching of the gospel, which he had
carried out in so many regions – though *impleverim* [I have fulfilled] or *com-
pleverim* [I have completed] would be more appropriate than *repleverim* [fill
up again, replenish]. I believe that a similar figure underlies the statement
in the Gospel, 'before you have finished all the cities,' meaning 'before you
have gone through all the cities.'[4] Chrysostom has observed that [Paul] did
not say he had preached, but that he had fulfilled,[5] that is, that he had left
nothing undone that belonged to the work of a keen and faithful evangelist.

> 1 I have ... evangelist.] The entire annotation was added in 1535. In the
> 1535 edition, this annotation on 15:19 follows the annotation on 15:20 ('but
> thus have I preached'). LB has reversed the order of 1535, thus making the
> sequence of annotations conform to the sequence of biblical verses.
> 2 In the Greek the ἐμέ identifies Paul as subject in an infinitive clause: ὥστε
> με ... πεπληρωκέναι 'so that I have fulfilled.' In both the Vulgate and
> Erasmus' translation the subject is made clear in the verb; consequently,
> neither translates this Greek pronoun with a corresponding Latin pronoun.
> 3 See eg the annotation on Matt 20:23 (*non est meum dare vobis*) and Eph 6:4 (*et
> vos patres*).
> 4 Matt 10:23 (where the Greek, however is τελέσητε), on which verse see the
> annotation *non consummabitis civitates*, where Erasmus attacks the Vulgate
> translation.
> 5 Chrysostom *Hom in Rom* 29.2 PG 60 656

15:21 [ER *et qui non audierant intelligent* 'and those who had not heard
will understand']
[VG] *et qui non audierunt de eo intelligent* 'and those who have not heard
of him will understand.' 'Of him' is redundant, though it is understood
from[1] the preceding clause.[2]

> 1 from ... clause] Added in 1519
> 2 Cf the preceding clause:
> ER VG *quibus non est annuntiatum de eo videbunt* 'those will see to whom no
> announcement of him was made'
> Erasmus follows the preferred Latin reading, which agrees with the Greek in
> omitting *de eo* from 15:21b (the cue phrase); see Wordsworth and White II
> 143 21n.

15:22 [ER *quapropter et praepeditus sum saepe* 'wherefore also I[1] have often
been prevented']
[VG] *propter quod impediebar plurimum* 'on account of which I was greatly

hindered'; διὸ καὶ ἐνεκοπτόμην τὰ πολλὰ τοῦ ἐλθεῖν,[2] that is, 'wherefore also I was hindered many times.' For τὰ πολλά used as an adverb has this meaning also [that is, 'many times']. So interpret the Greek scholia,[3] specifically[4] and clearly Chrysostom and Theophylact.[5] For [Paul] tried very often, and work always stood in his way to hold him back. Besides, 'I was hindered' is ἐνεκοπτόμην, which signifies that a matter begun is interrupted; 'I[6] was restrained' or 'prevented' would have been more suitable – as[7] in Acts [Paul], intending to set out for Bithynia, was prohibited by the Holy Spirit.[8]

1 I have been prevented] First in 1519; in 1516, impeditus sum 'I have been hindered'.
2 LB adds to the Greek the words πρὸς ὑμᾶς, and to the translation, 'from coming to you.' The additional words are not found in the editions published during Erasmus' lifetime.
3 Cf Pseudo-Oecumenius Comm in Rom 15:22 PG 118 624B.
4 specifically ... Theophylact] Added in 1519, except for the reference to Chrysostom, which was added in 1535
5 Cf Chrysostom Hom in Rom 29.3 PG 60 657; Theophylact Expos in Rom 15:22 PG 124 544C–D.
6 'I ... suitable] Added in 1519
7 as ... Spirit] Added in 1535
8 Acts 16:7. Titelmans had objected to Erasmus' earlier interpretation that it was the Apostle's busy life that prevented him from going to Rome, and thought Paul was prevented rather by a divine directive, as in Acts 16:7. Cf Responsio ad collationes LB IX 1013A–B.

15:23 [ER cum non amplius habeam locum 'since I no longer have a place']
[VG] locum non habens 'having no[1] place'; μηκέτι τόπον ἔχων, that is, 'since I no longer have a place.' He is thinking of a place that was free, which he was seeking so that there should be more fruit, as he had said before.[2]

1 no] Added in 1535. In 1516 only, the order of this and the next annotation was reversed.
2 Cf Rom 1:13.

15:23 [ER multis iam annis 'for many years now']
[VG] ex[1] multis iam praecedentibus annis 'from many years now past'; ἀπὸ πολλῶν ἐτῶν, that is, 'for many years' or[2] 'for many years now.' I do not see why the Translator found it necessary to add anything,[3] since the passage cannot refer to years yet to come.

1 ex] First in 1535; until then, ab in the cue phrase. The Vulgate printed in 1527 reads ex. For the position of this annotation in 1516, see the preceding annotation, n1.
2 or ... come] Added in 1519
3 The Vulgate's praecedentibus 'past' has no clear equivalent in the Greek.

15:24 [ER *quandocumque iter instituero in Hispaniam* 'whenever I undertake[1] the journey to Spain']

[VG] *cum in Hispaniam proficisci coepero* 'when I begin to set out for Spain'; ὡς ἐὰν πορεύωμαι εἰς τὴν Σπανίαν, ἐλεύσομαι πρὸς ὑμᾶς: 'So that if I set out for Spain, I shall come to you.'[2] But some Greek codices have ἕως [until],[3] not ὡς [so that]. If[4] [ὡς ἐάν] is read as two separate words, it means 'so that if'; if as a single phrase, it could be rendered 'as soon as,'[5] to indicate that this will happen soon.

Greek writers,[6] following Paul, cheat 'Spain' of its first syllable,[7] which [Spaniards] normally add to words of this kind, saying *espero* for *spero*, and *exspecto* for *specto*;[8] [the Greeks] do[9] the same with this word as we Latins do with 'Iscariot.'[10]

1 I undertake] First in *1519*; in *1516, fuero profectus* 'I shall set out'
2 So Valla *Annot in Rom* 15 (I 860); cf the annotation on 15:24 ('that in passing by') n3.
3 No such reading is listed in Tischendorf II 447 24n.
4 If . . . soon.] Added in *1535*
5 Cf eg 1 Cor 11:34. For ὡς ἄν or ὡς ἐάν 'as soon as' see ὡς IV c in BAG.
6 writers . . . Paul] Added in *1522*; before then, simply 'The Greeks cheat'
7 The Greek Σπανία (*Spania*) lacks the first syllable of the Latin *Hispania*.
8 This comment evoked a strong reaction from Zúñiga, who thought Erasmus was criticizing the linguistic skills of the Spanish. See *Apologia ad annotationes Stunicae* ASD IX-2 176–80. In *De recta pronuntiatione* CWE 26 445 Erasmus notes French speakers also who prefix an *e* to words like *specto*.
9 do . . . Iscariot'] Added in *1519*
10 In the preferred text, the Vulgate generally omits the initial *I*, though variants with *I* do appear; see, on Matt 10:4 and John 6:72, Weber II 1539 and 4n, and 1670 and 72n.

15:24 [ER *spero enim fore ut istac iter faciens videam vos* 'for I hope, while journeying that way, to see you']

[VG] *spero enim quod praeteriens videam vos* 'for I hope that in passing by I may see you'; ἐλπίζω γὰρ διαπορευόμενος θεάσασθαι ὑμᾶς, καὶ ὑφ᾽ ὑμῶν προπεμφθῆναι ἐκεῖ. Since I see that Lefèvre is offended by the language,[1] it could be rendered into good Latin thus: 'For I hope, while journeying that way, to see you and to be led on (or, escorted there) by you.'

1 language] First in *1527*; until then, *latinitate* 'by the Latinity.' Lefèvre wished to omit the *quod* of the Vulgate, and to turn the Greek participle into a Latin gerund (*Pauli epistolae* fol 104 recto). Lefèvre translated: *spero enim pertranseundo videre vos* 'for I hope in passing through to see you' (ibidem fol 11 recto).
For the position of this annotation in *1516*, see the next annotation, n1.

15:24 [ER *ut istac iter faciens* 'while journeying that way']

[VG] *quod praeteriens* 'that in passing by';[1] διαπορευόμενος, that is, 'passing through' or 'journeying that way.' The words[2] ἐλεύσομαι πρὸς ὑμᾶς [I shall come to you] appear to have been added,[3] if only from the fact that Chrysostom does not touch upon them[4] – though they are added in Theophylact.[5] Ambrose reads: 'When I have begun to set out for Spain I shall see you, and to be sent on there by you.' If the passage is free from error Ambrose construes thus: 'Having a desire to come to you for many years now (when I have begun to set out for Spain) and to be escorted there by you,' so that both verbs – 'to come' and 'to be escorted' – depend on the noun 'desire.'[6] But I conjecture that the text is mutilated. There is nothing awkward in the passage if we remove the Greek conjunction γάρ [for], which is not in the Latin, so that ὡσάν taken as a single phrase[7] relates to the preceding words in the following manner: 'Since I do not have a place that is free in these regions, and in any case have been eager for many years now to come to you as soon as I set out for Spain, I hope that in passing I shall see you and, proceeding on, be escorted there by you.'

The Translator has a custom of rendering verbs of future time with a word that indicates 'beginning'; but here the Greek reads ὡς ἂν πορεύωμαι.[8] Further, προπεμφθῆναι is badly rendered as *praemitti* [to be sent on] – whoever [the translator] was (for so Ambrose reads) – since it is a matter of courtesy to 'escort' one setting out on a journey.[9] The translator of Origen construes differently in his exposition, but still without adding the conjunction [γάρ 'for']: 'When I set out for Spain I hope that I will see you.'[10] And the words ἐλπίζω γὰρ διαπορευόμενος θεάσασθαι ὑμᾶς [for I hope, in passing by, I will see you] are in Chrysostom,[11] but are not added in Theophylact, either in the biblical text or in the exposition,[12] just as they are not in Ambrose.[13] I perceive that, in matters which do not seem to have much relevance to apostolic dogma, the ancients have allowed themselves too much [freedom] in changing Scripture. Hence so many variant readings in the Acts of the Apostles and the Apocalypse.[14] And the Greeks have been reluctant to include the Epistle to Philemon among the apostolic Epistles, because it seems to treat [only] human matters.[15] But I wish we had three hundred epistles like it!

1 This appeared as a separate annotation in all editions published in Erasmus' lifetime, though in LB it is conflated with the immediately preceding annotation. In 1516 it was placed before the preceding annotation, thereafter it followed.

2 The words ... like it!] This remaining portion of the annotation was added in 1535.

3 Tischendorf (II 447 24n) notes these words as a minor variant reading.
Erasmus, following Valla (*Annot in Rom* 15 [I 860]), printed these words in
the first edition, and retained them even in his final edition, though already
in 1529 he had noted that they are not found in Chrysostom (*Responsio ad
collationes* LB IX 1013B).

The discussion has for its context the whole of 15:23–4. In his translation,
Erasmus read the verses thus: 'Since I no longer have a place in these parts,
but have had a desire now for many years to come to you, when I undertake
the journey to Spain, *I shall come to you*, for I hope, while journeying there, to
see you, and to be escorted thither by you, if first I shall in part be satisfied
through my association with you.'

In the *1535* portion of this annotation Erasmus seeks to find a way to
construe the passage, following his textual evidence, without the words that
are italicized above. This, he proposes, can be done if 'for' (in 'for I hope') is
omitted, and 'when' is understood in the sense of 'as soon as.'

In passing he notes the reading of Ambrosiaster, which omits both the italicized words and the words 'for I hope, while journeying there.' See n6 below.

4 Chrysostom *Hom in Rom* 29.3 PG 60 657

5 Theophylact *Expos in Rom* 15:24 PG 124 544D

6 Ambrosiaster *Comm in Rom* 15:23–4. In the CSEL edition, the full text of the
passage discussed here reads: '... having a desire to come to you for many
years now, but when I have begun to set out for Spain, I shall see you, and
to be sent on there by you ...'

7 Cf, just above, the annotation on 15:24 ('when I begin to set out for Spain'),
where Erasmus shows that the Greek here should be read 'as a single phrase.'

8 Cf the Vulgate translation of the Greek verb μέλλειν 'to be about to' by the
Latin *incipere* 'to begin' (eg Acts 18:14, 19:27, 27:30), and the annotation on
Acts 18:14 (*incipiente autem Paulo*). Here, however, the verb is not future, but
subjunctive, which Erasmus understands in the sense of 'as soon as I set out
for Spain,' so that the Vulgate's *coepero* 'when I shall begin' is inappropriate.
But for the few witnesses to the verb in the future see Tischendorf II 447 24n
and Wordsworth and White II 143 24n.

9 Compare the translations of the Vulgate, *deducar* 'I shall be escorted' and of
Erasmus, *producar* 'I shall be conducted, led forward.'

10 Origen *Comm in Rom* 10.13 PG 14 1271B

11 Chrysostom *Hom in Rom* 29.3 PG 60 657

12 Cf Theophylact *Expos in Rom* 15:24 PG 124 544D. In Migne, the words are
found in the biblical text, but play no part in the exposition.

13 Cf n6 above; in Ambrosiaster, the missing words are, more precisely, 'for I
hope in passing by.'

14 Erasmus elsewhere also notes the variety of readings in Acts – cf the
annotation on Acts 1:1 (*primum quidem sermonem*) LB VI 433D – and,
frequently, in the Apocalypse – cf eg the annotations on 3:2 (*qui aperit et nemo
claudit*) 4:8 (*sanctus, sanctus, sanctus*). ˙

On the problems of the text, for Acts see Metzger 259–72, for the Apocalypse,
H.C. Hoskier *Concerning the Text of the Apocalypse: Collations of all Existing
Greek Documents* (London 1929). On Erasmus' text of the Apocalypse see
Bentley *Humanists* 128.

15 In the annotations on Acts 1:1 and Rev 4:8 cited above (n14), Erasmus notes that the Greeks scarcely accept the Apocalypse as canonical, but in these passages he makes no comment on the Epistle to Philemon. However, for ancient critics of the book see Chrysostom *In epistulam ad Philemonem homiliae* 1.1 PG 62 702; Theodore of Mopsuestia *In epistolas Pauli commentarii* ed H.B. Swete 2 vols (Cambridge 1880–2) II 258; and Jerome *Commentarius in epistulam ad Philemonem* prologus PL 26 (1883) 635–8.

15:24 [ER *fuero expletus* 'I shall be satisfied']

[VG] *fruitus fuero* 'I shall enjoy'; ἐμπλησθῶ, that is, 'I shall be satisfied,'[1] which is more suggestive in expressing Paul's great desire. And to intensify further he adds 'in part,' suggesting an insatiable desire.

> 1 Valla (*Annot in Rom* [1 861]) suggested *impletus fuero* 'I shall be satisfied, satiated,' and was followed by Lefèvre, who suggested also *satiatus fuero* (with much the same meaning) and so translated (*Pauli epistolae* fol 104 recto and fol 11 recto).

15:25 [ER *nunc autem proficiscor* 'but now I am setting out']

[VG] *nunc igitur proficiscar* 'now then I shall set out'; πορεύομαι, that is, 'I am setting out.' It is in the present tense,[1] as is also the participle which follows, διακονῶν, that is, 'ministering';[2] for he was already doing this.[3] We are[4] indeed said to 'be doing' that which we are preparing to do. In this statement, the Apostle is excusing the delay of his departure to Spain. For they could have said: 'If for your part there is nothing to delay you, why do you put off your visit to us?' 'Now,' he says, 'I am setting out for Jerusalem.' If he had said, 'I shall set out,' he would have increased their suspicion of a longer delay. And so the verb in the present tense is more suited to the Apostle's meaning. But I cannot imagine why the Translator changed the participle into an infinitive, unless perhaps he read [the infinitive] διακονεῖν.[5]

> 1 So Valla *Annot in Rom* (1 861)
> 2 Compare the translations of Erasmus and the Vulgate:
> ER *nunc autem proficiscor Hierosolymam ministrans sanctis* 'but now I am setting out for Jerusalem, ministering to the saints'
> VG *nunc igitur proficiscar Hierosolymam ministrare sanctis* 'now then I shall set out for Jerusalem to minister to the saints'
> 3 In his reply to Titelmans Erasmus noted that Paul had been for some time collecting money for the 'saints,' and this was already to minister to them (*Responsio ad collationes* LB IX 1013C).
> 4 We are ... the Apostle's meaning.] Added in *1535*
> 5 Ie 'to minister' in place of 'ministering.' Titelmans reminded Erasmus of a previous annotation, in which he had claimed that in Greek the participle was sometimes used in place of the infinitive (cf the annotation on Matt 11:1 [*cum consummasset praecipiens*]). Erasmus replied that this was not always the case, and certainly not here in the case of πορεύομαι, where the Greek

participle should be translated by a Latin participle (*Responsio ad collationes* LB IX 1013B–C).

15:26 [ER *visum est enim Macedoniae* 'for it seemed good to Macedonia']
[VG] *probaverunt enim Macedones* 'for the Macedonians[1] approved'; εὐδόκησαν, that is, 'they gave assent,' and 'so it seemed good to them.' But immediately he translates the same word as 'it pleased them'[2] – such a wicked offence did the Translator judge it to repeat the same word, though Paul himself had no scruples in doing so. Further, εὐδοκεῖν does not mean only 'to approve,' but 'to approve enthusiastically' – whenever something is not just merely pleasing, but when it pleases us heartily and well. Thus we understand that gifts of this kind,[3] if freely offered, ought to be accepted by those who need them, but should not be demanded, for Paul himself preferred to work with his hands rather than live off the food of others.[4]

1 Macedonians] The Vulgate printed in 1527 reads *Macedonia*, which is the preferred reading; see Wordsworth and White II 144 26n.
2 Ie in Rom 15:27: 'For so it seemed good to them, and they are debtors.' See the annotation next below, n7. Lefèvre noted the same variation in the Translator's rendering (*Pauli epistolae* fol 104 recto).
3 Ie such as the contributions for the poor of Jerusalem (15:26)
4 others] In 1516 only, there followed here a number of lines that were placed in 1519 in the succeeding annotation; see the next annotation, n3.

15:26 [ER *communicationem* 'a sharing of the common goods']
[VG] *collationem* 'a collection'; κοινωνίαν, that is, 'a sharing'[1] or a 'sharing of the common goods' – for so he calls the alms sent, a term[2] of courtesy, no doubt, as though to help with money were not a favour, but [is simply] to impart to those in need the wealth we hold in common with them. In rendering[3] 'for the poor of the saints,'[4] the Translator was too literal, as though he would express both the form and the idiom of the Greek. Otherwise he should have said 'for the poor saints,' so that no one would imagine that the saints had poor people who were not saints. For since[5] all Christians were at that time called saints, there was no need of the possessive case to distinguish poor pagans from the faithful.[6]

One should note that Paul seems to join two contradictory words, εὐδόκησαν [they gave assent] and ὀφειλέται [(they are) debtors].[7] For whoever offers voluntarily and with heartfelt affection does not seem to owe; hence he calls the divine kindness towards mankind εὐδοκία [good will].[8] But although he seems to have included this out of politeness rather than conviction, nevertheless he adds this one reason, that the [Jews] had bestowed spiritual gifts [on the gentiles], as though otherwise nothing would be owed. But today none require more tyrannically the tithes than those who bestow nothing spiritual. For it is the gospel teaching that Paul calls 'spiritual.'[9]

1 So Valla *Annot in Rom* 15 (I 861) and Lefèvre *Pauli epistolae* fol 104 recto
2 a term ... them] This part of the sentence was added in *1519*.
3 In rendering ... 'spiritual.'] Apart from the *1535* addition noted below (n5) this remaining portion of the annotation was, in *1516* only, the conclusion to the preceding annotation; see the previous annotation, n4.
4 Erasmus rendered 'to make some sharing of the common goods for the poor saints [*in pauperes sanctos*],' the Vulgate, 'to make a collection for the poor of the saints [*in pauperes sanctorum*].'
5 For since ... faithful.] Added in *1535*
6 Titelmans had argued that the possessive in the Latin was distributive – 'the poor among the saints,' but Erasmus noted that as a distributive the Latin required a different form of expression (*Responsio ad collationes* LB IX 1013C–D).
7 The discussion turns to the first part of 15:27:
    ER *nam ita visum est ipsis et debitores illorum sunt* 'for so it seemed good to themselves, and they are their debtors'
    VG *placuit enim eis et debitores sunt eorum* 'for it pleased them, and they are their debtors'
8 Cf eg Eph 1:5, 9.
9 Cf also 1 Cor 9:11, 10:4.

15:27 [ER *si spiritualia sua communicaverunt gentibus* 'if they have shared their spiritual goods with the nations']

[VG] *si spiritualium illorum participes facti sunt gentiles* 'if[1] the gentiles have become partakers of their spiritual goods.' The Greek reads εἰ γὰρ τοῖς πνευματικοῖς αὐτῶν ἐκοινώνησαν τὰ ἔθνη. Paul uses this word κοινωνεῖν [to share] in two senses – with reference sometimes to the one who gives, sometimes to the one who receives. In Galatians 6 he has used it in the sense of 'impart': κοινωνείτω δὲ ὁ κατηχούμενος τὸν λόγον τῷ κατηχοῦντι [6:6].[2] Here [in 15:27] he seems to understand ἐκοινώνησαν in the sense of 'were partakers' – it is concerned with 'receiving,' unless you read αὐτῶν with an aspirated alpha, and take τὰ ἔθνη as an accusative.[3] It makes no difference to the meaning which way you read. For – to take the expression as written – because the Law and the gospel and Christ arose first from the Jews, just as we are in debt to the descendants[4] for the favour received from [their] ancestors, so the descendants are said to have imparted to us what came to them from their progenitors. Chrysostom, continuing on [in the passage], uses, somewhat imprecisely, κοινωνῆσαι [to share] and μεταδοῦναι [to give a part] in explaining that Paul said λειτουργῆσαι [to minister].[5] Chrysostom has also observed that Paul adds αὐτῶν [their][6] to 'spiritual goods,' because these goods belong to the individual. He did not add [your] to 'carnal goods' because the supply of these belongs not only to the possessor but to everyone in need.[7]

1 if ... need.] The entire annotation was added in *1535*, evidently in response to Titelmans, who asked how the 'poor saints' at Jerusalem were in a position to communicate the gospel to the gentiles; see *Responsio ad collationes* LB IX 1013D–E.

2 'Let the one who is taught the word share with his teacher.'

3 On the first alternative, Erasmus evidently intends to read 'If the gentiles have been made partakers in their [ie the Jews'] spiritual goods'; on the second, 'If they have made the gentiles sharers in their spiritual goods.' Erasmus' translation, established in *1516*, appears to take the verb in the sense of 'impart,' the Vulgate in the sense of 'receive.' For the two meanings of the verb see Cranfield II 773. In the annotation on 12:13 ('sharing in the needs of the saints') Erasmus stressed the reciprocal relationship of giving and receiving implied by the verb.

4 A reference to the first part of 15:27; see the immediately preceding annotation, n7.

5 Cf Chrysostom *Hom in Rom* 30.1 PG 60 662. Chrysostom, commenting on the last clause of 15:27 ('they ought to minister to them in carnal things') notes that gentiles ought 'to share and give the Jews a part' of their carnal things. Chrysostom uses these verbs to explain the verb λειτουργῆσαι, but adds that this verb, more properly, means 'to minister.'

6 In Migne, αὐτῶν, but in *1535*, with the aspirated alpha, αὑτῶν 'their own'

7 Chrysostom writes: '[Paul] did not speak of "your" carnal goods as he had spoken of "their" [the Jews'] spiritual goods, for the spiritual goods are theirs, carnal goods belong to all'; *Hom in Rom* 30.1 PG 60 662.

15:28 [ER *ubi perfecero* 'when I have completed']
[VG] *cum consummavero* 'when I have fulfilled'; ἐπιτελέσας, that is, 'when I have completed.'[1]

1 For Erasmus' criticism of the Vulgate *consummare* see the annotations on 15:19 ('I have replenished the gospel of Christ') n4, and on 9:28 ('bringing to completion the word').

15:28 [ER *et obsignavero* 'and have sealed']
[VG] *et assignavero* 'and have marked'; σφραγισάμενος, that is, 'I have sealed' or 'I have[1] delivered under seal,' for in this way money is usually delivered. Paul means that he wishes to deliver this gift with care and with demonstrable honesty, because in every case the handling of money tends to arouse suspicion, especially among money-grasping Jews. Theophylact[2] suggests something of this kind.

1 'I have' is idiomatic English for the Latin future perfect 'I shall have,' as in the cue phrase.

2 Theophylact ... kind.] Added in *1519*; cf Theophylact *Expos in Rom* 15:28 PG 124 548A. Theophylact speaks only of Paul's desire to keep the money in a safe place.

15:28 [ER VG] *fructum hunc* 'this[1] fruit.' Chrysostom and[2] Theophylact refer [the word] 'fruit' not to those who would receive, but to those who had contributed,[3] as though in Christian acts of charity the gain lies with the one who gives, not with the one who receives. Now if Paul had delivered this money safe and sound, the result would be that to the Macedonians and the others who had given it, it would appear like a treasure stored up in safe-keeping. I have pointed this out so that the reader may understand that the pronoun 'them' refers to the Greeks, not to the saints.[4]

    1 this ... saints.] Except for a brief addition in *1535* (see n2 below) this annotation was added in *1519*, and as a separate note, though in LB it is conflated with the preceding annotation.
    2 Chrysostom and] Added in *1535*
    3 Chrysostom *Hom in Rom* 30.1 PG 60 662; Theophylact *Expos in Rom* 15:28 PG 124 548A
    4 Though some commentators, ancient and modern, have referred 'them' to the gentiles, it is probable that it refers to the Jerusalem Christians; hence, 'when I have delivered under seal to them this fruit,' not 'when I have delivered under seal for them this fruit.' Cf Cranfield II 774 n3.

15:29 [ER *cum plenitudine benedictionis etc* 'with[1] the fullness of the blessing etc']
[VG] *in plenitudine benedictionis etc* 'in the fullness[2] of the blessing etc'; ἐν πληρώματι εὐλογίας τοῦ εὐαγγελίου τοῦ Χριστοῦ, that is, 'in the fullness[3] of the blessing of the gospel.'[4] Paul sometimes calls alms a 'blessing.'[5] And here he seems modestly to suggest that the Romans also should offer a gift. And yet[6] Chrysostom prefers that [the word] here refer generally to every kind of virtue and duty, especially because 'of the gospel' is added;[7] but what is given in the name of the gospel is the εὐλογία [the blessing] of the gospel. They called alms given with kind words a εὐλογία [blessing] by a figure of speech similar to that in which the banquet customarily given to the poor is called an ἀγάπη [a love-feast]. Some[8] read 'of the gospel of Christ'; this is read in Chrysostom's [biblical] text, but in his exposition he shows that he read only 'of the gospel.'[9] It is also added in Theophylact, but only in his text.[10] Like Ambrose, our Translator has only 'in [...] the blessing of Christ';[11] such, too, is the reading in Ambrose' exposition;[12] Origen reads likewise.[13]

    1 with] First in *1519*; in *1516*, with the Vulgate, 'in'

2 The Vulgate printed in 1527 reads *abundantia* 'abundance,' which is the correct reading. Wordsworth and White (II 144 29n) do not offer *plenitudine* even as a variant. Valla, whose Vulgate read *abundantia*, wrote, 'the Greek is *in plenitudine* [in the fullness]' (*Annot in Rom* 15 [I 861]); see n3 below. In 1516 Erasmus concluded the annotations on this chapter with a version of the annotation here, where, however, *abundantia* appears in the cue phrase. *Plenitudine* here, then, appears to be a mistake. See below the annotation on 15:31 ('may become acceptable unto Jerusalem') n6.

3 Valla recommended the Latin *plenitudine* here, and Lefèvre so translated; cf Valla (cited in preceding note) and Lefèvre *Pauli epistolae* fol 11 recto.

4 Here LB adds the words 'of Christ,' but they are found in no edition published in Erasmus' lifetime.

5 Cf 2 Cor 9:5, where Paul speaks of the gift of the Corinthians 'for the saints' (2 Cor 9:1 RSV) as a εὐλογία (Vulgate *benedictio*, DV 'blessing,' RSV 'gift'). Valla had noted that some people called the offerings (*oblationes*) made in church a 'blessing'; cf Valla *Annot in Rom* 15 (I 861).

6 And yet ... ἀγάπη.] Added in 1527

7 Chrysostom *Hom in Rom* 30.1 PG 60 662

8 Some ... likewise.] Added in 1535

9 Chrysostom *Hom in Rom* 30.1 PG 60 662

10 Theophylact *Expos in Rom* 15:29 PG 124 548B

11 For the entire clause, the Vulgate of 1527 read: 'I shall come in the fullness of the blessing of Christ'; Erasmus read: 'I shall come in the fullness of the blessing of the gospel of Christ.' For the Vulgate, the shorter reading is the better attested one (Wordsworth and White II 144 29n); likewise in the Greek text the shorter reading has strong support (Tischendorf II 449 29n; Metzger 537).

12 For biblical citation and commentary see Ambrosiaster *Comm in Rom* 15:29.

13 Origen *Comm in Rom* 10.14 PG 14 1272B, 1275C–1276A

15:30 [ER *obsecro autem vos* 'now I beseech you']
[VG] *obsecro ergo vos* 'I beseech you therefore'; παρακαλῶ δέ,[1] that is, 'now I urge you,' though in this passage, at least, 'beseech' is not particularly unsuitable because of what follows – 'through our Lord Jesus Christ.'[2]

1 LB adds ὑμᾶς 'you,' without warrant from the editions 1516–1535.
2 Cf the annotation on Rom 12:1 ('I beseech you').

15:30 [ER *per dilectionem spiritus* 'through the love of the Spirit']
[VG] *per charitatem sancti spiritus* 'through the love of the Holy Spirit.' 'Holy' is an addition.[1] διὰ τῆς ἀγάπης τοῦ πνεύματος, that is, 'through the love of the Spirit.'

1 Though 'Holy Spirit' is the reading of the Vulgate in 1527, 'Spirit' is the preferred reading in the Latin manuscripts (cf Wordsworth and White II 144–5 30n) and is the only Greek reading given by Tischendorf (II 449 30 and 30n).

15:30 [ER *ut me laborantem adiuvetis* 'that you help me in my labour']

[VG] *ut adiuvetis me* 'that you help me'; συναγωνίσασθαι, which is 'to bring aid,' but to one who is struggling and labouring. Origen[1] has observed this before me, but he distorts the intent [when he says] that in prayer there is a struggle with impious demons, who are accustomed to interrupt the prayers of the pious.[2] Ambrose reads, 'that you may share solicitude.'[3] The Translator has expressed it more correctly than Ambrose, at least in my opinion. He says 'in prayers' for 'through supplications.'[4] This form of speech[5] should now be familiar to us.

> 1 Origen ... of the pious.] Added in *1519*
> 2 Origen *Comm in Rom* 10.15 PG 14 1276C–1277A. Origen explained that Paul's labour was a struggle with demons who opposed him in prayer.
> 3 Ambrosiaster *Comm in Rom* 15:30
> 4 In *1516* Erasmus translated, with the Vulgate, *in orationibus* 'in prayers'; from *1519, precationibus* 'with supplications.'
> 5 Ie the use of *in* to express means; cf the annotation on 1:4 ('in power').

15:31 [ER *ministerium hoc meum* 'this[1] my ministry']

[VG] *obsequii mei oblatio* 'the offering of my service'; καὶ ἵνα ἡ διακονία μου, that is, '[and that][2] my ministry.' Ambrose reads 'that the offering of my gifts' – as though explaining [ministry].[3] And yet it seems to me he read something different, perhaps προσφορά , a word which [the Apostle] used before,[4] since a little above also [Paul] used a word suited to sacrifice, λειτουργῆσαι, which the Translator renders 'to minister.'[5] I[6] have added the pronoun 'this,' 'that this my ministry,' because of the Greek article, ἵνα ἡ διακονία μου.

> 1 this] Added in *1519*. Lefèvre also translated *ministerium meum* (*Pauli epistolae* fol 11 recto).
> 2 and that] *et ut*, though in LB, is not found in any edition from *1516* to *1535*. Erasmus had, however, included the expression in his translation, 'and that this my ministry.'
> 3 Ambrosiaster *Comm in Rom* 15:32 (for 15:31)
> 4 before] First in *1527*; previously, 'above.' See Rom 15:16 and the annotation 'sanctifying the gospel of God.' Some witnesses read δωροφορία, 'the bringing of a gift,' which is evidently the source of Ambrosiaster's reading; cf Metzger 537–8.
> 5 In 15:27; but cf also 15:16 and the annotation 'sanctifying the gospel of God.'
> 6 I ... μου.] Added in *1519*

15:31 [ER *quod exhibebo Hierosolymis acceptum sit* 'which I shall offer at Jerusalem[1] may be acceptable']

[VG] *accepta fiat in Hierusalem* 'may become acceptable unto Jerusalem.' There is some difference in the readings of the Greek codices here. Some read καὶ ἵνα ἡ διακονία μου, ἡ εἰς Ἰερουσαλὴμ εὐπρόσδεκτος γένηται τοῖς ἁγίοις, that is, 'and that my ministry, which is "to" or "towards" Jerusalem, may be acceptable to the saints.' One codex reads ἡ διακονία μου ἡ Ἰερουσαλήμ, that is, 'my ministry which is Jerusalem.'[2] But[3] Theophylact does not add this phrase[4] either in his text or in his exposition, and neither does Chrysostom.[5] He speaks modestly of his ministry, since he is only a minister of the generosity of others.[6]

1 at Jerusalem] First in 1519; in 1516, in Hierusalem 'unto Jerusalem'
2 This reading is not found in Tischendorf II 449–50 31n.
3 But ... Chrysostom] First in 1527; in 1516, 'Vulgarius omits "Jerusalem" altogether'; in 1519 and 1522, 'Vulgarius [1522 Theophylact] seems not to have added the phrase in his exposition'
4 Ie the phrase 'which is to Jerusalem'
5 Cf Theophylact Expos in Rom 15:31 PG 124 548D and Chrysostom Hom in Rom 30.2 PG 60 663. In Migne the phrase appears in the biblical citation in both authors ('which is to Jerusalem' in Theophylact, 'in Jerusalem' in Chrysostom), but neither comments on the phrase in his exposition.
6 In 1516 there followed at this point a further annotation:
  [ER in plenitudine benedictionis 'in the fullness of the blessing']
  [VG] in abundantia benedictionis 'in the abundance of the blessing'; πληρώματι εὐλογίας. The Translator sometimes used 'blessing' for 'alms.' Hence here, too, he seems to have modestly suggested to the Romans that they do the same as Greece had done to help the saints in Jerusalem.
The annotation clearly duplicates the earlier annotation on 15:29 ('in the fullness of the blessing etc') and was omitted in all editions subsequent to 1516.

CHAPTER 16

16:1 [ER *quae est ministra* 'who is a minister']

[VG] *quae est in ministerio* 'who is in the ministry'; οὖσαν διάκονον, that is, 'who is a minister.'[1] It is thought that the Epistle was delivered to the Romans by this 'Phoebe.'

> 1 So Valla *Annot in Rom* 16 (I 861)

16:1 [ER *Cenchreensis* 'of the Cenchrean']

[VG] *quae est Cenchris* 'which is at Cenchrae.' The Greek is Κεγχρεαῖς, Cenchreïs [at Cenchreae], or,[1] as it is written in some manuscripts, Κεχρεαῖς [*Cechreais*], a word[2] of three syllables; I have translated this *Cenchreensis* [Cenchrean]. Several places have this name: a town in the Troad, and another in Italy; but it is more reasonable that Paul is thinking of Cenchreae, the Corinthian harbour,[3] since it is clear that this Epistle was sent from Corinth. Origen[4] has pointed this out; he says[5] in the preface to his commentary on this Epistle, 'Cenchreae refers to a place in the neighbourhood of Corinth, in fact the harbour of Corinth itself.'[6]

> 1 or ... manuscripts] Added in *1519*. Only a few witnesses support the reading Κεχρεαῖς; cf Tischendorf II 450–1 1n.
> 2 a word ... syllables] Added in *1527*. The three syllables are evident in Cenchreïs, the Latin locative Erasmus gives as the equivalent of the Greek dative.
> 3 On Cenchreae see CWE 42 7 n15. Pauly-Wissowa *Realencyclopädie* XI-1 165–70 identifies several towns of this name, including one in Troas, but none in Italy.
> 4 Origen] After the word 'Origen' Erasmus added, in *1516* only, 'or perhaps it was someone else.'
> 5 he says ... itself'] Added in *1535*
> 6 Origen *Comm in Rom* praefatio PG 14 835B

16:2 [ER *ita ut decet sanctos* 'so as befits the saints']

[VG] *digne sanctis* 'worthily of the saints'; ἀξίως τῶν ἁγίων. This could have been translated 'as befits the saints' or 'as is worthy of the saints.' He[1] has made the noun depend on an adverb.[2]

> 1 He ... adverb.] Added in *1535*
> 2 The Translator follows the Greek text literally in writing 'worthily of the saints.'

16:3 [ER VG] *Priscam et Aquilam* 'Prisca[1] and Aquila.'[2] Origen thinks that 'Prisca' is the same woman whom Luke calls 'Priscilla' in Acts 18 [:2], whose husband was Aquila, a native of Pontus, but Jewish in religion[3] and racial origin, ὁμότεχνος with Paul,[4] that is, a tent-maker, and, as Origen explains, a 'cobbler.'[5] Origen questions how Aquila could have been at Rome when the Emperor Claudius had driven out all [the Jews], as recorded in the chapter just cited.[6] But it is possible that once the severity of the edict had been mitigated Aquila left Corinth and returned to Rome, for later Paul himself came upon many Jews there.[7] This is clear from the narrative in the last chapter in that book.

1 Prisca ... book.] The entire annotation was added in 1519.
2 Between the previous annotation ('worthily of saints') and the annotation on 16:7 ('Andronicus and Julia') both the sequence and the number of annotations varied in the editions printed in Erasmus' lifetime as follows:

1516	1519–1527	1535
'worthily of the saints'	'worthily of the saints'	'worthily of the saints'
'who has laboured much among you'	'Prisca and Aquila'	'Prisca and Aquila'
'their necks'	'their necks'	'their necks'
'and the domestic church'	'who has laboured much among you'	'and the domestic church'
'Greet Ephenetus'	'but also all the churches of the gentiles'	'Greet Ephenetus'
'who is the first'	'and the domestic church'	'who is the first of the church of Asia'
'of the church of Asia'	'Greet Ephenetus'	'of the church of Asia'
'Andronicus and Julia'	'who is the first of the church of Asia'	'who has laboured much among you'
	'of the church of Asia'	'Andronicus and Julia'
	'Andronicus and Julia'	

LB conflates 'of the church of Asia' with 'who is the first of the church of Asia,' without support, however, from any of the editions. In 1535 the annotation 'but also all the churches of the gentiles' appeared later in the chapter (16:16) with a new cue phrase 'the churches of Christ greet you.'
3 religion and racial origin] In all the editions from 1519 to 1535; in LB, 'origin and religion'
4 Ie having the same trade as Paul
5 See Origen Comm in Rom 10.18 PG 14 1278C–1279B. Origen cites Acts 18:1–3, which concludes, 'for by trade they were tent-makers' (RSV); to which Origen adds hoc est sutores. Sutor, normally 'a cobbler,' seems here to have its root meaning, 'one who stitches.'
6 Ie Acts 18:2. For the expulsion of the Jews from Rome see Suetonius Claudius 25. For the historical problems raised by our sources of information on this event, see E. Mary Smallwood The Jews under Roman Rule from Pompey to Diocletian (Leiden 1976) 210–16.
7 So Origen (n5 above)

16:4 [ER *suam ipsorum cervicem* 'their very own neck']

[VG] *suas cervices* 'their necks';[1] τὸν ἑαυτῶν τράχηλον, that is, 'their very own neck.'

1 For the sequence of this annotation see the preceding annotation, ('Prisca and Aquila') n2.

16:5 [ER *item quae in domo (illorum) est congregationem* 'likewise the congregation which is in (their) house']

[VG] *et domesticam ecclesiam* [*eorum*] 'and [their] domestic church';[1] καὶ τὴν κατ᾽ οἶκον αὐτῶν ἐκκλησίαν. He calls the Christian household and those who had joined in with it a 'church'; hence I have chosen to use the term 'congregation' because[2] of those thickheaded persons who think a 'church' is a sacred building.[3] It should not seem unbecoming if someone describes an assembly of Christians as a 'congregation,' since the Translator in the second chapter of Second Thessalonians calls the entire gathering of the faithful into Christ a 'congregation' [2:1].

1 For the sequence of this annotation see the annotation on 16:3 ('Prisca and Aquila') n2.
2 because ... 'congregation'] Added in *1535*
3 Erasmus had made the point earlier in his reply to Titelmans; he did not want anyone to suppose there was a 'building within a building' (*Responsio ad collationes* LB IX 1014A).

16:5 [ER *salutate Epaenetum* 'greet Epenetus']

[VG] *salutate Ephenetum* 'greet Ephenetus.'[1] The word is 'Epaenetus,' Ἐπαι-νετός, not 'Ephenetus.' This means in Latin *laudatus* [praised] or *laudabilis* [praiseworthy].

1 For the sequence of this annotation see the annotation on 16:3 ('Prisca and Aquila') n2.

16:5 [ER *qui est primitiae Achaiae* 'who is the first-fruits of Achaia']

[VG] *qui est primitivus ecclesiae Asiae* 'who is the first of[1] the church of Asia'; ἀπαρχή, that is, 'the first-fruits'[2] either because he was the first of the Achaians whom Paul converted to Christ, or because he was distinguished. Ambrose[3] seems to think that this refers to the position of honour the man enjoyed, for he says: 'He did not fail to mention also the honourable position then held by this Epaenetus, in order to show that even the distinguished were believers, and to invite the foremost of Romans to the faith.'[4] So Ambrose. However, it is the custom that whatever is best is separated off as first-fruits. Then follows:[5]

1 of ... Asia] Added in 1519. For the sequence of this annotation see the
  annotation on 16:3 ('Prisca and Aquila') n2.
2 So Valla *Annot in Rom* 16 (I 861)
3 Ambrose ... first-fruits.] Added in 1535
4 Ambrosiaster *Comm in Rom* 16:5 (4). Valla (n2 above) also notes that some
  'think the word refers to dignity.'
5 Then follows:] Added in 1519

16:5 [ER *Achaiae* 'of Achaia']

[VG] *ecclesiae Asiae* 'of the church of Asia'[1]; τῆς Ἀχαίας, that is, 'of Achaia,'
according to the Greek, not[2] 'of Asia,' though the very old codex of Saint
Paul's disagrees. Chrysostom and Theophylact read 'of Achaia.'[3] Origen[4]
reads 'of Asia,'[5] and Jerome so cites it in several places.[6] Those who changed
'Asia' into 'Achaia' appear to have been struck by the improbability that
'Epaenetus' was 'first' in all Asia Minor, whether through honour or conversion, for Asia Minor was divided into many regions. But it is clear that
whenever 'Asia' is spoken of without qualification, the part of Asia Minor
is meant in which Ephesus is situated.[7]

'Of the church' is not added in the[8] Greek manuscripts or in the old
Latin copies,[9] or even in Ambrose.[10] Now [Paul] adds 'in Christ,' no doubt
to explain why he had called [Epaenetus] 'first-fruits.'

1 For the sequence of this annotation and its conflation in LB see the annotation
  on 16:3 ('Prisca and Aquila') n2.
2 not ... 'of Achaia'] Added in 1519, except for 'Chrysostom and,' added in 1527
3 Chrysostom *Hom in Rom* 31.1 PG 60 667–8; Theophylact *Expos in Rom* 16:5
  PG 124 552A
4 Origen ... situated.] Added in 1535
5 Origen *Comm in Rom* 10.19 PG 14 1279B
6 Jerome does not appear to cite this passage. The preferred reading is 'of
  Asia.' For the Greek witnesses, see Tischendorf II 452 5n and for the Latin,
  Wordsworth and White II 146 5n.
7 Cf the *Responsio ad collationes* LB IX 1013F: 'If Asia is understood as the whole
  region that, under a general name, is called Asia Minor, then it includes
  "Achaia," but if it is understood as the part specifically called "Asia" it is
  different from Achaia.'
  The term 'Asia Minor' is attested first in Orosius (fl c 420) (cf *Historiae* 1.2
  PL 31 679A), and came to refer to the western Asiatic peninsula. It is to be
  distinguished from the Roman province of Asia (of which Ephesus became
  the administrative centre) organized in the peninsula shortly after the death
  in 133 BC of Attalus III of Pergamum, who had bequeathed his kingdom
  to the Romans. The Roman province of Achaia was in Greece, not in Asia
  Minor, as Erasmus elsewhere seems to know; cf eg the paraphrase on Acts
  19:1 and the annotation on Acts 16:6 (*loqui verbum in Asia*).
8 in the ... Ambrose] Added in 1519
9 *ecclesiae* is a minority reading in the Latin manuscripts (cf Wordsworth
  and White II 146 5n); it is not cited as a Greek variant in Tischendorf II

452 5n. Like Erasmus, Lefèvre omitted 'of the church' (*Pauli epistolae* fol 11 verso).

10 Cf Ambrosiaster *Comm in Rom* 16:5.

16:6 [ER *quae multum laboravit erga nos* 'who has laboured much for us']
[VG] *quae multum laboravit in vobis* 'who has laboured much among you';[1]
εἰς ὑμᾶς, that is, 'for you.' This[2] is sufficiently evident from Origen's interpretation, even clearer in Ambrose, most obvious from Theophylact.[3] But I am aware that some of the Greek codices have the reading εἰς ἡμᾶς [for us],[4] for in [writing] these words scribal error is extremely easy. In[5] Chrysostom, the scribe included both words; it is not clear from his exposition what he read, except that ἡμᾶς, first person, fits better.[6]

1 For the sequence of this annotation see the annotation on 16:3 ('Prisca and Aquila') n2.
2 This ... easy.] Added in *1519*
3 Cf Origen *Comm in Rom* 10.20 PG 14 1279C–1280A; Ambrosiaster *Comm in Rom* 16:6; Theophylact *Expos in Rom* 16:6 PG 124 552B–C. In the Merlin edition of Origen (fol CCXXI verso), the text is cited as *in nobis* 'among us,' and the commentary leaves the interpretation of the phrase ambiguous; Migne reads *in vobis* but cites *in nobis* as a variant; Ambrosiaster reads *in vobis*, and notes that Mary 'had laboured for their [ie the Romans'] encouragement'; Theophylact (in Migne) cites the text 'for us' and writes that Mary 'laboured not only on her own behalf ... but for us.'
4 Wordsworth and White (II 146–7 6n) print *in vobis* 'among you.' In Greek the better attested reading is 'for you'; cf Tischendorf II 452 6n. Valla notes that either 'among us' or 'for us' should be read (*Annot in Rom* 16 [I 861]).
5 In ... better.] Added in *1535*
6 Chrysostom *Hom in Rom* 31.1–2 PG 60 668–9. In Migne's text Chrysostom cites the phrase both as 'for you' and 'for us,' and notes that Paul praises Mary for labouring on behalf of apostles. In his reply to Titelmans, Erasmus had argued that the first person accords better with the 'civility' of Paul, who includes himself among those served by Mary, so that 'the Romans should not think he was casting a reproach on the kindness of a woman' (*Responsio ad collationes* LB IX 1014B).

16:7 [ER *Andronicum et Iuniam* 'Andronicus and Junia']
[VG] *Andronicum et Iuliam* 'Andronicus and Julia'; Ἰουνίαν, that is, 'Junia.'[1]
He gives Julia her own place later on.[2] The[3] very old codex furnished from the church of Constance agreed with the Greek manuscripts.

1 So Valla *Annot in Rom* 16 (I 861)
2 In 16:15
3 The ... manuscripts.] Added in *1527*. The Greek manuscripts support the reading 'Junia,' and Junia is the preferred reading of the Latin text, though a very large number of Latin manuscripts have 'Julia'; cf Tischendorf II 452 7n and Wordsworth and White II 147 7n. The Vulgate printed in *1527* reads 'Junia.'

16:7 [ER *qui sunt insignes* 'who are distinguished']

[VG] *qui sunt nobiles* 'who are noble'; ἐπίσημοι, that is, 'distinguished.' No one[1] should suppose he is talking about class.

> 1 No one ... class.] Added in *1519*

16:8 [ER *Ampliam* 'Amplia']

[VG] *Ampliatum* 'Ampliatus'; Ἀμπλίαν, that is, 'Amplia,' unless[1] perhaps [Paul] altered the Roman word to accord with the Hebrew pronunciation. And it is not 'most beloved,' but 'beloved,' ἀγαπητός.[2]

> 1 unless ... pronunciation] Added in *1527*
> 2 The Vulgate read 'Ampliatus most beloved to me,' Erasmus, 'Amplia my beloved.' For the Greek as a positive rather than a superlative see the annotation on 11:28 ('but according to the election most dear').

16:10 [ER *salutate Apellam* 'greet Apella'[1]]

[VG] *salutate Apellem* 'greet[2] Apelles.' Origen is undecided whether this is Apollos, the Alexandrian, a man well versed in the Scriptures, who is mentioned in the eighteenth chapter of the Acts of the Apostles.[3]

> 1 Apella] First in *1519*; in *1516*, Apelles
> 2 greet ... Apostles.] The annotation was added *1519*.
> 3 Origen *Comm in Rom* 10.23 PG 14 1281A–B. For the scriptural reference see Acts 18:24.

16:10 [ER *ex Aristobuli familiaribus* 'of Aristobulus' household']

[VG] *ex Aristobuli domo* 'of Aristobulus' house'; τοὺς ἐκ τῶν Ἀριστοβούλου, that is, 'those who belong to Aristobulus,' pronounced with the acute accent on the penult, for it is a diphthong [ου] in Greek. The name[1] means 'excellent counsel.' 'House'[2] was not added in the manuscript provided at Constance. Likewise[3] Horace: 'We came to Vesta's'[4] – 'temple' understood; [and] the Greeks [say] ἐν ᾅδου [in Hades] understanding τόπῳ [in Hades' place]. We might say, not inappropriately, 'I'll come to Easter,' meaning the festival of Easter.

> 1 The name ... 'excellent counsel.'] Added in *1519*. On the accent, see *De recta pronuntiatione* CWE 26 415, and 432 n304.
> 2 'House' ... Constance.] Added in *1527*
> 3 Likewise ... Easter.] Added in *1535*
> 4 Cf Horace *Satires* 1.9.35.

16:14 [ER *Asyncritum, Phlegontem* 'Asyncritus, Phlegon']

[VG] *Asyncretum, Plegontam* 'Asyncretus, Plegonta.'[1] This should be read 'Asyncritus, Phlegon:[2] Ἀσύγκριτον, Φλέγοντα. Asyncritus[3] means 'incomparable,' Phlegon, 'burning.'

1 In *1516* this annotation appeared below, after the annotation 'Olympias.'
2 In the Vulgate printed in *1527*, the text has Phlegonta, not Plegonta.
3 Asyncritus ... 'burning.'] Added in *1519*

16:14 [ER *Hermam, Patrobam, Mercurium* 'Hermas, Patroba, Mercury']
[VG] *Herman, Patrobam, Hermen* 'Hermas, Patroba, Hermes.' These are [two] different names: the first is Ἑρμᾶς, 'Hermas'; the second is Ἑρμῆς [Hermēs], which in Latin means 'Mercury'; and so I have rendered, lest by chance in these matters anyone ξενίζηται [should find the foreign term strange]. Origen[1] in his book Περὶ ἀρχῶν [*On First Principles*] thinks this 'Hermes' is the author of the apocryphal book called *The Shepherd*;[2] he frequently quotes passages from it and thinks it was written by divine inspiration, although he admits that many have no regard for it.[3] In these matters, there was an astonishing credulity – or civility – in the ancient [writers], who gave such weight to the books we have under the name of Clement, though the forgery of the man who wrote such things appears so evident in them.[4]

    1 Origen ... in them.] The remainder of this annotation was added in *1527*.
    2 *Pastor Hermae* is an apocryphal apocalyptic work written sometime prior to the mid-second century AD by a certain Hermas of Rome (but not the Hermas of Rom 16:14 as Origen thought), once a slave, then a freedman. See M.H. Shepherd Jr 'Hermas' in IDB II 583–4 and Graydon F. Snyder ed *The Shepherd of Hermas* (London 1968) 1–26.
    3 Cf Origen *De principiis* 1.3.3 and 4.11 PG 11 148A and 366A.
    4 For the Pseudo-Clementine literature see the annotation on Rom 3:5 ('is God unfair who inflicts wrath') n16.

16:15 [ER *Olympam* 'Olympas']
[VG] *Olympiadem* 'Olympias.' Greek Ὀλυμπᾶν, 'Olympas.' It appears that these[1] were men, not women, due to the two Greek pronouns, αὐτοῦ [his] and σὺν αὐτῷ [with him].[2] But you can't make a man out of 'Olympias.'

    1 Ie those previously mentioned in 16:15: Philologus and Nereus
    2 Both pronouns are masculine: αὐτοῦ in the phrase 'Nereus and *his* sister'; but in place of σὺν αὐτῷ [with him] Erasmus, in his text, prints σὺν αὐτοῖς [with them], where the pronoun remains masculine.

16:16 [ER *salutant vos ecclesiae Christi* 'the churches of Christ greet you']
[VG] *salutant vos omnes ecclesiae Christi* 'all[1] the churches of Christ greet you.' Origen questions how Paul could send greetings in the name of all the churches; for it is improbable that they were all present at Corinth when this letter was written. But since [Paul] knew the devotion of all to the Romans, he greets them in the name of all.[2]

1 all ... you] This cue phrase was added in 1535, when the annotation was
moved to its position here from its earlier position in the editions from 1519
(when the annotation was added) to 1527. In the earlier editions it appeared
with the cue phrase (taken from Rom 16:4):

> [ER VG] *sed et cunctae ecclesiae gentium* 'but also all the churches of the
> gentiles'

Cf the annotation on 16:3 ('Prisca and Aquila') n2.
2 For Origen's question see *Comm in Rom* 10.34 PG 14 1283A.

16:18 [ER *per blandiloquentiam et assentationem* 'through smooth speaking
and flattery'[1]]

[VG] *per dulces sermones et benedictiones* 'through soft words and benedictions'; διὰ τῆς χρηστολογίας καὶ εὐλογίας. No one[2] should think [here]
of the 'benedictions' – as they are commonly called – of bishops.[3] There
are two words in the Greek – χρηστολογία [*chrēstologia*] which really means
'smooth speaking' or 'flattering speech.' Accordingly, we are told that certain Caesars, with more good will in their speech than in their actions, were
commonly called *chrestologos*.[4] And εὐλογία [*eulogia*] does indeed mean literally 'well-speaking,' but in this instance it is used for 'praise' or 'adulation.'
He has repeated the same term[5] due to his hatred of the vice, namely of
flattery.

1 flattery] First in 1519; in 1516, *benedicentiam* 'compliments'
2 No one ... 'adulation.'] Added in 1519. In place of this, 1516 read 'that is,
  through flattering speech and compliments.'
3 Cf the annotation on 1:25 ('who is blessed').
4 The word was applied to the emperor Pertinax (193 AD), 'who was smooth
  of speech rather than good in deed'; cf the *Historia Augusta*, 'Pertinax' 13.5.
5 term] Added in 1527. The two words *chrēstologia* and *eulogia* here mean much
  the same thing, and both contain the same Greek term *'logia.'*

16:18 [ER *corda simplicium* 'the hearts of the guileless']

[VG] *corda innocentium* 'the hearts[1] of the innocent.' The Greek is ἀκάκων,
which signifies the guileless, and those without any cunning, rather than
the innocent. For in Latin, one is called 'innocent' whose life is free from
all crime; [one is] ἄκακος who is free from deception and distrust. In fact,
'innocence' is one of the words that Cicero says has no equivalent in Greek.[2]

1 the hearts ... Greek.] This annotation was added in 1519.
2 Cicero *Tusculan Disputations* 3.8.16

16:19 [ER *nam vestra obedientia* 'for[1] your obedience']

[VG] *vestra enim obedientia* 'your obedience, in fact.' 'For your obedience'
would be more appropriate to this passage.[2] To the tacit question of why

he said 'the hearts of the guileless,' there suggests itself: 'For [the obedience of] you who are wise' etc.

1 for] First in *1519*; in *1516*, *enim* 'in fact'
2 For the distinction between *nam* and *enim* see Allen and Greenough 324h: *nam* introduces 'a real reason, formally expressed, for a previous statement; *enim* ... a less important explanatory circumstance put in by the way.'

16:21 [ER *Timotheus cooperarius meus* 'Timothy my fellow worker']
[VG] *Timotheus adiutor meus* 'Timothy my helper'; ὁ συνεργός μου, which in Greek signifies an 'associate' and 'partner in work,' as though you said 'colleague' or 'fellow worker.' Ambrose[1] appropriately translates *consors laborum meorum* [partner in my labours].[2]

1 Ambrose ... *meorum.*] Added in *1519*
2 Ambrosiaster *Comm in Rom* 16:21

16:22 [ER *ego Tertius* 'I Tertius'[1]]
[VG] *ego Terentius* 'I Terentius.'[2] The reading is 'Tertius,' Τέρτιος, not 'Terentius,' though in some sources 'Terentius' is found. Ambrose reads 'Tertius,'[3] for he adds 'in name, not in number.' And so reads Chrysostom, and[4] Theophylact, the Greek interpreter.[5] For[6] he is named 'Tertius' in the same way that Romans were named 'Sextus,' 'Quintus,' and 'Decimus.'[7]

1 Tertius] First in *1519*; in *1516*, 'Terentius.' 'Terentius' is cited by Tischendorf (II 455 22n) as a minor variant; it is not cited by Wordsworth and White (II 150 22n), and the reading of the Vulgate of *1527* is 'Tertius.'
2 In *1516* only, this annotation appeared in the sequence 'Timothy my helper,' 'city treasurer,' 'I Terentius.' For the sequence in later editions see the next annotation, n2.
3 Ambrosiaster *Comm in Rom* 16:22
4 Chrysostom and] Added in *1527*
5 Chrysostom *Hom in Rom* 32.2 PG 60 677 and Theophylact *Expos in Rom* 16:22 PG 124 557C
6 For ... 'Decimus.'] Added in *1522*
7 *Tertius* is the Latin ordinal 'third'; *Sextus, Quintus, Decimus* the ordinals, 'sixth,' 'fifth,' and 'tenth.' All were used frequently as proper names.

16:23 [ER *et ecclesiae totius* 'and of the whole church']
[VG] *et universae ecclesiae* 'and all[1] the churches.'[2] The Latin expression is ambiguous, since it is not clear whether Gaius, Paul's host, sends greetings, together with the whole congregation, to the Romans, or whether Gaius is to be understood as the host not only of Paul, but of the whole church. Only the latter sense is possible in the Greek, and so I have translated 'my host, and [the host] of the whole church.'[3]

1 and all ... church.'] The entire annotation was added in 1519.
2 The Vulgate printed in 1527 read *universa ecclesia*: all the church.
   From 1519 to 1527 this annotation appeared in the sequence: 'Timothy my
   helper,' 'I Terentius,' 'city treasurer,' 'and all the churches,' 'the grace of our
   Lord,' etc. The sequence in LB, represented in our text, was adopted first in
   1535. For the sequence of annotations in 1516 see the preceding annotation,
   n2.
3 The Greek is unambiguous: 'Gaius, my host and the host of the whole
   church.' The Latin of the cue phrase could read either as the Greek does
   or 'Gaius, my host, and all the churches greet you.' Ambrosiaster clearly
   understood the latter (*Comm in Rom* 16:23 [1]); a Vulgate variant modified the
   text to *universa ecclesia*, requiring the reading 'Gaius and the whole church
   greet you' (Wordsworth and White II 150 23n; the variant appears in the
   Vulgate of 1527). Lefèvre also noted the ambiguity and read, like Erasmus,
   'of the whole church' (*Pauli epistolae* fol 12 recto and fol 105 verso).

16:23 [ER *quaestor aerarius civitatis* 'quaestor of the city treasury']
   [VG] *arcarius civitatis* 'city treasurer';[1] ὁ οἰκονόμος, that is, 'the controller.'
   So I have translated 'quaestor of the treasury.'[2] Theophylact[3] thinks he was
   a prefect;[4] and certainly, to this extent [that he controlled the treasury] he
   was a prefect.[5] I think[6] a prefect of the treasury is meant.

   1 For the sequence of this annotation, see the preceding annotation, n2.
   2 The quaestor was a Roman magistrate in charge of financial matters.
   3 Theophylact ... prefect.] Added in 1519
   4 Theophylact *Expos in Rom* 16:23 PG 124 557D
   5 A prefect was one who had been made an overseer; the term was used of
     both civil and military offices; hence a superintendent, director, commander.
   6 I think ... meant.] Added in 1527

16:24 [ER VG] *gratia domini nostri* etc 'the grace[1] of our Lord etc.' Since almost
   the same words were used just a little above,[2] they are not repeated here in
   Ambrose and Origen,[3] or[4] in the very old codex that the library of Constance
   provided. In Chrysostom[5] [the words] are not added in the first instance,[6]
   either in the text or in his exposition, but only at the end, after the doxology,[7]
   and he points out that it is appropriate that our speech take its beginning
   from the grace of God, and end in the recollection of grace.[8] Theophylact
   agrees with Chrysostom.[9]

   1 The grace ... Origen] Added in 1519, when the annotation first appeared
   2 In 16:20
   3 Cf Ambrosiaster *Comm in Rom* 16:24 and Origen *Comm in Rom* 10.42–3 PG 14
     1289C–1290A. The verse (16:24) is absent from the best Greek witnesses; see
     Tischendorf II 455 24n and Metzger 540.
   4 or ... In Chrysostom] Added in 1527, when, however, the text read: 'or in
     Chrysostom, or in the very old codex that the library of Constance provided'

5 In Chrysostom ... agrees with Chrysostom.] Added in 1535 (but see n4
  above for the words 'In Chrysostom' in 1527)
6 Ie 16:20
7 Cf Chrysostom *Hom in Rom* 32.1–2 PG 60 677–8, where, in the Migne edition,
  however, Chrysostom comments on the benediction as it is found in the
  biblical text both at 16:20 and 16:24. The doxology, in the Migne edition,
  appears after 14:23.
8 Cf Chrysostom's comments on 16:24 in *Hom in Rom* 32.2 PG 60 678.
9 Cf Theophylact *Expos in Rom* 16:20 and 24 PG 124 557A–B and D. Theophylact,
  like Chrysostom, comments on the benediction in both passages, while the
  doxology follows after 14:23.

16:25 [ER VG] *ei autem qui potens* 'now to him who is able.' This is the part that is
not added in most Greek manuscripts.[1] In some it is added in another place,
namely,[2] the end of chapter 14, as we indicated at that point.[3] In a few, it
is placed at the end of the Epistle,[4] as I, too, have done, especially since the
Latin manuscripts concur,[5] even[6] the old ones; and with these, Ambrose
also, and Origen.[7] [Origen] informs us that not only this part was cut away
by Marcion, who rejected in their entirety some of the letters written by
Paul and cut short and mutilated others,[8] but also everything that follows
from the point where Paul said 'for whatever is not of faith is sin,' that
is, from the end of the fourteenth chapter[9] – because the rest (occupied
only with admonishments and greetings) scarcely seemed to accord with
the seriousness of Paul.[10] But what good is it to refute his opinion, which
has now long since been discredited by everyone?

But how this part came to be moved from its proper place, I find
puzzling. For if it was moved from its position because it did not fit very
neatly with what preceded and followed, it does not fit here either. That
the thought does not follow an orderly sequence either in the Greek or
in the Latin is not so surprising in Paul, where we frequently encounter
difficulties of this sort. Even if we overlook the hyperbaton, the phrase 'to
whom' prevents the 'honour and glory'[11] added at the end from referring
to [the words] 'but to him who' etc at the beginning of the doxology[12] –
as even Thomas[13] also noted, following Augustine.[14] [Aquinas] explains as
best he can the other difficulty in construction, that 'through Jesus Christ'
does not refer to [the words] 'wise God' (for God the Father should not
seem wise through the Son), but to what follows, 'be honour and glory';
for by his death the Son caused the Father's glory to shine among men. But
what will we do with that 'to whom' there?[15] – for such is the idiom of
that Aquinas.[16] It has so persistently held a place in all the Greek and Latin
codices that it could be removed only with the greatest impudence. But if
the passage is preserved, neither the earlier nor the later part fits, and for

myself, at least, I find nothing here to say, except frankly to admit that Paul, in his customary way, has left the sentence incomplete, so that we should understand 'let us give thanks,' or something similar. Ambrose joins the first part with the last, 'be honour and glory'; ignoring the syntactical difficulty that offended Thomas.[17] But[18] long before him, Augustine, in the third book *Against Maximinus the Arian Bishop*, the thirteenth chapter, supposes it can be construed thus: 'To him [be] the glory, to whom through Jesus Christ [is] the glory.' He admits, however, that if 'to whom' is omitted, the language is more normal.[19]

Our reading, 'through the Scriptures of the prophets,'[20] is in Greek διά τε γραφῶν προφητικῶν, that is, '*and* through the prophetic Scriptures' – since nothing precedes to which the conjunction τέ can refer, nor does καί (usually joined with it) follow, unless the force of a second conjunction is implied in the 'now.'[21] This is the sense we should follow, for the mystery is revealed now through the gospel, and was revealed long ago by the prophetic writings.

1 manuscripts] In *1519* and *1522* only, there followed at this point the words 'For Theophylact, the commentator, mentions this part in neither place – in the middle or at the end.' In the Migne edition Theophylact comments on the doxology after 14:23 (*Expos in Rom* 14:24–6 PG 124 533A–C).

2 namely ... chapter 14] Added in *1519*

3 at that point] Added in *1519*. See the annotation on 14:24 ('now to him who is able').

4 of the Epistle] Added in *1527*

5 The Greek witnesses strongly support the position of the doxology at the end of chapter 16; see Metzger 533–6 and Cranfield I 5–11, II 808–9. A majority of the Latin manuscripts also place the doxology here; see Wordsworth and White II 150 25–7n. Valla had found that only a very few Greek codices had the doxology here (*Annot in Rom* 16 [I 861]).

6 even ... writings] With the exceptions noted below (nn13, 14, 16, 18) this remaining portion of the annotation was added in *1519*.

7 Cf Ambrosiaster *Comm in Rom* 16:25–7 and Origen *Comm in Rom* 10.43 PG 14 1290A–B. Origen notes, however, that some manuscripts did indeed have the doxology at the end of chapter 14.

8 Marcion was a radical Paulinist of the second century who sharply distinguished the 'God of law' of the Old Testament, the creator God, and the 'God of love' of the New Testament, the redeemer God. Marcion formed his own canon of the Scriptures, which rejected the whole of the Old Testament and included as its center the Pauline Epistles and the Gospel of Luke, both of which he revised, principally by deletion. The pastoral Epistles were not included in his Pauline canon probably because they were unknown to him. Marcion's Scripture, the first New Testament canon, in large measure prompted the early church to form its own canon. See H. Koester *Introduction to the New Testament* 2 vols (Philadelphia 1982) II *History and Literature*

of Early Christianity 8–11, 328–34; A. Harnack *Marcion: Das Evangelium vom fremden Gott* Texte und Untersuchungen 45, 2nd ed (Leipzig 1924); and Joseph R. Hoffmann *Marcion on the Restitution of Christianity* (Chico, CA 1984).

9 14:23. Cf Origen *Comm in Rom* 10.43 PG 14 1290B.

10 The reason given here appears to be Erasmus' gloss on Origen.

11 So the Vulgate printed in *1527*. Erasmus translated simply 'glory.'

12 The hyperbaton here arises from the distant separation of the phrases: 'to him who is able ... to the only wise God' in 16:25–7. Further, the passage concludes without a main clause, since in the Greek the final clause is relative: 'To the only wise God through Jesus Christ to whom the glory forever and ever' (so also DV; but AV, RSV render verse 27 as a main clause).

13 Thomas] First in *1522*; in *1519*, 'St Thomas'

14 following Augustine] Added in *1522*. For the reference, see n19 below.

15 Thomas Aquinas *Super Rom lect* cap 16 lectio 2.1228–9

16 Aquinas] Added in *1535*; previously 'of that one.' By noting the idiom, Erasmus appears to ridicule Thomas' use of *ly* (in the phrase *ibi ly cui*). *Ly* is a medieval form of the article developed from the Latin pronoun *ille* 'that.'

17 Cf Ambrosiaster *Comm in Rom* 16:25–7 (1–3). Ambrosiaster understands: 'To him who is able to establish you according to ... the revelation of the mystery which ... has now been manifested through the prophetic Scriptures ... [a mystery] known to the only wise God, through Jesus Christ, to whom [be] glory forever.' Ambrosiaster notes that the praise ascribed by this doxology is given to God through Jesus Christ, but he makes no comment on the incomplete sentence.

18 But ... normal.] Added in *1522*

19 Augustine *Contra Maximinum haereticum Arianorum episcopum* 2.13.2 PL 42 769–70. Augustine asks how the phrase 'through Jesus Christ' functions in the sentence. Does one understand 'to the only God who is wise through Jesus Christ, to him be glory' or 'to the only wise God, to him be the glory through Jesus Christ'? He adopts the latter alternative, explaining that one understands 'to him be glory to whom glory comes through Christ.' On this reading it would have been enough to omit the 'to whom' and read simply 'to him be the glory [through Christ].'
Though 'to whom' is omitted in a very few manuscripts, whether or not it should be included in the text is debated. Cf Metzger 540; Cranfield II 813–14.

20 Compare the translations of Erasmus and the Vulgate:
ER *manifestati vero nunc et per scripturas propheticas* 'but manifested now and through the prophetic Scriptures'
VG *quod nunc patefactum est per scripturas prophetarum* 'which now has been disclosed through the Scriptures of the prophets'

21 Though the text reads only τε 'and,' Erasmus suggests that here in 16:26 νῦν ... τε has the force of a τε ... καί ('both ... and') sequence: both now and in the past.

16:25 [ER *missa fuit a Corintho* 'was sent from Corinth'[1]]

[VG **omitted**]. I have added this [subscription] from the Greek manuscripts, except that I have translated ἐγράφη [was written] as 'was sent.' 'It was sent through Phoebe,' but written by the hand of Tertius[2] and dictated by Paul. Meanwhile, this strikes me as a matter for wonder, what kind of envoys those who were truly the chief[3] pontiffs then employed, when Paul sent to the Romans,[4] who were still at the height of their power, a letter on such weighty themes – through a mere woman.

Next, one wants to laugh at the unexpected diligence of Nicholas of Lyra, who, though Origen and St Jerome[5] and all the ancients with them confirm that this letter was sent from Corinth, nevertheless for his part has doubts, apparently because Haymo[6] wrote that it was sent from Athens.[7] But see with what great dexterity our marvellous craftsman unravels this more-than-Gordian knot. He says: 'Part of it he wrote at Athens; then he added the rest at Corinth; and he sent it from there to Rome.'[8] What a fine fellow! He would prefer, I suppose, that Paul[9] make a journey, however roundabout, just so that Haymo's authority[10] should not be impaired, as though he might slip[11] in one or two places.[12]

1 Though the annotation begins with a cue phrase (*missa fuit a Corintho*), it is clear from Erasmus' remarks that he did not read the subscription in his Vulgate Bible, and the Vulgate printed in *1527* did not carry it; for the subscription in the Latin manuscripts see Wordsworth and White II 151. The full subscription according to Erasmus' translation from the Greek reads: 'To the Romans. [The letter] was sent from Corinth through Phoebe, a minister of the church at Cenchreae.' For the subscription in Greek see Metzger 541. A subscription follows 16:27 in AV.

2 Tertius] First in *1519*; in *1516*, 'Terentius'; see the annotation on 16:22 ('I Terentius').

3 chief] Added in *1527*

4 to the Romans ... power] First in *1519*; in *1516*, 'Rome, which was still at the height of its power'

5 Cf Origen *Comm in Rom* praefatio PG 14 835B–C; Jerome apparently offers no explicit statement that Paul wrote his letter to the Romans from Corinth.

6 Haymo] In *1516* and *1519* only, there followed the words 'a weighty author, no doubt.'

7 According to the Migne text of Haymo, Lyra appears to be in error. Haymo, bishop of Halberstadt, a medieval commentator (d 853) wrote in the preface to his commentary on Romans that the Epistle was written from Corinth (PL 117 361C, and cf 504D). The Migne text reproduces the 1519 Strasbourg edition of Haymo *In divi Pauli Epistolas ... expositio*, of which see the praefatio and fol xliiii verso.

8 Cf Lyra's prologus to the Epistle to the Romans *Postilla* IV fol aa recto.

9 Paul] Added in *1519*

10 authority] First in 1522; previously, 'greatness'
11 slip] First in 1522; previously, 'be out of his wits'
12 These satirical comments were severely criticized by Titelmans, who thought
   Erasmus should have much more reverence for a man who might now be in
   heaven beholding the face of God. Erasmus countered that Titelmans often
   disagreed with Valla, who was more probably reigning in heaven than Lyra
   (*Responsio ad collationes* LB IX 1014B–D).

End of the Annotations on the
Epistle to the Romans

WORKS FREQUENTLY CITED

SHORT-TITLE FORMS FOR ERASMUS' WORKS

INDEX OF BIBLICAL AND APOCRYPHAL
REFERENCES

INDEX OF CLASSICAL REFERENCES

INDEX OF PATRISTIC, MEDIEVAL, AND
RENAISSANCE REFERENCES

INDEX OF GREEK AND LATIN WORDS CITED

GENERAL INDEX

WORKS FREQUENTLY CITED

This list provides bibliographical information for works referred to in short-title form in this volume. For Erasmus' writings see the short-title list following.

Allen
:   P.S. Allen, H.M. Allen, and H.W. Garrod eds *Opus epistolarum Des. Erasmi Roterodami* (Oxford 1906–47) 11 vols plus index by B. Flower and E. Rosenbaum (Oxford 1958)

Allen and Greenough
:   *Allen and Greenough's New Latin Grammar for Schools and Colleges* ed J.B. Greenough, G.L. Kittredge, A.A. Howard, and Benjamin L. D'Ooge (Boston 1931), cited by section number

Ambrosiaster *Comm in Rom*
:   *Ambrosiastri qui dicitur commentarius in epistulas Paulinas. Pars I: In epistulam ad Romanos* ed Henry Joseph Vogels CSEL 81/1 (Vienna 1966)

ASD
:   *Opera omnia Desiderii Erasmi Roterodami* (Amsterdam 1969–)

BAG
:   *A Greek-English Lexicon of the New Testament and Other Early Christian Literature*, a translation and adaptation of the fourth revised and augmented edition of Walter Bauer's *Griechisch-deutsches Wörterbuch zu den Schriften des Neuen Testaments und der übrigen urchristlichen Literatur* by William F. Arndt and F. Wilbur Gingrich (Chicago 1957); 2nd ed revised and augmented by F. Wilbur Gingrich and Frederick W. Danker from Walter Bauer's 5th ed, 1958 (Chicago 1979)

Bentley *Humanists*
:   Jerry H. Bentley *Humanists and Holy Writ: New Testament Scholarship in the Renaissance* (Princeton 1983)

CCL
:   *Corpus Christianorum series Latina* (Turnhout 1953)

Chantraine *Dictionnaire*
:   Pierre Chantraine *Dictionnaire étymologique de la langue grecque* (Paris 1968) 2 vols

Chomarat *Grammaire et rhétorique*
:   Jacques Chomarat *Grammaire et rhétorique chez Erasme* (Paris 1981) 2 vols

Chrysostom *Hom in Rom*
:   John Chrysostom *In epistulam ad Romanos homiliae* PG 60 385–682

Colet *Enarratio*
:   John Colet *Enarratio in epistolam B. Pauli ad Romanos* ed and trans J.H. Lupton (London 1873; repr Ridgewood, NJ 1965)

Colet *Expositio literalis*   John Colet *Epistolae B. Pauli ad Romanos expositio literalis* ed and trans J.H. Lupton (London 1876; repr Ridgewood, NJ 1966)

Contemporaries   *Contemporaries of Erasmus: A Biographical Register of the Renaissance and Reformation* ed Peter G. Bietenholz and Thomas B. Deutscher (Toronto 1985–7) 3 vols

Cranfield   C.E.B. Cranfield *A Critical and Exegetical Commentary on the Epistle to the Romans* (Edinburgh 1975, 1979) 2 vols

CSEL   *Corpus scriptorum ecclesiasticorum Latinorum* (Vienna 1866–   )

CWE   *Collected Works of Erasmus* (Toronto 1974–   )

GCS   *Die griechischen christlichen Schriftsteller der ersten drei Jahrhunderte* (Berlin-Leipzig 1897–   )

Godin *Erasme*   André Godin *Erasme lecteur d'Origène* (Geneva 1982)

Holborn   *Desiderius Erasmus Roterodamus: Ausgewählte Werke* ed Hajo Holborn and Annemarie Holborn (Munich 1933; repr 1964)

IDB   *Interpreter's Dictionary of the Bible* ed George Arthur Buttrick et al (New York 1962) 4 vols

Kelly *Doctrines*   J.N.D. Kelly *Early Christian Doctrines* 5th revised ed (London 1977)

Lausberg   Heinrich Lausberg *Handbuch der literarischen Rhetorik* (Munich 1960), cited by section number

LB   *Desiderii Erasmi Roterodami opera omnia* ed J. Leclerc (Leiden 1703–6; repr 1961–2) 10 vols

Lefèvre *Pauli epistolae*   Jacobus Faber Stapulensis *S. Pauli epistolae* XIV *ex Vulgata, adiecta intelligentia ex Graeco, cum commentariis* (Paris 1512; facsimile ed Stuttgart-Bad Canstatt 1978)

L&S   Charlton T. Lewis and Charles Short *A Latin Dictionary* (Oxford 1879; repr 1975)

LSJ   *A Greek-English Lexicon* compiled by Henry George Liddell and Robert Scott, revised and augmented by Sir Henry Stuart Jones, 9th ed with supplement (Oxford 1968)

Lyra *Postilla*	Nicolaus de Lyra *Postilla super totam bibliam* (Strasbourg 1492; facsimile ed Frankfurt am Main 1971) 4 vols
Merlin	Jacobus Merlin *Operum Origenis Adamantii tomi duo priores*, cum tabula et indice generali. Venundantur cum duobus reliquiis eorundem tomis in edibus Joannis Parvi et Jodocii Badii Ascensii (Paris 1512) 4 vols in 2
Metzger	Bruce M. Metzger *A Textual Commentary on the Greek New Testament* (London and New York 1971)
Michel	Otto Michel *Der Brief an die Römer* 12th ed (Göttingen 1963)
NPNF	A Select Library of Nicene and Post-Nicene Fathers of the Christian Church (New York 1887–1900)
Niermeyer	Jan Frederik Niermeyer *Mediae Latinitatis lexicon minus: A Medieval Latin-French/English Dictionary* (Leiden 1954)
Oberman *Harvest*	Heiko Oberman *The Harvest of Medieval Theology: Gabriel Biel and Late Medieval Nominalism* revised edition (Grand Rapids, MI 1967)
OLD	*Oxford Latin Dictionary* ed P.G.W. Glare (Oxford 1982)
Opuscula	*Erasmi Opuscula: A Supplement to the Opera Omnia* ed Wallace K. Ferguson (The Hague 1933)
Origen *Comm in Rom*	Origen *Commentarii in epistulam B. Pauli ad Romanos* PG 14 837–1292
Payne *Erasmus: His Theology*	John B. Payne *Erasmus: His Theology of the Sacraments* (Richmond, VA 1970)
Pelagius *Expos in Rom*	*Pelagi expositio in epistulam ad Romanos* in Souter II 6–126
PG	*Patrologiae cursus completus ... series Graeca* ed J.-P. Migne (Paris 1857–86) 162 vols
PL	*Patrologiae cursus completus ... series Latina* ed J.-P. Migne (Paris 1844–84) 221 vols
Pseudo-Oecumenius *Comm in Rom*	Pseudo-Oecumenius *Commentarii in epistulam Pauli ad Romanos* PG 118 307–636
Quasten *Patrology*	Johannes Quasten *Patrology* (vols I–III Utrecht 1950–60; vol IV ed Angelo di Berardino, trans Placid Solari, Westminster, MD 1986)

Rahlfs

Septuaginta: id est Vetus Testamentum Graece iuxta LXX *interpretes* ed Alfred Rahlfs (Stuttgart 1935) 2 vols

Rummel *Erasmus' 'Annotations'*

Erika Rummel *Erasmus' 'Annotations' on the New Testament: From Philologist to Theologian* (Toronto 1986)

Schelkle

Karl Herman Schelkle *Paulus Lehrer der Väter: Die altkirchliche Auslegung von Römer 1–11* 2nd ed (Düsseldorf 1959)

Seeberg

Reinhold Seeberg *Text-book of the History of Doctrines* trans Charles E. Hay (Grand Rapids, MI 1961) 2 vols

Smyth

Herbert Weir Smyth *A Greek Grammar for Colleges* revised Gordon M. Messing (Cambridge, MA 1980 [1956]), cited by section number

Souter

Alexander Souter *Pelagius's Expositions of Thirteen Epistles of Paul* Texts and Studies 9 (Cambridge 1922–31) 3 vols: I *Introduction* (1922); II *Text and Critical Apparatus* (1926); III *Pseudo-Jerome Interpolations* (1931)

Swete

Henry Barclay Swete *The Old Testament in Greek according to the Septuagint* 3rd (vol II) and 4th (vols I and III) eds (Cambridge 1907–12) 3 vols

Theophylact *Expos in Rom*

Theophylact *Expositio in epistulam ad Romanos* PG 124 319–560

Thomas Aquinas *Super Rom lect*

Thomas Aquinas *Super epistolam ad Romanos lectura* in Thomas Aquinas *Super epistolas S. Pauli lectura* ed P. Raphaelis Cai OP, 2 vols, 8th ed revised (Turin 1953) I 5–230

Thompson *Colloquies*

The Colloquies of Erasmus ed and trans Craig R. Thompson (Chicago and London 1965)

Tischendorf

Novum Testamentum Graece ed Constantinus Tischendorf, 8th ed (Leipzig 1869–72) 2 vols; *Prolegomena* (vol III) ed C.R. Gregory (Leipzig 1894)

Trigg *Origen*

Joseph Wilson Trigg *Origen: The Bible and Philosophy in the Third-Century Church* (Atlanta 1983)

Valla *Annot in Rom*

Laurentius Valla *Annotationes in epistolam Pauli ad Romanos* in *Opera omnia* (Basel 1540; repr Turin 1962) 2 vols, I 855–61

Weber

Biblia sacra iuxta vulgatam versionem ed Robertus Weber with Bonifatio Fischer OSB et al, 3rd ed (Stuttgart 1983) 2 vols

Wordsworth and White

Novum Testamentum ... Latine secundum editionem Sancti Hieronymi ed John Wordsworth and Henry J. White et al (Oxford 1889–1954) 3 vols

Titles following colons are longer versions of the same, or are alternative titles. Items entirely enclosed in square brackets are of doubtful authorship. For abbreviations, see Works Frequently Cited.

Acta: Academiae Lovaniensis contra Lutherum *Opuscula* / CWE 71
Adagia: Adagiorum chiliades 1508, etc (Adagiorum collectanea for the primitive
    form, when required) LB II / ASD II-4, 5, 6 / CWE 30–6
Admonitio adversus mendacium: Admonitio adversus mendacium et obtrecta-
    tionem LB X
Annotationes in Novum Testamentum LB VI
Antibarbari LB IX / ASD I-1 / CWE 23
Apologia ad Caranzam: Apologia ad Sanctium Caranzam, or Apologia de
    tribus locis, or Responsio ad annotationem Stunicae ... a Sanctio Caranza
    defensam LB IX
Apologia ad Fabrum: Apologia ad Iacobum Fabrum Stapulensem LB IX
Apologia adversus monachos: Apologia adversus monachos quosdam His-
    panos LB IX
Apologia adversus Petrum Sutorem: Apologia adversus debacchationes Petri
    Sutoris LB IX
Apologia adversus rhapsodias Alberti Pii: Apologia ad viginti et quattuor libros
    A. Pii LB IX
Apologia contra Latomi dialogum: Apologia contra Iacobi Latomi dialogum de
    tribus linguis LB IX / CWE 71
Apologiae contra Stunicam: Apologiae contra Lopidem Stunicam LB IX / ASD IX-2
Apologia de 'In principio erat sermo' LB IX
Apologia de laude matrimonii: Apologia pro declamatione de laude matri-
    monii LB IX / CWE 71
Apologia de loco 'Omnes quidem': Apologia de loco 'Omnes quidem resurge-
    mus' LB IX
Apologia qua respondet invectivis Lei: Apologia qua respondet duabus invectivis
    Eduardi Lei *Opuscula*
Apophthegmata LB IV
Appendix respondens ad Sutorem LB IX
Argumenta: Argumenta in omnes epistolas apostolicas nova (with Paraphrases)
Axiomata pro causa Lutheri: Axiomata pro causa Martini Lutheri *Opuscula* /
    CWE 71

Carmina: poems in LB I, IV, V, VIII / CWE 85–6
Catalogus lucubrationum LB I
Ciceronianus: Dialogus Ciceronianus LB I / ASD I-2 / CWE 28
Colloquia LB I / ASD I-3
Compendium vitae Allen I / CWE 4
Conflictus: Conflictus Thaliae et Barbariei LB I
[Consilium: Consilium cuiusdam ex animo cupientis esse consultum] *Opuscula* /
    CWE 71

De bello Turcico: Consultatio de bello Turcico (in Psalmi)

De civilitate: De civilitate morum puerilium LB I / CWE 25

Declamatio de morte LB IV

Declamatiuncula LB IV

Declarationes ad censuras Lutetiae vulgatas: Declarationes ad censuras Lutetiae vulgatas sub nomine facultatis theologiae Parisiensis LB IX

De concordia: De sarcienda ecclesiae concordia, or De amabili ecclesiae concordia (in Psalmi)

De conscribendis epistolis LB I / ASD I-2 / CWE 25

De constructione: De constructione octo partium orationis, or Syntaxis LB I / ASD I-4

De contemptu mundi: Epistola de contemptu mundi LB V / ASD V-1 / CWE 66

De copia: De duplici copia verborum ac rerum LB I / ASD I-6 / CWE 24

De immensa Dei misericordia: Concio de immensa Dei misericordia LB V

De interdicto esu carnium: Epistola apologetica ad Christophorum episcopum Basiliensem de interdicto esu carnium LB IX / ASD IX-1

De libero arbitrio: De libero arbitrio diatribe LB IX

De praeparatione: De praeparatione ad mortem LB V / ASD V-1

De pueris instituendis: De pueris statim ac liberaliter instituendis LB I / ASD I-2 / CWE 26

De puero Iesu: Concio de puero Iesu LB V / CWE 29

De puritate tabernaculi: De puritate tabernaculi sive ecclesiae christianae (in Psalmi)

De ratione studii LB I / ASD I-2 / CWE 24

De recta pronuntiatione: De recta latini graecique sermonis pronuntiatione LB I / ASD I-4 / CWE 26

Detectio praestigiarum: Detectio praestigiarum cuiusdam libelli germanice scripti LB X / ASD IX-1

De taedio Iesu: Disputatiuncula de taedio, pavore, tristicia Iesu LB V

De vidua christiana LB V / CWE 66

De virtute amplectenda: Oratio de virtute amplectenda LB V / CWE 29

[Dialogus bilinguium ac trilinguium: Chonradi Nastadiensis dialogus bilinguium ac trilinguium] *Opuscula* / CWE 7

Dilutio: Dilutio eorum quae Iodocus Clithoveus scripsit adversus declamationem suasoriam matrimonii

Divinationes ad notata Bedae LB IX

Ecclesiastes: Ecclesiastes sive de ratione concionandi LB V / ASD V-4

Elenchus in N. Bedae censuras LB IX

Enchiridion: Enchiridion militis christiani LB V / CWE 66

Encomium matrimonii (in De conscribendis epistolis)

Encomium medicinae: Declamatio in laudem artis medicae LB I / ASD I-4 / CWE 29

Epistola ad Dorpium LB IX / CWE 3 / CWE 71

Epistola ad fratres Inferioris Germaniae: Responsio ad fratres Germaniae Inferioris ad epistolam apologeticam incerto autore proditam LB X / ASD IX-1

Epistola ad graculos: Epistola ad quosdam imprudentissimos graculos LB X

Epistola apologetica de Termino LB X

Epistola consolatoria: Epistola consolatoria virginibus sacris LB V

Epistola contra pseudevangelicos: Epistola contra quosdam qui se falso iactant evangelicos LB X / ASD IX-1

Euripidis Hecuba LB I / ASD I-1

Euripidis Iphigenia in Aulide LB I / ASD I-1

Exomologesis: Exomologesis sive modus confitendi LB V

Explanatio symboli: Explanatio symboli apostolorum sive catechismus LB V / ASD V-1

Ex Plutarcho versa LB IV / ASD IV-2

Expositio concionalis (in Psalmi)

Formula: Conficiendarum epistolarum formula (see De conscribendis epistolis)

Hyperaspistes LB X

In Nucem Ovidii commentarius LB I / ASD I-1 / CWE 29

In Prudentium: Commentarius in duos hymnos Prudentii LB V / CWE 29

Institutio christiani matrimonii LB V

Institutio principis christiani LB IV / ASD IV-1 / CWE 27

[Julius exclusus: Dialogus Julius exclusus e coelis] *Opuscula* / CWE 27

Lingua LB IV / ASD IV-1A / CWE 29

Liturgia Virginis Matris: Virginis Matris apud Lauretum cultae liturgia LB V / ASD V-1

Luciani dialogi LB I / ASD I-1

Manifesta mendacia CWE 71

Methodus (see Ratio)

Modus orandi Deum LB V / ASD V-1

Moria: Moriae encomium LB IV / ASD IV-3 / CWE 27

Novum Testamentum: Novum Testamentum 1519 and later (Novum instrumentum for the first edition, 1516, when required) LB VI

Obsecratio ad Virginem Mariam: Obsecratio sive oratio ad Virginem Mariam in rebus adversis LB V

Oratio de pace: Oratio de pace et discordia LB VIII

Oratio funebris: Oratio funebris in funere Bertae de Heyen LB VIII / CWE 29

Paean Virgini Matri: Paean Virgini Matri dicendus LB V

Panegyricus: Panegyricus ad Philippum Austriae ducem LB IV / ASD IV-1 / CWE 27

Parabolae: Parabolae sive similia LB I / ASD I-5 / CWE 23

Paraclesis LB V, VI

Paraphrasis in Elegantias Vallae: Paraphrasis in Elegantias Laurentii Vallae LB I / ASD I-4

Paraphrasis in Matthaeum, etc (in Paraphrasis in Novum Testamentum)

Paraphrasis in Novum Testamentum LB VII / CWE 42–50

Peregrinatio apostolorum: Peregrinatio apostolorum Petri et Pauli LB VI, VII
Precatio ad Virginis filium Iesum LB V
Precatio dominica LB V
Precationes LB V
Precatio pro pace ecclesiae: Precatio ad Iesum pro pace ecclesiae LB IV, V
Psalmi: Psalmi, or Enarrationes sive commentarii in psalmos LB V / ASD V-2, 3
Purgatio adversus epistolam Lutheri: Purgatio adversus epistolam non sobriam
    Lutheri LB IX / ASD IX-1

Querela pacis LB IV / ASD IV-2 / CWE 27

Ratio: Ratio seu Methodus compendio perveniendi ad veram theologiam (Methodus
    for the shorter version originally published in the Novum instrumentum of
    1516) LB V, VI
Responsio ad annotationes Lei: Liber quo respondet annotationibus Lei LB IX
Responsio ad collationes: Responsio ad collationes cuiusdam iuvenis gerontodidas-
    cali LB IX
Responsio ad disputationem de divortio: Responsio ad disputationem cuiusdam
    Phimostomi de divortio LB IX
Responsio ad epistolam Pii: Responsio ad epistolam paraeneticam Alberti Pii, or
    Responsio ad exhortationem Pii LB IX
Responsio ad notulas Bedaicas LB X
Responsio ad Petri Cursii defensionem: Epistola de apologia Cursii LB X / Allen
    Ep 3032
Responsio adversus febricitantis libellum: Apologia monasticae religionis LB X

Spongia: Spongia adversus aspergines Hutteni LB X / ASD IX-1
Supputatio: Supputatio calumniarum Natalis Bedae LB IX

Tyrannicida: Tyrannicida, declamatio Lucianicae respondens LB I / ASD I-1 /
    CWE 29

Virginis et martyris comparatio LB V
Vita Hieronymi: Vita divi Hieronymi Stridonensis *Opuscula* / CWE 61

Index of
Biblical and Apocryphal References

This index lists the citations and allusions made by Erasmus, but not those added by the translators for explanation or illustration.

Index of Classical References

Aristophanes
- *Knights* 91 n11 (twice), 217 n9
- *Plutus* 326 n2, 396 n8
Aristotle
- *Magna moralia* 390 n3
- *Nicomachean Ethics* 63 n4, 82 n1, 328 n13
Athenaeus *Deipnosophistae* 362 n8 (twice)

Caesar *De bello civili* 6 n6, 129 n15
Cicero
- *De finibus* 56 n2
- *De inventione* 7 n9, 201 n3, 365 n18
- *De officiis* 8 n2
- *De oratore* 79 n2, 365 n21
- *Epistulae ad Atticum* 85 n2
- *In Verrem* 120 n7
- *Orator* 353 n7, 364 n13
- *Pro Caecina* 353 n12
- *Tusculan Disputations* (1.2.4) 397 n8; (3.27.66) 336 n13; (3.4.7–9) 56 n2; (3.6.13–3.10.22) 65 n3; (3.8.16) 430 n2; (3.9.19) 110 n7; (4.5.10) 56 n2; (4.13.29–30) 65 n2; (4.15.34) 65 n2; (5.20.60) 54 n6
Curtius Rufus, Quintus *History of Alexander* 41 n3

Dionysius of Halicarnassus *De Demosthenis dictione* 85 n2

Euripides
- *Alcestis* 19 n4
- *Andromache* 307 n4
- *Hecuba* 397 n7
- *Medea* 45 n4
- *Trojan Women* 63 n7

Gellius, Aulus *Noctes Atticae* 157 n51, 331 n7
Greek Anthology 336 n13

Hesychius *Lexicon* 91 n10, 94 n3
Hippocrates *Aphorisms* 7 n2
Historia Augusta 430 n4
Homer
- *Iliad* 26 n30 (twice), 403 n11
- *Odyssey* 14 n9
Horace
- *Ars poetica* 356 n5
- *Epistles* 277 n3
- *Odes* 56 n3, 236 n3, 285 n5, 356 n6
- *Satires* 240 n4, 369 n6, 428 n4

Josephus *Jewish Antiquities* 8 n6, 123 n4, 254 n11
Julius Pollux *Onomasticon* 63 n6
Juvenal *Satires* 30 n3, 44 n3, 65 n6, 91 n12, 343 n1

Livy *Ab urbe condita* 268 n3
Lucian
- *De mercede conductis* 343 n1
- *Hermotimus* 285 n6

Martial *Epigrams* 265 n6, 343 n1 (twice)

Ovid *Remedia amoris* 155 n21

Plato
– *Crito* 345 n4
– *Laws* 82 n1
– *Phaedrus* 155 n35
– *Republic* 54 n6, 345 n4
– *Symposium* 362 n7
Plautus *Miles gloriosus* 63 n1
Pliny (the Elder) *Naturalis historia* 213 n2, 331 n7
Pliny (the Younger) *Letters* 30 n1 (three times), 343 n1
Plutarch *Moralia* 8 n2, 332 n1

Quintilian *Institutio oratoria* (1.5.40) 253 n3; (1.16.3) 331 n7; (3.10.4) 58 n4; (4.1.5–51) 7 n9; (5.11.22) 168 n7; (5.11.22–4) 365 n18; (5.11.31) 121 n3; (5.11.34) 168 n7; (6.1.1) 355 n4; (6.2.8) 56 n2; (6.2.24) 235 n14; (8.2.11) 8 n3; (8.3.88) 235 n14; (8.6.4) 363 n17; (8.6.21) 253 n3; (8.6.34–6) 365 n21; (8.6.62–7) 22 n21; (9.1.33) 353 n12; (9.2.6) 235 n15; (9.2.64) 8 n3; (9.2.104) 235 n14; (9.2.106) 79 n2; (9.3.12) 119 n10; (9.3.54–5) 235 n12; (9.3.54–7) 133 n5; (9.3.66) 66 n3; (9.3.71) 235 n13; (9.3.77) 365 n16; (9.3.78–9) 365 n20; (9.3.90) 79 n2; (9.4.122–4) 353 n7;

(12.10.58) 235 n16; (12.10.58–9) 363 n13

Rhetorica ad Herennium 133 n5, 235 n13, n14, n15, n16, 291 n3, 345 n7, 353 n12, 364 n13

Seneca
– *De beneficiis* 73 n5
– *Epistulae morales* 61 n2 (three times), 73 n5, 82 n1, 111 n7, n17, 182 n6, 397 n8
Sophocles *Antigone* 82 n1
Suetonius
– *Augustus* 236 n3
– *Claudius* 424 n6
– *Galba* 6 n6
– *Vespasian* 5 n6, 136 n3

Terence
– *Adelphi* 223 n2
– *Andria* 123 n4
– *Hecyra* 186 n7
Thucydides *Peloponnesian War* 120 n8

Virgil
– *Aeneid* 207 n10, 240 n6
– *Georgics* 14 n9

Index of

Patristic, Medieval, and Renaissance

References

References are to the notes. Individual entries are not given for passages from the commentaries on Romans most frequently quoted by Erasmus, namely, those of Ambrosiaster, John Chrysostom, Lefèvre d'Etaples, Origen, Theophylact, Thomas Aquinas, and Valla; nor are citations given for Edward Lee's and Frans Titelmans' detailed criticisms of Erasmus' *Annotations*. Lee and Titelmans are usually cited in the commentary according to Erasmus' replies to them in, respectively, the *Responsio ad annotationes Lei* and the *Responsio ad collationes*.

Ambrose of Milan *Expositio evangelii secundum Lucam* 348 n7

Aquinas. *See* Thomas Aquinas

Athanasius *Ad Serapionem* 208 n10

Augustine. *See also* Pseudo-Augustine
- *Confessions* 158 n59
- *Contra adversarium legis et prophetarum* 241 n3
- *Contra duas epistulas Pelagianorum* 152 n4, 160 n72, 198 n20, 265 n2, 267 n8
- *Contra Faustum Manichaeum* (3.3) 221 n4, 240 n4; (9.2) 304 n3, 305 n2; (11.4) 9 n4; (12.3) 241 n2; (13.18) 392 n8; (21.2) 267 n6; (22.27) 253 n8; (22.89) 270 n4, 271 n21
- *Contra Julianum* 58 n3, 153 n5 (twice), 160 n73 (twice), n74, n76, n77
- *Contra Maximinum haereticum Arianorum episcopum* 435 n19
- *De baptismo contra Donatistas* 304 n3
- *De catechizandis rudibus* 393 n26, n27
- *De civitate dei* 83 n5, 208 n6, 237 n6, 325 n3

- *De correptione et gratia* 225 n8, n15, 228 n22 (twice), 312 n2
- *De diversis quaestionibus ad Simplicianum* 192 n7 (twice)
- *De diversis quaestionibus* LXXXIII 219 n3, 265 n12, n2
- *De doctrina christiana* (2.12.17) 304 n3; (2.16.23) 5 n13; (3.3.6) 232 n8, 274 n2; (4.7.11) 133 n7, n8; (4.18.35–4.30.63) 364 n14; (4.20.40) 345 n6, 352 n3, 353 n8, 364 n6; (4.20.43) 229 n3, 230 n6, 235 n11, 237 n7
- *De dono perseverantiae* 292 n5, 312 n2 (twice)
- *De gratia Christi et de peccato originali* 101 n2, 152 n3
- *De gratia et libero arbitrio* 192 n9
- *De natura boni* 319 n6
- *De natura et gratia*: 58 n3, 159 n69, 206 n4
- *De nuptiis et concupiscentia*: 160 n73, n74, 170 n6, 198 n21
- *De peccatorum meritis et remissione et de baptismo parvulorum* (1.11.13) 165 n8, 166 n16; (1.12.15) 170 n9; (1.20.77) 159 n66; (1.24.34) 159 n66;

Index of Greek and Latin Words Cited

This is a selective index. It includes those words that Erasmus undertakes at some point and in some manner to explain. For Greek conjunctions and prepositions see grammar in the General Index.

καιρός 133–4, 356
κακία 42, 61
κακοήθεια 62
καλέω 5
καλλιέλαιος 305, 308
κατάγω 281
καταισχύνω 131, 275, 280
κατάλαλος 62
κατάνυξις 297
καταράομαι 337, 338
καταργέω 92, 104, 116, 186
καταρτίζω 267
κατασκάπτω 292
κατέναντι 118
κατηχέω 84
κάτοπτρον 48
καύχημα 106
καύχησις 106, 405
κειμήλιον 239
κλητός 5, 30, 225
κλῖμαξ 132
κοινωνέω 417
κοινωνία 416
κοίτη 256–7, 258 n4
κρῖμα 350
κρίνω 15 n24, 58, 73, 93, 371, 380
κτίσις 48
κυριεύω 177, 183
κωλύω 39
κωμάζω 362
κῶμος 361–2
κωμῳδία 362 n6
λατρεία 33, 34 n2, 55 n3, 241, 321,
    405 n8
λατρεύω 33, 55
λέγω 326, 398
λειτουργέω 417, 421
λειτουργός 404
λογίζομαι 103, 107, 109, 125, 162, 179,
    214–15
λογικός 322
λόγιον 90–1
λόγος 255, 272
λυπέω 381
μακαρίζομαι 110, 111 n15
μακαρισμός 110
ματαιόομαι 51
μάταιος 51

ματαιότης 217
μείζων 260
μέλλω 125, 168, 216, 414 n8
μέμφομαι 262
μετάνοια 74
μικρολογία 362
μνεία 34
μόρφωσις 85–6
μυστήριον 308
ναί 103
νεκρόω 123
νήπιος 85
νομοθεσία 241
νόμος 184
νοῦς 59, 318, 323, 373
οἰκονόμος 432
οἰκτείρω 260
ὀκνηρός 334
ὁμοθυμαδόν 395
ὁμοιόπτωτον 363
ὁμοιοτέλευτον 363
ὁμοίωμα 164, 166 n14, 201
ὄντα. See εἰμί
ὁρίζω 10–12, 266
ὁριστικός 12, 15 n21, 350
ὅρος 12, 14 n21
ὀφειλέτης 40
ὀψώνιον 181, 182
πάθημα 187, 188
πάθος 56, 204 n4
παιδευτής 85
παντοκράτωρ 272
παραζηλόω 288, 297, 301–2
παρακαλέω 320, 420
παράκλησις 331, 394
παράπτωμα 162, 163 n14, 301
παρεισέρχομαι 172
πάρεσις 102
παρίστημι 179, 320–1, 379
παῦλα 3
παύω 3
πειθαρχέω 347
πείθω 347, 381, 401
περισσός 90
περιτομή 111
πίπτω 298, 301
πιστεύω 90, 120
πίστις 42–4, 385

General Index

Abelard, Peter, theological method of 161 n83

Abraham: his name 106–7; two Abrahams in one 117

accommodation, principle of 339, 340, 367, 389

Acts. *See* Bible, canon of

Adam, earthly and heavenly 117

Aldine. *See* Bible, editions of

Alexander the Great 3

allegory. *See* Scripture, hermeneutics of; Origen, 'philosophizes'

Allen, P.S., editor of Erasmus *Opus epistolarum* 296 n10, 348 n10, 352 n14. *See also* Erasmus, original works, letters

alms. *See under* Erasmus, views of

ambiguity. *See under* Scripture

Ambrose of Milan: not distinguished from Ambrosiaster 335 n7; his commentary on Luke 348 n7; interpretation of Rom 7 198 n17

Ambrosiaster: identified with Ambrose of Milan xii–xiii, 334, 335 n7; his knowledge of Greek 334, 335 n7; twists Scripture 165

Anabaptists 167 n25

Anselm of Canterbury, on sin 153 n11

Anselm of Laon, contributor to the *Gloss* 335 n9

Apocalypse. *See* Bible, canon of

apostle(s): meaning of word 5; language of 6, 17, 32, 252 n15, 297, 322, 332. *See also under* Paul

Aquila, translator of the Bible 272, 273 n16

Aquinas. *See* Thomas Aquinas

Arianism, Arians: derived from Origen 244; history of 247 n6; doctrine of 247 n6, 249; interpretations of: (John 1:15) 10 n9; (Rom 1:3) 10 n9; (Rom 9:5) 243–6, 247 n2; Erasmus accused of xiii; condemned by Erasmus 245–6

Arius. *See* Arianism

Asia Minor, distinguished from Asia 426

Athanasius: Theophylact's commentary falsely attributed to 12, 15 n25, 92; cited by Lefèvre 362 n4

Athenaeus, author of *Deipnosophistae* 362 n8

Augustine of Hippo: esteemed by Erasmus 372; concerned with *minutiae* of Scripture 362; follows Greek 119; fails to follow Greek 371; twists Scripture 165, 197; acknowledged mistakes 28; taken for Pseudo-Augustine 211, 212 n13; conflict with Pelagians 139, 152 n5; views of: on predestination 227; on sin 139, 149–50, 153 n8, 161 n81; on baptism of infants 157 n55; interpretations of: (Rom 7) 198 n17; (Rom 10:6–7) 282 n4

Baal, meaning of name 293

This book

was designed by

ANTJE LINGNER

based on the series design by

ALLAN FLEMING

and was printed by

University

of Toronto

Press